Lecture Notes in Computer Science 12787

More information about this subseries at http://www.springer.com/series/7409

Qin Gao · Jia Zhou (Eds.)

Human Aspects of IT for the Aged Population

Supporting Everyday Life Activities

7th International Conference, ITAP 2021
Held as Part of the 23rd HCI International Conference, HCII 2021
Virtual Event, July 24–29, 2021
Proceedings, Part II

Springer

Editors
Qin Gao
Tsinghua University
Beijing, China

Jia Zhou
Chongqing University
Chongqing, China

ISSN 0302-9743   ISSN 1611-3349   (electronic)
Lecture Notes in Computer Science
ISBN 978-3-030-78110-1   ISBN 978-3-030-78111-8   (eBook)
https://doi.org/10.1007/978-3-030-78111-8

LNCS Sublibrary: SL3 – Information Systems and Applications, incl. Internet/Web, and HCI

This Springer imprint is published by the registered company Springer Nature Switzerland AG
The registered company address is: Gewerbestrasse 11, 6330 Cham, Switzerland

Foreword

Human-Computer Interaction (HCI) is acquiring an ever-increasing scientific and industrial importance, and having more impact on people's everyday life, as an ever-growing number of human activities are progressively moving from the physical to the digital world. This process, which has been ongoing for some time now, has been dramatically accelerated by the COVID-19 pandemic. The HCI International (HCII) conference series, held yearly, aims to respond to the compelling need to advance the exchange of knowledge and research and development efforts on the human aspects of design and use of computing systems.

The 23rd International Conference on Human-Computer Interaction, HCI International 2021 (HCII 2021), was planned to be held at the Washington Hilton Hotel, Washington DC, USA, during July 24–29, 2021. Due to the COVID-19 pandemic and with everyone's health and safety in mind, HCII 2021 was organized and run as a virtual conference. It incorporated the 21 thematic areas and affiliated conferences listed on the following page.

A total of 5222 individuals from academia, research institutes, industry, and governmental agencies from 81 countries submitted contributions, and 1276 papers and 241 posters were included in the proceedings to appear just before the start of the conference. The contributions thoroughly cover the entire field of HCI, addressing major advances in knowledge and effective use of computers in a variety of application areas. These papers provide academics, researchers, engineers, scientists, practitioners, and students with state-of-the-art information on the most recent advances in HCI. The volumes constituting the set of proceedings to appear before the start of the conference are listed in the following pages.

The HCI International (HCII) conference also offers the option of 'Late Breaking Work' which applies both for papers and posters, and the corresponding volume(s) of the proceedings will appear after the conference. Full papers will be included in the 'HCII 2021 - Late Breaking Papers' volumes of the proceedings to be published in the Springer LNCS series, while 'Poster Extended Abstracts' will be included as short research papers in the 'HCII 2021 - Late Breaking Posters' volumes to be published in the Springer CCIS series.

The present volume contains papers submitted and presented in the context of the 7th International Conference on Human Aspects of IT for the Aged Population (ITAP 2021) affiliated conference to HCII 2021. I would like to thank the Co-chairs, Qin Gao and Jia Zhou, for their invaluable contribution in its organization and the preparation of the Proceedings, as well as the members of the program board for their contributions and support. This year, the ITAP affiliated conference has focused on topics related to designing for and with older users, technology acceptance and user experience of older users, use of social media and games by the aging population, as well as applications supporting health, wellbeing, communication, social participation and everyday activities.

I would also like to thank the Program Board Chairs and the members of the Program Boards of all thematic areas and affiliated conferences for their contribution towards the highest scientific quality and overall success of the HCI International 2021 conference.

This conference would not have been possible without the continuous and unwavering support and advice of Gavriel Salvendy, founder, General Chair Emeritus, and Scientific Advisor. For his outstanding efforts, I would like to express my appreciation to Abbas Moallem, Communications Chair and Editor of HCI International News.

July 2021   Constantine Stephanidis

HCI International 2021 Thematic Areas and Affiliated Conferences

Thematic Areas

- HCI: Human-Computer Interaction
- HIMI: Human Interface and the Management of Information

Affiliated Conferences

- EPCE: 18th International Conference on Engineering Psychology and Cognitive Ergonomics
- UAHCI: 15th International Conference on Universal Access in Human-Computer Interaction
- VAMR: 13th International Conference on Virtual, Augmented and Mixed Reality
- CCD: 13th International Conference on Cross-Cultural Design
- SCSM: 13th International Conference on Social Computing and Social Media
- AC: 15th International Conference on Augmented Cognition
- DHM: 12th International Conference on Digital Human Modeling and Applications in Health, Safety, Ergonomics and Risk Management
- DUXU: 10th International Conference on Design, User Experience, and Usability
- DAPI: 9th International Conference on Distributed, Ambient and Pervasive Interactions
- HCIBGO: 8th International Conference on HCI in Business, Government and Organizations
- LCT: 8th International Conference on Learning and Collaboration Technologies
- ITAP: 7th International Conference on Human Aspects of IT for the Aged Population
- HCI-CPT: 3rd International Conference on HCI for Cybersecurity, Privacy and Trust
- HCI-Games: 3rd International Conference on HCI in Games
- MobiTAS: 3rd International Conference on HCI in Mobility, Transport and Automotive Systems
- AIS: 3rd International Conference on Adaptive Instructional Systems
- C&C: 9th International Conference on Culture and Computing
- MOBILE: 2nd International Conference on Design, Operation and Evaluation of Mobile Communications
- AI-HCI: 2nd International Conference on Artificial Intelligence in HCI

List of Conference Proceedings Volumes Appearing Before the Conference

1. LNCS 12762, Human-Computer Interaction: Theory, Methods and Tools (Part I), edited by Masaaki Kurosu
2. LNCS 12763, Human-Computer Interaction: Interaction Techniques and Novel Applications (Part II), edited by Masaaki Kurosu
3. LNCS 12764, Human-Computer Interaction: Design and User Experience Case Studies (Part III), edited by Masaaki Kurosu
4. LNCS 12765, Human Interface and the Management of Information: Information Presentation and Visualization (Part I), edited by Sakae Yamamoto and Hirohiko Mori
5. LNCS 12766, Human Interface and the Management of Information: Information-rich and Intelligent Environments (Part II), edited by Sakae Yamamoto and Hirohiko Mori
6. LNAI 12767, Engineering Psychology and Cognitive Ergonomics, edited by Don Harris and Wen-Chin Li
7. LNCS 12768, Universal Access in Human-Computer Interaction: Design Methods and User Experience (Part I), edited by Margherita Antona and Constantine Stephanidis
8. LNCS 12769, Universal Access in Human-Computer Interaction: Access to Media, Learning and Assistive Environments (Part II), edited by Margherita Antona and Constantine Stephanidis
9. LNCS 12770, Virtual, Augmented and Mixed Reality, edited by Jessie Y. C. Chen and Gino Fragomeni
10. LNCS 12771, Cross-Cultural Design: Experience and Product Design Across Cultures (Part I), edited by P. L. Patrick Rau
11. LNCS 12772, Cross-Cultural Design: Applications in Arts, Learning, Well-being, and Social Development (Part II), edited by P. L. Patrick Rau
12. LNCS 12773, Cross-Cultural Design: Applications in Cultural Heritage, Tourism, Autonomous Vehicles, and Intelligent Agents (Part III), edited by P. L. Patrick Rau
13. LNCS 12774, Social Computing and Social Media: Experience Design and Social Network Analysis (Part I), edited by Gabriele Meiselwitz
14. LNCS 12775, Social Computing and Social Media: Applications in Marketing, Learning, and Health (Part II), edited by Gabriele Meiselwitz
15. LNAI 12776, Augmented Cognition, edited by Dylan D. Schmorrow and Cali M. Fidopiastis
16. LNCS 12777, Digital Human Modeling and Applications in Health, Safety, Ergonomics and Risk Management: Human Body, Motion and Behavior (Part I), edited by Vincent G. Duffy
17. LNCS 12778, Digital Human Modeling and Applications in Health, Safety, Ergonomics and Risk Management: AI, Product and Service (Part II), edited by Vincent G. Duffy

38. CCIS 1420, HCI International 2021 Posters - Part II, edited by Constantine Stephanidis, Margherita Antona, and Stavroula Ntoa
39. CCIS 1421, HCI International 2021 Posters - Part III, edited by Constantine Stephanidis, Margherita Antona, and Stavroula Ntoa

http://2021.hci.international/proceedings

7th International Conference on Human Aspects of IT for the Aged Population (ITAP 2021)

Program Board Chairs: **Qin Gao,** *Tsinghua University, China*, **and Jia Zhou,** *Chongqing University, China*

- Bessam Abdulrazak, Canada
- Inês Amaral, Portugal
- Panagiotis Bamidis, Greece
- Alan H. S. Chan, China
- Alex Chaparro, USA
- Honglin Chen, China
- José Baptista Coelho, Portugal
- Fausto Colombo, Italy
- Loredana Ivan, Romania
- Hirokazu Kato, Japan
- Chaiwoo Lee, USA
- Jiunn-Woei Lian, Taiwan
- Hai-Ning Liang, China
- Eugene Loos, Netherlands
- Yan Luximon, Hong Kong
- Lourdes Moreno, Spain
- Sergio F. Ochoa, Chile
- Peter Rasche, Germany
- Marie Sjölinder, Sweden
- Patrice Terrier, France
- Wang-Chin Tsai, Taiwan
- Ana Veloso, Portugal
- Nadine Vigouroux, France
- Tingru Zhang, China
- Yuxiang (Chris) Zhao, China

The full list with the Program Board Chairs and the members of the Program Boards of all thematic areas and affiliated conferences is available online at:

http://www.hci.international/board-members-2021.php

HCI International 2022

The 24th International Conference on Human-Computer Interaction, HCI International 2022, will be held jointly with the affiliated conferences at the Gothia Towers Hotel and Swedish Exhibition & Congress Centre, Gothenburg, Sweden, June 26 – July 1, 2022. It will cover a broad spectrum of themes related to Human-Computer Interaction, including theoretical issues, methods, tools, processes, and case studies in HCI design, as well as novel interaction techniques, interfaces, and applications. The proceedings will be published by Springer. More information will be available on the conference website: http://2022.hci.international/:

General Chair
Prof. Constantine Stephanidis
University of Crete and ICS-FORTH
Heraklion, Crete, Greece
Email: general_chair@hcii2022.org

http://2022.hci.international/

Contents – Part II

Supporting Health and Wellbeing

Supporting Communication, Social Participation and Everyday Activities

Contents – Part I

Technology Acceptance and User Experience Studies

Aging and Social Media

Aging: Games and Leisure Activities

The Belief in Health Benefits of Digital Play Modulates Physiological Responses to Games: A Repeated-Measures Quantitative Study of Game Stress in Older Adults Playing Different Game Genres

Atousa Assadi[1], Sasha Elbaz[2], and Najmeh Khalili-Mahani[1,2,3(✉)]

[1] Department of Electrical and Computer Engineering, Concordia University, Montreal, QC, Canada
atousa.assadi@mail.mcgill.ca, najmeh.khalili-mahani@concordia.ca
[2] engAGE Centre for Studies in Aging, Concordia University, Montreal, QC, Canada
s.elba@live.concordia.ca
[3] PERFORM Centre, Concordia University, Montreal, QC, Canada

Abstract. To create games that target older adults' interests in engaging in cognitively-boosting activities is a rising trend. However, the novelty of the digital medium of play, as well as the implicit expectation of cognitive performance can create stressful experiences for them. To address this question, we have previously proposed an empirical framework, Affective Game Planning for Health Applications (AGPHA). Drawing on Lazarus's Transactional Theory of Stress Appraisal and Coping, AGPHA deploys an iterative evaluation of interactions between primary appraisal (PA) and secondary appraisal (SA) of the game challenge in relation to individual beliefs, as well as cognitive and physiological abilities, to predict whether players choose to learn and master the game further. In this study, we focused on the PA of health benefits of digital games (even before the games were introduced), and showed its effect on biomarkers of stress, namely cortisol, electrodermal activity (EDA), and heart rate (HR) during play. Furthermore, we showed that physiological variations explained differences in SA of the games benefits related to mental health and cognitive stimulation, but not related to the perception of game difficulty. Finally, we showed that interactions between physiological and SA factors were more sensitive predictors of the desire to replay than physiology or SA alone. Our findings show that AGPHA provides a suitable framework for investigating complex interindividual variations in physiological and perceptual experience of different games.

Keywords: Cognitive games · Theory of stress · Interindividual differences · Serious games · Older adults · Human computer interface · Cognitive and emotional arousal · Physiological monitoring · Cortisol

© Springer Nature Switzerland AG 2021
Q. Gao and J. Zhou (Eds.): HCII 2021, LNCS 12787, pp. 3–22, 2021.
https://doi.org/10.1007/978-3-030-78111-8_1

1 Introduction

Playing digital games is an important and beneficial activity for older adults [1, 2]. Digital games offer a playful and enjoyable strategy for health intervention [3–7]. They can serve as personalized diagnostic tools in digital healthcare [8, 9]. Leisure and enjoyment are important motivations for play as well [10, 11]. The challenge is in the fact that to engage with digital games is not very common among many isolates and health-wise challenged seniors, who need them most. Especially in the COVID-era, to design and create interactive and engaging digital experiences for older adults has become imperative.

As far as older-play is concerned, games are often promoted to serve as preventive strategies against cognitive decline [3]. Several independent studies indicate that to play for cognitive stimulation is a primary motivation for older players [2, 12], albeit variations exist depending on the context of the study[13]. Besides cognitive games, exercise games offer social benefits [5], as well as functional improvements in physical balance, confidence, mobility, executive functions, and processing speed [7].

The fact that the medium of game produces a complex interactive experience which is not only mechanical, but also aesthetic and sociocultural [1], is the reason why many researchers are trying to find a category of game that is both beneficial, and easily accessible/playable to be adopted into the seniors' daily lifestyle [14].

To believe that games are beneficial may not be sufficient to overcome the barriers of exploring various genres of available games [15]. In 2013, one of the most impactful scientific studies to date, conducted by the neurologist Adam Gazzaley's team showed that a multi-tasking car-racing game produced longer-lasting cognitive improvements than normal cognitive training tasks did [4]. Nevertheless, in a study of the preferred experiences with different cognitively stimulating games, car racing games were rated as the least favorite [10].

In our experience, we find that many seniors approach digital games with trepidation. Skepticism about risks of game violence and addiction is more prevalent in older adults [16].

In addition, to tie playing games to cognitive and physical performance can in and of itself become a great source of stress, as it poses a challenge to their self-efficacy and competence, preventing them from approaching game. We have previously shown that those who have a negative appraisal about the games, are less likely to participate in gaming studies [17].

The question is how to tip the primary appraisal of the games into favorable? Undeniably, to increase enjoyment is going to be important [11], and there are several qualitative methods that can reliably assess the flow and positive affect during the playing experience. But if the game is to deliver specific health benefits, then pleasure and motivation alone are not sufficient, and physical and physiological interactions of the game with the player must be also accounted for.

To address this need, we have recently proposed an empirical framework, AGPHA, to evaluate the relationship between players' appraisal of the game as a moderator of stress experienced in the course of learning to play, and as a predictor of the desire to play again [18]. AGPHA builds on the Transactional Theory of Stress Appraisal and Coping by Lazarus and Folkman [19].

According to this theory, individuals cope with any challenge through *primary appraisal* (PA) of the stressful challenge (*irrelevant, benign-positive,* and *stressful*). If the stressor is *irrelevant,* then they will not engage with it, if it is *benign- positive* then they will explore it, but if it is *stressful* (i.e. it threatens them physically, psychologically, or socially--e.g., an exam or public speech), then their coping strategy will be a function of the *secondary appraisal* (SA) process: how to cope successfully? At this stage, the availability of resources (e.g., physical energy, knowledge, tools, etc.) as well as personality of the individual will modulate the psychophysiological "stress" responses that can be measured from body signals such as heart rate, skin conductance, or neuroendocrine cortisol response (even to passive viewing of films [20]).

So far, we have tested the AGPHA model in two independent studies. In one study, we showed that positive game appraisal (in terms of personal preferences for game type) was associated with increased analgesia in the course of an experimental pain condition [21]. In another analysis of this current dataset, we showed that differences in cognitive abilities were associated with differences in both reflective and reflexive game-related stress [22].

The aim of the current study is to examine the sensitivity of the AGPHA framework to detect a relationship between PA of the health-benefits of digital play and subsequent physiological responses to the game experience, in explaining SA variations in subjective game stress and the desire to replay.

2 Materials and Methods

2.1 Experimental Design and Data Collection

In the AGPHA framework, we have proposed collecting various data in order to create a comprehensive profile of the personal traits, and perceptual and physiological states of participants that would predict their differences in stress-sensitivity (See Table 1 for details).

Table 1. Psychological and physiological characteristics that predict stress-sensitivity

Personal Factors	
General Self Efficacy	10-item measure to assess optimistic self-beliefs to cope with a variety of difficult demands in life, especially that one's actions are responsible for successful outcomes. GSE is positively correlated with positive affect, optimism, work satisfaction, and negatively with negative affect, stress, health complaints

(continued)

Table 1. (*continued*)

Personal Factors	
Perceived Stress Scale [23]	A 14-item measure, based on Lazarus' transactional model, designed to measure the degree to which situations in one's life are appraised as stressful, namely how unpredictable, uncontrollable, and overloaded respondents find their lives
UCLA loneliness Index [24]	A 20-item measure that assesses how often a person feels disconnected from others
MoCA [25]	Montreal Cognitive Assessment is a test of cognitive impairment that is administered by a trained individual and assesses short term memory, visuospatial abilities, executive function, attention, concentration and working memory, language, orientation to time and place
Perceptual Factors	
State-trait anxiety [26]	STAI-6 is a 6-item questionnaire to measure the state of anxiety characterized by subjective feelings of tension, apprehension, nervousness, and worry as a result of an event (game sessions)
Primary Appraisal (PA)	"Playing games is important for keeping healthy." *Yes* vs *No/I don't know*
Secondary Appraisal (SA)	Subjective rating of game experience administered after each game session, to evaluate the positive and negative impressions, and the desire to play again (See Table 3 and [17, 22] for more details.)
Physiological Factors (Stress variables)	
Heart Rate	HR (Beats/min) was measured from a wrist-worn photoplethysmogram (in E4 device). HR is a quantitative measure of workload while fully engaged in an activity [27]
Electrodermal activity	EDA is measured on the surface of the skin, and is a proxy measure for nervous system's response to emotional arousal, increased cognitive workload or exertion [28]
Salivary Cortisol	HR and EDA measure momentary autonomic responses to a stressor, but slower adaptive responses manifest by neuroendocrine signaling cascade that can be non-invasively measured from salivary cortisol, a hormone that modulates the metabolic resources available to coping with a stressor [29]

The experiment was a repeated measures study, with three game interventions involving brain training games, a car racing game and an exergame (Fig. 2) played by each participant. We informed participants (see Table 3 for sample characteristics) that the study was designed to present the games in increasing degrees of complexity and difficulty.

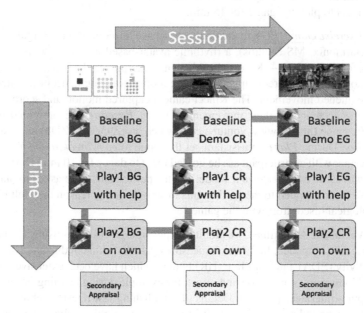

Fig. 1. Experimental Design: Repeated measures, non-randomized, longitudinal (3 sessions with incrementally difficult games in each session, and 3 consecutive Epochs per Session). EDA and HR were continuously monitored by a wristband and data was averaged over the duration of each Epoch per Session. Salivary cortisol was measured at the beginning of each Epoch.

Session 1 (Reference) MindGames (MG): This session involved playing a simple so-called 'brain training' game on an iPAD (_MindGames_, v2.5, by Tom Lake). During **Baseline** we offered a demo of the game, during **Play1** they played _Reaction, Match and Pattern_ for about three minutes each. We also administered a simple cognitive tasks that is sensitive to acute stress, with the objective of comparing the game effect across three sessions, but this data is not within the scope of this current analysis, and is reported elsewhere [20]. Finally, during **Play2**, the participants were given about 15 min to play block-match puzzles or MindGames (MG). This Sessions serves as a reference for comparison of two less familiar, and cognitively and physically more intense types of games.

Session 2 Car Race (CR): In the second session we introduced a free car racing simulation game (_Real Racing 3, v 5.4.0, Electronic Arts Inc._) an iPad. In this game, players used the iPad as a wheel to steer the car, thus minimizing efforts to learn control buttons. During **Baseline**, we played the official commercial video of the gameplay (https://www.youtube.com/watch?v=nEmc53kZPMY&t=349s) on a 42 inch TV monitor, while an assistant explained the rules of the game by pointing to the TV screen. During *Play1*, participants played the game in *Amateur* mode by help from our research assistant. During *Play2*, participants played the game in competitive mode and had to finish a short track by ranking lower than the third place, else be eliminated and have to restart the game. During the free play session, the assistant was present but at a distance and left the players to play the game for 15 min.

Session 3 Exercise Game (EG): In the final session, we introduced the Exergame, *Dance Central* (Harmonix, MS Studios), a rhythmic avatar-based and semi-adaptive routine developed for X-Box360 + Kinect. In this game, the players had to watch and copy the moves of a virtual choreographer while the motion tracking Kinect evaluated them against the queued movement. The Kinect camera captured motion and scored players based on the accuracy of their movements. During *Baseline*, we presented a video demo of the game (https://www.youtube.com/watch?v=IZ95rWRSZD8) and explained the gameplay. During *Play1* an assistant set the game to *easy/break it down* mode and played together with a participant as she guided them to dance for 10 min. During *Play2* the game was set to *easy/perform it* mode, and the participants were asked to play up to 15 min. We recommended to the participants to stop if for any reason they felt physical or psychological discomfort with the game.

"Stress" Variables. At all times, we monitored physiological signals using a light wrist-band device E4 (Empatica, Inc), which measures galvanic skin conductance or electro-dermal activity (EDA) and heart rate (HR) both of which have been extensively used as surrogate biomarkers of attention and effort, for example during learning or interaction with computer interfaces [30, 31]. Details of establishing test-retest reliability of these metrics were reported previously [22]. The values used in this analysis were averaged over the course of *Baseline, Play1*, and *Play2*, for each session. We also measured cortisol, shown to be a biomarker of stress during visuomotor activities [32], at the end of the *Baseline, Play1* and *Play2* sessions. In total, we had 162 physiological samples (18 x 3 Sessions x 3 Epochs).

Personality Variables in this study included General Self Efficacy (10-item) [33]), Perceived Stress Scale (10-item) [23], UCLA Loneliness Index [24] and the Montreal Cognitive Assessment Test to assess cognitive abilities [25]. These psychometric variables were assessed as control variables to account for interindividual variations in stress sensitivity and desire to replay. The first three questionnaires were administered during screening and the MoCA was administered prior to start of the experiment in the first session. At the end of each experiment, we also administered the STAI-6 to asses emotional states after each play session [26]. These variables allow to control for trait variables that would explain individual differences in stress-sensitivity due to the experiment.

Primary Appraisal (PA) Variable in this study is response to the question "Playing games is important for health" (n = 11, Agree; n = 7, Do not agree).

Secondary Appraisal (SA) Variables are listed in Table 2. As it can be noted, over-all the majority of the sample had a positive attitude towards all games. As we have shown before the reason for this may be that those who have generally negative attitudes towards gaming self-excluded themselves after the screening (when the primary appraisal questionnaire was administered) [17]. Because almost everyone found all experiences enjoyable and interesting, we exclude these from further analyses.

Table 2. Frequencies of subjective response to each game

SA variables	MindGame (MG) (yes/no)	CarRace (CR) (yes/no)	Exergame (EG) (yes/no)
Positive Appraisal			
The experience was enjoyable	17/1	18	17/1
These games are cognitively stimulating	16/2	17/1	16/2
This game helps improve mental health	15/3	13/4	14/4
The experience was interesting	17/1	17/1	17/1
The game is intense	12/6	15/3	12/6
Negative Appraisal			
The experience was frustrating	3/15	5/13	6/12
The experience was stressful	3/15	9/9	7/11
The game was difficult	13/5	12/6	11/7
This game is useless	2/16	2/16	3/15
I did not like the experiment	2/16	2/16	4/14
Final Appraisal			
I would like to play the game again	16/2	15/3	10/8
I will play the game again	14/4	12/6	10/8

2.2 Statistical Analyses

Figure 2 illustrates the AGPHA model we used to test two hypotheses:

H1: We expected that if an individual considered playing digital games to be important for health (positive PA), then they would be increasing their attention to the game and engage with the game more intensely. As a result, we hypothesized to observe higher levels of physiological response (as measured by increased cortisol, increased EDA and increased heart rate). Conversely, if the PA was negative, we did not expect the players to "stress" themselves by trying out the game.

H2: We expected that if higher levels of "stress" (i.e. physiological response) were associated with positive SA (e.g. stimulating and enjoyable experience), then this would predict an increased chance of desire to play again. Conversely, if higher levels of "stress" (i.e. physiological response) were associated with negative SA (e.g. difficult and uselessness), then this would reduce the odds of a desire to replay.

To examine the effect of PA (health benefits) on "stress" outcomes we performed an omnibus test of generalized estimating equation (GEE) with PA by Epoch by Session as

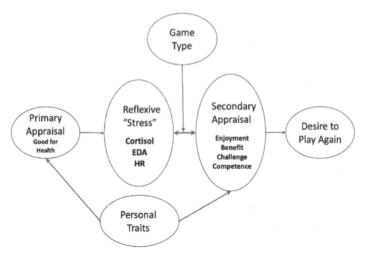

Fig. 2. The overall AGPHA model tested in this study focused on the relation between Primary and SA of three different games and reflexive responses measured by physiological variable assessed during **Baseline** (pre-game), **Play1** (training), **Play2** (practice), and their prediction of the expressed desire to play those games again.

model factors. In our model, the first session during which players tried MG, served as the Session reference. Within each Session, the first measurement (Baseline) served as the Epoch reference.

To explore effects of "Stress" variables on SA (Difficult, Intense, Stressful, Frustrating) we performed an omnibus logistic GEE test with each SA variable as dependent variables and "Stress" (EDA, HR and cortisol) and Session as model factors.

Finally, in order to investigate the added value of accounting for reflexive (physiological), reflective (SA), and personal state and emotional factors on the desire to replay, we performed a logistic GEE test with the *Desire to Play Again* as the dependent variable, and physiological measures, SA and Personal variables as predicting factors.

Parametric group differences were investigated using a t-test, and non-parametric group comparisons using a Chi-square test. *Posthoc* statistics are reported at 95% confidence intervals.

All statistical analyses were performed using SPSS 21 (IBM, Inc.) for MAC OS. Graphs were generated with Prism 7.0 (Graphpad, Inc.)

3   Results

3.1   Demographic and Psychometric Characteristics of Participants with Respect to PA

Nineteen older adults (65+) volunteered for the experimental study, but one participant dropped out after the first visit, due to extreme physical discomfort which forced her to eat and drink (thus rendering the cortisol sampling invalid). Participant characteristics are presented in Table 3. We did not observe any statistically significant differences with regards to the PA variable "To play is important for health".

Table 3. Sample characteristics with respect to PA and personal trait factors

Personal Characteristics	Good for Health?		Statistical Difference
	Yes	No	
Gender (M/F)	2/9	4/3	$\chi^2 = 2.9$, p = .09
Age (mean, sd)	71.2, 4.8	70.0, 4.2	t = .53, NS
General Self Efficacy	34.7, 2.6	33.6, 2,7	t = .39, NS
Perceived Stress Scale	15.8, 3.7	19.4, 2.3	t = −2.3, p = .036
UCLA Loneliness Index	9.91, 2.98	8.57, 22	t = .36, NS
Montreal Cognitive Assessment Scores	26.6, 2.4	27.0, 2.3	t = −.32, NS

3.2 The Relation Between PA of Health Benefits of Play and "Stress" Variables

Results of the omnibus GEE test of the interactions between PA (belief in health benefits), and Session are summarized in Table 4 and Fig. 3. We found a significant effect of game type on all physiological factors which was expected given the fact that the EG and even CR were physically more demanding than MG. Consistent with H1, PA was associated with differences in EDA and cortisol levels. Irrespective of Session, those with positive PA had higher EDA (95% CI:,22 to 5.06, p = .032). In Session 3 (EG), we observed a significant elevation of EDA from the **Baseline** during **Play1** (95%CI .75 - 5.07, p = .008) and **Play2** (95%CI 1.04 - 5.39, p = .004). This corroborates H2 that to have

Table 4. Omnibus GEE test of effect of Session × Time × PA (PA) on physiological variations caused by games.

Model Factor	Average EDA (muS)			Average HR (bpm)			Cortisol (nmol/mL)		
	Wald χ^2	df	Sig.	Wald χ^2	df	Sig.	Wald χ^2	df	Sig.
(Intercept)	30.07	1	.000	5867	1	.000	35.479	1	.000
PA[a]	4.48	1	**.034**	1.726	1	.190	4.368	1	**.037**
Epoch[b]	2.05	2	.359	16.06	2	**.000**	7.574	2	**.023**
Session[c]	16.37	2	**.000**	128.1	2	**.000**	6.266	2	**.044**
Epoch × PA	.902	2	.637	1.516	2	.470	2.342	2	.310
Epoch × Session	21.66	4	**.000**	217.2	4	**.000**	3.445	4	.486
PA × Session	2.27	2	.320	7.55	2	**.023**	3.396	2	.183
PA × Epoch × Session	6.10	4	.192	11.18	4	**.025**	8.385	4	.078

a Play is important for health > otherwise
b **Play1** and **Play2** > **Baseline**
c CR and EG > MG

found the new challenge positive would have increased the drive to engage with it--thus increasing exertion to beat the challenge.

Irrespective of Session and Epoch, those with positive PA had higher overall cortisol levels, most pronounced in Session 2 (95% CI .243 to 5.4, p = .032). For those with positive PA, the reduction of cortisol from baseline after *Play1* was significant in Sessions 2 (CR) (95% CI: −2.5 to −.26, p = .016) and 3 (EG) (95% CI: −4.7 to −.38, p = .021) but flat for the other group, again corroborating H1 that PA predicted pre-game psychophysiological differences in players. This is further supported by observing reduced HR in Session 2 in those with negative PA (95% CI: −10.56 to −.49) and increased HR in Session 3 in those with positive PA (95% CI: 5.25 to 29.1, p = .005), suggesting disengagement of those with negative PA.

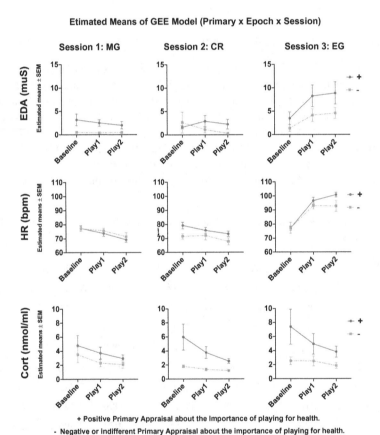

Fig. 3. Effects of PA (health benefits) on physiological variables.

3.3 The Relation Between Final SA of Desire to Re-play and "Stress" Variables

Results of the omnibus GEE test of the interactions between PA, and session are summarized in Table 5 and Fig. 4.

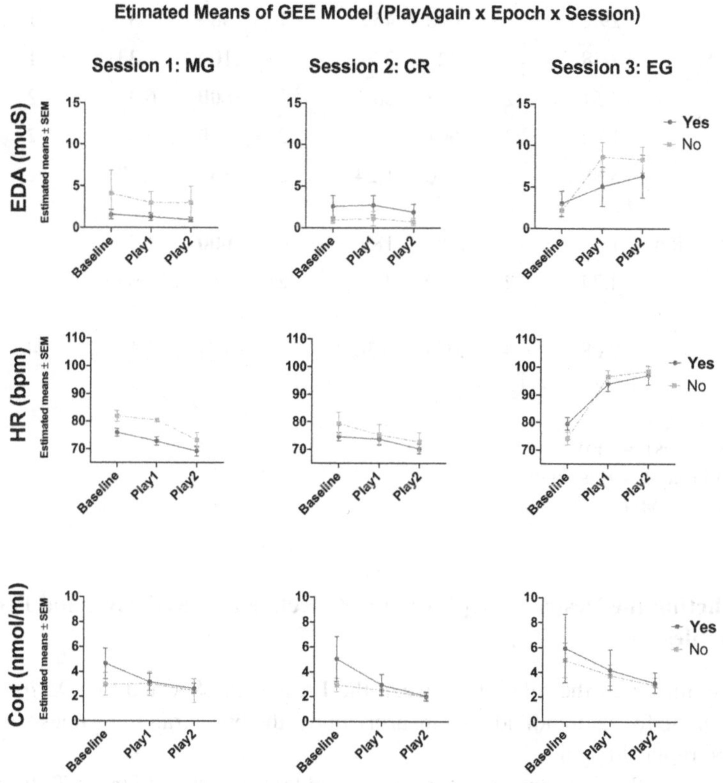

Fig. 4. Effects of final SA on physiological variables.

Contrary to our expectation, we did not find any significant physiological differences related to the final appraisal (desire to play again). However, Epoch by Session interactions were significant especially in Session 3 (EG, compared to CR & MG), again showing a steady increase in those who desired to play again and flat response in those who did not (consistent with H2, that positive appraisal would be associated with increased engagement.) The lack of group differences during the Session 1 and 2 is hypothetically related to the fact that games played on mobile devices are most preferred by older adults [10, 14]. Therefore, it should be considered that the desire to play again was not necessarily a function of how interesting the experience was, but how accessible and realistically available it was to them.

Table 5. Omnibus GEE test of effect of Session x Time x Final SA (like to play again) on physiological variations caused by games.

Source	Average EDA (muS)			Average HR (bpm)			Cortisol (nmol/mL)		
	Wald χ^2	df	Sig.	Wald χ^2	df	Sig.	Wald χ^2	df	Sig.
(Intercept)	29.25	1	.000	4597	1	.000	33.3	1	.000
PlayAgain[a]	.638	1	.42	2.7	1	.100	.331	1	.57
Epoch[b]	3.51	2	.173	20	2	**.000**	6.35	2	**.042**
Session[c]	14.28	2	**.001**	137	2	**.000**	4.4	2	.110
Epoch × PlayAgain	3.98	2	.136	1.24	2	.53	3.17	2	.205
Epoch × Session	18	4	**.001**	189	4	**.000**	1.22	4	.88
PlayAgain × Session	4.24	2	.120	4.4	2	.110	.085	2	.96
Epoch × PlayAgain × Session	9.08	4	.059	6.36	4	.174	2.10	4	.72

a PlayAgain (yes) > (no)
b Play1 and Play2 > Baseline
c CE and EG > MG

3.4 Predicting the Desire to Replay from Reflective and Reflexive, and Personal Variables

Figure 5 summarizes the relation between the PA and the SA and the *Desire to Play Again* the game for each individual. Unsurprisingly, the brain training games were more likely to be replayed again.

In terms of reflective game experiences, the odd ratios (OR) of *Desire To Play Again* were lowered with *Disliking* the experiment (95%CI OR: = .002 to .21, p < .001), finding it *Useless* (95%CI OR = .03 to .94, p = .04) and *Frustrating* (95%CI OR = .045 to .69, p = .01), but significantly increased with finding it *Good for Mental Health* (95%CI OR = 2.77 to 60.6, p < .001) and *Cognitively Stimulating* (95%CI OR = 1.77 to 178, p < .002). Interestingly, the odds of *Desire to Play Again* did not differ in relation to gender, cognitive abilities (measured by MoCA), PA, finding the game *Difficult*, or *Stressful*.

In terms of reflexive response to game experiences, we did not observe any significant effect of physiological interactions with game type on SAs that would be subjectively interpreted as stress (*Difficult, Intense, Frustrating*). However physiological responses predicted SAs of finding the game *Stressful, Good for Mental Health,* and *Cognitively Stimulating*, as well as the *Desire to Play Again*, albeit depending on the session (Table 6).

In Session 1: higher HR lowered the odds of finding the *MG* games *Stressful*. Conversely, higher EDA increased the odds of finding the *MG Stressful* and lowered the

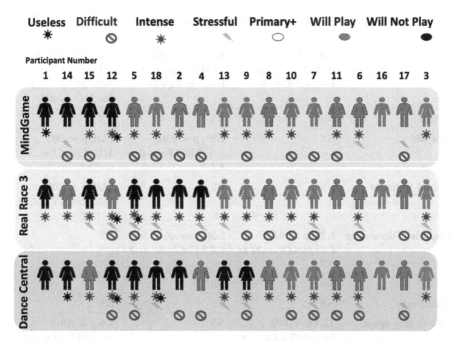

Fig. 5. Individual characteristics in terms of general PA and SA variables of each game.

odds of finding the *MG Good for Mental Health*. EDA also lowered the odds of *Desire to Play Again (MG)*. Interestingly, in Session 1, higher levels of cortisol were associated with lower odds of *Desire to Play Again*, which is paradoxical to having higher cortisol associated with positive PA about health benefits. A possible explanation may be that the game was not challenging-enough for those few who did not wish to play it again. The CR game in Session 2 was considerably more stimulating and indeed we found that higher levels of cortisol and HR in this session predicted higher likelihood of finding the game *Cognitively Stimulating*. In Session 3: higher HR lowered the odds of finding the exergame *Stressful* as well (Table 6). Overall, these findings point to the fact that the individuals' responses to different types of games are specific and individual preferences as well as physical or cognitive abilities to engage with a particular game type must be carefully modeled.

Indeed, when we explored the relationship between psychometric indices of state stress after each game (obtained from STAI-6), general PSS, and UCLA loneliness, as predictors of playing the game again, we found that those with higher loneliness scores were less likely to play again (95%CI OR:1.016 to 1.214, p = .021). Although there were interaction trends, anxiety (STAI-6) and stress sensitivity (PSS) were not significant predictors of desire to replay (Fig. 6).

Table 6. Logit GEE test of the effect of physiological responses on SA

Subjective post-game evaluations (SA)	Cortisol $Wald\ \chi^2_{(df=2)},\ p$ Posthoc: Exp(B) [a]	Heart Rate (HR) $Wald\ \chi^2_{(df=2)},\ p$ Posthoc: Exp(B)	Eletrodermal activity (EDA) $Wald\ \chi^2_{(df=2)},\ p$ Posthoc: Exp(B)
Difficult	NS[b]	NS	NS
Stressful	NS	**7.99, p < 0.02** *EG: 95%CI = 1.0 to 1.1*	**12.0, p < .002** *MG: 95% CI = .57 to .98*
Mental Wellness	NS	NS	**12.9, p < .002** *MG: 95% CI = 1.15 to 1.74*
Cognitive Stimulation	**6.29, p = .043** *CR: 95%CI = .21 to .77*	**5.58, p = .06** *CR 95%CI: .68 to .99*	NS
Intense	NS	NS	NS
Frustrating	NS	NS	NS
Like to play again	**12.4 p < .002** *MG: 95% CI = .1 to .48*	NS	**4.6 p < .10** *MG: 95% CI = 1.06 to 1.42*

a *OR > 1: increasing physiological response decreases the likelihood of SA being a "yes" and OR < 1: increasing physiological response increases the likelihood of SA being a "yes"*
b *NS: statistically not significant p > 0.1*

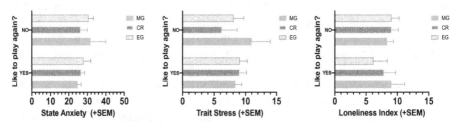

Fig. 6. Effects of personal traits on final SA. State anxiety was measured from SATI-6 at the end of each session. Trait stress was measured from PSS questionnaire and Loneliness from UCLA loneliness index.

4 Discussion

4.1 Principle Findings

This repeated measures crossover study design (Fig. 1) deployed AGPHA model [18] (depicted in Fig. 2) across different stimuli in a within-subject analysis to extend our previous work [17, 22] and illustrate that the PA and SAs of the health benefits of digital playing produce quantifiable physiological effects that correlate with individuals' engagement with the gaming experience.

We hypothesized (H1) that if an individual considered digital games to be important for health (positive PA), then they would be paying more attention and effort to the game and elicit stronger physiological responses. Indeed, we observed significant differences in cortisol and EDA levels even prior to engaging with the game (Fig. 3). Differences in PA of health benefits were also associated with personal differences in PSS (although there was no relation between PSS and final appraisal of desire to replay). This confirms our expectation that higher anticipation of health benefits, together with higher sensitivity to stress would be associated with higher levels of stress for which cortisol and EDA are surrogate variables. In contrast, the relationship between physiological variables and final SA (Fig. 4) were not as clearly distinct as were the relationships between physiological variables and PA (Fig. 3).

It has to be noted that in the short run, stress is not necessarily a maladaptive phenomenon, and it should rather be interpreted as a state of readiness to take on the physical and cognitive demands of a new challenge. According to Lazarus' theory, it is not just this physiological response, but the secondary appraisal of the challenge that moderate this initial physiological response.

Therefore, we also hypothesized (H2) that if higher levels of physiological response were caused by increased effort and were associated with positive SA (*Stimulating, Good for Mental Health*), then we would observe increased desire to replay. Conversely, if increased physiological response were associated with negative SA (*Difficult, Stressful, Frustrating, Useless*), then we would expect a reduced desire to replay.

We found a game-dependent support for H2 (Table 5) that further corroborated the appraisal theory (Table 5): higher EDA during MG (Session 1, the most familiar type of game with highest anticipation of cognitive relevance) increased the *Stressful* SA and lowered the likelihood of finding MGs *Good for Mental Health*. In this session, higher EDA and cortisol also lowered the *Desire to Play Again*. These relationships were not found for other game types.

This observation is concordant with our early assumption that the connotation of cognitive fitness with game-training put pressure on the player's self-esteem and become stressful experiences. According to Lazarus, individuals cope with stress differently: some avoid it (those who would be stressed by the game and decide to not play again), and some approach it (those who try harder to overcome it.) The changes in physiological variables (especially HR) in relation to SA elucidate this point: Higher HR during MG and EG decreased the likelihood of finding the brain training games *Stressful*. Higher HR during CR was associated with finding the game *Cognitively Stimulating*. These suggest that increased physiological arousal was not necessarily related to increased self-evaluative stress, but due to increases engagement with the challenge of the game. This underlines the importance of avoiding reductionist and purely quantitative or purely qualitative methods in design and evaluation of health technologies.

4.2 Implications for Digital Health Game Design

At present, given the small and homogenous sample (in terms of education, ethnicity, cognitive and physical abilities), we will avoid speculations about the direction and significance of our physiological findings. As others have shown as well, interpretations of physiological variations, must account for variations that arise from individual coping characteristics [30, 32]. We suffice to emphasize that our study also shows that perceptual and coping strategies are important moderators of physiological responses. Even when the same individual is tested repeatedly, physiological factors alone could not fully explain variations that arise from experiencing different game types (Fig. 5). The transactional theory of stress appraisal and coping [19] may provide a more comprehensive empirical framework for game design and evaluation in healthcare contexts.

Previous studies of older player's preferences have repeatedly shown that casual games and digital puzzles (such as those played in Session 1) are more preferred by older adults than simulation games like CR or physical games like our EG [10, 14, 34]. The CR and EG were less familiar to our players, and their cognitive and physical 'toll' varied with participants' attitudes (SA) and how much each player took interest in engaging with them. For example, EG was not considered *Useless*, and those who put more effort in it (evidenced by increased HR) were less likely to find it *Stressful*, yet nearly half of the sample did not wish to play it again.

This observation raises the question: To what extent can a transactional model of stress appraisal predict older adults' desire to replay a game? There are several theoretical frameworks that often deploy flow or self-determination theories to address this question. We have looked at the problem from a different perspective and have found that subjective variables that link to challenge, competence and enjoyment are not sufficient to explain individual variations in desire to replay.

For instance, we found no statistically significant relationship between the SA variables such as finding the game *Difficult*, *Frustrating*, *Stressful* or *Intense* and the *Desire to Play Again*. Instead, SAs of *Good for Mental Hea*lth or *Cognitively Stimulating* were both better predictors of interest in replaying, and also associated with physiological responses, albeit only in Session 1 (Table 6). The type of game that individuals like to play can also depend on social factors such as loneliness (Fig. 6). Thus, in studying complex media such as digital games, not only the momentary experience of the play, but also the entire context in which the game finds meaning within one's lifestyle and phenomenological experience must be accounted for.

We should also note that the fact that the majority of the participants found the experiences 'enjoyable' was confounded by the fact that they were enjoying the social interactions and learning about new topics while returning to each session. This is corroborated by the fact that anticipatory stress (Session 1) was more obvious in the first encounter with our team.

Design factors that inform game design for older adults emphasize pleasure and connection [35, 36], cognitive stimulation and mastery [37], and physical accessibility [38]. Martsen et al. have conducted several scoping reviews of the application of games in digital health to highlight that while many studies focus on functional applicability of presumably beneficial games few quantitative studies pay attention to **what** older adults wish to play [34, 39]. Because games are communication media, games for older adults must be designed for cultural [15, 40] and socioeconomic [40] inclusiveness too. On the other hand, there is a lack of experimental frameworks that would enable researchers to cross-compare the efficacy of different genres of games in different health domains [13, 39]. We propose that the mixed methods approach in AGPHA can inform design and personalization of digital games intended for healthcare applications for older adults.

We have so far tested the AGPHA framework from two different perspectives arising from Lazarus' transactional theory. In the first analysis, we focused on cognitive abilities (namely differences in MoCA scores) as predictors of primary and secondary appraisal of the games, as well as physiological responses to each [22]. In this current analysis, we focused on PA of the potential health benefits of playing (which were not dependent on MoCA) yet predicted differences both in appraisal and in physiological response to different games. Both these studies reveal quantifiable differences that arise from variations in personal factors (such as MoCA, loneliness and PA of game benefits) together with experiential responses (game-dependent appraisals and physiological reactions).

5   Conclusions, Limitations and Future Work

The aim of this pilot study was to examine the sensitivity of the AGPHA framework to test the hypotheses that differences in PA of the health-benefits of digital play predict variations in physiological response to the game (H1), and that interactions between appraisal and physiological response to the game predict the desire to replay (H2). The most important finding of this study is that PA of the game's benefits (in the case of this study framed in the context of cognitive health) was associated with significant differences in stress states (as measured by cortisol and EDA) even prior to engaging with the game. Our observations support the appraisal theory and underline the importance of continuous and iterative monitoring of perceptual and physiological responses in determining the playability, as well as acceptability of different games to the same individual.

Given the small sample size, we acknowledge that our findings may not be fully immune to the problem of multiple comparisons. While a repeated-measures study mitigates the small sample size to some extent, the fact that older adults are a heterogeneous group with diverse cognitive and physical abilities, or medical history, complicates studies such as this. An important bias in the current study arises from the fact that, as we have shown in previous work, the participant in this study had already higher opinions about the advantages of digital gaming. To have a positive attitude is likely to have mitigated the magnitude and the dynamics of the negative affect caused by playing non favorite games. Another limitation comes from the study design, which was not randomized, and therefore we expect that the levels of anticipatory stress were diminished by becoming increasingly familiar with our protocol.

In future work, we must repeat these experiments over a longer period of time, to validate the AGPHA framework by testing the interactions between familiarity and practice of favorite and non-favorite genres of digital games.

Acknowledgements. This paper is part of an empirical investigation of Finding Better Games for Older Adults supported by the seed funding from Concordia University's Office of Research and PERFORM Centre. We thank the following research assistants who were involved in data collection, Mahsa Mirgholami, Kate Li and Anna Smirnova. Logistic support from McGill Centre for Integrative Neuroscience (mcin-cnim.ca), the Ageing + Communication + Technologies (ACT) network (http://actproject.ca/), and Technoculture, Arts and Games (TAG) Centre (tag.hexagram.ca) is acknowledged.

References

1. De Schutter, B., Malliet, S.: The older player of digital games: a classification based on perceived need satisfaction. Communications **39**(1), 67–88 (2014)
2. Kaufman, D., et al.: Older adults' digital gameplay. Simul. Gaming **47**(4), 465–489 (2016)
3. Narme, P.: Benefits of game-based leisure activities in normal aging and dementia. Geriatr. Psychol. Neuropsychiatr. Vieil. **14**(4), 420–428 (2016)
4. Anguera, J.A., et al.: Video game training enhances cognitive control in older adults. Nature **501**(7465), 97–101 (2013)
5. Li, J., et al.: The social effects of exergames on older adults: systematic review and metric analysis. J. Med. Internet Res. **20**(6), e10486 (2018)
6. Taler, V., Deary, I.J., Altschul, D.M.: Playing analog games is associated with reduced declines in cognitive function: a 68-year longitudinal cohort study. J. Gerontol.: Ser. B **75**(3), 474–482 (2020)
7. Zhang, F., Kaufman, D.: Physical and cognitive impacts of digital games on older adults. J. Appl. Gerontol. **35**(11), 1189–1210 (2016)
8. Coughlan, G., et al.: Toward personalized cognitive diagnostics of at-genetic-risk Alzheimer's disease. Proc. Natl. Acad. Sci. U.S.A. **116**(19), 9285–9292 (2019)
9. Mandryk, R.L., Birk, M.V.: The potential of game-based digital biomarkers for modeling mental health. JMIR Ment. Health **6**(4), e13485 (2019)
10. Chesham, A., et al.: What older people like to play: genre preferences and acceptance of casual games. JMIR Serious Games **5**(2), e8 (2017)
11. Loos, E., Zonneveld, A.: Silver gaming: serious fun for seniors? In: Zhou, J., Salvendy, G. (eds.) Human Aspects of IT for the Aged Population. Healthy and Active Aging. LNCS, vol. 9755, pp. 330–341. Springer, Cham (2016). https://doi.org/10.1007/978-3-319-39949-2_32
12. Blocker, K.A., Wright, T.J., Boot, W.R.: Gaming preferences of aging generations. Gerontechnology **12**(3), 174 (2014)
13. Loos, E., Kaufman, D.: Positive impact of exergaming on older adults' mental and social well-being: in search of evidence. In: Zhou, J., Salvendy, G. (eds.) Human Aspects of IT for the Aged Population. Applications in Health, Assistance, and Entertainment, vol. 10927, pp. 101–112. Springer, Cham (2018). https://doi.org/10.1007/978-3-319-92037-5_9
14. Kaufman, D., et al.: Benefits of digital gameplay for older adults: does game type make a difference? Int. J. Aging Res. (2019)
15. Khalili-Mahani, N., et al.: For whom the games toll: a qualitative and intergenerational evaluation of what is serious in games for older adults. Comput. Games J. **9**(2), 221–244 (2020). https://doi.org/10.1007/s40869-020-00103-7
16. Ferguson, C.J.: Clinicians' attitudes toward video games vary as a function of age, gender and negative beliefs about youth: a sociology of media research approach. Comput. Hum. Behav. **52**, 379–386 (2015)
17. Khalili-Mahani, N., de Schutter, B., Sawchuk, K.: The relationship between the seniors' appraisal of cognitive-training games and game-related stress is complex: a mixed-methods study. In: Stephanidis, C., Antona, M., Gao, Q., Zhou, J. (eds.) HCI International 2020 – Late Breaking Papers: Universal Access and Inclusive Design. LNCS, vol. 12426, pp. 586–607. Springer, Cham (2020). https://doi.org/10.1007/978-3-030-60149-2_45

18. Khalili-Mahani, N., De Schutter, B.: Affective game planning for health applications: quantitative extension of gerontoludic design based on the appraisal theory of stress and coping. JMIR Serious Games 7(2), e13303 (2019)
19. Lazarus, R.S., Folkman, S.: Transactional theory and research on emotions and coping. Eur. J. Pers. 1(3), 141–169 (2020)
20. Hubert, W., de Jong-Meyer, R.: Autonomic, neuroendocrine, and subjective responses to emotion-inducing film stimuli. Int. J. Psychophysiol. 11(2), 131–140 (1991)
21. Goodman-Vincent, E., Roy, M., Khalili-Mahani, N.: Affective game planning for playing the pain. In: Extended Abstracts of the 2020 Annual Symposium on Computer-Human Interaction in Play, pp. 122–128 (2020)
22. Khalili-Mahani, N., et al.: Reflective and reflexive stress responses of older adults to three gaming experiences in relation to their cognitive abilities: mixed methods crossover study. JMIR Ment. Health 7(3), e12388 (2020)
23. Cohen, S.: Perceived stress in a probability sample of the United States. In: The social Psychology of Health, pp. 31–67. Sage Publications, Inc., Thousand Oaks (1988)
24. Russell, D.W.: UCLA Loneliness Scale (Version 3): Reliability, validity, and factor structure. J. Pers. Assess. 66(1), 20–40 (1996)
25. Nasreddine, Z.S., et al.: The montreal cognitive assessment, MoCA: a brief screening tool for mild cognitive impairment. J. Am. Geriatr. Soc. 53(4), 695–699 (2005)
26. Marteau, T.M., Bekker, H.: The development of a six-item short-form of the state scale of the Spielberger State—Trait Anxiety Inventory (STAI). Br. J. Clin. Psychol. 31(3), 301–306 (2011)
27. Roscoe, A.H.: Heart rate as a psychophysiological measure for in-flight workload assessment. Ergonomics 36(9), 1055–1062 (1993)
28. Critchley, H.D.: Review: electrodermal responses: what happens in the brain. Neuroscientist 8(2), 132–142 (2016)
29. Kirschbaum, C., Hellhammer, D.H.: Salivary cortisol in psychobiological research: an overview. Neuropsychobiology 22(3), 150–169 (1989)
30. Christopoulos, G.I., Uy, M.A., Yap, W.J.: The body and the brain: measuring skin conductance responses to understand the emotional experience. Organ. Res. Methods 22(1), 394–420 (2016)
31. Dedovic, K., et al.: The montreal imaging stress task: using functional imaging to investigate the effects of perceiving and processing psychosocial stress in the human brain. J. Psychiatry Neurosci. 30(5), 319–325 (2005)
32. Vine, S.J., Moore, L.J., Wilson, M.R.: An integrative framework of stress, attention, and visuomotor performance. Front. Psychol. 7, 1671 (2016)
33. Luszczynska, A., Scholz, U., Schwarzer, R.: The general self-efficacy scale: multicultural validation studies. J. Psychol. 139(5), 439–457 (2005)
34. Marston, H.R., Smith, S.T.: Interactive videogame technologies to support independence in the elderly: a narrative review. Games Health J. 1(2), 139–152 (2012)
35. De Schutter, B., Brown, J.A.: Digital games as a source of enjoyment in later life. Games Cult. 11(1–2), 28–52 (2015)
36. Genoe, R., et al.: E-leisure and older adults: findings from an international exploratory study. Ther. Recreat. J. 52(1), 1–18 (2018)
37. Boot, W.R., Souders, D., Charness, N., Blocker, K., Roque, N., Vitale, T.: The gamification of cognitive training: older adults' perceptions of and attitudes toward digital game-based interventions. In: Zhou, J., Salvendy, G. (eds.) Human Aspects of IT for the Aged Population. Design for Aging, vol. 9754, pp. 290–300. Springer, Cham (2016). https://doi.org/10.1007/978-3-319-39943-0_28

38. Gerling, K.M., Schulte, F.P., Smeddinck, J., Masuch, M.: Game design for older adults: effects of age-related changes on structural elements of digital games. In: Herrlich, M., Malaka, R., Masuch, M. (eds.) Entertainment Computing. LNCS, vol. 7522, pp. 235–242. Springer, Heidelberg (2012). https://doi.org/10.1007/978-3-642-33542-6_20

39. Marston, H.R., Kroll, M., Fink, D., Poveda, R., Gschwind, Y.J.: Digital game technology and older adults. In: Marston, H.R., Freeman, S., Musselwhite, C. (eds.) Mobile e-Health. HCIS, pp. 149–171. Springer, Cham (2017). https://doi.org/10.1007/978-3-319-60672-9_7

40. Vale Costa, L., Veloso, A.I., Loos, E.: Age stereotyping in the game context: introducing the game-ageism and age-gameism phenomena. In: Zhou, J., Salvendy, G. (eds.) Human Aspects of IT for the Aged Population. Social Media, Games and Assistive Environments. LNCS, vol. 11593, pp. 245–255. Springer, Cham (2019). https://doi.org/10.1007/978-3-030-22015-0_19

Designing a Somatosensory Interactive Game of Lower Extremity Muscle Rehabilitation for the Elderly

Chien-Hsiang Chang[1], Kao-Hua Liu[2(✉)], Hiroyuki Kajihara[3], Wei-Chih Lien[4], Peng-Ting Chen[5], Atsushi Hiyama[2], Yang-Cheng Lin[1], Chien-Hsu Chen[1], and Masahiko Inami[2]

[1] Department of Industrial Design, National Cheng Kung University, Tainan 70101, Taiwan
{lyc0914,chenhsu}@mail.ncku.edu.tw
[2] Research Center for Advanced Science and Technology, The University of Tokyo, Tokyo 153-8904, Japan
{maarkliu,hiyama,inami}@star.rcast.u-tokyo.ac.jp
[3] Department of Leisure Regimen Management, College of Tourism, Tainan University of Technology, Tainan 710302, Taiwan
tq0016@mail.tut.edu.tw
[4] Department of Physical Medicine and Rehabilitation, National Cheng Kung University Hospital, Tainan 70403, Taiwan
lwclwhab@ms8.hinet.net
[5] Department of Biomedical Engineering, National Cheng Kung University, Tainan 70101, Taiwan
chen@ncku.edu.tw

Abstract. Somatosensory game-based rehabilitation has recently experienced rapid increases in demand and scale in the health promotion market. However, the existing research on this topic mostly focuses on treatment efficacy rather than game usability, experience feedback, and the needs of the elderly when experiencing the games. To fill this knowledge gap, we designed a somatosensory interactive game focusing on lower extremity rehabilitation, explored the intention and motivation of elderly patients, and documented the difficulties and needs of these patients in using the game. We enrolled 15 elderly subjects with lower extremity degeneration and collected data using a one-group pre-test and post-test experiment. For the pre-test, the subjects were treated with a traditional lower extremity rehabilitation program for 1 min, followed by a 5-min questionnaire survey. Next, the subjects were asked to play the somatosensory interactive game for 1 min, followed by 15 min of post-test questionnaire survey and interview. The results showed a significant difference between the two types of rehabilitation in the us-ability constructs of "fun", "liking", "self-expression", "self-understanding", "intention", and "fatigue" in elderly subjects with no prior rehabilitation experience, indicating that, compared to the traditional ones, the rehabilitation game performed better in introducing rehabilitation to the elders, enhancing their motivation, intention, and increasing their self-confidence. The results also showed that the status of lower extremity disease in elderly users did not affect gameplay. Lastly, we provide suggestions for further improvements in

© Springer Nature Switzerland AG 2021
Q. Gao and J. Zhou (Eds.): HCII 2021, LNCS 12787, pp. 23–37, 2021.
https://doi.org/10.1007/978-3-030-78111-8_2

the design of the operational interface, software, and hardware of lower extremity rehabilitation-dedicated somatosensory interactive games.

Keywords: Somatosensory interactive game · Exergame · Lower extremity · Rehabilitation

1   Introduction

Due to the aging of the global population, the increasing prevalence of degenerative diseases such as degenerative arthritis and sarcopenia, and the increasing number of trauma patients in need of rehabilitation have resulted in an increasing demand for rehabilitation in elderly people. The estimated global market value of rehabilitation equipment was USD 10.53 billion in 2016 and is projected to rise at a compound annual growth rate of 6.0% from 2014 to 2025 [1]. In particular, the integration of somatosensory or video games with rehabilitation is increasingly valued, the effectiveness of which has been verified [2]. Research on the application of somatosensory games to lower extremity motor rehabilitation in elderly people has mostly focused on treatment efficacy and seldom analyzed the operational difficulty and use intention of elderly users, rarely analyzing their needs regarding the content and form of rehabilitation regimens. Therefore, this study designed a somatosensory game-based rehabilitation method based on the rehabilitation needs of elderly people and compared it to a traditional rehabilitation method to provide deeper insight into the response and feedback of elderly people to somatosensory game-based rehabilitation. In addition to rehabilitation treatment, the elderly subjects in this study were surveyed by questionnaires, observed, and interviewed, with quantitative analyses of the questionnaire data of different subject groups performed in conjunction with qualitative analysis of the interview results to reveal the factors influencing elderly rehabilitation. The analysis results of this study may provide a reference for the development of rehabilitation games to promote the health of elderly people. The results of this study will ultimately lead to the formation of a somatosensory interactive game-based rehabilitation system with tunable parameters that is suitable for lower extremity rehabilitation of elderly people. Lastly, this study proposed several design recommendations as a reference for relevant research.

2   Literature Review

From a theoretic perspective and with a focus on the research issue, a literature review was conducted on the global status of elderly care and game markets and on degenerative arthritis, providing a research context for the design of the somatosensory game-based rehabilitation system in this study. Based on literature compilation and analysis, the illness characteristics and rehabilitation needs of elderly people were retrieved, which were then integrated with video games and somatosensory technology to develop a prototype of a somatosensory game-based rehabilitation system.

2.1 Global Status

With the increasing proportion of elderly people in the population, industrial development and financial investment have long been made in various fields relevant to the health
of the elderly. In recent years, due to the rapid development of various hardware technologies, relevant information and communication technology (ICT) has been introduced to
various elderly populations, forming a popular field with products aimed at middle-aged
and elderly people gradually emerging on the market. Zion Market Research reported
that the global market for disabled and elderly assistive technology was worth an estimated USD 18.7 billion in 2017, and is projected to reach USD 30.82 billion by 2024,
with a compound annual growth rate of 7.4%. This market includes products such as
walkers, wheelchairs, hoists, bathroom safety and assistive products, hearing aids, readers, and activity monitors [3]. In addition to product use in general medical institutions,
product use for home care also accounts for a large market share that is soon expected
to generate higher income.

At present, the global elderly care market mainly comprises two product types;
namely, 1) home and assistive devices and 2) medicines. In 2018, the market share
of home and assistive devices was the highest, with a compound annual growth rate
projected to reach 6.6% by 2025. Meantime, the global elderly care market can be
divided into three parts: home care, institutional care, and adult daycare. In 2018, home
care accounted for the largest market share and is expected to have the highest compound
annual growth rate by 2025. Home care is further subdivided into health care and non-
health care, with the former referring to physical therapy, telemedicine, conservative
treatment, and hospice care and the latter referring to personal care and rehabilitation.

In contrast, regarding the global game market, 1 billion players across the globe are
willing to pay for games and players had a spending power of USD 108.9 billion in
2017, with digital revenue accounting for 87% of the market value. Mobile and tablet
games increased by 19% year on year to USD 46.1 billion, accounting for 42% of the
market. Moreover, mobile and tablet games are important tools for exercise game-based
weight loss, rehabilitation of chronic patients, and adjustment of sedentary lifestyles and
have been widely adopted by all age populations, gradually becoming mainstream in the
market. The main health-related game categories include rehabilitation, cognitive brain
training, health management, and weight loss management.

However, the health industry, which includes interactive technical equipment, rehabilitation technologies, and medical equipment for long-term care or home care of
middle-aged and elderly populations, is an integrated and interdisciplinary industry in
which innovative technologies and products initially developed in other industries are
often tentatively applied. For instance, ICT is currently being applied—tentatively on
a large scale—to value-added activities in the health industry such as preventive health
care, exercises and fitness activities, and medical treatment, leading to the establishment
of intelligent long-term care, rehabilitation, and healthcare, covering daily activities of
middle-aged and elderly populations such as leisure, social intercourse, diets, studying, travel, and security, as well as various activity spaces such as homes, communities,
institutions, and hospitals.

As shown above, with the continued aging of the global populations, the elderly health
industry has become the main direction for market development and investment. In recent

years, with the rapid development of various hardware technologies, the introduction of related ICT to various types of equipment for the elderly has also become a popular trend. However, the statistics reported in the literature also clearly show, that as far as the current global elderly care market is concerned, home and assistive devices account for the highest market share, mostly due to the development of the game industry. This indicates that the integration of assistive rehabilitation devices with games presents an essential development mode, which is the research focus of the present study.

Rehabilitation equipment is divided into four product categories: body support, exercise, mobile, and daily assistive equipment. The market for home rehabilitation products and services is divided into several segments: positioning devices, general assistive devices, body support devices (e.g., walkers, canes, crutches, and arm and shoulder slings), and wheelchairs. The global market for home rehabilitation products and services was worth an estimated USD 88 billion in 2017 and the is estimated to increase by a compound annual growth rate of 8.3% over in 2018–2026 to reach a projected market value of USD 160 billion by 2026 (Transparency Market Research, 2018), namely considerable output values and profits.

2.2 Degenerative Arthritis (DA)

DA, also known as osteoarthritis, is the most common form of arthritis [4]. It is a pathological phenomenon in which excessive articular cartilage wear results in increased bone formation at the joint surfaces and consequent narrowing of the joint space. DA most commonly occurs at the knee joint [5]. The knee joint cartilage is composed of chondrocytes, their surrounding extracellular matrix, and interstitial water [6]. A normal knee joint contains three articular surfaces formed by the femur, tibia, and patella; namely, one surface between the medial femur and tibia, one between the lateral femur and tibia, and one between the femur and the patella. When the knee joint is subject to repeated wear, the cartilage surfaces are damaged or even peeled off [7]. When the knee articular cartilage has problems, it cannot bear loads and will fail to act as a cushion to distribute compressive forces, resulting in a series of changes in the articular cartilage and, in turn, causing wear of the articular surfaces and, eventually, degenerative knee arthritis. The knee joint is the largest weight-bearing joint in the human body, serving to bear loads and provide high motility. Therefore, patients with this disease often present with the following symptoms of physical discomfort:

Pain. Knee joint pain is one of the most common symptoms and is also the leading reason for clinic visits. The continuous wear of the articular surface leads to the formation of osteophytes. With swelling and deformation of the knee joint and loosening of the peripheral ligaments, the knee joint becomes unstable, which aggravates articular surface wear, initiating a vicious cycle in which the patients suffer [8].

Stiffness. The knee joint is often stiff after long periods of motionlessness, especially after sitting for a long time or when waking, which is often mitigated by movement of the knee joint [9].

Swelling. The soft tissue around the patient's knee joint is swollen, either intermittently (increased synovial liquid) or constantly (thickening of the articular capsule or extensive osteophyte formation).

Deformation. The cartilage becomes roughened when worn and the joint gradually undergoes deformation, which decreases joint mobility so that it cannot be straightened, especially the medial knee joint, which is prone to wear, causing O-shaped legs.

Muscular Atrophy. Activity is reduced due to pain, causing atrophy of the quadriceps and hamstrings and consequent different thigh thicknesses. At this time, excessive use of the healthy side for activities will cause overload on that side, leading to degenerative knee arthritis.

Activity Restriction. Due to low knee joint mobility, patients often experience constraints such as difficulty in squatting, walking instability, and higher difficulty in going down stairs compare to up, which prevents them from engaging in daily functional activities such as jogging, resulting in poor quality of life [10].

Given that current treatment regimens aim to reduce joint pain and stiffness, improve mobility, reduce psychological stress, and maintain patient independence [11], this study outlines five major non-pharmacological rehabilitation methods for degenerative knee arthritis.

Cryotherapy and Thermotherapy. Cryotherapy can be used to relieve swelling and pain due to acute joint inflammation and swelling. In the case of chronic inflammation, stiff but not swollen joints may be treated with thermotherapies such as a heated blanket or hot water. In the hospital, deep thermotherapy such as infrared and ultrasound treatment can also be used to promote blood circulation, relax muscles, and improve collagen extensibility [12].

Hydrotherapy. Hydrotherapy provides many beneficial effects for arthritis such as reducing edema, relieving pain, and reducing loads [13].

Acupuncture, Electrical Stimulation, and Interference Current Therapy. These treatment methods can block the signal transduction pathways of pain-sensing nerves and stimulate the brain to produce natural endorphins to reduce the feeling of pain.

Assistive Devices. The use of assistive devices such as knee pads, crutches, and walkers can reduce pain, maintain function, and avoid joint deformation to ensure patient safety [14].

Exercises. Therapeutic exercises cover a range of targeted physical activities intended to improve muscle strength, neuromotor control, joint motion range, and aerobic fitness. One of the main purposes of exercises is to improve muscle strength, as lack of muscle strength is a common knee joint weakness. Enhancing lower extremity strength can reduce load on the knee joint, reduce pain, and improve physical function [15].

2.3 SG and Muscle Strength Rehabilitation of Lower Limbs

As Taiwan's population ages, it is necessary to design products and services related to elders' demand to achieve the promotion of physical and mental health. Kristof and

Satran [16] indicated that interactive design must include three elements: (1) the information design, content, and the organization between users and products; (2) the interactive design, the interactive type of the product; and (3) the perception design, which integrates the above elements into the story script and storyboard, which is the contextual effect [17]. In conclusion, to attract the target group, an interactive device must not only have good interaction but also possess an acceptable appearance design. With modern digital technology, interactive devices have had multiple applications. Applying SGs to the medical field can improve patients' quality of life and motivation for rehabilitation, increase patients' attention, and convey knowledge and information through the games [18].

Recent studies have proved that video games (including SGs) can help patients in rehabilitation to recover motion function through high-intensity exercises [19]. For example, Nintendo WiiFit has been used for the rehabilitation of lower limb function [20]. In addition to the existing vehicles on the market, several studies developed their own rehabilitation devices.Taking a somatosensory rehabilitation game developed by Fietsgame (Dutch for cycling game), making the rehabilitation system more interesting through the game plots and visual effects. Adopting video games in lower limb rehabilitation has been studied for rehabilitation goals of improving balance and function recoveries such as walking ability and muscle strength. Different from the monotonous traditional rehabilitation, the somatosensory games can stimulate patients to have more motivation and sense of accomplishment. It can be conducted at home alone, which helps to improve the effect of in-home rehabilitation.

3   Experimental Methodology

This section addresses the game design concept and living lab procedure.

3.1   Game Flow Design

The game flow design was intended to integrate a fun Parkour game with a muscle sensor-based somatosensory device to mitigate mental fatigue during rehabilitation through game enjoyment. The game flow comprised four steps: (1) wearing a somatosensory knee pad; (2) selecting a game mode; (3) setting parameters; and (4) playing the game (Fig. 1). Then, using the Somatosensory Interaction and nostalgic game to provoke elders emotional resonance, and then increase their rehabilitation motivation. (Fig. 2).

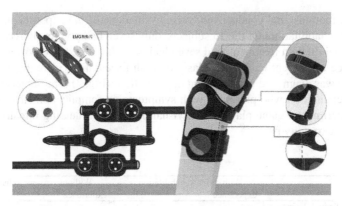

Fig. 1. Somatosensory knee pad developed in this study

Fig. 2. In-game scene

3.2   Usability for Elderly Persons

This study aimed to explore and analyze the rehabilitation intention, motivation, operational difficulty, and use needs of elderly people using lower extremity rehabilitation-dedicated somatosensory interactive games. This experiment used five-point questionnaires to quantify their subjective perceptions, while a semi-structured interview was used to collect qualitative data.

Subjects. This study was conducted at Meiyou Day Care in Tainan, Taiwan, which referred subjects suitable for this study. This study enrolled a total of 15 subjects, consisting of 5 males and 10 females with an average age of 78.4 years, all having normal expression and communication skills. The subject inclusion criteria were: subjects aged over 60 years who could autonomously flex and extend the knee with normal expression and cognitive abilities. Due to the need to engage in somatosensory interactive games during the treatment course, the patients were required to have normal cognitive abilities to understand and cooperate with the researchers, follow game instructions for required motions, and conduct subjective evaluations of the experiments after the game-based rehabilitation. Of the 15 subjects, only seven had previously received conventional rehabilitation treatment, and seven had been diagnosed with lower extremity disease (three underwent knee arthroplasty on both knees, three were diagnosed with DA, and one was diagnosed with hip joint degeneration) (Fig. 3). The subject exclusion criteria were: subjects who presented with symptoms or complications that interfered with the experimental game play such as visual impairment, hearing impairment, and severe lower-extremity pain.

	With prior rehabilitation experience		Without prior rehabilitation experience	
With confirmed diagnosis of lower extremity disease		3 females		4 females
	0 males		0 males	
Without confirmed diagnosis of lower extremity disease		1 female		2 females
	3 males		2 males	

Fig. 3. Study subjects

Experimental Design. This study adopted a one-group pre-test and post-test experimental design. Questionnaire items were designed on the basis of modifications of the System Usability Scale (SUS) consisting of 10 usability constructs; namely, "fun," "liking," "performance," "stress," "convenience," "necessity," "understanding," "complexity," "intention," and "fatigue," each scored on a five-point Likert scale. The objectives of this study were to explore and analyze the rehabilitation intention, motivation, operational difficulty, and use needs of elderly people using lower extremity rehabilitation-dedicated somatosensory interactive games. As detailed below, the experimental process was divided into three stages: (1) traditional lower extremity rehabilitation; (2) somatosensory interactive game-based rehabilitation; and (3) semi-structured interview.

Questionnaire Survey After Traditional Lower Extremity Rehabilitation. In the traditional lower extremity rehabilitation, the knee-straightening exercises included asking the subjects to raise their legs while being seated. The subjects sat on comfortable chairs with their feet relaxed and placed perpendicularly on the ground as the researchers assisted the subjects in wearing knee pads. After the researchers provided instruction, the subjects performed the leg-raise exercises for one minute, followed by a data collection step in which the researchers used a five-point questionnaire to ask the subjects about their experiences or feelings regarding the traditional lower extremity rehabilitation, with responses such as "I think the traditional mode is interesting." The subjects responded orally and the researcher assisted them in completing the questionnaire (Table 1).

Table 1. Questionnaire for traditional rehabilitation

Questionnaire for traditional rehabilitation
1. I think the traditional mode is interesting
2. I don't like to exercise in the traditional mode
3. I think I performed well during the exercise
4. I feel stressed when exercising in the traditional mode
5. I think it is convenient to use the traditional mode for exercises
6. I think I have to do this exercise, but it is not the exercise I prefer
7. I feel that the traditional mode allows me to understand my exercise status
8. I think this rehabilitation method, process, and wear are too complicated
9. Overall, I would be willing to continue to use the traditional mode for exercise
10. In the long run, this training method will make me tired

Questionnaire Survey After Somatosensory Interactive Game-Based Lower Extremity Rehabilitation. Before the experimental gameplay, the researchers orally explained to the subjects the game operation and allowed the subjects to practice the game by playing one to two times to ensure that the subjects correctly understood how to operate the game. This explanation-practice step took approximately 3 min. Next, the subjects sat in a comfortable chair with their feet relaxed and placed perpendicular to the ground. The researchers assisted the subjects in wearing the knee pads (Fig. 4) and projected a game screen on the wall in front of the subjects. The types of games in the experiment were randomly selected. When the subjects saw a crocodile/eagle moving within a specified range, they were required to kick the foot of the leg wearing the knee pad as if they were kicking a ball to move the animal away, so that the knee joint underwent angular movement. It took one minute to complete a game and the subjects were permitted to play it one more time, depending on their physical strength and intention. During the game, the caregivers of the daycare center accompanied the subjects and assisted the researchers in explaining and asking questions to the subjects. The researcher asked the subjects to speak aloud their thoughts or questions while they were playing the game; meanwhile, the researcher also made close observations and recorded data. After the game, the researchers used a five-point questionnaire to ask the subjects about their experiences or feelings regarding the somatosensory interactive game-based lower extremity rehabilitation. The subjects responded orally and the researcher assisted them in completing the questionnaire (Table 2).

Semi-structured interview. The semi-structured interview included four constructs; namely, usability, feedback function, game interface, and home rehabilitation, that were used to understand the users' needs and ideas for rehabilitation games. The interview topics were as follows:

1. What do you think about the comfort of knee pads?
2. Do you pay attention to the game achievement after each game?

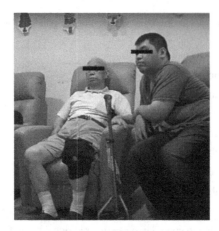

Fig. 4. Study subject

Table 2. Questionnaire for somatosensory interactive game-based rehabilitation

Questionnaire for somatosensory interactive game-based rehabilitation
1. I think the game mode is interesting
2. I don't like to exercise using the game
3. I think I performed well during the exercise
4. I feel stressed when exercising in the game mode
5. I think it is convenient to use the game mode for exercises
6. I think I have to do this exercise, but it is not the exercise I want
7. I feel that the game mode allows me to understand my exercise status
8. I think this rehabilitation method, process, and wear are too complicated
9. Overall, I would be willing to continue to use the game mode for exercise
10. In the long run, this training method will make me tired

3. Does the game achievement have any effect on rehabilitation?
4. What's your opinion on the music or audio feedback of the game?
5. Is the screen easy to understand?
6. When kicking, does the picture respond accordingly?
7. What's your opinion on home rehabilitation instead of hospital rehabilitation?

4   Results

4.1   Quantitative Analysis (Questionnaire Data)

The quantitative analysis compared responses to the two types of rehabilitation methods between subjects who had prior rehabilitation experience and those who did not.

Among elderly subjects with prior rehabilitation experience, no significant difference was observed between the traditional and the video game-based rehabilitation techniques except for a difference in the degree of fun. Among elderly subjects without prior rehabilitation experience, significant differences were observed in the degree of fun, liking, self-expression, self-understanding, intention, and fatigue. The results showed that the video game-based rehabilitation method designed in this study performed equally well as the traditional method in subjects with prior rehabilitation experience except for the degree of fun, which was higher for the game-based method. Compared to traditional rehabilitation, the video game-based rehabilitation was accepted to a greater extent in elderly subjects without prior rehabilitation experience; it was more likely to trigger them to perform rehabilitation, reduce their resistance to long-term rehabilitation, and increase their rehabilitation intention.

In addition, this study also investigated the effect of a history of lower extremity disease on 10 usability constructs for each type of rehabilitation. The results showed no differences in usability constructs regardless of rehabilitation type or history of extremity disease (Tables 3 and 4). This finding further indicated that the use of the video game-based rehabilitation method designed in this study was independent of the history of lower extremity disease, that is, the game would not add difficulty or pressure to elderly users with a confirmed diagnosis of lower extremity disease. As with traditional rehabilitation, the video game-based method would not be unusable in elderly patients with certain health conditions. By adjusting game parameters, the game can be adapted to meet the varying needs of elderly users under different conditions, including those at different health levels.

Table 3. Independent sample T-tests for differences in 10 usability constructs between traditional and video game-based rehabilitation in subjects with prior rehabilitation experience versus subjects without.

Item	With prior rehabilitation experience p-value (two-sided)	Without prior rehabilitation experience p-value (two-sided)
Fun	0.003798221*	1.15248E-05*
Liking	0.783514876	0.025601259*
Self-expression	0.078730157	0.025656717*
Stress	0.551719095	0.196182975
Convenience	0.511563864	0.325787003
Necessity	0.796157301	0.79418593
Self-understanding	0.361496547	0.001135702*
Complexity	0.589289349	0.79418593
Intention	0.681847941	0.025601259*
Fatigue	0.182716763	0.043572454*

Table 4. Independent sample t-tests of the differences in 10 usability constructs between subjects with and without lower extremity disease for each type of rehabilitation

Item	Traditional rehabilitation p-value (two-sided)	Somatosensory interactive game-based rehabilitation p-value (two-sided)
Fun	0.095066	0.345726
Liking	0.875606	1
Self-expression	0.688606	0.233688
Stress	0.934908	0.535839
Convenience	0.458748	0.424868
Necessity	0.84688	0.458748
Self-understanding	0.156901	0.743406
Complexity	0.735007	0.223854
Intention	0.665818	0.212493
Fatigue	0.185071	0.61616

4.2 Qualitative Analysis

A semi-structured interview was conducted to provide insight into the subjective perception of somatosensory interactive game-based lower extremity rehabilitation in elderly people.

The results of the qualitative analysis revealed that the somatosensory interactive game developed in this study was easy to understand, with approachable cartoon characters such as ducks, crocodiles, eagles, and birds in bright and easily identifiable colors. Moreover, two game themes with adjustable game levels were available for selection. These characteristics allowed elderly users to undergo rehabilitation through a fun game as opposed to the boring and repetitive exercises of traditional therapy. The real-time feedback and scoring system provided by the game allowed elderly users to clearly understand their performance. Meantime, the game-based rehabilitation method helped the users to develop their concentration and improve their rehabilitation motivation and interest.

- "It's fun so I want to kick when I see the screen, and I can also understand my situation."
- "This is really fun. It will be really nice if this game can be used by the people in the rehabilitation center. By playing the game, the rehabilitation process can last long."
- "Use this eye to watch, and if you see the animal approaching quickly you must kick it, but please do not kick randomly as you need to focus"
- "Yes, if we have this kind of course here, we would install it for everyone to use, and everyone will rush to play"
- "If the system tells me that I score high in the game play, I will of course be happy"
- "When failing to hit the target, I feel lost, but I am happy when passing the game level."

This study also aimed to provide a deeper understanding of the difficulties faced by elderly users during the game-based rehabilitation and to analyze their needs regarding the form and content of lower-extremity somatosensory games to improve the humanistic value of these games. The semi-structured interview indicated the following improvements to the game-based rehabilitation method:

"I prefer the traditional rehabilitation method I have been using, as it involves both foot and waist movement, in contrast to this game-based method in which only such kicking movement is required."
"Have no idea to what extent I have exercised."

In addition, the interviews revealed that the intention of elderly people to continually undergo rehabilitation was largely dependent on persuasion from doctors and family members, even for traditional rehabilitation without much entertainment:

- "I will do what the doctor tells me to"
- "I will do it upon request, as this will be beneficial to me, and they ask me to do it because it is good to my health"
- "The game is fun, and I am also open to the traditional method while it is not much fun"
- "I am willing to try both methods"

5   Conclusion

This study conducted a semi-structured interview of elderly subjects to inform the design of the operational interface of the lower extremity rehabilitation-dedicated somatosensory interactive game to better meet the needs of these patients. The results of the qualitative analysis suggested the following improvements in the design of the operational interface, software, and hardware of lower extremity rehabilitation-dedicated somatosensory interactive games.

5.1 Operational Interface

Somatosensory interactive games are different from traditional rehabilitation tools in design. Simple and straightforward operational surface design are required to allow the easy operation of somatosensory interactive games.

5.2 Software

The software design parameters of lower extremity rehabilitation-dedicated somatosensory interactive games should be adjustable according to the needs of the patients, such as the ability to store rehabilitation data and adjust game time and speed, to assist rehabilitation practitioners or nursing staff in assessing individual situations of elderly patients and, in turn, track the rehabilitation status of these patients. In the future, additional rehabilitation exercises should be introduced to meet the rehabilitation needs of different body parts.

5.3 Hardware

Most subjects provided positive feedback on the comfort of the knee pads used for the somatosensory interactive game. As the muscle sensors may have had too high a sensitivity due to software design problems or individual differences, resulting in false-positive responses, a positioning system such as nine-axis sensors should be included in the hardware to increase stability and reduce game misoperation.

References

1. Grand View Research: Rehabilitation Devices/Equipment Market Size, Industry Report, 2025 (2017). https://www.grandviewresearch.com/industry-analysis/rehabilitation-products-marke. Accessed 20 April 2019
2. Lewis, G.N., Rosi, J.A.: Virtual reality games for movement rehabilitation in neurological conditions: how do we meet the needs and expectations of the users? Disabil. Rehabil. **34**, 1880–1886 (2012)
3. Zion Market Research (2019). https://www.giichinese.com.tw/publisher/zmr.shtml
4. Grelsamer, R.P., Loebl, S.: The Columbia Presbyterian Osteoarthritis Handbook: The Complete Guide to the Most Common Form of Arthritis. Wiley, New York (1997)
5. Kee, C.C., Harris, S., Booth, L.A., Rouser, G., McCoy, S.: Perspectives on the nursing management of osteoarthritis. Geriatr. Nurs. **19**, 19–28 (1998)
6. Monteforte, P., Rovetta, G.: Sonographic assessment of soft tissue alterations in osteoarthritis of the knee. Int. J. Tissue React. **21**, 19–23 (1999)
7. Fishkin, Z., Ritter, C., Ziv, I.: Changes in human knee ligament stiffness secondary to osteoarthritis. J. Orthop. Res. **20**, 204–207 (2002)
8. Wu, J., Epstein, M.: Joint contact mechanics in early stage of osteoarthritis. Med. Eng. Phys. **22**, 1–12 (2000)
9. Felson, D.T., Lawrence, R.C., Hochberg, M.C., McAlindon, T., Dieppe, P.A.: Osteoarthritis: new insights: part 2: treatment approaches. Ann. Intern. Med. **133**, 726–737 (2000)
10. Kaufman, K.R., Hughe, S.C., Morrey, B.F., Morrey, M., An, K.N.: Gait characteristics of patients with knee osteoarthritis. J. Biomech. **34**, 907–915 (2001)
11. Bradley, J.D., Brandt, K.D., Katz, B.P., Kalasinski, L.A., Ryan, S.I.: Treatment of knee osteoarthritis: relationship of clinical features of joint inflammation to the response to a nonsteroidal antiinflammatory drug or pure analgesic. J. Rheumatol. **19**, 1950–1954 (1992)
12. Oddis, C.V., Pennsylvania, P.: New perspectives on osteoarthritis. Am. J. Med. **100**, 10s–15s (1996)
13. Foley, A., Halbert, J., Hewitt, T., Crotty, M.: Does hydrotherapy improve strength and physical function in patients with osteoarthritis—a randomised controlled trial comparing a gym based and a hydrotherapy based strengthening programme. Ann. Rheum. Dis. **62**, 1162–1167 (2003)
14. Hsieh, L.F., Che, W.S., Chuang, C.C.: Arthritis rehabilitation. Fu-Jen J. Med. **2**, 17–43 (2004)
15. Fransen, M., McConnell, S., Harmer, A.R.: Exercise for osteoarthritis of the knee: a Cochrane systematic review. Br. J. Sports Med. **49**, 1554–1557 (2015)
16. Kristof, R., Satran, A.: Interactivity by Design: Creating and Communicating With new Media. AdobePress, Mountain View (1995)
17. Colautti, L., et al.: CREC:the role of serious games in improving flexibility in thinking in neuropsychological rehabilitation. Br. J. Educ. Technol. **49**, 717–727 (2018)
18. Ling, Y., Meer, L.P.T., Yumak, Z., Veltkamp, R.C.: Usability test of exercise game designed for rehabilitation of elderly patients after hip replacement surgery : pilot study. Advancing Digital Health and Open Science, vol 5, pp. 1–21 (2017)

19. Fung, V., Ho, A., Shaffer, J., Chung, E., Gomez, M.: Use of Nintendo Wii Fit in the rehabilitation of outpatients following total knee replacement: a preliminary randomised controlled trial. Physiotherapy. **98**(3), 183–188 (2012). https://doi.org/10.1016/j.physio.2012.04.001
20. Adlakha, S., Chhabra, D., Shukla, P.: Effectiveness of gamification for the rehabilitation of neurodegenerative disorders. Chaos, Solitons Fractals **140**, 1–11 (2020)

Tangible Chess for Dementia Patients – Playing with Conductive 3D Printed Figures on a Touchscreen

Christian Eichhorn[1]([✉]), David A. Plecher[1], Oleksandr Golovnya[1], Dorothee Volkert[2], Atsushi Hiyama[3], and Gudrun Klinker[1]

[1] Chair for Computer Aided Medical Procedures and Augmented Reality,
The Technical University of Munich, Munich, Germany
{christian.eichhorn,alex.golovnya}@tum.de, {plecher,klinker}@in.tum.de
[2] Institute for Biomedicine of Aging, Friedrich-Alexander-Universität
Erlangen-Nürnberg, Erlangen, Germany
Dorothee.Volkert@fau.de
[3] INAMI.HIYAMA Laboratory, The University of Tokyo, Tokyo, Japan
Hiyama@star.rcast.u-tokyo.ac.jp

Abstract. In the area of dementia care, Serious Games are seen as an opportunity to boost cognitive capabilities and to stabilize the ability to independently perform Activities of Daily Living (ADLs). We developed a Serious Game based on the popular boardgame chess to target the elderly and dementia patients through incorporating dementia relevant requirements. We analyzed multiple chess variants, which use a smaller board size with less pieces to reduce the game complexity. This results in a new chess version, that helps players to understand the core mechanics of the game and allows them to get into the flow of playing with chess figures. Included are different training scenarios as well as a virtual opponent, that adjusts towards the cognitive skill level of a dementia patient. The game's visual appearance can be tailored to any person and preference by e.g. adjusting the board color theme to address color blindness or changing between 2D and 3D modes. Another core aspect of our game concept focuses on custom 3D printed chess pieces. They are made from conductive material and have a unique finish with additional accessories to distinguish individual pieces from each other. This results in a natural, tangible playing experience on a touchscreen device, a so-called Tangible User Interface. Besides connecting to the feeling of playing real chess, such an approach has the potential to reduce the fear towards modern devices, a well-known entry barrier for this target group. In a retirement home a small pilot study with dementia patients is performed. Furthermore, by utilizing a user-centered approach, we can identify additional insights into the concept of a supported boardgame with tangible game figures which can overcome fear towards modern technology.

Keywords: Tangible User Interface · Serious Games · Tangibles · 3D printing · Chess · Cognitive training · Dementia · Alzheimer · HCI · AI

© Springer Nature Switzerland AG 2021
Q. Gao and J. Zhou (Eds.): HCII 2021, LNCS 12787, pp. 38–57, 2021.
https://doi.org/10.1007/978-3-030-78111-8_3

1   Introduction

With the ageing population, the amount of people with dementia increases. Worldwide, every 3 s, a new case of dementia is diagnosed and by prognosis, the total amount of people with dementia will triple until the year 2050, surpassing 150 million [4]. There is no cure for this disease, but a supporting therapy to prolong independent living exists that utilizes Serious Games (SGs). The focus of such games lies not solely on entertainment, but on training and improvement of physical and cognitive abilities [15]. However there are challenges such as the fear of technology, apathy and bad cognitive and physical condition, which are common for this target group.

Chess belongs to the oldest and also to the most popular games. It was invented to train strategic and tactical thinking for military purposes [24]. Until today it represents an outstanding training for the human brain. Chess is currently experiencing a very strong increase in interest triggered by the Covid-19 pandemic on the one hand and the Netflix series "The Queen's Gambit" on the other [9]. Since the basic rules of the game are widely known, we think it is especially suitable as a SG to help elderly people to train their cognitive abilities and thus continue to maintain a largely self-determined life. The serious use case of supporting cognitive training for PwD in combination with the changes of the game to make it playable for such a target group, builds the foundation of chess becoming a SG. It is a well-known game for its stimulation of various cognitive abilities such as pattern-recognition, decision-making and planning. But the high complexity and the lack of an equally strong partner hinder People with Dementia (PwD) to play it. With this work we want to also address an entry barrier for the elderly to utilize modern technology, apathy and in general fear. We propose the solution of hybrid board games with a tangible Natural User Interface (NUI). Custom conductive chess pieces for playing on a touchscreen have been developed. Hybrid board games are promising to get rid of limitations of virtual games and not losing advantages of the versatile nature of touchscreen applications.

The complexity is reduced by analyzing existing chess variants on a smaller board with fewer pieces and introducing a modified variant. Additionally, to make the game understandable for PwD, different tutorials and training scenarios are implemented, which teach the player the rules and strategies they can utilize in playing against an virtual or human opponent. Furthermore, a companion is added that guides and motivates the player to interact with the game. To adjust for personal preferences or visual impairments, the player can switch between digital 2D and 3D modes and change the color scheme of the board to find the most suitable and enjoyable appearance.

2   Related Work

SGs are a well-received method of treating dementia and there are plenty of studies for the effect of SGs on PwD. For example, the researchers Tárraga et al. [30]

paired the daily typical cognitive stimulation treatment with the SG Smartbrain. Results showed that Smartbrain provided an improvement of cognitive skills of patients with Alzheimer's disease above and beyond what could have been achieved with state-of-the-art cognitive stimulation alone [30]. SGs for PwD differ from each other in goals, functions and features, which allows caregivers to choose the most suitable game to train a certain skill in a particular patient. Most SGs for dementia care have been developed to either train cognitive functions or to improve the quality of life of PwD by helping them maintain their autonomy [15]. In the following subsections we present important aspect of SGs development for PwD and elderly-friendly design guidelines adapted for SGs [17].

2.1   Flow Zone Model

Lack of motivation to do something, lack of interest to anything and total indifference are symptoms of apathy. Sooner or later it affects about 90% of PwD and accelerates the progression of the disease [8]. Improving skills requires repetition of tasks on a regular basis, but the patient's apathy and boredom have a negative effect on the desire to continue. Games that are able to create a reaction from players usually guarantee their interest and motivation [28]. In order to ensure positive results from playing, a SG has to be based on a Flow Zone Model, thus making it enjoyable to play and improving their learning experience [15]. To reach the flow zone (state of mind), a game should contain four important elements: Clear goals, constant feedback, possibility to focus on tasks and possibility to complete tasks [6].

2.2   Difficulty Level

PwD have a hard time learning new concepts, hence the game must be straightforward, easy to learn and not too difficult in order to avoid confusion and frustration of the player. The SG must adapt the difficulty to the player, and reward him positively in order to provide a positive gameplay experience [15]. It is possible to automatically regulate the difficulty level or adjust it as soon as certain progress conditions are met. For example, the scientists Tárraga et al. [30] increased the difficulty level when performance was over 80% or decreased it when performance was below 20% in some consecutive sessions. However, the SG also has to offer the possibility to manually regulate the difficulty. Since the cognitive and motor functions of PwD may differ every day, it is almost impossible for the program to estimate the correct difficulty level, regardless of previous results [15]. Caregivers work with their patients everyday and can observe their cognitive and physical abilities. So, they have more experience than the system in order to determine a perfect difficulty level for the player [14].

2.3   Positive and Immediate Feedback

Many people with dementia suffer from anxiety of failure and are scared to perform actions when they are unsure of the outcome [17]. To reinforce learning strategies and the rehabilitation of cognitive functions, providing immediate and positive feedback on performance and outcome is important. This could prevent PwD from frustration and the loss of motivation, while also increasing their self-esteem [28]. To make feedback understandable, it has to be adapted to the player's visual and hearing abilities, e.g. by giving audio feedback for PwD with visual impairments and vice versa [14]. For example, showing an encouraging picture when a correct answer is given [22] or decreasing negative outcomes [10].

In order to prevent an overload and keep the motivation high, introductory levels might be needed. Starting levels using the concept of errorless learning, e.g. with dynamic cue stimuli, should explain the game, the equipment, give first insights into what the player will experience and will help to learn new skills [14,15,28].

2.4   Assistance

Since PwD have problems with their long-term and especially short-term memory, it is a challenge for them to remember the objectives and rules of game, so the assistant system is the most important component of SGs for PwD. The assistance should be accessible at all times and the instructions have to be short and easy to understand. PwD may have various, not only cognitive, but also sensory and motor impairments and to satisfy this, the SG should minimize actions that require complicated movement or quick reactions and contain visual scenes which are as simplistic as possible. Such as feedback, the instructions and cues should repeatedly use different modalities (audio, text, pictures, etc.) [11,28]. A study was carried out, where participants were asked, if SGs are adapted to be used by PwD alone, or together with a therapist, a family caregiver, a professional caregiver or a robot. The results showed, that only PwD in the early stages of dementia can play alone [28] and for PwD in the later stages it's almost impossible to play without a caregiver, who assists them with handling the technical equipment and helps them progress in the game if they get stuck. That means, written explanations within the game alone seem to be not sufficient [14].

2.5   Natural User Interface

Popular touchscreen devices without external accessories like keyboards, mice or control panels allow to realize the NUI, that "exploits skills that we have acquired through a lifetime of living in the world, which minimizes the cognitive load and therefore minimizes the distraction" [7, time in the video: 13:45] and might be the most appropriate way of interaction for PwD [20]. Familiar gestures, like grabbing and moving physical (tangible) objects make the interaction with digital devices even more intuitive and natural, which lightens the cognitive and physical load and helps the player to focus on the game instead of on how to control it. Combining NUI with tangible objects will make technologies more convenient for elder people [29]. In recent years various researchers have shown interest in combining modern technology with tangible objects. For example, the University of Applied Sciences Dusseldorf created a Tangible Multimedia Book to stimulate memory [19].

In a small prototype they connected a paper book with corresponding sound and music for each double page spread. The conclusion of the experiment was, that a combination of digital multimedia content with familiar physical objects may be an effective way to improve the therapy for PwD.

3   Early Prototype

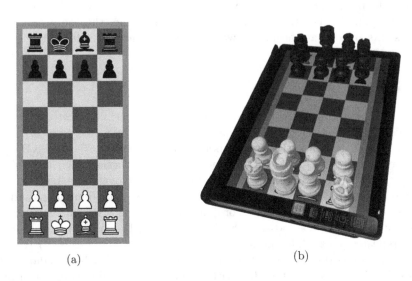

(a)   (b)

Fig. 1. 4 × 8 setup for the early reduced chess prototype (a), Stone chess pieces with conductive paint used on the touchscreen (b)

Around the world chess and its ancient variations are well known, hence allowing us to build on existing knowledge of a lot of participants. Elderly people tend to prefer traditional games, which they can more easily associate with. Board games were especially popular and have a social component in the form of interactions with the other players. The chance of developing dementia was 15% lower for active board game players as discovered by Dartigues et al. [13]. This could indicate, that playing board games and having social connections have a positive impact on the cognitive reserve and thus may prevent or slow down dementia.

In previous studies we received positive feedback with mobile games [15], but in most cases there was a noticeable rejection rate at before actually starting the game. The elderly felt uncomfortable when interacting with modern technology. A typical opinion was, that they haven't used a touchscreen device before and wouldn't profit from it. Others were afraid to embarrass themselves when not knowing how to handle the device. Therefore, we think, to overcome such an entry barrier, the negative feeling of being confronted with these devices must be addressed. Our concept is to combine the advantages of a virtual SG with the natural, tangible interactions of playing figures. This means, the tablet will be placed in the background and function as a smart game board, where the figures are placed on, called a Tangible Interface. The idea of using a Tangible Interface for SGs with the elderly has only been looked at sparsely, e.g. de la Guía et al. [18] developed a SG by equipping everyday objects with NFC tags. These objects then needed to be placed close to a mobile device which recognized them. Results were positive, indicating that the combination of physical objects with virtual elements can stimulate motivation. Another term for such games is hybrid board games, e.g. False Prophets [23] is played on a tabletop display and physical figures are recognized by the system when being placed on it.

Table 1. Analysis of movement patterns of chess pieces

Figure	Advantages	Disadvantages
Pawn	Protects own figures, predictable movement patterns, disposable figure	Specific capture pattern, promotion rules
Rook	Simple movement pattern (vertical/horizontal)	Opponent can easily counter it
Bishop	Simple movement pattern (diagonally on the same color)	Zick-zack pattern needed to make the piece work
Knight	Enhances game balance, few movement options	Complicated movement pattern
Queen	Can save the situation, diversity in movement strategies	Overwhelming movement possibilities, too dominant
King	Simple movement pattern	Limited range

For the early chess prototype, a 2D version has been developed with a 4×8 tile layout as seen in Fig. 1. Therefore, each tile had roughly a size of at least 3 cm $\times$ 3 cm on the screen. For the figures an simplistic analysis of the complexity of their role in the game took place to sort out those who were either too complex or too powerful in a reduced chess version (see Table 1).

After analyzing the pieces, the knight and queen were considered the best choices to be sorted out, since the bishop and rook have a simpler movement pattern. The rook was deemed as the best figure to use for PwD because of its intuitiveness. The bishop had the advantage of staying on one color of the tiles and offers a diagonal pattern. Additionally, the pawns are necessary to slow down the game. The pawn promotion rule was kept in order to prevent these figures getting stuck at the other side of the board.

Physical figures were introduced to help shifting the focus on a known and natural interaction concept (NUI). A figure-based game allows the transfer of all active game elements to the real world, only support elements such as the

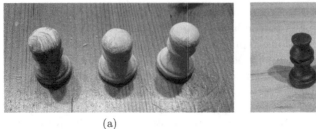

(a)   (b)

Fig. 2. Overspraying the black conductive paint with various layers of thickness, here one to three layers of white acrylic paint (a), Accessories to distinguish the figures from each other, left figure is a bishop, the middle one the queen and on the right a crown was added for the king (b)

tiles are still being virtually represented. Because physical figures have the disadvantage that another person has to move the opponents figures in the case of a single-player mode, it was opted to use the physical figures when playing against another player. The figures have a size about 2.5 cm × 2.5 cm in area and are between 3.3 cm and 5.3 cm high. The material of the chess pieces is stone which makes them heavier compared to standard wooden figures, resulting in weights around 23 g in the case of the smaller pieces like pawn or knight up to 47 g for the queen or the king. Since they are handmade, there are minor differences in optics and weight, but only noticeable on a closer inspection. This could add some difficulties for PwD to distinguish individual types of figures, also the height of some of types of pieces can be similar, hence accessories have been added on specific pieces such as the king (see Fig. 3a). The chess pieces were covered with black conductive paint. Additionally, a varnish spray and white water-based acrylic paint were used to overspray the black conductive paint (see Fig. 2). Experiments were made to identify the ideal solution on how to guarantee a contact point of the paint with the touchscreen on various mobile devices. The result was to have a bump of paint in the center bottom area to keep the contact surface small, without making the whole figure wobbly.

A solely virtual 3D mode has been implemented too. It is possible to view the chess board looking down from an angle on the left corner side (see Fig. 3b), which makes the chess pieces more easily to distinguish. It is possible to choose between different chess board sizes and switch between 2D and 3D mode. Playing with the physical chess pieces only works well with the 2D top down mode and by tapping a figure, the player can see viable movement patterns.

3.1 Pilot User Study

With a prototype at hand, two successive visits in a retirement home with PwD were made before the outbreak of the Covid-19 pandemic. The same open-ended questions in the form of a self-made survey were asked and notes have been taken as in most cases PwD aren't able to fill out a questionnaire themselves.

Fig. 3. 3D virtual chess pieces modeled after the stone pieces and their accessories with Blender (a), Customizable 3D mode, here with full chess setup (b)

One elderly man felt engaged with the game because the figures reminded him about playing the game earlier in his life. Afterwards, the 3D mode was tested, the interaction with the figures was more inconsistent due to the rotation of the chess board. However the visual appearance of the models was perceived as better than when using the 2D mode. Another participant had trouble interacting with the touchscreen, he mainly used his nails to tap on the chess pieces. When using the physical pieces, the situation noticeably improved. The next participant was curious and played with the physical pieces, but just wanted to watch others playing.

Both visits weren't really fruitful or conclusive, but it was important to get some first reactions and to see, if such a concept actually can reach this user group. It was quite visible, whenever the physical pieces were used, there was more connection to the actual game and PwD were less stressed. The virtual game mode wasn't rejected either, but as this prototype was quite rough, some more thoughts needed to be given to better support the player.

4   Advanced Prototype

We felt confident in the game concept, but also saw the need to rework the physical chess pieces and further enhance the depth of the virtual User Interface (UI). Three distinct focus points were addressed:

1. The reduced chess variation of the early prototype did lead to one-dimensional strategies as it had been solely based on the thought to reduce complexity. For that reason, we wanted to have a look at various existing compact chess setups which are typically used to introduce chess to beginners. This will allow us to enhance the diversity of the game, hence keep PwD in the flow zone [6].
2. The physical stone pieces are hard to distinguish even with their accessories. Furthermore, the white acrylic paint is reducing the conductivity. Therefore,

we planned on 3D printing our own chess pieces out of conductive polylactides (PLA) and experiment with spray color.

3. An elderly-friendly UI with a support system needs to be implemented in such a way, that it will be possible to play the SG without a caregiver around [28]. Thereby, we can rely on our extensive guideline research, specifically targeting PwD [17].

4.1 Chess Variant Analysis and Selection

Since chess is a complicated game, PwD will have a difficult time keeping track of the chess pieces, concentrating for longer periods of time and finding tactics. For the advanced prototype multiple existing chess variants on a smaller board with fewer pieces were analyzed in order to find the most fitting one for PwD. The following variants were underwent testing to estimate their strengths and weaknesses: Silvermann 4 × 4, Silvermann 4 × 5, Microchess, Gardner, Chess Attack, Los-Alamos, Demi-Chess [27] and the variant proposed in the first prototype (see Sect. 3). The analysis criteria were:

- The game is perceived as similar to chess and seen as balanced
- It does not cause too much stress through piece trades or imminent closeness to the opponent
- The mobility of a piece is limited
- The board dimensions allow to involve tactics
- There is no optical division into flanks that require more attention
- Most games do not end in a draw and thus are not being perceived as boring
- The white site is the first moving player and has no major advantages or disadvantages
- The games finish fast

As Table 2 shows, the Demi–Chess variant is the most suitable for PwD. To reduce the number of possible draws, both bishops have to be positioned on the same color. This can be achieved through mirroring the black pieces or through removing one line, thus making the board 4 × 7 squares.

The reduced board size also solves other challenges. Since the opponent is one line closer, the number of moves before attacking is reduced, which accelerates the game, but both players still have enough space to reposition their pieces. Another balancing improvement, that a smaller board provides is, that knights now restrict each other (for example after 1. Nb3 and Nb5, the square d4 is controlled by both, thus preventing either knight from accessing it), which is a common theme in classical chess (e.g. knights on f3 and c6 restrict each other on squares d4 and e5). So, for the simplified chess variant for PwD, a modified variant of Demi–Chess on a 4 × 7 board was used.

4.2 Physical 3D Printed Chess Pieces

The device to play and test the game on was an "Acer Switch 3" notebook with a 12.2 in. display size.

Table 2. Chess variants analysis results

	Silvermann 4×4	Silvermann 4×5	Microchess	Gardner	Chess Attack	Los-Alamos	Demi-Chess	Chess early prototype see chapter 3
Similar to chess	✗	✓	✓	✓	✓	✓	✓	✓
Stress-free Game	✗	✗	✗	✗	✗	✗	✓	✓
Limited piece mobility	✓	✓	✓	✓	✗	✗	✓	✓
Enough space for strategies	✗	✗	✗	✗	✓	✓	✓	✓
No board division into flanks	✓	✓	✓	✓	✗	✗	✓	✓
Not draw-heavy	✓	✓	✗	✓	✓	✓	✗	✗
Fair chances for both players	✗	✗	✓	✗	✓	✓	✓	✓
Fast games	✓	✓	✓	✓	✗	✗	✓	✗

A combination of real objects with a digital environment is a good approach for SGs for PwD, so physical chess pieces will be used as an option. Today almost all smartphones and tablets use projected, capacitive touchscreens which return a signal if a capacitive object touches it (e.g. finger, aluminum etc.), so the chess pieces have to be capacitive.

It is important for a comfortable and interesting game of chess, to find the right proportions of the sizes of squares and chess pieces. Since the beginning of official chess tournaments, specific guidelines were established regarding the proportions of the pieces: The king's base diameter should be between 40–50% of the king's height and roughly 75–80% of the size of a square [2].

The screen size of 12.2 in. with the physical pixel size of 0.136 cm of the used device doesn't allow for the square size to be bigger than 30 mm. However, since the chosen variant has no queen in the starting setup, and she can only appear in the endgame when most pieces are already gone, it was decided to make the base of the king and queen pieces bigger in order to make them more distinguishable.

In the classical chess set, the rook is the smallest of all pieces with the exception of the pawn. But since the chosen setup has no queen, the rook becomes the strongest piece and to emphasize its power, it was made taller than the knight. Making it taller than the bishop was unnecessary because it already looks massive due to its width. The final chosen sizes are shown in Table 3.

The 3D models were created according to the sizes in Table 3 and are shown in Fig. 4. The focus lied on creating familiar classical forms, absence of sharp edges, comfortable usage and good recognition from all angles. To ensure better positioning of the physical pieces on the touchscreen, a small contact field with a height of 2 mm and diameter of 8 mm was added below each piece. To isolate

Table 3. The table shows the final sizes of the chess pieces in millimeters

	King	Queen	Bishop	Knight	Rook	Pawn
Base diameter, mm	28	28	25	25	25	22
Height, mm	80	70	60	49	54	40

the remaining bottom area, and ensure stability, a thick felt will be glued to the bottom. The pieces were then printed with conductive filament *Proto-pasta* using a 0.8 hardened steel nozzle.

Fig. 4. The 3D models of the chess pieces with a rounded contact surface on the bottom for better conductivity

Since the 11th century in Europe, a white-red chess board contained white and red chess pieces, later in the middle of the 13th century, red was changed to black, first only the board squares and later also the pieces [25]. Currently by terms of "black chess pieces", people understand either black or brown colors. But these colors don't allow for easily recognizing details, which can be seen in Fig. 5, when comparing the first and the last pawns. Thus, it was decided to paint the "black" pieces red because red has a high enough contrast to white, highlights small details and helps to keep the attention for longer periods of time, than blue or green colors.

For the table app, the basic functions such as the creation of the chessboard, rules, pieces and their movement and highlighting of all viable moves were implemented in accordance to a tutorial [1]. The function to find all viable moves of a selected piece was extended and all moves that would result in the own king being in check were excluded. In order to avoid frustration from bad or accidentally played moves, the board state is additionally saved after every move, thus allowing for take-backs. After every move the game also checks, if the next player is able to move and determines whether it is a stalemate, mate or the game can go on. A promotion chess rule was introduced to let the player decide to what

Fig. 5. Four pawns in different stages: 1. after printing, 2. after grinding, 3. after priming and grinding, 4. after painting the pawn in red (Color figure online)

piece he wants to promote a piece to, if it reaches the first line of the opponent. But to make the interaction of the player with the game simpler, the pawn will automatically promote to a queen because other pieces are rarely chosen. Additional rules from classical chess were ignored, as they were not suitable. To lessen the cognitive load on PwD, the selected piece and all its possible moves are highlighted. Because small highlight shapes could be covered by the pieces, especially in the 3D mode, it was decided to mark the whole square. Additionally, after every move, the current and previous squares of the moved piece are highlighted in another color. Trying to perform illegal moves such as selecting an opponent's piece, selecting the own piece that can't move or moving a selected piece on an illegal square, will cancel the selection and audio feedback is played to signal the impossible move (multi-modal, direct feedback [14]). Trying to place the selected piece on its own square will just cancel the selection.

4.3   User Interface

To lessen the cognitive load on the user, the UI must be intuitive. For the game interface language we recommend the mother tongue, hence for evaluation purposes, German is used for the chess game.

To immerse the player into the game atmosphere, a bright, colorful approach for the interface was chosen along with a light background color. Used colors are mostly associated with positive emotions, draw and help to keep the player's attention and are kept consistent in every menu [21]. Furthermore, the colors were tested in a Color Blindness Simulator [3] and each one was picked to look distinguishable in every scenario. Each single button press provides audio feedback.

The main menu (see Fig. 6a) contains three scenario buttons and gives access to the options and statistics. If the player moves to the main menu before completing his game, two buttons will appear for continuing the game or aborting it (see see Fig. 6b).

When choosing the tutorial or training scenarios in the main menu, a secondary menu opens, where the player can quickly start the first uncompleted level or select a specific level from the scenario (see Fig. 7a and Fig. 7b respectively). Completed levels are marked with a checkmark, but are still available for replay. Clicking the play scenario in the main menu allows to choose a computer

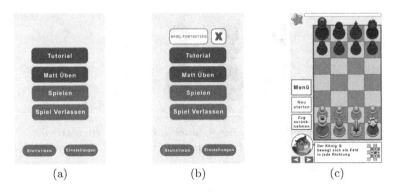

Fig. 6. Main Menu (a,b) and Game Scene (c).

Fig. 7. Tutorial (a), Training (b) and Play (c) Menus

opponent of three difficulty levels or play against another player (see Fig. 7c). Every secondary menu has a button to return back to the main menu.

The game window consists of the 4 × 7 chess board, a progress bar at the top, the companion at the bottom and control buttons on the left that allow the player to take the move back, restart the level or go back to the main menu (see Fig. 6c).

4.4 Game Modes

To adapt the game for different mental capabilities, it contains three scenarios: The tutorial, training and play scenario. In order to guide and support the PwD, a companion was added that provides information and helpful tips on how to complete the goals of each level, or reminds the player of the rules. The main menu additionally includes the settings, where color, board themes and 2D or 3D modes with custom models, can be changed and the statistics, where the progress of the player in the current game session is tracked.

Computer Opponent: To make this game more convenient to play and get rid of the requirement to move the other players' pieces, a computer opponent was developed. It is present on every level, apart from the player vs. player level. The game uses two types of computer opponents, namely Random AI and MinMax AI [5].

The Random AI first takes a random piece with at least one possible move and then randomly decides a square for it. This approach makes the probability of moving minor pieces or pawns equal to the probability of moving major pieces like the queen or rook. The estimation of this AI's strength was declared to be weak, making it an easy opponent for PwD.

The MinMax AI uses an evaluation function of the board state, which counts how much material is on the board according to the classical chess evaluation in Table 4, with positive values for white and negative for black, and additionally returns 0 in case of a stalemate. Usually this evaluation function is bad to use as a guideline against healthy players because it disregards good positioning, attacking opportunities and weaknesses. But it is ensuring an interesting and not complicated game for PwD. Since the evaluation function is symmetrical, it enables the AI to play as any color.

Table 4. Classical chess evaluation

	Pawn	Bishop	Knight	Rook	Queen	Mate
Value	$+/-1$	$+/-3$	$+/-3$	$+/-5$	$+/-10$	$+/-$infinity

As the name implies, the MinMax AI uses the minmax algorithm [5] to determine the move after a certain depth with the best evaluation according to Table 4. Since the strength depends on the calculation depth D, many games against different depths were played to estimate good strength variations for PwD:

– $D = 1$ was, as expected, just taking every piece it could take without regarding the consequences and played worse than the Random AI.
– $D = 2$ and $D = 4$ played very defensively, making the games last longer than needed.
– $D = 3$ played more aggressive, but made many mistakes, that could easily be punished.
– $D = 5$ was a decent opponent, it made some surprising moves and is creating interesting positions, where longer thinking is required.

As a mediocre AI opponent for PwD, MinMax AI $D = 3$ and as hard opponent, MinMax AI $D = 5$ were chosen.

Scenarios: To make the game more interesting for people with different levels of cognitive impairments, three varying scenarios were designed, the tutorial,

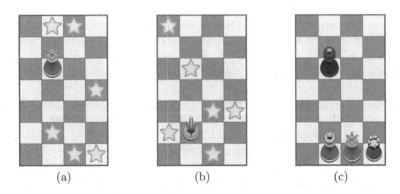

Fig. 8. Queen Tutorial (a), Knight Tutorial (b), Training (c)

training and play scenario. The tutorial uses the concept of errorless learning (similar to the possibility of completing a task [12]) and is the easiest scenario [14, 15, 28]. It contains six different levels, and each is dedicated to a different piece: the king, rook, bishop, queen, knight and pawn. On each level, the player is given one piece and has to collect stars positioned on game tiles (focus on tasks [12]). The number of moves is not limited and the stars do not move. This way the player learns the capabilities of each piece. The examples of the levels are shown in Fig. 8a and Fig. 8b. Upon collecting a star and completing the level, positive audio feedback is provided, the progress bar is filled and the player is suggested to play the next level.

In the training scenario, six different levels are included which introduce the player to various strategies. The goal of each level is to mate the enemy king. Each level provides many opportunities, and in some cases even excessive material to make it even easier. An example of the levels is shown in Fig. 8c. The play scenario provides an opportunity to test the player's skills against an AI of three difficulty levels or play against another person.

Companion: The companion's design is based on the owl from the Disney cartoon 'Bambi' from 1942. A familiar connection to the player should be established, as there is a high chance, that the player knows this cartoon from their childhood. Also, an owl usually symbolizes wisdom and knowledge, which are both fitting traits for chess. The name was kept the same as in the cartoon, namely "Freund Eule", so that the player could recognize this character more easily. This companion is present on every level. He states the task of the level and provides helpful information via speech bubbles (constant feedback [6]). Below him, navigation buttons are located that lead to the next or previous speech bubble (see Fig. 9).

The letter size has been chosen as big as possible, to ensure good legibility. In the text there are symbols of the chess pieces included, to help the player better understand which piece is talked about (see Fig. 9a). In the tutorial levels, small pictures of the movement options for each piece are provided, as well as pictures

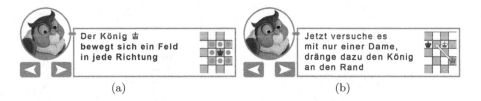

(a)   (b)

Fig. 9. Example companion messages

on how to complete the level through collecting stars (see Fig. 9a). The training levels also contain pictures that explain the concepts of mate and stalemate, and show some example mates (see Fig. 9b). In the play levels against the AI or another person, the companion repeats the rules of the game, in case the player forgot them.

Customization: Providing an option menu allows the player or their caregiver to adapt the SG to their personal player preferences (see Fig. 10a). There is a toggle for 2D and 3D modes to select the desired variation of the chess pieces. Green, grey, blue and brown color themes are provided for the chessboard. All used colors, including highlights for possible moves of pieces, were specifically chosen to look distinguishable for every form of color blindness and were tested in a Color Blindness Simulator [3]. It is also possible to change the color themes and the mode at any time when playing and resume the game afterwards. In the tutorial and training scenarios, the player can only play with white pieces, but in the play scenario, he can choose between "White" and "Black". Changing the own color is only possible, if there is currently no game running, so the player must first complete or abort his game.

Statistics: The progress of the current session is tracked and shown in the Statistic menu (see Fig. 10b). This would allow the caregivers to keep track of the success of the player, and also encourage the player to try and improve their results. Currently the statistics show the number of moves played, the amount of take-backs, how many unique levels were completed and the number of victories, draws and losses the player had.

Physical Game Mode: An example of how the game could be played with physical pieces is shown in Fig. 11. In the training or play scenarios, additional help of a caregiver might be needed to move the enemy pieces on the screen.

5   Future Work

The game can be extended in many directions to further enhance the benefits for both the elderly people and caregivers.

(a)   (b)

Fig. 10. Option Menu (a) and Statistics (b) (Color figure online)

5.1 Game Modifications

Currently six levels with different board setups for the tutorial and training scenarios are implemented. Adding random appearing game setups will exclude the possibility that after some sessions, the player will memorize the moves and hence stops investing time thinking about a strategy, thus not training the cognitive functions anymore.

The stars collected in the tutorial scenario and rewarded upon victory in other scenarios can be further utilized for some extra motivation and rewards.

As mentioned previously, the MinMax AI uses a low complexity evaluation function. It can be modified to also consider the positioning of the pieces, for example giving a higher score for pieces that control the center squares or are closer to the enemy king. This would result in the AI playing more consistent, making it more enjoyable to play against.

Player profiles could have the function to save the progress over multiple sessions and hence help the caregivers and doctors to monitor the progress over long periods of time. Additionally, the statistics can be saved in a local database and illustrate the progress via graphs.

5.2 Physical Pieces

A different coating for the physical chess pieces would be helpful because sanitizers may act as a dissolver for the used paint and are common in care centers. Especially during the Covid-19 pandemic (focusing on hygiene is important).

Further enhancing the quality of the detection (at the moment 9 out of 10 times the interaction is reliably detected) for the figures on the touchscreen is important to enable the elderly to play on their own. Therefore, testing different contact surface forms, touchscreen types, conductive materials for the figures and improving the error handling of the software still has additional potential.

Fig. 11. Physical pieces on tablet

5.3   Evaluation

We plan to perform a user study in a retirement home environment to test the chosen strategies. Thereby, similarly to the small pilot study (see Sect. 3.1), we want to figure out, if the physical chess pieces can enhance the openness towards the game compared to a solely digital gameplay experience. As we are working with PwD, we want to involve a similar approach as with our previous user study by first categorizing the progress of dementia with the Mini Mental Status Test (MMST) to get a better understanding in which way groups of the elderly respond towards the SG [16, 26].

6   Conclusion

In this paper, we describe the successful development of a chess-based Serious Game for elderly people and patients with dementia, which targets the goal to improve cognitive abilities. The combination of conductive, 3D printed chess pieces with a digital chessboard (touchscreen) creates an intuitive gameplay experience, called a Natural User Interface which is able to motivate the target group to interact with modern technology. We describe in detail, how to adapt a board game for dementia patients. The difficulty and complexity can be configured through the beginner-friendly chess variants and the tips given by the supportive companion provide an anchor to not get lost. The variety of game scenarios keep the experience interesting and challenging for people in all stages of dementia.

Acknowledgment. Thank you to Andreas Holzner for supporting this project.
The preparation of this paper was supported by the enable cluster and is catalogued by the enable steering committee as enable **70** (http://enable-cluster.de). This work was funded by a grant of the German Ministry for Education and Research (BMBF) **FK 01EA1807A.**

References

1. Chess Game Tutorial. https://bit.ly/380Prak. Accessed 30 Nov 2020
2. Chessboard Dimensions. https://bit.ly/382nlew. Accessed 30 Nov 2020
3. Cobis. https://bit.ly/2WZooWk. Accessed 30 Nov 2020
4. Dementia. https://bit.ly/3n9Mk4h. Accessed 30 Nov 2020
5. Min-Max Algorithm. https://bit.ly/34WkPos. Accessed 30 Nov 2020
6. Meaning and Happiness: "In the zone": enjoyment, creativity, and the nine elements of "flow" (2008). https://bit.ly/3amsga7. Accessed 03 June 2020
7. NUI with Bill Buxton (2010). https://channel9.msdn.com/Blogs/LarryLarsen/CES-2010-NUIwith-Bill-Buxton. Accessed 03 June 2020
8. Beating Apathy in Dementia: Alzheimer's & Dementia Weekly. Support & Insight for the Autumn of Life (2015). http://www.alzheimersweekly.com/2015/06/beating-apathy-indementia.html. Accessed 16 June 2020
9. Checkmate! The chess business is suddenly booming (2020). shorturl.at/svHOS. Accessed 30 Nov 2020
10. Benveniste, S., Jouvelot, P., Péquignot, R.: The MINWii project: renarcissization of patients suffering from Alzheimer's disease through video game-based music therapy. In: Yang, H.S., Malaka, R., Hoshino, J., Han, J.H. (eds.) ICEC 2010. LNCS, vol. 6243, pp. 79–90. Springer, Heidelberg (2010). https://doi.org/10.1007/978-3-642-15399-0_8
11. Bouchard, B., Imbeault, F., Bouzouane, A., Menelas, B.-A.J.: Developing serious games specifically adapted to people suffering from Alzheimer. In: Ma, M., Oliveira, M.F., Hauge, J.B., Duin, H., Thoben, K.-D. (eds.) SGDA 2012. LNCS, vol. 7528, pp. 243–254. Springer, Heidelberg (2012). https://doi.org/10.1007/978-3-642-33687-4_21
12. Csikszentmihalyi, M.: Toward a psychology of optimal experience. Flow and the Foundations of Positive Psychology, pp. 209–226. Springer, Dordrecht (2014). https://doi.org/10.1007/978-94-017-9088-8_14
13. Dartigues, J.F., et al.: Playing board games, cognitive decline and dementia: a French population-based cohort study. BMJ Open **3**(8), 1–7 (2013)
14. Dietlein, C., Bock, B.: Recommendations on the design of serious games for people with dementia. EAI Endorsed Trans. Serious Games **5**(17), 1–12 (2019)
15. Eichhorn, C., et al.: Innovative game concepts for Alzheimer patients. In: Zhou, J., Salvendy, G. (eds.) ITAP 2018. LNCS, vol. 10927, pp. 526–545. Springer, Cham (2018). https://doi.org/10.1007/978-3-319-92037-5_37

16. Eichhorn, C., et al.: THe innovative reminder in senior-focused technology (THIRST)—evaluation of serious games and gadgets for Alzheimer patients. In: Zhou, J., Salvendy, G. (eds.) HCII 2019. LNCS, vol. 11593, pp. 135–154. Springer, Cham (2019). https://doi.org/10.1007/978-3-030-22015-0_11

17. Eichhorn, C., et al.: Combining motivating strategies with design concepts for mobile apps to increase usability for the elderly and Alzheimer patients. In: Gao, Q., Zhou, J. (eds.) HCII 2020. LNCS, vol. 12208, pp. 47–66. Springer, Cham (2020). https://doi.org/10.1007/978-3-030-50249-2_4

18. de la Guía, E., Lozano, M.D., Penichet, V.M.: Increasing engagement in elderly people through tangible and distributed user interfaces. In: Proceedings of the 8th International Conference on Pervasive Computing Technologies for Healthcare, pp. 390–393 (2014)

19. Huldtgren, A., Mertl, F., Vormann, A., Geiger, C.: Reminiscence of people with dementia mediated by a tangible multimedia book. In: ICT4AgeingWell, pp. 191–201 (2016)

20. Joddrell, P., Astell, A.J.: Studies involving people with dementia and touchscreen technology: a literature review. JMIR Rehab. Assist. Technol. **3**(2), e10 (2016)

21. Jones, G.M., van der Eerden, W.J.: Designing care environments for persons with Alzheimer's disease: visuoperceptual considerations. Rev. Clin. Gerontol. **18**(1), 13–37 (2008)

22. Lee, G.Y., Yip, C.C., Yu, E.C., Man, D.W.: Evaluation of a computer-assisted errorless learning-based memory training program for patients with early Alzheimer's disease in Hong Kong: a pilot study. Clin. Interv. Aging **8**, 623 (2013)

23. Mandryk, R.L., Maranan, D.S.: False prophets: exploring hybrid board/video games. In: CHI 2002 Extended Abstracts on Human Factors in Computing Systems, pp. 640–641 (2002)

24. Murray, H.J.R.: A History of Chess. Clarendon Press (1913)

25. Pastoureau, M., Gladding, J.: Black: The History of a Color, vol. 170. Princeton University Press, Princeton (2009)

26. Plecher, D.A., et al.: Interactive drinking gadget for the elderly and Alzheimer patients. In: Zhou, J., Salvendy, G. (eds.) HCII 2019. LNCS, vol. 11593, pp. 444–463. Springer, Cham (2019). https://doi.org/10.1007/978-3-030-22015-0_35

27. Pritchard, D.B., Beasley, J.D.: The Classified Encyclopedia of Chess Variants. J. Beasley (2007)

28. Robert, P., et al.: Recommendations for the use of serious games in people with Alzheimer's disease, related disorders and frailty. Front. Aging Neurosci. **6**, 54 (2014)

29. Spreicer, W.: Tangible interfaces as a chance for higher technology acceptance by the elderly. In: Proceedings of the 12th International Conference on Computer Systems and Technologies, pp. 311–316 (2011)

30. Tárraga, L., et al.: A randomised pilot study to assess the efficacy of an interactive, multimedia tool of cognitive stimulation in Alzheimer's disease. J. Neurol. Neurosurg. Psychiatry **77**(10), 1116–1121 (2006)

Designing a Dementia-Informed, Accessible, Co-located Gaming Platform for Diverse Older Adults with Dementia, Family and Carers

Paula Gardner[1]([⊠]), Stephen Surlin[1], Adekunle Akinyemi[1], Jessica Rauchberg[1], Caitlin McArthur[3], Yujiao Hao[1], Rong Zheng[1], and Alexandra Papaioannou[2]

[1] McMaster University, Hamilton, ON, Canada
gardnerp@mcmaster.ca
[2] GERAS Centre for Aging Research, McMaster University, Hamilton, ON, Canada
[3] Dalhousie University, Halifax, NS, Canada

Abstract. The ABLE.family project deploys disability and crip approaches and universal design, to create a platform that engages diverse older adults with dementia (OAD) and their carers in social engagement and play. Our prototyped gaming platform, created with OAD stakeholders and carers aims to decrease loneliness and despair experienced by OAD and carers during the COVID-19 pandemic, by increasing opportunities for intergenerational family engagement. Pleasurable interactions are encouraged through real-time collaborative play (e.g. art and turn based games) and real-time video-calling embedded in the platform. Our human-centered design approach works with OAD and their carer networks to design the platform interface with features that can be used to effectively collaborate, interact and produce sustainable platforms for OAD and their carer community. This project is supported generously by funding from CABHI (Centre for Aging and Brain Health Innovation), the Alzheimer Society of Hamilton and Halton, and MIRA (the McMaster Institute for Research on Aging); resources and spaces supporting this work are provided by Pulse Lab (funded by the Asper Foundation) and McMaster University.

Keywords: Co-design · Gaming · Dementia

1 Introduction

Prior to the COVID-19 pandemic, growing research demonstrated the importance of engaging diverse older adult stakeholders in technology research to ensure it is usable, accessible, valued and effective for diverse populations. In pre-pandemic times, researchers seeking to enhance the engagement of older adults in research struggled to adhere to best practices for informed, sustained, and effective engagement of older adults; in dementia research, these challenges are yet amplified by the unique communication experiences and needs of diverse older adult populations.

Accelerated by the import of social movements for equity and inclusion, researchers are beginning to recognize, and funding bodies are beginning to demand, that researchers

© Springer Nature Switzerland AG 2021
Q. Gao and J. Zhou (Eds.): HCII 2021, LNCS 12787, pp. 58–77, 2021.
https://doi.org/10.1007/978-3-030-78111-8_4

adjust their enhanced human centered approaches to center diverse older adults, particularly older adults with dementia (OAD) in health technology design. Engaging older adults also makes common sense: engaging diverse older adults in design increases the possibility that technologies created will be broadly accessible, desired, sustainable and effective for diverse users. Government agencies also increasingly recognize the value of focusing research on diverse older adults via human centered approaches. To wit, a key strategy of the Canadian Dementia Strategy [1] is to rigorously engage OAD and stakeholders to ensure that they inform the development of communication and assistive technologies based on lived experience. Contrary to popularly held beliefs, research shows that older adults are keen to engage with and participate in developing health and communication technologies. However, best practices for engaging older adults, particularly diverse OAD and their carers (now commonly referred to as carers) in research developing assistive and other health technologies, remains an under-researched area.

These realities were evident amongst researchers, funding and regulatory bodies, when the COVID-19 pandemic struck; at that moment, research teams and service provision groups working with OAD (such as the Alzheimer's Society) pivoted programming and research to remote communication platforms such as Zoom. Research and service teams immediately recognized a lack of proven practices for engaging older adults in research via remote technologies. While this research is slowly compiling, many human-focused research continues to under-represent diverse OAD, a problematic resulting from historic systems of inequity and access and cultural research practices that routinely marginalize BIPOC, remote and under resourced older adult participants in health systems and health and technology research.

This paper discusses our team's efforts to inform our critical, intersectional, human-centered approach to research. Our approach brings critical human-machine communication (HMC) theory, disability and "crip" research, and transdisciplinary, community-driven practices to normative human computer interaction (HCI) practices; in doing so we aim to create effective practices for research engaging older adults in meaningful ways via remote communication technologies[1]. The paper also discusses our efforts to employ that critical approach as we build ABLE.Family, as an accessible, interactive, intergenerational web-based gaming platform. The platform aims to offer opportunities for social engagement and play among diverse OAD, their families and carers, to combat loneliness and to produce an array of mood and health benefits. ABLE.Family is also

---

[1] Our team is currently working with stakeholders from organized community and university-supported dementia organizations and programs. We recognize that these programs struggle to serve diverse BIPOC, remote, under-resourced and indigenous folks, as well as diverse OAD experiencing varying levels of cognitive impairment. In this study, our stakeholders (primarily carers and service providers) offer their experiences with existing participants in this program, who are normally white, middle class, resourced, Canadians, but do reflect diverse spectrums of cognitive impairment. In this and other dementia research projects, we are working with organizations including Alzheimer Society of Hamilton and Halton, as well as the Hamilton Council on Aging and the Dementia-Friendly Communities, Hamilton, to investigate and redress the lack of engagement by diverse OAD, due to many factors including lack of security, lack of access to services and resources, and structural discrimination due to historic white supremacy and racial and ethnic bias; in future publications we will report on these efforts.

designed to relieve burdens on carers, who represent a significant population in need of support—a situation that has dramatically worsened since the pandemic.

2   The Challenge to Support Older Adults with Dementia and Their Carers

Canada is experiencing an epidemic of dementia. Over 1/2 million Canadians live with dementia, 90% of whom are cared for by spouses and adult children [2]. The COVID pandemic has created a crisis, where isolation due to public health measures has worsened the physiological, psychological, and quality of life of older adults with dementia (OAD) and their exhausted caregivers (hereto referred to as carers). Alongside the large proportion of OADs and CPs in remote areas, addressing the needs of those who are black, indigenous and people of colour (BIPOC) [3], of lower income, and other under-represented groups must be considered in the design of any initiatives aimed at this population. We contend that dementia-informed digital health technologies can offer highly accessible, affordable, effective, and pleasure-driven solutions when designed with engaged, diverse OAD and carer participants.

Older adults with dementia (OAD) suffer a range of debilitating health issues (physical, cognitive and affective), arising from isolation, immobility and loneliness. Social isolation can exacerbate certain dementia symptoms in older adults, resulting in sharp declines in physical and cognitive health, aggression, and worsening mood. Additionally, physical distancing can place increased demands on family and/ other carers, leading to greater amounts of burnout [4, 5]. Untreated symptoms lead to physical, cognitive and mood decline and often hospitalization and institutionalization which strain OAD and contribute to mounting government health costs exceeding $12 billion for this care [6]. Recent research assessing the impact of the pandemic on ageing research seeking to apply technology solutions for older adults. Sixsmith finds ongoing barriers include: structural impediments to large-scale implementation, the need to focus on service rather than crisis management, and to address the digital divide. The COVID-19 pandemic has created a heightened crisis reflecting these barriers, while social isolation yet worsens their impacts on physiological, psychological, and quality of life of OAD and their burdened carers.

3   The Promises of Digital Health, Activity and Gaming Technologies for OAD

While not a panacea, recent developments in dementia-friendly digital technologies offer approaches that can improve the quality of everyday life of those with OAD, their carers and families and aim to surmount some of the aforementioned barriers via enhanced digital service and supported access.

While the progression of disease cannot be reversed, regular physical activity and lifestyle choices for people with dementia can significantly slow disease progression and reduce depression. Research shows for example that telehealth and healthcare technologies designed *for* older adults (specifically, OAD) and their carers can significantly impact the well-being and health of older adults and relieve carer burdens. Typical approaches to telehealth for persons with dementia however often render OAD as passive users who are not agentic and whole [4, 7]. Such styles can result in symptoms of agitation and aggression for OAD, placing a heavier burden for at-home carers, especially for those who are spouses of OAD or family members [5]. A critical, more inclusive approach to telehealth for OAD is possible when OAD and care networks are conceptualized as agentic stakeholders from the beginning.

Important research in telehealth lends advice regarding best practices for engaging OAD with communication technologies. For instance, [8] researchers suggest making brief, plain language how-to guides or videos to ease OAD through the telehealth process. Additionally, healthcare providers can embrace dementia-friendly approaches to care, such as rephrasing questions or giving OAD time to respond, can ease the digital communication between providers and OAD [9]. Telehealth providers find they may need to assess racial, cultural or linguistic barriers in care: emerging research emphasizes that working with culturally-safe practices can provide possibilities for comfort, trust, and agency for OAD from marginalized racial, cultural, or linguistic groups can ease the care process for older BIPOC and migrant groups who experience medical racism and discrimination [3, 10, 11]. By amplifying and designing telehealth and aging technology alongside OAD and care networks, OAD interdependence is enhanced, creating much-needed respite for at-home carers. As the COVID-19 pandemic continues, physical therapists, gerontologists, and other healthcare providers working with OAD may find it beneficial to adopt such practices into their telehealth conferencing [12].

Also important is research showing that creative activity, especially in regard to physical movement and sense of self can benefit physical, cognitive, and social wellness in OAD. Exercise programs can enhance emotional well-being, and social interaction; range of motion interventions reduce risks of falls and boost dual task ability [13, 14] and improve on global cognition for OAD [15]. Additionally, light physical activity, such as walking exercises, can improve balance and mobility [16, 17]. Other forms of gamified light activity, such as low-impact aerobics, walking activities, or tai-chi and meditation, can also relieve agitation and aggression, which may increase the possibility of falls for OAD [18–20]. Similarly, arts-based initiatives adding creativity and multisensorial engagement are shown to enhance mood and reduce loneliness and have become popular with those living with dementia. Dance programs can improve balance and offer culturally-safe practices for physical activity [21, 22]. As well, physical activity, combined with social interaction and art have synergistic effects, producing physical, cognitive and emotional benefits for older adults with dementia [23–25]. There are enormous possibilities to be gained in merging technology with these arts-based initiatives, but research must radically shift to ensure these platforms are designed in partnership with OADs and their families [26].

Recently, digital approaches to serious gaming reveal the cognitive and social benefits of co-design with OAD and their care networks. Research shows that haptic matching games designed for older adults can have significant health and mood benefits, such as increases in memory and word recall for household or everyday objects [27, 28]. Serious gaming mobile applications can also present opportunities for intergenerational play and connection between OAD and young adults, creating new networks and possibilities for social interaction and care as interfaces center the unique access needs of OAD, while providing nodes of contact and connection [29, 30]. Co-design approaches to serious gaming can promote physical therapy as a fun, engaging digital experience. Noting the popularity of exergame platforms in the early 2010s, many projects co-design serious gaming for OADs that position physical therapy and other forms of low-intensity activity with video game consoles such as Nintendo's Wii Fit [31] or Microsoft's Xbox Kinect systems [32, 33]. These efforts at gamification work to promote balance and cognition, in addition to providing a space for OAD to practice memory, word-recall, and specific types of physical movement (e.g.: raising arms). Recent studies reveal the important potential of serious gaming and/or social networking applications, for the physical, cognitive, and social health of older adults with dementia [34–36]. As the COVID-19 pandemic continues, halting the reopening of day programming for OAD, serious gaming or social media-based interventions can facilitate digital networks of interdependence and social interaction. While there is great promise in engaging digital technologies including gaming to gain multiple benefits for OAD, few technology solutions have been designed by and for OAD, and even fewer seek to deliver benefits to carers.

4 Incorporating OAD in Technology Design

Highly impactful digital health and communication technologies can be developed with approaches that recognize the unique physical, cognitive, and social health needs of People with Disabilities, in our case, OAD (older adults with dementia.) [34–36]. Participant-driven or deeply informed approaches are particularly effective, focusing on lateral knowledge sharing (across older adults, stakeholders and research team members), and engaging interdisciplinary teams focused on solution-driven methods; these enable agile and curious problem-solving, rather than addressing user needs via disciplinary approaches [37].

As noted, OAD tend to be positioned in research as individuals requiring care, rather than as offering lived expertise, skills, and abilities essential to advancing knowledge and treatment of dementia. Research on dementia disease and interventions has typically been developed focusing on a narrow white, upper middle-class population [38], leaving out knowledge from diverse OAD, that is crucial for ensuring solutions address the wide range of OAD and carer needs.

There are a multitude of reasons that older adults are absented or positioned as "users" and not as designers in technology design research. Older adults are stereotypically portrayed as technophobic and unable to engage with healthcare technologies and mobile communication devices. As a result, many age-related digital divides such as health and activity trackers, like media devices, such as smartphones, are incompatible with or fail to address older adults' unique needs, diverse cultural experiences, and fail to offer sustainable long-term assistance affordances [3, 39, 40] such as health monitoring or exercise incentives. A clear digital divide presents barriers to health technology adoption and use by individuals who are under-resourced and marginalized [41]. Many scholars [42] have warned that researchers tend to overlook diverse populations during health technology *implementation*, for example, failing to address how digital literacy and/or collective or nuclear family living impacts technology adoption.

While technology adoption is a serious barrier, our team focuses on the problematic absenting of diverse (e.g., BIPOC, cognitively diverse OAD, etc.) populations in technology *design research*. Developing technology with diverse older adults at the table allows for inclusive design of the interface and the interaction to fit into the lifestyle, flow and to anticipate trust and security needs of projected BIPOC users. It is not enough to include individuals from underserved and under-represented populations—rather, the structure of the research itself must seek to correct historic normative research practices that make BIPOC, differently abled and other marginalized folks reluctant, fearful and skeptical. Models are available to assist researchers in working with marginalized populations to create tools that are accessible, desired, and accommodate their lived realities of. Universal design is an approach that can design effectively across populations (of high to low digital 'literacy'. However, approaches must also take into account: participants' comfort with and access to digital health tools and remote health care provider services; reliable Internet access; and possessing an appropriate space to engage with these technologies, etc. [43]. It is essential that teams address issues of trust arising from historic marginalization and unethical treatment by medical communities; users won't consider using health devices (designed for low digital literacy) if they fear they are designed for privileged, white people but represent security and safety risks for themselves [3, 10, 44].

Finally, human technology development research driven by disciplinary and top-down approaches often alienate targeted user groups, in failing to explore fully the needs of diverse older adult participants and stakeholders, or sequentially distributing user problems to discreet team members [4, 7, 44]. Methods are available to help teams to enhance rigorous interdisciplinarity to support universal design and meet the needs of diverse OAD stakeholders.

5 Pivoting with COVID-19: Best Practices for Remote Research with Diverse Older Adults

The COVID-19 pandemic presents new challenges for health and technology research [42, 45] The rush to invent new health technologies or onboard individuals to new tools, for example, remote health monitoring, smartphone and web-based symptom tracking, virtual care via the "virtual hospital" (telemedicine practices, online prescriptions), raises concerns over risks to users. While digital tools can be effective in addressing mounting public health needs, they can be unethical (intrusive), unsafe (erode individual freedoms) and fail to reach at-risk and vulnerable populations [42]. Research to develop technologies for diverse OAD must ensure that such ethical concerns are embedded in their research questions and approaches.

Sixsmith's [6] review of the Canadian Ageing and Technology research network identifies key areas to target to support appropriate technology solutions for older adults via remote communication technologies. Technology, for example, should not be a "bandage" but should support long term care interventions. It is essential that we address systemic inequities in care provision and avoid enhancing the digital divide. In so doing, more OAD can remain at home, which both abides their wishes, and prevents decline and the risks associated with congregate living in long term care facilities. We must create policy change to foreground digital citizenship, and to the right affordable Internet access. In the immediate, however, our team seeks to create technology suitable for immediate and longer-term care provision, and to create an accessible and free platform with a low barrier to entry. In working with NGOs invested in providing cheap digital technologies to OA (such as digital tablets), we hope to intervene effectively at this moment of the pandemic, offering a gaming platform that will sustain OAD's family and social engagement, and that over time, policy changes will produce greater access to digital technologies and Internet access to support the use of such digital health and activity platforms.

6   ABLE.Family: Intergenerational Gaming for Older Adults with Dementia and Carers

The ABLE.Family project seeks to engage diverse OAD and stakeholders in rigorous co-design to create a gaming platform for families participating via remote technology. Our research approach centres OAD and carers in the development of the interface and game interaction to meet diverse needs and interests, and to ensure sustained use and benefits.

The goals of ABLE.Family platform are to: reduce loneliness and isolation; increase socialization & pleasurable interactions, particularly intergenerational play; reduce carer stress and depression; investigate how the interactions might aid memory, cognitive and mood enhancement; to restore a sense of self, identity and family role for OAD, and to restore close relations among OAD and family members. Our interface and interaction design strategies reflect emerging research on dementia, and the needs and experiences of those living with dementia and their carers, as outlined earlier.

Our design process has the following objectives, further explained below:

1 Diverse OAD and stakeholders will offer rich personal experiences to inform the interface and gaming elements of the ABLE.Family gaming platform
2 The online game platform will be highly accessible to diverse OAD and intergenerational family members; it should, for example, offer opportunities for non-verbal interaction and other dementia-informed approaches to enhance the accessibility and effectiveness of the platform for OAD
3 The game platform should provide activity and playful interactions that enhance the well-being and increase the cognitive engagement of OAD.
4 The platform games should engage OAD in motor learning, supporting consistent game play using the platform.
5 The online game platform will aim to increase interaction to reduce dementia symptoms in OAD, provide stress relief to carers, and enhance family and friendship bonds among players.

7   Fortifying an OAD-Friendly Human-Centered Design Approach

In pursuit of these diverse objectives, our team draws on our multiple experts, and engages in interdisciplinary practice. We bring distinct skill sets in aging (reflecting diverse needs of older adults with frailty and dementia and their carers); platform and sensor design, code design, and data analytics; occupational therapy and rehabilitation with older adults; and frailty-informed co-design, user interaction design and disability theory. Our interdisciplinarity practice is informed by research and experience. Four years of team-based work has taught us to embrace the following key practices: comprehensive engagement with and sharing of data acquired in co-design with stakeholders; blending our diverse disciplinary methods; critical approaches to remote research collaboration across the team and with stakeholders; community engagement, knowledge sharing and translation; and a ongoing reflexive review of our mission and objectives. To support remote collaboration, our team employs new digital tools including an iterative design map to track planning, documentation and timelines (as these change, routinely) and to facilitate the persistent transfer of learnings and knowledge among all team members.

8 Pivoting from ABLE Music to ABLE.Family's Web-based Platform

Iterative design is key to our development; over the past four years we have developed ABLE platform versions with distinct interactions (using gesture and wearable technologies) to meet different needs (e.g. movement, mood enhancement) all of which draw on arts and game-based interaction. With the pandemic, we pivoted to designing a web-based gaming platform, to meet the needs of OAD, carers and multigenerational family members isolated at home. To date we have produced a beta version of ABLE.Family as a co-located, interactive platform to combat the extended isolation, loss of cognitive and activity and socialization. Research shows that loss of socialization produces loneliness, loss of identity, and depressed mood. The platform is designed with approaches drawn from dementia therapy, disability studies, and successful technology and game research for OAD. The Able.Family platform aims to create opportunities for family play and cognitive engagement.

In response to the COVID-19 crisis, we have adapted our design process to work with stakeholders (e.g. physical and occupational therapists, Gerontologists, recreation therapists, and carers), rather than OAD. Engage in research that is ethical, accessible and rewarding with stakeholders, prior to engaging OAD them in remote participation. Our team-based work and testing has leaned more toward participatory (or human centered) design, as we are unable to maintain consistent rigorous co-design approaches via remote communication tools [46]. However, we maintain a commitment to ensuring that the games and interface are dementia-friendly and fully accessible for a diverse population, taking into account potential technology, physical, emotional and cognitive barriers.

9 A Disability and Crip-Informed Research Approach

The ABLE.Family platform is informed by crip theory (a branch of critical disability studies) and disability justice activism, aiming to subvert ableism, or the oppressive practice of assuming all disabled people should be made able. Crip theory rejects cure, rehabilitation, and assimilation [47–51] and understands disability as a cultural experience and a political category. Crip approaches call for interdependence among disabled people and for coalition building among different disability groups; it foregrounds intersectionality [52], mapping how disability and race are shaped by systems of ableism and white supremacy in cultural institutions, such as education and healthcare [53, 54]. Crip approaches to OAD do not seek to 'cure' or rehabilitate but invite OAD to define their own goals and definitions of wellness. This aligns with the demands made by disability rights movements for self-leadership by those living with multiple tiers of 'disability' (e.g. neurodivergent people, older adults, and BIPOC and queer/trans disabled people) [55, 56]; the mission to eradicate ableism thus shares aims with movements to disrupt white supremacy, settler-colonialism, and the medical industrial complex [57].

Recent projects in human-computer interaction, science and technology studies, and media studies have used crip and disability justice-informed critiques, illustrating the important applied and theoretical contributions of these frameworks. Crip approaches to technoscience reveal the benefits of design teams working with disabled stakeholders to meet diverse needs and goals [44], to provide access rather than recovery, and to challenge positioning OAD as cognitively deficient [7], instead prioritizing the wholeness of OAD [4, 9, 57]. These approaches inform our co-design processes for ABLE.Family, which complement our ongoing efforts to embed elements of speculative and emotional design in our human centered design approaches [46, 58] to ensure participants drive research goals and practices, project the future they wish to see for themselves, and achieve benefits from the research experience.

10   Dementia, Crip and Accessibility-Informed, Intergenerational Game Design

In this section, we will discuss the key conceptual ideas that drive our interaction and interface designs, always filtered via dementia and crip-informed and participatory, community-based research [7]. We position OAD and their carers as experienced thinkers, tinkerers, creators, and makers [44] whose design expertise is crucial to team success. In our co-design approach, we rework the platform goals in iterative design to re-center OAD goals, preferences and crucially, their diverse interests, while focusing on objectives to meet diverse needs, and not to cure disability [26].

The game choices rely on OAD's (often strong) long term memory [25, 29, 59] to increase pleasure and reduce discomfort. We aim for games to be familiar and colours to be bright, reflecting reminiscence (memory) theory, and language/colour recognition approaches [27, 60]. We reference familiar interface and game options, reflecting principles of accessible and universal design. We endeavour to offer opportunities for OAD to recall memories of music, and to reminisce, or create personal stories, known to be comforting to OAD. [30, 61, 62]. The platform allows users to save a drawn picture as a.png file, to be printed as memento or used as a screensaver, which is beneficial for recall [63] and re-instills a sense of identity for family members, such as grandparenting.

We implement accessibility design principles to maximize usability, and support the diverse needs and abilities of users. Following a responsive design approach, we aim for ease of navigation, offering simple and intuitive interaction. The platform aims to respond and adapt to multiple devices, allowing users to access the platform in their preferred format. The design platform includes text and icons that are easy to read and understand by diverse users. The interface calls upon Zoom and tablet interaction skills that OAD already possess. To increase accessibility, we added roll-over text that appears when a user places their mouse or finger over a button or symbol, to explain in plain language the feature's purpose. We offer text below buttons and other features to increase redundancy, and ease of use for people with sight disabilities or colour blindness. Certain buttons have an activation colour, denoting a mode or setting, e.g. selecting draw mode, using the pencil or eraser, etc. These features reference mechanical systems that may be recognizable to OAD users, such as a latching button or switch used to turn on a household device.

Dementia-friendly principles drive us to design with clear and concrete instructions. To wit: we have created the platform as a sparsely populated space; use navigational colours and symbols (drawing on long term memory); offer short duration game options; level play difficulty; and offer multiple options befitting different levels of cognitive impairment engagement (e.g. observing, responding, guessing, making/active playing). Larger buttons are used to focus OAD's attention on the most important features for play. As well, the platform (and our instruction manual) invites trusted carers to choose and even customize game interactions that will be most pleasurable and least frustrating for their OAD. One key challenge given Canada's diversity is to offer games that reflect diverse cultural, ethnic and regional experiences. To this end, we have designed open-ended games (such as group drawings) which allow for cultural expression, and have planned customized features allowing families for example to upload a familiar pictures to "paint" or favourite songs to sing with. In this way, families can "curate" their game experience to reflect their family's traditions and OAD needs.

The following images demonstrate how these principles (clarity, clean interface, color coding, game options, etc.) are instituted in our present prototype. Note that as testing and iterative design occurs, we are yet minimizing button options on the interface and plan a highly minimal view (1 play pad, 2 buttons) for OAD players in future iterations. Each frame will be discussed following the images (Fig. 1 and 2).

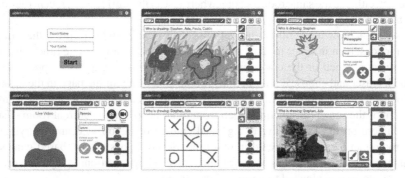

Fig. 1. Mockup images of the ABLE.Family platform in its desktop computer version used in a web browser.

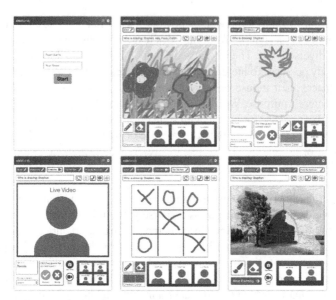

Fig. 2. Mockup images of the ABLE.Family platform in its iPad or Tablet device version used in a web browser.

11   Detailed Interface Review

The above images depict each screen or mode that can be used in the current iteration of the ABLE.Family platform. From screen one (viewing left to right and then row by row), screens/modes consist of:

- Login – The login screen is the first thing a user sees after going to the ABLE.Family platform URL on their web browser. A user is asked to enter a room name and their name, which will be used to identify each user while using the app. The room name connects all users that entered the same room. This allows people connected to the Internet, either in the same room or somewhere else in the world, to interact in real-time with each other in their own private virtual room.
- Draw – The draw mode allows users to use their mouse, stylus or press their finger on a touchscreen in order to draw pictures on the canvas at the same time. The user can select a pencil or the eraser and select a wide array of colours by pressing the pencil, eraser and choose colour buttons (in the upper right of the page in the desktop layout and bottom left of the iPad layout). Live video feeds can be seen to the right or bottom of the screen, displaying video from other people in the current room. Using the camera on the user's device, e.g. iPad camera or laptop webcam, everyone in the room can be seen and heard in real-time. Several types of turn based games or collaborative drawing can be done to encourage intergenerational play. The drawn picture can be downloaded to be shared or viewed later.
- Pictionary – This mode is based on the popular game where a person draws out a secret word while their teammates try to guess what it is before the timer runs out. On the ABLE.Family platform, a user can select a category from the dropdown menu and

then start drawing out the word it supplies. In the image above, the word pineapple has been given in the "Your Word" box. None of the other users can see the word in the "Your Word" box until the person drawing selects the green check mark of red "X" to signal to players if they have guessed correctly or incorrectly. Connecting red and green colours to buttons can help an OAD to understand the actions initiated by the button. The game is reset by selecting another category and receiving a new word.

- Charades – This mode is based on the popular game similar to Pictionary; instead of drawing, the user acts out the word while the rest of the players try to guess what it is. In this mode, the drawing canvas is turned into a larger video screen enabling everyone to see the player acting out the word. Other buttons allow players to take a screenshot of the live video or start a recording of everyone playing to share or watch later.
- Tic-Tac-Toe – In this mode, two or more users can play the game Tic-Tac-Toe. In this turn-based game, one player draws an X in a box while another player places an O. In order to win, players need to draw three of their own symbols in a row in any direction. This game encourages intergenerational play through its familiarity and enables OAD to teach strategy to child or younger players.
- Paint by Numbers – This mode is based on the popular painting trend in 1950's and 1960's North America, where players could paint a white canvas with faint outlines, by following the numbers found in each segment and selecting the corresponding colour. In our app, the outlines can be seen, though no numbers are present. The user can paint on the canvas to virtually apply paint to the image and the colour is chosen automatically. This is both a beneficial sensory (eg tactile) engagement for OAD, and reduces anxiety associated with painting within the lines and allows for cooperative game play to reveal the image. The game offers various images to choose from and will add a feature where users can upload images familiar and comforting to OAD (eg. family cottages, favourite events, pets, etc.). This mode can stimulate reminiscence and storytelling known to be beneficial and comforting to OAD. As well, as images appear, participants can invite OAD to narrate what they see for cognitive enhancement. This practice also offers opportunities to restore grandparents as roles as teachers and family historians while it builds family bonds.

12 Planning Future Iterations: Music, Matching and Dementia-Informed Movement Games

Future iterations plan music games including "Name that Tune" (where players guess recognizable songs) and "Sing Alongs", a popular experience in long term care facilities, where OAD sing along and motion to old tunes such as "The Itsy Bitsy Spider", and "The Wheels on the Bus".[2]) Research is well-established noting that music referencing long term memory is cognitively and affectively beneficial for OAD.

Notably, the simple games we have included are chosen because they are pleasurable for OAD, recognizable to older adults children and fun for smaller children (and grand-children.) We anticipate that the "Sing Alongs", group drawing, "Pictionary" (drawing

---

[2] Our team has past music intervention experiences for OAD; these new ideas come from conversations with IM Hope (Hamilton, Ontario), who advise the project.

guessing game) and Charades games will be engaging for young children, who might in fact drive the play, allowing OAD to observe, cheer, and congratulate them, and in so doing, restore a sense of identity and family roles, which is a goal of dementia-friendly research. Future iterations will test the interest and enjoyment for OAD and small children in playing interactive puzzle, matching and guessing games.

We are currently exploring the integration of movement into this interface. As discussed in past publications [58], the Able Music project intended to exploit the synergistic effects that come from platforms offering movement, art and social interaction, which are shown to beneficially impact older adults physiologically, cognitively and to improve mood. We are engaging an expert in dance and movement therapy, with experience teaching dance to older adults via remote platform during the pandemic to create options for low level and intensity movement, such as Tai Chi, with proven benefits [19, 64]. The movement will not replicate physical therapy but in some cases will seek to simulate some of the movements of physical therapy exercises while feeling like play.

An additional key approach of the platform, which we will further implement in the future, is engaging motor learning to allow OAD to return each time to the platform and know (from experience) how to engage and play. From a motor learning perspective, OAD learn and re-learn best through procedural or implicit learning where they "learn by doing" in contrast to declarative or explicit learning which requires conscious awareness and knowledge [65–67]. Implicit learning means the OAD learn through repetition and skill practice without deliberate cognitive oversight (e.g., awareness, reflection, attention). In the ABLE.Family platform, OAD can engage in familiar tasks that allow them to learn and re-learn motor tasks which do not require explicit cognitive oversight.

13 Future Machine Learning Approaches to Gesture and Game Design

As noted [46], the previous ABLE Music platform sought to transform movement into play and art creation; we were employing wearable sensors to capture and translate user movement data to create artful and gaming interactions. Though we pivoted to a web-based platform with Able.Family, we plan to offer gesture-capture as a platform add-on tool that allows for non-verbal interaction (gesture rather than hand tools such as touchpads, mice, and tablet pens) in advanced future iterations. To this end, we have ideated a gesture-based interaction in Pictionary where players would draw a shape (in the air); images drawn would be captured by a wearable sensor and then revealed in computer renderings visible on the computer screen. This ideation is in the early stages of development and of course requires that we further pursue our efforts to train the sensor via machine learning techniques. We have begun this research, as described below.

Free painting in the air with a wrist-worn sensor is a non-trivial task if no limits are imposed. Research on Google Quick Draw shows that 86% of Americans draw circles counterclockwise while 80% of Japanese draw them clockwise [68]. To address the problem of drawing from different directions, we have formulated the problem as a 2-step pattern matching. In the first step, a machine learning model will help recognize a sequence of pre-defined meta-gestures painted by the user. Then a simple matching step will compare the predicted sequence with predefined templates and output the corresponding ID of the sketched object. The predefined meta-gestures and objects to be recognized are shown in Fig. 3.

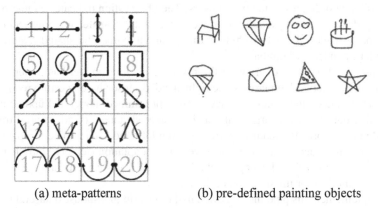

(a) meta-patterns   (b) pre-defined painting objects

Fig. 3. To limit the scope of painting, we define (b) sketched objects to be recognized by the machine learning model and further decompose them into (a) basic meta-patterns. To allow users to paint from any direction and paint in any order, the template is defined as a set that includes all possible meta-patterns. E.g., a template of a smiling face is defined as {5, 6, 19, 20}.

To recognize meta-patterns in a free painting, it is necessary to segment data into one-stroke pieces. As an IMU sensor records data continuously, it is difficult to implement data segmentation by post-processing. Thus, we simplify the problem by asking the user to make a 1 s stop when they finish each stroke of paint. Then with a 1 s length sliding window, the neural network can predict the corresponding meta-patterns contained in it.

Another issue to be considered is that the target users may have different dominant arms and thus wear IMU at either wrist. Such using habits divergence will lead to dramatically different sensor signal patterns. The painting habit matters more than simply rotating the sensor or augmenting the recorded data; a straightforward example is given in Fig. 4.

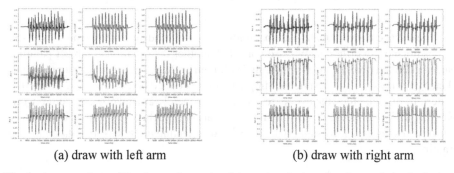

(a) draw with left arm   (b) draw with right arm

Fig. 4. A comparison of 3-axis accelerometer data captured when drawing a circle clockwise with different arms. Each data trial includes 10 repetitions.

From Fig. 4, it is clear that exchanging the sign of x and y-axis in (a) respectively, though they share similarities, will not make the signal pattern match with that in (b). This procedure simulates the rotation of the sensor around the z-axis for 180 degrees and aligns the coordinates of the two sensors. The observation indicates a meta-pattern painted by different hands should be treated separately. Transfer learning techniques [69] can be utilized to help a machine learning model extract the shared feature for a given pattern painted by both hands.

The proposed pipeline of training the machine learning model has 3 steps. First, pre-train a neural network on large-scale right-handed sensor-based gesture recognition dataset; second, keep the feature extractor of the pre-trained model and update it with right-handed data from the target dataset; last, take advantage of adversarial training proposed in [70], force the features extracted from lefthanded data to be inseparable to that of the right-handed ones. Note: the adversarial adaptation step here only helps the left-handed model to take advantage of the large-scale right-handed data; we still have two separate models for inference on each hand.

We implemented this pipeline and evaluated it on a small in-house dataset. Data was collected from 2 subjects painting each meta-pattern for 10 times with both hands. Then it was randomly split 80% for model adaptation and 20% for test. The confusion matrix for the test on each hand shows in Fig. 5.

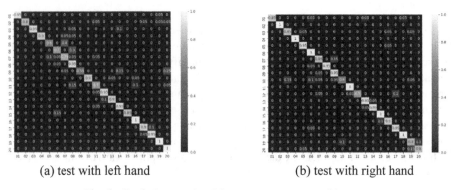

(a) test with left hand   (b) test with right hand

Fig. 5. Confusion matrix of the meta-pattern recognition test.

The test accuracy for meta-pattern painting is >80%, and the confused meta-patterns for each hand are different. We also collected another data trial on 1 subject painting each predefined object 3 times with both hands then evaluated the accuracy of predicting sketch paintings with it. Despite the simplicity of predefined objects and their distinctive pattern from each other, the overall test accuracy is merely around 60%. As future work we plan to revise the design of the machine learning pipeline and further improve its performance by enriching supported objects and collecting more sensory data for model training.

14 Conclusion and the ABLE.Family Future

In this paper, we have reviewed key outcomes and plans for future development of the ABLE.Family gaming platform designed for OAD and their carers, which firmly centers diverse OAD and the carers as experts in their experiences of the world and how they wish to navigate it via technology. To ensure diverse input into the platform, our team is working with regional dementia-engaged organizations to broaden the diversity OAD who participate in this research. Many of these organizations also work to enhance access to digital technologies and Internet access for diverse OAD. For our work to succeed, we recognize the need for policy changes to redress systemic discrimination, bias against and neglect of marginalized populations, due to historic racial and ethnic biases and white supremacy. Canadian health care providers and researchers must amplify calls for policy changes that will improve access to telehealth, digital healthcare technologies, and Internet service for diverse populations, particularly the many and growing numbers of OAD and their carers.

As researchers, it is also our responsibility to integrate theory and methods (such as disability and crip theory, and universal and co-design methods) to ensure that we are designing *with* OAD and carers, to create technology with universal accessibility and to produce tools that are desired, inviting, sustainable and innovative, affordable and meet the health and wellness goals of diverse OAD. In these efforts, interdisciplinary teams and approaches are key. Our team's diverse expertise in gerontology, computer science and machine learning, art and design, and disability and "crip" methods has allowed us to address challenges posed by COVID-19, to create a gaming platform that combats long-term isolation and loneliness of OAD. We are inspired by and grateful for the creative ideas and engagements offered by participating OAD carers and stakeholders. Their ongoing insights and challenges have productively 'broken' the ABLE.Family platform many times over, offering us the opportunity to create a truly accessible platform to combat loneliness and despair, and to enhance opportunities for play and pleasure among intergenerational family members. We look forward to continuing to update and modify the platform, and in the spirit of universal design, and dementia- and crip-informed approaches, to continue to improve and add features to the platform. As well, we look forward to launching this as a free, accessible, and *living* platform (that will be continually updated and evolved) in the near future.

References

1. Canada Public Health Service. A dementia strategy for Canada: together we aspire. https://www.canada.ca/en/public-health/services/publications/diseasesconditions/dementia-strategy.html. Accessed 9 April 2020
2. Canada Institute for Health Information (CIHI). Dementia in Canada Summary (2021). https://www.cihi.ca/en/dementia-in-canada/dementia-in-canada-summary
3. Starblanket, D., O'Connell, M.E., Gould, B., Jardine, M., Ferguson, M., Bourassa, C.: Defining technology user needs of older Indigenous adults requiring dementia care. Gerontechnology **18**(3), 142–155 (2019). https://doi.org/10.4017/gt.2019.18.3.002.00
4. Bennett, C.L., Rosner, D.K.: The promise of empathy: design, disability, and knowing the 'other'. In: Proceedings of the 2019 CHI Conference in Human Factors in Computing System, pp. 1–13 (2019). https://doi.org/10.1145/3290605.3300528

5. Bosch, L.B.J., Kanis, M.: Design opportunities for supporting informal caregivers. In: Proceedings of the 2016 CHI Conference Extended Abstracts on Human Factors in Computing Systems, pp. 2790–2797 (2016). https://doi.org/10.1145/2851581.2892354
6. Sixsmith, A.: COVID-19 and AgeTech. Qual. Ageing Older Adults (2020). https://doi.org/10.1108/QAOA-07-2020-0029
7. Lazar, A., Edasis, C., Piper, A.M.: A critical lens on dementia and HCI. In: Proceedings of CHI 2017, pp. 1–14 (2017a). http://doi.org/10.1145/3025453.3025522
8. Costa Costanho, T., et al.: Assessing cognitive function in older adults using a video conferencing approach. EBioMedicine **11**, 278–284 (2016)
9. Cridland, E.K., Philipson, L., Brennan-Horley, C., Swaffer, K.: Reflections and recommendations for conducting in-depth interviews for people with dementia. Qual. Health Res. **26**(13), 1774–1786 (2016). https://doi.org/10.1177/1049732316637065
10. Jacklin, K., et al.: Developing the Canadian indigenous cognitive assessment for use with indigenous older adults in Ontario Canada. . Innov. Aging **4**(4), 1–13 (2020). https://doi.org/10.1093/geroni/igaa038
11. Salma, J., Salami, B.: "We Are Like Any Other People, But We Don't Cry Much Because Nobody Listens:" the need to strengthen aging policies and service provision for minorities in Canada. Gerontologist **60**(2), 279–290 (2020)
12. Lee, A.C.: COVID-19 and the advancement of digital physical therapist practice and telehealth. Phys. Ther. **100**(7), 1054–1057 (2020). https://doi.org/10.1093/ptj/pzaa079
13. Kayama, H., Okamoto, K., Nishiguchi, S., Yamada, M., Kuroda, T., Aoyama, T.: Effects of a kinect-based exercise game on improving executive cognitive performance in community-dwelling elderly: case control study. J. Med. Internet Res. **16**(2), e61 (2014). https://doi.org/10.2196/jmir.3108
14. Webster, D., Celik, O.: Systematic review of Kinect applications in elderly care and stroke rehabilitation. J. Neuroeng. Rehabil. **11**(108) (2014). https://doi.org/10.1186/1743-0003-11-108
15. Sanders, L.M.J., Hortobágyi, T., la Bastide-van Gemert, S., van der Zee, E.A., van Heuvelen, M.J.G.: Dose-response relationship between exercise and cognitive function in older adults with and without cognitive impairment: a systematic review and meta-analysis. PLoS ONE **14**(1), e0210036 (2019). https://doi.org/10.1371/journal.pone.0210036
16. Spartano, N.L., et al.: Association of accelerometer-measured light-intensity physical activity with brain volume: the framingham heart study. JAMA Netw. **2**(4), 1–12 (2019)
17. Suwabe, K., et al.: Rapid stimulation of human dentate gyrus function with acute mild exercise. PNAS **115**(41), 10487–10492 (2018). https://doi.org/10.1073/pnas.1805668115
18. Tse, A.C.Y., Wong, T.W.L., Lee, P.H.: Effect of low-intensity exercise on physical and cognitive health in older adults: a systematic review. Sports Med. **1**(37), 1–13 (2015)
19. Hsieh, C., et al.: The effectiveness of a virtual reality-based Tai Chi exercise on cognitive and physical function in older adults with cognitive impairment. Dement. Geriatr. Cogn. Disord. **46**(5–6), 358–370 (2017). https://doi.org/10.1159/000494659
20. Sungkarat, S., Boripuntakul, S., Chattipakorn, N., Watcharasaksilp, K., Lord, S.R.: Effects of Tai Chi on cognition and fall risk in older adults with mild cognitive impairment. J. Am. Geriatr. Soc. **65**, 721–727 (2016)
21. Guzmán-García, A., Mukaetova-Ladinska, E., James, I.: Introducing a latin ballroom class to people with dementia living in care homes, benefits and concerns: a pilot study. Dementia **12**(5), 523–535 (2013). https://doi.org/10.1177/1471301211429753
22. Abreu, M., Hartley, G.: The effects of salsa dance on balance, gait, and fall risk in a sedentary patient with alzheimer's dementia, multiple comorbidities, and recurrent falls. J. Geriatr. Phys. Ther. **36**(2), 100–108 (2013)

23. Nagahata, K., Fukushima, T., Ishibashi, N., Takahashi, Y., Moriyama, M.: A soundscape study: what kinds of sounds do elderly patients with dementia recollect? Noise Health **6**(24), 63 (2004)

24. Camic, P.M., Tischler, V., Pearman, C.H.: Viewing and making art together: a multi-session art-gallery-based intervention for people with dementia and their carers. Aging Ment. Health **18**(2), 161–168 (2014). https://doi.org/10.1080/13607863.2013.818101

25. Savulich, G., et al.: Cognitive training using a novel memory game on an iPad in patients with amnesiac Mild Cognitive Impairment (aMCI). Int. J. Neuropsychopharmacol. **20**(8), 624–633 (2017). https://www.academic.oup.com/ijnp/article/20/8/624/3868827

26. Lazar, A., Edasis, C., Piper, A.M.: Supporting people with dementia in digital social sharing. In: Proceedings of CHI 2017, pp. 1–14 (2017b)

27. Seah, C.L.E., Tan, M.T.B.K.: MatchLink- a multi-sensorial game for persons with dementia. In: Proceedings of the International Design Conference 2018, pp. 2311–2312 (2018)

28. Ferreira, C.D., Gadelha, M.J.N., de Fonsêca, E.K.G., da Silva, J.S.C., Torro, N., Fernández-Calvo, B.: Long term memory of haptic and visual information in older adults. Aging Neuropsychol. Cognit. **28**, 65–67 (2021)

29. Chesham, A., et al.: Search and mask task: development of a taskified match-3 puzzle game to assess and practice visual search. JMIR Serious Games **7**(2), 1–19 (2019)

30. Welsh, D., et al.: Ticket to talk: supporting conversation between young people and people with dementia through digital media. In: Proceedings of the 2018 CHI Conference on Human Factors in Computing Systems, pp. 1–13 (2018). https://doi.org/10.1145/3173574.3173949

31. Rendon, A.A., Lohman, E.B., Thorpe, D., Johnson, E.G., Medina, E., Bradley, B.: The effect of virtual reality gaming on dynamic balance in older adults. Age Ageing **45**, 549–552 (2012)

32. Gerling, K., Mandryk, R.: Custom-designed motion-based games for older adults: a review of literature in human-machine interaction. Gerontechnology **12**(2), 68–80 (2014)

33. Dove, E., Astell, A.: The kinect project: group motion-based gaming for people living with dementia. Dementia **18**(6), 2189–2205 (2019)

34. Franz, R.L., Munteanu, C., Barbosa Neves, B., Baecker, R.: Time to retire old methodologies?: Reflecting on conducting usability evaluations for older adults. In: MobileCHI 2015: Proceedings of the 17th International Conference on Human-Computer Interaction with Mobile Devices and Services Adjunct, pp. 912–915 (2015)

35. Foley, S., Welsh, D., Pantidi, N., Morrissey, K., Nappey, T., McCarthy, J.: Printer pals: experience-centered design to support agency for people with dementia. In: CHI 2019: Proceedings of the 2019 Conference on Human Factors in Computing Systems, pp. 1–13 (2019)

36. Karimi, A., Neustadter, C.: From high connectivity to social isolation: communication practices of older adults in the digital age. In: CSCW 2012: Proceedings of the ACM 2012 Conference on Computer Supported Cooperative Work Companion, pp. 127–130 (2012)

37. Tait, J., Lyall, C.: Short Guide to Developing Interdisciplinary Research Proposals. ISSTI (Institute for the Study of Science, Technology and Innovation) Briefing Note (Number 1) March 2007

38. Dilworth-Anderson, P., Moon, H., Aranda, M.P.: Dementia caregiving research: expanding and reframing the lens of diversity, inclusivity, and intersectionality. Gerontologist **60**(5), 797–805 (2020). https://doi.org/10.1093/geront/gnaa050

39. Nimrod, G.: Technophobia among older adult internet users. Educ. Gerontol. **44**(2–3), 148–162 (2018). https://doi.org/10.1080/03601277.2018.1428145

40. Andrews, J.A., Brown, L.J.E., Hawley, M.S., Astell, A.J.: Older adults' perspectives on using digital technology to maintain good mental health: interactive group study. J. Med. Internet Res. **21**(2), e11694 (2019). https://doi.org/10.2196/11694

41. Mackert, M., Mabry-Flynn, A., Champlin, S., Donovan, E.E., Pounders, K.: Health literacy and health information technology adoption: the potential for a new digital divide. J. Med. Internet Res. **18**(10), e264 (2016)
42. Fagherazzi, G., Goetzinger, C., Rashid, M.A., Aguayo, G.A., Huiart, L.: Digital health strategies to fight COVID-19 worldwide: challenges, recommendations, and a Call for Papers. J. Med. Internet Res. **22**(6), e19284 (2020). https://doi.org/10.2196/19284
43. Benjamin, R.: Race After Technology: Abolitionist Tools for the New Jim Code. Polity Press, Cambridge (2019)
44. Hamraie, A., Fritsch, K.: Crip technoscience manifesto. Catalyst Feminism Theory Technosci. **5**(1), 1–31 (2019). https://doi.org/10.28968/cftt.v5i1.29607
45. Sastry, S., Basu, A.: How to have (critical) method in a pandemic: outlining a culture-centered approach to health discourse analysis Front. Health Commun. **14** (2020) https://doi.org/10.3389/fcomm.2020.585954
46. Gardner, P., et al.: ABLE music: arts-based exercise enhancing longevity. In: Stephanidis, C., Antona, M., Ntoa, S. (eds.) HCII 2020. CCIS, vol. 1294, pp. 450–454. Springer, Cham (2020). https://doi.org/10.1007/978-3-030-60703-6_58
47. Schalk, S.: Coming to claim crip: disidentification with/in disability studies. Disabil. Stud. Q. **33**(2) (2013). http://dx.doi.org/10.18061/dsq.v33i2.3705
48. Clare, E.: Brilliant Imperfection: Grappling with Cure. Duke University Press, Durham (2017)
49. Kafer, A.: Feminist, Queer, Crip. Indiana University Press, Bloomington (2013)
50. McRuer, R.: Crip Theory: Cultural Signs of Queerness and Disability. NYU Press, New York (2006)
51. Crenshaw, K.: Mapping the margins: intersectionality, identity politics, and violence against women of color. Stanf. Law Rev. **43**, 1241–1299 (1990)
52. Erevelles, N., Minear, A.: Unspeakable offenses: untangling race and disability in discourses of intersectionality. J. Literary Cultural Disability Stud. **4**(2), 127–146 (2010). https://doi.org/10.3828/jlcds.2010.11
53. Bailey, M., Mobley, I.A.: Work in the intersections: a black feminist disability studies framework. Gend. Soc. **33**(1), 19–40 (2018)
54. Berne, P.: What is disability justice? 16 June 2020. Retrieved https://www.sinsinvalid.org/news-1/2020/6/16/what-is-disability-justice.
55. Piepzna-Samarasinha, L.L.: Care Work: Dreaming Disability Justice. Arsenal Pulp Press, Vancouver (2018)
56. Mingus, M.: Medical industrial complex visual, 6 February 2015. Retrieved https://leavingevidence.wordpress.com/2015/02/06/medical-industrial-complex-visual/
57. Spiel, K., et al.: Nothing about us without us: investigating the role of critical disability studies in HCI. In: Proceedings of CHI EA 2020: Extended Abstracts of the CHI 2020 Conference on Human Factors in Computing Systems, pp. 1–8 (2020)
58. Gardner, P., et al.: Employing interdisciplinary approaches in designing with fragile older adults; advancing ABLE for arts-based rehabilitative play and complex learning. In: Zhou, J., Salvendy, G. (eds.) HCII 2019. LNCS, vol. 11592, pp. 3–21. Springer, Cham (2019). https://doi.org/10.1007/978-3-030-22012-9_1
59. Yang, Y., Kwak, Y.T.: Improvement of cognitive function after computer-based cognitive training in early stage of Alzheimer's Dementia. Dement. Neurocogn. Disord. **16**(1), 7–11 (2017)
60. Gomes, G.P.R., et al.: *Healing spaces*: feasibility of a multisensory experience for older adults with advanced dementia and their caregivers. In: PETRA 2020: Proceedings of the 13th ACM International Conference on PErvasive Technologies Related to Assistive Environments, pp. 1–9 (2020). https://doi.org/10.1145/3389189.3392607
61. Subramaniam, P., Woods, B.: Digital life storybooks for people with dementia living in care homes: an evaluation. Clin. Interv. Aging **11**, 1263–1276 (2016)

62. Houben, M., Brankaert, R., Bakker, S., Kennig, G., Bongers, I., Egan, B.: The role of every day sounds in Dementia care. In: CHI 2020: Proceedings of the 2020 CHI Conference on Human Factors in Computing Systems, pp. 1–14 (2020)
63. Tong, T., Chan, J.H., Chignell, M.: Serious games for Dementia. In: WWW 2017 Companion: Proceedings of the 26th International Conference on the World-Wide Web, pp. 1111–1115 (2017). https://doi.org/10.1145/3041021.3054930
64. Pandit, S., et al.: ExerciseCheck: a scalable platform for remote physical therapy deployed as a hybrid desktop and web application. In: PETRA 2019: Proceedings of the 12th ACM International Conference on PErvasive Technologies Related to Assistive Environments, pp. 101–109(2019). https://doi.org/10.1145/3316782.3321537
65. Patterson, J.T., Wessel, J.: Strategies for retraining functional movement in persons with Alzheimer disease: a review. Physiother Can. **54**, 274–280 (2002)
66. van Halteren-van, T.I.A.D.A., Scherder, E.J.A., Hulstijn, W.: Motor-skill learning in Alzheimer's disease: a review with an eye to the clinical practice. Neuropsychol. Rev. **17**(3), 203–212 (2007). https://doi.org/10.1007/s11065-007-9030-1
67. Vidoni, E.D., Boyd, L.A.: Achieving enlightenment: what do we know about the implicit learning system and its interaction with explicit knowledge? J. Neurol. Phys. Ther. JNPT. **31**(3), 145–154 (2007). https://doi.org/10.1097/NPT.0b013e31814b148e
68. Thu-Huong Ha, N.: How do you draw a circle? We analyzed 100,000 circles to show how culture shapes our instincts. Quartz2021. https://qz.com/994486/the-way-you-draw-circles-says-a-lot-about-you/. Accessed 10 Feb 2021
69. Torrey, L., Shavlik, J.: Transfer learning. In: Handbook of Research on Machine Learning Applications and Trends: Algorithms, Methods, and Techniques. IGI Global, pp. 242–264 (2010)
70. Tzeng, E., Hoffman, J., Saenko, K., et al.: Adversarial discriminative domain adaptation. In: Proceedings of the IEEE Conference on Computer Vision and Pattern Recognition, pp. 7167–7176 (2017)

NEONEO Balance Ball: Designing an Intergenerational Interaction Exergame for In-home Balance Training

Emiran Kaisar, Ren Bo Ding, Ting Han, and Shi Qiu[✉]

Department of Design, Shanghai Jiao Tong University, Shanghai, China
{imarsemiran,drbdrb,hanting,qiushi11}@sjtu.edu.cn

Abstract. This paper describes a tangible interactive prototype, aiming at reducing the risk of falling in older adults and ensure their adherence to the in-home balance training. The design of the prototype derived from our research on the effectiveness of different training modes in balance. An exergame created for this prototype, appealing to youngsters, might result in them (older adults and young people) playing together. This may not only provide motivation to exercise but also a platform increasing communication between two generations, which is beneficial to older adults' mental health. Therefore, perceiving benefits aforementioned, older adults could get more interested and even develop a long-term habit of playing such exergame. Researches had been done regarding the older adults' perspective when designing intergenerational games or exergames. Here, our concept focuses on involving both older adults and young people to play the exergame together. In this paper, an experimental plan has been designed to gain insights from young people for better solutions to motivate them to play the game with older adults.

Keywords: Balance training · Older adults · Tangible serious game · Intergenerational interaction

1 Introduction

Aging is associated with the decline in mobility and balance, rising the rate of falling in older adults, causing huge threats to their functional independence and health [1]. Falling is the most common injuries to elderlies which will bring burden on medical care, family, or society level [2]. Many population-based studies showed that every third senior (over 65) falls once a year and half of those are recurrent fallers [3]. Previous studies revealed that the proper training with the focus on balance could reduce the risk of falls [4]. The in-home Otago Exercise Program has seen a 35% reduction in falls rates and injurious falls [2]. In addition, the in-home exercise program is important as it's cost-effective and many older adults are reluctant to or unable to attend group exercise classes [5]. Therefore, in-home balance training plays an important role in reducing the rates of falling in society. However, evidence suggests that there is a problem with the adherence to rehabilitation at home [6]. This means that many fallers do not fulfill the recommended

Q. Gao and J. Zhou (Eds.): HCII 2021, LNCS 12787, pp. 78–89, 2021.
https://doi.org/10.1007/978-3-030-78111-8_5

amount of exercise per week and the benefits of exercise will disappear when exercise is halted [7]. Low confidence to the exercise program can result in the decline of interest [8]. There are also other factors influencing adherence such as motivation and nature of the exercise program [9, 10]. Although there are still debates concerned with the factors contributing to the low adherence in-home training, previous studies revealed the increments in interests and adherence in functional training with the use of exergames.

This paper presents a novel design of an exergame and an experimental design on the prototype. Our concept is to motivate older adults' training by adding appealing features to our exergame that older adults can keep up training for a long duration. Social interaction in the game attracts players and they play for a long time due to the social connectedness of such games [11]. Some studies revealed that intergenerational communication of the game can be an attraction for older adults [12, 13]. Older adults can be motivated more when they play exergame with young people [14]. The participants will be recruited from the university. Our preliminary test will be taken from the youth's perspective because as an important part of our concept, their interests and ideas to the scenario are crucial in designing an exergame that they will play willingly and really have conversations with older adults. So, our aim in this experiment is to get an insight into a scenario that can motivate young people to join in.

2 Related Work

Related work in exergames and intergenerational communication game was really inspiring while carrying out our project.

2.1 Balance Training Exergame for Older Adults

Uzor et al. [15]studied the effects of long-term involvement in exergames compared with the traditional training, and found promising outcomes in motivating training at home with long duration. Donker et al. [16] showed with the interactive tiles for balance training, that real time visual feedback improved the motivation on balance rehabilitation, and also suggested personalization to individual patient training needs.

While focusing on the aspects that could attract elderlies' adherence, the effectiveness of the exergame shouldn't be neglected. Morat et al. [17] highlighted the importance of unstable surface in balance training that requires motor skills relevant to preventing falls.

2.2 Intergenerational Communication Game

Playing multiplayer mode (cooperative or competitive) with partners enhances game enjoyment compared to playing alone [18], and people are more likely to play the social games for a long duration[11]. Both old and young generations think highly of the social game, while younger adults unanimously shared the intention to play more with the older adults in their families [19–23]. Pecchioni et al. [24] argued that playing video games together can be a platform for the expansion of family relationships. Promising results have been seen in co-located exergame playing between grandparent and grandchild [25]. Fuchsberger et al. [12] showed a novel online-intergenerational game for geographically separated grandparent and grandchild.

3 Prototype

The prototype has been implemented to be qualified for our preliminary test. During our implementation, fast iteration was very helpful in putting on a better solution for the prototype. In total, there were two generations of our hardware and many adjustments to the game.

3.1 Design Concept

The NEONEO Balance Ball was designed to motivate older adults to train their balance for a long duration. According to the researches mentioned above, two factors may help us achieve our goals: gamification and intergenerational interaction. Participants would be asked to talk out their feelings about the exergame and scenarios we designed.

User Needs. Older adults need an easily comprehensive system, while their interests in the game are important that they would be willing to learn to play the game despite some barriers in the way [12]. However, youth would get upset sometimes when older adults keep asking questions [26]. Therefore, both of theirs need should be considered during the design and the trade-off be met after our research.

Attributes. Based on the reasons mentioned above, our design should acquire the following features. By doing this research, we want to know how we can better integrate these features into our design.

Unstable Surface. Improvement in balance is very important, and unstable surface is proven to be effective while balance training [17].

Gamification. This game should provide interesting gaming experience that attract both generations.

In-home Usage. Our equipment should be space-efficient and suitable for older adults to use at home.

Easily Comprehensive. There should be a trade-off between comprehensions and attractions concerning both generations. and that's what we need to find out during our research.

Intergenerational Communication. Our exergame should be able to provide chances for two generations (old and young) to communicate.

Use Scenario. It is usually the case in China that three consecutive generations living together in the same household [27]. Therefore, our first scenario presents old and young playing together in the living room. In addition, elderlies can choose to play with their offspring (geographically separated) or other young people through the internet. There'll be two kinds of multiplayer modes (cooperative and competitive). While motor ability and cognitive competence will be considered in game design to narrow the performance gap in competitive mode, the different tasks will be given in cooperative mode that two generations both make their own contributions to the team goal. Figure 1. Presents competitive mode in living room scenario.

Fig. 1. Competitive mode in one physical space.

3.2 Implementation

When reading articles in this field, we encountered a prototype (ActivBOSU) presented by Caltenco et al. [28], having one feature we desired (unstable surface). However, there were problems mentioned in their preliminary test that players found it frustrating to look down for the visual feedback. Therefore, we made some changes to the original design, making it a readily comprehensive exergame with visual feedbacks of their tilt angles on the gaming screen and the scores reflecting their performances. USB cable was removed because we used portable battery to supply power and blue-tooth to transmit signals. In addition, by providing the feedbacks at eye-level which is important in balance training[16] and increasing the stability of the surface, we removed the safety support handlebar to simplify the equipment and made it more space-efficient and suitable for elderly's using at home.

Fig. 2. NEONEO Balance Ball Prototype 1.

Iteration 1. The first generation was made quickly equipped with the sensor designed and made by our team Fig. 2. There's a copper ball inside of the PVC tube, rolling to the side according to the tilt direction of the tube, and it will send signals when it touches either side Fig. 3. The Arduino controller receives and processes these signals, then it can detect the tilt direction of the platform. Figure 4. presents the realization of our sensors placed right-angle with each other to detect two dimensional directions.

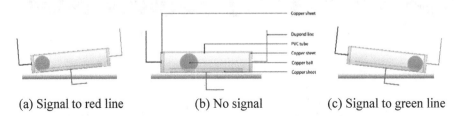

(a) Signal to red line   (b) No signal   (c) Signal to green line

Fig. 3. Mechanism of self-designed sensor.

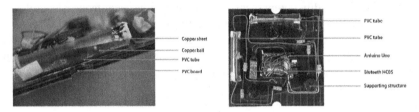

Fig. 4. Self-Designed sensor.

We tested the first prototype by playing the exergame ourselves and found out that without safety handle bars, it's hard to keep balance on the NEONEO 1.0 even after deflating the BOSU ball, which is indicating potential threats to the older adults. After discussions and debates, still resisting the handle bars, we replaced the BOSU ball with four small elastic balls supporting the unstable surface, which might provide enough stabilities. The iteration went well, and the whole exergame system was optimized that it is ready for the preliminary test.

Iteration 2. The final version of our prototypes consists of one acrylic layer (5 mm thick) on the top for players to step on, which is laser cut to roundness ($\Phi = 460$ mm), with foot-shaped non-slip mat indicating the right position for standing Fig. 5.there are four small hemispheroids ($\Phi = 160$ mm, H = 80 mm) cross positioned under the acrylic layer. So far, it's much more stable than the traditional BOSU, fitting our design requirements. The digital system consists of an Arduino microcontroller, a blue-tooth device, a gyroscope, and a power-bank Fig. 6. The tilt angle and direction detected by the gyroscope will be sent to the Arduino microcontroller to process, then Arduino will transfer this information to computer games by blue-tooth. Additionally, with a self-carried portable battery supplying power, there is no need for wires to connect the digital system with computers. We managed to get rid of wires due to our attempt to

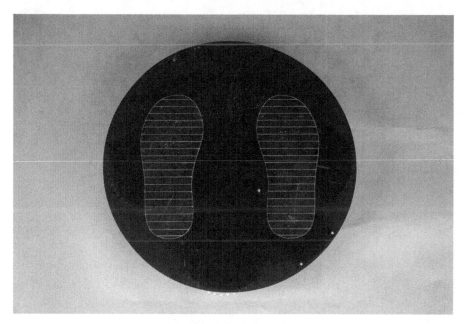

Fig. 5. NEONEO balance ball prototype 2.

meet the required features we made earlier, the same as the reason for discarding safety handlebars, that our training equipment should be easy-to-use and convenient in the home environment.

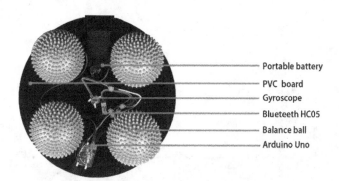

Portable battery
PVC board
Gyroscope
Blueteeth HC05
Balance ball
Arduino Uno

Fig. 6. The structure of the NEONEO Balance Ball

Older adults, putting their feet at the suggested position, which is two pieces of foot-shaped non-slip mat, could control the game character on the screen by changing the dip direction and angle of the board Fig. 7. The game character can move both horizontally and vertically, depending on the tilt direction of the board. And players could speed up the game character by creating a large angle, vice versa (small angle means slow movement).

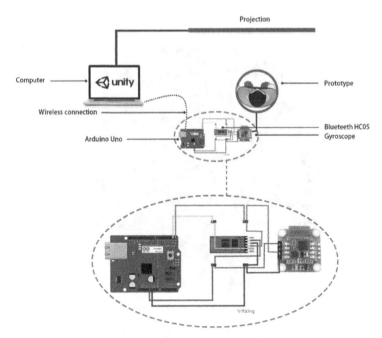

Fig. 7. System overview.

Fig. 8. User interface.

we minimized the UI elements in the game to prevent the frustration caused by overwhelming information, allowing the players to focus on one main task [10]. A screenshot of the game GUI with one player mode can be seen in Fig. 8. The objective of the game is to collect yellow stars, which are randomly positioned vertical, drifting from right to left. Besides collecting stars, players also need to avoid purple heart-shaped icons which minus the points. In the experimental design for this paper, young adults will be playing this one player mode.

4 Experimental Design

In our plan, we will conduct the user experiments in two stages. In the first stage, we design an experimental plan to test the usability of the prototype, focusing on the perspective of young people. In the second stage, we will come up with a solution that two generations can play together for a long duration. We will recruit both older adults and young people to evaluate social interactions between them.

4.1 Participants

In the primary test, we will recruit 20 university students (10 female and 10 male) with the age from 18–25. Recruitments will be hold on the website: https://tongqu.sjtu.edu.cn/ and WeChat. The experiment will take around 40 min and each participant will be reward 40 RMB.

4.2 Setup

The experiment will be conducted in NEO Bay at Shanghai Jiao Tong University. Figure 9. shows the experimental setup which contains all the components with distances and scales. Participants will stand on the NEONEO Balance Ball, 2 m away from the screen, can ask for help from the assistant sitting in front of the computer. And this assistant will also go through the game menu for participants.

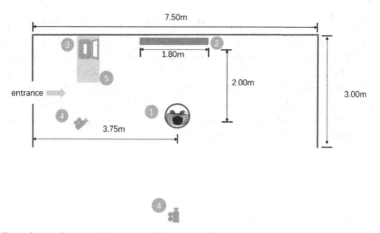

Fig. 9. Experimental setup: (1) the participant standing on NEONEO Balance Ball; (2) screen; (3) computer; (4) camera; (5) table.

4.3 Measurement

We will use subjective questionnaires to measure the usability of the system and the feelings change of the participants after playing the game. Pretest posttest design will be deployed in this experiment using the Positive and Negative Affects Schedule (PANAS)[29] to evaluate and compare participants' affects before and after playing the game. The questionnaire consists of 10 items with five-point Likert-type scale (from not at all true to very true).

Before pretest PANAS questionnaire, demographic information will be collected along with open questions about participant's former experience of gaming, entertainment, and exercise. Example items are "What games have you played sbefore?" "Have you had joint entertainment with older adults?" "What stop you from exercising?".

After posttest PANAS questionnaire, the participant will fill out the Post-Study System Usability Questionnaire (PSSUQ) [30], giving an overall evaluation of the system with seven-point Likert-type scale. The questionnaire consists of 19 items categorized into three subscales: system usefulness (SYSUSE), information quality (INFOQUAL), and interface quality (INTERQUAL). There will be open-questions to the participant about his/her perceptions to play the exergame and communicate with elderlies. Thirteen questions will be asked from three aspects: game experience, kinaesthesis, and social presence, such as "How do you think we can improve this game?" "How does gamification affect your exercise?" "How do you think of intergenerational exergame?".

Qualitative data will be collected from the semi-structured interviews and analyzed by thematic analysis [31]. Some of the interesting items from open-questions will be asked during the eventual semi-structured interview, supplemented with the participant talking freely about their perceptions to our topics. All interviews will be conducted and recorded in Chinese.

4.4 Procedure

First, the participant will read and sign the informed consent form before a pre-test questionnaire using PANAS. Then the researcher will start the game and go through the menu for the participant when he or she is standing on the NEONEO Balance Ball and ready to play. Each participant will be asked to play five minutes before getting scores of the performance. After that, there will be a post-test questionnaire containing PANAS for the evaluation of emotion, PSSUQ on system usability, and open-questions. At last, the semi-structured interview will be conducted to get more insights into the evaluation. Table.1 illustrates the experimental procedure.

Table 1. Experimental procedure.

Experimental Procedures		User Tasks
Before Experiment (10 min)	Signing the informed consent	The participants will fill in the informed consent form, understand the experimental procedure, experimental content and confidentiality agreement, and sign the informed consent forms
	Filling in the pre-test questionnaire	The participants will fill in the paper version of the pre-experimental questionnaire (i.e., demographic information and the PANAS questionnaire)
In Experiment (15 min)	Standing on the prototype	The participant will stand on the prototype
	Starting the game	The assistant will turn on the game for the participant
	Playing the game	The participant will control the characters in the game through interactive devices
After Experiment (15 min)	Filling in the post-test questionnaire	The participant will fill in the questionnaire after the end of the experiment
	Conducting the interview	The researcher will conduct an interview with open questions
Total: 40 min		

5 Discussion and Conclusion

In this paper, we presented an exergame (featuring intergenerational interaction) aiming at reducing the risk of falling in older adults. We hypothesized that the features of our exergames such as intergenerational interaction and interesting gaming experience could make it possible to provide older adults with a platform to play the exergame for a long-duration which is beneficial to their physical and mental health.

An experimental plan from the perspective of young adults (first stage) was presented. In the future, there will be the second stage experiment involving both generations (old and young) to help us gain insights and better integrate desired features into our design.

Acknowledgements. . We thank our team members Chew Wei Jing Charissa, Xiang Yi Wu to design GUI of the game interface and their efforts in our earlier stage research. This work is supported by the [Shanghai Pujiang Program] under Grant [2020PJC071]; [Shanghai Jiao Tong University] under Grant [WF220543011].

References

1. Rees, S.S., Murphy, A.J., Watsford, M.L.: Effects of whole body vibration on postural steadiness in an older population. J. Sci. Med. Sport **12**(4), 440–444 (2009). https://doi.org/10.1016/j.jsams.2008.02.002
2. Robertson, M.C., Campbell, A.J., Gardner, M.M., Devlin, N.: Preventing injuries in older people by preventing falls: a meta-analysis of individual-level data. J. Am. Geriatr. Soc. **50**(5), 905–911 (2002). https://doi.org/10.1046/j.1532-5415.2002.50218.x
3. Rubenstein, L.Z.: Falls in older people: epidemiology, risk factors and strategies for prevention. Age Ageing **35**(suppl_2), ii37–ii41 (2006). https://doi.org/10.1093/ageing/afl084
4. Sherrington, C., et al.: Exercise for preventing falls in older people living in the community. Cochr. Database Syst. Revi. **40**(2), 204–205 (2019). https://doi.org/10.1002/14651858.CD012424.pub2
5. L., Yardley, et al.: Older people's views of falls-prevention interventions in six European countries. Gerontologist **46**(5), 650–660 (2006). https://doi.org/10.1093/geront/46.5.650
6. Nyman, S.R., Victor, C.R.: Older people's participation and engagement in falls prevention interventions: Comparing rates and settings. Eur. Geriatr. Med. **5**(1), 18–20 (2014). https://doi.org/10.1016/j.eurger.2013.09.008
7. Sherrington, C., Tiedemann, A., Fairhall, N., Close, J.C.T., Lord, S.R.: Exercise to prevent falls in older adults: an updated meta-analysis and best practice recommendations. N. S. W. Public Health Bull. **22**(3–4), 78–83 (2011). https://doi.org/10.1071/nb10056
8. Cumming, R.G., Thomas, M., Szonyi, G., Frampton, G., Salkeld, G., Clemson, L.: Adherence to occupational therapist recommendations for home modifications for falls prevention. Am. J. Occup. Ther. **55**(6), 641–648 (2001). https://doi.org/10.5014/ajot.55.6.641
9. Jurkiewicz, M.T., Marzolini, S., Oh, P.: Adherence to a home-based exercise program for individuals after stroke. Top. Stroke Rehabil. **18**(3), 277–284 (2011). https://doi.org/10.1310/tsr1803-277
10. Radomski, M.V.: More than good intentions: advancing adherence to therapy recommendations. Am. J. Occup. Ther. **65**(4), 471–477 (2011). https://doi.org/10.5014/ajot.2011.000885
11. Never too old to play: the appeal of digital games to an older audience. Games Cult. **6**(2), 155–170 (2011). https://doi.org/10.1177/1555412010364978
12. Fuchsberger, V., Sellner, W., Moser, C., Tscheligi, M.: Benefits and hurdles for older adults in intergenerational online interactions. In: Miesenberger, K., Karshmer, A., Penaz, P., Zagler, W. (eds.) ICCHP 2012. LNCS, vol. 7382, pp. 697–704. Springer, Heidelberg (2012). https://doi.org/10.1007/978-3-642-31522-0_104
13. Kow, Y.M., Chen, Y.: Designing online games for real - life relationships: examining QQ farm in intergenerational play, pp. 613–616 (2012). https://doi.org/10.1145/2145204.2145297
14. Xu, X., Theng, Y.-L., Li, J., Phat, P.T.: Investigating effects of exergames on exercise intentions among young-old and old-old. In: Proceedings of the 2016 CHI Conference Extended Abstracts on Human Factors in Computing Systems, pp. 2961–2968 (2016). https://doi.org/10.1145/2851581.2892296
15. Uzor, S., Baillie, L.: Investigating the long-term use of exergames in the home with elderly fallers. In: Proceedings of Conference on Human Factors Computing System, pp. 2813–2822 (2014). https://doi.org/10.1145/2556288.2557160
16. Donker, V., Markopoulos, P., Bongers, B.: REHAP balance tiles: a modular system supporting balance rehabilitation. In: Proceedings of 2015 9th International Conference on Pervasive Computing Technological Health PervasiveHealth 2015, pp. 201–208 (2015). https://doi.org/10.4108/icst.pervasivehealth.2015.259278

17. Morat, M., et al.: Effects of stepping exergames under stable versus unstable conditions on balance and strength in healthy community-dwelling older adults: a three-armed randomized controlled trial. Exp. Gerontol. **127**, 110719 (2019). https://doi.org/10.1016/j.exger.2019.110719

18. Schmierbach, M., Xu, Q., Oeldorf-Hirsch, A., Dardis, F.E.: Electronic friend or virtual foe: exploring the role of competitive and cooperative multiplayer video game modes in fostering enjoyment. Media Psychol. **15**(3), 356–371 (2012). https://doi.org/10.1080/15213269.2012.702603

19. De la Hera, T., Loos, E., Simons, M., Blom, J.: Benefits and factors influencing the design of intergenerational digital games: a systematic literature review. Societies **7**(3), 1–18 (2017). https://doi.org/10.3390/soc7030018

20. Costa, L., Veloso, A.: Being (grand) players: review of digital games and their potential to enhance intergenerational interactions. J. Intergener. Relatsh. **14**(1), 43–59 (2016). https://doi.org/10.1080/15350770.2016.1138273

21. Osmanovic, S., Pecchioni, L.: Family matters: the role of intergenerational gameplay in successful aging. In: Zhou, J., Salvendy, G. (eds.) Human Aspects of IT for the Aged Population. Healthy and Active Aging: Second International Conference, ITAP 2016, Held as Part of HCI International 2016 Toronto, ON, Canada, July 17–22, 2016, Proceedings, Part II. Springer International Publishing, Cham (2016)

22. Lin, M.-C., Harwood, J., Bonnesen, J.L.: Conversation topics and communication satisfaction in grandparent-grandchild relationships. J. Lang. Soc. Psychol. **21**(3), 302–323 (2002). https://doi.org/10.1177/0261927X02021003005

23. Zhang, F., Kaufman, D.: A review of intergenerational play for facilitating interactions and learning. Gerontechnology **14**(3), 127–138 (2016). https://doi.org/10.4017/gt.2016.14.3.002.00

24. Pecchioni, L.L., Osmanovic, S.: Play it again, grandma: effect of intergenerational video gaming on family closeness. In: Zhou, J., Salvendy, G. (eds.) ITAP 2018. LNCS, vol. 10926, pp. 518–531. Springer, Cham (2018). https://doi.org/10.1007/978-3-319-92034-4_39

25. Abeele, V.V., De Schutter, B.: Designing intergenerational play via enactive interaction, competition and acceleration. Person. Ubiquit. Comput. **14**(5), 425–433 (2010). https://doi.org/10.1007/s00779-009-0262-3

26. Zhang, F.: Intergenerational play between young people and old family members: patterns, benefits, and challenges. In: Zhou, J., Salvendy, G. (eds.) ITAP 2018. LNCS, vol. 10926, pp. 581–593. Springer, Cham (2018). https://doi.org/10.1007/978-3-319-92034-4_44

27. Sheng, X., Settles, B.H.: Intergenerational relationships and elderly care in China: a global perspective. Curr. Sociol. **54**(2), 293–313 (2006). https://doi.org/10.1177/0011392106056747

28. Caltenco, H.A., et al.: Designing interactive systems for balance rehabilitation after stroke. In: TEI 2017 – Proceedings of 11th International Conference on Tangible, Embed. Embodied Interaction, pp. 511–516 (2017). https://doi.org/10.1145/3024969.3025084.

29. Watson, D., Clark, L.A., Tellegen, A.: Development and validation of brief measures of positive and negative affect: the PANAS scales. J. Personal. Soc. Psychol. **54**(6), 1063–1070 (1988). https://doi.org/10.1037//0022-3514.54.6.1063

30. Lewis, J.R.: IBM computer usability satisfaction questionnaires: psychometric evaluation and instructions for use. Int. J. Hum. Comput. Interact. **7**(1), 57–78 (1995). https://doi.org/10.1080/10447319509526110

31. Braun, V., Clarke, V.: Using thematic analysis in psychology. Qual. Res. Psychol. **3**(2), 77–101 (2006). https://doi.org/10.1191/1478088706qp063oa

MEMORIDE: An Exergame Combined with Working Memory Training to Motivate Elderly with Mild Cognitive Impairment to Actively Participate in Rehabilitation

Xin Li, Ting Han[✉], Enjia Zhang, Wen Shao, Liang Li, and Chenye Wu

School of Design, Shanghai Jiao Tong University, Shanghai, China
hanting@sjtu.edu.com

Abstract. Chronic diseases such as mild cognitive impairment have severely affected the quality of life of the elderly worldwide, both physically and psychologically. Working memory training is an intervention method that has been widely used in clinical treatment. However, memory decline, decreased physical function and psychological resistance to the training prevent seniors from gaining an ideal training outcome. Researchers use gamification methods to help the therapists improve the effect of rehabilitation training to solve the problem. This research is based on working memory training in cognitive rehabilitation and developed an exergame for seniors with mild cognitive impairment called MEMORIDE. Using the method of participatory design (PD), researchers design the Chinese classical garden's training scene that caters to the hobbies of the elderly. Moreover, a positive feedback mechanism was used to encourage the elderly to participate actively. This study recruited 10 participants with mild cognitive impairment over 65 years old (MMSE scores between 21 and 26) who used MEMORIDE for 30-min rehabilitation training. The post-experiment interview showed that most participants had a pleasant experience and willing to continue trying this training method. The research results verified the acceptance of gamified rehabilitation training for seniors. The study proves that gamification can improve training compliance and relieve training pressure in elderly rehabilitation. In further research, longer-term experiments will be carried out to verify this training method's cognitive function enhancement effect.

Keywords: Exergame · Mild cognitive impairment · Rehabilitation training · Aging design

1 Introduction

There were 703 million persons aged 65 years or over in the world in 2019 [1]. Chronic diseases of the elderly and related psychological problems launch a huge challenge to the global medical service system [2]. China's elderly population (60 years old and above) has reached 18.1% of the total population in 2019, and such a rapid growth rate of the elderly population will continue until 2040. The aging population poses a huge

© Springer Nature Switzerland AG 2021
Q. Gao and J. Zhou (Eds.): HCII 2021, LNCS 12787, pp. 90–105, 2021.
https://doi.org/10.1007/978-3-030-78111-8_6

challenge to China's medical security system and the sustainable development of the economy. As the body functions continue to decline with age, the elderly are more prone to chronic diseases and physical disabilities. These diseases that affect daily life not only give the elderly a physical level of distress but also cause them to develop psychological problems such as depression and a sense of fear [3]. For this reason, scientists have been trying to use information technology to increase the well-being of the elderly and improve the quality of life in their later years. Cognitive impairment is a chronic diseases that seriously decrease the quality of life of the elderly [4]. Scientists proposed mild cognitive impairment (MCI), refers to a group of clinical conditions that have obvious memory impairment or mild other cognitive impairment but do not affect daily life, and are between normal old age and mild dementia [5]. Mild cognitive impairment is the key stage to delay the weakening of cognitive function. Without timely intervention, there is a very high risk of progression to Alzheimer's disease (conversion may be about 10–15% per year and increasing annually), with irreversible impairment of cognitive and motor function [6]. Studies have shown that early intervention with rehabilitation training can effectively improve the cognitive ability of patients [7, 8]. Current research in the treatment of mild cognitive impairment focuses on both pharmacological [9] and non-pharmacological treatments [10]. In the actual treatment, medications for AD are usually used to intervene with insignificant effects. Therefore, non-pharmacological interventions regarding MCI rehabilitation have become a hot research topic in the field in recent years.

Sports training has been widely used in the cognitive rehabilitation field, but the elderly's memory, physical function, and psychological issues may lead to low partic-ipation in training, especially in the home environment [11]. To this end, researchers designed exergames with entertaining graphical interfaces and tasks to help the elderly recover [12].

This research uses a framework of gamification to develop an exergame to motivate elderly patients with mild cognitive impairment to actively participate in rehabilitation training. This study focuses on participatory design and usability evaluation to obtain and validate the preferred gamification approach of Chinese older adults. Unlike previous games, this research combines exercise therapy with working memory training certified by professional therapists to achieve better user experience and compliance.

2 Related Works

Exercise games (Exergame) are a combination of exercise and video games that enable interaction by detecting the body's motor responses. Exergames are a more enjoyable, safe and engaging form of exercise and can also be referred to as somatic games. In past research, exergames have shown great potential in the field of exercise rehabili-tation. Exergames can directly promote the user's motor abilities. Studies have proven that timely intervention with rehabilitation training can also be effective in improving the cognitive level of patients [7, 8]. Besides, exergames can motivate users to exercise both endogenously and exogenously[13], allowing them to actively engage in exer-cise. Exergames help people generate pleasurable and positive experiences and develop healthy behaviors. Exergames can positively impact participants' physical, cognitive, improve mental health, increase social connectedness, encourage interaction with others.

In commercial applications, exergames have gained consumer and market recognition. Companies such as Nintendo, Microsoft, and Sony have developed body-sensing devices that are widely used, and most exergames in past research are developed based on these platforms. These products use body sensors or image recognition algorithms to capture the user's movements and interact with the game on-screen in real-time. For example [14], Nouchi uses somatosensory games developed by Nintendo to promote motor and cognitive function in older adults.

While exergames have shown great potential in the field of rehabilitation, it is undeniable that the vast majority of sports games are designed for younger players. The physical condition, age-related injuries and educational background of older people can affect their use of exergames. Therefore, we must consider the needs and characteristics of the older population in the design process. Several theoretical frameworks have been proposed by scholars regarding the design of exergames for the elderly population. MIDE design framework proposed by Yirou li et al. [15]. emphasizes the need for designers to interact with all stakeholders such as the elderly, healthcare professionals, and family members through observation and co-design methods. The need to reflect user preferences and needs using literature review and building user personas. bob De Schutter proposes guidelines for designing digital games for older players [16], emphasizing the need to consider the playability of the game itself, to view aging in older adults as a process of growth and decline, and to use as much positive and inclusive discourse as possible during the process. Especially for older players who have not been exposed to digital games, the gamification content should be closely related to the player's personal growth and identity background to evoke empathy.

In our past research, we investigated how gamification can improve the mental health of older adults by designing a jigsaw puzzle game [17]. The results show that gamification design is capable of reducing anxiety symptoms, enhancing social communication and satisfying their desire for expression. This finding also supports our idea of using gamification elements in combination with cognitive-motor training. In previous experiments, we have collected suggestions from older adults for improving the game such as increasing sound stimulation due to declining vision ability and using a slower game pace with natural and soothing music to reduce the stress of older adults while playing the game.

3   Materials and Methods

3.1   User Research on Game Content

In previous studies, game elements are considered to be key factors affecting game experience [18]. When designing games for special populations, the physical condition, cognitive preferences, and cultural background of the population need to be fully considered first, and the rules, difficulty, and other elements of the game should be designed based on them [19].

To fully understand the game element preferences of the Chinese elderly population, this study uses participatory design (PD) [20] and UCD design methods to actively involve the elderly in the creation of interactive game content. Considering that some older adults with declining physical abilities have difficulty completely expressing their opinions and ideas in the standard participatory design process, we developed a design framework with three workshops to stimulate the elderly to express themselves. Researchers guide and observe them to achieve the research purposes.

The objectives of the user study focused on four aspects: (1) to understand the current stage of rehabilitation training methods and training satisfaction of Chinese older adults; (2) to know the motor and cognitive ability levels of the elderly population living in healthcare institutions; (3) to understand the cultural background and preferences of Chinese older adults for game content; (4) to assess the motivation and incentive effects of older adults in single/multiplayer, competitive/cooperative type of game activities.

The workshops were conducted at a local healthcare center, and seniors voluntarily signed up for one or more workshops, with two weeks between each activity. 58 seniors participated in the activities in total, and three activities were conducted to investigate the seniors' opinions about the game mechanics, game narratives, and game difficulty adaptation. After the collective activity participation, the researcher invited some senior players for interviews and obtained findings on game design for seniors.

Workshop 1: Creation and Competition (Fig. 1). In this activity, each senior was given a free hand to paint a vase within an hour, and the researchers provided the seniors with plenty of paints and brushes. Also, some graphic elements for reference are provided. In this activity, we wanted to find out if there is a certain uniformity in the visual and color preferences of Chinese seniors, as well as the decision between speed and quality of completion.

Fig. 1. Workshop 1: vase painting.

Visual Element Preference. Natural elements such as flowers, zodiac (animals), and clouds appeared repeatedly in the completed paintings. Abstract graphic elements appeared in the works as decorative or complementary elements such as pentagram elements and circles. When the seniors embarked on their paintings, they would tend to refer to the pattern elements we provided and alter them (simplify them). Most of the participants exceeded our expectations for the quality of their paintings. The feedback from the interviews showed that the seniors loved the rewards of this activity, but would still spend more time perfecting their creative works.

Color Preference. There was no designated color reference for this workshop, and paints were filled by the seniors freely. Green, red and yellow were the most used colors from the finished artworks. Green was used to depict the ground and vegetation in realistic natural scenes, and two bright colors, red and yellow, were chosen to fill in visual themes such as animals; when depicting non-living elements such as sunlight, water, and plants, the seniors usually used colors of established impressions conservatively. While depicting animals, people and flowers, the elderly usually use more abstract colors and rich patterns to express personality.

Workshop 2: Creation and Narrative (Fig. 2). In this workshop, the elderly were invited to make their props for the Shadow Puppet Play. The researcher prepared a collage of printed Chinese historical figures for the elderly, and the elderly cut out their favorite characters and assembled movable limbs and handheld objects to create a storytelling image. In this activity, the seniors were invited to volunteer to narrate their Shadow Puppet Play for us. We were hoping to both understand their interest in traditional elements with strong Chinese characteristics and assess their logical thinking and hands-on skills.

Fig. 2. Workshop 2: The shadow puppet play works created by the elderly.

Findings. Most of the elderly could understand the correspondence between characters and figures, but there existed a small percentage of elderly with speech impairment or cognitive impairment who were unable to fully express the interaction between the characters created. When making hand-made paper cuts, it was difficult to concentrate resulting in rougher works, which was caused by the declining motor function of the upper limbs. it is noteworthy that the older adults did not care much about whether their work matched the historical story of the character, but created it primarily from matching visual elements. The researchers believe that the cognitive impressions of historical figures are hardly associated with graphics, and when faced with something unfamiliar, it is difficult for the elderly to match it with their past experiences or knowledge. The senior users prefer realistic, playful elements that have clues in their lives. The abstract elements serve more as decoration and personalization than for expressing narrative content that needs to be understood by the elderly.

Workshop 3: Game Type. In the third activity, the researcher arranged four different types of games for 24 elderly people including passing ball, ping pong, Rock-Paper-Scissors and stroop game. The first two games correspond to the two main forms of group games: cooperation and confrontation. The passing ball game requires players to cooperate to reach the endpoint as fast as possible, and the ping pong game is a confrontation between teams to avoid dropping the ball in their area. The other two games both challenge players' reaction speed, the difference lies in the different sources that send out judgment signals. Rock-Paper-Scissors requires two players to act simultaneously, while stroop game only requires one-way access to signals, which is equivalent to a single-player game, without competition or cooperation with actual players (Fig. 3).

Fig. 3. Workshop 3: The elderly were playing stroop game.

Findings. Older adults showed very high interest in both cooperative/confrontational games, and had higher enthusiasm and performance than usual during rehabilitation training to complete the game tasks. however, it is worth noting that the physical condition of older adults varies widely, and when playing group confrontation games, some people will participate less actively or refuse to participate because of the fear of affecting the group performance. compared to confrontation games, cooperative and single-player games can be played more smoothly because of less psychological pressure. When designing the mechanics of group games, it is necessary to consider whether the participants have similar physical abilities. the complexity of the rules should also be minimized, and detailed prompts are needed to guide them.

Through three workshops with older adults, we collected opinions from older users related to exergame design, including preferences for visual elements, game mechanics, and narrative style. Overall, older people's vision, hearing, and motor coordination are aging, and the design of sports games need to minimize tasks that require precise manipulation and use contrasting colors for key elements. According to the Flow Theory [21], if the game task is too difficult, it will affect the trainer's self-confidence and generate negative emotions of anxiety and tension; if the difficulty is too low, it will cause the training effect to be substandard. In terms of content narrative, we tend to use the most familiar elements from the past experiences of the elderly as the story content, so that the elderly will have a natural sense of affinity and cause emotional resonance. The rules of the game should not be complicated, and before the formal start of the challenge, we should leave seniors with warm-ups and tutorials to reduce the learning difficulty. In terms of game mechanics, if a multiplayer game is to be designed, attention should be paid to the disparity in physical abilities of the participants to avoid negative effects on one of them.

3.2 Exergame Design: MEMORIDE

Based on the inspiration and insights gained during the participatory design and user research phases, we designed an exergame: MEMORIDE. MEMORIDE is a rehabilitation training game that uses an engaging and interactive approach to stimulate the active participation of older people. MEMORIDE uses computer-assisted technology and IoT sensors to simulate the experience of riding in nature (Fig. 4), allowing users to immerse themselves and enjoy each training session. In between the exercise, users need to recall the buildings and routes that appeared before to complete the memory training questions, thus reaching motor and cognitive improvement.

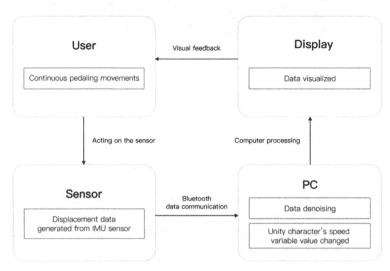

Fig. 4. Components of MEMORIDE system

The MEMORIDE prototype consists of three parts (Fig. 5), which are the physical pedal bike, the motion sensor and the virtual sports game developed based on Unity3D engine. The user completes the motion task by pedaling the bike, the sensor installed at the pedal to identify the user's pedaling frequency, using low-power Bluetooth to transfer this part of the motion data to the PC in real-time, with the Arduino data processing code to convert the original data into the current speed of the ride, assigned to the unity game character. The final visual feedback to the user through the screen backward of the surrounding objects, giving the virtual ride a sense of reality.

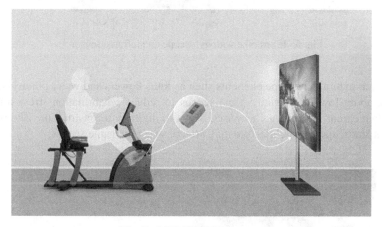

Fig. 5. MEMORIDE diagram

Exercise Equipment (Fig. 6). Studies have shown that aerobic exercise can help people improve cognitive function memory capacity and psychosocial problems such as anxiety and depression [22, 23]. The researchers wanted to use a safe aerobic exercise combined with cognitive tasks to improve the existing rehabilitation training. By interviewing rehab therapists at a local senior facility, pedaling will be the proper movement for this exergame, as pedaling is appropriate for most older users, even those with walking impairments. Because sitting on an adequately protected cushion, the pedal movement reduces the risk of falling during exercise.

Sensors. In the prototype design, we used infrared sensors. A LED probes fixed in the bike's frame, while a black and white baffle fixed on rotatable pedals. When the user stepped on the pedal, each time the baffle swept over the LED probe, the sensor counts once, the number of sweeps per unit of time can be counted to get the user's riding speed.

Interactive Content Developed in Unity3D. Through the preliminary research of senior Chinese users, we chose the Chinese classical garden "Zhuozheng Garden" as the main scene of the game (Fig. 7), one of China's most reputable classical gardens. When mentioning the "Zhuozheng Garden", seniors can associate it with the impression of nature, leisure, and healthy. Based on this familiar and historical scene, which represents Chinese architecture and culture, we hope to establish a connection with the past experiences of the elderly. Simultaneously, the Zhuozheng Garden's clear topography,

Fig. 6. Fixed bike with gyroscope and infrared sensor

with its rich natural landscape elements such as lotus flowers and water ponds, is ideal for developing low-stimulation virtual scenes to reduce rehabilitation stress training to a certain extent. The researchers used Maya to digitally reconstruct the Zhuozheng Garden's landscape and architecture in 3D to construct the game scenes.

Fig. 7. Traditional Chinese garden training scene

In the MEMORIDE video game, the researchers have built-in three types of cognitive training that focus on the elderly's ability to remember words, directions, and objects (Fig. 8). When reaching a checkpoint, the user is asked about the location they have passed, and the user needs to select an answer using buttons on the armrest of the bike. If the answer is correct, positive feedback will be given, including a scoring sound effect and a poem about the building. If the answer is incorrect, the game will not give direct negative feedback. Instead, a visual tip will appear on the screen to hint the player to make a new choice. During the game, players will not get frustrated by mistakes and avoid breaking their sense of self-identity.

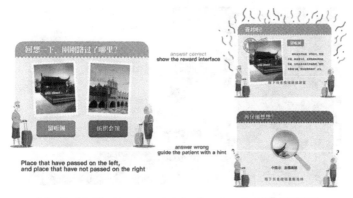

Fig. 8. Working memory training interface in MEMORIDE

3.3   Usability Evaluation

Usability evaluation is an important research method to verify product functionality and help product iteration [24]. To evaluate the satisfaction of Chinese elderly users of MEMORIDE exergames, the researcher used the usability evaluation method. Referring to Rita.W.L.Yu's research that five categories of elements can influence user behavioral intention [25]. This study was modified based on this model to obtain the target users' attitudes and suggestions about the MEMORIDE program in four dimensions: perceived ease of use, challenge, enjoyment, and perceived usability.

Participants. Ten older adults residing in Shanghai and Harbin, China, aged 65–80 years with a mean age of 73.5 years, were invited for this study's usability assessment. There were three males ($N = 3$) and seven females ($N = 7$), and all participants could walk independently, were free of serious illness, and were conscious enough to take care of themselves on a daily basis, with their vision and hearing at normal aging levels. All participants were experiencing exercise games for the first time. Six of the participants had a secondary school education background, and four had an elementary school education background.

Process. Each participant underwent a usability assessment of approximately 30 min, including a task introduction, completion of the game task, and a semi-structured interview (Fig. 9). The process of the game tasks was as follows:

The process of the game tasks was as follows:

1. click on the start game button.
2. start riding according to the screen instructions.
3. arrive at checkpoint one and answer the upcoming question.
4. click on the confirmation button to return to the ride screen after receiving feedback on the answer.
5. continue riding to checkpoint two and complete the second question.
6. when the question is completed, click the confirm button to return to the ride screen.

Fig. 9. Senior participant taking MEMORIDE training

7. continue riding to checkpoint three and complete the third question.
8. when the question is completed, click the confirm button to return to the ride screen.
9. complete the entire cycling loop.
10. Get the feedback that the training is over and click the button to end the game.

Usability was assessed using a fixed bike and a stepper as exercise equipment, and a television projecting a computer screen was used to provide visual feedback to the participants. After completion or discontinuation of the game task, the researcher asked the participants how they felt about the experience using a five-point Richter scale from the four dimensions described above, with the following questions (Table 1):

Table 1. A post-trail questionnaire on four dimensions of experience

Factor	Number	Discription
Perceived ease of use (PEOU)	Q1.1	I can master controls for MEMORIDE
	Q1.2	I do not need any more instructions for MEMORIDE
	Q1.3	I feel easy to perform the game control as I want
	Q1.4	I can play MEMORIDE alone without the help of others
Challenge (CH)	Q2.1	I think MEMORIDE is challenging
	Q2.2	I am proud when I reached the checkpoint in MEMORIDE
	Q2.3	Playing MEMORIDE involves my muscles and reaction practice
	Q2.4	I want to acheive better performance in MEMORIDE

(continued)

Table 1. (continued)

Factor	Number	Discription
Enjoyment (EN)	Q3.1	I enjoy playing MEMORIDE
	Q3.2	I feel that time passes quickly when I play MEMORIDE
	Q3.3	I think that playing MEMORIDE is a good form of exercize
	Q3.4	I feel relaxed when I was playing MEMORIDE
Perceived usefulness (PU)	Q4.1	I think my physical performance can be improved by MEMORIDE
	Q4.2	I think playing MEMORIDE can improve my social relationships
	Q4.3	I believe that the benefits of playing MEMORIDE outweigh the costs
	Q4.4	I think MEMORIDE makes me more committed to exercise

4 Results and Discussion

During the evaluation, one participant discontinued the task while completing the second checkpoint for physical reasons; the rest completed the entire ride within 30 min. To understand which part of the task caused the ride to be terminated, the researcher still invited this participant to fill out the questionnaire and interview. The results of the questionnaire are shown in the Fig. 10.

Factor	Number	Totally disagree		Disagree		Neutral		Agree		Totally agree	
		N	%	N	%	N	%	N	%	N	%
	Q1.1	0	0	0	0	0	0	7	70	3	30
Perceived	Q1.2	1	10	1	10	0	0	6	60	2	20
ease of use (PEOU)	Q1.3	0	0	0	0	0	0	7	70	3	30
	Q1.4	0	0	0	0	1	10	6	60	3	30
	Q2.1	0	0	1	10	0	0	5	50	4	40
Challenge (CH)	Q2.2	0	0	0	0	1	10	7	70	2	20
	Q2.3	0	0	0	0	0	0	3	30	7	70
	Q2.4	0	0	0	0	0	0	5	50	5	50
	Q3.1	0	0	0	0	0	0	4	40	6	60
Enjoyment (EN)	Q3.2	0	0	1	10	2	20	6	60	1	10
	Q3.3	0	0	0	0	0	0	6	60	4	40
	Q3.4	0	0	1	10	2	20	5	50	2	20
	Q4.1	0	0	0	0	0	0	3	30	7	70
Perceived usefulness (PU)	Q4.2	1	10	0	0	2	20	7	70	0	0
	Q4.3	0	0	0	0	1	10	8	80	1	10
	Q4.4	0	0	0	0	0	0	5	50	5	50

Fig. 10. Subjective outcomes from participants

Overall, the results of all four experience factors met expectations, and the majority of seniors expressed their enjoyment of riding the MEMORIDE and their willingness to continue to try it for exercise.

Perceived Ease of Use (PEOU)
The concept of perceived ease of use is derived from the TAM model [26]. Typically, when designing for older adults, we need to increase perceived ease of use as much as possible. High perceived ease of use lowers the threshold for users to start using the product, and the perceived ease of use increases as the experience increases, so we need to reduce confusion for the first time. The beginning steps of MEMORIDE are straightforward so that participants can get into the game quickly. We simulated real riding actions and established a connection with the immersive game so that older people can interact naturally and react unconsciously and quickly with instinctive responses.

Challenge (CH)
Challenge refers to the physical and cognitive level required to complete the ride and memory tasks. Maintaining an appropriate level of challenge can motivate older adults to sustain active participation in the activity. When designing the challenge of MEMO-RIDE, we did not want the difficulty to be so high that seniors would become anxious and thus less motivated to participate in the exercise. Simultaneously, we did not want the difficulty to be so low that older adults could easily accomplish their goals, which would reduce the enjoyment of the game and lack willingness to accomplish the purpose. For this reason, we use a bicycle that can change the resistance so that the elderly can adjust freely according to their physical condition, and when the questions are answered incorrectly, we give hints to reduce the difficulty of the questions instead of negative feedback.

Enjoyment (EN)
Enjoyment is an essential factor for gamification design to be able to attract users. From the user study conclusion, we found that the elderly prefer visual elements of natural scenery. We used a game scenario full of outdoor riding to cater to seniors' preferences, and with the help of classical Chinese gardens, we hope to find resonance among the elderly population. From the usability evaluation results, most seniors found MEMORIDE fun and felt that time became faster during the game because they were fully engaged in the exercise, and the natural, low-stimulation scenery helped create a relaxing game atmosphere.

Perceived Usefulness (PU)
The concept of perceived usefulness is also derived from the TAM model[26]. Although the user's perceived usefulness does not fully represent the objective effect, the feeling increases the user's motivation to use the product voluntarily. MEMORIDE invites therapists to participate in the task design so that the elderly can feel that long-term training will improve their physical condition. However, there are still a small number of participants who think MEMORIDE does not affect improving interpersonal relationships, probably because MEMORIDE is a single-player game and there is no Non-Player Character (NPC) and real player interaction. We hope that MEMORIDE can help older

adults improve psychosocial issues, including interpersonal relationships, so in future iterations, we will focus on improving the multiplayer experience.

4.1 Interview Findings

In the semi-structured interviews, we also got some comments from older people about MEMORIDE. For example:

1.*Some icons (icons indicating the type of task) have unclear representation, and it is difficult for the elderly to understand the meaning when using it for the first time.*
2.*In the text interface that needs to be read, users would like to get voice feedback.*
3.*People would like to have a game mode of racing with other characters and play with friends.*
4.*The game scenes of classical gardens can further enhance the sense of realism instead of using a low-polygon modeling style.*
5.*We hope to add media elements related to personal experiences, evoking positive emotions in the elderly.*
6.*The memory training questions' design can be more closely integrated with cycling, the current questions appear rather abruptly, and users may need tutorials or examples to understand how to answer the questions.*

5   Conclusion

According to the participants' feedback, most people expressed interest in the content of the game, obtained a relaxing and enjoyable experience, and were willing to continue to try this training method. This result indicated the acceptance of gamification rehabilitation training and improved compliance of seniors with mild cognitive impairment. This study can motivate seniors to actively participate in rehabilitation training and achieve higher scores. MEMORIDE is especially meaningful for older people affected by the covid-19 epidemic or who are physically inconvenient to go out. This research is in cooperation with a local hospital. Future research will focus on verification and effectiveness between regular rehabilitation training and the combination of working memory training and aerobic exercise games.

Acknowledgments. The research is supported by National Social Science Fund (Grant No. 18BRK009).

References

1. Nations, U.: World Population Ageing 2019 Highlights. World Population Ageing (2019)
2. Frieden, T.R.: Asleep at the switch: local public health and chronic disease. Am. J. Publ. Heal. **94**(12), 2059–2061 (2004). https://doi.org/10.2105/AJPH.94.12.2059
3. Moussavi, S., et al.: Depression, chronic diseases, and decrements in health: results from the World Health Surveys. The Lancet **370**(9590), 851–858 (2007)

4. Leroi, I., et al.: Cognitive impairment in Parkinson disease: impact on quality of life, disability, and caregiver burden. J. Geriatr. Psychiatry Neurol. **25**(4), 208–214 (2012)
5. Petersen, R.: Mild cognitive impairment: transition between aging and Alzheimer's disease. Neurologia **15**(3), 93–101 (2000)
6. Petersen, R.C., et al.: Mild cognitive impairment: clinical characterization and outcome. Arch. Neurol. **56**(3), 303–308 (1999)
7. Finn, M., McDonald, S.: Repetition-lag training to improve recollection memory in older people with amnestic mild cognitive impairment. A randomized controlled trial. Aging, Neuropsychol. Cogn. **22**(2), 244–258 (2015). https://doi.org/10.1080/13825585.2014.915918
8. Redick, T.S.: The hype cycle of working memory training. Curr. Dir. Psychol. Sci. **28**(5), 423–429 (2019)
9. Fink, H.A., et al.: Pharmacologic interventions to prevent cognitive decline, mild cognitive impairment, and clinical Alzheimer-type dementia: a systematic review. Ann. Intern. Med. **168**(1), 39–51 (2018)
10. Song, D., et al.: The effectiveness of physical exercise on cognitive and psychological outcomes in individuals with mild cognitive impairment: a systematic review and meta-analysis. Int. J. Nurs. Stud. **79**, 155–164 (2018)
11. Balaam, M., et al.: Motivating mobility: designing for lived motivation in stroke rehabilitation. In: Proceedings of the SIGCHI Conference on Human Factors in Computing Systems (2011)
12. McCallum, S.: Gamification and serious games for personalized health. In: pHealth (2012)
13. Whitehead, A., et al.: Exergame effectiveness: what the numbers can tell us. In: Proceedings of the 5th ACM SIGGRAPH Symposium on Video Games, pp. 55–62. Association for Computing Machinery, Los Angeles, California (2010)
14. Nouchi, R., et al.: Brain training game improves executive functions and processing speed in the elderly: a randomized controlled trial. PLoS ONE **7**(1), e29676 (2012)
15. Li, Y., Muñoz, J., Mehrabi, S., Middleton, L., Cao, S., Boger, J.: Multidisciplinary iterative design of exergames (MIDE): a framework for supporting the design, development, and evaluation of exergames for health. In: Fang, X. (ed.) HCII 2020. LNCS, vol. 12211, pp. 128–147. Springer, Cham (2020). https://doi.org/10.1007/978-3-030-50164-8_9
16. De Schutter, B.: Gerontoludic design: extending the mda framework to facilitate meaningful play for older adults. Int. J. Gaming Comput. Mediat. Simul. (IJGCMS) **9**(1), 45–60 (2017)
17. Muroi, F., Tao, X., Han, T.: A Study on the Effect of Gamification on Alleviation Anxiety Levels of the Elderly in China. Springer International Publishing, Cham (2020)
18. Amory, A., et al.: The use of computer games as an educational tool: identification of appropriate game types and game elements. Br. J. Edu. Technol. **30**(4), 311–321 (1999)
19. Soldati, M., et al.: Create Video Games to Promote Well-Being of Elderly People – A Practice-Driven Guideline. Springer International Publishing, Cham (2020)
20. Schuler, D., Namioka, A.: Participatory design: Principles and practices. CRC Press, Boco Raton (1993)
21. Csikszentmihalyi, M., Csikzentmihaly, M.: Flow: The Psychology of Optimal Experience, vol. 1990. Harper & Row, New York (1990)
22. Zheng, G., et al.: Aerobic exercise ameliorates cognitive function in older adults with mild cognitive impairment: a systematic review and meta-analysis of randomised controlled trials. Br J Sports Med **50**(23), 1443–1450 (2016)
23. Redwine, L.S., et al.: An exploratory randomized sub-study of light-to-moderate intensity exercise on cognitive function, depression symptoms and inflammation in older adults with heart failure. J. Psychosom. Res. **128**, 109883 (2020)
24. Branaghan, R.J., O'Brian, J.S., Hildebrand, E.A., Bryant Foster, L.: Usability evaluation. In: Humanizing Healthcare – Human Factors for Medical Device Design, pp. 69–96. Springer, Cham (2021). https://doi.org/10.1007/978-3-030-64433-8_4

25. Yu, R.W.L., et al.: Acceptance Level of Older Chinese People towards Video Shooting Games. Springer International Publishing, Cham (2020)
26. Davis, F.D.: Perceived usefulness, perceived ease of use, and user acceptance of information technology. MIS Q. **13**(3), 319 (1989). https://doi.org/10.2307/249008

Promoting Active Aging Through Location-Based Games: A Survey of Older Pokémon Go Players

Jesse Nery Filho[1,2(✉)] [ID] and Ana Isabel Veloso[2] [ID]

[1] Instituto Federal Baiano, Estrada da Igara s/n, Senhor do Bonfim, 48970-000 Bahia, Brazil
jesse.filho@ifbaiano.edu.br
[2] DigiMedia, Departamento de Comunicação e Arte, Universidade de Aveiro. Campus Universitário de Santiago, 3810-193 Aveiro, Portugal
aiv@ua.pt

Abstract. Technologies have contributed to increase the average life expectancy, through medical care support, early diagnosis, psycho-physical-cognitive rehabilitation and, more recently, digital games, which have played a key role in the general well-being. However, the aging process embodies multiple-facets that determine the level of self-dependency on economic, social, cultural, physical, personal, behavioral and health services (WHO, 1998). Thus, this research identifies the location-based game components that can impact on active aging based on the lived experiences of Pokémon Go players aged 50 and over. This paper reports on an online survey carried out in Portugal between August and October 2020 (N = 78). Results show low and moderate degrees in Pearson's correlations coefficient between the players' experiences (immersion and level of game enjoyment) and the variables of active aging ($0.2 < R < 0.5$; $p < 0.05$), with the exception of accessibility issues relating to the physical environment.

Keywords: Active aging · Location-Based Games · Pokémon Go · Survey

1 Introduction

Digital games have evolved a lot in the last decades and in the year 2020 with the effects of the Covid-19 pandemic, the market grew and raised about $ 1.59Bi dollars reaching the mark of 2.7Bi players worldwide [1]. At the same time, the first players such as the Atari generation, for example, aged but continued to play. Reports show that about 10% to 15% of players in the US are 55 or older [1, 2]. Thus, in the coming years these numbers will increase and digital games will become part of the daily lives of people in different contexts and at all ages, whether in education, quality of life or health [3–5].

The studies of games and the applications of games in the lives of seniors are fields that have grown considerably, as games are not only intended for entertainment. There is research that intersect games and seniors in several areas, namely, well-being and quality of life [4, 6]; intergenerational involvement [7, 8], social participation [9] and physical exercise [10, 11].

© Springer Nature Switzerland AG 2021
Q. Gao and J. Zhou (Eds.): HCII 2021, LNCS 12787, pp. 106–123, 2021.
https://doi.org/10.1007/978-3-030-78111-8_7

Aging involves not only health changes but also a series of other aspects that must be taken into account, such as: learning, participation in society, access to rights and security that determine the increase in the activity of individuals, i.e. active aging. "The word "active" refers to continuing participation in social, economic, cultural, spiritual and civic affairs, not just the ability to be physically active or to participate in the labor force. Older people who retire from work and those who are ill or live with disabilities can remain active contributors to their families, peers, communities and nations" [12].

Despite being an 18-year-old concept, thinking about the applicability of active aging has only more recently aroused the interest of game researchers and producers. For example, the study by Costa and Veloso [13] shows that games and intergenerational issues raised in the scientific community in 2002. In this same context, a recent study [14] shows the existence of only 5 works, until March 2019, that intersect Location-Based Games (LBGs), the senior public and the issues of active aging when studied in an isolated way. In addition to this study, we conducted further research, crossing the keywords "Active Aging" and "Games", in the databases of Scopus, Web of Science and ACM library, obtaining only one study in 2020 addressing Geocaching (an LBG) and active aging [15].

Location-based games emerged with the popularization of mobile devices and location-based technologies, mainly with the Global Positioning System (GPS). These games create an interface between the physical and cyber environments and one ends up influencing the other. The urban space, for example, becomes an element of the game, as well as the city, monuments, people, among others [16]. With this, the LBGs provide several game dynamics that can range from physical displacement in space, to cooperation or competition, similar to city-scale chess. Pokémon Go has been a great success until today since its release and many studies have been conducted in several areas, but little is known about the relationships between these games and active aging.

Given the scarcity of studies on this subject and the importance of promoting active aging, this research seeks to look deeper into the relationship between the experiences of Pokémon Go (PoGo) players, over 50 years old, and aspects related to active aging. PoGo was chosen because it is still the most played LBG in the world [17] and Niantic[1] provides constant updates to keep players on the platform. If we observe that each year a generation of Pokémon is released within Pokémon Go, at this rate the last generation will only be launched in 2022, which makes this game a great field for research.

Thus, the hypotheses to be observed are mainly related to mobile games based on location and the senior audience, where we seek to find evidence, based on sociodemographic conditions, player experiences and self-assessments on the pillars of active aging related to playing Pokémon Go. Therefore, we have the following hypothesis related to the target audience and active aging:

H1 – The sociodemographic conditions of Pokémon Go players over 50 years old correlate with perceptions about location-based mobile games promoting active aging.

The game has many mechanics that require walking, battles between players, player cooperation to complete certain missions, attention to more complex activities or remembering the attributes of each type of Pokémon. In this sense, the diversity of these activities

---

[1] Company that developed Pokémon Go together with Nintendo and The Pokémon Company.

can alienate or attract players, as well as the possibility of players preferring one part of the game over another. In this regard, the following hypotheses will be observed:

H2 – There is a correlation between how much players like Pokémon Go and active aging.

H3 – There is a variation between player preferences (polarization) and perceptions about location-based mobile games that promote active aging.

The players' history, the number of similar games and how they learned to play Pokémon Go are also variables that can influence perceptions, as familiarity with the game and the learning of mechanics allows the player to have a better relationship with the game. Therefore, we also intend to verify whether these conditions are related in any way to the variables of active aging:

H4 – There is a correlation between the level of experience with similar games, how they learned to play Pokémon Go and active aging.

H5 – There is a variation (polarization) between the gaming experience, how they learned to play Pokémon Go and perceptions about location-based mobile games promoting active aging.

Finally, there are two other hypotheses related to the players' immersion, i.e. how much time is invested by the players, the moments they play and how much they have progressed in the game. Observing these variables makes us perceive in a segmented way the experiences of the players that influence the perception of the subjects in relation to the potential of the games for active aging. Therefore, we came to the following hypotheses:

H6 – There is a correlation between how much players are immersed in Pokémon Go and active aging.

H7 – There is variation between player immersion (polarization) and perceptions about location-based mobile games that promote active aging.

This paper is structured in three further parts. In addition to the introduction, the second part presents the methodology, the participants and the procedure. In the third part, the results will be shown with the characterization of the sample, the results and the quantitative and qualitative analyses. Finally, the conclusions of this research, along with the limitations and future work will be presented.

2   Methodology

2.1   Research Methodology

In order to understand the behaviors of Pokémon Go players who are over 50 years old and their perspectives, the strategy adopted to obtain a sample of a wide geographical distribution, in a short period of time and with few resources [18] was the Survey Research. However, there are numerous aspects that lead to a research of this nature to have scientific rigor, as says Ponto: "survey research has developed into a rigorous approach to research, with scientifically tested strategies detailing who to include (representative sample), what and how to distribute (survey method), and when to initiate the survey and follow up with nonresponders (reducing non-response error), in order to ensure a high-quality research process and outcome." [19].

In a Survey Research, there are fundamental elements that must be strictly respected, such as the design of the research, including thought about the sample to be studied, choosing the method of data collection, writing the questions that collect sufficient information, observing the conditions of the participants, reviews and testing data collection tools [20].

The instruments for data collection in this research integrated closed-ended questions of a quantitative nature while the open-ended fields (qualitative) were implemented in order to provide a better understanding of the investigative questions. The data collection instrument chosen was an online questionnaire, using the LimeSurvey Platform installed on the web servers of the research institution to implement, with robustness and reliability, the data protection law (RGPD UE 2016/679).

2.2 Data Collection Instruments

The questionnaire design was based on similar research that studies Pokémon Go, mobility and well-being [21, 22], physical activity [23–25], social [26], psychic [27] and the senior public [28]. As a result, the questions were inspired by well-being assessment instruments such as WHO-5 [29] and even other instruments that have a wide range of questions thus eliminating factors not applied to this study [30].

The online questionnaire was divided into three sets of questions based on the categories of this study: The target audience and its sociodemographic characterization, the players' experiences and a self-assessment on the issues of active aging related to the experience of playing Pokémon Go:

- Section 1 (16 questions). In order to know the target audience of the study, questions related to sociodemographic data were asked: Age, Gender, Marital Status, Education, Job Status (JobStatus), Number of children (Children), Number of grandchildren (Grandchildren), City, Type of Home (Home), Who do you live with? (LivesRx), Interaction with ICT (ICTRx), What does ICT do? (DoICTRx), Devices you play? (EquipGameRx), play other LBGs (LBGRx), ICT experience (ICTBefore andICTAfter).
- Section 2 (12 questions). This section was intended to gather information about the players' profile and habits regarding the Pokémon Go game: Difficulty learning PoGo (LearnPG), How did you learn Pogo? (LearnRx), Game Difficulties (HardSx), Other difficulties (HardOpen), How long have you been playing PoGo? (Time), Game level (Level), average time per day playing (AvgTime), When you play (WhenRx), Where you play (WhereRx), What do you like best about PoGo? (LikeSx), How many Pokémons have you captured? (Catch) and What event do you like the most? (EventOpen - Qualitative).
- Section 3 (12 questions). This section brought together questions about active aging and the interconnections with the Pokémon Go game: Well-being (WellbeingGeneral, WellbeingSx), Cognition (CognitionSx), Physical exercise (ExerciseSx), Social questions (SocialSx), Security (SecuritySx), City Accessibility (AccessibilitySx), Break idleness (end1), PoGo is entertaining and healthy (end2), I feel fulfilled (end3), Difficulties (DifficultiesOpen - Qualitative) and Well-being (WellBeingOpen - Qualitative).

In Sect. 3, self-assessment questions were chosen to understand the seniors' relationship with the game, for example, if they perceive that the game stimulates physical exercises and whether exercises are performed by virtue of the game. The same questions were also asked with the other pillars of active aging such as: learning, participation, health and safety. Finally, before ending the online survey, the participant, voluntarily, could provide the contact to participate in other meetings and/or participate in a prize draw for having answered the questionnaire online, gifts that could be used to buy credits on the same game.

A strategy used to facilitate reading and avoid abandonment by participants was to create questions mainly of multiple choices, dichotomous or on a Likert scale, but open questions were also made available for participants to describe what difficulties they have while playing and whether the game stimulates well-being, as well as what they feel when playing. Before proceeding to the dissemination stage of the online survey, in order to maintain the quality of the research, cycles of review and validation of the data collection instrument were carried out by researchers in the field of health and/or games, Pokémon players and other people over 50.

Scalar data needs to be adequate for better statistical robustness, both for calculating correlation and even for testing variances between mean values. Thus, variables were created using an additive approach [31, 32], taking into account that the new variables accumulate the values of a certain category. Below we present the additive variables based on the response codes previously presented.

$$ICT = \sum_{x=1}^{5} ICTRx + \sum_{x=1}^{8} DoICTRx + \sum_{x=0}^{4} EquipGameRx$$

$$Learn\_Games = \sum_{x=1}^{5} LBGRx + \sum_{x=1}^{6} LearnRx$$

$$Like\_PoGo = \sum_{x=1}^{5} LikesSx$$

$$Cognition = \sum_{x=1}^{8} CognitionSx$$

$$Wellbeing = \sum_{x=1}^{9} WellbeingSx$$

$$Excercice = \sum_{x=1}^{2} ExcerciceSx$$

$$Social = \sum_{x=1}^{4} SocialSx$$

$$Security = \sum_{x=1}^{6} SecuritySx$$

$$Participation = \sum_{x=1}^{6} ParticitationSx$$

$$Accessibility = \sum_{x=1}^{5} AccessibilitySx$$

$$Wellbeing2 = WellbeingGeneral + End1 + End2 + End3$$

$$PoGo_{Immersion} = \sum_{x=1}^{6} WhenRx + \sum_{x=1}^{5} WhereRx + Time + AvgTime$$

We have grouped these variables into larger categories: Sociodemographic, experiences with Pokémon Go and Active Aging. These groups of variables allow the analysis of the influences of ones in relation to the others, i.e. the Sociodemographic and Pokémon Go independent variables have some influence on Active Aging (dependent variable) as shown in Fig. 1.

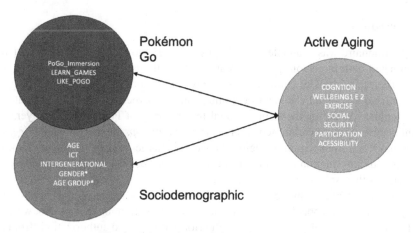

Fig. 1. Independent and dependent variables.

2.3 Ethical Issues

This study is part of a doctoral research entitled "Mobile games based on location and active aging: the study of Pokémon Go in the lives of seniors", which was approved by the ethics committee of the University of Aveiro (opinion 15-CED/2020) that ensures: the informed consent of participants aged 50 or over; voluntary participation; the commitment of the research team in the process of data collection, storage and treatment, according to the GDPR (EU 679/2016), and that the risks of participating in the study do not exceed the risks associated with the participants' daily lives. The research is part of a larger project called "SEDUCE 2.0 - Use of Communication and Information in the miOne online community by senior citizens" which aims to assess the impact of psychosocial variables and Online Sociability of senior citizens using the Information and Communication Technologies.

2.4 Participants

The objective of this research was to observe the perceptions of Pokémon Go players, who are over 50 years old, regarding the potential of the game interaction to promote active aging. Thus, the inclusion criteria, to accept a valid answer for the analysis, were centered on the over 50-year-old being a Pokémon Go player and living in Portugal. While the exclusion criteria were those who answered that they were less than 50 years old, in addition to those who did not complete the form (a part of those who accessed the form when realizing that in the first question, age was restricted to those over 50 years old).

The form had 163 accesses, but only 83 answered all questions. Following the exclusion criteria, 6 respondents were under 50 years old, which accounted for 78 valid entries.

2.5 Procedure

The questionnaire was available from August 13, 2020 to October 16, 2020 and was disseminated both in person (pamphlets at events, daily gatherings) and on social networks. The main forms of communication between players were studied (as the game does not have an official channel of communication between users) to disseminate the survey online. At the moment, in Portugal the majority of Pokémon Go players use instant social communication networks such as *WhatsApp*, *Messenger* and *Telegram*, which may vary from region to region. However, a large number of players look for asynchronous information on social networks like *Facebook*, in groups created by the communities themselves, usually by region.

In instant social communication networks, Telegram is the most used application, mainly because of the bots for organizing various information. In view of this, we were able to publish in 36 Telegram groups, with prior warnings and authorizations from the administrators of each group, reaching around 14 thousand users in these groups and cities from north to south of the country. Likewise, the dissemination was made on the social network Facebook, following the same strategies of regionalization and ethical issues, reaching approximately 65 thousand users on this platform and groups related to Pokémon Go.

At the end of the application period, those who agreed to participate in the gift card raffle were contacted and received registration numbers and instructions on how the selection would be made. This strategy was used to enhance the participation of the target audience and according to the collected data there were no people who could give a false positive, due the fact that to receive the gifts they would have to provide a contact.

3 Results

3.1 Characterization of Participants

The data were extracted from LimeSurvey and imported into SPSS 27, making the adjustments according with the exclusions criteria previously described. The samples' mean age was 55 years old ($N = 78$, $SD = 4.91$; minimum $= 50$; maximum $= 76$), of these 67% were men. Most of them have a relationship (62% married and 10% non-marital partnership), 85% have at least one child and 21% at least one grandchild. Regarding education, 60% of respondents have a degree or postgraduate degree and 76% work full time. In addition, the geographic distribution of the sample was very heterogeneous, from which we obtained responses from various locations in Portugal, such as: Lisbon Region, Porto Region, Faro, Braga, Coimbra, Aveiro, Covilhã, Mirandela and Funchal.

In terms of technologies, respondents frequently use Laptops (64%) and/or Desktop Computers (32%), and generally use digital devices to read e-mails (69%), watch news (62%), work (60%), play (58%), for social networks (55%). The data does not show a significant number of the use of other platforms to play (tablets - 27%, computer - 22% and consoles - 15%). However, they demonstrate that there was an improvement in ICT learning after they started playing Pokémon Go (see Table 1).

Table 1. ICT skills before and after playing Pokémon Go.

How do you consider your experience with communication and information technologies (Internet, social networks…)				
	Before playing Pokémon Go		After playing Pokémon Go	
	N	%	N	%
Great	23	29.5	28	35.9
Good	**46**	**59.0**	**48**	**61.5**
Poor	9	11.5	2	2.6
Total	78	100.0	78	100.0

Most respondents stated they have been playing for more than 2 years (79%) and that they are already at a higher level[2] (71%) and that always or almost always have all Pokémons released in the game (88%). Regarding the learning of the game, the responses varied with friends/players (46%), with children/grandchildren (45%) or alone (42%). The Fig. 2 shows the proportions of the number of hours played per day by the players, showing that 70% play more than one hour per day - players considered hardcore, i.e. different from those who play casually [33].

---

[2] The highest level when the questionnaire was applied was level forty (40).

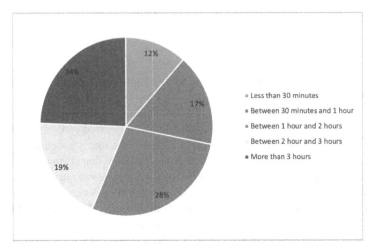

Fig. 2. Daily time spent playing Pokémon Go.

According with players testimonials, the most frequent place to play is in the neighborhood or at home (77%) and the most frequent bracket of time are at the weekends (60%) or when they go to work/study (59%). These data allow us to understand how much the sample knows or immerses in the game, and to complement this, they were also asked about the main aspects of the game they like most, resulting in Fig. 2.

The categories that respondents (Fig. 3) evaluated were as follows: 1 - Complete the Pokémon collection; 2 - Get Shiny Pokémon (Shiny); 3 - Collect the general medals of the profile; 4 - Get very rare Pokémon (100% iv, unown …); 5 - Collect Gym Badges (gold, silver, bronze); 6 - Raid with other people,; 7 - Visit new PokéStops and gyms; 8 - Battle with other players; and 9 - Do Pokémon exchanges. We can see that in most of these categories the players showed to like a lot or a little, and we have an opposite emphasis for points 5 and 8: the "Collect Gym Badges" case is due to the fact that the players generally like elements that give good benefits to the player and the Gym Badge collection is not such a good return; the "Battle with other players" case concerns the battles that demand a complexity and a hypothesis (that will not be tested in this work) for the players not liking it so much is because they have to create a good team of Pokémons, have a good battle strategy (agility, memory, attention …) or mainly due to the low victory rewards.

3.2 Quantitative Analysis

In addition to the additive variables created previously, a dichotomous age variable was also created, being classified as 50–55 years old and over 55 to perform some other tests. The additive variables, gender, age, age over 55 were analyzed through Pearson's correlation, observing a significant correlation of $p < 0.05$.

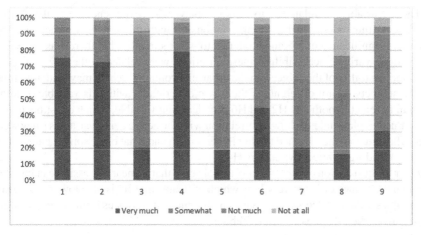

Fig. 3. Categories that players like most on PoGo.

Initially, as expected, the active aging variables showed correlations with each other. These variables showed a correlation with a significance of 1% and classified between moderate (between 30% and 50%) and strong (greater than 50%) [34]. The variables related to sociodemographic data, on the other hand, did not show any correlation between the other variables, with the exception of "Aged 55 and over" and "Participation" ($r = -0.257$, $p < 0.05$), with a difference in the responses of these groups regarding the contribution category of "Participation" and "Active Aging" (Table 2).

Table 2. Correlation analyzes of socioeconomic variables, experiences and active aging.

		1	2	3	4	5	6	7	8	9	10	11	12	13	14	15	16
Gender (1)	Pearson's Cor.	1	.163	.191	-.006	-.093	-.096	-.184	.060	.033	-.085	-.115	.006	-.079	-.082	.090	.045
	Sig. (2-tailed)		.153	.094	.958	.417	.404	.106	.601	.775	.462	.318	.958	.492	.475	.436	.698
Aged 55 and over (2)	Pearson's Cor.			.727**	.086	-.049	.006	.000	.062	-.012	-.038	.002	-.189	-.153	.004	-.257*	-.025
	Sig. (2-tailed)			.000	.453	.667	.956	1.000	.591	.920	.739	.983	.098	.182	.973	.023	.831
Age (3)	Pearson's Cor.				.376**	-.092	-.013	.043	-.058	-.008	.055	-.075	-.168	-.037	.095	-.079	.062
	Sig. (2-tailed)				.001	.425	.910	.711	.612	.944	.635	.513	.142	.750	.410	.491	.588
Intergenerational (4)	Pearson's Cor.					.118	.089	.116	-.081	.150	.174	.144	.113	.152	.216	.080	.205
	Sig. (2-tailed)					.303	.438	.312	.480	.189	.127	.210	.325	.184	.058	.488	.072
ICT (5)	Pearson's Cor.						-.110	.175	-.031	.192	.095	.144	.249*	.103	-.067	.030	.006
	Sig. (2-tailed)						.339	.125	.790	.093	.409	.207	.028	.369	.559	.793	.961
Like PoGo (6)	Pearson's Cor.							.019	.250*	.426**	.399**	.370**	.280*	.308**	.221	.441**	.140
	Sig. (2-tailed)							.868	.027	.000	.000	.001	.013	.006	.051	.000	.220
Learn PoGo (7)	Pearson's Cor.								.229*	.061	.054	.033	.108	-.123	.120	-.012	.083
	Sig. (2-tailed)								.044	.597	.640	.777	.348	.284	.295	.915	.468
PoGoImmersion (8)	Pearson's Cor.									-.237*	-.475**	-.240*	-.231*	-.291**	-.298**	-.150	-.186
	Sig. (2-tailed)									.037	.000	.034	.042	.010	.006	.191	.104
Well-being (9)	Pearson's Cor.										.584**	.587**	.386**	.472**	.416**	.536**	.332**
	Sig. (2-tailed)										.000	.000	.000	.000	.000	.000	.003
Wellbeing2 (10)	Pearson's Cor.											.557**	.530**	.491**	.492**	.623**	.353**
	Sig. (2-tailed)											.000	.000	.000	.000	.000	.002
Cognition (11)	Pearson's Cor.												.470**	.353**	.307**	.492**	.185
	Sig. (2-tailed)												.000	.002	.006	.000	.106
Exercise (12)	Pearson's Cor.													.316**	.243*	.534**	.128
	Sig. (2-tailed)													.005	.032	.000	.266
Social (13)	Pearson's Cor.														.439**	.541**	.298**
	Sig. (2-tailed)														.000	.000	.008
Security (14)	Pearson's Cor.															.417**	.298**
	Sig. (2-tailed)															.000	.008
Participation (15)	Pearson's Cor.																.397**
	Sig. (2-tailed)																.000
Acessibility (16)	Sig. (2-tailed)																

**The correlation is significant at 0.01 (2 extremities).
* The correlation is significant at 0.05 (2 extremities)

The variables related to the players' experience, "Like_PoGo" and "PoGo_Immersion", had a strong relationship with the variables of active aging (minimum significance of 5% and moderate to weak strength), but there was an exception with the variable accessibility (these questions were related to the physical space and the accessibility of the subjects in the urban environment) which may lead us to infer that the subjects do not differentiate their own experiences with this variable, leading us to fail to reject hypotheses H2 and H6. The learning variable, which questioned how they learned to play, did not show a correlation with the active aging variables (they were asked who and how they learned to play Pokémon Go and what other similar games they also play) leading to reject hypothesis H4.

After the correlation checks, we can also observe that a linear regression can be ruled out when the values of R are very low, which indicates that R^2 is also low. Afterwards, the variables were divided into 2 groups and the mean differences of these groups were verified using the t-Test, as shown in Table 3.

Table 3. Analysis of the t-Tests of the Like_PoGo variable and the Active Aging variables.

		Levene Test for Equality of Variances		t-Test for Equality of Means					95% Confidence Interval in the Difference	
		Z	Sig.	t	df	Sig. (2-tailed)	Mean difference	Difference standard error	Inferior	Superior
Cognition2	Equal Variances Assumed	.175	0,677	3.573	76	0,001	2.057	.576	.910	3.203
	Equal Variances not Assumed			3.637	73.072	0,001	2.057	.565	.930	3.183
Acessibility	Equal Variances Assumed	1.261	0,265	1.890	76	0,063	1.566	.829	-.085	3.216
	Equal Variances not Assumed			1.834	60.848	0,072	1.566	.854	-.141	3.273
Participation	Equal Variances Assumed	1.847	0,178	3.340	76	0,001	2.859	.856	1.154	4.563
	Equal Variances not Assumed			3.263	62.760	0,002	2.859	.876	1.108	4.609
Security	Equal Variances Assumed	.112	0,739	1.716	76	0,090	1.295	.755	-.208	2.798
	Equal Variances not Assumed			1.706	67.629	0,093	1.295	.759	-.220	2.810
Social	Equal Variances Assumed	.137	0,712	2.796	76	0,007	1.349	.483	.388	2.311
	Equal Variances not Assumed			2.794	68.969	0,007	1.349	.483	.386	2.313
Exercise	Equal Variances Assumed	.819	0,368	2.047	76	0,044	.691	.338	.019	1.363
	Equal Variances not Assumed			2.093	73.875	0,040	.691	.330	.033	1.349
Well-being	Equal Variances Assumed	.618	0,434	3.366	76	0,001	2.414	.717	.986	3.842
	Equal Variances not Assumed			3.426	73.025	0,001	2.414	.705	1.010	3.818
Cognition	Equal Variances Assumed	1.127	0,292	3.640	76	0,000	4.071	1.118	1.843	6.298
	Equal Variances not Assumed			3.721	73.791	0,000	4.071	1.094	1.891	6.251

Firstly, it is necessary for the t-Test to find out whether the variances are equal. In this case, the Levene test is used for equality of variances where the null hypothesis is that the variances are homogeneous. In the case of Table 3 in all lines we fail to reject (p > 0.05) the null hypothesis and we assume that the variances are homogeneous. Regarding the t-Test, the null hypothesis is that the mean values of the groups are equal and, in these cases, the Accessibility and Security variables (p > 0.05) fail to reject the null hypothesis, i.e. only in these categories the groups of those who like and dislike did not show a difference in the mean value of the answers whereas in the other variables, the groups diverged in the answers.

This analysis is in agreement with the results observed in the correlation analyses leading to fail to reject hypothesis H3. Likewise, t-Tests were performed with the Learn_PoGo and PoGo_Immersion variables with the Active Aging variables. The first variable did not show any difference in the observed mean values of the Active aging variables. Whilst the variable of the players who are more or less immersed in the game showed different mean values in the responses regarding the general well-being (questions such as: I consider Pokémon a healthy leisure activity, I feel fulfilled when playing Pokémon Go, I believe that the game provides you with health-related well-being). Thus, we reject hypotheses H5 and H7.

3.3 Qualitative Analysis

To complement the quantitative analyses, open-ended questions were inserted for the participants to express questions about certain experiences, difficulties /discomforts and whether the games provide well-being. The data were inserted in MS Excel for a better visualization, afterwards categorized and then grouped in common themes to allow analysis of the number of responses.

The first question "What events did you like most about PoGo? Please explain" was mandatory. However, there was still a lack of response (3%) or a lack of justification for choosing a particular event (36%). The relevance of this question is not related to the interest in the event, but to the experience it provided.

From what can be seen in Table 4, five categories emerged: Elements and game mechanics (rare Pokémon, game news) (38%, N = 28 responses); Social issues that include meetings and socializing with other players (18%, N = 14 responses); Intergenerational interaction (3%, N = 2 responses); adequacy of the schedule that allows participation in events and in the game itself (4%, N = 3 responses); and, finally, mobility (travel from home, neighborhood and countries) (6%; N = 5 responses).

Table 4. Analysis of responses regarding the preference of events (EventOpen variable).

Category	N	%	Coding examples
Did not explain	28	36%	
No moment	2	3%	
On account of the game (New Pokémon, shinies, rare, legacy attacks)	30	38%	"Community Day All events that can give new Pokémons or shinies all the news in the game are welcome"
Gather, socialize	14	18%	"Raid hour and Community Day, because there is always a fun group"
Intergenerational	2	3%	"Community Day. An event that allows the whole family and friends to get together on long walks."
Because it is a good time/day or the possibility to participate in events	3	4%	"Legendary time because it usually always has a good time and I have time to play"
Leaving home or going to other places or countries	5	6%	"Go fest, I end up visiting other countries" or "Community Day, leaving home and playing is beautiful"

Table 5. Analysis of responses regarding well-being in the game (WellBeingOpen variable).

Category	N	Frequency	Frequency answered	Coding examples
Did not answer	55	71%	–	
Collect	3	4%	13%	"Everything in the game the news the missions find 100 percent new pokemons shines"
Exercise, walking	8	10%	35%	Encourages daily walking and socializing with other players
Occupation, personal fulfillment	5	6%	22%	The fact of having goals to achieve and being very dynamic that prevents moments of leisure
Play with other people, social networks, socializing	10	13%	43%	Have a goal to leave home and meet people not related to work

The other two questions were not mandatory but allowed the counting of the number of responses and illustration of some statements of the participants. The first case was with the question "What else has provided you with well-being in the game?" where only 29% (N = 23) of respondents answered.

With the data collected, the following four categories emerged associated to well-being in the game (see Table 5): act of collecting (4%, N = 3); promotion of physical activity (10%, N = 8) through walking to reach points suggested by game; occupation of free time in which the respondents (6%, N = 5) believe that the game does provide an occupation and does fulfil players; finally, the question regarding socialization that includes playing with others, the use of social networks and interaction(13%, N = 10).

The third question "Leave a comment about difficulties or discomforts while playing" had only 12 responses from participants, which revealed some situations in which participants experienced stereotypes regarding games - game-ageism[3]. Although most respondents answered that they did not know whether or not they felt excluded by age (78% of respondents) some cases reported (in the open-ended responses) that they were excluded.

"As I had already explained I play alone and I don't know anyone who plays so my interaction with other players is done exclusively with the friends I have added, whilst giving and receiving gifts. If I am on the street and see someone playing, I don't even feel comfortable talking to these people due to my age."

Player X

---

[3] This term referring to the discrimination of older people and digital games [35].

According to player X, his interaction is primarily digital, probably established on social networks, where player codes and gifts are exchanged in the game (a way to obtain items and increase the ranking of friends by establishing digital friendships. However, these relationships do not help with other issues in the game where players are needed to battle bosses. The problem here is that the player himself feels excluded, due to his age, and is unable to approach the players in person.

Player Y also states that he feels pressured, stating "The fact that friends and family think that I waste a lot of time playing and don't understand/nor accept that". These statements are some examples of situations that discourage older players from having an active aging mainly mediated by digital games. The general population plays an active role in active aging, including friends and family.

4   Final Discussions and Considerations

The results of the correlation analysis showed that there is no correlation between sociodemographic variables and perceptions about location-based mobile games that promote active aging, leading us to reject hypothesis H1. The non-correlation, in this sense, shows us that there is no differentiation in this sample whether it be by age, gender, marital status or education, directing attention to the relationship of the players' experience and active aging.

Before proceeding with the discussion, it is observed that the additive variables (values on the vertical axis in Fig. 4 that represent the accumulation of responses related to the category) of active aging, when the box plot graphs are generated, show that the data are well distributed, creating a polarity in the hypothesis that the determinants of active aging can be stimulated with the interaction of Pokémon Go.

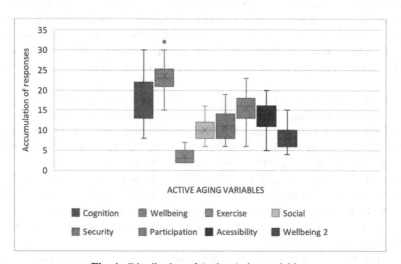

Fig. 4. Distribution of Active Aging variables.

The perceptions of the players, those who like the most (Like_PoGo variable) and the least, explain this polarization in the variables of active aging variables, as observed in the t-Test table (Table 3). Once the players know the mechanics and advance in the game, they can understand whether the activities performed are associated with the determinants of active aging. This group consists of non-casual players, i.e. different from those who play occasionally or give up. It was not possible to verify whether the way the players learned (Learn_PoGo variable) or immersed in the game (PoGo_Immersion) could be related to or influence the perceptions of active aging. In the same way, some authors show that the immersion and increase in ICT or LBG skills provide potentialities to aspects of active aging [7, 9, 10, 36].

In addition, the Accessibility variable, one of the eight determinants of active aging, did not show a correlation with the other variables ($p > 0.05$), whether socioeconomic or from the players' experiences. As can be seen in Fig. 4, the opinions of the players differ regarding the relationship between the game and the accessibility issues whether physical or informational. Some participants do not believe that physical means or info-communicational access can support gaming experiences. However, LBG can, for all ages and unconsciously, provide access to information about spaces, relationships with spaces and change behavior in public spaces, aligned also with other studies [37–39].

Thus, we reject the hypotheses: H1 – The sociodemographic conditions of Pokémon Go players over 50 years old correlate with perceptions about location-based mobile games promoting active aging. H4 – There is a correlation between the level of experience with similar games, how they learned to play Pokémon Go and active aging. H5 – There is a variation (polarization) between the gaming experience, how they learned to play Pokémon Go and perceptions about location-based mobile games promoting active aging. H7 – There is variation between player immersion (polarization) and perceptions about location-based mobile games that promote active aging.

Moreover, we fail to reject the hypotheses: H2 – There is a correlation (with a minimum significance of 5% and moderate to weak strength) between how much players like Pokémon Go and active aging. H3 – There is a variation between player preferences (polarization) and perceptions about location-based mobile games that promote active aging. H6 – There is a correlation (with a minimum significance of 5% and moderate to weak strength) between how much players are immersed in Pokémon Go and active aging.

We can say that the experiences of non-casual Pokémon Go gamers (who like and emerge) over 50 years of age recognize that location-based mobile games promote active aging. Many of them may not explicitly think that all categories of active aging will be enhanced by the game, but they do believe that they generally create goals such as exercising, socializing, being more active, breaking idleness, among others.

The next challenge is to think how the group of casual players can perceive the use of Pokémon Go for well-being, socialization, participation and for active and healthy aging. This task must be carried out by everyone, and even break barriers amongst those who see games as a villain or who discriminate older players, as was observed in the statements of some respondents.

Thinking about these strategies to disseminate the perceptions of the players themselves who think about active aging is part of this challenge. Of course, thinking about the problems that games can bring about is also part of this activity. With that, we think as future work to monitor more closely groups of players to confront with the data already obtained. As one of the pillars for active aging is education, as with access to information you have access to other pillars of aging, a proposition would be to build an intergenerational platform or strategy for older players to share experiences and attract groups that are not so familiar with the world of games.

We are aware that this work has limitations, one of them being a not very expressive number of participants. However, the data allow us to describe the community of older Pokémon Go players in Portugal and think about next steps of this research. We cannot observe a cause-effect in this study, but we found correlations that give us clues for future work. This work is pioneering and can bring a worldwide focus on the Gerontology and Games research scene, considering about how to combine digital technologies in favor of the well-being and health of those aged 50 and over. We intend to carry out field observations with the subjects for a better understanding of the influence of location-based games on active aging.

Acknowledgements. The authors would like to thank the participants of this study. To the Federal Institute Baiano for a doctorate license. This work was supported by DigiMedia Research Centre, Fundação para a Ciência e Tecnologia, I.P., COMPETE 2020, Portugal 2020 and European Union, under the European Regional Development Fund – the research project SEDUCE 2.0 - Use of Communication and Information in the miOne online community by senior citizens, POCI-01-0145-FEDER-031696.

References

1. NEWZOO, Key insights from Newzoo's gamer motivation study (2020)
2. Entertainment Software Association. Essential Facts About the Video Game Industry in July 2020 (2020)
3. Prensky, M.: Aprendizagem Baseada Em Jogos Digitais. SENAC SP (2007)
4. Costa, L.V., et al.: Games for active ageing, well-being and quality of life: a pilot study. Behav. Inf. Technol. **37**(8), 842–854 (2018). https://doi.org/10.1080/0144929X.2018.1485744
5. Veloso, A.I., Carvalho, D., Sampaio, J., Ribeiro, S., Vale Costa, L.: Footour: designing and developing a location-based game for senior tourism in the mione community. In: Gao, Q., Zhou, J. (eds.) HCII 2020. LNCS, vol. 12208, pp. 673–687. Springer, Cham (2020). https://doi.org/10.1007/978-3-030-50249-2_48
6. Scase, M., Kreiner, K., Ascolese, A.: Development and evaluation of cognitive games to promote health and wellbeing in elderly people with mild cognitive impairment. In: Studies in Health Technology and Informatics, pp. 255–262 (2018)
7. Kopeć, W., et al.: A location-based game for two generations: teaching mobile technology to the elderly with the support of young volunteers. In: Giokas, K., Bokor, L., Hopfgartner, F. (eds.) eHealth 360°. LNICST, vol. 181, pp. 84–91. Springer, Cham (2017). https://doi.org/10.1007/978-3-319-49655-9_12
8. Comunello, F., Mulargia, S.: My grandpa and I "Gotta Catch 'Em All." a research design on intergenerational gaming focusing on *Pokémon Go*. In: Zhou, J., Salvendy, G. (eds.) ITAP 2017. LNCS, vol. 10298, pp. 228–241. Springer, Cham (2017). https://doi.org/10.1007/978-3-319-58536-9_19
9. Kopeć, W., et al.: LivingLab PJAIT: towards better urban participation of seniors. arXiv preprint arXiv:1707.00030 (2017). https://doi.org/10.1145/3106426.3109040

10. Birn, T., Holzmann, C., Stech, W.: MobileQuiz: a serious game for enhancing the physical and cognitive abilities of older adults. In: Stephanidis, C., Antona, M. (eds.) UAHCI 2014. LNCS, vol. 8515, pp. 3–14. Springer, Cham (2014). https://doi.org/10.1007/978-3-319-074 46-7_1

11. Hino, K., Asami, Y., Lee, J.S.: Step counts of middle-aged and elderly adults for 10 months before and after the release of Pokémon GO in Yokohama, Japan. J. Med. Internet Res. 21(2), (2019). https://doi.org/10.2196/10724

12. Saúde, O.M.: Active ageing – A policy framework, Second United Nations World Assembly on Ageing, Madrid, Spain, pp. 1–59 (2002)

13. Costa, L., Veloso, A.: The gamer's soul never dies: review of digital games for an active ageing. In: 2015 10th Iberian Conference on Information Systems and Technologies (CISTI) (2015). https://doi.org/10.1109/cisti.2015.7170614

14. Nery Filho, J., Ana Isabel, V.: Location-based games on active aging: a systematic review. In: 14ª Conferência Ibérica de Sistemas e Tecnologias de Informação, Coimbra (2019)

15. Fornasini, S., et al.: Using geocaching to promote active aging: qualitative study. J. Med. Internet Res. 22(6) (2020). https://doi.org/10.2196/15339

16. Lemos, A.: Jogos móveis locativos: Cibercultura, espaço urbano e mídia locativa. Revista USP 0(86) (2010). https://doi.org/10.11606/issn.2316-9036.v0i86p54-65

17. Iqbal, M.: Pokémon GO Revenue and Usage statistics (2020). https://www.businessofapps. com/data/pokemon-go-statistics/. Accessed 30 Oct 2020

18. Leeuw, E.D.: Choosing the method of data collection. In: de Leeuw, E.D., Hox, J.J., Dillman, D.A. (eds.) International Handbook of Survey Methodology. Taylor & Francis Group/Lawrence Erlbaum Associates, New York, pp. 113–135 (2008). https://doi.org/10. 4324/9780203843123.ch7

19. Ponto, J.: Understanding and evaluating survey research. J. Adv. Pract. Oncol. 6, 168–171 (2015). PMID: 26649250

20. Campanelli, P.: Testing survey questions. In: de Leeuw, E.D., Hox, J.J., Dillman, D.A. (eds.) International handbook of survey methodology, pp. 176–200. Taylor & Francis Group/Lawrence Erlbaum Associates, New York (2008)

21. Zach, F.J., Tussyadiah, I.P.: To Catch Them All—The (Un)intended consequences of Pokémon GO on mobility, consumption, and wellbeing. In: Schegg, R., Stangl, B. (eds.) Information and Communication Technologies in Tourism 2017, pp. 217–227. Springer, Cham (2017). https://doi.org/10.1007/978-3-319-51168-9_16

22. Nikou, S., Tarvoll, J., Öörni, A.: Impact of playing Pokémon Go on wellness. In: Proceedings of the 51st Hawaii International Conference on System Sciences, p. 10 (2018). https://doi. org/10.24251/hicss.2018.240

23. Ma, B.D., et al.: Pokemon GO and physical activity in Asia: multilevel study. J. Med. Internet Res. 20(6), (2018). https://doi.org/10.2196/jmir.9670

24. Kim, H., et al.: Replacing self-efficacy in physical activity: unconscious intervention of the AR Game, Pokémon GO. Sustainability 10(6) (2018). https://doi.org/10.3390/su10061971

25. Khamzina, M., et al.: Impact of Pokémon Go on physical activity: a systematic review and meta-analysis. Am. J. Prev. Med. 58(2), 270–282 (2020). https://doi.org/10.1016/j.amepre. 2019.09.005

26. Finco, M.D., et al.: Let's Move! the social and health contributions from Pokémon GO. Int. J. Game Based Learn. 8(2), 44–54 (2018). https://doi.org/10.4018/ijgbl.2018040104

27. Hsieh, C.Y., Chen, T.: Effect of Pokémon GO on the cognitive performance and emotional intelligence of primary school students. J. Educ. Comput. Res. 57(7), 1849–1874 (2019). https://doi.org/10.1177/0735633119854006

28. Bengs, A., et al.: Designing for suburban social inclusion: a case of geo-located storytelling. IxD&A 25, 85–99 (2015)

29. WHO. Wellbeing measures in primary health care: the DepCare project: report on a WHO meeting. Stockholm (1998)
30. Santo, R.P.S.E.: Bem-estar Psicológico: Validação da Escala Psychological General Wellbeing para a população portuguesa. In: Faculdade de Psicologia, Educação e Desporto, p. 55. Universidade Lusófona do Porto, Porto (2015)
31. Johns, R.: SURVEY QUESTION BANK: Methods Fact Sheet 1: LIKERT ITEMS AND SCALES. 2010. https://www.sheffield.ac.uk/polopoly_fs/1.597637!/file/likertfactsheet.pdf
32. Trochim, W.M.K.: Research methods knowledge base (2020). https://conjointly.com/kb/likert-scaling/
33. Kuittinen, J., et al.: Casual games discussion. In: Proceedings of the 2007 Conference on Future Play. Association for Computing Machinery, Toronto, Canada (2007). https://doi.org/10.1145/1328202.1328221
34. Filho, D.B.F., Junior, J.A.S.: Desvendando os mistérios do coeficiente de correlação de pearson (r). Revista Política Hoje, vol. 18, p. 32. https://periodicos.ufpe.br/revistas/politicahoje/article/view/3852
35. Vale Costa, L., Veloso, A.I., Loos, E.: Age stereotyping in the game context: introducing the game-ageism and age-gameism phenomena. In: Zhou, J., Salvendy, G. (eds.) HCII 2019. LNCS, vol. 11593, pp. 245–255. Springer, Cham (2019). https://doi.org/10.1007/978-3-030-22015-0_19
36. Baez, M., Nielek, R., Casati, F., Wierzbicki, A.: Technologies for promoting social participation in later life. In: Neves, B.B., Vetere, F. (eds.) Ageing and Digital Technology, pp. 285–306. Springer, Singapore (2019). https://doi.org/10.1007/978-981-13-3693-5_17
37. Nika, C., Varelas, I., Bubaris, N., Kasapakis, V.: Interactive spatial storytelling for location-based games: a case study. In: Liapis, A., Yannakakis, Georgios N., Gentile, M., Ninaus, M. (eds.) GALA 2019. LNCS, vol. 11899, pp. 585–594. Springer, Cham (2019). https://doi.org/10.1007/978-3-030-34350-7_56
38. Leorke, D.: Location-based gaming: play in public space, pp. 1–266 (2018). https://doi.org/10.1007/978-981-13-0683-9
39. Papangelis, K., et al.: Conquering the city: understanding perceptions of mobility and human territoriality in location-based mobile games. Proc. ACM Interact. Mob. Wearable Ubiquit. Technol. 1, 1–24 (2017). https://doi.org/10.1145/3130955

Fostering Senior Community-Based Cyclotourism Using Transmedia: A Proposal

Cláudia Ortet$^{(\boxtimes)}$ (iD), Ana Isabel Veloso(iD), and Liliana Vale Costa(iD)

DigiMedia, Department of Communication and Art, University of Aveiro, Aveiro, Portugal
{claudiaortet,aiv,lilianavale}@ua.pt

Abstract. The general decrease in fertility rates and the increase in longevity allow the incessant aging of the world population. Furthermore, senior citizens are becoming better consumers of tourism products, leading to the need to meet their context, demands, and preferences while avoiding overtourism. Although a boom is observed in this field, there is a lack of information and products that address cyclotourism, senior tourism and its impact on citizens' well-being and formation of communities. Community-based tourism, alongside media convergence culture, relies on the use of information and communication tools to inform purchase decisions and reinforce the connections among people relative to both place-making and place-visiting. The purpose of this position paper is to discuss the potential of transmedia to foster participatory strategies in cyclotourism to encourage active aging. In specific, it proposes the delivery of an integrated cyclotourism experience targeted to senior citizens that result from the convergence of community-based, induced, and transmedia tourism.

Keywords: Cyclotourism · Senior citizens · Convergence culture · Transmedia · Participatory culture

1 Introduction

Digital convergence is defined as the content's flow across numerous media platforms, the cooperation with multiple media industries, and the migratory behavior of media audiences seeking the types of entertainment experiences that meet their expectations [1]. Emphasis is placed on the willingness of the audiences to the adherence to such experiences, highlighting the importance of developing engagement strategies. The concept can be applied to different areas and its definition will change accordingly. Regarding cultural convergence, this occurs from the emergence of new forms of creativity at the intersection of digital media with users, fostering a new participatory culture by giving the common person the ability to appropriate, change, and redistribute content [2].

One of the most important characteristics in convergence culture is whether the introduction of new media derives from the use of old media in new contexts, which often leads to changes in human behavior. Meanwhile, the phenomenon of demographic aging has also had a significant impact on society and the use of technological devices by different generations has been asymmetric. Therefore, recent developments have

© Springer Nature Switzerland AG 2021
Q. Gao and J. Zhou (Eds.): HCII 2021, LNCS 12787, pp. 124–134, 2021.
https://doi.org/10.1007/978-3-030-78111-8_8

increased the need for a participatory culture and collective intelligence, as well as reinventing strategies for sustainable active aging and healthier lifestyles [3].

More than ever, concepts such as sustainability, inclusion, media convergence, collective and integrated participation, collective intelligence, sharing, flexibility, and transparency are terms to be implemented as public policies by government entities towards the tourism sector. Such implementation is needed because of the new consumer profile that is continually demanding, responsible, and aware of the representation of destinations through the "circulation of media content – across different media systems, competing media economies, and national borders – [that] depends heavily on consumers' active participation" [1: p. 3].

Tourism has become one of the most robust activities in the world with marked economic developments while connecting people [4]. It has been growing globally with a boom, but the economic benefits are questioned and the environmental damage of overtourism is pointed out (*i.e.* the impact of tourism on a destination that excessively and negatively influences the perception of citizens' quality of life and/or the quality of visitor experiences).

Tourists are consumers and producers of media products, which makes them highly influential in the reproduction of the tourism space. A consequence of a continuous convergence is that the tourism circuit will be less predictable and more multifaceted in the future. In fact, the development of products aimed at the tourism market has led to the need to meet new sociodemographic challenges. The age groups of 50 to 55 years and 60 to 65 years have been an important segment to address in the tourism industry, given its significant proportion in the total population (*i.e.* in Portugal the proportion will be 317 senior citizens per 100 young people until the year 2080 [5]). Senior tourists also tend to have greater power related to the consumption of leisure and tourism products in contrast to younger tourists, mainly because they tend to have the highest incomes when compared to other age groups.

Thus, cyclotourism is an activity that could combine the goals sets for active aging and tourism. If in the past cycling was considered just an exercise activity linked to the health and fitness sector, recently it has come to play an important role in mobility, transport, and tourism sector. Given this fact, cyclotourism is an unexploited sector with great potential for environmental and economical sustainability [6], as well as health promotion, participation, and social inclusion.

The purpose of this position paper is to identify convergence culture's strategies, some of them adopted in the undermentioned case studies, aiming at applying those to senior cyclotourism and promoting active aging, and sustainable tourism.

The position paper is structured as follows: Sect. 1 is introductory and exposes the problem of an aging population, the tourism boom, and the need to reinvent strategies for active aging and sustainable tourism; Sect. 2 addresses the convergence culture presented by Jenkins [1, 2] and their influence on tourism; Sect. 3 defines the term 'senior citizens' and presents cyclotourism as a motivating activity for this audience; Sect. 4 focuses on case studies' strategies and proposes a transmedia senior cyclotourism strategy in a participatory culture; and finally, Sect. 5 reveals some concerns and possible study contributions.

2   Convergence Culture and Tourism

The emergence of digital convergence is directly linked to the technological paradigm in which we live. Although the technology reflects and amplifies several social aspects, it does not convergence *per se*, since this is a cognitive process occurring in the individual consumers' brains that results from environment interactions [1]. This potential for interaction within individuals' actions and decision-making is essential for the success of a convergence culture.

Convergence, within media theory, initially focused more on the technological convergence of media production. However, the term convergence now encompasses a multitude of different ongoing processes. For Jenkins [1], convergence represents a paradigm shift, in which a change in the specific content of the medium that flows through various media channels arises. In general, there is a greater interdependence of communication systems, various forms of accessing media content and increasingly complex relationships between corporate media (*i.e.* top-down) and participatory culture (*i.e.* bottom-up). In other words, the convergence culture in the media is being defined top-down by decisions taken at company meetings and bottom-up by any independent consumer. They are shaped by the desire of media conglomerates to expand their empires on various platforms and by the desire of consumers to have the media they want, when they want, where they want and in the format they want.

A participatory culture contrasts with older notions of passive media viewers. It is a culture with relatively low barriers to artistic expression and civic involvement, providing strong support to create and share creations, in which participants believe that their contributions are important and feel some degree of social connection with each other [7]. Users are no longer isolated, passive and predictable entities, since their "silent and invisible" activity are now public and noisy [1]. Indeed, users make themselves heard, ensuring their satisfaction becomes an unavoidable goal for content providers. Also, the success or failure of this premise has immediate repercussions since the users are now part of a network where opinions circulate rapidly. Given the myriad of options available, it is possible to presume that the users are the true focus of participatory culture "in a convergent communication environment, [where] audiences have participated further and have taken advantage of the opportunities opened up by new media technologies" [8: p. 24]. At the same time, the content generated by users gains significant relevance centered on the possibility for each one to interact and participate in its development.

Although digital literacy is important, the use of digital platforms for the (re)creation of content allows each user to contribute, suggest, comment and distribute a scale that is comfortable for them since the participatory culture changes the emphasis of literacy from individual expression to community involvement [2]. This involvement is realized through the idealization, construction and application of new forms of connection, coordination, collaboration and creation [1]. Collective intelligence can be seen as an alternative source of media power [1], where pieces can be put together, resources combined and skills merged, because none can know everything, but each one knows something, and the knowledge is widespread in society. In this way, the convergence culture in the media lead to the production of personal and distinct content by a diversity of creative and diligent users, which favors the growth of complex open networks and intellectual property is not always controlled but shared by all stakeholders – agents that are active [9], being comparable to specialists, since the latter no longer have the exclusivity of knowledge [10].

Media convergence can be a highly intentional trading process where the goal is to get as many media platforms as possible, to influence potential consumers (*e.g.* tourists) and their interaction. In this case, tourists are active in the production of media products - making reproductions, transforming content or creating products - so that others can interact with. In addition, the media products of tourists tend to be relevant for marketing spaces. Any media product, alone or combined with other products, can be an entry point for the consumption of tourist spaces [11]. Consumption, in a convergent environment, creates the opportunity to consume a new media product and intertextual references, in discernment of other media products. Convergence may, therefore, be one of the reasons for the fast rise to fame of some places as popular destinations, while others are still unknown or uninteresting to tourists. It can be considered that the interaction between the physical visit and the media product is only the beginning of the crossover, as tourists continue to act after visiting a place (*e.g.* publishing on social networks, commenting on blogs).

A convergence strategy for media products in tourism may focus on transmedia. Transmedia, by itself, simply means 'through the media', where there is a connection between different media (analog or digital) in order to give a new view on certain content. The transmedia narrative represents a process in which integral elements of a fiction are systematically dispersed across various distribution channels in order to create a unified and coordinated entertainment experience. Ideally, each medium makes a distinct and valuable contribution to the history unfolding through the principles of radical intertextuality (*i.e.* movement between texts or textual structures within the same media, where texts are created from existing ones) and multimodality (*i.e.* how different media involve different representations with different possibilities of interaction).

In an evident prosumer culture with an increasing need for interaction and involvement, tourists increasingly desire to co-create memorable experiences and take on more active roles [12] to fight against massified tourism (*i.e.* overtourism). This may lead to the development of a creative tourism [13], so that tourists be able to enjoy an authentic experience and explore new ways of socialization with the people and places they visit.

3   Senior Citizens and Cyclotourism

Although there is no consensus on the definition of the chronological dimension of aging, (*e.g.* the retirement age in Portugal is 66 years old whereas the World Health Organization [14] considers the age of 60 and over to define the third age, and lately a citizen with 55 years and over has also been considered a senior citizen, since it is common to find people of that age in Universities of the Third Age and nursing homes). According to the World Health Organization [14: p. 12], Active Aging can be defined as "the process of optimizing opportunities for health, participation and security in order to enhance quality of life as people age". Being active does not only refer to physical functional capacity, but also incorporates the willingness of individuals to participate in other activities (*e.g.* social, economic, cultural, spiritual and civic).

The senior citizen represents a constantly growing age group and many of them are in good health and highly inclined to travel, as well as tend to have greater consumption power for leisure and tourism products in relation to younger tourists, because they usually have higher yields [15]. In the continuously expanding tourism market, there is an increasing need to find innovative solutions to improve the tourism experience, perceived well-being and meet the needs of tourism and leisure for different age groups.

Tourism is important due to its multifunctionality associated with the consumer's impulses, and thus exercising the following functions: (i) recreational, where there is a concentration of places characterized by a strong tourist activity, which is not always a positive aspect (*e.g.* overtourism) – this fact may cause an imbalance in the regions' development, especially in rural areas where there is a lower concentration; (ii) patrimonial, in which discovery of natural and cultural attractions and activities are likely to attract urban consumers; (iii) pedagogical, wherein tourists seek knowledge and learn more about the visited place; and (iv) social, so that tourism can generate new social ties and cultivate a relationship of proximity between the visitors and local residents.

Regarding its multifunctionality, when thinking about a tourist activity that can also contribute to the pillars of active aging, cyclotourism arises, since a large part of the population considers the use of bicycles as a tendency of preference [16]. Cyclotourism represents a niche market linked to broad mobility practices and changes in social practices produced in association with rising debates around sustainability, quality of life and participation. Not only it is theoretically associated with issues of sports tourism, slow tourism, and cultural identification, but it also draws the recognized intersection of leisure, recreation and tourism into policies and analyses of everyday mobility practices [17].

The association of cycling with tourism can be characterized by (i) the use of bicycles as a fundamental means of transportation for tourism, as well as (ii) the tradition of cycling events as tourist destinations or as events to be attended and observed [18]. Thus, the cyclotourist is defined as an individual who, throughout their stay, uses the bicycle as the main travel resource or simply for leisure purposes. It tends to have a greater environmental awareness, resulting in a less negative impact on fauna and flora compared to other types of rural and sustainable tourism [6].

Today's cyclotourism differs from cyclotourism in the last century, regarding the fact that technological development has facilitated and improved bicycle use, leading to enormous facilities for cycling practitioners and improving bicycles and bike products in the market. Such advancements have led to the evolution of bicycles and diversity of types of bicycles according to the context of use (*e.g.* mountain, road, track, electric), development of bicycle routes, and equipment used by cyclo-tourists.

Based on the results obtained in the study of Ortet and colleagues [19, 20], some current market-oriented digital apps can address cyclotourism, such as Strava[1] and Zwift[2], and can be used via PC or MAC and Android or IOS devices – although Strava is used outdoors and Zwift is used indoors. Even if these apps can be applied to the tourism sector, they were not specifically designed for that, relying more on fantasy with virtual characteristics and sport. A general lack of work related to physical exercise and tourism combined with users' participation has been found, which opened up an opportunity to

---

[1] https://www.strava.com/ [Accessed: January 2021].

[2] https://www.zwift.com/ [Accessed: January 2021].

approach this issue – concerning senior citizens and the adaption to their needs and preferences – with the creation of a gamified app from and for active aging [20].

Hence, the senior citizens' motivations for cyclotourism refer to physical and mental health, economic impact, ease and convenience of transportation, physical exercise itself, relationships formed when practicing the activity, pleasure inherent in cycling and the surrounding scenery at a landscape and cultural level [19, 20]. Also, in this study, it was possible to observe the appreciation of the senior citizens' opinion in co-design techniques, interviews and usability tests - points that important to take part in participatory culture.

4 Participatory Culture and Transmedia: Adaptation and Replication

People fall into the misconception that tourists are consumers of passive media, seen only as users of media products. This is limiting, as it neglects the action of tourists in the creation of new media products and their active participation which enables them to be highly influential [21]. As tourist markets and modes of travel become increasingly differentiated, the boundaries between tourism and other spheres of experience and practice become more open, allowing direct influence from media prosumers.

Through a participatory culture and strategies inherent to the convergence culture, it is possible to transform places that are little visited into tourist destinations, while valuing culture and making the environment (physical and economic) sustainable. Overtourism must be reconfigured according to new criteria of cultural management, in order to decentralize and differentiate its activities. This is imperative because tourism can significantly shape natural landscapes and social relationships, so that there is an urgency to implement the power of tourism to do good to communities, as well as to benefit tourists and the natural environments where people and species live [22].

For the proposal presented in this article, the strategies of two case studies are studied, since it seems appropriate to adapt and replicate to senior cyclotourism:

Exploring Outcomes of Community-Based Tourism on the Kokoda Track, Papua New Guinea: A Longitudinal Study of Participatory Rural Appraisal Techniques [23] – in the development of eco-trekking on the Kokoda trail in Papua New Guinea, a participatory rural assessment approach was used, supported by community-based tourism, social mapping and awareness patrol. Through media articles, newsletters and forums for collaborative studies, the opportunity arose to create small businesses based on tourism through a bottom-up approach;

Finding Nemo's Spaces: Defining and Exploring Transmedia Tourism [21] – through a case study of the Disney-Pixar franchise "Finding Nemo", it addressed how spatial experiences and intertextual references were generated in various coded tourist attractions. It was intended to explore the world-building opportunities offered by different attractions and to map the intertextual dissemination of transmedia content in the tourism sector in virtual and physical spaces.

Based on these case studies, it is assumed that community-based tourism involves local communities in the planning process for sustainable tourism, honoring and incorporating their knowledge and opinions; and that transmedia tourism is part of the growing intersections between the experience economy, the culture of convergence and the tourism sector.

The proposal must diversify experiences incorporating creative activity and self-expression, linking to the meaningful and mindful travel niche, as well as the growing desire for personal well-being. Therefore, it must be and must be seen as a reciprocal exchange between the region, residents and tourists, that gives the opportunity of citizens recognition, quality of life improvement, awareness of cultural and natural heritage, and development of the destinations' image.

4.1 Proposal for Senior Cyclotourism

In terms of strategies, three were selected, from the aforementioned case studies, that are linear with senior cyclotourism: (i) **induced tourism** – cyclotourism can be motivated by economic, sporting or ecologically sustainable reasons, as well as by thematic issues through the intertextuality of the intellectual property of those involved (*e.g.* stories or local legends related to cycling or the region); (ii) **community-based tourism** - locals (*i.e.* residents and shopkeepers) must promote tourism routes and transmedia narratives, with or without intertextuality, that preserve and/or improve the economy and the environment, as well as valuing the location; and (iii) **transmedia tourism** - taking advantage of physical and virtual environments, indoor and outdoor, through various media and narratives for a diverse audience (*i.e.* senior citizens who are physically and mentally healthy, but also those unable to travel due to physical and/or psychological limitations, weather conditions or external factors).

In line with the selected strategies, a transmedia solution for senior cyclotourism, that encompasses a participatory culture to promote sustainable tourism and active aging, is proposed. For this solution, it is suggested to use an application that is interconnected with other platforms, such as email, website, social networks, software and hardware (*e.g.* smart bicycle rollers or elliptical bicycles with sensors). It is also recommended the development of the application in co-design, as it is a cooperative and participative technique that develops a shared sense of ownership of the project – resulting from a set of applied theories and practices that involve the end user in activities that inform, test and drive the development of digital products and services, encouraging them to be co-designers. Thus, the key points are as follows:

Participatory Culture and Collective Intelligence – Senior Citizen, residents, shopkeepers and companies operating in a network, sharing opinions, stories and local commerce through their own channel (*e.g.* website or email). This application aims to link tourism at the national level – not promoting just one city – so the use and connection, for instance, of the RUTIS network[3] (*i.e.* network of all Portuguese Universities of Third Age) with CICLOVIA[4] (*i.e.* Portugal's official bicycle paths) could lead to the use of the

---

[3] http://www.rutis.pt/ [Accessed: January 2021].
[4] http://www.ciclovia.pt/ [Accessed: January 2021].

intertextuality, inherent to regions' history and culture, for the creation of narratives. The use of this application will aim not only to attract tourists induced by cycling or cycling events, sustainable tourism and easier and better ways to get to know the places, but also residents, shopkeepers and companies induced by the creation of routes that promote local commerce and do not contribute to overtourism. One way to bring together the different audiences (*i.e.* the local people - including residents, shopkeepers and companies - and tourists) would be through social networks, forums and the app's website.

Transmedia – A transmedia narrative storytelling has great potential to enable the intertextuality of (i) stories from the region, (ii) from residents and possible cyclists amongst them or (iii) from companies. These stories can be used in external environments (*e.g.* at the place of visit) and virtual environments (*e.g.* at home, through the computer or virtual reality system); the creation of virtual characters (*e.g.* relevant figures who can accompany or tell the story); augmented reality at points of interest (*e.g.* highlighting historical, cultural or natural facts of a particular location). It is also proposed to use gamification with augmented and virtual reality for outdoor environments; as well as exergames, aimed, not exclusively, at a public that cannot go out and experience tourism on the venue (*e.g.* senior citizens in nursing homes, people with physical limitations and even users unable to leave due to weather conditions or external factors such as the COVID-19 pandemic). In this way, it is intended to include a range of profiles of senior citizens to reach the pillars of active aging.

The main challenge to materialize the proposal would be to recruit and provide a participatory environment that reshapes interactions between communities and companies for transmedia narrative, as well as their integration in the solution. Nevertheless, it is considered that the narrative can be seen as: a democratic and inclusive planning model; which offers space to a variety of stakeholders with their own experiences and emotions; which allows stakeholders to build shared understandings of what their situation is and what can be done [24]. It is also believed that narrative gerontology (*i.e.* a process in which senior citizens tell their story by memory) brings many benefits and improves the sense of well-being through sharing, thus enhancing the social participation and inclusion inherent to active aging.

Regarding the option of using gamification, it is justified by the forecast of being a major trend for tourism in the coming years, influencing and shaping behaviors [19, 20]. In addition, the main motivations reported for using a gamified tourism application are: (i) to obtain accurate information about a destination before, during, and after the experience; and (ii) being able to interact with other people [25]. For this, combining physical and digital spaces is important to merge the virtual and the reality in the users' mentality, not only to enhance digital inclusion but also to support content development, build knowledge, reinforce network formation, and spread local history, traditions and cultural expression.

Exergaming, on the other hand, provides pleasure and involvement in the short and medium term, integrating physical exercise in the daily lives of users [19]. As for the use of exergames, it is suggested that senior citizens can participate in cycling trips online with several users, using elliptical bikes or smart rollers. Specifically, users can ride a bicycle in virtual environments that represent outdoor locations in certain locations (*e.g.* riding in a park or by the sea). The goal is for the exergame to be executed using software

- in which cities and routes are being gamified to motivate people to ride on virtual roads in indoor environments, with or without structured exercises and forming social groups - that works via a platform or web browser of the application, on a tablet mounted on the handlebar or with a television or computer, to project the route map, textual information and miniature photos of other cyclists' avatars.

This proposal includes inclusive and innovative characteristics, which may enhance not only the involvement of communities in the social integration of senior citizens, but also the planning of strategies for sustainable tourism in order to promote regions, local commerce and network decision-making (*i.e.* not being exclusively top-down and allowing bottom-up participation). Also, succeeding Ortet and colleagues' study [19, 20], it is relevant that the proposal follows some of the endorsements suggested at different experiment stages, such as: (i) pre-experience – weather forecast and route recommendation; (ii) in loco – route directions, gamification and narrative elements; and (iii) post-experience – feedback and social engagement.

5   Final Considerations

Traditionally, it was believed that content spreading over multiple media would generate a rich experience of reality, but nowadays it is known that information circulation on multiple platforms is not enough. It is only by giving a new vision, expanding current knowledge, and introducing something new with the dissemination of this content in new media that an immersive and reliable experience is provided.

This may imply that media products can be produced by both consumers and traditional media producers. In the context of tourism destination marketing, tourists have become consumers-users-producers, complementing the specialized content often shared by Destination Marketing Organizations. In a convergence culture, this distinction between producers and consumers has become blurred.

Digital convergence is an inevitable process in constant evolution and mutation, occurring in a network society (*i.e.* flow space), an environment in constant transformation, where the users and their needs have become the focus of digital information and communication [26].

This convergence occurs in a network ecosystem, which can be transformed, evolved, and restructured with possible implications on both individual and collective entities. As socio-cultural disruptions within this network ecosystem occur, addressing the individual context in place-making and place-vising with the use of media is also essential [1]. In this sense, providing a personalized experience may enable active participation and informed choice-making by senior tourists.

Transmedia approaches favor the consolidation of contextual and participatory models that consider social factors, the dialogue, and interaction between the agents of the info-communication process from a relational perspective. Transmedia strategies are consistent with community-based tourism, in which communities are associated with a commercial and social value of natural and cultural heritage in tourism, promoting the conservation of community-based resources. The exchange of knowledge in science and society may also foster public participation and decision-making power.

It is worth noting that a considerable number of people share happy memories of cycling despite the fact that most do not have the opportunity to ride a bicycle again due to functional limitations related to the aging process, increased road traffic or access to convenient motorized transport, but also because of fears and external factors (*e.g.* COVID-19 pandemic). The proposed solution aims to address the lack of social participation of senior citizens in communities to promote active aging and sustainable cyclotourism through transmedia. In this position paper, some examples were given to encourage community-based cyclotourism as an integrated part of participatory culture. The proposal would enable the recognition of senior citizens' contribution to society, which may lead to a broader acceptance and inclusion.

Despite this, it is important to take into account that the adaptation and replication of strategies from other cases, the approach to senior citizens, their acceptance and inclusion in a network society, and participatory culture involves care and precautions. It is necessary to build strategies in accordance with the profile of senior citizens (*e.g.* exergaming for users in nursing homes or physical rehabilitation), paying special attention to their needs and preferences. Even so, it is considered that the proposal may contribute to the promotion of active aging, especially with a focus on the pillars of health and participation; encourage economy growth; improve infrastructures and develop sustainable tourism.

Acknowledgments. The study reported in this publication was supported by FCT – Foundation for Science and Technology (Fundação para a Ciência e Tecnologia) nr. 2020.04815.BD and the project SEDUCE 2.0 - Use of Communication and Information in the miOne online community by senior citizens, funded by FCT – Fundação para a Ciência e a Tecnologia, I.P., COMPETE 2020, Portugal 2020 and European Union, under the European Regional Development Fund, POCI-01-0145-FEDER-031696 SEDUCE 2.0.

References

1. Jenkins, H.: Convergence Culture. Where Old and New Media Collide. New York University Press, New York (2006)
2. Jenkins, H.: Confronting the Challenges of Participatory Culture: Media Education for the 21st Century. The MIT Press, Cambridge (2009)
3. Costa, L., Grist, H.: Ageing in a network society: an introduction. Netw. Knowl. J. MeCCSA Postgrad. Netw. **10**(1), 1–4 (2017)
4. Rastegaeva, T.E., Kazakov, I.S.: Tourism – a social and economic phenomenon of modern-day. Krasnoyarsk Sci. **0**(1), 107 (2016). https://doi.org/10.12731/2070-7568-2016-1-107-118
5. INE - Instituto Nacional de Estatística: Report of the INE of Estatísticas Demográficas 2016 [Demographic Statistics 2016]. 76th edition of the thematic yearbook on Demography, published by Statistics Portugal (INE, IP) (2016)
6. Gazzola, P., Pavione, E., Grechi, D., Ossola, P.: Cycle tourism as a driver for the sustainable development of littleknown or remote territories: the experience of the Apennine regions of Northern Italy. Sustainability **10**(6), 1863 (2018). https://doi.org/10.3390/su10061863
7. Jenkins, H., Ito, M., Boyd, D.: Participatory Culture in a Networked Era: A Conversation on Youth, Learning, Commerce and Politics. Polity Press, Cambridge (2016)
8. Arango-Forero, G., Roncallo-Dow, S., Uribe-Jongbloed, E.: Rethinking convergence: a new word to describe an old idea. In: Lugmayr, A., Dal Zotto, C. (eds.) Media Convergence Handbook - Vol. 1. MBI, pp. 17–28. Springer, Heidelberg (2016). https://doi.org/10.1007/978-3-642-54484-2_2

9. Hartley, J.: From the Consciousness Industry to Creative Industries. Blackwell, Oxford (2008)
10. Nichols, T.: The Death of Expertise: The Campaign Against Established Knowledge and Why it Matters. Oxford University Press (2017)
11. Månsson, M.: Mediatized tourism. Ann. Tour. Res. **38**(4), 1634–1652 (2011). https://doi.org/10.1016/j.annals.2011.02.008
12. Campos, A., Mendes, J., do Valle, P., Scott, N.: Co-creation of tourist experiences: a literature review. Curr. Issues Tour. **21**(4), 369–400 (2015). https://doi.org/10.1080/13683500.2015.1081158
13. OECD: Tourism and the Creative Economy. OECD, Paris (2014)
14. WHO: Active Ageing: A Policy Framework. A Contribution of World Health Organization to the Second United Nations World Assembly of Ageing, Madrid, Spain (2002). https://doi.org/10.1080/713604647
15. Aln, E., Dominguez, T., Los, N.: New opportunities for the tourism market: senior tourism and accessible tourism. Vis. Glob. Tour. Ind. Creating Sustain. Competit. Strateg. (2012). https://doi.org/10.5772/38092
16. FPC – Fundação Portuguesa de Ciclismo: Ciclismo e Dinamização da Atividade Turística (2016). http://business.turismodeportugal.pt/pt/Conhecer/estrategia-turismo/programas iniciativas/Paginas/programa-portuguese-trails.aspx. Accessed Dec 2020
17. McKibbin, D.: Cycling for leisure, recreation and tourism. Research and Information Service Briefing Paper (2015). http://www.niassembly.gov.uk/globalassets/documents/raise/publicati ons/2015/regdev/2415.pdf
18. Gantar, A., Kočiš, D., Pehnec, M.: How to develop cycle tourism? Project-Bicy.Eu. Maribor (2012)
19. Ortet, C.P., Costa, L.V., Veloso, A.I.: Jizo: a gamified digital app for senior cyclo-tourism in the mione community. In: Zagalo, N., Veloso, A.I., Costa, L., Mealha, Ó. (eds.) VJ 2019. CCIS, vol. 1164, pp. 195–207. Springer, Cham (2019). https://doi.org/10.1007/978-3-030-37983-4_15
20. Ortet, C., Veloso, A.I., Costa, L.V.: A Gamified app to promote senior cyclo-tourism: a pilot study. In: 21st Annual European GAMEON® Conference (GAME-ON®'2020) on Simulation and AI in Computer Games (2020, in Press)
21. Garner, R.: Finding Nemo's spaces: defining and exploring transmedia tourism. JOMEC J. **14**, 11–32 (2019). https://doi.org/10.18573/jomec.195
22. Matteucci, X., Gnoth, J.: Elaborating on grounded theory in tourism research. Ann. Tour. Res. **65**, 49–59 (2017). https://doi.org/10.1016/j.annals.2017.05.003
23. Reggers, A., Grabowski, S., Wearing, S.L., Chatterton, P., Schweinsberg, S.: Exploring outcomes of community-based tourism on the Kokoda Track, Papua New Guinea: a longitudinal study of Participatory Rural Appraisal techniques. J. Sustain. Tour. **24**(8–9), 1139–1155 (2016). https://doi.org/10.1080/09669582.2016.1145229
24. van Hulst, M.: Storytelling, a model of and a model for planning. Plan. Theory **11**, 299–318 (2012)
25. Xu, F., Weber, J., Buhalis, D.: Gamification in tourism. Inf. Commun. Technol. Tour. **2014**, 525–537 (2014). https://doi.org/10.1007/978-3-319-03973-2_38
26. Castells, M.: The Rise of the Network Society: The Information Age: Economy, Society, and Culture, vol. 1. Wiley (2011)

A Goal Oriented Storytelling Model for Improvement of Health Game Experiences Among Older Adults

Zhengxiang Pan[1,2(✉)], Hao Zhang[2], Yaming Zhang[2,4], Cyril Leung[2,3], and Chunyan Miao[2,4]

[1] Interdisciplinary Graduate School, Nanyang Technological University, Singapore, Singapore
panz0012@e.ntu.edu.sg
[2] Joint NTU-UBC Research Centre of Excellence in Active Living for the Elderly, Nanyang Technological University, Singapore, Singapore
{zhang.h,zhangym,cleung,ascymiao}@ntu.edu.sg
[3] Department of Electrical and Computer Engineering, University of British Columbia, Vancouver, Canada
[4] School of Computer Science and Engineering, Nanyang Technological University, Singapore, Singapore

Abstract. As part of efforts to promote health game adoption among older adults, the Goal Oriented Storytelling Model (GSM) is proposed to improve their health game experiences. In GSM, coaching is presented as an approach that helps older adults with low prior experience with digital technology to nevertheless enjoy digital health games and the benefits they provide. Propp's theory in storytelling is used to structure while persuasion, goal setting and familiarity augments the set of available coaching strategies. With GSM, a coached gameplay session is crafted on top of the Pumpkin Garden health game. This form of health game coaching is then evaluated through a small-scale phenomenological study. Effects of GSM-driven coaching were positively exhibited by our older players, proving that GSM is a viable way to coach older adults to enjoy health games.

Keywords: Health game · Coaching · Storytelling · Persuasion · Familiarity · Goal setting

1 Introduction

1.1 Research Motivation

Aging as a global challenge requires solutions to ensure that healthy aging societies are in place, which enhances societies' ability to function. Existing literature repeatedly supports the potential of serious health games as a mediator for creating a healthy aging population. Hence, it is necessary to develop methods to increase serious health game adoption among older adults, especially those who are illiterate with technology.

Q. Gao and J. Zhou (Eds.): HCII 2021, LNCS 12787, pp. 135–152, 2021.
https://doi.org/10.1007/978-3-030-78111-8_9

1.2 Research Problem: Age-Related Factors Forming Digital Barriers

Although games were gaining popularity among older adults [1], they still only prefer a certain subset of games. The report titled "2019 Essential Facts About the Computer and Video Game Industry" [2] reported that *boomer gamers* aged between 55–64 prefer card games, puzzle games and virtual board games. This significantly differs from other age groups' favorite genres like racing, sports, and first-person shooters, which tend to be more action-packed.

Hence, we see the player's age to be a major influencer in this distinct gaming preference. Aged-related attributes and characteristics that cause the shift in preference include physical degeneration, cognitive impairment and extra psychological needs (e.g. loneliness, inferiority, menopause) [3]. Older adults who suffer from degradation of eyesight and movement dexterity also make more mistakes than younger users [4]. Sensory degeneration causes difficulty when reading at close distances, while weakened motor functions results in loss of flexibility and coordination [5] which games may sometimes require. The higher rate of error, compounded with difficulty understanding what they did wrong from the ensuing error messages, causes frustration and inability to perform well when using technology products [6, 7]. As a study put it, *"for some, initial enthusiasm soon faded away and was replaced by tardiness, discomfort and trepidation"* [8, p. 543].

These "digital barriers" cause older adults to have an entirely different set of preferences and constraints from other age groups. Despite elderlies' willingness to engage with easier games [9], it is important to take measures to help older adults to overcome the digital barriers they may face due to their age. This makes it possible for health games to be widely accepted by older adults with a level of success comparable to commercial games.

1.3 Research Question: How Do We Shape a Positive Health Game Experience for Older Adults?

Researchers have suggested learning from the commercial games industry to improve health game adoption, stating that *"if the user is sufficiently entertained to regard the process as a game rather than a rehabilitative program, then the chances of continued engagement are increased"* [10, p. 7]. After all, commercial video games are valued in terms of the positive experience they create for the player [11], and industries will seek to design the optimal game experience for their players. Improving game experiences can be a holistic approach to overcome the digital barrier; an alternate route to health game adoption on top of existing approaches focusing on HCI and game design [12].

Coaching is proposed as a promising method to improve the health game experience for older adults, especially those with low digital literacy. Older adults with low prior experience to technology perceive guidance as a very important factor when using digital applications [13, 14]. The positive impact of an effective guide to older adults' daily activities has been proven in various other domains. For example, a majority of older adults displayed inadequate inhaler use technique due to lack of proper guide, and the guide design technique outlined in the study had led to significant improvement in older adults' inhaler use technique [15]. Another study on a virtual supervisor for older adults' physical exercise using monitoring, feedback, and motivational elements has received much appreciation [16]. Thus, there is a need to properly guide and encourage older adults to overcome their natural decline in cognitive abilities [17] and participate technology-related behaviors that are beneficial to them (e.g. health games). Referencing commercial games' successful approach, we propose to provide better game experience for older adults playing health games to encourage health game adoption (Fig. 1).

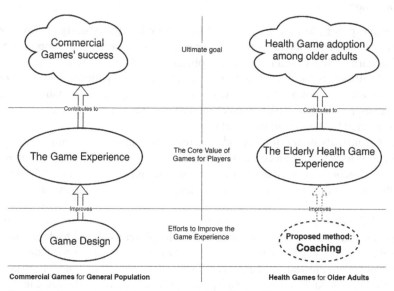

Fig. 1. Learning from commercial games: improving the health game experience among older adults

This paper presents the Goal Oriented Storytelling Model (GSM) as a methodology to coach older adults through an unfamiliar realm of digital health games. Given a health game, GSM helps researchers or healthcare workers craft an engaging gameplay session for older adults that ultimately provides a positive game experience.

The organization of the paper is as follows: Familiarity (Sect. 2.1), goal setting (Sect. 2.2) and persuasion (Sect. 2.3) helps derive coaching techniques to handle specific scenarios. Propp's 31 Functions for storytelling lays out a structure to the events that are anticipated to take place during a health game session (Sect. 2.4). A phenomenological study is then introduced (Sect. 3.1) and results (Sect. 3.3) provide initial support for the GSM's feasibility. GSM is then concluded in Sect. 4.

2 Components of the GSM Coaching Model

Research provides support to the use of coaching practices into providing better game experience for older adults. For instance, a phenomenological study revealed that elderlies are interested to learn about digital technology if they are provided with one-to-one learning sessions [18]. Thus, there is potential for coaching practices to produce better health game experiences for older adults.

The GSM aims to improve existing question-and-answer approaches employed in current research [19]. Several concepts that constitute the GSM are reviewed in a bottom-up approach. Familiarity, Goal Setting and Persuasion is presented first as components of health game coaching, while Storytelling is presented last as a structure to depict the entire gameplay coaching process.

2.1   Familiarity

In a previous paper [20], the author investigated how familiarity design helps provide better human computer interactions. 3 dimensions of familiarity were proposed. Symbolic familiarity refers to placing everyday objects from the user's world into the game. Cultural familiarity is similar but involves concepts, artefacts, patterns, traditions, or rituals from the user's culture, instead of from their day-to-day life. Actionable familiarity means the user is familiar with computer interactions that are similar to other activities often conducted by the user in their real life.

The 3 familiarity dimensions can also be relevant in terms of coaching, seeing that GSM's role is to function as a coaching framework. Hence, the 3 familiarity dimensions above can be recontextualized from "what in-game design elements can help" into "how might the coach utilize familiar elements to enhance the health game experience".

- Cultural familiarity may translate into the gameplay coach's appearance, spoken language, attire etc. so that they can appeal to the player's cultural background.
- Symbolic familiarity emphasizes on utilizing the player's existing knowledge towards certain objects to illustrate the health game's benefits, or lending strength from familiar objects to handhold the player through particularly tricky parts of the game that would have otherwise made them lose their patience.
- Actionable familiarity encourages the coach to enquire more about the physical activities that the subject is familiar with. The coach can then attempt to associate subsequent game task requirements to something the player has done before in the past. This is even potentially applicable to utilizing the coach's knowledge base, suggesting the coach to share more about their past relevant experience with the activity on hand to help the player visualise the actions in a real-world context.

We present some actionable thoughts on utilizing familiarity in the implementation guide on page 9.

2.2   Goal Setting

Goal setting theory is very relevant in the context of coaching, especially when tailoring various in-game tasks for older adults.

One of Locke's earliest research concludes that clear goals (specific goals that require effort and high competence) tend to generate better performance from individuals compared to easier goals (goals that simply state "do your best"), on the premise that the goal is not too hard for the individual [21].

Thus, regulating the task difficulty at an optimal level is important. When designing a game session using a specific health game, the amount of challenge that is inherent to specific game tasks should be considered. As a coach, we could constantly monitor the amount of assistance required. Players can be left to overcome in-game challenges if they have the ability; on the contrary they should be coached closely when the challenges are significant. This helps regulate participants' perceived challenge, keeping it at an optimal level.

The coach is a core mediator that sets goals for the player. Although goals can be set in several distinct ways like self-set, collaborative, group-set, guided and assigned, only the last 2 methods are preferred since aged players tend to be more often illiterate with digital technology and games. Given an existing health game, the coach (as an expert) should clearly define several segments of the game for older players. During gameplay, the coach obtains feedback on individuals by observing how well they are playing. The coach will then scale the goal according to the individual's abilities. This provides a tailored, positive game experience in health games.

2.3 Persuasion

Setting proper goals alone may sometimes not be enough to garner interest from older adults who perceive digital games as foreign. The Elaboration Likelihood Model (ELM) [22] is leveraged in GSM as a persuasion mechanism to drive the user towards the set goals, especially when signs of defiance begin to emerge.

ELM studies how persuasion works on individuals through two different routes. The "central" route describes how likely an individual can scrutinize and elaborate on a piece of information, while the "peripheral" route involves providing cues that help increase the perceived credibility of messages, usually on a subconscious level. In more applicable terms, the game coach has to assess the subjects' likelihood of attempting to elaborate messages. If elaboration likelihood is high, the coach should employ central route of persuasion; otherwise, the coach should employ peripheral route of persuasion.

2.4 Storytelling

Vladimir Propp was a Russian structuralist who, through the study of Russian folk tales, established the concept of an atomic unit of character types and events. After analyzing and breaking down a massive number of Russian traditional fairytales into their smallest narrative units, he generalized the types of events into 31 irreducible functions and types of characters into 7 main archetypes [23]. Propp's theory is well-received for his two key findings: all the fictional parts have basically the same structure underneath; and that a story can be generated through a sequence of abstract plot elements.

Similar to how Vladimir Propp himself breaks down folklores into discrete narrative units, the storytelling mechanism in GSM segments out different points in the coached gameplay process. In this gameplay process, the player is viewed as the "hero in their lived story at this very moment" and their ultimate quest is to "finish the game session with a good game experience". Propp's functions is, in our case, reinterpreted in context of playing a health game. Despite Propp's statement *"all functions known to the tale will arrange themselves within a single tale, and none will fall out of order"* [24, p. 10], we

Table 1. Reinterpretation of Propp's functions in GSM

Current Function	Original Context in Propp's Theory	Recontextualized Description in GSM	Action Items for the Coach	Possible Transition(s) and Condition(s)
		Scenario 1: Introduction of the Health Game		
Interdiction	Hero is warned	Player is informed to play pumpkin garden	Tell the player they need to go through the minigames in Pumpkin Garden to complete the session	The player appears to not want to play the game: **Violation of Interdiction** The player immediately agrees to play the game: **Departure**
		Scenario 2: Persuading the Player to Continue		
Violation of Interdiction	Warning is violated	Player does not want to play the game	Ask for the reason that they don't want to play.	Proceed to **Complicity**
Villainy/Lack	Need is identified	Coach identifies reason player rejects playing the game	Attempt to *persuade* them (ELM), promise to guide them throughout the game • highlight health game objective: improve PD detection tool (central processing) • offer encouragement, highlight the game will be simple and quick to finish (peripheral cue)	Proceed to **Mediation**
Mediation	Hero discovers lack and approached with a request; hero is dispatched	Player considers; they are asked to play the game again.	Ask whether the player agrees to play	When player still refuses to play: **Violation of Interdiction** When player expresses interest in playing: **Counteraction**
Counteraction	Hero chooses positive action	Player is successfully persuaded to play the game	Hand the device to the player to commence the play session	Player starts to play: **Departure**
		Scenario 3: Completing a Game Goal		
Departure	Hero leaves on mission	Player starts to play the game with a specific goal set out for them	Observe the player's playthrough until they encounter a problem	Player encounters problem while playing: **Absentation** Player completes a round without problems: **Acquisition**

(continued)

Table 1. (*continued*)

Current Function	Original Context in Propp's Theory	Recontextualized Description in GSM	Action Items for the Coach	Possible Transition(s) and Condition(s)
Absentation	Something goes missing	Knowledge is missing in player that makes them unable to play the game	-	Proceed to **Testing**
Testing	Hero is challenged	Player encounters a problem when playing the game	Observe if player tries to overcome by themselves; intervene if they ask for help	Player asks for help: **Reaction** Player gives up: **Violation of Interdiction**
Reaction	Hero responds to challenges	Player shows difficulty when attempting to resolve challenges.	Investigate problems encountered. Guide the player through the challenge, set dynamic goals by lowering the passing criteria if necessary	Player is making progress in the challenge: **Acquisition**
Acquisition	Hero gains magical item	Player is able to overcome the problem encountered	The problem on hand is resolved; observe for additional problems	Player encounters another problem: **Absentation** Player completes the assigned game goal: **Guidance**
Guidance	Hero reaches destination	Player achieves their current game goal	Set the next game goal for the player to play and achieve	The next task is the final challenge: **Struggle** The next task is a regular game segment: **Departure**
		Scenario 4: The Final Challenge		
Struggle	Hero battles villain	Player has to finish the challenging round without giving up	Observe player until they finish the challenging round. Only help out when asked.	Player finishes: **Victory** Player gives up: **Violation of Interdiction**
Victory	Villain is defeated	Player is able to complete the final challenge without giving up	Applaud the player for completing the game session.	-

found it necessary to group certain functions together into re-arrangeable *coaching scenarios* to describe the gameplay situation more accurately. The full re-contextualization of Propp's function in health game coaching is presented in Table 1 below:

Player's Perspective: Coaching Scenarios
The four identified scenarios in Table 1 form a logical sequence that enables older adults unfamiliar with digital technology to enjoy health games. Details are presented below:

- the player is first requested to complete several in-game tasks (Introduction of Health Game, Interdiction),
- they may need to be persuaded to embark on the learning journey (Persuading the Player to Continue, Violation to Counteraction),
- they complete the challenge one by one (multiple iterations of "Completing a Game Goal", Departure to Acquisition),
- they complete a segment of more challenging gameplay as a final challenge to finish off a game session (The Final Challenge, Struggle to Victory).

Game Coach's Perspective: GSM Implementation Guide
The same set of coaching scenarios serve as a guideline for game coaches to design health game sessions for a particular health game. Here we summarize the mechanisms presented above as an actionable step-by-step guide when implementing GSM-driven coached gameplay sessions for a particular health game:

1. Prepare a convincing set of relevant facts to help players perceive personal benefits from playing the health game. These health facts can be used in the introduction, or the persuasion process to motivate older players who may initially refuse.
2. With understanding towards the health game, divide its gameplay into several segments with clearly defined goals.

   a. It is recommended to have more shorter segments to increase flexibility when coaching the player through the gameplay session.
   b. The goals for each segment should be simple enough for the player, yet difficult enough to engage them.
   c. Some games that feature minigames or well-defined rounds (e.g. Pumpkin Garden [25] or Ping Ping Pong Pong exergame [20]) are more easily segmented, while other health games with less segmentation may need to be redesigned to fit the purpose of conducting GSM game sessions.

3. Set aside a gameplay segment to serve as the "final challenge" in a gameplay session.

   a. The amount of challenge should be relatively higher in the "final challenge".
   b. No new gameplay elements should be introduced in the "final challenge" so that the player may focus on reapplying familiar gameplay knowledge gained beforehand.

The coach should also prepare for the coaching session with the guidelines below:

- Familiarize with in-game elements

  - It enables the coach to associate in-game elements with objects familiar to the player.
  - Prepare a convincing set of health game facts relevant to the health game to help players perceive personal benefits from playing the health game. These health facts can be used in the introduction, or the persuasion process to motivate the player to play the health game.

- Build a knowledge base for each player. Probe for and note down traits that help us work on personalizing the game experience:

  - Cultural background (work culture, ethnicity etc.)
  - Objects that the player is familiar with
  - Player's prior knowledge towards some different topics
  - Their ability to process messages

2.5 Summary of the GSM

The proposed Goal Oriented Storytelling Model (GSM) highlights coaching is a viable method to counteract the digital barrier between technology and older adults through facilitating a better health game experience for them. Propp's 31 Functions in storytelling inspires a set of events termed as "coaching scenarios" that describe and anticipate interactions between the older players and the health game. From these coaching scenarios, the coach's role is then clarified. With reference to existing theories on familiarity, persuasion and goal setting, measures to design the game session (pre-game preparation) or handle various reactions by older players (mid-game reaction) are proposed.

This integrative, step-by-step approach to improving the health game experience among older adults is put into test in a phenomenological study. Procedures and results are reported below.

3 Phenomenological Study on the Health Game Experience Under GSM-Driven Coaching

3.1 Study Participants and Procedure

This study aims to evaluate GSM's effectiveness as a coaching model to improve game experience for older adults with low digital literacy. Hence for this study, we randomly selected 5 older adults from the community who had little to no prior experience with digital technology. A game session is conducted with them under GSM-driven coaching, carried out by the researcher.

Players are first briefed about the Pumpkin Garden health game and its health values (Parkinson's Disease early detection [25]). Then, they play through a game session. The Pumpkin Garden game is segmented into several tasks that the players play through sequentially to finish the game session. First, they are required to play 3 iterations of the water wheel minigame using 3 different tools in the listed order: their fingers, the Microsoft Arc Mouse, and the Apple Pencil. Each iteration consists of 6 rounds, and participants are required to switch hands between rounds. Then, participants will be required to play 1 iteration of the weed-clearing minigame with their fingers, which consists of 5 rounds of static gameplay (participants clear weeds spanning 1 screen) and 1 round of "final challenge" (participants are challenged to clear weeds as they grow in real-time). Throughout the 4 iterations of minigames, the researcher assists the participants to complete the required rounds by applying the 4 coaching scenarios: introducing the game, guiding them to finish the game tasks, persuading them to continue (if needed), and encouraging them through the final challenges. Players are finally interviewed, sharing with us the game experiences they just had through an open-ended discussion. We used the following few questions as a starting point for each participant:

- How do you feel after playing the Pumpkin Garden game? Would you like to share your game experience?
- Do you recall encountering challenges when you played just now? What do you think enabled you to finish the game?

3.2 Phenomenological Approach to Evaluate the GSM

Phenomenology is deemed to be a suitable method to observe and interpret how exactly GSM-driven coaching can help create a good game experience for aged players. If a mechanism present in GSM can be linked to a good game experience felt by most of our players, more validity and confidence can be gained on the mechanism, allowing it to become an integral part of the GSM model. The phenomenon under study is: "What is the game experience of our older players under GSM-driven coaching?"

3.3 Results and Findings

Although certain coaching scenarios were planned (page 9) based on certain storytelling patterns, the sequence of events in the gameplay session are still unique to each player. Below we presented the lived experiences of the players based on observations.

Coaching Scenario 1: Introduction
The researcher started by addressing an Interdiction to the hero, which comes as a prompt to try out the game in order to complete the "quest" (study). Some participants felt nervous as they are not well-trained in using touchscreen devices. In the interview, P2 shared that when he is asked to play initially, he felt pressured to play well. Others are more carefree as they are confident the researchers will guide them well. When we asked P5 if she is nervous when we handed her the iPad, she responded with "not at all, I'll follow what you say". The contrasting reaction resembles how different heroes would have reacted to the same Interdiction.

Since participants has been told about the Pumpkin Garden game's health benefits, they tend to oblige and attempt to play the game when prompted, thus fast-forwarding us to the Departure stage.

In the Departure stage, participants proceed with a minigame by themselves after receiving a briefing on how to play the minigame. For the water wheel minigame, they are told to place a finger on the red dot and use another hand to turn circles, following the shape of either the small or the big wheel (requirements alternate between different rounds of the same minigame). For the weed-clearing minigame, they are simply told to use both hands to gesture along the shape of the weeds. This briefing is deemed necessary as they would not have been able to start playing otherwise and could be thought of as "packing up before the journey". After "sending them off to begin the journey", we observe them until they encounter difficulties. Figure 2 below sums up the common path taken by all 5 observed participants.

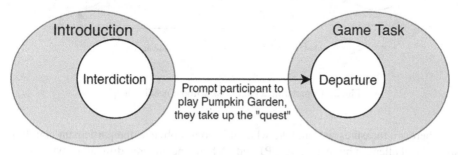

Fig. 2. Introduction and associated Propp functions

According to Propp's Character Archetypes, the game coach in this segment acts simultaneously as a *Helper* and a *Dispatcher*. Helper for providing initial help to the hero by giving them direction, and Dispatcher for sending the hero onto the journey.

Coaching Scenario 2: Completing a Game Task

A game session requires participants to complete a number of tasks. However, knowledge barriers are present when player interacts with digital games, especially for participants with little or no prior exposure to digital games. When P5 first started to play the water wheel minigame with the mouse, he does not possess prior knowledge on using the computer mouse. Hence, we observed a troubled expression on his face. At this point in the gameplay session, the knowledge required to complete the game task on hand is absent, hence he is unable to proceed with the game task. This knowledge gap manifests as challenges he has to overcome.

As participants eventually encounter challenges, they will try to overcome the test. This phenomenon can be mapped to Testing in Propp's functions. Here is where we paid attention to how they cope with the test and whether they are able to cope with the test by themselves.

It is oftentimes best to let the participants overcome the problems themselves if they have the ability to do it. P3 felt challenged when he uses a computer mouse to play the water wheel minigame, which is evident through his extremely slowed down gameplay and his look of concentration. He also reported the feeling of being challenged in the subsequent interview. However, he did not show signs of quitting; instead, he was able to complete the 3 rounds of the game through self-motivation and, as he put it, "staying immersed and focused". Hence, in each round, he has proceeded to the Acquisition stage without the need of our assistance. Figure 3 below indicates the path P3 has taken.

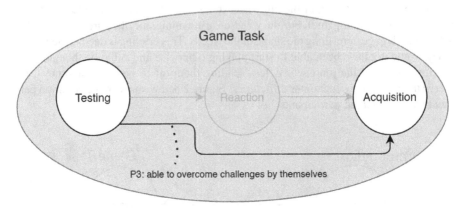

Fig. 3. Completing a game task without needing help

There are measures we can take when it becomes obvious the participant couldn't solve the challenges by themselves. P1 and P5 both encountered difficulties when synchronizing their fingers in the weed clearing minigame. For more than half a minute, they not making any progress; in their perspective the screen seemingly did not react to their inputs which is a source of frustration. Now in the Reaction stage, we explained the step-by-step process to her on how to synchronize the fingers and move upwards together, at the same time providing real-time feedback by asking them to go back when her fingers have slid too far ahead without registering progress. With specific instructions to help them break a problem down into understandable goals, their performance improved, and they are able to complete the first 5 rounds of the weed clearing minigame. Figure 4 below indicates the path P1 and P5 have taken.

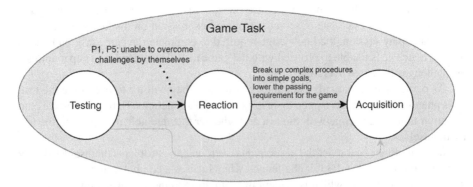

Fig. 4. Completing a game task with help

An interesting story usually features the hero facing off with challenges hard enough for them to develop their character, and achievable enough for them to survive the challenges. The role of the coach in this case is the *Donor* who provides assistance (albeit sparingly[1]), in the process producing an optimal level of challenge to maximize satisfaction. This act is also known as dynamic game balancing [26] and is in line with how goal setting recommends tasks which are "difficult enough to stimulate performance and fair/reasonable enough to obtain commitment" [27].

Coaching Scenario 3: The Final Challenge
The game session concludes with a challenging round 6 of the weed clearing minigame where it is possible to lose by getting overrun by the weeds, known as the hero's Struggle. We described the round as the ultimate challenge of what participants has learnt in the previous rounds of the weed clearing minigame. Upon the warning, all participants assumed a ready stance to chase the weeds as they grow on-screen, appearing to be within reach visually. P2, P3, P4 successfully caught up to the growing weeds and won the round in a short amount of time. P1 and P5 had the same issues they had before; they could not clear the weeds as fast as the others. With our encouragement, they tried their best and managed to eventually catch up with the constantly growing number of weeds. We applauded them for achieving Victory in our game session, and they too showed smiles of relief in return (Fig. 5).

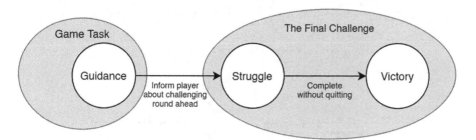

Fig. 5. Ending a game session with a final challenge

By applauding the player for their dedication towards completing the game session, we draw their learning journey to a close by providing the reward (the *Princess*) that the Hero has proved worthy of.

Coaching Scenario 4: Persuading Player to Continue
Participants' motivation to play the game appears to be hampered if the unsatisfaction persists for too long. When turning the water wheel, P2 has stopped a few times mid-game, which presents a Violation of Interdiction. We asked what is wrong and she vaguely expressed about not wanting to continue playing. Upon further inquiry, the

---

[1] The *Donor* and *Helper*, although alike in functionality, differs in the way that the donor attempts to put the hero through some kind of test before rewarding them (hence the *Testing* function); whereas the helper may help the hero without their knowledge. .

Villainy/Lack is made known. She said, *"my reaction is very slow, I don't know how to play."* From our interaction, we noticed that she reacts better to cues and prompts rather than logic and reasoning, hence we encouraged her through a peripheral route. *"You played very well just now, keep it up."* After the encouragement, she continued to play but still mumbled on her unsatisfactory performance, which we prompted with *"you are doing great, go on and you should complete it in no time."* After spending some time in Mediation, she chose positive action (Counteraction), and continued to play subsequent rounds without further complaint (Departure).

P1 when first playing with the weed clearing minigame asked if she can choose not to play the part, as she found it challenging and unsatisfying (Villainy/Lack). She seemed like a fact-driven rational individual. In ELM's terms, the need for cognition is high, thus we decided to go through the central route of persuasion. We explained that her gameplay result is part of our data gathering process to improve the game's detection capabilities, hence her gameplay data is valuable to improve the game and help future PD patients in their diagnosis. She thought about it (Mediation) and agreed to continue despite the foreseeable production of unsatisfying results (Counteraction).

Figure 6 below indicates the path P1 and P2 has taken in the above 3 scenarios.

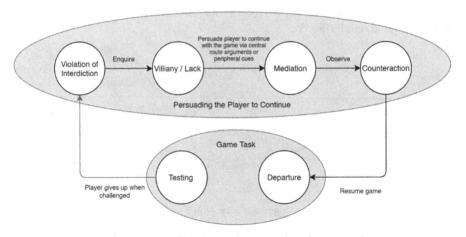

Fig. 6. Breaking off and resuming gameplay after persuasion

Unlike Propp's theory, the Violation of Interdiction in GSM's context typically do not occur after Interdiction (i.e. Hero asked to play). Rather, it only comes after an initial Departure (i.e. started to play for the first time) which the Hero withdraws after discovering the significant challenges presented ahead of them in the game session. The coach in this case has to complete his duty as a *Dispatcher* by leveraging ELM persuasion techniques.

In the above analysis, we did not explicate the False Hero nor the Villain; although one could argue the health game to þe a source of challenge for our players (like the Villain), we nevertheless played down that aspect avoid attaching a negative stigma to the health games they are supposed to enjoy. Another interesting "potential Villain" can be the player's pre-existing unwillingness to participate in health games; an abstract "dark

Table 2. Summary of the coached game experience in Propp's theory terms

Coaching scenario	Propp functions	Segment description from hero's perspective	Coach's character archetype
Introduction	Interdiction to Departure	Setting off for the journey	Helper and Dispatcher
Completing a Game Task	Departure to Guidance	Completing a Game Task	Observer
Overcoming a Challenge	Testing to Acquisition	Encountering and overcoming difficulties	Donor
Persuading the Player to Continue	Violation to Counteraction	Regaining interest towards the game	Dispatcher (using persuasion)
The Final Challenge	Struggle to Victory	A stretch of unassisted gameplay as a final challenge	Donor (more conservative with providing help)

side of the self". While not explicated in this study, it may be an interesting coaching technique to personify a player's unwillingness to themselves in future studies.

Table 2 above summarizes the GSM *storytelling mechanism* as observed in real life. It has shown that Propp's theory of storytelling is a viable method to chart down our aged player's gameplay learning journey as a story of their experiences. The following section discusses how goal setting, familiarity and persuasion mechanisms are applied in our study.

Goal Setting, Familiarity, Persuasion Mechanisms
Different mechanisms worked in different stages of the study to provide our participants with a positive health game experience.

When coaching participants to play the Pumpkin Garden game, we heeded goal setting's recommendation to pose adequate challenges and regulated our intervention frequency. We allowed P3 to find his own way around a problem and helped out P1 and P5 when things get too hard for them. Based on P3's description of feeling relaxed and satisfied after the challenge and P1's appreciation towards our "helpfulness", we can recognize that they appreciated the dynamic scaling of the challenge tailored to them.

"I saw the goal, I saw your (water wheel) bar! You are very encouraging."
(P1, Female, 64 years old)

"How do you motivate yourself to continue playing, when you notice you are losing focus on the game?"
"I just try my best to maintain my performance and try to draw faster whenever possible. I never thought of giving up."
(P3, Male, 72 years old)

Familiarity was observed and utilized during the gameplay when we drew relevance of game task to real life. When P4 had issues when playing with the mouse, the relevance of the pen to her everyday life helped her regain the interest towards the game.

"Which tool (pen, mouse, finger) do you prefer the most to play the water wheel minigame?"

"I prefer to use the pen as it is easier to play. When using my finger, I need to apply more force. I dislike the mouse the most."

(P5, Male, 66 years old)

P3 also attributed his hobbies when asked about his good performance in the weed-clearing minigame.

"How do you find the weed-clearing game?"

"That one is easy. I play Ukulele! That's why I can coordinate my hands. I am now trying to learn piano, self-taught through online. I find it very difficult… have to keep on trying."

(P3, Male, 72 years old)

During "Violation to Counteraction" when we persuaded participants not to give up, we applied central and peripheral routes of persuasion onto P1 and P2 respectively. They were, as a result, able to finish the game and have a better overall game experience for knowing they accomplished the game without quitting.

"I tried to coordinate but (I was) not able to. It is quite frustrating… But I stayed positive and kept trying, and you encouraged me to play on."

(P1, Female, 64 years old)

"I lose control easily while playing the water wheel minigame. But I still try to keep playing to finish it… I try my best to complete the game even if I face challenges."

(P2, Female, 70 years old)

Quotes from our players presented above illustrates how familiarity, goal setting and persuasion mechanisms work within the storytelling framework to maintain player's interest (i.e. persuading players back into continuing with the game) and tackle in-game challenges with a positive attitude (i.e. embrace and enjoy the challenging process).

3.4 Summary

In this study, the player's learning journey is painted as a story and examples are put forward to describe GSM coaching scenarios. These real-world observations were presented to detail how each GSM mechanism contributed to player's positive game experience. From their interview responses and quotes, real-world relevance is also drawn for persuasion, goal setting and familiarity mechanisms.

4   Conclusion

This paper proposes coaching as a viable approach in helping older adults accept and enjoy health games, which in turn allows health game benefits to take their intended effect. The Goal Oriented Storytelling Model (GSM) is presented with storytelling, persuasion, goal setting and familiarity as its theoretical building blocks. Coaching scenarios built from to Propp's functions are proposed. Structured like a story, a coached health game session conceptualizes game tasks to be completed by the player, suggests the need for a final challenge, and feature numerous strategies to overcome in-game challenges and player noncompliance.

This integrative approach is then tested and evaluated in a phenomenological study. 5 players' gameplay process and sharing are closely inspected and analysed. Evidence support the GSM and its mechanisms' feasibility in helping improve the health game experience among older adults. Future research can seek to improve the model by testing out if health game adherence is improved through the use of GSM.

Acknowledgements. This research is supported by the Interdisciplinary Graduate School, Nanyang Technological University, Singapore. This research is also supported, in part, by the National Research Foundation, Prime Minister's Office, Singapore under its IDM Futures Funding Initiative and the Singapore Ministry of Health under its National Innovation Challenge on Active and Confident Ageing (NIC Project No. MOH/NIC/HAIG03/2017).

References

1. Gaming Attitudes and Habits of Adults Ages 50-plus. AARP research (2019)
2. 2020 Essential Facts about the Video Game Industry. Entertainment Software Association (2020)
3. Liu, Y., Tamura, R.: Application of game therapy in the health of future elderly: an experience design perspective. In: Stephanidis, C., Antona, M., Gao, Q., Zhou, J. (eds.) HCII 2020. LNCS, vol. 12426, pp. 608–625. Springer, Cham (2020). https://doi.org/10.1007/978-3-030-60149-2_46
4. Blackler, A., Mahar, D., Popovic, V.: Older adults, interface experience and cognitive decline. In: Proceedings of the 22nd Conference of the ComputerHuman Interaction Special Interest Group of Australia on ComputerHuman Interaction (2010)
5. Vasconcelos, A., Silva, P.A., Caseiro, J., Nunes, F., Teixeira, L.: Designing tablet-based games for seniors: the example of CogniPlay, a cognitive gaming platform. In: Proceedings of the 4th International Conference on Fun and Games, Toulouse, France (2012)
6. Kurdoghlian, S.: Designing Technology With the Older Population in Mind. The UX Collective, 17 March 2020. https://uxdesign.cc/designing-technology-with-the-older-population-in-mind-8a6a4f920bec. Accessed 16 Sept 2020
7. Kane, L.: Usability for Seniors: Challenges and Changes. Nielsen Norman Group, 8 September 2019. https://www.nngroup.com/articles/usability-for-senior-citizens/. Accessed 16 Sept 2020
8. Namazi, K.H., McClintic, M.: Computer use among elderly persons in long-term care facilities. Educ. Gerontol. **29**(6), 535–550 (2003)
9. Salmon, J.P., et al.: A survey of video game preferences in adults: building better games for older adults. Entertain. Comput. **21**, 45–64 (2017)

10. Ushaw, G., Davison, R., Eyre, J., Morgan, G.: Adopting best practices from the games industry in development of serious games for health. In: The 5th International Conference (2015)
11. Tan, E.S., Jansz, J.: 23 - The game experience. In: Product Experience, San Diego, Elsevier, pp. 531–556 (2008)
12. Brox, E., Fernandez-Luque, L., Tøllefsen, T.: Healthy gaming - video game design to promote health. Appl. Clin. Inform. **2**(2), 128–142 (2011)
13. Barnard, Y., Bradley, M.D., Hodgson, F., Lloyd, A.D.: Learning to use new technologies by older adults: perceived difficulties, experimentation behaviour and usability. Comput. Hum. Behav. **29**(4), 1715–1724 (2013)
14. de Oliveira Santos, L.G.N., Ishitani, L., Nobre, C.N.: Casual mobile games for the elderly: a usability study. In: Simpósio Brasileiro de Games e Entretenimento Digital, São Paulo (2013)
15. Abley, C.: Teaching elderly patients how to use inhalers. A study to evaluate an education programme on inhaler technique, for elderly patients. J. Adv. Nurs. **25**(4), 699–708 (1997)
16. Bleser, G., et al.: A personalized exercise trainer for the elderly. J. Ambient Intell. Smart Environ. **5**(6), 547–562 (2013)
17. Garcia Vazquez, J.P., Rodriguez, M.D., Andrade, A.G.: Design dimensions of ambient information systems to assist elderly with their activities of daily living. In: Proceedings of the 12th ACM international conference adjunct papers on Ubiquitous computing - Ubicomp '10, Copenhagen (2010)
18. Betts, L.R., Hill, R., Gardner, S.E.: "There's not enough knowledge out there": examining older adults' perceptions of digital technology use and digital inclusion classes. J. Appl. Gerontol. **38**(8), 1147–1166 (2019)
19. Oppl, S., Stary, C.: Game-playing as an effective learning resource for elderly people: encouraging experiential adoption of touchscreen technologies. Univers. Access Inf. Soc. **19**, 295–310 (2020)
20. Pan, Z., Miao, C., Yu, H., Leung, C., Chin, J.J.: The effects of familiarity design on the adoption of wellness games by the elderly. In: IEEE/WIC/ACM International Conference on Web Intelligence and Intelligent Agent Technology (WI-IAT), Singapore (2015)
21. Locke, E.A.: Toward a theory of task motivation and incentives. Organ. Behav. Hum. Perform. **3**(2), 157–189 (1968)
22. Petty, R.E., Cacioppo, J.T.: The Elaboration Likelihood Model of Persuasion, pp. 141–172. Springer, New York (1986)
23. Propp, V.: Morphology of the Folktale, 2nd edn. University of Texas Press (2010)
24. Exceprt of Vladímir Propp Morphology of the Folk Tale. The American Folklore Society and Indiana University (1968). http://web.mit.edu/allanmc/www/propp.pdf. Accessed 5 Jan 2020
25. Liu, S., Miao, C., McKeown, Martin J., Ji, J., Shen, Z., Leung, C.: Pumpkin garden: a mobile game platform for monitoring parkinson's disease symptoms. In: Zhou, J., Salvendy, G. (eds.) ITAP 2018. LNCS, vol. 10927, pp. 546–560. Springer, Cham (2018). https://doi.org/10.1007/978-3-319-92037-5_38
26. Andrade, G., Ramalho, G., Santana, H., Corruble, V.: Extending reinforcement learning to provide dynamic game balancing. In: IJCAI 2005 Workshop on Reasoning, Representation, and Learning in Computer Games (2005)
27. Latham, G.P., Locke, E.A.: Goal setting—a motivational technique that works. Organ. Dyn. **8**(2), 68–80 (1979)

A Brief Study on Excessive Online Game Playing Among Older Adults

Haijing Tang and Qin Gao[(✉)]

Department of Industrial Engineering, Tsinghua University, Beijing, China
tanghj19@mails.tsinghua.edu.cn, gaoqin@tsinghua.edu.cn

Abstract. Recently, there have been increasing games designed for older adults and growing concerns about older people's excessive online gaming. Since games require a high degree of commitment and time investment from the players to the detriment of occupational, social, and other recreational activities and relations, a few factors have been linked to excessive online gaming in older adults. We interviewed and surveyed 6 current older game users regarding their gaming behavior, living conditions, problems as consequences of gaming, and game motivations. Results indicated that older game users are significantly more likely to experience gaming-related problems and that some types of gaming motivations significantly predicted excessive gaming. Low connectedness to family, having friends with habitual gaming behavior and living in rural areas also had discriminative effects on older game users' investment. We also give some advice about game design for older adults. The findings support the necessity of offering guidelines for older users' game design and emphasize the importance of preventing older adults from being damaged by games specially designed for them.

Keywords: Older adults · Excessive game playing · Risk factors

1 Introduction

Older People are the fastest-growing segment of the population worldwide and it is predicted that a total of 2.1 billion people aged $\geq$60 years will appear in 2050 (Ackland et al. 2017). Despite the increase of the population, aging brings many physical challenges for older people, including sensory decrements, cognitive impairments, declines in motor skills, and chronic illnesses (Gerling et al. 2012). Thus, activities that require manual dexterity or memory, for instance, become more difficult for older people to perform (Vasconcelos et al. 2012). Furthermore, those changes affected older adults' lifestyles from all aspects, such as social activities, entertainment, and learning (Cota et al. 2015).

A solution for mitigating the bad effect is the digital game, as some studies have suggested that engaging with digital games has a positive impact on the mental and physical well-being of older people (Jung et al. 2009). Nowadays, more and more gaming products become available for older people, which promotes the trend of older people playing games, especially mobile games as they are easier to learn and operate for older people than the traditional online games (Cota et al. 2015). However, addiction to games

© Springer Nature Switzerland AG 2021
Q. Gao and J. Zhou (Eds.): HCII 2021, LNCS 12787, pp. 153–163, 2021.
https://doi.org/10.1007/978-3-030-78111-8_10

or excessive game playing has been one of the most prominent aspects discussed in the public and scientific debate about computer and video games. Many studies imply that excessive game playing does harm people, which appears in adolescents mostly (Kuss et al. 2012). As more and more older people begin their interaction with the mobile game, suggestions for them avoiding excessive game playing should be investigated and put forward.

To explore the factors for game addiction and excessive game playing, researchers conducted a lot of researches. Initially, people play digital games based on different motivations and factors. Older people invest in the game because they want to have social activities and entertainment and cultivate their skills that suffer from aging (Cota et al. 2015). From the perspective of factors, many researchers suggest that personality traits, demographic variables, social relationships can be important factors for game addiction for adolescents and young adults (Yen et al. 2009). However, studies on the factors for older people's excessive game playing is few. For older people, social isolation is a significant feature of the aging life among various age-related changes, which typically refers to objective separation from other people and lack of social activities (Tomaka et al. 2006). Despite the evidence demonstrating the effect of social isolation on adolescents' excessive game playing, the effect of social isolation for older mobile game users remains understudied. This gap warrants an investigation on the relationship between the older mobile game user' excessive game playing and their social isolation.

Generally, games for older adults are becoming more and more widespread. Thus, it implies us excessive game playing deserved a study and exploration for that older adults could play the game in the right way and prevent the potential risk and damage from excessive game playing. Thus, this paper aims (1) to describe typical excessive online game playing behaviors and present warning signs among Chinese older adults; (2) to examine the possible factors on excessive online game playing among Chinese older adults. (3) to provide guidelines for preventing older adults from problematic online game playing and designing online games for older adults.

2　Literature Review

2.1　Excessive Game Playing

Excessive gaming has been identified as a specific subtype of Internet addiction (Block 2008). In many situations, excessive game playing is strongly associated with online game addiction. Previous studies focus on online game addiction in aspects of features of behaviors and personalities, potential factors, and possible effects on addicts' life, most of them conducted among adolescents.

Many studies present typical behaviors and motives for excessive game playing. An investigation, based on 7069 gamers, revealed the addictive potential of gaming as well as the relationship between excessive gaming and aggressive attitudes and behavior (Grüsser et al. 2006). Another behavioral study presents that people may show some warning signs for potential game addiction, including a preoccupation with gaming, lying or hiding gaming use and loss of interest in other activities, social withdrawal, defensiveness and anger, psychological withdrawal, using gaming as an escape and continued use despite its consequences (Young 2009). In the term of motives, mechanics, relationship, escapism, advancement, competition, socializing, roleplaying seem to have a strong positive effect on game use (Kuss et al. 2012). Especially, s number of gaming motives have been linked to excessive online gaming in adolescents and young adults.

Studies on potential factors suggest personal traits, demographic variables, and social-cognitive factors affect game addiction/excessive game playing. Also, there are other categories for the factors. Some personalities, including neuroticism, sensation seeking, trait anxiety, state anxiety, and aggression, show a significant correlation with excessive game playing (Mehroof and Griffiths 2010). In another study, a total of 8941 adolescents were surveyed to explore the multi-dimensional discriminative factors for Internet addiction among adolescents regarding gender and age (Yen et al. 2009). Other factors, like gender, age, other demographical variables, depression, and low family monitoring, are also summarized in some studies.

To identify game addiction and excessive game playing, some diagnostic scale has been designed to measure addicted behaviors. One of the digital addiction scale measures behaviors in five aspects: deprivation, impulsivity, underperformance, low self-perception, and social isolation (Dilci 2019). Another classical game addiction scale measures the game behaviors from salience, tolerance, mood modification, relapse, withdrawal, conflict, and problems (Lemmens et al. 2009). These scales are modified in many studies to adapt to the characteristic of the population. For older adults, the scales should be modified slightly.

Excessive game playing may impact individuals and families negatively and seriously. Online gaming is an emotionally draining and time-consuming activity. To create more time for the computer, gaming addicts neglect sleep, diet, exercise, hobbies, and socializing. They let their health go as they do not get the proper rest and nutrition they need. They may suffer some health problems from back strain, eye strain, carpal tunnel syndrome, and repetitive stress injury (Hussain and Griffiths 2009; King et al. 2010; Young 2009).

2.2 Motivations for Game Playing by the Elderly

Various researches have focused on the motivation and reasons for the use of video games by the elderly. In general, motivations can be divided into external motivation and internal motivation. External motivation refers to the external motivation of the subject, such as the financial benefits obtained by completing a task. Internal motivation is related to a person's expectation, interest, and taste, which comes from the internal factors of the individual (Frey and Osterloh 2001).

The elderly usually have different internal motivations to play video games, and the motivations will change with the extent of game exposure, and physical and cognitive ability (Brown 2012). By summarizing the previous studies, the internal motivations of games for the elderly can be classified into four types: social interaction, entertainment needs, functional/skill training, and other motivations (Boyle et al. 2012; Cota et al. 2015; Festl et al. 2013; Miller 1996).

First of all, for the elderly, social isolation is an important feature of their life, usually referring to the objective isolation from others and the lack of social activities (Tomaka et al. 2006). The reasons for this kind of social isolation are complex, such as inconvenience to take activities due to physical reasons, shrinking social circle, etc.

Therefore, playing games can provide a kind of "virtual society" for the elderly, and thus breaking the state of social isolation. Many elderly people start playing games with such expectations. At the same time, the elderly usually possess a lot of free time, so they look forward to activities that can bring fun and kill time. Playing games as a wide range of public entertainment thus also attracts many elderly users for entertainment. Besides, some elderly people are worried about age-related changes, such as the decline of perception, cognitive function, and motor skills. As a result, many people began to play video games to develop and exercise these skills.

In cases of external motivations to play video games for the elderly, mechanism and element design of the game take a major part, and taking pride and getting communication with different generations also attribute to motivations. For the mechanism and element design of the game itself, some researches show that people prefer to play games on social networks for the following motivations: providing asynchronous games without establishing a daily commitment to the activity; allowing contact with other people in the game; providing rewards for each task; simulating competition; supporting state sharing and publishing, etc. (Omori and Felinto 2012). Other researches showed that immersion, fun, and entertainment of activities, increasing challenges and unexpected feedback of ongoing operations brought by games can also bring more external motivation to users (Boyle et al. 2012). A study that provides guidance on game design for the elderly points out that, in addition to the general principles of game design, cognitive challenges to make the elderly proud of their abilities can bring stronger external motivation (De Carvalho et al. 2012). Also, studies have shown that communication and proximity with different generations have also become the external motivation of some elderly people to play games, such as the elderly and children (Al Mahmud et al. 2010). The type of game is also an important factor affecting the game motivation of the elderly. For example, the incentive effect of reasoning games is stronger than an action game, and the incentive effect of games is stronger for exercising the memory ability and perception ability of the elderly (Cota et al. 2015). The women who have received higher education and the elderly paying attention to the development of cognitive function tend to play cognitive or strategic games (Alonso-Diaz et al. 2019).

The internal motivation of the old people to use games comes from their life characteristics, such as physiological and psychological changes, increased leisure time, and narrowed social scope, while the external motivation is closely related to the design of games and needs to be considered in combination with the internal motivation.

There are also studies on the motivation of the elderly to play games according to different types of games, and among them, one of the most various studied types is the massively multiplayer online role-playing games (MMORPGs). For MMORPGs, motivations for the elderly to play can be divided into mainly three parts: achievement, society, and immersion (see Table 1) (Yee 2007). The achievement motivation involves advancement, analyzing game mechanics, and competition. The sociality motivation involves helping and chatting with other players, developing meaningful relationships, and teamwork. The immersion motivation involves discovery, role-playing, avatar customization, and escapism. The analysis of motivations for MMORPGs assesses players' motivations.

Table 1. Three motivational components for playing MMORPGs (Yee 2007).

Motivation		Definition
Achievement	Advancement	The desire to gain power, progress rapidly and accumulate in-game symbols of wealth or status
	Mechanics	Having an interest in analyzing the underlying rules and system to optimize character performance
	Competition	The desire to challenge and compete with others
Sociality	Socializing	Having an interest in helping and chatting with other players
	Relationship	The desire to form long-term meaningful relationships with others
	Teamwork	Deriving satisfaction from being part of a group effort
Immersion	Discovery	Finding and knowing things that most other players don't know about
	Role-playing	Creating a persona with a background story and interacting with other players to create an improvised story
	Customization	Having an interest in customizing the appearance of their character
	Escapism	Using the online environment to avoid thinking about real-life problems

In the game design for the elderly, how to consider the external motivation and internal motivation, so that the game design can meet the deep needs of the elderly, is a process still needing a systematic review of the current research, and repeatedly verifications.

3   Method

3.1   Procedure

6 participates are gathered by contacting older game users whom the researchers already knew. They are all over 52 years old, with 5 of them retired and 1 still working (4 male and 2 females). They play different games, with their times for the game ranging from 0–5 h/day. When they came to the study, a questionnaire was used to assess background variables, game playing behaviors, and personalities, firstly. Then, a deep semi-structured interview was conducted. Table 2 shows the basic information about the six participates.

3.2   Measurements

Background Variables. The first questionnaire assessed demographics, including questions about age, gender, and education. Moreover, it included questions about habitual behaviors as well as game use, and computer game preference, weekly time spent on gaming, and the highest number of hours spent in a single gaming session.

Table 2. Basic information about the three participates

Code	Sex	Age	Time for Game/D	Login Times/D	Game type	Education	Occupation
1	M	58	2.5 h	5	Online card games	Bachelor	Designer
2	M	65	5 h	Over 10	Online chess games and card games	Bachelor	Manager
3	M	62	4 h	Over 10	Online shooting games	Bachelor	Teacher
4	M	57	1.5 h	5	Online card games	Middle School	Worker
5	F	52	0.5 h	3	Casual puzzle games	High School	Worker
6	F	82	0.5 h	2	Casual puzzle games	Middle School	Manager

Excessive Game Playing Behavior. To assess problems with gaming, the 21-item Game Addiction Scale (Lemmens et al. 2009) was translated from English into Chinese, and the consistency of translations was checked by yet another party to ensure the translated questionnaire's representation validity. The 21-item GAS assesses seven dimensions of game-related problems, including salience, tolerance, mood modification, relapse, withdrawal, conflict, and problems.

Personalities. To assess the participants' personality, the Mini-IPIP Scales (Donnellan et al. 2006) was translated from English into Chinese, and the consistency of translations was checked by yet another party to ensure the translated questionnaire's representation validity. The Mini-IPIP Scales assesses five dimensions of personality, including extraversion; agreeableness, conscientiousness, neuroticism, and intellect/imagination.

3.3 Semi-structured Interview

A semi-structured interview was conducted with every older game user to know their game use, life states, motivations, attitudes, potential factors for excessive game playing, impacts, and expectations for the game. The shortest time for the interview is 30 min and the longest time for the interview is 70 min. The interview was recorded and turned into a manuscript and was analyzed.

Generally, the outline was divided into three parts: game experience, older life, and excessive game playing. In the part of game experience, general game use, motives/reasons for game playing, interactions and experiences in the game, and impacts of game playing were questioned. In the second part, we mainly focused on daily activities, social life, health condition, psychological well-being, and personality. In the last part, we mainly questioned their self-assessment for game playing, self-control for game playing, alternatives for the game, and attitudes towards the game for older adults. When interviewing, the subject put questions according to the outline mainly and made a detailed inquiry for possible other phenomena, factors, and reasons. Thus, lots of detailed inquiries are conducted according to the answer in the practical interviewing process.

4 Results

4.1 Game Experiences

The six participants have different game experiences, which represents several typical game playing patterns.

Interview 1 is 58 years old, whose occupation is an interior designer, living with a son. He began to play games about 3–4 years ago, lasted for 2 years, stopped playing the game because of his wife's disease, and played again after his wife's death. Now, he plays the game about 2.5 h/day recently, usually in the morning and in the evening. One of the reasons for his excessive game playing is escaping from reality and releasing a bad mood. When he takes the self-assessment, he thinks he is under control. If something has to be done, he can stop playing games immediately. Also, he has some other hobbies that are more important than playing a game, like a cricket fighting. Interview 2 is 65 years old, whose occupation is a manager, living with wife and granddaughter. He began to play the game for killing time and obtaining achievements. Recently, he played the game about 5 h/day, usually all day long except time for meals, housework, and looking after granddaughter. He often plays the game until 1 a.m. and once felt uncomfortable because of excessive game playing. When losing too many game currencies, he feels angry. In reality, he is active in some community activities, like voluntary activities. Generally, he is looking for more offline activities for older adults. Interview 3 is 62 years old and is a retired teacher, living with his wife. He began to play games about 1 year ago, for killing time, continue to play for achievements and stimulations. One of the important features of him is that he enjoys the opponent process. Recently, he plays the game about 4 h/day, usually all day long except time for meals, housework, and exercise. He often feels unsatisfied with the age-related physical changes and concerns about the older life. Thus, he wants to obtain achievements and stimulations through online games to make him believe in himself and overcome the sense of loss and depression. Interviewee 4 and 5 are 57 years old and 52 years old, who are a couple and both workers. They began to play games about 5 months ago because their son recommended the game to them considering that the couple lacks entertainment. However, they play the game for little time every day. Interviewee 6 is 82 years old, whose previous occupation was a manager in government. She began to play the game after she was introduced to the game in the hospital. Limited to her health condition, she cannot play the game for too long in daily life. She mentioned that she may feel uncomfortable when she interacts with people who are younger than her, which prevents her from interacting with others. Also, limited time for the game is a struggle.

In summary, all six interviewees believe that their game playing behaviors are under control. The direct reason for game playing is killing time but deep reasons and motives are different. Achievements and fun from games are important roles for them. Alternatives for games are not available enough for them. Some individual difference indicates some different guidelines.

4.2 Typical Excessive Game Playing Behaviors for Older Adults

Based on the results of the interview, we can summary some typical excessive game playing behaviors for older adults.

Firstly, the older adults' time for the game is quite long. This is because they usually have more free time, with no work and less sleep. Secondly, the games that they are playing are relatively traditional and easy. Next, they may be more immersed in the game since they have more time for learning and experiencing new games. Besides, the older adults claim to have more reliable self-control for not excessive game playing. Thus, they are generally open-minded to other activities while playing games. Also, there are some warning signs of excessive game playing for older adults, including some physical changes after long-time game playing, delays for meals and housework, and conflicts with families.

Several situations may lead to excessive game playing for older adults. The first situation is the resilience of adversity among older adults. As Interviewee 1 implies, he must release the bad mood after his wife's death. The second situation is the tries to new things, especially smartphones. And the third situation is the observations for other people playing the game. In these situations, older adults show different motives for excessive game playing, including the pursuit of stimulation and challenge, loyalty for the game, the pursuit of achievements, and escaping from reality.

Finally, we summarized several possible factors for older adults' excessive game playing, including depression, loss of families, low connectedness with peers, low connectedness with the community, and little community activities. Also, there are some risks for adults, such as irritable personality is dangerous for bringing out illness, like hypertension and delays in having meals, taking medicine, and exercising.

4.3 Guidelines for Preventing Excessive Game Playing for Older Adults

Based on the results of the current study, we believe that some guidelines for preventing older adults from problematic online game playing and designing online games for older adults can be put forward. For the improvement of the problem, we can discuss that from the aspect of community and the aspect of technology.

From the perspective of the community, more off-line activities that are different from games should be organized. One of the major reasons for older adults playing games is to kill time. The deeper cause is that they face no other meaningful activities so that they choose to kill time in the virtual world. The participants of the current study suggest that off-line activities can be combined with their necessary activities, such as shopping in the supermarket, walking in the park, and taking care of their grandchildren. Once the real activities occupied their free time, they can decrease their time for game playing.

From the perspective of technology, there are some design suggestions. Firstly, more design elements that improve older adults' social interactions in the game should be considered since older adults imply that they are looking for more real and deep social interactions in the virtual game. Secondly, a system for reminding of important things like having meals or taking medicine can be added in the game design, which will be a helpful way for preventing causes that will harm their health. Finally, the game mechanics should be proper for older adults. For example, it should be smoother when it comes to competition in the game since older adults are hard to affording huge losses or gaining.

Generally, game design for older adults can be meaningful but difficult. Thus, it deserves more attention to older adults' game playing behaviors and their challenges.

5 Conclusions

In this study, we interviewed and surveyed 6 current older game users regarding their gaming behavior, living conditions, problems as consequences of gaming, and game motivations. Results indicated that older game users are significantly more likely to experience gaming-related problems and that some types of gaming motivations significantly predicted excessive gaming. Low connectedness to family, having friends with habitual gaming behavior, and living in rural areas also had discriminative effects on older game users' investment.

Specifically, typical excessive game playing behaviors for older adults include a long time spent on the game, immersing in the game. However, they may hold more reliable self-control for not excessive game playing and an open-mind to other activities while playing games. Also, three situations and motives are presented in the brief study. Furthermore, we find that depression, loss of families, low connectedness with peers, low connectedness with community, little community activities may be some possible factors for older adults' excessive game playing. From the perspective of impact, there are some risks for older people that irritable personality is dangerous for bringing out illness, like hypertension. Also, it may bring delays in having meals, taking medicine, and exercising. Thus, the game designed for older adults may be smoother in competition. And a system for reminding of important things like having meals and taking medicine can be added to the game.

To conclude, understanding the behaviors and motivations associated with the development of excessive behaviors related to playing online games will promote future research and will pave the way for addiction prevention and treatment approaches for older adults. Discerning motivations for addictive game behaviors serve the purpose of informing clinical practice and research in the new field of problematic online gaming of older game users. The reasons for playing online games serve as a first step to understand how initial high engagement can develop into a potential behavioral addiction. Moreover, understanding that specific situations may lead to excessive game playing for older adults is important. The above findings support the necessity of offering guidelines for older users' game design and emphasize the importance of preventing older adults from being damaged by games specially designed for them.

References

Ackland, P., Resnikoff, S., Bourne, R.: World blindness and visual impairment: despite many successes, the problem is growing. Commun. Eye Health **30**(100), 71 (2017)

Al Mahmud, A., Mubin, O., Shahid, S., Martens, J.-B.: Designing social games for children and older adults: two related case studies. Entertain. Comput. **1**(3–4), 147–156 (2010)

Alonso-Diaz, L., Yuste-Tosina, R., Mendo-Lázaro, S.: Adults video gaming: key competences for a globalised society. Comput. Educ. **141**, (2019)

Block, J.J.: Issues for DSM-V: internet addiction (2008)

Boyle, E.A., Connolly, T.M., Hainey, T., Boyle, J.M.: Engagement in digital entertainment games: a systematic review. Comput. Hum. Behav. **28**(3), 771–780 (2012)

Brown, J.A.: Let's play: understanding the role and meaning of digital games in the lives of older adults, pp. 273–275 (2012)

Cota, T.T., Ishitani, L., Vieira Jr., N.: Mobile game design for the elderly: A study with focus on the motivation to play. Comput. Hum. Behav. **51**, 96–105 (2015)

De Carvalho, R.N.S., Ishitani, L., Nogueira Sales De Carvalho, R.: Motivational factors for mobile serious games for elderly users. In: Proceedings of XI SB Games (2012)

Dilci, T.: A study on validity and reliability of digital addiction scale for 19 years or older. Univ. J. Educ. Res. **7**(1), 32–39 (2019)

Donnellan, M.B., Oswald, F.L., Baird, B.M., Lucas, R.E.: The mini-IPIP scales: tiny-yet-effective measures of the Big Five factors of personality. Psychol. Assess. **18**(2), 192 (2006)

Festl, R., Scharkow, M., Quandt, T.: Problematic computer game use among adolescents, younger and older adults. Addiction **108**(3), 592–599 (2013)

Frey, B.S., Osterloh, M.: Successful Management by Motivation: Balancing Intrinsic and Extrinsic Incentives. Springer Science & Business Media, New York (2001)

Gerling, K.M., Schulte, F.P., Smeddinck, J., Masuch, M.: Game design for older adults: effects of age-related changes on structural elements of digital games. In: Entertainment Computing-ICEC 2012, pp. 235–242 (2012)

Grüsser, S.M., Thalemann, R., Griffiths, M.D.: Excessive computer game playing: evidence for addiction and aggression? Cyberpsychol. Behav. **10**(2), 290–292 (2006)

Hussain, Z., Griffiths, M.D.: The attitudes, feelings, and experiences of online gamers: a qualitative analysis. CyberPsychol. Behav. **12**(6), 747–753 (2009)

Jung, Y., Li, K.J., Janissa, N.S., Gladys, W.L.C., Lee, K.M.: Games for a better life: effects of playing Wii games on the well-being of seniors in a long-term care facility. In: IE '09: Proceedings of the Sixth Australasian Conference on Interactive Entertainment, pp. 1–6 (2009)

King, D.L., Delfabbro, P.H., Griffiths, M.D.: Cognitive behavioral therapy for problematic video game players: conceptual considerations and practice issues. J. CyberTherapy Rehabil. **3**(3) (2010)

Kuss, D.J., Louws, J., Wiers, R.W.: Online gaming addiction? Motives predict addictive play behavior in massively multiplayer online role-playing games. Cyberpsychol. Behav. Soc. Netw. **15**(9), 480–485 (2012)

Lemmens, J.S., Valkenburg, P.M., Peter, J.: Development and validation of a game addiction scale for adolescents. Media Psychol. **12**(1), 77–95 (2009)

Mehroof, M., Griffiths, M.D.: Online gaming addiction: the role of sensation seeking, self-control, neuroticism, aggression, state anxiety, and trait anxiety. Cyberpsychol. Behav. Soc. Netw. **13**(3), 313–316 (2010)

Miller, W.R.: Motivational interviewing: research, practice, and puzzles. Addict. Behav. **21**(6), 835–842 (1996)

Omori, M.T., Felinto, A.S.: Analysis of motivational elements of social games: a puzzle match 3-games study case. Int. J. Comput. Games Technol. **2012**(3) (2012). https://doi.org/10.1155/2012/640725

Tomaka, J., Thompson, S., Palacios, R.: The relation of social isolation, loneliness, and social support to disease outcomes among the elderly. J. Aging Health **18**(3), 359–384 (2006)

Vasconcelos, A., Silva, P.A., Caseiro, J., Nunes, F., Teixeira, L.F.: Designing tablet-based games for seniors: the example of CogniPlay, a cognitive gaming platform, pp. 1–10 (2012)

Yee, N.: Experimental motives for playing online games. J. CyberPsychol. Behav. **9**(6), 772–775 (2007)

Yen, C., Ko, C., Yen, J., Chang, Y., Cheng, C.: Multi-dimensional discriminative factors for Internet addiction among adolescents regarding gender and age. Psychiatry Clin. Neurosci. **63**(3), 357–364 (2009)

Young, K.: Understanding online gaming addiction and treatment issues for adolescents. Am. J. Family Therapy **37**(5), 355–372 (2009)

ZhiTu: A Smartphone Photo Managing Application for the Elderly

Mei Yang, Qin Gao[(✉)], and Qiang Liu

Department of Industrial Engineering, Tsinghua University, Beijing, China
gaoqin@tsinghua.edu.cn

Abstract. As an important tool of photo management, current smartphone photo managing applications are not supportive enough for the elderly. In order to provide more support for photo management to the elderly, this research designed a smartphone photo managing application called ZhiTu. Focusing on four activities of photo management, which were photo collecting, photo organizing, path recalling and photo finding, four innovative features were introduced: (1) organizing structure, (2) seeking paths, (3) sharing, (4) treatments of special photo types. The application was evaluated using the method of cognitive walkthrough. The results showed that only five of the eleven tasks evaluated were agreed consistently to be suitable for elderly people. Information expression and the understandability of conceptual model are the main problems needed to be solved before further evaluation of functions with elderly people. Nevertheless, the conceptual ideas of this application were mostly approved. Comparing to existing solutions, polished follow-up version of ZhiTu was expected to provide more friendly user experiences of smartphone photo management for the elderly.

Keywords: Photo managing tool · Elderly people · Smartphone application

1 Introduction

With the development of camera module on smartphones, it has become easy for elderly people to take photos at any time. The amount of photos produced every day has ushered in an explosion [1]. To address the problem, cloud storage was introduced to enlarge storage space. Image analysis was also applied to automatic photo sorting, reorganizing and search. In recent years, smartphone photo managing applications with usage of these technologies have become more and more popular.

However, existing smartphone photo managing applications are still unsatisfying to elderly users in four activities: photo collecting, photo organizing, path recalling and photo finding. First, it is too tiring for the elderly to collect a large number of photos due to their reduced operating abilities [2]. Second, for the elderly, keeping a large number of photos organized requires too much time, effort and skills. Third, the decline of nonverbal memory makes it difficult for elderly people to recall key information they used to organize photos [3]. Fourth, they may also feel inconvenient to find photos by

© Springer Nature Switzerland AG 2021
Q. Gao and J. Zhou (Eds.): HCII 2021, LNCS 12787, pp. 164–175, 2021.
https://doi.org/10.1007/978-3-030-78111-8_11

glancing over a large number of thumbnails in an album because of weakened vision and lengthened reaction time [4].

In order to provide more support for photo management to the elderly, a smartphone photo managing application called ZhiTu was developed, which focused on four features corresponding to the four activities mentioned above. Semi-structured interviews, focus group discussion and online survey were conducted to gather user needs. Then the requirements were summarized combing the result of user study and an analysis of existing products. After that, the application was designed and a high-fidelity prototype was developed. Finally, the application was evaluated using the method of cognitive walkthrough.

2 Related Works of Photo Managing Tools for the Elderly

Several works had been carried out to explore solutions for four activities of photo management: photo collecting, photo organizing, path recalling, and photo finding.

Photo sharing between friends is the most common way of collecting photos for elderly users apart from taking photos directly. Social media such as WeChat and Facebook, is the main medium for photo sharing for the elderly. However, users need to save photos one by one, which is very tiring. Also, these photos are often saved to the secluded default path of application, leading to strange folder name. Besides, advanced users collect photos from web pages or online disks, but technical problems ensue in this case. To simplify this activity, Holloway explored the possibility of adopting Facebook as public family photo album [5]. Unfortunately, problems arose in ownership and maintenance work. Furthermore, it was difficult to determine whether embarrassment or invasion of privacy will occur when choosing photos to share. It became worse when they found that elderly users always act only as recipients in such group sharing activities, which was contrary to the original intention of this attempt. In essence, public albums will eventually be centrally managed. Personal photo storage with simplified sharing method is still a better choice by comparison.

Database and narrative are the two main types of organizing tools for digital photos [6]. Among database-type tools, most of the galleries that come with operating systems determine storage path by default based on the source. Although reorganizing photos by creating folders and moving photos between folders manually is allowed, it is too cumbersome to deal with a large number of photos. At present, photo classifying service according to people, time and events are fairly common with the development of image recognition and analysis technology. More intelligent examples like speeding up photo managing process with the help of geographical analysis, image similarity analysis and face recognition provided by Pang et al. also exists [7]. But instead of serious database interface, understandable expressions should be designed to increase elderly users' acceptance toward database tools. Different situations arise for narrative tools, which are usually a side function of social media such as Facebook and WeChat. This type of organizing tools preserves the actual life experience and communication history to the greatest extent, at the expense of concentrated display and freedom of modification. It is also worth noting that managing photos in social media leads to risk of privacy leakage, especially for elderly people who have insufficient knowledge. Some researchers introduced a narrative recording method based on database, to gather the advantages of two organizing types. Hu et al. designed a smart photo album named Fond Memories, which involves written messages, voices and music in real-time communication [8]. Dialogues about photos can be carried out so that users can share memories with their family. Another example called PhotoFlow not only builds up photo organizing structure through storytelling in family reminiscence, but also visualizes it by imitating the activity of sorting out photos on a table top [9]. However, these applications ask for big screen devices and a mass of speech resources, which is not realistic for daily photos in smartphones.

Users are always required to recall photo paths based on previous organizing structure. Otherwise, they can only find photos through inefficient traversal methods. However, unnatural or changed organizing structure, ambiguous keywords or fuzzy memory may lead to failure of path recalling. Elsweiler summarized the common causes and countermeasures of lapse in daily life. Accordingly, a photo managing interface on computer called PhotoMemory was designed, which showed contextual fragments of seeking history [10]. After applying filters each time, inappropriate photos will only become smaller instead of being removed, in case that users need to be reminded again. In the case of smartphones, it is hard to show such content on the screen. Nonetheless, the research has inspired that information of impressive dimensions and connection between photos play an important role in path recalling.

The premise of finding a target photo is that the user recognizes it. For elderly people with dementia, Schoneveld et al. developed an augmented reality photo album [11], which could reconstruct the scene in photos to improve recognition. In general situation, the biggest difficulty for the elderly is to find photos in thumbnails. Cleaning up junk photos and increasing thumbnail size can palliatively relieve their visual load. However, meaningful photos that will not be cleaned are still the majority. Visual simplification methods considering photo features are expected.

Although defects can be found, valuable guidance and inspiration are provided in existing works. In this study, we will try to put forward improved solutions and innovative ideas of these photo managing activities.

3   Requirements Gathering

To collect detailed requirements of smartphone photo managing tools for elderly users, we conducted a two-stage user study. In the first stage, a focus group discussion with four elderly people aged above 65 and semi-structured interviews with seven elderly people aged above 65 were carried out for qualitative research. In the second stage, an online questionnaire toward 207 middle-aged and elderly people was used for extensive and prospective statistics. Among them, the proportion of people aged 45–54 was 61.35%, 55–64 was 32.85%, and people above 65 was 17.25%.

Most of the participants use galleries that come with their own smartphones. Less than 10% of participants use narrative tools in social media as their main photo managing tools. To the participants, the main purpose of using smartphone photo managing tools is to view photos. It is worth noting that, compared with direct search, they are more inclined to trace back the initial path of collecting to find specific photos. The participants organize photos every once in a while, but still expect quicker or automated operations. Photo sharing may happen occasionally, and backup is the least. When sharing photos, their shared objects are generally fixed, such as friends and family members. Backing up photos or cleaning up smartphone memory rarely happens, as it is difficult to distinguish the storage location and status of photo files for the elderly.

As for the basic functions of photo managing tools, more than 90% of the participants understand delete, and more than 50% understand copy, move, and create a new album. Cancel and sorting are relatively unfamiliar. Most of the functions that are known can also be used, except for search. Because they are not sure if they can provide an accurate description. For the functionality of the photo management tool, we found different voices such as "only a few functions are needed" and "more supportive intelligent functions should be developed". The safety and misuse of photos are also concerned. It can be seen that the functionality of current photo managing tools and the users' needs are misaligned.

Table 1. Summary of requirements.

Category	Description
Presentation	Interface should be concise and informative
	Provide large interface elements, text and margins
	Photo thumbnails and album covers should be representative enough
	Simplify the display of similar photos
Interaction	Provide adequate feedback, error prevention and recovery
	Simplify operation gestures and task steps
	Enlarge hot zone and reduce requirements of operational precision
Functionality	Increase the degree of automation
	Provide more photo display and search methods
	Replace manual operations with intelligent organizing services
	Provide basic internal sharing for small social circles
User characteristics	Vision-friendly for the elderly
	Provide understandable instructions
	Keep enough information on interfaces to reduce mental workload
	Consider the emotional needs of users
	Reduce the requirements of technical knowledge

The physiological characteristics of the elderly also lead to more requirements of interface and interaction. Decline in vision and memory makes it difficult to identify photos with thumbnails. The delicate operations are also too demanding. These factors cause an increase in ineffective use time, visual fatigue and mental workload.

Up to two-thirds of the participants had more than 300 photos on their smartphones. According to the content, their photos can be divided into three main categories: people and activities, objects and scenery, knowledge and notifications. Among them, photos of people and activities occupy the largest proportion in number, as well as in degree of importance. These photos are precious records of the past, which are usually checked and reviewed. Photos of objects and scenery are used to represent less memory, and therefore a relatively low frequency of use. Photos of knowledge and notifications are always regarded as tools for storing information, which will only be used when needed. In a word, there are obvious differences in users' attitudes toward these categories, which should be noticed by the designers. In addition, junk photos caused by application caching or other reasons are not welcomed. For similar photos, users also hope to reduce the burden of distinguishing them without deleting them directly.

After a brief supplementary evaluation of commonly used products mentioned by the participants, requirements of smartphone photo managing applications for elderly people are summarized in Table 1.

4   ZhiTu: A Smartphone Photo Managing Application for the Elderly

According to the above requirements, we designed a smartphone photo managing application for the elderly called ZhiTu. The four main activities of photo management are supported by the four features introduced: (1) organizing structure, (2) seeking paths, (3) sharing, (4) treatments of special photo types.

4.1   Organizing Structure

Tags. ZhiTu proposes an organizing structure that organizes photos through multi-dimensional tags. Instead of using common practice of mapping photos to folders, it maps tags to photos. Through image recognition, key information of each dimension,

Fig. 1. Interface screenshots: (1) detail information of a photo, (2) people tags, (3) the homepage of a people tag, (4) quick selection when creating a new tag.

such as people and activities, will be tagged by the system (see Fig. 1(1)). For each photo, tags in various dimensions, personalized descriptions and sources are recorded. Users no longer need to copy or move photos between folders. In the high-fidelity prototype, we provided example tags in the most commonly used dimensions: people and activities (see Fig. 1(2)). Dimensions and tags can also be added by users. On the homepage of a people tag, all photos containing him and all activities he participated in are shown (see Fig. 1(3)). Similarly, the homepage of an activity tag also shows all the photos and contacts that participated in the activity.

Quick Selection. In addition to existing tags, ZhiTu can also detect the same characteristics of the photos selected. The system will provide several recommended keywords with photo batches that can be selected in one click for the users (see Fig. 1(4)). It is especially useful when selecting photos manually in scenarios such as creating new tags.

4.2 Seeking Paths

In ZhiTu, the most impressive information of photos like time, people, activities and contexts [10] can be used as clues to recall photo paths. When seeking photos in ZhiTu, what users should do is to only provide any one of the above that related to the photo, rather than determine the exact source folder. The information required for photo seeking is substantially reduced. In other words, more possible paths are provided. Therefore, the success rate and efficiency of photo seeking can be improved. In our design, ZhiTu provides five paths to seek specific photos:

- Seeking for photos by browsing all photos directly. This method is available as the entrance of "all photos" is still reserved. There is no doubt that it is the best method to find recent photos.
- Seeking for photos by browsing tags. Browsing tags is commonly used when information of people, activities or other dimensions is certain. Users can turn to interface of the dimension, then find out the tag and the photos they are looking for. The tags can be sorted by creation date and popularity.
- Seeking for photos in memory view. This view provides a photo catalog focusing on events according to a timeline, which not only provides a story-like experience when viewing the photos, but also helps to find clues in memories when looking for photos (see Fig. 2(1)). It is useful when facing old photos, photos of specific dates, or photos received close to big events. It allows users to see references on time and events.
- Seeking for photos by searching. Searching is appropriate for users who have a lot of photos and want to search precisely. Both existing tags and input words can be used as search conditions.
- Seeking for photos through association with other photos. It is convenient to find other relative photos on the detail page of a photo. Users can jump to the homepage of relative tags directly to seek for other relative photos.

Fig. 2. Interface screenshots: (1) memory view, (2) contacts of a tag, (3) sharing record, (4) similar photos that are folded and unfolded.

4.3 Sharing

Sharing Methods. Two types of sharing are available in ZhiTu: manually sharing and automatic sharing through tags. Automatic sharing through tags is introduced to reduce workload of manual sharing. For all related contacts of a tag, all photos in tags can be automatically synchronized (see Fig. 2(2)). In other words, when new photos are added to the tag, these photos will be automatically shared by the system to contacts of the tag. Photos that are automatically shared can only be used by receivers themselves and cannot be shared anymore. This service is very useful for collective activities that produce a large number of photos. Certainly, automatic sharing permission of each contact can be turned off by the user.

Sharing Records. Sharing records clearly shows the history of photo sharing (see Fig. 2(3)). Records of manual sharing, automatic sharing and photo reception are classified. Photo sharing to others can be withdrawn in a short time in case of misoperation. When receive new photos, the user will be prompt to view and sort them out, which prevents work from accumulation. New photos will be recognized and tagged by the app first. After confirmation and modification of the results, the photos will be officially added to storage.

4.4 Treatments of Special Photo Types

Photos that are indistinguishable and seldom used are omitted to help users find photos through the thumbnails. For special photo types, different treatments are implemented:

- Store photos of knowledge and notifications separately. Photos of knowledge and notification are rarely used, but should be found quickly when needed. We store these photos separately to satisfy this requirement. Timed reminders can be added, to show photos to the user at a specific time. The system can also extract information from the photos to generate notes.

- Fold similar Photos. Similar photos that appear continuously occupy large interface space, which brings inconvenience to browse and operation. They are also difficult to distinguish in thumbnail view. Therefore, we fold similar photos by default to make it more refreshing visually (see Fig. 2(4)). The folded photos will be unfolded when click the collection of similar photos.

5 Evaluation

5.1 Method

Cognitive walkthrough was used as the method to evaluate the four features of ZhiTu. The evaluation was conducted based on the high-fidelity prototype introduced above. Three students of human-computer interaction were invited as evaluators.

Participants. The three evaluators were students of the Human Factors Laboratory of Tsinghua University, who were post-doctoral, the fourth-year doctoral and the fourth-year undergraduate respectively. They all had an educational background of interaction design and research experience in interaction design for the elderly.

Table 2. Tasks of cognitive walkthrough.

Features	Tasks
Organizing structure and seeking paths	T1-Find a photo of a given activity
	T2-Find a photo of given person and activity
	T3-Find a photo of given time and activity
	T4-Find a photo of the same activity from a given photo
	T5-Edit a photo itself, its tags and description
	T6-Create a new tag and add photos to it
Sharing	T7-Find related contacts of a given tag and edit their sharing permission
	T8-Add received photos to your storage
	T9-Share some photos to a contact manually
Treatments of special photo types	T10-Find a similar photo of a given photo
	T11-Find the notebook and edit one of the timed reminders

Procedure. A brief introduction of ZhiTu was provided at first. Then 11 tasks on four features (see Table 2) and an experimental record table are introduced. During the cognitive walkthrough, the evaluator was asked to find out solutions of the given 11 tasks and answer the following five questions for each task from the perspective of the elderly:

- Q1: Will the users know what they should do?
- Q2: Will the users notice the availability of operation?
- Q3: Will the users operate correctly?
- Q4: Can the users judge the progress of task through the feedback of system?
- Q5: Will the users feel it easy to use as it only requires minimum time and effort?

For the solution of task, the evaluators were asked to determine whether it is suitable for the elderly. Finally, the overall comments and suggestions for the three features were also interviewed.

5.2   Results

Results of Cognitive Walkthrough. The results are shown in Table 3. For each task, we summarized the answer of each question and the number of evaluators who approved of the solution. Due to space limitations, only the categories of negative opinions and the times they were mentioned are displayed.

Among the solution of 11 tasks evaluated, only five were agreed to be adopted by all the three evaluators, which are T1, T4, T5, T6 and T8. T2, T9 and T10 got two votes and the others got even fewer. In T2, one evaluator pointed out that the gesture of "fold up" in the search options bar might be unexpected, resulting in blocked search feedback. In T3, T7, T10 and T11, the evaluators thought it difficult to find the target plates because of the inappropriate icons or the unexpected functional structure of ZhiTu. In T9, one evaluator worried that the omitted steps may bring uncertainty to the task progress. In addition to these fatal issues, there were also suggestions that worth attention. All the evaluators reminded that the preview interface before sharing lacked the necessary information in T9. Inconvenient operations including tedious operation and inappropriate hot zone setting, were found in T7, T9, T10 and T11. In T2, T6, T7, T8 and T9, poor visibility of interface elements and feedback occurred.

From the longitudinal results, the main problems of the existing design were found. The most mentioned problems in total are inappropriate icon (7 times) and unexpected functional architecture (5 times). Then followed missing steps, unobvious feedback and lack of information (3 times). Usage of icons, display of feedback and content of interface are all issues about information presentation, which should be improved in further iterations. However, we should pay more attention to the other two problems. Instead of improving efficiency, the simplification of some operating steps may cause uncertain of task procedures because of the inherent impression of task flow. Unexpected information structure also implied the misunderstanding of conceptual models.

Attitudes Towards Features. Evaluators have different attitudes toward the four features. Two evaluators highly recognized the organizing structure and seeking paths of ZhiTu. They agreed that dimensions like activities and people which take important

Table 3. Summary of evaluation results.

Tasks	N	Q1 (times)	Q2 (times)	Q3 (times)	Q4 (times)	Q5 (times)
T1	3					
T2	2			Unexpected gestures (1)	Unobvious feedback (1)	
T3	1	Unexpected functional architecture (1)	Inappropriate icon (2)			No automatic jump (1)
T4	3		Unclear interactivity (1)			
T5	3	Missing steps (2)				
T6	3	Inappropriate wording (1)			Unobvious feedback (1)	
T7	0	Unexpected functional architecture (2)	Unclear interactivity (1) Visibility (1)			Tedious operation (1)
T8	3				Unobvious feedback (1)	
T9	2	Missing steps (1)	Visibility (1)	Concentrated hot zone (1)	Lack of information (3)	
T10	2		Inappropriate icon (2)			Limited hot zone (1)
T11	1	Unexpected functional architecture (2)	Inappropriate icon (3)			Tedious operation (1)

Note: Number of evaluators who agreed that the task was suitable for the elderly (N).

parts of older people's lives are effective classification indicators. Another evaluator questioned the difficulty of learning unless additional instruction is provided. Two evaluators also said that the various photo seeking paths provided by ZhiTu are very helpful. Besides, one evaluator worried that the elderly would feel resistant to intelligent photo recognition, hoping to provide the option of turning it off.

For photo sharing, two evaluators stated that the automatic sharing function may only be used by expert users. But it is indeed practical for activity organizers or others who need to share a large amount of photos in groups. Another evaluator suggested adding options for photo reception to prevent interruptions. The cross-user impact of operation on shared photos should also be clarified.

The treatments of special photo types ZhiTu provided were approved by all evaluators. However, photos of knowledge and notification are suggested to be stored in a tag, rather than in a notepad on the homepage. One evaluator suggested to set unfolded as default state of similar photo collections to prevent users from misunderstanding. But it goes against with the original intention of reducing the visual and operational burden.

6 Discussion and Conclusion

Noticing the lack of supportive smartphone photo managing applications for the elderly, this study designed ZhiTu, which provides four innovative features for the four activities of photo management.

For photo organizing and path recalling, ZhiTu introduces multi-dimensional tags, which not only gives meaning to the organizing structure, but also allows more possible seeking paths. According to Axtell's advice, both narrative and database interactions should be considered [6]. Different from the storytelling idea that is of excessive workload [9], ZhiTu takes the advantage of image recognition technology to directly tag the default photo paths with photo information. On one hand, it leads to more natural organizing structure while maintaining logic of database tools. On the other hand, five paths to seek specific photos are allowed due to the special mapping method, which is far more than existing products. Therefore, ZhiTu will be able to perform better facing elderly users with less memory and skills.

For photo collecting, ZhiTu reduces the burden of manual operation through automatic sharing within contactors of tags. For the elderly, photo sharing happens frequently after collective activities with several friends or family members. If large amount of photos are produced, effective solutions such as cloud disks and hard drives automatic sharing service require technical knowledge, while manual sharing on social media is too cumbersome [5]. In these scenarios, automatic sharing within contactors group built according to activity tags provided by ZhiTu can be very helpful.

For photo finding, treatments of special photo types are proposed to improve conciseness of thumbnail view. As a supplement to existing practices such as cleaning up junk photos, we focus on similar photos and photos of knowledge and notifications that are both difficult to distinguish for the elderly in thumbnail view. According to their characteristics, ZhiTu proposes different treatments without affecting the normal use.

However, information expression and users' understandability are found to be potential obstacles from practical application. Few references can be found, leading to poor expressions, such as the form of similar photo collections. How to typeset a large number of tags that may appear on the small screen of smartphone is also an unresolved problem. We are also worried about the elderly users' understandability of multi-dimensional tags and automatic sharing through tags. The current design has obvious flaws. Therefore, more adjustments and iterations are needed. Simplifying conceptual model, optimizing interface design and adding user guidance are recommended directions.

This study has the following limitations. First, many interface design problems like information expression can be discovered, which have nothing to do with the features that ZhiTu proposed. These questions might be so attention-grabbing in the assessment that they cover up other questions. They could also reduce the learnability and performance of the application, which may lead to deviations in results. Secondly, only a cognitive walkthrough involving three evaluators was implemented as a staged evaluation, which cannot completely replace user tests with the elderly.

The first work of future study is to solve the interface design problems that have been discovered. Afterwards, adjustment of functional structure and task steps for the current issues raised will be carried out, according to research of the elderly. After eliminating these interferences, we will conduct user tests on the elderly to evaluate their acceptance and the actual effects of the features, with the help of iterated prototype.

References

1. Jiang, J., Zhang, W., Jeung, J.: Preliminary exploration of interface design for senior citizens: a study of smartphone camera usage for people above 50. In: Marcus, A., Rosenzweig, E. (eds.) HCII 2020. LNCS, vol. 12201, pp. 277–293. Springer, Cham (2020). https://doi.org/10.1007/978-3-030-49760-6_20

2. Blackler, A., Popovic, V., Mahar, D.: Investigating users' intuitive interaction with complex artefacts. Appl. Ergon. **41**(1), 72–92 (2010). https://doi.org/10.1016/j.apergo.2009.04.010

3. Hawthorn, D.: Possible implications of aging for interface designers. Interact. Comput. **12**(5), 507–528 (2000). https://doi.org/10.1016/S0953-5438(99)00021-1

4. Czaja, S.J., Boot, W.R., Charness, N., Rogers, W.A.: Designing for Older Adults: Principles and Creative Human Factors Approaches, Third edn. Taylor and Francis, Milton Park (2019)

5. Holloway, D., Green, L.: Mediated memory making: the virtual family photograph album. Commun. **42**(3) (2017). https://doi.org/10.1515/commun-2017-0033

6. Axtell, B., Munteanu, C.: Back to real pictures: a cross-generational understanding of users' mental models of photo cloud storage. Proc. ACM Interact. Mob. Wearable Ubiquit. Technol. **3**(3), 1–24 (2019). https://doi.org/10.1145/3351232

7. Pang, W.-M., Wong, K.-H.: Sensor-rich smart personal photo organization. In: Proceedings of 2nd International Electronic Conference on Sensors and Applications, E003 (2015). https://doi.org/10.3390/ecsa-2-E003

8. Hu, H.-J., Wu, P.-F., Tsai, W.-C.: A conceptual design for a smart photo album catered to the elderly. In: Zhou, J., Salvendy, G. (eds.) ITAP 2017. LNCS, vol. 10298, pp. 42–52. Springer, Cham (2017). https://doi.org/10.1007/978-3-319-58536-9_4

9. Axtell, B., Munteanu, C.: PhotoFlow in action: picture-mediated reminiscence supporting family socio-connectivity. In: Extended Abstracts of the 2019 CHI Conference on Human Factors in Computing Systems, pp. 1–4 (2019). https://doi.org/10.1145/3290607.3313272

10. Elsweiler, D., Ruthven, I., Jones, C.: Towards memory supporting personal information management tools. J. Am. Soc. Inf. Sci. Technol. **58**(7), 924–946 (2007). https://doi.org/10.1002/asi.20570

11. Schoneveld, J.: Augmented reality photo album for people with dementia, p. 106 (2020)

Gamification Design of Health Apps for the Elderly Based on the Kano Model and Conjoint Analysis Method

Tongyao Yuan and Yongyan Guo[✉]

School of Art Design and Media, East China University of Science and Technology, Shanghai 200237, People's Republic of China

Abstract. With the aging of population over the world, more and more old people try to learn something about health in health apps. However, they often encounter troubles, e.g., mistake touch and unreasonable interface design. It would be useful to consider gamification design when developing health apps for the elderly. Therefore, the preference of old people for the gamification function in health apps were studied. In this paper, the functional attributes and attribute levels of gamification design were summarized according to references. Then, kano model and focus group discussion were conducted to determine the attributes and attribute levels, and conjoint analysis was used to obtain the importance of all attributes and the utility value of attribute levels . The results of data analysis show that older people of different ages and genders have different preferences for the level of attributes, but these older people have the same preference for the three attributes, which are reward function, winning status and feedback function in turn.

Keywords: Kano model · Conjoint analysis method · The elderly · Health app · Prototype design

1 Introduction

It is known to all that the aging phenomenon is becoming more and more serious in China. By the end of 2020, there will be 167 million elderly people, 24% of the elderly population of world [1]. Keep health is the most important thing for old people. Nowadays, some old people begin using health apps to learn something about health, e.g., stroke, heart disease and osteoporosis, thanks to the improvement of people's health consciousness and smart phones. However, the body functions of people, such as learning ability and memory, declining after peaking in youth. For the elderly, the decline is more noticeable, which leads to some problems when using health apps. Firstly, the elderly usually touch screen by mistake or ignore some important functions in apps due to the complication of user interface. Then, older people often suffer from presbyopia or are insensitive to changes in color, which makes it difficult for them to locate the target article exactly and quickly, especially when the color is not conspicuous or the layout is not special [2]. In addition, interface design is unreasonable and operational logic lacks consistency and

© Springer Nature Switzerland AG 2021
Q. Gao and J. Zhou (Eds.): HCII 2021, LNCS 12787, pp. 176–190, 2021.
https://doi.org/10.1007/978-3-030-78111-8_12

synchronization for most health apps [3]. It is difficult for old people to learn something about health.

Fortunately, gamification design in health apps can be employed in the health app so as to help old people know the information efficiently [4]. Gamification is an emerging research field in business and information systems [5]. Gamification is user goal-oriented, encourage users to promote continuously by setting up some practical challenges, engage and motivate users to achieve their goals in emotional level [6]. The experience and stickiness of users are strengthened by applying the gamification design elements to the scenes without game. It is very potential to design health apps for the elderly based on gamification.

Both gamification design and the difficulties encountered by old people in using apps have been studied a lot. However, there are little research about gamification design of health apps for the elderly. Chen and Wang [7] summarized and applied the design strategy of gamification to the healthy eating app, which aimed for the young people whose diet are unhealthy. Research shows that the design strategy can change diet structure of people and enhance sense of accomplishment and pleasure. Li [8] thought that game can be a breakthrough point in the field of health and can be used to carry out the idea of smart endowment. Wang [3] analyzed the influence factors and existing problems of the interface design of health apps for the elderly, proposed the basic methods to improve the interface design of health apps for the elderly based on user experience. Xu and Li [9] adopted the kano model to classify the design attributes of apps user interface, and designed the app interface for the elderly in a targeted way to improve user satisfaction. Many scholars have started to study gamification design and health apps, but few scholars directly extract gamification design elements and applied them to the design of health knowledge apps for the elderly. Therefore, this paper aims to use a quantitative research method to study the gamification design of health knowledge apps for the elderly.

In this study, the gamification functions associated with health apps were selected from published references. The functional attributes of gamification design were filtered by the kano model and the attribute levels were obtained by the focus group discussion. Then, conjoint analysis method was used to analyze acceptance and preference of old people to gamification design elements of health apps. Consequently, the first objective of this paper was to help the elderly use health apps conveniently and understand the knowledge about hygiene and health efficiently by optimizing user experience. The second objective was to give some suggestions about the design of health apps for the elderly.

2 Methods

The kano model is presented by Noriaki Kano in 1984 and is a useful tool for classifying and prioritizing user needs [10]. In kano model, user satisfaction is surveyed by two-factor questionnaire and the effect of user need on user satisfaction is analyzed. The nonlinear relationship between product performance and user satisfaction can be found.

Conjoint analysis method, a multivariate and quantitative statistical analysis method, has been largely used in the field of market research. The procedure of conjoint analysis method is shown in Fig. 1. It is assumed that the product consists of a series of basic attributes and every attribute includes some attribute levels. The importance degree of these attributes and attribute levels are quantitatively evaluated by mathematical statistics. All attribute levels are arranged and combined so as to generate many virtual product models. Then, orthogonal analysis method is used to select some appropriate product models. The users can evaluate these selected virtual products according to their preferences. The results of conjoint analysis method based on evaluation of users are shown, that is, we can know the evaluation of users to attributes and the ideal expectations for the product.

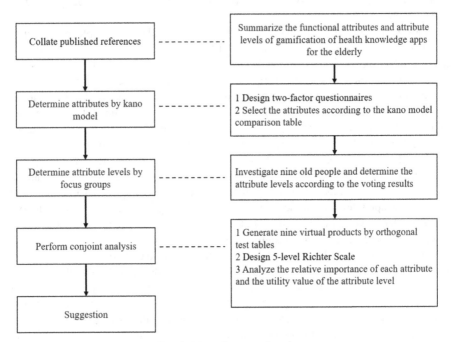

Fig. 1. Flow diagram of study.

2.1 Confirming Attributes

As shown in Table 1, gamification elements can be classified into dynamics, mechanics and components elements. Dynamics elements, which are most abstract, are inherent reason for the user to continue. Mechanics elements are the methods to promote the game process and enhance the user experience [11]. Components elements are the representation of the dynamics and mechanics elements [12]. Game mechanics is the structural relationship and operation mode among gamification elements. Therefore, these mechanics elements were chosen as the functional attributes of gamification design of health apps for the elderly. Additionally, the component elements were used for attribute levels of three functional attributes. In order to find three of most useful function attributes, the kano model was used to determine the gamification functions which are acceptable for the elderly when using health apps from mechanics elements of gamification design.

Table 1. Classification of gamification elements.

Category	Elements
Dynamics	Constraint, emotion, narrative, progression, relationship
Mechanics	Challenge, chance, competition, cooperation, feedback, resource acquisition, reward, trading, turn, winning status
Components	Achievement, avatar, badge, boss fight, collection, combat, content unlocking, gifting, leaderboard, level, point, quest, social graph, team, virtual good

As shown in Fig. 2, two-factor questionnaires were designed for all mechanics elements in Table 1. The two-factor questionnaires were named Q1. For every gamification function attribute, both positive and negative dimensions were considered, which means that the satisfaction degree was shown when the function is provided or not. There are five options in questionnaire: very useful, very practical, indifferent, not applicable, and very impractical.

How would you feel if this gamification function attribute is provided?				
Very useful	Very practical	Indifferent	Not applicable	Very impractical
◯	◯	◯	◯	◯
How would you feel if this gamification function attribute is not provided?				
Very useful	Very practical	Indifferent	Not applicable	Very impractical
◯	◯	◯	◯	◯

Fig. 2. Two-factor questionnaire.

The explanation of "very useful" is that the existence of a certain gamification design function in app can extremely please users and help them to use the app better. By analogy, the meaning of "very practical" is that the function is indispensable for the users because it can make users happy and read the article easily. Next, "indifferent" means that users do not care whether app contains the given function or not, and that the presence or absence of the function has no effect on reading and the mood of the users. "Not applicable" means that the users reluctantly accept it even though they do not like it. The final option is "very impractical", which means that this function is very annoying and unacceptable for users.

All two-factor questionnaires were recollected, invalid of which are excluded. In this survey, 85 valid questionnaires were recollected. Based on the results of questionnaires, all gamification function attributes were divided into Attractive, One-dimensional, Must-be, Indifferent and Reverse, as displayed in Table 2. The Attractive, One-dimensional and Must-be attributes were reserved. The Indifferent and Reverse attributes could be negligible owing to the behaviors and habits of users. Finally, the attributes that are acceptable for old people were carefully picked, that is feedback, reward, winning status.

Table 2. Evaluation and classification of demand in kano model.

		Not providing this function				
		Like very much	Well	Just as well	Accept reluctantly	Dislike
Providing this function	Like very much	Q	A	A	A	Q
	Well	R	I	I	I	M
	Just as well	R	I	I	I	M
	Accept reluctantly	R	I	I	I	M
	Dislike	R	R	R	R	Q

2.2 Confirming Attribute Levels

Attribute levels need to be determined previous to conjoint analysis. In this paper, focus group discussion was applied to determine attribute levels, by the way that nine old people were required to select three attribute levels for each attribute. The attribute levels of feedback, rewards and winning status were figured out by investigating existing health apps. In order to make users more intuitive understanding of these attribute levels, this paper designed some interactive prototypes. The prototypes of gamification design were designed on the basis of the survey results and other health apps, as shown in Fig. 3.

The results of vote of the focus group on these attribute levels are shown in Table 3. Three attribute levels were chosen for every attribute based on numbers of vote. The final attribute levels were color highlighting feedback, identity feedback and graphical symbol feedback in the feedback attribute. Reward attributes included cash rewards,

Table 3. Vote of attribute levels.

Attribute level	Text feedback	Color highlighting feedback	Identity feedback		Graphical symbol feedback
Vote	4	9	5		9
Attribute level	Cash reward	Virtual currency reward	Medal award		Random gift reward
Vote	8	6	5		8
Attribute level	Status hierarchy change	Social sharing	Leaderboards	Text congratulations popover	Personal achievements
Vote	4	8	6	6	3

First : Specific performance of feedback function in health knowledge APP

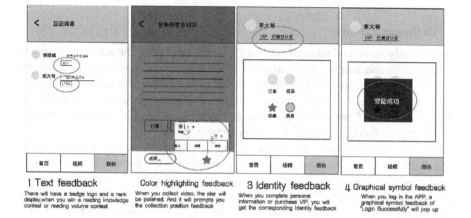

1 Text feedback
There will have a badge logo and a rank display,when you win a reading knowledge contest or reading volume contest

Color highlighting feedback
When you collect video, the star will be polished. And it will prompts you the collection position feedback

3 Identity feedback
When you complete personal information or purchase VIP, you will get the corresponding identity feedback

4 Graphical symbol feedback
When you log in the APP, a graphical symbol feedback of "Login Successfuly" will pop up

Second : Specific performance of reward function in health knowledge APP

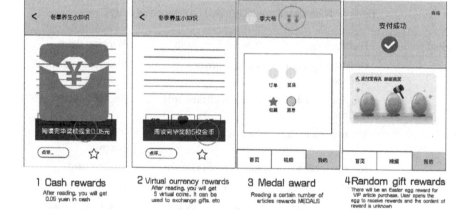

1 Cash rewards
After reading, you will get 0.05 yuan in cash

2 Virtual currency rewards
After reading, you will get 5 virtual coins. It can be used to exchange gifts, etc

3 Medal award
Reading a certain number of articles rewards MEDALS

4 Random gift rewards
There will be an Easter egg reward for VIP article purchase. User opens the egg to receive rewards and the content of reward is unknown

Thirdly : Specific performance of winning status in health knowledge APP

1 Status hierarchy change
There will have a badge logo and a rank display, when you win a reading knowledge contest or reading volume contest

2 Social sharing
The top five readers will receive a winning status display. And you can forward the circle of friends to share

3 leaderboard
The first most-read user can dominate the leaderboard cover of their friends

4 Text congratulations popover
When the reading volume of user reaches a certain level, the upgrade popups and rewards will be displayed

5 A record of personal achievements
Displays the learning progress of users.

Fig. 3. Prototype design of attribute levels.

virtual currency rewards and random gift rewards. The attribute levels of winning status attribute were social sharing, leaderboard and text congratulations popover.

2.3 Orthogonal Design

Conjoint analysis method takes all attributes and attribute levels into account to combine these attributes and attribute levels to generate a series of virtual products. In this paper, total contour analysis was used to generate virtual products. A combination consisting of a level of all attributes is called a profile, and each profile is represented by a single card [13]. For example, Card for Virtual Product 1 represents graphical symbol feedback, virtual currency feedback, and text congratulation popover.

There are three attributes and nine corresponding attributes levels in present study. These attribute levels could be permuted and combined to produce 27 ($3 \times 3 \times 3$) virtual products. But the fact that the elderly is asked to rate 27 virtual products is beyond rational judgment of consumers. Therefore, orthogonal design was considered to reduce the number of virtual products. The orthogonal module in SPSS was used to reduce the number of cards to 9. Each card in the orthogonal design table represents a virtual product, and the corresponding attribute levels are shown in Table 4.

Table 4. Nine virtual products based on orthogonal design.

Virtual product	Feedback	Reward	Winning status
1	Graphical symbol feedback	Virtual currency rewards	Text congratulations popover
2	Graphical symbol feedback	Random gift rewards	Social sharing
3	Identity feedback	Cash rewards	Text congratulations popover
4	Identity feedback	Random gift rewards	Leaderboards
5	Identity feedback	Virtual currency rewards	Social sharing
6	Color highlighting feedback	Random gift rewards	Text congratulations popover
7	Color highlighting feedback	Cash rewards	Social sharing
8	Graphical symbol feedback	Cash rewards	Leaderboards
9	Color highlighting feedback	Virtual currency rewards	Leaderboards

2.4 Questionnaire Design and Collection of Data

Then, the questionnaire that collects people's preference for these virtual products was designed and named as Q2. The first part of questionnaire includes questions about basic information of people. In the second part, the background of questionnaire and the scoring criteria of Likert Scale are briefly introduced.

The third part is the topic of the questionnaire. In this part, the elderly was asked to rate the virtual products by using the 5-level Richter Scale according to their preferences. Likert scale has five options including Strongly agree, Agree, No matter, Disagree and Strongly disagree. The scores are 5, 4, 3, 2, 1, and the score represents their preference for each virtual product.

In this study, the people surveyed are older than 55 years old and can use smart phone. The questionnaires were conducted and collected online. In order to increase the credibility of survey, people who participated in focus group discussion before were required to fill in the questionnaire. In this survey, 46 valid questionnaires were recollected.

3 Results

3.1 Descriptive Analysis

Basic information about respondents is listed in Table 5. Among the people surveyed, 43.48% were male and 56.52% were female. 60.87% of the people were older than 55

Table 5. Basic information of respondents.

Characteristic	Category	Number	Percentage
Gender	Male	20	43.48%
	Female	26	56.52%
Age	55–70 years old	28	60.87%
	>70 years old	18	39.13%
Profession	Civil servant	11	23.91%
	Doctors, lawyers, drivers, and other professional technical personnel	1	2.175%
	Doctoral, master, and other advanced education personnel	3	6.52%
	Entrepreneurs, individual businesses, and other private enterprises	3	6.52%
	The peasant class, the working class, and other social backbone groups	11	23.91%
	The rest of the population	3	6.52%
	Retired group	14	30.43%
Wage	Less than 2000	10	21.74%
	2000–5000	18	39.13%
	5000–8000	11	23.91%
	More than 8000	7	15.22%
Education background	Primary school	13	28.26%
	Junior high school	9	19.57%
	Senior high school	9	19.57%
	Undergraduate	10	21.74%
	Master	4	8.7%
	Doctoral degree or above	1	2.17%

years old but younger than 70 years old, which indicates that the majority of smartphone-using old people are between 55 and 70 years old. From the perspective of occupation, most people were civil servants, farmers and workers. The monthly income of people was evenly distributed from 2000 to 8000 RMB, accounting 84.78% of the total population. As for educational level, most of old people had a bachelor's degree or less.

3.2 Utility Value and Attribute Relative Importance Analysis

Based on the scores of nine products obtained from the questionnaire survey, the conjoint analysis method was used to analyze the preference of the elderly for various attributes and attribute levels in gamification design. The importance of attribute and the utility value of attribute level can be calculated. The higher the importance is, the more valuable the attribute is. The higher the utility value is, the more consumer prefers a certain attribute level.

Credibility Analysis. In conjoint analysis method, the Pearson correlation coefficient and Kendall correlation coefficient were calculated to verify the credibility of questionnaire results. The larger the correlation coefficient is, the better model fitting is. The Pearson correlation coefficient was 0.964 and Kendall correlation coefficient was 0.873. Significance of two-tailed test of Pearson's R and Kendall's tau were 0.000 and 0.001, respectively. Therefore, two correlation coefficients passed statistical test (Table 6).

Table 6. Values of correlation coefficients.

	Pearson's R	Pearson's R Sig	Kendall's tau	Kendall's tau Sig
Value	0.964	0.000	0.873	0.001

Attribute Importance. Table 7 are the importance of gamification functional attributes, which represents preference of old people to attributes. Reward function was the most important for the elderly among three attributes, with importance 54.412%. The importance of feedback function and winning status were 22.059% and 23.529%, respectively. The percentage of reward function was more than half, which indicates that most older people like reward function very much. Therefore, more rewards can be included in gamification design so as to enhance the motivation of the elderly to read articles and learn new things.

Table 7. Importance of attributes.

Attribute	Feedback	Reward	Winning status
Importance	22.059%	54.412%	23.529%

Utility Value of Attribute Levels. The utility value of attribute level is related to user preference. The higher the utility value is, the more users prefer it [14]. Analyzed by conjoint analysis method, all utility values are shown in Table 8. The utility value of color highlight feedback, identity feedback and graphical symbol feedback were −0.07, 0.4 and 0.3, respectively. Obviously, the elderly prefers identity feedback and graphical symbol feedback. Considering reward function, the utility value of cash reward was 0.15, while the utility value of virtual currency reward and random gift reward were −0.03 and −0.12, respectively. The older users prefer cash reward to virtual currency and random gift reward. As for winning status attribute, the utility value of text congratulation popover was as low as −0.7. The utility value of social sharing and leaderboard were 0.2 and 0.5, respectively. It is apparent that the elderly desires social sharing and ranking list.

Table 8. Utility value of attribute levels.

Attribute	Attribute level	Utility value
Feedback	Color highlighting feedback	−0.07
	Identity feedback	0.4
	Graphical symbol feedback	0.3
Reward	Cash reward	0.15
	Virtual currency	0.03
	Random gift reward	−0.12
Winning status	Text congratulation popover	−0.7
	Social sharing	0.2
	Leaderboard	0.5

Analysis According to Different Characteristics of Samples. Conjoint analysis was conducted according to different characteristics of the samples to study the influence of gender and age on gamification design. The acceptance and preference to gamification design among elderly people aged between 55 to 70 years old, people over 70 years old and older people of different genders were compared.

Firstly, the samples were classified according to gender and the questionnaire data of male and female were analyzed, respectively. It can be seen from Table 9 that views of both elderly male and elderly female to three functional attributes were basically the same, preferring the reward function. More exactly, elderly female was fond of reward function compared with elderly male. As seen in Table 10, both elderly male and elderly female favored the identity feedback function, with the utility value 0.144 and 0.029, respectively. Graphical symbol feedback caught more fancy of elderly male compared with elderly female, with the utility value 0.012 and −0.066, respectively. For reward function, it could be seen that the cash reward is the most important one for the elderly. Elderly men also liked virtual currency reward. But for winning status, elderly women's attitude was diametrically opposed to older men. Female elderly people preferred the leaderboard and text congratulations popover, with utility values 0.144 and 0.045, respectively. However, male elderly people favored in social sharing function, with utility value 0.099.

Table 9. Importance of attributes when age and gender is different.

Characteristic	Category	Attribute	Importance
Gender	Male	Feedback	14.286%
		Reward	46.429%
		Winning status	39.286%
	Female	Feedback	24%
		Reward	40%
		Winning status	36%
Age	55–70 years old	Feedback	38.776%
		Reward	28.571%
		Winning status	32.653%
	>70 years old	Feedback	22.727%
		Reward	65.909%
		Winning status	11.364%

Then, the samples were divided based on age and analyzed by conjoint analysis method, showing a great difference. Results revealed that people aged between 55 to 70 years old tend to feedback and winning status function. They cared more about something caused by their behaviors. The elderly over 70 years old were more favor of reward function and the value of importance of reward function attribute was 65.909%. As shown in Table 10, the elderly aged 55 to 70 years old preferred the identity feedback and graphic symbol feedback, while people older than 70 years old chosen identity feedback and color highlighting feedback. That may be because older people more likely suffer from presbyopia, cataract and glaucoma, so bright colors attract their attention more easily. As for reward function, no matter how many years old they are, people would choose cash as reward first. For people between 55 and 70 years old, the favorite attribute level in winning status was the leaderboard feature, whose utility value is 0.111. In addition to the leaderboard function, people older than 70 years old were also fond of the text congratulations popover, with utility value 0.006.

Table 10. Utility value of attribute levels when age and gender is different.

Characteristic	Category	Attribute	Attribute level	Utility value
Gender	Male	Feedback	Color highlighting feedback	−0.041
			Identity feedback	0.029
			Graphical symbol feedback	0.012
		Reward	Cash reward	0.99
			Virtual currency	0.29
			Random gift reward	−0.129
		Winning status	Social sharing	0.099
			Leaderboard	−0.006
			Text congratulation popover	−0.094
	Female	Feedback	Color highlighting feedback	−0.078
			Identity feedback	0.144
			Graphical symbol feedback	−0.066
		Reward	Cash reward	0.206
			Virtual currency	−0.041
			Random gift reward	−0.165
		Winning status	Social sharing	−0.189
			Leaderboard	0.144
			Text congratulation popover	0.045
Age	55–70 years old	Feedback	Color highlighting feedback	−0.123
			Identity feedback	0.111
			Graphical symbol feedback	0.012
		Reward	Cash reward	0.086
			Virtual currency	0.000
			Random gift reward	−0.086
		Winning status	Social sharing	−0.086
			Leaderboard	0.111
			Text congratulation popover	−0.025
	>70 years old	Feedback	Color highlighting feedback	0.023
			Identity feedback	0.076
			Graphical symbol feedback	−0.099
		Reward	Cash reward	0.269

(*continued*)

Table 10. (*continued*)

Characteristic	Category	Attribute	Attribute level	Utility value
			Virtual currency	−0.029
			Random gift reward	−0.240
		Winning status	Social sharing	−0.047
			Leaderboard	0.041
			Text congratulation popover	0.006

4   Discussion and Suggestion

4.1   Discussions

All questionnaires were studied with conjoint analysis method to get importance of attributes and utility value of attribute levels. The effects of gender and age on preference for these attributes and attribute levels were also studied. On the whole, preference of the elderly for three gamification design functions was health apps are different. The reward function was number one, the winning status was number two and the third was feedback function. The most popular attribute level in the feedback function was identity feedback, followed by graphical symbol feedback. The favorite attribute level in the reward function was cash reward. The most preferred attribute level in winning status was leaderboards, social sharing next. The preference of the elderly for functional attributes were not affected by their gender and age, but the preference for attribute levels did. Men preferred the combination of cash reward, social sharing and identity feedback, while women liked the combination of cash rewards, leaderboards and identity feedback. Male and female were opposite when it comes to graphical symbols, virtual currency rewards and text congratulatory popover. Older people of different ages chosen the same combination of levels: cash rewards, leaderboards and identity feedback. However, their attitudes towards other attribute levels were different. In addition to identity feedback, people over 70 years old also favored color highlighting feedback, while the elderly between 55 and 70 years old preferred graphical symbol feedback. Compared with people between 55 and 70 years old, those older than 70 years old were very cautious about virtual currency but were fond of text congratulation popover.

4.2   Suggestions

Based on above results and analysis, some suggestions are provided for the gamification design prototype of health apps for the elderly in this paper. First, the user interface of health apps should be clean and organized. The elderly has difficulty in dealing with complex information. Simple information would be more helpful for old people to use apps, which can largely reduce the learning cost in using apps and their wrong operations. Second, the gamification functions should be organized proportionally and appropriately. In the development process of apps, feedback function, reward function and winning status function are chosen and designed according to the importance of three attributes.

More precisely, for every attribute, the proportion of the attribute level is determined by utility value of the attribute level. Higher the utility value of attribute level is, more important and more percentage the attribute level should be. Third, it is necessary to carry out personalized customization for different groups. The app can be compatible with user habits and preference of different people by changing the proportions of three attributes and selecting combinations of different attribute levels according to age and gender of user. In this way, everyone will possess their own health app.

4.3 Conclusions

In this paper, the kano model was used to determine the preference attributes of old people and the focus group discussion was carried out to select the attribute level. The importance of attribute and the utility value of the attribute level were calculated by conjoint analysis method in software SPSS. Moreover, the effects of their gender and age on choice preference for different attributes and attribute levels were studied. Finally, some suggestions were offered for the gamification design prototype of health apps for the elderly. However, these old people surveyed are differ in educational level, wage and living area. These differences have not been separately analyzed in present study and more questionnaires need to be collected for further research. Furthermore, more prototypes will be designed and experiment such as eye tracker will be conducted to verify the results.

Acknowledgements. The authors acknowledge the financial support of the Ministry of Education Humanities and Social Sciences Foundation of China (nos. 71672017).

References

1. Yao, J.: Interface interactive design of information products for the elderly from the perspective of experience. Packag. Eng. **36**(02), 67–71 (2015)
2. Shi, W.: APP design for the elder based on AHP. Packag. Eng. **38**(08), 126–131 (2017)
3. Wang, J.: Study of Elderly Health APP Interface Design Based on User Experience. Jingdezhen Ceramic Institute, Jingdezhen (2015)
4. Shen, Y.: Gamification: a new paradigm of information literacy education for graduate students from the perspective of information science. Mod. Intell. **039**(011), 107–112 (2019)
5. Mullins, J.K.: Gamification: a cognitive-emotional view. J. Bus. Res. **106**, 304–314 (2020)
6. Burke, B.: Gamify. Bibliomotion, Brookline (2014)
7. Chen, S.: Research on healthy eating app design based on gamification. Pop. Arts Arts **477**(03), 141–142 (2020)
8. Li, H.: Design of brain training game system for the elderly based on kinect. Inf. Syst. Eng. **000**(005), 130–131 (2019)
9. Xu, Y.: Design of the elderly smart phone APP user interface based on Kano model. Packag. Eng. **38**(16), 163–167 (2017)
10. Wang, S.: Research on customer requirements' target system based on Kano model. Packag. Eng. **27**(4), 209–210 (2006)
11. Lu, Y.: Gamification design components of preschoolers' mathematics education APP of mobile terminal. Packag. Eng. **40**(02), 172–176 (2019)

12. Xi, Q.: Gamification design model of MOOC: from the perspective of scenario approach. Distance Educ. China **40**(12), 24–33+92–93 (2019)
13. Chen, L.: Research on consumer preference of remanufactured products based on joint analysis method. Shanghai Manag. Sci. **42**(03), 46–53 (2020)
14. Guan, Y.: A conjoint value analysis of tourism preference for Hainan Tangka culture. Tour. Forum **10**(06), 63–73 (2017)

Supporting Health and Wellbeing

DemSelf, A Mobile App for Self-administered Touch-Based Cognitive Screening: Participatory Design with Stakeholders

Martin Burghart[1]([✉]) [ID], Julie L. O'Sullivan[2] [ID], Robert Spang[1] [ID], and Jan-Niklas Voigt-Antons[1,3] [ID]

[1] Quality and Usability Lab, Technische Universität Berlin, Berlin, Germany
m.burghart@campus.tu-berlin.de, jan-niklas.voigt-antons@tu-berlin.de
[2] Institut für Medizinische Soziologie und Rehabilitationswissenschaft,
Charité - Universitätsmedizin Berlin, Berlin, Germany
[3] German Research Center for Artificial Intelligence (DFKI), Berlin, Germany

Abstract. Early detection of mild cognitive impairment and dementia is vital as many therapeutic interventions are particularly effective at an early stage. A self-administered touch-based cognitive screening instrument, called DemSelf, was developed by adapting an examiner-administered paper-based instrument, the Quick Mild Cognitive Impairment (Qmci) screen.

We conducted five semi-structured expert interviews including a think-aloud phase to evaluate usability problems. The extent to which the characteristics of the original subtests change by the adaption, as well as the conditions and appropriate context for practical application, were also in question. The participants had expertise in the domain of usability and human-machine interaction and/or in the domain of dementia and neuropsychological assessment.

Participants identified usability issues in all components of the Dem-Self prototype. For example, confirmation of answers was not consistent across subtests. Answers were sometimes logged directly when a button is tapped and cannot be corrected. This can lead to frustration and bias in test results, especially for people with vision or motor impairments. The direct adoption of time limits from the original paper-based instrument or the simultaneous verbal and textual item presentation also caused usability problems. DemSelf is a different test than Qmci and needs to be re-validated. Visual recognition instead of a free verbal recall is one of the main differences. Reading skill level seems to be an important confounding variable. Participants would generally prefer if the test is conducted in a medical office rather than at a patient's home so that someone is present for support and the result can be discussed directly.

Keywords: Mild cognitive impairment · Dementia · Computerized cognitive screening · Usability · Self-assessment

© Springer Nature Switzerland AG 2021
Q. Gao and J. Zhou (Eds.): HCII 2021, LNCS 12787, pp. 193–209, 2021.
https://doi.org/10.1007/978-3-030-78111-8_13

1   Introduction

Currently there are no pharmacological treatments available for mild cognitive impairment (MCI) and most causes of dementia [17,26]. The diagnosis of potentially progressive cognitive impairment can cause fears and affected people often feel stigmatized and marginalized by society. These arguments can be put forward against an early diagnosis of MCI and dementia. Nevertheless, in the view of most experts, the arguments for a diagnosis outweigh [13]: every patient has the right to be honestly informed about his or her health status. A diagnosis along with professional consultation can help family members better understand the behaviors they are experiencing. Early detection of MCI and dementia is vital as many therapeutic and preventive approaches – such as consultation, cognitive training, and physical exercise – are particularly effective at an early stage [26]. Such approaches can reduce the need for care and the burden on the patient and their caregivers.

Hence, there is a need for fast, reliable, and affordable screening instruments. The use of mobile devices such as tablets promises to better meet these requirements. Possible advantages include better standardization, automatic scoring, a digital test result, dynamic adaptation to the test person, or more accurate measurement of time and other factors. A person can also perform some tests without a trained medical professional, making cognitive testing less expensive and more accessible [4,32]. DemSelf is an attempt to adapt a validated paper-based instrument so that it can be performed independently on a touch-device. An expert evaluation provides insights into usability issues, differences to the original test and the appropriate context of use.

2   Related Work

For an average person, cognitive decline begins in the third decade and continues throughout life [18]. Cognitive aging affects domains such as attention, memory, executive functions, language, and visuospatial abilities [20]. Dementia is a brain syndrome associated with a decline of cognitive functioning that is "not entirely attributable to normal aging and significantly interferes with independence in the person's performance of activities of daily living." [35]. The most common form of dementia is due to Alzheimer's disease (AD), but dementia can occur in a number of different circumstances and diseases, such as vascular diseases, Parkinson's disease or Lewy body dementia [17]. Cognitive decline is the clinical hallmark in dementia and memory impairment is the most prominent symptom in most patients. A key feature of dementia is that everyday skills such as using public transport or handling money are affected. AD in particular has a progressive course. In severe dementia, patients are almost completely dependent on help from others. In the course of research on cognitive aging, some people have been found to be in a "gray area between normal cognitive aging and dementia" [33, p. 370]. A person shows cognitive decline that is beyond normal ageing, but functional activities of daily living are not affected. MCI is one of the most widely used and empirically studied terms to describe this state. A precise and universal definition of MCI has not yet been established [17]; see [33] for a discussion on similar concepts such as Mild Neurocognitive Disorder. In some cases, MCI can be a pre-clinical stage of dementia, particularly AD [17]. Early identification of MCI would allow interventions at an early stage which may influence the course of the disease. However, people with MCI often remain undiagnosed [7].

An early step in diagnosing cognitive impairment is often a brief cognitive screening instrument. The administration usually takes only a few minutes and allows assessment of different cognitive domains such as attention, memory, orientation, language, executive functions, or visuospatial abilities. A cognitive screening instrument provides information on the presence and severity of cognitive impairment in patients with suspected dementia or MCI. There is a multitude of different cognitive screening instruments. Recent systematic reviews and meta-analyses are available [2,27,34]. The right choice depends on numerous factors: "Clinicians and researchers should abandon the idea that one screening instrument ... can be used in every setting, for all different neurodegenerative diseases and for each population." [27, p. 11].

Most available cognitive screening instruments are primarily paper-based and administered by healthcare professionals. However, computers, tablets, or similar devices can also be used to administer, score, or interpret a cognitive test.

Computerized cognitive screening instruments offer several potential advantages over paper-based instruments, such as increased standardization of scoring, ease of administering in different languages, reduced costs, remote testing, adaption, and more precise measurement of time- and location-sensitive tasks [4,32]. A self-administered web-based test Brain on Track, for example, uses random elements to minimize learning effects in longitudinal tests [28]. Other computerized tests are designed as mini-games to achieve a more relaxed testing environment and to reduce the drop-out rates in longitudinal testing [37], or use scoring algorithms similar to principal components analysis to improve sensitivity [29]. Individual factors like technical experiences, attitudes towards technology, or non-cognitive impairments such as motor or sensory disabilities may affect interaction with the computer interface and bias the test result. A computerized screening instrument might therefore not be suitable for certain people. Test developers should consider such factors during validation and report their influences on the test [4]. Computerized cognitive assessment already has a long tradition and a variety of instruments is available [2,27,38]. Nevertheless, they are still used much less frequently in practice than paper-based tests [32]. The lack of normative population data is one problem, making it difficult to choose the right instrument.

Usability is another crucial aspect in self-assessment by elderly users with possible cognitive and other impairments, posing a potential barrier to the practical use of self-assessment instruments. Mobile devices with touch displays are often used for computer-based testing as they allow direct manipulation of information, which can feel very natural to the user [8]. However, most applications do not take into account the needs of the elderly. Several age-related factors affect interaction with touch interfaces in mobile applications [3,10]. Older people can have trouble identifying thin lines, reading small and low-contrast text, or distinguishing between visually similar icons. Fine movements, time critical gestures (e.g. double taps), or complex multi-touch gestures can also be problematic. Other studies have shown that mobile devices such as tablets can be successfully integrated into the lives of people with dementia - for example, to assess quality of life [12], to improve quality of live via cognitive training games or communication with staff and family members [1,6], or to improve outpatient dementia care by fostering guideline-based treatment [14,15]. Usability aspects should be considered early on in the development of a new instrument. Some authors have chosen cognitive training exercises as subtests where high usability has already been confirmed [28]. In general, however, the usability must be evaluated specifically for the new instrument. Various methods of expert-based evaluation and tests with users are available for this purpose. For example, some authors had organized focus groups with doctors and healthy older people and asked them to rate the usability of their instrument with a list of 12 statements based on the System Usability Scale [37]. Usually, several cycles of re-design and evaluation are necessary to achieve high usability, since not all problems are discovered in one pass and a new design may also reveal or create new problems [21].

3   Methods

We conducted five semi-structured interviews with usability and domain experts to determine which usability problems exist in the DemSelf app and how they could be solved. The extent to which the characteristics of the original subtests change by the adaption, as well as the conditions and appropriate context for practical application, were also in question.

3.1   Participants

The participants had expertise in the domain of usability and human-machine interaction and/or in the domain of dementia and neuropsychological assessment. The average age was 29.6 years ($SD = 1.34$). All participants were female and had a university degree as their highest completed level of education. Three participants worked as research assistants in an MCI-research domain, while two participants were professionals in usability and user experience. Participants had an average of 7.2 years ($SD = 2.5$) of professional experience in human-machine interaction or usability. Three participants reported practical experience in the diagnosis of MCI and dementia. Only one participant reported practical experience with computerized digital screening instruments. All participants reported practical experience in assessing the usability of touch-based software. Two participants reported practical experience in assessing the usability of touch-based software specifically for elderly people.

3.2 Procedure

Four interviews were conducted in person. Participants operated the DemSelf app on an iPad (6th Generation). One interview was conducted remotely via telephone call. Here, the app was simulated in Xcode on an iPad (6th Generation) and operated remotely via TeamViewer. The average interview duration was 71 min.

Participants were informed about dementia, MCI, and the purpose of cognitive screening instruments. Each participant then completed the DemSelf testing process twice. We first presented a scenario in which an elderly patient is asked by a physician to perform the test alone. Participants were asked to put themselves in that person's position and to solve the test as correctly as possible. We encouraged participants to think aloud during the first round. This procedure is a form of cognitive walkthrough [16] in the sense that a usage context, a user, and a task were specified. The goal was to uncover usability problems when the test is performed for the first time as this is the most common use of a screening instrument.

In the second round, participants could try alternative inputs and make typical mistakes. We asked participants to clarify comments made in the first round of thinking aloud and asked further questions regarding usability and differences between the original and the adapted subtests. After completing the second round, participants could comment on the adequate context of use and conditions for using the app as a cognitive screening instrument.

3.3 Apparatus

We developed a self-administered touch-based cognitive screening instrument, called DemSelf, by adapting an examiner-administered paper-based instrument, the Quick Mild Cognitive Impairment (Qmci) screen. The goal of DemSelf is to classify whether a person has normal cognition, MCI, or dementia. The test is to be performed independently on a mobile device such as a tablet.

The Qmci was selected based on the following criteria: high accuracy in detecting MCI, short administration time (under 10 min), and detailed instructions for administration and scoring. The Qmci was originally published in 2012 and is specifically designed to differentiate MCI from normal cognition [22]. Two recent systematic reviews show reliable results for detecting MCI [11,27]. It is a short (3–5 min) instrument composed of six subtests – Orientation, Word Registration, Clock Drawing, Delayed Recall, Word Fluency, and Logical Memory. There are cut-off scores for MCI and dementia adjusted for age and education. The Qmci covers the cognitive domains orientation, working memory, visuospatial/construction, episodic memory and semantic memory/language [23].

We translated the items from the Qmci into German and based the instructions and scoring system of DemSelf on the Qmci guide [19]. In the Qmci there is a verbal interaction between the test administrator and the subject. In a self-assessment, speech recognition would come closest to this interaction, but was considered too error-prone. The Qmci subtest Word Fluency, in which as many animals as possible are to be named in one minute, is therefore not included in DemSelf. Keyboard input was identified as a major difficulty for older people and a frequent source of errors in another self-assessment screening instrument [28]. Therefore, most user input in DemSelf is done by tapping large, labeled buttons that represent either correct answers or distractors. Thus, the answer choices are limited in DemSelf – this is one of the key differences from Qmci. Answer choices are randomly distributed for repeated testing.

Consent. DemSelf first requires informed consent from the patient. To limit the demands on working memory and attention, each screen contains only a few short sentences with information about the risk of a false result, the data collected, the duration of the test, and the option to stop the test at any time. Subjects are encouraged to talk to a physician if they have any doubts about the test. Any isolated cognitive screening instrument is insufficient for a diagnosis of MCI or dementia [2]. The Qmci guide recommends verbally clarifying the purpose and indicating that the subject can stop at any time [19]. In DemSelf, this comprehension is tested with the questions: Does the test provide a reliable diagnosis of dementia (No)? Can you stop the test after each task (Yes)? Subjects can continue only if both questions are answered correctly and if they agree to take the test (see Fig. 1).

Test Environment. The aim of cognitive testing is to achieve the best possible performance to ensure that deficits are not caused by internal or external confounding factors [25]. The subject is therefore instructed to perform the test in a quiet environment without distractions and to use a hearing aid and wear glasses if necessary. The volume setting and the reading aloud function can be tested in advance. The physiological and emotional state of the person being tested can cause the test result to be biased [24]. A subject is therefore asked whether he or she feels well, is not in pain, is not emotionally upset, and is not tired (see Fig. 1). The answers are reported in the test result for the healthcare professional.

Subtest Orientation. DemSelf asks five questions about the country, year, month, date (for the day), and day of the week. There are 12 answer choices for country and year including the correct answer and 11 distractors: 7 countries are randomly selected European countries (testing was assumed to take place in Germany). The remaining 4 countries are randomly selected from a list of all countries on earth. The distractors for the current year are randomly selected from a span of ±20 years. For month, date, and day of the week all available options are given as possible answers. There is a 10 s time limit for answering before the next question appears.

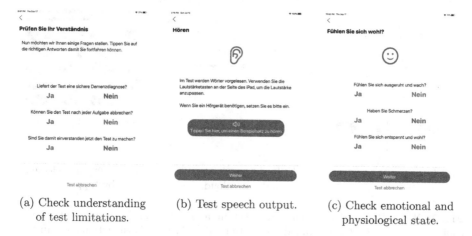

(a) Check understanding of test limitations.

(b) Test speech output.

(c) Check emotional and physiological state.

Fig. 1. Selection of screens before the test begins. See Sect. 3.3 for a detailed description. Translation of instructions: (a) Now we would like to ask you some questions. Tap on the correct answers so that you can continue. Does the test provide a reliable diagnosis of dementia? Can you stop the test after each task? Do you agree to take the test now? (b) In the test, words are read aloud. Use the volume buttons on the side of the iPad to adjust the volume. If you need a hearing aid, please insert it. (c) Do you feel rested and awake? Are you in pain? Do you feel relaxed and comfortable?

Subtest Word Registration. In Word Registration, DemSelf displays 5 words on the screen and consecutively reads each word aloud. The Swift class AVSpeechSynthesizer was used for speech synthesis with a German female voice. The speech rate was set to 0.40 throughout the app with a pause of 1/2 s before and after each utterance. The subject is then asked to tap the previously presented words in any order. The 16 answer options include 11 distractors which are randomly selected from a list of semantically and syntactically related words. If the subject does not select the correct words, the items are presented again up to 3 times and the subject must select the words again.

Subtest Clock Drawing. Clock Drawing is a common subtest in cognitive screening instruments with variations in administration and scoring systems [9]. In DemSelf, all input in Clock Drawing is made by tapping and drawing with a finger. An empty circle is provided as in the Qmci. Numbers and hands can be entered inside the circle and in a quadratic area surrounding it. The subject is first asked to put in all the numbers and then draw the hands into this clock face in a subsequent step. Drawing is done with one finger and creates a straight line between the start and end points.

Numbers are added by (1) tapping on a location in the rectangular area (2) entering a number in the appearing number pad (3) confirming the number which closes the number pad (see Fig. 3). A number can be modified by tapping on it – the number pad reappears, and the number can be deleted or changed. When a number is selected this way, it can be relocated by either tapping on a new location or by dragging it to a new location (Fig. 2).

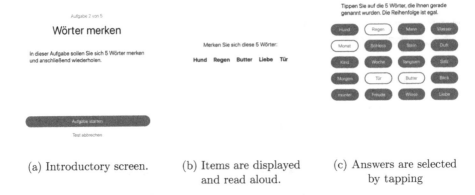

(a) Introductory screen.   (b) Items are displayed   (c) Answers are selected
                                 and read aloud.   by tapping

Fig. 2. Word Registration: item presentation and selection from different answer choices. See Sect. 3.3 for a detailed description. Translation of instructions: (a) In this task you are supposed to remember and then repeat 5 words. (b) Remember these 5 words. (c) Tap on the 5 words you were just told. The order does not matter.

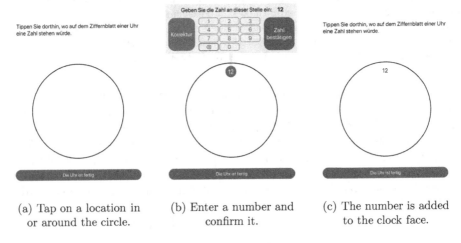

(a) Tap on a location in   (b) Enter a number and   (c) The number is added
    or around the circle.   confirm it.   to the clock face.

Fig. 3. Clock Drawing: steps to add a number to the clock face. See Sect. 3.3 for a detailed description. Translation of instructions: (a) Tap where a number would be on the face of a clock. (b) Enter the number at this point.

The target areas for numbers and hands are shown in Fig. 4. The numbers 12, 3, 6 and 9 must be located inside a section of 30° and the numbers 1, 2, 4, 5, 7, 8, 10 and 11 must be located inside the corresponding quadrant to be correct. The numbers are also accepted in a limited range outside the circle. Numbers are scored as in the Qmci [19]: 1 point for each correct number and minus 1 point for each number duplicated or if greater than 12. Incorrectly placed numbers which are not duplicates or greater than 12 are ignored.

Hands need to be drawn at 10 min past 11. Drawing with the finger creates a straight line between start and end point. A hand is considered correct if its end point lies within one of the hand sections shown in Fig. 4. An additional point is given, if both inner end points of the hands lie within the inner circle.

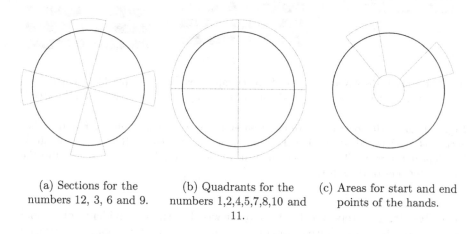

(a) Sections for the numbers 12, 3, 6 and 9.

(b) Quadrants for the numbers 1,2,4,5,7,8,10 and 11.

(c) Areas for start and end points of the hands.

Fig. 4. Clock Drawing: target areas for scoring numbers and hands

A subject could rotate the device while entering the numbers and hands. The Qmci guide asks the human evaluator to maximize the score by lining up the scoring template at "12 o'clock" [19]. In DemSelf, the target areas are rotated and lined up at the location of the number 12 (if 12 is missing, 3, 6, or 9 are used respectively). The maximum of the unaligned or aligned score is selected.

Subtest Delayed Recall. In Delayed Recall, test subjects are asked to repeat the words that have been presented in the subtest Word Registration. Again, there are 16 answer choices with 11 randomly selected distractors.

Subtest Logical Memory. Logical Memory tests the recall of a short story. Instead of free verbal recall, repeating the story is divided into 9 steps. For each step, there are 6 answer choices with the correct story component and 5 distractors. The distractors were chosen to (1) have the same syntactic structure, (2) be semantically related, and (3) be used with a similar frequency in German as the original item. A new story component is added to the answer by tapping on the according button. The current answer is displayed on the screen (Fig. 5).

(a) The story is displayed and read aloud.

(b) Subject taps the beginning of the story.

(c) The story is completed step by step.

Fig. 5. Logical Memory: item presentation and repeating a story in several steps. See Sect. 3.3 for a detailed description. Translation of instructions: (a) Remember this story. (b) Repeat the story. Tap the beginning of the story. (c) Repeat the story. Tap the next component of the story.

Test Result. It is reported to the subject whether there is evidence of normal cognition or risk for cognitive impairment. Subjects are once again encouraged to speak with a physician if they have any concerns. Test results can be sent to the physician who initiated the testing or saved on the tablet.

A more detailed test result is intended for medical professionals. The test score and the cut-off scores are displayed on a bar plot. We used the original cut-off scores from Qmci, but scaled down because the Verbal Fluency subtest was missing. Additional information such as the test date, start time and duration, as well as the subject's age and education are displayed. The subject's answers about the test environment and current physiological and emotional status are also reported. Further details can be displayed for each subtest, including the subject's responses, an explanation for the subtest's scoring system, and additional information such as the time taken to complete the subtest.

4   Results

Below we present some of the feedback on the DemSelf instrument that was mentioned by two or more participants or was considered particularly important.

4.1   Usability

Participants identified usability issues in all components of the DemSelf app. In this section, we present a selection of important usability issues noted by two or more participants.

Participants generally supported the idea to test a subject's understanding that the test result alone does not provide a diagnosis and can be inaccurate. However, hiding the button to proceed to the next screen until the user has answered correctly without providing any feedback was considered bad practice (see Fig. 1). Leaving the application to make adjustments in the device settings or to get more information about cognitive impairments in the browser may cause problems, as subjects may not be able to find their way back. In addition, reading about dementia and commonly used cognitive tests could lead to priming effects that influence behavior on the test. The buttons for changing volume on the iPad might be difficult to find for subjects unfamiliar with tablets. Participants suggested displaying arrows on the screen pointing to the volume buttons. Participants also missed an indicator of how many screens are displayed before the actual test begins.

The confirmation of answers in the subtests was not consistent. Responses are sometimes logged directly when tapping a button and can no longer be changed, such as in the Orientation and Logical Memory subtests. This can be particularly frustrating for people with vision or motor impairments who accidentally touch the wrong button. Such operating errors also lead to bias within the test result. In the Word Registration and Delayed Recall subtests, the screen changes automatically when five words have been logged in, so that the fifth word cannot be changed. Previous answers can be deselected by tapping on them. This behavior was irritating and inconsistent. Participants suggested adding a global confirmation button to all subtests that logs in the selected answers and switches to the next screen. In the Orientation subtest, the next question appears after a time limit of 10 s, which was considered a serious usability problem. Subjects may feel they are loosing control. As a result, some participants also falsely assumed a time limit in the following subtests. Scores may still depend on reaction time, but the end of a time limit should not result in an automatic screen change. When items are presented both in text form and verbally, new text passages should be displayed step-by-step and synchronously with the spoken word, as the speed of reading and following the verbal presentation may differ.

In Clock Drawing, almost all participants initially overlooked the buttons to confirm a number or hand and add it to the clock. Instead, participants tapped a new location in the clock circle or began drawing a new hand. The confirmation process intended by the system was unexpected, since no input had to be explicitly confirmed in the previous subtests. Numbers can be relocated on the clock by drag-and-drop, which was perceived as intuitive for younger people. However, dragging a number across the screen requires fine motor skills that many elderly people do not have. The mechanism also was not explicitly mentioned, which could influence the test result. A subject's arm and hand will partially cover the clock while using the number pad (see Fig. 3). A position below the clock circle would prevent this and correspond to the common conventions for mobile devices.

4.2   Adaption

DemSelf is a different test than Qmci and needs to be re-validated. This section presents important changes that were introduced by the adaption as self-administered touch-based instrument. Visual recognition and selection between several answer options instead of a free verbal recall is one of the main differences between the Qmci and DemSelf, with implications on the involved cognitive processes and the subtest difficulty. In all subtests besides Clock Drawing, users provide answers by tapping on labeled buttons and no longer have to verbally recall the items. This changes the nature of the task. Overall, there was no clear consensus on how many or what type of distractors are appropriate.

Reading skills, visual memory abilities, or visual impairments are new confounding variables in DemSelf. Items are presented in text form for a certain period, and a fast reader can scan the words several times. The same applies to labeled answer buttons when there is a time limit, such as in the Orientation subtest. Different questions in Orientation will likely require different time limits as different amounts of text are displayed. We reported in the previous section that people with non-cognitive impairments, such as tremor or visual impairments, could unintentionally give wrong answers by tapping on wrong buttons. Participants therefore raised doubts about whether Orientation is valid and really tests whether subjects know the answer.

For the Clock Drawing subtest, participants reported that important aspects from the paper-based version such as spatial orientation and understanding the clock are also tested in the adapted version. Many typical errors also seemed possible in the adapted version. Experience with touchpads and mobile devices could be an important factor for this subtest, as some interaction options are not explicitly mentioned, such as dragging a number to change the position. In the paper-based version of Clock Drawing, it is common to draw auxiliary lines or a dot in the middle of the clock before filling in the numbers. This is not possible in DemSelf, nor is drawing curved hands.

Scoring in Logical Memory is based on the number of target words recalled, which makes sense for free verbal recall. However, in the adapted version, a correct story component with two target words such as "Der rote Fuchs" [The red fox] may actually be easier to remember than a story part like "im Mai." [in May] with only one target word, and thus should not score higher.

4.3   Acceptance

Participants were generally cautious about self-assessment in practical application. Participants assumed that many older people would not be able to self-administer the test due to a lack of technical experience. However, as mobile devices are increasingly used by older people, this problem will decrease in the future. For now, an assisting person should be present at least to start the app and to adjust volume and brightness. Participants would generally prefer if the test is conducted in a medical office rather than at a patient's home so that someone is present for support, and the result can be discussed directly. Healthcare professionals may also hesitate to use DemSelf because they lack information from observation and interaction with the patient. It was therefore positively noted that the state of the subject is reported in the test result as fatigue and pain can affect the test result, which means that the subject should be retested. Reporting the test result directly to the subject in the app was viewed very negatively. It would not be ethical to leave individuals alone with an unexpected test result about MCI or dementia that may also be incorrect. DemSelf could also be used in a traditional context with a human administrator to automatically score a test and save the results. Given the current trend towards digitizing patient data, automatic scoring and digital test results are beneficial for clinical practice. Because DemSelf is a different test than Qmci, participants agreed that DemSelf needs validation to be used in practice. Validation must also clarify which requirements a test person must fulfil in order to use DemSelf. Subjects must at least be able to read and must not have a severe visual or motor impairment. For people who can perform the test, DemSelf is a promising direction for application and research.

5   Discussion

Developing a self-assessed cognitive screening instrument is challenging. Psychometric properties must be ensured, taking into account a variety of technical and human factors [4]. This study provides some insights for the development, validation and practical application of self-administered cognitive screening instruments. DemSelf is still a rather traditional instrument as it is directly based on a validated paper-based instrument. Some potential benefits of computerized tests, such as adapting to individual performance or the use of machine-learning algorithms to interpret test performance [6,32,36], are not part of the instrument. A high level of usability is a prerequisite for successful practical use. Test subjects should immediately feel confident in using the device, as the test takes only a few minutes and is not repeated. However, it is in the nature of a standardized cognitive test that certain usability heuristics are hard to fulfill. Items can, for example, be presented only once because otherwise the test results would no longer be comparable. This rigidity can also be a problem for computerized tests. The confirmation of inputs should be handled consistently throughout the subtests. Subjects must be able to change an answer, just as in a human-administered test, where a subject can revoke a statement or cross out a number or hand. Errors that are not due to cognitive impairment, such as manually missing the right button should be avoided. An open question is still to what extent the measurement of time limits can be used as in the Qmci. Automatic change of screens after 10 s during orientation questions was one of the most criticized usability issues. Even if the screens do not change automatically, differing reading abilities and visual or motor impairments add a lot of variance to the time it takes to answer a question that is not related dementia or MCI.

One of the main differences between the original Qmci and DemSelf was recall vs. recognition. A comparison of free recall and either yes/no recognition or three-alternative forced-choice recognition in cognitively-impaired subjects found that yes/no recognition was the best predictor of MCI and early AD [5]. Yes/no recognition could therefore be used in an updated version of DemSelf. A digital pen was suggested for the Clock Drawing subtest to make it more similar to the original paper-based version. [30] successfully used such a digital pen as well as a machine learning approach for evaluation of the Clock Drawing test. In the DemSelf implementation, users only need to tap a certain location to enter numbers and can only draw straight lines. The reduced vulnerability to motor impairments in the DemSelf implementation could be a strength of the instrument. User testing is required to determine if DemSelf is appropriate for certain subpopulations – for example, for those who are uncomfortable using a tablet or have certain limitations such as aphasia, poor reading skills, or hemiparesis [4]. Some factors can affect a self-assessed computerized screening instrument differently than an examiner-administered paper-based instrument. For example, technology use and commitment towards technology has been shown to affect test scores when the same test is administered on paper or on a tablet [31]. Technical experience, reading skills, and motor impairments were mentioned as possible confounding factors for DemSelf.

The expert interviews revealed possibilities for improving the prototype. By completing the test twice, participants could explore different ways of interaction and discover usability problems that would otherwise have gone unnoticed. The involvement of stakeholders from dementia and MCI research allowed us to evaluate the acceptability of the instrument for practical use and to identify usability issues that are specific to elderly and cognitively-impaired users. In a future study, screen capture or video recordings can help to better analyze the interaction with complex tasks like the clock drawing test. One limitation of this study is that no users from the target group were involved. Until then, the presented comments on usability remain partly speculation. Similar to [37] the next step in the evaluation of DemSelf could be focus group interviews with healthy and cognitively-impaired elderly users. A study comparing the test performance in Qmci and DemSelf would shed more light on the discussed differences between the instruments. In the future, we hope to allocate more funding in order to further our research on the usability and validity of computerized cognitive screening instruments.

6   Conclusion

Early detection of MCI and dementia is vital as many therapeutic and preventive approaches are particularly effective at an early stage. Cognitive screening instruments are primarily paper-based and administered by healthcare professionals. Computerized cognitive screening instruments offer a number of potential advantages over paper-based instruments, such as increased standardization of scoring, reduced costs, remote testing and a more precise measurement of time- and location-sensitive tasks [4].

We presented a touch-based cognitive screening instrument, called DemSelf. It was developed by adapting an examiner-administered paper-based instrument, the Quick Mild Cognitive Impairment (Qmci) screen. Usability is a key criterion for self-assessment by elderly users with potential cognitive and other impairments. We conducted interviews with experts in the domain of usability and human-machine interaction and/or in the domain of dementia and neuropsychological assessment to evaluate DemSelf. The expert interviews revealed possibilities for improving the prototype. Developers should consider barriers for elderly and inexperienced users, such as not being able to reverse an answer or leaving the application without finding their way back. Time limits cannot be taken directly from a paper-based test version and should not lead to automatic screen changes. Visual recognition instead of a free verbal recall is one of the main differences between the Qmci and DemSelf. Reading skills, technical experience, and motor impairments seem to be important confounding variables. Further research is needed to determine validity and reliability of computerized versions of conventional paper-based tests. Healthcare professionals may hesitate to use DemSelf because they lack information from observation and interaction with the patient – that could also be evaluated electronically in the long-term. Participants would generally prefer if the test is conducted in a medical office rather than at a patient's home so that someone is present for support and the result can be discussed directly. In view of the current trend towards digitization of patient data, automatic scoring and digital test results are beneficial for clinical practice. Computerized instruments like DemSelf also have the potential to reduce costs and provide early support for people with MCI and dementia.

References

1. Antons, J.N., et al.: PflegeTab: enhancing quality of life using a psychosocial internet-based intervention for residential dementia care. In: ISRII 8th Scientific Meeting - Technologies for a Digital World: Improving Health Across the Lifespan. International Society for Research on Internet Interventions (ISRII), p. 1 (2016)
2. Aslam, R.W., et al.: A systematic review of the diagnostic accuracy of automated tests for cognitive impairment. Int. J. Geriatr. Psychiatry **33**(4), 561–575 (2018). https://doi.org/10.1002/gps.4852
3. Balata, J., Mikovec, Z., Slavicek, T.: KoalaPhone: touchscreen mobile phone UI for active seniors. J. Multimodal User Interfaces **9**(4), 263–273 (2015). https://doi.org/10.1007/s12193-015-0188-1
4. Bauer, R.M., Iverson, G.L., Cernich, A.N., Binder, L.M., Ruff, R.M., Naugle, R.I.: Computerized neuropsychological assessment devices: Joint position paper of the American academy of clinical neuropsychology and the national academy of neuropsychology. Arch. Clin. Neuropsychol. **27**(3), 362–373 (2012). https://doi.org/10.1093/arclin/acs027
5. Bennett, I.J., Golob, E.J., Parker, E.S., Starr, A.: Memory evaluation in mild cognitive impairment using recall and recognition tests. J. Clin. Exp. Neuropsychol. **28**(8), 1408–1422 (2006). https://doi.org/10.1080/13803390500409583
6. Cha, J., et al.: Finding critical features for predicting quality of life in tablet-based serious games for dementia. Qual. User Exp. **4**(1) (2019). https://doi.org/10.1007/s41233-019-0028-2
7. Cordell, C.B., et al.: Alzheimer's association recommendations for operationalizing the detection of cognitive impairment during the medicare annual wellness visit in a primary care setting. Alzheimer's Dement. **9**(2), 141–150 (2013). https://doi.org/10.1016/j.jalz.2012.09.011

8. Daniel Wigdor, D.W.: Brave Nui World: Designing Natural User Interfaces for Touch and Gesture. Morgan Kaufmann Publishers, Burlington (2011)

9. Ehreke, L., Luppa, M., König, H.H., Riedel-Heller, S.G.: Is the clock drawing test a screening tool for the diagnosis of mild cognitive impairment? a systematic review. Int. Psychogeriatr. 22(1), 56–63 (2009). https://doi.org/10.1017/s1041610209990676

10. Fisk, A.D., Rogers, W.A., Charness, N., Czaja, S.J., Sharit, J.: Designing for Older Adults (2004). https://doi.org/10.1201/9781420023862

11. Glynn, K., Coen, R., Lawlor, B.A.: Is the Quick Mild Cognitive Impairment Screen (QMCI) more accurate at detecting mild cognitive impairment than existing short cognitive screening tests? A systematic review of the current literature. Int. J. Geriatr. Psychiatry (2019). https://doi.org/10.1002/gps.5201

12. Junge, S., et al.: Quality of life in people with dementia living in nursing homes: validation of an eight-item version of the QUALIDEM for intensive longitudinal assessment. Qual. Life Res. 29(6), 1721–1730 (2020). https://doi.org/10.1007/s11136-020-02418-4

13. Knopman, D.S., Petersen, R.C.: Mild cognitive impairment and mild dementia: a clinical perspective. Mayo Clin. Proc. 89, 1452–1459 (2014)

14. Lech, S., O'Sullivan, J., Voigt-Antons, J.N., Gellert, P., Nordheim, J.: Tablet-based outpatient care for people with dementia: guideline-based treatment planning, personalized disease management and network-based care. In: Abstracts of the 14th International Congress of the European Geriatric Medicine Society, pp. 249–250. Springer International Publishing (2018)

15. Lech, S., O'Sullivan, J.L., Gellert, P., Voigt-Antons, J.N., Greinacher, R., Nordheim, J.: Tablet-based outpatient care for people with dementia. GeroPsych 32(3), 135–144 (2019). https://doi.org/10.1024/1662-9647/a000210

16. Mahatody, T., Sagar, M., Kolski, C.: State of the art on the cognitive walkthrough method, its variants and evolutions. Int. J. Hum.-Comput. Interact. 26(8), 741–785 (2010). https://doi.org/10.1080/10447311003781409

17. Maier, W., Deuschl, G.: S3-Leitlinie Demenzen [S3 guideline dementia]. In: Leitlinien für Diagnostik und Therapie in der Neurologie. Deutsche Gesellschaft für Neurologie (2016). https://www.dgn.org/images/red_leitlinien/LL_2016/PDFs_Download/038013_LL_Demenzen_2016.pdf

18. Mayr, U.: Normales kognitives Altern [normal cognitive aging]. In: Karnath, H.O., Thier, P. (eds.) Kognitive Neurowissenschaften, pp. 777–788. Springer, Heidelberg (2012). https://doi.org/10.1007/978-3-642-25527-4_72

19. Molloy, W., O'Caoimh, R.: Qmci The Quick Guide. New Grange Press, Waterford (2017)

20. Murman, D.: The impact of age on cognition. Semin. Hear. 36(03), 111–121 (2015). https://doi.org/10.1055/s-0035-1555115

21. Möller, S.: Usability engineering. In: Möller, S. (ed.) Quality Engineering, pp. 59–76. Springer, Heidelberg (2017). https://doi.org/10.1007/978-3-662-56046-4_4

22. O'Caoimh, R., et al.: Comparison of the quick mild cognitive impairment (Qmci) screen and the SMMSE in screening for mild cognitive impairment. Age Ageing 41(5), 624–629 (2012). https://doi.org/10.1093/ageing/afs059

23. O'Caoimh, R., Molloy, D.W.: The quick mild cognitive impairment screen (Qmci). In: Larner, A.J. (ed.) Cognitive Screening Instruments, pp. 255–272. Springer, Cham (2017). https://doi.org/10.1007/978-3-319-44775-9_12

24. Overton, M., Pihlsgård, M., Elmståhl, S.: Test administrator effects on cognitive performance in a longitudinal study of ageing. Cogent Psychol. 3(1) (2016). https://doi.org/10.1080/23311908.2016.1260237

25. Pentzek, M., Dyllong, A., Grass-Kapanke, B.: Praktische Voraussetzungen und Hinweise für die Durchführung psychometrischer Tests - was jeder Testleiter wissen sollte [practical requirements and tips for conducting psychometric tests - what every test administrator should know]. NeuroGeriatrie **7**(1), 20–25 (2010)

26. Petersen, R.C., Caracciolo, B., Brayne, C., Gauthier, S., Jelic, V., Fratiglioni, L.: Mild cognitive impairment: a concept in evolution. J. Intern. Med. **275**(3), 214–228 (2014). https://doi.org/10.1111/joim.12190

27. Roeck, E.E.D., Deyn, P.P.D., Dierckx, E., Engelborghs, S.: Brief cognitive screening instruments for early detection of Alzheimer's disease: a systematic review. Alzheimer's Res. Ther. **11**(1) (2019). https://doi.org/10.1186/s13195-019-0474-3

28. Ruano, L., et al.: Development of a self-administered web-based test for longitudinal cognitive assessment. Sci. Rep. **6**(1) (2016). https://doi.org/10.1038/srep19114

29. Shankle, W.R., et al.: Methods to improve the detection of mild cognitive impairment. Proc. Natl. Acad. Sci. **102**(13), 4919–4924 (2005). https://doi.org/10.1073/pnas.0501157102

30. Souillard-Mandar, W., Davis, R., Rudin, C., Au, R., Penney, D.L.: Interpretable machine learning models for the digital clock drawing test. In: 2016 ICML Workshop on Human Interpretability in Machine Learning (WHI 2016) (2016)

31. Steinert, A., Latendorf, A., Salminen, T., Müller-Werdan, U.: Evaluation of technology-based neuropsychological assessments in older adults. Innov. Aging **2**(suppl_1), 504 (2018). https://doi.org/10.1093/geroni/igy023.1874

32. Sternin, A., Burns, A., Owen, A.M.: Thirty-five years of computerized cognitive assessment of aging–where are we now? Diagnostics **9**(3), 114 (2019). https://doi.org/10.3390/diagnostics9030114

33. Stokin, G.B., Krell-Roesch, J., Petersen, R.C., Geda, Y.E.: Mild neurocognitive disorder: an old wine in a new bottle. Harv. Rev. Psychiatry **23**(5), 368–376 (2015). https://doi.org/10.1097/hrp.0000000000000084

34. Tsoi, K.K.F., Chan, J.Y.C., Hirai, H.W., Wong, S.Y.S., Kwok, T.C.Y.: Cognitive tests to detect dementia. JAMA Intern. Med. **175**(9), 1450 (2015). https://doi.org/10.1001/jamainternmed.2015.2152

35. World Health Organization: ICD-11 for mortality and morbidity statistics (2020). https://icd.who.int/browse11/l-m/en

36. Yim, D., Yeo, T.Y., Park, M.H.: Mild cognitive impairment, dementia, and cognitive dysfunction screening using machine learning. J. Int. Med. Res. **48**(7), 030006052093688 (2020). https://doi.org/10.1177/0300060520936881

37. Zeng, Z., et al.: Towards long-term tracking and detection of early dementia: a computerized cognitive test battery with gamification. In: Proceedings of the 3rd International Conference on Crowd Science and Engineering - ICCSE 2018. ACM Press (2018). https://doi.org/10.1145/3265689.3265719

38. Zygouris, S., Tsolaki, M.: Computerized cognitive testing for older adults. Am. J. Alzheimer's Dis. Other Dement. **30**(1), 13–28 (2014). https://doi.org/10.1177/1533317514522852

A Compact Automated Tablet Dispensing & Packaging System for Community Healthcare Facilities to Provide Unit Dose Repackaging Service

Yiming Chen and Zhenyu Gu[✉]

Shanghai Jiao Tong University, 800 Dongchuan RD. Minhang District, Shanghai, China
zygu@sjtu.edu.cn

Abstract. Unit dose packaging is a gradually promoted medicine packaging form, which has been widely proved to improve the convenience, compliance and safety of patients. Especially for the elderly patients with chronic diseases, who need to take a variety of drugs and their cognitive ability is reduced, providing unit dose packaging is a very effective service. At present, the large-scale automatic production mode of unit dose packaging is not suitable for community healthcare facilities, while the manual mode has low safety and high workload. Therefore, on the basis of investigation and analysis, this research designed a compact automated tablet dispensing & packaging system for these facilities, and built a prototype, and tested the performance and availability of the system in the laboratory. In this way, the workload of staff will be reduced, and the level of unit dose drug packaging service provided by these facilities will be improved. In a word, designing the service-oriented products based on a wide range of existing community facilities is an enlightening innovative way for welfare for the elderly.

Keywords: Unit dose · Medical product · Medical service · Medication compliance · Community service

1 Introduction

A large number of patients with chronic diseases, especially the elders, need to take a variety of pills. Due to the complexity of medicines, they often miss or take wrong pills, which leads to the decline of curative effect and increase the risk of danger [1]. The ability to take and manage medication is considered to meet the basic needs of older people all over the world [2]. Reading drug labels and understanding prescriptions have a significant impact on drug compliance [3]. Therefore, reducing the complexity of drug packaging and the cognitive burden of obtaining accurate drugs can effectively improve the ability of medication management.

Unit dose package is a packaging form which is gradually adopted in hospitals or central pharmacies. It repackages multiple solid oral drugs taken at a time according to prescriptions, and patients only need to take one package when taking medicine.

© Springer Nature Switzerland AG 2021
Q. Gao and J. Zhou (Eds.): HCII 2021, LNCS 12787, pp. 210–222, 2021.
https://doi.org/10.1007/978-3-030-78111-8_14

This has been proved that the convenience, compliance and treatment effect of taking medicine can be significantly improved [4, 5]. There are several packaging forms for dose dispensing, of which sachet packs and blister packs are two most widely used forms [5]. Traditionally, before patients use unit dose package, they need to manually prepack drugs by themselves or others, which is a troublesome and unsafe work.

With the implementation of the Unit Dose Dispensing System (UDDS) [6] in hospitals, large-scale automation equipment has been developed and deployed in the inpatient department of large hospitals, and then gradually extended to central pharmacies [7]. In recent 20 years, some Nordic countries such as Finland and Sweden have implemented Automated dose dispensing (ADD) service for primary healthcare patients to improve the medication compliance of patients while reducing the workload of pharmacists and medication cost [8].

However, the Automated Tablet Dispensing & Packaging System (ATDPS) on the market is extremely expensive and bulky, which is not suitable for community healthcare facilities such as clinics, nursing homes or pharmacies. A large number of such facilities still rely on manual or simple packaging equipment to complete the repackaging, so the staff are under great pressure and prone to errors [9, 10]. In addition, in some areas, unit dose repackaging service is not provided to outpatient patients, but it is widely welcomed, especially for elderly patients [11]. Therefore, in order to popularize the unit dose repackaging service to community primary healthcare, it is necessary to make adaptive changes to its process or product.

This paper focuses on using design to help community healthcare facilities to provide unit dose repackaging service to patients to improve their medication experience and safety. Because of the economic, space and staff limitations of these facilities, a new compact ATDPS and new service procedure are established, which are expected to achieve the following contributions:

Firstly, the equipment should be able to accurately complete the packaging of unit dose products. A universal drug dispensing method is used to greatly reduce the cost and volume of the equipment. It reminds pharmacists to complete the standard operation process through interaction, and they are expected to have more pharmaceutical communication with patients in the community, rather than repeated mechanical labor.

Secondly, this paper provides an inclusive unit dose repackaging service mode, which provides services through decentralized community healthcare facilities. It has lower trial cost for facilities and patients as well as better flexibility than the central pharmacy service mode.

2 Investigation and Analysis

2.1 Related Works

After decades of development and people's increasing attention to medication management, the service mode of unit dose medicine presents diversification. The scene of providing services expanded from the initial hospital inpatient department to nursing homes, clinics, community pharmacies [12], online pharmacies [13] and family drug management terminals [14, 15]. The dispensing methods used include integrated automated, decentralized automated and manual dispensing. The automated dispensing technologies used include special dispensing mechanism and universal dispensing mechanism. Packaging methods also include automated, semi-automated and manual packaging. Unit dose packaging form includes disposable sachet, disposable blister and reusable container. The following will summarize different production methods of unit dose from the perspective of dispensing and packaging equipment, technical features, costs, scenarios and products provided to patients.

Automated Dispensing Method Which Drug and Device Structure Must Be One to One Matched. This method is the most common automated drug dispensing method, which requires one drug corresponding to one dispenser module. In the dispenser, a turntable with a slot corresponding to the size of the drug is used to make a drug fall into the slot by rotation, and then fall out of the gap at the bottom, so as to dispense a drug from multiple drugs. Therefore, each type of drug needs a dispenser with customized structure, and a large number of drugs need to be put into the corresponding dispenser before use, so types of drugs cannot be adjusted flexibly.

Hospitals often adapt large-scale ATDPS, which integrates a large number of dispensers for commonly used drugs [16]. The system collects the drugs sorted out by different dispensers into continuous disposable sachets printed with prescription information, and then heat seals them. This production method has high efficiency, but also high cost and large volume. It needs to be customized for the list of commonly used drugs, and complex cleaning and maintenance needs to be performed on a regular basis. The drugs stored in the dispensers cannot be stored for a long time. Therefore, the scenarios of this method are inpatient departments with a large number of rapidly updated prescriptions, or large pharmacies and Internet pharmacies with large drug consumption.

Some pharmacies do not have high requirements for efficiency. They will use an equipment [17], which needs the staff to manually place a dispenser on the host machine. According to the prescription, different drugs are dispensed into blisters in batches. The specification of the blisters is usually 4 * 7 doses, which provides patients with 4 times a day and 7 days a week. After the drug completely dispensed into the blister, the label with prescription information is manually pasted on the blister for sealing. This production method reduces the degree of automation and is more suitable for universal pharmacy for reducing the cost and volume. However, the management and maintenance of a large number of dispensers is still a complex activity.

Universal Automated Dispensing Method. Some dispensing methods are used as the supplementary dispensing methods of the large-scale ATDPS mentioned above. The drugs added temporarily would be dispensed by complex mechanisms such as tilt rotation, baffle limit or vibration, and electronic control systems for different drugs.

Another dispensing method uses the way of negative pressure suction to get a tablet. It extends the suction cup into the drug container through the movement mechanism to absorb the required drugs, and then moves to the outlet to release the drugs. This method can sort out a drug without the influence of drug appearance, but has complex mechanical structure, high cost, and lower dispensing efficiency than the first method. At present, there are mainly two kinds of scenarios adapting this method. One is the large-scale equipment with a large number of kinds of drugs built into the equipment used in the pharmacy, and the released drugs can be packaged into continuous sachets or blisters after concentration. The other one is a home device with a small number of kinds of drugs built in. The released drugs are concentrated in a cup and taken out by users in time.

Manual Dispensing Method. This method relies on the combination of hands and eyes of employees to put a variety of drugs taken at one time into a container. Drugs can be dispensed into small plastic boxes with lids or blisters with a capacity of one week or one month, and then packaged with wrapping paper. Some products give interactive auxiliary methods for the scene of manual dispensing, which can guide users to accurately put drugs in the right position through light, thus reducing the burden of attention. Another scene is to manually dispense drugs into the lattice of the rotating disk above the drug packaging machine, and then use the automated rotation to release all the drugs of a unit dose into the packaging bag, and then heat seal drugs into continuous sachets. This manual dispensing method has the lowest cost, is the most flexible, and can also be assisted by some devices. However, there is high mental pressure at work, which takes up a lot of pharmacists' time, and the high error rate will affect the medication safety of patients.

To sum up, there is no suitable automated unit dose dispensing method for community healthcare facilities. The universal dispensing method and partial automation may be effective solutions to emancipate the manual in an appropriate cost and volume. It is suitable to use continuous sachets and blisters as the form of unit dose packaging.

2.2 User Interview

In order to better understand the current situation of unit dose repackaging service in community healthcare facilities, this paper conducted a visit for some nursing homes and pharmacies in Shanghai, China, and conducted semi-structured interviews with the staff.

The interview found that pharmacists in these facilities would download the prescription information uploaded by the hospital from the medication system and check with the paper prescriptions provided by patients. However, it is difficult for them to obtain the unit dose drugs packed according to the prescription, and the drug distribution company only provides the whole package of drugs. At present, pharmacies do not provide unit dose packaged drugs, but provide multi dose drugs packaged in boxes. Pharmacies sell simple unit dose portable medicine box which needs users to dispense drugs by hand, but they are not popular, especially for elderly patients who think dispensing drugs by themselves adds extra burden. Prescriptions of elderly patients is relatively stable, and the elderly who come to pharmacies to buy drugs are often familiar with the drugs they need to take. Some customers (especially the relatives of the elderly patients) have expressed the hope that pharmacies will provide unit dose drug repackaging service to help the elderly take medicine correctly.

Nursing homes strictly implement the Unit Dose Dispensing System for the hospitalized elderly, and the pharmacists would manually dispense each patient's oral medicine of the next day to a small plastic box (see Fig. 1) and place it according to the name according to the prescription every night. During the medication period, the nurses checked the dispensed unit dose drugs and distributed them to the patients. Pharmacists need to dispense hundreds of doses of drugs every day, which is inefficient cumbersome and error prone, wasting the limited medical human resources. Patients in nursing homes often take less than six kinds of drugs, and because most of them suffer from chronic diseases, their prescriptions often lasts more than two weeks. Nursing homes have expressed their limited budget cannot afford the high cost for automation, but they still hope to improve the efficiency and quality of dispensing and reduce the workload.

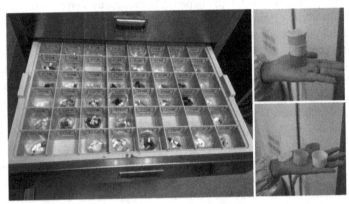

Fig. 1. Investigation in nursing homes about dispensing and repackaging pills manually.

Based on the above research and user interviews, this paper summarized the needs of community healthcare facilities to provide unit dose repackaging services as follows: automatic dispensing, appropriate cost and volume, easy cleaning and maintenance, high-quality unit dose drug packaging and good operation experience.

To sum up, the design is defined as a solution to provide unit dose repackaging service for community healthcare facilities, including a low-cost and compact Automated Tablet Dispensing & Packaging System (ATDPS) and a service procedure for patients or customers. This design aims to improve the surrounding residents' convenience of medication by providing unit dose repackaging services through a large number of existing distributed community healthcare facilities. This design is also expected to promote the communication between patients and local pharmacists.

3   Design and Implementation

3.1   Design Concept

The Compact ATDPS
In this paper, a compact ATDPS is designed, which is used to dispense and package drugs from the original multi dose packages into unit dose packages according to the patient's prescription. In order to be suitable for community healthcare facilities, products need to be designed to be low-cost and easy to use, so there will be a balance between automation and user needs. The prescription of community patients is different from

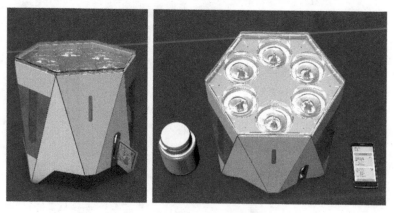

Fig. 2. Concept rendering of the compact ATDPS.

that of inpatients. A prescription will last for a long time, so there is no need to prepare a large number of drugs at any time. This design uses the method of temporarily adding needed drugs to the equipment when processing a prescription. The drugs are still in the original packages when they are not purchased, so as to reduce the cost and volume of the system, as well as benefit the preservation of drugs. Therefore, it is necessary to use the universal drug dispenser. In order to improve work efficiency, the equipment is equipped with six universal drug dispensers to meet the requirements of dispensing multiple kinds of drugs in a prescription at the same time. The dispenser adopts the patented technology previously developed by the authors' research group, realizes the dispensing of different kinds of drugs with few parts contacting drugs, so it is easy to clean and maintain. In addition, in order to improve the convenience of patients taking medicine, reduce the process of equipment operators, and protect the environment, the degradable disposable continuous packaging sachets are used for unit dose packaging of drugs, and the corresponding prescription information needs to be printed on each dose of sachet to remind patients to take medicine correctly (Fig. 2).

In the aspect of HCI design, the three key points are the user's input and processing of the patient's prescription, the correct placement of drugs into the corresponding dispenser and the display of the production status of unit dose packaging. Considering the prescription information needs word processing and the cost of the device, the smart phone is designed as the interface terminal, Bluetooth is used to connect the equipment and the smart phone, and the native lighting effect and mechanism of the equipment are also used to provide information for users. The following will be a brief introduction to the use of the system.

When a pharmacist obtains a user's prescription, he or she needs to input the drug information that needs to be repackaged in unit dose on the App according to the prescription. After typing and filling in the basic information of the patient on the App, the drug information will be obtained by scanning the bar code on the original medicine packages. When a prescription label of a drug appears on the interface, the user should enter the dosage, frequency and taking method of the drug in the sticker. Repeat the above steps until all the drugs in the prescription are entered, and then click the "check

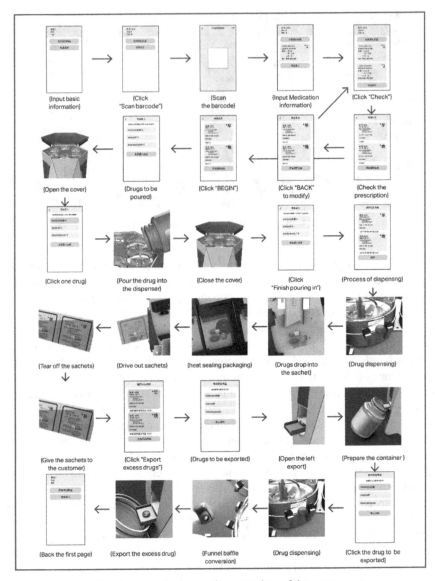

Fig. 3. A standard operation procedure of the system.

prescription" button to check the information. At this time, the interface displays the medication information printed on the unit dose package. If the information is wrong, return to modify. If the information is correct, click the "start dispensing" button to activate the equipment. Open the cover of the equipment and click a drug label on the interface. A dispenser on the equipment will produce flashing light to instruct the user to remove the original package of the drug and pour it into this dispenser. Repeat the step of placing drugs until all drugs are placed. After clicking the "placement complete" button, the dispenser will start dispensing drugs, and the process of each drug will be displayed on the interface. After different drugs are dispensed, concentrated and packaged according to the prescription in the equipment, the continuous unit dose sachets will be gradually transported out of the equipment from the right outlet. After a prescription is packaged, the user can tear off the finished sachets to give to the customer. If there are still redundant drugs in dispensers, click the "export redundant drugs" button on the app, select the label of the drug to be exported, and then the drugs can be exported from the export to containers one by one. The above is a complete standard operation process of unit dose drug repackaging. Figure 3 is a visualization of the standard operation procedure.

Service Design. The ultimate service objec of unit dose repackaging is customers or patients in community healthcare facilities, and the equipment is only a part of the service process completed by pharmacists alone. Service processes of different kinds of facilities are different, but the unit dose repackaging procedure using the equipment is almost the same. Therefore, a set of service processes was constructed in the form of service blueprint [18], which covered different branches of community pharmacies (see Fig. 4), clinics (see Fig. 5) and nursing homes (see Fig. 6).

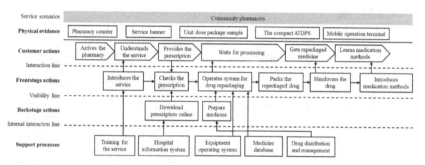

Fig. 4. Service blueprint for community pharmacies.

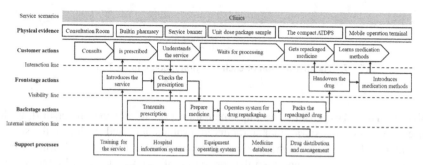

Fig. 5. Service blueprint for clinics.

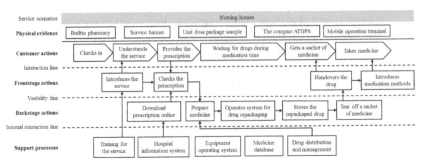

Fig. 6. Service blueprint for nursing homes.

3.2 System Implementation

The design concept of the system involves the following main functional components: universal drug dispenser, drug concentration funnel, medication information printer, heat sealing packaging mechanism and interactive interface. Through the reasonable spatial layout, each function is integrated into a desktop level compact equipment, and the user interface is provided by the mobile app. The core functions of the system are as follows (see Fig. 7 and Fig. 8).

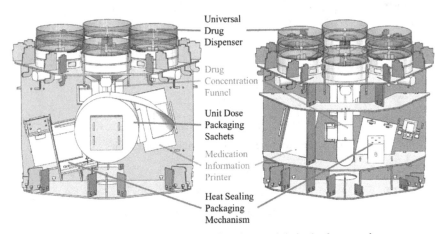

Fig. 7. The distribution of each function module in the framework.

Universal Drug Dispenser. The implementation principle of the universal drug dispenser is as follows: a spiral track and curved turntable are used to change the support and friction of the drugs in the process of rotation, so that the mixed drugs can be dispersed along the track, and then the separation of drugs is detected by the infrared photoelectric detection at the outlet, and the accurate separation of single drug is realized by the timely stop of the turntable. The types of solid oral drugs that can be separated include tablets, pills and capsules, and the design size of the dispenser covers most of the existing drug sizes. The medicine contacting part of the structure has only two parts:

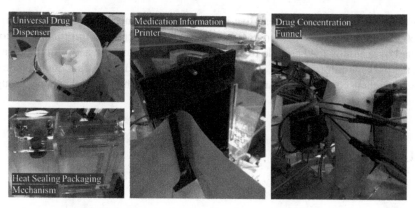

Fig. 8. Prototype implementation of core function modules.

track and turntable, which can be easily taken out and cleaned. There is a light under the turntable. When using, pour the medicine into the track from above according to the instructions of app and flashing light.

Drug Concentration Funnel. The drug concentration funnel is used to concentrate the dispensed drugs into the packaging sachets, as well as discharge the excess drugs from the equipment. Therefore, the drug concentration funnel is arranged in the middle of the equipment to connect the outlet of six drug dispensers and the packaging sachets. The funnel adopts the double outlets form, and a motor is used to control a baffle to switch the drug flow direction: vertically downward into the packaging sachets, or obliquely downward from the left side outlet of the equipment. There is another baffle controlled by the motor at the left side outlet of the equipment, which will be opened when there is excess medicine.

Medication Information Printer. Due to the removal of the information on the original package, the information of the drug contained in the unit dose package needs to be reprinted, and the patient information, medication time and other information need to be added to facilitate patients. Traditionally, ATDPS uses ribbon transfer printing, which is bulky and needs to be replaced frequently. In this design, a small thermal printer is used to print without replacing printing consumables, but a thermal coating is needed on one side of the continuous packaging sachets. The thermal printer communicates with the host computer through TTL serial port. During the operation, a section of packaging sachets would be printed with the information of a dose, and then transmitted to the bottom of the funnel to receive the dispensed drugs.

Heat Sealing Packaging Mechanism. When the dispensed drugs enter the packaging sachet, the sachet will be transported to the next stage. An inverted U-shaped electric heating frame driven by an electromagnet is pressed on the packaging sachet for heat sealing. There is also a serrated steel sheet on the frame, and the dotted line will be cut on the sachet to facilitate tearing off sachets. At the end of the mechanism is a driving wheel, which transports the continuous packaging bag to the right outlet of the equipment.

Interactive Interface. The interactive interface includes mobile app and device light effect. The mobile app is written based on Web. The prescription information is constructed by scanning the bar code to access the medicine database and form input, and then the package information of each unit dose is generated. Each function module of the equipment is controlled by Arduino, which interacts with the mobile phone through a Bluetooth module.

4   Usability Test

4.1   Performance Test

In this study, the performance of universal drug dispensing process and unit dose packaging process were tested.

First, three kinds of capsules, two kinds of oval tablets and two kinds of round tablets were randomly selected and divided into seven groups, 30 same pills in each group. Put each group into the drug dispenser, record the time and correct number, and calculate the average time and correct rate. The results show that the average time for each drug is 0.91 s (SD 1.26), except for the first drug (5.37 s in average, SD 3.55), which is mainly due to the uneven distribution of drugs on the track. The correct rate of round and oval drugs was 100%, and the correct rate of capsule drugs was 98.7%. The reason for the error was that the shells of the two capsules were locked in the process of moving side by side and fell together at the exit.

Two kinds of drugs were randomly selected and packaged according to the random prescription (one type of drug in a dose less than 4, continuous 21 doses). The experiment was repeated for three times. Record the production time, printing, sealing and cutting results of unit dose packaging. The results show that the average time of repackaging 21 doses is 103 s, the thermal printing occasionally appears incomplete, and the package sealing and cutting occasionally appear incomplete, which is due to the instability of the prototype system.

4.2   User Test in Lab

Five college students (3 males, 2 females, average age 21.4, SD 1.03) were invited to use the system in the laboratory, and the users were told how to use the system before the experiment. A same task is set for each user: using the system to dispense and package two types of drugs into the unit dose package, release and store the redundant drugs. After the experiment, we observed the results of the operation, recorded the operation time and problems, and then interviewed them (Fig. 9).

All participants successfully completed the task. They expressed that the process is easy to operate and the cognitive burden is low. Two participants believed that some drugs need to be stripped from the original packaging, which is inconvenient. They hoped to optimize this process. One participant expressed doubts about how to deal with the temporary change of prescription in the form of unit dose sachets.

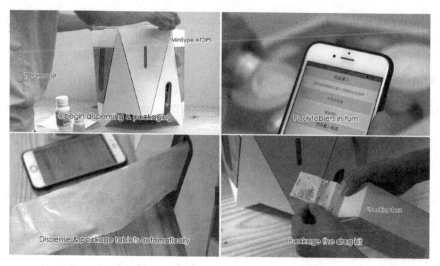

Fig. 9. Scenarios of users using the system.

5 Discussion

This paper focuses on the problem of taking multiple medicines at the same time. From the perspective of medicine packaging, this paper hope to provide unit dose package to simplify the patients' medication. Therefore, a compact Automated Tablet Dispensing & Packaging System (ATDPS) and service modes for community healthcare facilities (such as pharmacies, nursing homes and clinics) were designed. This design does not adapt the way of providing Internet services based on the existing dispensing equipment, but based on the widely distributed offline facilities to provide more direct and timely services for patients and customers. Therefore, a cost and function balanced equipment is essential to optimize the service process of these facilities.

Although the design of this paper has gone through a relatively complete stage of investigation, design, prototype production and testing, due to the limitation of technical ability and research time, the system is still relatively rough, and the long-term stability, medication safety and operability need further research. Moreover, the system has not been used and tested by professionals, and the economic value and business model of the solution also need to be evaluated. More detailed, the functional modules also need to be further improved. The universal drug dispenser needs to solve the problem of capsule locking and reduce the time wasted by uneven drug distribution. Printing and heat sealing packaging modules need higher stability. Whether the form of disposable continuous packaging sachets is suitable for long course prescription is also worth further discussion.

The original intention of the study is to simplify medication and help patients, especially the elder, in a way of community cooperation. It is hoped that a practical system and practical experiments in the community can be further researched. In the future, the system will also be combined with more internet medical services. Strengthening local processing capacity and broadening Internet channels are complementary to community medical services.

References

1. Donzé, J.D., et al.: International validity of the HOSPITAL score to predict 30-day potentially avoidable hospital readmissions. JAMA Intern. Med. **176**(4), 496–502 (2016)
2. World Health Organization. Decade of healthy ageing: Baseline report (2021)
3. Song, S., Lee, S.M., Jang, S., et al.: Mediation effects of medication information processing and adherence on association between health literacy and quality of life. BMC Health Serv. Res. **17**, 661 (2017)
4. Hersberger, K.E., Boeni, F., Arnet, I.: Dose-dispensing service as an intervention to improve adherence to polymedication. Expert Rev. Clin. Pharmacol. **6**(4), 413–421 (2013)
5. Conn, V.S., Ruppar, T.M., Chan, K.C., Dunbar-Jacob, J., Pepper, G.A., De Geest, S.: Packaging interventions to increase medication adherence: systematic review and meta-analysis. Curr. Med. Res. Opin. **31**(1), 145–160 (2015)
6. Tousignaut, D.R.: Joint Commission on Accreditation of Hospitals' 1977 standards for pharmaceutical services. Am. J. Hosp. Pharm. **34**(9), 943–950 (1977)
7. Spinks, J., Jackson, J., Kirkpatrick, C.M., Wheeler, A.J.: Disruptive innovation in community pharmacy–impact of automation on the pharmacist workforce. Res. Soc. Adm. Pharm. **13**(2), 394–397 (2017)
8. Sinnemäki, J., Sihvo, S., Isojärvi, J., et al.: Automated dose dispensing service for primary healthcare patients: a systematic review. Syst. Rev. **2**, 1 (2013)
9. Aldhwaihi, K., Schifano, F., Pezzolesi, C., Umaru, N.: A systematic review of the nature of dispensing errors in hospital pharmacies. Integr. Pharm. Res. Pract. **5**, 1 (2016)
10. Freato Gonçalves, A.M.R., Almeida Campos, M.S., Bernardes, A., Gabriel, C.S., Pereira, L.R.L.: Development and validation of an instrument to measure the professional's knowledge of dispensing medication (CDM-51) in community pharmacies. PLoS ONE **15**(3), e0229855 (2020)
11. Wiedyaningsih, C., Rahmawati, F., Lukitaningsih, E.: Consumer perception and experience regarding medicine packaging systems: a survey of medicine dispensing for outpatients. J. Generic Med. **16**(4), 153–160 (2020)
12. DISPILL Homepage. https://dispill-usa.com/, last accessed 2021/2/12
13. PillPack Homepage. https://www.pillpack.com/. Accessed 3 Feb 2021
14. HERO Health. homepagehttps://herohealth.com/. Accessed 12 Feb 2021
15. MedaCube Homepage. https://www.medacube.com/. Accessed 12 Feb 2021
16. JVM ATDPS NSP. https://www.myjvm.com/en/product/view.php?idx=7&ckattempt=1. Accessed 12 Feb 2021
17. J.H. V-21MT PRO. http://jh.pgo.tw/?id=1044#pgo. Accessed 12 Feb 2021
18. Holdford, D.A., Kennedy, D.T.: The service blueprint as a tool for designing innovative pharmaceutical services. J. Am. Pharm. Assoc. **39**(4), 545–552 (1999)

A Conceptual Design and Research of Automatic Blood Sampling Device

Ran Chen[1], Jing Luo[1(✉)], and Yan Luximon[2]

[1] School of Arts and Design, Shenzhen University, Shenzhen, Guangdong, China
luojng@szu.edu.cn
[2] School of Design, The Hong Kong Polytechnic University, Kowloon, Hong Kong SAR

Abstract. With the continuous development of science and technology, informatization has begun to blend into people's daily lives. In today's era, medical treatment has also begun to develop in the direction of digitalization and informatization. Blood sample collection is a common detection method in clinical treatment. At present, blood sample collection is still dominated by manual collection. Since the last century, there have been a number of researchers in the field of venous location and venipuncture, to assist medical personnel to carry out puncture or to achieve the purpose of robotic venipuncture. At this stage, robotic puncture is already technically possible. However, the current design of automatic blood collection device does not consider the user's psychological level and using the process, which is easy to bring psychological pressure to the user. Therefore, from product design point of view, this project designs an automatic blood sampling device with the consideration of ergonomics and user journey. The device can not only reduce the working pressure and training cost of medical staff, but also improve the user's experience.

Keywords: Ergonomics · Blood sampling · Automatic

1 Introduction

Blood routine test is a commonly used means of clinical detection, and its results have important reference value in the clinical diagnosis, treatment and prognosis evaluation of many diseases [1]. In current clinical practice, blood sample collection is a common basic operation in clinical nursing. Currently the blood sample collection method is still using the manual way. A tourniquet is usually attached to the patient to make the blood vessels stand out and allow for puncture. Artificial methods of finding blood vessels are visual recognition or touch of veins, which have a certain error rate. In a survey with a sample size of 2,861, 20.78% of nurses had been injured in the past year [2]. The occurrence of needle puncture injury greatly increases the risk of infection with blood-borne infectious diseases among caregivers. Especially during the 2019-nCoV, health care workers are prone to fatigue and drowsiness in high-risk, high-stress work environments. This not only affects their sense of control and accuracy in the work process [3], but also increases the probability of being scratched. With the continuous

© Springer Nature Switzerland AG 2021
Q. Gao and J. Zhou (Eds.): HCII 2021, LNCS 12787, pp. 223–233, 2021.
https://doi.org/10.1007/978-3-030-78111-8_15

development of information technology, intelligent medical treatment has a very broad prospect, which is of great significance to reduce the medical cost and relieve the pressure of medical staff [4].

With the continuous development of medical science and technology, a variety of venipuncture auxiliary methods have been invented. In the early days, researchers designed a skin patch based on the characteristic that the temperature of the body's veins is higher than the surrounding skin. The patch is attached to a material that displays different colors depending on the temperature. But the patch is very unstable, and it is easy to cause infection of the patient [5]. Later, some researchers proposed another method. Because red blood cells in the blood absorb part of visible light more efficiently, the veins would appear darker than the rest of the skin by shining bright light on the skin's surface. Using this principle, researchers have created a vene-locator called the Veinlite. However, it still has the disadvantage of stability, and for people with dark skin color, the error is large [6]. Similar to its principle, blood vessels have a higher absorption rate of infrared light than other human tissues, so the visualization of blood vessels can also be realized by proactively providing infrared light source projection. But the heat of high-power infrared light source is too large, so it is not suitable for widespread use [6]. Near-infrared venous projector is a combination of near-infrared imaging and image algorithm to project the computed venous image onto the skin surface. The formed vein image projection can help the auxiliary medical staff to identify the vein and play the role of auxiliary puncture [7]. A research team has designed a vein imaging device using a single-chip microcomputer to control a red-orange mixed light source. This device improves the clarity and accuracy of venous imaging. However, the device needs to be applied to the user's skin, which can cause a certain amount of pressure on the skin surface. This pressure can cause the veins to deform, which can interfere with the medical staff's ability to carry out the puncture [8]. Researchers have also proposed a vein imaging device based on optical imaging. The device mainly uses dual-color laser scanning method to carry out venous imaging, to detect and locate the patient's blood vessels. Its positioning is clear and accurate, but its realization method mainly benefits from the application of laser technology, so the cost is very high [9]. In addition to optical imaging, the use of ultrasonic technology for imaging devices has also been developed [10]. Sounds encounters different obstacles and produces different echoes. Ultrasonic echoes from blood vessels and other human tissues are also different. A handheld device called the Sonic Window (BK Ultrasound, Analogic, Inc) is based on this principle to image veins. The advantage of the device is that it can automatically adjust the sound wave intensity to different usage conditions to make the image clearer [11]. Intravenous imaging can also be achieved by combining photoacoustic imaging with optical imaging and acoustic imaging [12]. Kolkman RG et al. [13] have developed a set of photoacoustic imaging device for human forearm angiography. The device has unique advantages over pure optical or pure ultrasonic technology. However, the device is huge and expensive, so it is not suitable for normal venous imaging.

In the case of venipuncture robots, researchers have also made conceptual devices. Okuno et al. [14] first proposed a device for venipuncture through force feedback and tested it on rabbits' ears. Zivanovic et al. [15] proposed a device called BloodBot, which is more advanced than previous devices. The device mainly achieves puncture through force and position profile, but it has only one degree of freedom and the needle must be changed before each use. De Boer et al. [16] developed a six-degree-of-freedom automatic puncture device. The device first requires the clinician to manually place the device on the target position and then achieve puncture through ultrasound imaging and force induction. In the following study, Carvalho et al. [17] proposed a compact portable device called the PhleBot. It uses infrared monocular imaging to achieve venous imaging and force feedback to achieve puncture. Its imaging model is only linear, but in the actual venipuncture process, the form of human blood vessels is far more complex than a straight line.

There are also some researchers who have actually developed the design of venipuncture robot. For example, VeeBot uses industrial robotic arms and photoacoustic imaging technology to achieve venipuncture. Tests showed that the device found the right vein 83% of the time. But the device is large, and its shape is psychologically frightening [18]. In addition, Venouspro is also a system for automatic venipuncture. This system can not only improve the accuracy of puncture, reduce the diagnosis time, but also greatly reduce the responsibility of the medical staff [19]. In addition, a controlled trial on automatic venous blood collection and nurse venous blood collection was conducted jointly in Beijing Jishuitan Hospital and Beijing You' an Hospital affiliated to Capital Medical University. In the experiment, the success rate of automatic venous blood sampling robot was 94.44% (85 cases/90 cases), which was higher than that of nurses 82.22% (74 cases/90 cases) [20]. Under the existing technical conditions, a series of actions including blood vessel identification, precise positioning, automatic blood sampling, skin disinfection, arm banding and blood vessel pressing can be achieved by mechanical means. This makes it possible to replace manual blood sampling with automatic blood collection device at technical level.

Therefore, designing an automatic blood sampling device instead of manual blood sampling will not only help reduce the work pressure of medical staff, and decrease the training cost of health care workers, also benefit through improve the success rate of the blood to reduce waiting for inspection personnel due to factors such as nurse independent or involuntary vibration caused by the pain, optimize the use of quarantine personnel experience.

In the design process of medical devices, it has become a consensus to follow the design principle of human body as the center. On the one hand, it is necessary to ensure that the device fits the patient's body and will not cause secondary injury due to the use of the device. On the other hand, it is necessary to ensure the convenience of medical staffs in accessing, using and maintaining the equipment easily. In the design process of automatic blood sampling device, human factor engineering elements should be fully considered, and the safety and stability of the device should be guaranteed on the basis of guaranteeing the basic blood sampling function [21].

For the persons to be examined, the blood sample collection is the entire process from identity verification to collection and departure. If machine sampling is used instead of manual sampling, users may have fear due to the cold feeling and strangeness brought by machine. At the same time, if there is a lack of effective guidance in the whole process, it is easy for first-time users to make operational mistakes and panic. Therefore, in the design process of products related to medical devices, it is necessary to give full consideration to the user's psychology and relieve the user's tension through design.

On the basis of previous research, we designed an automatic blood sampling device based on human factors engineering and service system design. Based on the full understanding of human scale and user psychology, the design provides a more stable and convenient automatic collection method to improve user experience and collection efficiency. First of all, the methods of user research are observation and interview. The purpose of the research is to understand the user's behavior and psychology during the blood sample collection process. These methods can also identify human engineering issues that need to be addressed during the design process. And according to these design criteria, put forward the design scheme. This paper introduces in detail the application of human factor engineering principle in the design of automatic blood sample collection device.

2　User Research

User research includes two parts: (a) Observation: the designer mainly observes the behavior process of users in the current stage of manual blood collection, finds and summarizes the problems existing in the existing behavior process, and finds design insights based on it. (b) Interview: Through interviews with medical staff and patients, the design insights in part (a) are verified and more design concepts are explored.

2.1　Observation

The designer observed and recorded two complete blood sample collection processes participant A goes to the hospital for routine check-ups. Participant A completed a series of actions of payment, identity verification and receiving blood collection tube according to the prescription of blood routine check issued by the doctor, and then went to the blood sample collection window for collection. The first was the number, the personnel to be examined could choose to take the number through the automatic numbering machine, according to the number assigned to different windows for blood collection. The personnel to be tested could also choose to line up manually at the non-call window for blood sample collection. The second was the process of formal collection. The person to be examined extends his arm into the collection window, and the medical staff completes the whole process of arm binding, disinfection and blood sample collection. Finally, the medical staff will distribute cotton swabs to the testing staff, and the testing staff will press the injection point to stop bleeding. In this process, the designer found that the steps of blood sample collection by medical staff were relatively fixed, and the main operation process was the mechanical repetition process of the above process, which had the basic conditions for replacing manual labor with machine. Secondly, the height of the blood sample collection window is fixed and immutable, so it is not suitable for all people to collect blood samples.

Participant B is a special person who developed fever during the covid-19 and went to a fever clinic for taking a blood sample. During the covid-19, Chinese hospitals at all levels set up fever clinics for pre-testing and triaged all patients in accordance with the requirements of epidemic prevention and control, so as to eliminate the hidden danger of the spread of the epidemic. After participant B came to the fever clinic, blood samples were collected for nucleic acid testing according to the requirements of the clinic. The fever clinic had only one nurse, and needed to take care of both the information input of the waiting staff and the collection of blood samples. Even though there were only four persons waiting for examination when participant B arrived at the fever clinic, it still took more than half an hour for blood sample collection, which wasted a lot of time in the waiting process of participant B. In this process, the designer found that, at the present stage, there is still a shortage of medical staff, and the manual collection is not stable in time compared with the machine collection.

2.2 Interview

The designers interviewed the tested personnel and the medical staff respectively. Through interviews, users' views on manual blood sample collection and their expectations on automatic blood collection device, so as to facilitate further design and exploration. In the interview with the medical staff, the designer learned that the medical staff often cannot leave the test window for a long time and often work overtime because of the large number of waiting patients when collecting blood samples. For new medical staff, puncture failure caused by unskilled operation also causes tension between doctors and patients. Therefore, they hope to design an automatic blood collection device to reduce the work pressure of medical staff. Through the interview of the personnel to be inspected, it is found that they believe that intelligence is the inevitable trend of development. If the queue for manual detection is too long, they are willing to try automatic blood collection equipment for blood sample collection.

Through observation and interview, the designers drew user portraits and empathy maps of health care workers and prospective patients (Fig. 1) to analyze user behaviors and user psychology.

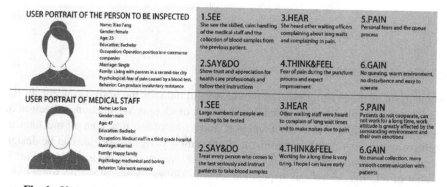

Fig. 1. User portraits and user empathy maps of prospective and healthcare personnel

The following are specific design problems that emerged from user research. First, they want the device to be easy to operate and clear with instructions that don't add extra learning costs. Secondly, the device should be adjustable to meet the requirements of the personnel in different ages and different physical conditions. Finally, the equipment can automatically collect the collected samples, and after each collection is completed, the equipment is closely sterilized.

3 Design Process

Through literature review and user research, we summarized the collection process of manual blood sample collection (Fig. 2).

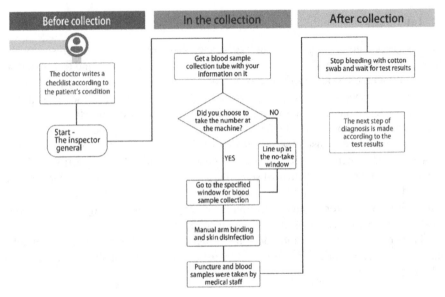

Fig. 2. Manual blood sample collection process

3.1 User Journey Map

The analysis of the existing process provides valid data for the design concept. In the analysis process, this research found that the work of identity verification, collection of test tubes, blood sample collection and post-collection of test tubes are all mechanical repetitive work. Therefore, an automatic blood sample collection device can be design to replace the manual operation. The optimized user journey mapping is shown in Fig. 3.

First of all, this device can inspect the identity authentication of the personnel and realize automatic arm tie. And it can automatically position and accurately pierce the needle into the blood vessel. Then, automatic disinfection can be completed after the collection of blood samples. At last, this product can automatically storage the blood samples after collection. Based on the above design requirements, the conceptual sketching is designed by brainstorm, as shown in Fig. 4.

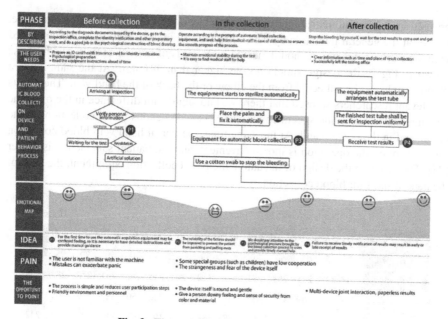

Fig. 3. The optimized user journey mapping

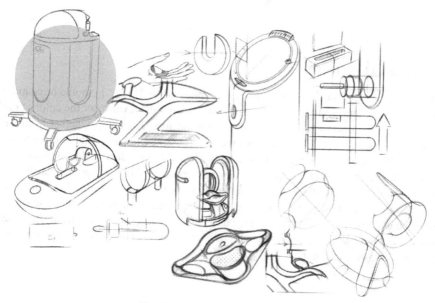

Fig. 4. The conceptual sketching

3.2 Human Body Data

Considering that the automatic blood collection device should have all functions of verification, detection and collection, and can meet the requirements of placing in the hospital space, the automatic blood collection device adopts the cabinet shaped structure. Based on the general human body data collected in Fig. 5 of Ref. [22] and combined with the working posture, it should meet the use needs of more than 95% of adults. As shown in Fig. 5, the design should not be higher than 591 mm. At the same time, a blood sample can be collected from the elbow or the back of the hand vein. The results of relevant researchers showed that there was no significant difference in the one-time puncture success rate and specimen pass rate between venous blood collections in the elbow and in the dorsal hand. At the same time, the dorsal hand vein blood collection time is shorter, the operation is more convenient, and the patient satisfaction is higher [23]. Therefore, in the design of the automatic blood collection equipment, the back of the hand is used for blood collection.

Units: mm

MEASURING PROJECT \ GROUPING PERCENTILE	Male (18 ~ 60 years old)							Female (18 ~ 55 years old)						
	1	5	10	50	90	95	99	1	5	10	50	90	95	99
SITTING CUBITS HIGH	214	228	235	263	291	298	312	201	215	223	251	277	284	299
ADD FULL HEIGHT TO YOUR CALVES	372	383	389	413	439	448	463	331	342	350	382	399	405	417
FOREARM LENGTH	206	216	220	237	253	258	268	185	193	198	213	229	234	242

Fig. 5. Body size (part)

3.3 Material Selection

The overall shape of the device is relatively complicated, and the style should be adapted to the environmental style of different hospitals. Neither the texture nor the color of the device can bring tension and oppression to the inspectors. Therefore, whether from the product processing technology or from the psychological fitness of the patient to be tested or from the point of view of the adaptability of the product to the environment, the overall shell material is suitable for the use of opaque plastic material. Translucent plastic material is used in the rear tube compartment, so that the medical staff can observe the remaining condition of the tube in real time and replace it in time. In the position of the arm band, take into consideration the band for frequent opening and closing, and the role of the band should be played to expose blood vessels. The final design prototype rendering is shown in Fig. 6.

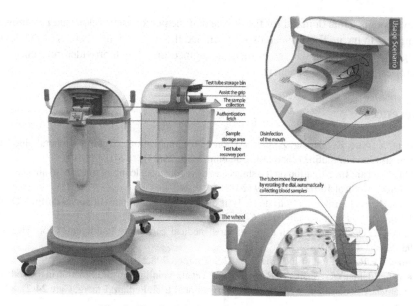

Fig. 6. The final design prototype renderings

4 Evaluation of Design

This design mainly put forward a conceptual model of automatic blood collection device to optimize the testing process of the personnel to be tested. Through the analysis of man-machine dimensions, it provides reference data for the design of the same type of products in the future. In the whole design, there are still the following deficiencies.

Firstly, there is no prototype test for the design, which is unpredictable for the problems that may be encountered in the actual use process.

Secondly, although the device has been designed to take into account the fear of the personnel to be examined because of the coldness and strangeness of the equipment itself, and the device has chosen a more rounded shape as far as possible, it cannot completely eliminate the strangeness of users to the design. In the subsequent design of related products, users' psychological factors should also be fully considered.

Finally, in the design process of products, there is the situation of neglecting one and losing the other. The automatic blood collection device adds a runner structure at the bottom for ease of movement, but the addition of this structure also introduces extra problems in the fixation of the product.

5 Conclusion

This study mainly focuses on the discussion of automatic blood collection device, with the purpose of replacing artificial blood sample collection with automatic blood collection device to improve the collection efficiency and reduce the risk of infection of blood-borne diseases caused by stab wounds of medical staff. According to the user survey, there is a real demand for the device and the person to be inspected has shown a willingness to try it. The project also determined the required dimensions of the device through the relevant knowledge of thermal engineering, which provided reference data for the design of similar products.

References

1. Ping, X., Xue, Z., Shuang, Z.: Observation on the application effect of peripheral blood and venous blood in routine blood test. Contemp. Med. **25**(24), 182–184 (2019)
2. Hui, L., et al.: Investigation on the status quo of venous needle injury in Chinese nurses. Chin. J. Infect. Control **16**(09), 816–819 (2017)
3. Lina, H., Jie, L.: Investigation and analysis of sleep and health status of nurses during COVID-19 epidemic. J. Changchun Univ. Chin. Med.
4. Shuo, T., et al.: Smart healthcare: making medical care more intelligent. Glob. Health J. **03**(03), 62–65 (2019)
5. Nosari, E.R.: Method of locating vein: U.S. Patent 3,998,210 (1976)
6. Katsogridakis, Y.L., Seshadri, R., Sullivan, C., et al.: Veinlite transillumination in the pediatric emergency department: a therapeutic interventional trial. Pediatr. Emerg. Care **24**(2), 83–88 (2008)
7. Steiner, J.W., Szmuk, P., Farrow-Gillespie, A., et al.: Skilled nurses are more successful when using standard techniques than the vein viewer for first attempt of intravenous cannulation in pediatric patients with difficult access. In: Anesthesiology 2011, Chicago, pp. 15–19 (2012)
8. Chengdong, L., Xiaoyong, H., Ma, Z.: Simple vein development instrument (2012)
9. Fan, Z., Xiangdong, L.: Subcutaneous vein display device based on dual-wavelength laser scanning (2010)
10. Brunette, W., Gerard, W., Hicks, M.A., et al.: Portable antenatal ultrasound platform for village midwives. In: Proceedings of the First ACM Symposium on Computing for Development, p. 23. ACM (2010)
11. Fuller, M.I., Owen, K., Blalock, T.N., Hossack, J.A., Walker, W.F.: Real time imaging with the sonic window: a pocket-sized, C-scan, medical ultrasound device. In: 2009 IEEE International Ultrasonics Symposium, pp. 196–199. IEEE (2009)
12. Xu, M., Wang, L.V.: Photoacoustic imaging in biomedicine. Rev. Sci. Instrum. **77**(4), 305–598 (2006)
13. Niederhauser, J.J., Jaeger, M., Frenz, M.: Real-time three-dimensional optoacoustic imaging using an acoustic lens system. Appl. Phys. Lett. **85**(5), 846–848 (2004)
14. Okuno, D., Togawa, T., Saito, H., et al.: Development of an automatic blood sampling system: control of the puncturing needle by measuring forces. In: Proceedings of the 20th Annual International Conference of the IEEE Engineering in Medicine and Biology Society, pp. 1811–1812 (2000)
15. Zivanovic, A., Davies, B.: The development of a haptic robot to take blood samples from the forearm. In: Niessen, W.J., Viergever, M.A. (eds.) MICCAI 2001. LNCS, vol. 2208, pp. 614–620. Springer, Heidelberg (2001). https://doi.org/10.1007/3-540-45468-3_74
16. De Boer, T., Steinbuch, M., Neerken, S., et al.: Laboratory study on needle–tissue interaction: towards the development of an instrument for automatic venipuncture. J. Mech. Med. Biol. **7**(03), 325–335 (2007)
17. Carvalho, P., Kesari, A., Weaver, S., et al.: Robotic assistive device for phlebotomy. In: ASME 2015 International Design Engineering Technical Conferences and Computers and Information in Engineering Conference. American Society of Mechanical Engineers (2015)

18. Perry, T.S.: Profile: veebot drawing blood faster and more safely than a human can. IEEE Spectr. **50**(8), 23 (2013)
19. Balter, M.L.: Robotic devices for automated venipuncture and diagnostic blood analysis. Rutgers The State University of New Jersey-New Brunswick (2017)
20. Zhigang, C., Ming, L., et al.: Clinical research of automatic venous sampling robot for automatic identification and location of blood vessels. Chin. J. Clin. Pharmacol. **36**(19), 3148–3150 (2020)
21. Qianwen, C.: Discussion on the application of ergonomics in medical device design. Sci. Technol. Innov. Her. **17**(15), 62–63 (2020)
22. Yulan, D.: Ergonomics. Beijing Institute of Technology, Beijing (2017)
23. Lili, Z.: Application of dorsal hand venous blood collection in group health examination. J. Community Med. **13**(06), 87–88 (2015)

Visualizing Wellness: The Myant Skiin System Connected Life App

Sara Diamond[1]([✉]), Ajaz Hussain[1], Renn Scott[2], Rittika Basu[1], Shunrong Cao[1], Manisha Laroia[1], and Veda Adnani[2]

[1] OCAD University, 100 McCaul Street, Toronto, ON M5T 1W1, Canada
sdiamond@ocadu.ca
[2] Myant Inc, 100 Ronson Drive, Etobicoke, ON M9W 1B6, Canada

Abstract. This paper presents a design study of the visualization interface to the Myant Skiin Connected Life App (Skiin), a family informatics application which will connect family members, friends, and caregivers, by engaging them together and enabling health and wellness related data sharing and support. It is based on Myant's highly accurate intelligent textiles garments which collect activity and related biomechanical data through knitted sensors on the garment. Our design seeks to deliver a seamless user experience between this complex of technologies through effective data presentation, visualization, and tool tips. One of Skiin's differentiators is the provision of a communication overlay (the Aura) which cues users to view metrics data and engage in dialogue around its meaning. We undertook a comprehensive literature review and examination of related work that included personal informatics, mHealth applications, and family informatics – motivation and social communication, wellness standards for older adults, technology adoption by older adults, effective design, and visualization strategies to support aging individuals, their family, friends, and support team, and issues of privacy. We used iterative prototyping to build and revise the visualization interface. We discuss our visualization methods, detail the resulting Skiin application, our usability testing strategy which combines personas, Talk Aloud and SUS approaches, research outcomes, and next steps.

Keywords: Data visualization · Visual analytics · Wearable technologies · Personal informatics · Family informatics · Seniors informatics · mHealth

1 Introduction

The Myant Skiin Connected Life App (Skiin) [1] is a family informatics application which will connect family members, friends, and caregivers, by engaging them together and enabling health and wellness related data sharing and support. Skiin differs from products such as Cocoon [2], the Alexa Care Hub [3], or the Medical Guardian smart watch app [4], or our previous Care and Condition Monitor [5] as it is based on Myant's highly accurate intelligent textiles garments which collect activity and related biomechanical data through knitted sensors on the garment. Data are transferred from the

© Springer Nature Switzerland AG 2021
Q. Gao and J. Zhou (Eds.): HCII 2021, LNCS 12787, pp. 234–250, 2021.
https://doi.org/10.1007/978-3-030-78111-8_16

garment pod to the mobile Skiin app via Bluetooth. Skiin began as a family informatics tool, intended to facilitate wellness initiatives and health monitoring for families, close friends, and caregivers. Myant has recently focused application development on senior engagement and care, recognizing the accelerating demand for seniors' health applications and older adults' isolation and need for health support that the COVID-19 pandemic has amplified.

Our design seeks to deliver a seamless user experience between this complex of technologies through effective data presentation, visualization, and tool tips. One of Skiin's differentiators is the provision of a communication overlay (the Aura) which cues users to view metrics data and engage in dialogue around its meaning. Data visualization is one of the core strategies that health and wellness applications use to allow individuals to manage, analyze and share their data, including for senior users, "For older adults, this has the potential of bridging the gap between the abstract collection of data and the tangible representation of integrated wellness" [6, pg. 923].

2 Related Work

2.1 Wellness and mHealth Applications, Family Informatics

The use of personal informatics technologies has grown significantly in the last decade. Rooksby et al. [7] describe the personal informatics context as, "lived informatics", and emphasize the ephemeral emotional qualities of personal data collection and sharing, including pleasure and sociality, enhanced self-esteem, and self-image. They recognize that people collect data across multiple platforms that need integration. Many studies indicate the difficulty in retaining users, requiring interface design to be engaging, easy to use, create reminders and prompts [8–11], and allow goal setting by the user [12]. Tools should connect users with support groups that provide "social sense-making", with "accountability partners" [13, pg. 6938] rather than an open social media platform which Epstein et al. [14] have shown can diffuse support and engagement. Bhargava and Nabi [15] demonstrate that analytics must provide "thorough and continuous analyses of past health status, present lifestyle, and long-term health goals of these users" [pg. 1355]. These strategies offered useful guidance for Skiin which enables users to curate their own support teams and offers varying temporalities of data slices. Family informatics are a variant of social fitness, wellness, and health applications. Research indicates that adherence, comfort and behaviours on platforms, whether health support or safety monitoring, are mediated by family dynamics and gender roles. In Colineau and Paris's [16] study mothers out-performed other family members in trying to reach and encourage collectively set goals. Technology adoption changes relationships, sometimes heightening a sense of security and shared responsibility, other times increasing, rather than alleviating anxiety and tension [17]. Healthy "biosemiotics" feedback and intimacy can be supplanted by tracking, [17, 18] and some individuals exercise control rather than closeness (for example over adult children). For these reasons Skiin allows custom sharing controls for each group and individual connection in order to respect the differences in relationships and different individual's desire for data sharing.

2.2   IT and Design for Older Users

Studies note the desire of seniors to be active agents who can give their best to the world [19]. Mendoza-Núñez et al. [20] stress the importance of independence and indicate that self-perception of well-being and health are critical to sustaining and improving health. A goal of Skiin is to empower older adults to play an active role in self-management of their health in order to sustain quality of life. Studies indicate that seniors' access to the Internet [21] and their adoption of mobile technologies, activity trackers, wellness, and safety monitoring in and outside seniors' homes is on the rise [21–23]. Etemad-Sajadi et al. [22] underscore the importance of perceived usefulness in seniors' willingness to accept a technology, linked to a sense of social presence for seniors, "that there is personal, sociable and sensitive human contact" [pg. 1165]. Seniors trade-off privacy concerns and utility of a technology – described as the "privacy calculus" by Schomakers and Ziefle [24, pg. 327]. Other studies indicate that seniors will trade privacy for effective support [6]. Users want to decide what, how, at what time, where, and to whom data is collected and transmitted. These dynamics are even more important given the impact of COVID-19 on seniors' health and enforced isolation.

Studies suggest that most mobile health (mHealth) applications (apps) do not take the needs and preferences of older adults into account. Documentation and user support are weak. Most smartphones have not been developed with seniors in mind. To address this challenge Morey et al. [25] provide usability design and visualization guidelines for mobile health apps for older users and suggest an approach where seniors can add levels of interactivity and complexity over time. A number of researchers emphasize the need for easy access to tool tips and troubleshooting and the lack of these in many mobile applications [26, pg. 371]. As with other demographics, seniors show a high level of initial adoption with a degradation of use over time if device interfaces are overly complex, or poorly designed and when the interpretive context of longitudinal data (for instance, whether the user is in decline) is unclear [27]. Skiin will eventually provide a chatbot with contextual information. Le et al.'s studies [6, 28, 29] establish that seniors find visualizations of value in assessing their cognitive, physiological, social, and spiritual well-being and to identify patterns where there was a change in health status. Seniors find the analysis only to be meaningful if connected to sources of information that help them to understand factors impacting change, to strategize interventions and hence they ask for annotations within the data. Le et al. observed, "Older adults were consistent in taking longer amounts of time to make assessments across both comparison and proportion tasks compared to the general population. However, this is offset by matching or even slightly better accuracy on the tasks" [28, pg. 55]. Visualizations are a viable means to support information sharing for seniors.

3   Methodology

3.1   Process Overview

We applied an iterative prototyping approach to building the interface, visualizations, and navigation strategy, developing and re-iterating components of each of the visualization sections and linking these using a user journey map [30]. We then undertook user testing and are now applying results to the revised user interface and visualization strategy; undertaking design and engineering sprints, with a future round of user testing focused on seniors.

3.2 Visualization Interface Design Approach

We drew from an ample data visualization vocabulary [31–33]. Of relevance were visualization methods applied to small data sets that are interpreted within a large-scale system that collects data from multiple individuals that it correlates and accrues over time [34]. Our goal was to guide users through a process of insight detection [35], - providing an overview, allowing adjustment and focus, supporting pattern detection, and then eliciting a mental model of their connections, activities, health data and locations. Fan [36] summarizes the challenge of visualization in a context where individuals are managing multiple types of personal information, "By changing the focus of visualizing personal data from visualizing in an engaging and optimized way, to also visualizing in the simplest and most relevant way, we can help users be more efficient, engaged, and enlightened in understanding their data" (pg. 4). This challenge is amplified by the need to manage and visualize complex data at both the granular and trend level, within the context of a small screen. Researchers have addressed this challenge. Noirhomme-Fraiture et al. [37] suggest the use of stacked bar charts, alternate bar charts and pixel bar charts. Summers et al. [38] provide the concept of semantic zooming where data visualizations are scaled up according to user navigation.

We used bar and line graphs to indicate the length and type of activity. and stacked graphs, such as our 'stacked, stacked' bar graph [39] to layer background analytics of comparative data with a graph that linked nodes. Graphs were accompanied by data tables when appropriate. We developed and tested a series of approaches to presenting group data, ensuring that individuals could compare their own state and status. Patient data represented in radial displays such as the work of Zhang et al. [40], provided a helpful example for representing complex data over time. We chose donut and circle graphs to compare individuals within a care group [41]. Lugmayr et al. [42] provide guidelines for simplifying health data without losing meaning. We considered and applied best practices in representing GIS data [43] creating maps that could show and compare individual activity pathways. These are particularly poignant when connections are undertaking planned activities together in different parts of the world or in lockdown sites at home or in care homes because of COVID-19.

4 Prototypes

Visualizations follow a user journey map (Fig. 1) which begins with individual log-on, moves to a personal Metrics page and then on to Connections which brings together all members of a support group.

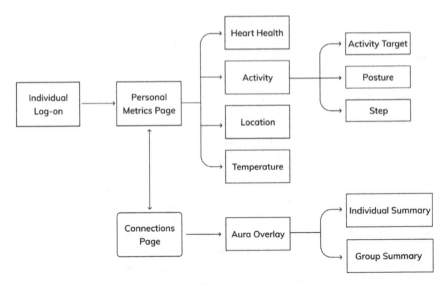

Fig. 1. Skiin user journey map

Users wear a Skiin biometric sensing garment in order to collect heart rate, location, activity, and body temperature data. They create a health profile, identity, and pair their Skiin Pod with the app, and then connect to their loved ones, friends, and caregivers, with whom they can share data and vice versa see the data that their connection decides to share with them. Through the Myant secure system individuals keep a log of symptoms, body temperature, medication, and mood. They can link to outside sites to access contextual data or use social networks to converse. Different views of the app provide the user's metrics, their diary, connections, and device management. The Metrics page offers their real time heart health, comparative resting heart rates, temperature, and activities (running, sitting, sleeping and other postures) measured in time and steps, and their location. The user can set activity and health goals and measure against these. They can access a location view and summary of where they have been for the day, week and month, and the types of activities there. The Connections functions of the app and the comparative visualizations encourage social connectedness, group activities and comparisons. A user can invite others to connect and form a group. Connections choose the kind of data that they will share (temperature, activity, location, heart rate). The app provides real time activity and summaries of each individual in the group's data and group summaries. Location data summaries show where group members are and where their activity is occurring.

Safety features including fall detection and geofencing were added in response to research suggesting that safety was a concern both for seniors and caregivers and should be an option in all products for seniors [44]. A senior or individual recovering from a health challenge can set a geofence with the expressed purpose of moving beyond this limit if they are feeling stronger. Geofencing is not automatic and seniors and other users can control who can set a geofence and turn sharing off and on at any time. A communication overlay or "Aura", indicates the continual status of each individual who is a Skiin user within the team. Skiin presents icons and associated actionable messages for trouble shooting to help users understand system level issues such as low battery, or lack of Bluetooth connection. See Figs. 2 and 3, first for individuals and then for group data.

Fig. 2. Sample visualizations: metrics data, active and resting heart rate, activity targets.

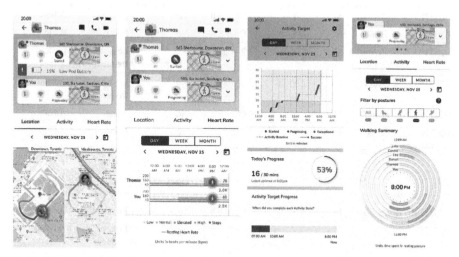

Fig. 3. Sample visualizations: aura overlay, steps one connection, activities (postures) and connections.

5   Usability/Usefulness Testing Process

Our goal was to obtain detailed feedback regarding the legibility and meaningfulness of each visualization and to assess their efficacy in the dual contexts of a family and seniors' wellness and collaborative care tracker and a mobile application that could effectively support senior care. We chose as diverse a sample as possible of usability test participants within three age demographics – seniors, children of seniors and adult grandchildren, providing a small, but rich sample of fourteen. The division into personas roughly matched the individuals' age. We recruited usability testers with the assistance of Myant, our industry partner from a large staff contingent and a volunteer group that has been recruited to test the garment interface and its application. Potential participants filled out the Skiin Pre-test Survey which provided demographic details: age, gender, technical capacity, perceived value in monitoring for health conditions (or not), and experience with health, sports, and wellness monitoring. We then chose as diverse a sample as possible within three age demographics – seniors, children of seniors and grandchildren, providing a small, but rich sample of fourteen. All personal data was anonymized and analyzed in relation to the user testing results (Table 1).

Table 1. Demographic overview of usability testers

Participant #	Age	Gender	Health condition	Device interaction	Use of health and Fitness app	Interaction with Health and Fitness app	Viz knowledge
202077P1	41–50	M	Y	Over 8 h	Yes	Frequent	Advance
202077P2	51–60	F	Y	Over 8 h	No	None	Basic
202077P3	Over 60	M	Y	2–4 h	Yes	Less frequent	Basic
202077P5	Over 60	F	Y	up to 1 h	No	Less frequent	Advance
202077P7	Over 60	M	Y	Over 8 h	No	None	Advance
202077P10	51–60	M	N	4–8 h	No	None	Advance
202077P13	Over 60	F	Y	4–8 h	Yes	Less frequent	Basic
202077P14	Over 60	F	Y	4–8 h	No	Less frequent	Advance
202077P15	26–30	M	N	Over 8 h	Yes	Frequent	Basic
202077P16	35–40	M	Y	Over 8 h	Yes	Less frequent	Advance
202077P18	21–25	F	Y	Over 8 h	Yes	Less frequent	Basic
202077P19	26–30	M	Y	Over 8 h	Yes	Less frequent	Basic
202077P20	35–40	M	Y	Over 8 h	Yes	Frequent	Advance
202077P21	26–30	M	Y	Over 8 h	Yes	Less frequent	Basic

We developed an experimental approach to user testing that used three methods. Participants were assigned goal-based, role-based personas [30, 45, 46] derived from Myant's prior market research, in order to elicit empathy and free the imagination of the participants. According to O'Leary et al. [47], "The power of the persona approach is due to the empathy which such well-designed characters can invoke in designers and other stakeholders in the design process" [pg. 2917]. The three personas from the family were a support-seeking active grandparent with a heart condition, adult child of grandparent, and young adult grandchild. We built specific interfaces for each persona around a unified scenario to understand the point of view and represent the behaviours of each persona.

We used a Talk Aloud, Think Aloud method [29, 48] in which the participants explored the visualizations, first with minimal guidance from the testing team in order to encourage "serendipitous" insights. Upon completion of a set of visualizations and related tasks, participants were asked to verbally rate their understanding of a task and quality of experience using a Likert scale. Video recording and transcription captured data of the task activities, and the Talk Aloud/Think Aloud commentary as testers engaged with each set of visualizations. Understanding that seniors may take longer to analyze visualizations [29] we did not time task performance as we were most interested in data exploration discoveries and commentary on the efficacy of the visualizations. We then applied the System Usability Scale [49] in an exit survey as it brings strength in analyzing learnability and usability and is able to manage small sample sizes. Participants undertook Talk Aloud, Think Aloud in their persona role and the SUS analysis outside of the personas according to their demographic data.

Participants accessed a web-browser simulation of the Skiin System Connected Life Test App through a link shared with them in an online Zoom session. They received an orientation to the product, the app and visualizations and were given a persona to role-play and a specific scenario that provided simulated data and visualizations for that persona, including their own data and group data of their family connections. For example, the Group Summary displays the primary user's data along with all the connections they have in a created group, hence a grandparent would see their data along with all members of their family who are using the app and are part of their 'family group'. The test app had four sections, the Metrics page, Aura Overlay, Individual Summary and Group Summary each corresponding to different data. In the scenario each lived in a different city and all were committed to increasing their own physical activity and supporting each other in doing so, while providing overall support to their grandparent. In the scenario the family had decided to undertake a walk although at different times and in different locations. The app indicated the activity, location, time, and related health data. Participants explored the interfaces, visualizations, identified theirs or others' data, located a shared walk activity and commented on both the usability of visualizations and the usefulness of components of the app to their persona.

6   Overall Findings, Conclusion, and Next Steps

6.1   Usability Outcomes

In alignment with our test process, we analyzed Talk Aloud and Likert scale task surveys by persona. We analyzed the SUS survey by overall response, gender, age, health and fitness app experience and interaction time with digital devices on a daily basis. Skiin met usefulness expectations as all users saw value in tracking their own data as well as viewing and acting upon the data within their connections. The majority of testers 85.7% (12 of 14) felt that they would use the application frequently. The two who disagreed were frequent fitness application users under forty who interact with electronics devices for more than eight hours a day.

Findings from the Scenarios and Likert Testing. The majority of users from each persona were able to locate their data in the application, understand the visualizations and relate symbols to the data types. All found that the sequence of information and navigation strategy was logical, although several suggested entering the app through the Connections page as social connection drives the application. The majority of participants in all personas found value in alerts regarding their or others' heart rate and that this data was provided in the context of activities. Users saw correlation of postures (standing, sitting, or walking activities) to wellness goals as useful. Posture (activity) summary circles in the Individual Summary that one could compare with a connected group member were a popular visualization. A participant lauded the tooltips which walked them through the Aura Overlay and some suggested these tooltips be implemented for other complex visualizations.

Under half, 42.8% (6 of 14) of participants found the icons were easy to understand, "Data is easy to understand and interpret. Icons are helpful." They appreciated the use of colour coding for icons in the Aura Overlay which indicated different ranges of the data, red for high, green for normal and blue for data not logged. A parent persona felt that icons would prompt their parents to charge their battery. Abstract icons were not always successful as 80% (12 of 14) across all personas found it difficult to understand the 'noisy signal' symbol for the wearable garment.

Not all users saw location mapping functions as useful as a record of their activities. Across all personas, some felt that maps could encourage group activity, yet many feared that geolocation would intrude into their privacy. A parent persona mentioned that their children would not be comfortable with a shared location feature if they were using the application together as a family. A grandchild participant remarked they would not want to reveal all of their locations to the other members of the family and especially not their parents. These findings align with Mancini et al. [17] records of families' discomfort with location tracking. In contradiction, individuals in the child and grandchild personas wished to monitor the grandparent's location although they did not want to share their own location data. Users in all categories wished to know what duration of presence was required for a location to be detected and how it would be shown on the maps. They also wanted an indication of how a senior family member (or the individual who was the focus of care) arrived at locations (walking, transit, driving). Privacy trade-offs in return for security [6] are evident in these comments.

We identified usability challenges. A small minority, 14.3% (2 of 14) of the participants agreed and 7.1% (1 of 14) of the participants strongly agreed that it was difficult to find data. 28.6% (4 of 14) of the participants disagreed that data was easy to understand. The overall view was that the Metrics pages were legible, but that Connections pages required simplification of data presentation and enhanced tooltips. Users of all personas identified challenges with Summary pages, with 42.9% (6 of 14) of the participants agreed and 7.1% (1 of 14) of the participants strongly agreed that the visualizations were difficult to decipher on this page. Participants across all personas found the weekly and monthly heart rate (HR) graphs difficult to decipher and understand, as the trend lines were hard to differentiate on the mobile screen view. Some users also asked for brighter colours, better colour differentiation and shading, echoing one of the grandparent personas who suggested, "The visuals are just too small. And there's not enough differentiation between the colors and I wish things were a little bit bigger. That said, it would be fairly easy to navigate, just making things clear."

Participants suggested providing more context for daily, weekly, and monthly heart health and for temperature, including trend lines rather than scatter plots. Some recommended simple pie-charts or bar-graphs instead of the circular visuals (used for Individual and Group summaries) and Kagi charts (used for the activity and postures data). Participants emphasized the value of showing an overall summary as a graph, followed by a tabular list of data and then a detailed explanation of the data, having a macro-view and a micro-view of data ensured there was one or the other visual that worked for each persona. The majority of users in each persona asked for a zoom lens function and for larger font size and image size. As one of the parent personas put it, "...zooming on the phone if this works because it's a touchscreen so one should be able to zoom on it so. You could consider the size of the graphics." Users felt that maps required enlarging and clear positioning of legends. Skiin is intended to be a communications tool with a seniors' focus more than an individual wellness application, hence addressing usability issues for the Connections and Group Summary pages will be of critical importance.

Participants suggested ways that the application could more effectively meet their support needs, and proposed building engaging social interaction around Connections pages, for example adding chat within a group challenge to motivate care groups to use the app to collaborate and share wellness goals. Three users from the grandparent persona on viewing their group connections' location and activity visualized in the Group Summary, exclaimed that they liked this feature where they could see everyone's status. This suggestion reinforces Etemad-Sajadi et al.'s [21] correlation of social presence and usefulness. Users wanted to personalize their graphical interface, select numerical charts versus graphs or more complex visualizations. Some wished to personalize their colours.

Individuals who assumed the child or grandchild persona expressed concern that their parent or grandparent would find the visualizations difficult to navigate. A number of younger users believed that the visualizations were too complex for senior users to deal with, indicating a bias about older adults and their understanding of technology. By contrast, a user in a grandparent persona felt confident reading the visual indications and prompts of each icon, "I didn't find any of them (the visualizations) difficult. I found they were pretty obvious, you know, heart rate, temperature. I like the running shoe icon size, the guys walking and the guy running it's like they were all guys working out."

SUS Survey Results. According to the SUS the majority of users found the various components of the application to be clear, and the data visualizations easy to use, not requiring previous visualization knowledge, or other prior knowledge, or professional support. Users with extensive fitness application experience felt that some functions of the application were redundant to applications that they already used, and that data was overly granular. A frequent user of health apps with advanced knowledge of visualizations commented, "just give me short insights and a summary, not this granular data which I have to then interpret." However, those that had little experience, including the seniors testing the application, were enthusiastic about the breadth of functions. The former would be better served by the ability to import their data from fitness apps to Skiin.

Female respondents gave more positive responses to the majority of survey questions than the male participants, although female users tended to express less confidence in their use of the application than males. Sixty-five percent of users whose interaction time with digital devices is over 8 h a day found the visualizations very cumbersome to use. In comparison, none of the users whose interaction time is less than eight hours with devices perceived the visualizations to be cumbersome. Our interpretation of this finding is that the overload of digital information in frequent users' lives could lead to exhaustion when deciphering the visualizations.

Older respondents enjoyed the application and found the visualizations learnable. We found grandparent personas who were also older participants by demographic analysis were engaged and positive about Skiin and able to navigate and interpret the visualizations as well as other participants. The charts below show that the majority of users who were over sixty strongly agreed that the visualizations were easy to use (60%), and none of them found this application cumbersome to use (Fig. 4, 5).

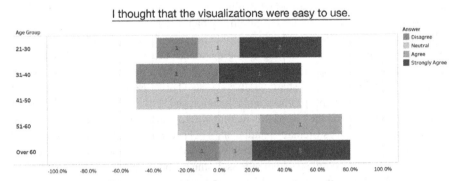

Fig. 4. Participant responses to the question: "I thought that the visualizations were easy to use."

The results showed that it was not as difficult for older participants to explore the complexity of visualizations as the younger participants presumed. Younger participants found the visualizations were harder to use than those who were older. Despite ranking Skiin as a valuable application that they would use, a significant minority of participants, including the senior users who enjoyed the app felt that the visualizations were not appropriate for seniors over 65 to use (40%). As this finding contradicts other answers,

I found the visualizations very cumbersome to use.

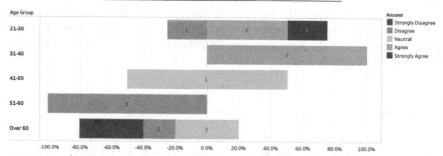

Fig. 5. Participant responses to the question: "I found the visualizations very cumbersome to use."

we infer that this finding is driven by usability issues that were discussed in detail in the Talk Aloud/Think Aloud process. According to the SUS survey, a majority of participants, including seniors, reported that the graphics were not the right size for them to see and understand (65%), and all SUS respondents requested larger graphics. This conforms to the Likert tables. We present the macro-overview of SUS responses below in Fig. 6.

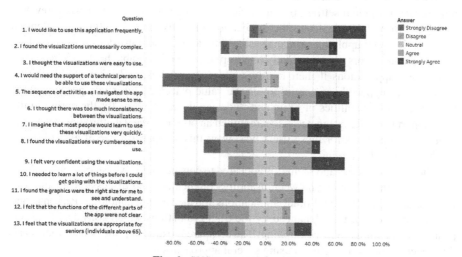

Fig. 6. SUS responses overview

Scenario, Likert Scale and SUS Summary. It is evident that most users validated the need for and value of Skiin, the data types collected and displayed and expressed relatability to the visualization of the data for their day-to-day experiences. Critical feedback focused on the details of the visualizations in sections where a large amount of data was being displayed. It was evident that having different visualizations summarizing the data with varying levels of details was helpful as eventually most users could understand the data but there was a learning curve. Users who observed the Metrics section with the individuals' data more carefully, were able to better relate to the Connections sections where the same data was compared with other people. Even for these users the Group Summary section with the more complex data visualizations was challenging due to information and cognitive load.

6.2 Conclusions

Users' response to our designs demonstrates the usefulness of a wearable technology visualization application that supports individual wellness and collaborative care for families and for seniors. Skiin's concept of a limited circle of curated connections is supported by research [13, 14]. As Rooksby et al. [7] note personal data comes from many different sources. In order for Skiin to engage all family members it will likely need to accept input data from users of other fitness and health informatics technologies. User testing supported the importance of social presence and connectivity in providing value to users. However, designs need to take privacy into account and adapt to different levels of user permissions, in relation to location data and medical data. For example, Skiin will need to support users who do not wish to share their location data but still wish to participate in group care. Enabling individual fitness regimes as well as family and group regimes, supported by diaries and information sharing may prove as valuable as group goal setting [16] Goal setting, prompts, challenges and support, and possible rewards may need to be integrated into the application more explicitly, replying to retention best practices and applying principles of gamification. The Talukder et al. study [50] indicated that seniors are more likely to accept the use of wearable health technologies and related applications if their family, colleagues, friends, and other members of a social circle support the use, reinforcing the value placed by our study participants in the connection capabilities of Skiin and to design the application for the entire family and support team. Redesign needs to strengthen an option to see data through trend lines over longer durations for those users who want this, supporting Lee et al.'s [27] and Pridham et al.'s [4] findings.

The use of personas and scenarios appeared to engage usability testers' imaginations and allowed them to move between usability commentary and discussions of the usefulness, improvements, and other applications for the Skiin technology. Personas and TalkAloud feedback were balanced by the SUS evaluations which considered participants' actual demographic positioning. The compared results provide consistencies and differences, suggesting value in using several approaches to usability testing.

6.3 Next Steps

Skiin was originally conceived as a family informatics tool and then pulled focus onto older adult users and their needs. Usability testing signaled means to design more effectively for this demographic. Visualization simplification and increased legibility were requested by all users. However, older adult test participants were some of the most engaged participants in the test, interested in the widest range of the application's capabilities. Hence, we need to pursue design simplification without compromising the app's analytics capabilities. We will apply researchers' suggestions [25, 26] that seniors require a simplified platform and the option to begin with basic tools and add levels of complexity with care, older adult users vary greatly in their capabilities. In fact, all users might want the ability to start with simple analysis, learn the app and then add more complexity. Tool tips will be an important factor in encouraging the adoption of the full range of capabilities.

We will refine the visualization strategy, fully applying Morey et al. [25] and Almao and Golpayegan's [26] principles of design for seniors, simplifying appropriate graphics elements and introducing zoom lens capabilities. We will explore interface personalization, strengthening the visibility of tool tips and social connectedness within the care circle and through a chatbot. Skiin is meant to encourage goal setting by individuals and groups and the current design sets the stage for future gamification and goal setting within the app. Improving design for senior users will address better human computer interaction and suite larger contexts of use for all users of Skiin.

Acknowledgements. This research is supported by the MITACS Accelerate program, Myant, OCAD University's Visual Analytics Lab, and the Canada Foundation for Innovation.

References

1. https://myant.ca/. (2020)
2. Cocoon - A private app for the most important people in your life (2020). https://www.pro ducthunt.com/posts/cocoon-6
3. Alexa Care Hub (2020). https://www.amazon.com/Alexa-Care-Hub/b?ie=UTF8&node=213 90531011
4. Freedom Guardian (2020). https://www.medicalguardian.com/medical-alert-systems/smart-watch-alert-app
5. Hudson, P., Anne, S., Steve, S., Diamond, S., Bhuvaneswari, A.: Fostering insight and collaboration in long-term healthcare through the collection and visualization of qualitative healthcare data. In: Mobile HCI 2014, Toronto, Ontario (2014)
6. Le, T.D., Chi, N.-C., Chaudhuri, S., Thompson, H.J., Demiris, G.: Understanding older adult use of data visualizations as a resource for maintaining health and wellness. J. Appl. Gerontol. **37**(7), 922–939 (2018)
7. Rooksby, J., Rost, M., Morrison, A., Chalmers, M.: Personal tracking as lived informatics. In: CHI 2014, One of a CHInd, Toronto, CHI 2014 (2014)
8. Duan, H., et al.: Using goal-directed design to create a mobile health app to improve patient compliance with hypertension self-management: development and deployment. JMIR Mhealth Uhealth **8**(2), e14466 (2020)
9. Cheng, V.W.S., Davenport, T., Johnson, D., Vella, K., Hickie, I.B.: Gamification in apps and technologies for improving mental health and well-being: systematic review. JMIR Mental Health **6**(6), e13717 (2019)
10. Druce, K.L., Dixon, W.G., McBeth, J.: Maximizing engagement in mobile health studies lessons learned and future directions. Rheum. Dis. Clin. N. Am. **45**, 159–172 (2019)
11. Johnson, D., Deterding, S., Kuhn, K.-A., Staneva, A., Stoyanov, S., Hides, L.: Gamification for health and wellbeing: a systematic review of the literature. Internet Interv. **6**, 89–106 (2016)

12. Munson, S.A., Consolvo, S.: Exploring goal-setting, rewards, self-monitoring, and sharing to motivate physical activity. In: 6th International Conference on Pervasive Computing Technologies for Healthcare (Pervasive Health) and Workshops, San Diego, pp. 25–32 (2012)

13. Puussaar, A., Wright, P.C., Clear, A.K.: Enhancing personal informatics through social sensemaking. In: CHI 2017, Denver. ACM (2017). ISBN: 978-1-45-034655-9

14. Epstein, D.A., Jacobson, B.H., Bales, E., McDonald, D.W., Munson, S.A.: From "nobody cares" to "way to go!": a design framework for social sharing in personal informatics. In: CSCW 2014, Vancouver (2015)

15. Bhargava, Y., Nabi, J.: The opportunities, challenges and obligations of Fitness Data Analytics. Procedia Comput. Sci. **167**, 1354–1362 (2020)

16. Colineau, N., Paris, C.: Family vs. individual profiles in a health portal: strengths and weaknesses. In: Proceedings of HCI 2011, The 25th BCS Conference on Human Computer Interaction (HCI) (2011)

17. Wang, J., O'Kane, A.A., Newhouse, N., Sethu-Jones, G.R., de Barbaro, K.: Quantified baby: parenting and the use of a baby wearable in the wild. In: PACM HCI, CSCW, vol. 1, p. 19 (2017). Article 108

18. Mancini, C., et al.: In the best families: tracking and relationships. In: CHI 2011, Vancouver, pp. 2419–2428. ACM (2011). ISBN: 978-1-45-030267-8

19. Holm, A.L., Severinsson, E.: A qualitative systematic review of older persons' perceptions of health, ill health, and their community health care needs. In: Nursing Research and Practice, p. 12 (2013). Article ID 672702

20. Mendoza-Núñez, V., et al.: Influence of the self-perception of old age on the effect of a healthy aging program. J. Clin. Med. **7**, 1–11 (2018)

21. Davidson, J., Schimille, C.: Evolving internet use among Canadian seniors. In: Social Analysis and Modeling Division, Statistics Canada, Analytic Studies Branch Research Paper Series, Ottawa (2019). 11F0019M No. 4272019015. ISSN: 1205-9153 ISBN: 978-0-66-031538-6

22. Etemad-Sajadi, R., Dos Santos, G.: Senior citizens' acceptance of connected health technologies in their homes. In: International Journal of HealthCare Quality Assurance, vol. 32, no. 8, pp. 1162–1174© Emerald Publishing Limited 0952–6862 (2019). https://doi.org/10.1108/IJHCQA-10-2018-02

23. Srugo, S.A., Jiang, Y., de Groh, M.: Living arrangements and health status of seniors in the 2018 Canadian community health survey. In: Health Promotion and Chronic Disease Prevention in Canada, vol. 40, no. 1. Public Health Agency of Canada, Ottawa (2018)

24. Schomakers, E.-M., Ziefle, M.: Privacy concerns and the acceptance of technologies for aging in place. In: Zhou, J., Salvendy, G. (eds.) HCII 2019. LNCS, vol. 11592, pp. 313–331. Springer, Cham (2019). https://doi.org/10.1007/978-3-030-22012-9_23

25. Morey, S.A., Stuck, R.E., Chong, A.W., Barg-Walkow, L.H., Mitzner, T.L., Rogers, W.A.: Mobile health apps: improving usability for older adult users. Ergon. Design **27**(4), 4–13 (2019)

26. Almao, E.C., Golpayegani, F.: Are mobile apps usable and accessible for senior citizens in smart cities? In: Zhou, J., Salvendy, G. (eds.) HCII 2019. LNCS, vol. 11592, pp. 357–375. Springer, Cham (2019). https://doi.org/10.1007/978-3-030-22012-9_26

27. Lee, B.C., Ajisafe, T.D., Vo, T.V.T., Xie, J.: Understanding long-term adoption and usability of wearable activity trackers among active older adults. In: Zhou, J., Salvendy, G. (eds.) HCII 2019. LNCS, vol. 11592, pp. 238–249. Springer, Cham (2019). https://doi.org/10.1007/978-3-030-22012-9_18

28. Le, T.D., Aragon, C., Thompson, H.J., Demiris, G.: Elementary Graphical Perception for Older Adults: A Comparison with the General Population in a Dissertation submitted in partial fulfillment of the requirements for the degree of Doctor of Philosophy University of Washington (2014)

29. Le, T.D.: Design and Evaluation of Health Visualizations for Older Adults, in a Dissertation submitted in partial fulfillment of the requirements for the degree of Doctor of Philosophy University of Washington (2014)
30. Nielsen, L.: Personas. In: Soegaard, M., Dam, R.F. (eds.) The Encyclopedia of Human-Computer Interaction, 2nd edn. The Interaction Design Foundation, Aarhus (2013). https://www.interaction-design.org/encyclopedia/personas.html
31. Meirelles, I.: Design for Information: An Introduction to the Histories, Theories, and Best Practices Behind Effective Information Visualizations. Rockport Publishers, Beverly Hills (2013)
32. Munzner, T.: Visualization Analysis and Design. A K Peters Visualization Series CRC Press, Boca Raton (2014)
33. Fekete, J.: The infovis toolkit. In: IEEE Symposium on Information Visualization, INFOVIS 2004, pp. 167–174 (2004)
34. Tulp, J.W.: Designing for small and large datasets. In: New Challenges for Data Design, pp. 377–390 (2014)
35. Yi, J.S., Kang, Y., Stasko, J.T., Jacko, J.A.: Understanding and Characterizing Insights: How Do People Gain Insights Using Information Visualization? BELIV 2008, Florence (2008)
36. Fan, C.: The future of data visualization in personal informatics tools. In: Personal Informatics in the Wild: Hacking Habits for Health & Happiness CHI 2013 Workshops. CHI 2013, Paris. ACM (2013). ISBN: 978-1
37. Noirhomme-Fraiture, M., Randolet, F., Chittaro, L., Custinne, G.: Data Visualizations on small and very small screens (2004). https://www.researchgate.net/publication/228872186_Data_visualizations_on_small_and_very_small_screens/citations
38. Summers, K.L., Goldsmith, T.E., Kubica, S., Caudell, T.: An experimental evaluation of continuous semantic zooming in program visualization. In: IEEE Symposium on Information Visualization, Seattle (2003)
39. Szigeti, S., Patrasc, J., Schnitman, D., Diamond, S.: Stacked-stacked bar graph: a new twist on an old visualization. In: InfoVis Conference Proceedings Sara. IEEE (2014)
40. Zhang, Z., et al.: The Five W's for information visualization with application to healthcare informatics. IEEE Trans. Vis. Comput. Graph. **19**, 1895 (2013)
41. Tapia, A., Beltrán, J., Caro, V.K.: Designing visualization tools to support older adults care process. In: ENC 2016: Mexican International Conference on Computer Science, Chihuahua, p. 4. ACM, New York (2016)
42. Lugmayr, A., Greenfeld, A., Zhang, D.J.: Selected advanced data visualizations: "The UX-Machine", cultural visualisation, cognitive big data, and communication of health and wellness data. In: 2017 International World Wide Web Conference Committee (IW3C2), WWW 2017 Companion, Perth. ACM (2017). ISBN: 978-1-45-034914-7
43. Gordon, M.A., Diamond, S., Zheng, M., Carnevale, M.: Compara. In: Encounters in Theory and History of Education, vol. 19. Digital Methods and Media (2018). https://ojs.library.queensu.ca/index.php/encounters/article/view/11867
44. Jiang, R., Zhang, Z., Xi, X.: A study of the needs and attitudes of elderly people and their caregivers with regards to assistive technologies. In: Zhou, J., Salvendy, G. (eds.) HCII 2019. LNCS, vol. 11592, pp. 200–211. Springer, Cham (2019). https://doi.org/10.1007/978-3-030-22012-9_15
45. Nielsen, L.: Personas - User Focused Design. Springer, New York (2012). https://doi.org/10.1007/978-1-4471-4084-9
46. Nielsen, L.: From user to character.an investigation into user-descriptions in scenarios. In: Proceedings DIS 2002 (2002)
47. O'Leary, C., Mtenzi, F., McAvinia, C.: Towards reusable personas for everyday design. In: CHI 2016, Extended Abstracts, San Jose. ACM (2016). ISBN: 978-1-45-034082-3

48. Saraiya, P., North, C., Duca, K.: An insight--based methodology for evaluating bioinformatics visualizations. IEEE Trans. Vis. Comput. Graph. **11**(4), 443–456 (2005)
49. Brooke, J.: SUS: a retrospective. J. Usability Stud. **8**(2), 29–40 (2013)
50. Talukder, M.S., Sorwar, G., Bao, Y., Ahmed, J.U., Palash, M.A.S.: Predicting antecedents of wearable healthcare technology acceptance by elderly: a combined SEM-Neural Network approach. Technol. Forecast. Soc. Chang. **150**, 119793 (2020)

Cognitive, Mental and Social Benefits of Online Non-native Language Programs for Healthy Older People

Blanka Klimova[✉]

University of Hradec Kralove, Rokitanskeho 62, 500 03 Hradec Kralove, Czech Republic
blanka.klimova@uhk.cz

Abstract. The older population groups are on their rise nowadays. In particular, the population aged 65 and over is growing faster than all other age groups. The purpose of this review is to investigate if there are any cognitive, mental and social benefits of online non-native language programs for healthy older people, which they may exploit in this COVID-19 pandemic. The methodology of this review was based on a literature search of peer-reviewed English written research articles found in Pub Med, Web of Science and Scopus. The findings of this review reveal that the research on the cognitive, mental and social benefits of online non-native language programs for healthy older individuals are rare. The results of this review indicate that the online non-native language programs may bring a lot of benefits for healthy elderly, especially as far as the enhancement of their cognitive (i.e. working memory) and mental (i.e. reduced depression) functions, are concerned. In fact, the stimulation of social and psychological wellbeing benefits of non-native language learning may consequently also generate multilingual cognitive gains in healthy older generation.

Keywords: Elderly · Cognitive skills · Mental functions · Social functions · Benefits · Online programs · Non-native language

1 Introduction

Currently, there is an increase in the number of aging population groups. Globally, the population aged 65 and over is growing faster than all other age groups [1]. The statistical data [2] indicate that in 1990, there were about 0.5 billion of older people at age of 60+ years living worldwide, while in 2100, the number of older populations should reach 3.1. billion (Fig. 1 below).

This presents many challenges to society, such as increased demands on healthcare systems, social security, or pension schemes. Generally, this ageing trend represents a significant economic and social burden for the entire society [3]. Aging also brings serious changes to an individual, such as deterioration of his/her physical, mental and cognitive abilities [4]. Aging also brings serious changes to an individual, such as deterioration of his/her physical, mental and cognitive abilities [4]. The most significant changes are declines in cognitive abilities which demand fast processing of information

Q. Gao and J. Zhou (Eds.): HCII 2021, LNCS 12787, pp. 251–259, 2021.
https://doi.org/10.1007/978-3-030-78111-8_17

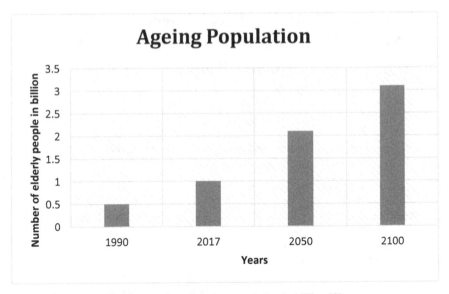

Fig. 1. Number of ageing population in billion [2].

or to making quick decisions [5]. Such changes are part of the normal aging process. More serious difficulties with memory, language, thinking or judgment may signify an age-related cognitive disorder, such as dementia [6].

Research findings have revealed that non-pharmacological strategies seem to contribute to the delay of the onset of age-related diseases, such as dementia [7–9]. In this sense, clear evidence has been confirmed by studies on physical activities [10–12], cognitive training [13, 14], and healthy diet [15, 16]. However, most recently, other non-pharmacological strategies have been employed. These include, for example, non-native language learning [17–19] or computerized cognitive training [20, 21], which might help enhance cognitive performance of older people.

Nevertheless, research findings [22–24] show that besides the cognitive benefits, there are also the non-cognitive benefits of these non-pharmacological strategies, such as improved mental and social health, i.e. thanks to these activities, older people tend to be less depressed and isolated. This then leads to their overall improved wellbeing,

In this COVID-19 era, older people's wellbeing is severely affected, especially their mental health [25]. Elderly people are being socially disconnected and isolated. As research [26–28] reveals, using the Internet may be beneficial for decreasing loneliness and increasing social contact among older adults. Therefore, online learning, in this case of non-native language, might serve as one of the preventive strategies in the COVID-19 pandemic. In fact, most of the elderly people at the age between 60 and 74 years nowadays possess relatively sufficient computer skills. They use computers for communicating with their relatives and friends, making appointments with a doctor, doing shopping, developing leisure and entertainment opportunities, or life-long learning habits [29, 30]. Moreover, they are willing to learn about computers and acquire new skills despite a general belief that the learning process is complicated or inaccessible. On the contrary, they think that they can learn so long as they remain healthy and have adequate levels of cognitive function [31].

The purpose of this review is to investigate if there are any cognitive, mental and social benefits of online non-native language programs for healthy older people, which they may exploit in this COVID-19 pandemic.

2   Methods

The methodology of this review was based on a literature search of peer-reviewed English written research articles found in Pub Med, Web of Science and Scopus. The articles were searched for the following keywords: second language learning AND elderly, second language learning AND elderly AND technologies, technologies AND older people AND foreign language learning, technologies AND elderly AND foreign language learning, online language courses AND elderly, online language courses AND older people, computer-based language programs AND elderly. The studies included healthy older individuals at the age of 55+ yrs who study/studied a non-native language using an online foreign language program. The search was not limited by any time period.

The author also performed a backward search, i.e., she searched the references of the detected studies for relevant research studies, which could be missed during her research. In addition, a Google search was conducted in order to detect the unpublished (gray) literature.

3   Findings and Discussion

Generally, empirical studies on this research topic are very rare. The author detected only seven studies. Those were three US studies [32–34]; a Canadian study [35]; a Dutch pilot study [36]; a French pilot study [37]; and a Chinese study [38]. The main topic was learning a foreign language, especially retention, by older healthy individuals and the use of technologies. In three cases, older adults were learning Latin, in two cases English and Spanish. The studies used standardized outcome measures, i.e., standardized tests for measuring cognitive functions, questionnaires, post-intervention, semi-directive interviews, or a content/theme analysis. However, methodologies of these studies significantly differ.

Cox [32] conducted a semi-randomized study with 43 monolingual (English) and bilingual (English/Spanish) seniors at the age of 60+ yrs to investigate learning basic Latin morphosyntax via computer. Half of the group received explicit grammar instruction prior to computer practice and the other half underwent only the computer practice. The participants were tested for multiple language skills, i.e. interpretation (written and aural), grammaticality of judgment and written production. Altogether they had three computer sessions with four pre-tests, four post-tests and four delayed tests. The findings of this study support the theory of lifelong bilingual advantage in the delay of cognitive decline. The results namely showed that bilinguals benefited from explicit instruction when transferring skills, and they also had better scores on interpretation regardless of instruction in comparison with the monolingual seniors. Otherwise, there were no other differences in learning. This study extends the findings of previous two studies [33, 34] on the acquisition of Latin morphosyntax with or without explicit feedback. These two studies were comparing learning outcomes of both older and younger adults and they found out that learning was not significantly different and older people did achieve the same learning outcomes as the younger adults. However, in comparison with the young people, older adults benefited more from less explicit feedback and would have appreciated more time for this feedback.

Marcotte and Ansaldo [35] explored the neural basis of second-language learning, particularly vocabulary retention, as a function of age, between younger (approx. 22 yrs old) and older people (approx. 70 yrs old) during a 5-day computer-based Spanish word learning program and subsequent training until they achieved 100% accuracy on the program. Their findings revealed that older people had relied more on episodic memory circuits (i.e. reflected in a larger retention of cognate words) and visual learning, while younger ones on control processing areas. There were no differences in learning gains, however, older people required more time to attain this accuracy on tasks.

Ware et al. [37] developed a technology-based English training program for 14 older French adults. The program was based on the assumptions provided by [39]. These assumptions involved various factors, such as that computer-based language training can be administered anywhere and at any time to suit learner's needs, the content can be adjusted and items can be repeated. In addition, learners can socialize. The average age of the participants was 75 yrs. The course lasted for four months and consisted of 16 two-hour sessions during which they used tablets. The participants found the program feasible, stimulating, and enjoyable, although some of them had difficulties with English. However, no gains on cognitive and mental performance was detected. Despite this, the authors believe that FLL can be a good therapeutic intervention. Nevertheless, the results also showed the need for computer training and the importance of social ties, which participants would appreciate.

Wong et al. [38] in their prospective randomized controlled study worked with 153 healthy seniors between the ages of 60 and 85 yrs from Hong Kong. The subjects were divided into three groups: 1. foreign language group, in which they learned basic English (experimental group); 2. games, in which subjects played cognitively stimulating activities, for example, puzzles (active control group); and 3. music appreciation group, in which subjects watched traditional and contemporary Chinese music videos (passive control group). All these intervention trainings lasted up to five hours per week for six months. In the experimental group, subjects used a computer-based language training software called Rosetta Stone [40], which helps learners speak English in conversations with bite-sized lessons that focus on delivering spoken words alongside visual and audio cues (Fig. 2 and 3 below). The findings of this study reveal that computer-based foreign language learning and games, but not music appreciation, improved overall cognitive abilities that were maintained at 3 months after training. In addition, FLL had a positive impact on the enhancement of working memory.

The improvement of working memory was also true for the participants of van den Berg's study [35]. She conducted an experiment on improving cognition through FLL in seven Dutch older adults at the age between 64 and 78 yrs who participated in a 10-day (one-hour lesson per day) online Spanish course. Van den Berg [36] also used Rosetta Stone software described above for FLL. Although the participants boosted their working

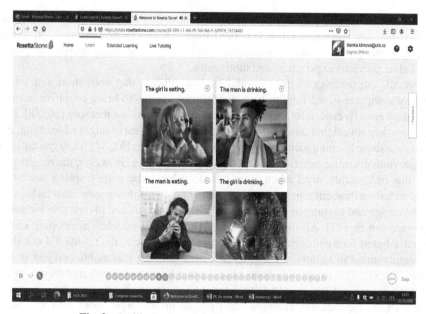

Fig. 2. An illustration of the Rosetta Stone program [40].

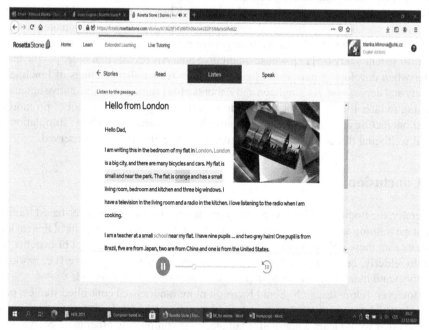

Fig. 3. An illustration of the Rosetta Stone program [40].

memory, they did not improve their attentional control and wellbeing. Additionally, she reported that her participants had benefited from visual-semantic information during learning, better preserved attention, memory, auditory processing, established linguistic knowledge, previous experience, and motivation.

Overall, the findings of the explored studies indicate that both short and longer intensive computer-based foreign language learning seems to bring cognitive benefits for healthy elderly, especially the enhancement of their working memory [36, 38]. Furthermore, they reveal that older individuals, particularly in early stages of learning, can achieve the same learning gains as their younger counterparts [33, 34]. They can build on their previous learning experience and linguistic knowledge. However, the results also show that older adults need much more time to achieve the same learning outcomes, would welcome frequent repetition and also more time on solving individual tasks; simply, the design and running of the whole course should be tailored to their specific needs as pointed out by [41]. All these aspects must be considered when developing such a computer-based foreign language program [35]. Nevertheless, the results did not show any improvement in seniors' wellbeing. In fact, wellbeing was mentioned just in two studies [36, 37]. This might have been caused either by a short duration of these courses or by a computerized aspect of FLL, which does not provide much space for socializing when learning individually, although older people might forget about their loneliness for the period of their studies and get involved by craving new knowledge. However, as Formosa [42] states, maintaining cognitive skills and expanding social contacts are the most common reasons for attending such a course. Klimova and Pikhart [43] emphasize particularly social and psychological wellbeing benefits of non-native language learning, which may consequently also generate cognitive gains. This has been also confirmed by the most recent study by [17], whose qualitative analysis reveals that older people learn better when developing new social ties, which can reduce their feelings of loneliness, anxiety and depression. As Singleton and Zaborska [44] summarize, non-native language learning in later life should not be considered only as a goal but as a tool of promoting social interaction and integration and because it is also partly through the stimulation of social wellbeing through which multilingual cognitive effects can be observed.

4 Conclusion

Generally, the findings of this review study reveal that the use of computer-based foreign language training among older people is not common. However, the results of this review indicate that these online non/native language programs may bring a lot of benefits for healthy elderly, especially as far as the enhancement of their cognitive (i.e. working memory) and mental (i.e. reduced depression) functions, are concerned.

However, future research should focus on more randomized controlled studies, particularly on those in which one group would be trained only in non-native language and the other would learn a non/native language via computer in order to detect whether there are any differences in effect sizes, as well as identify differences in wellbeing gains among both groups. In addition, besides providing an adequate training for elderly population, it would be desirable to offer them also a possibility of mutual communication and networking within these online non-native language programs.

Acknowledgements. This study is supported by the SPEV project 2021, run at the Faculty of Informatics and Management, University of Hradec Kralove, Czech Republic. The author thanks Lukas Sanda for his help with the data collection.

References

1. United Nations. Ageing. 2019. https://www.un.org/en/sections/issues-depth/ageing/. Accessed 22 Dec 2020
2. Ageing Population. https://www.un.org/development/desa/publications/graphic/wpp2017-ageing-population. Accessed 22 Dec 2020
3. Klimova, B., Maresova, P., Kuca, K.: Non-pharmacological approaches to the prevention and treatment of Alzheimer's disease with respect to the rising treatment costs. Curr. Alzheimer Res. **13**(11), 1249–1258 (2016)
4. Charles, S., Carstensen, L.L.: Social and emotional aging. Ann. Rev. Psychol. **61**, 383–409 (2010)
5. Murman, D.L.: The impact of age on cognition. Semin. Hear **36**(3), 111–121 (2015)
6. Klimova, B., Maresova, P.: Computer-based training programs for older people with mild cognitive Impairment and/or dementia. Front. Hum. Neurosci. **11**, 262 (2017)
7. Klimova, B., Kuca, K.: Alzheimer's disease: potential preventive, non-invasive, intervention strategies in lowering the risk of cognitive decline – a review study. JAB **13**(4), 257–261 (2015)
8. Li, B.Y., Wang, Y., Tang, H.D., Chen, S.D.: The role of cognitive activity in cognition protection: from bedside to bench. Trans. Neurodegener **6**, 7 (2017)
9. Rosenberg, A., Mangialasche, F., Ngandu, T., Solomon, A., Kivipelto, M.: Multidomain interventions to prevent cognitive impairment, Alzheimer's disease, and dementia: from finger to world-wide fingers. J. Prev. Alzheimers Dis. **7**, 29–36 (2020)
10. Chapman, S.B., et al.: Shorter term aerobic exercise improves brain, cognition, and cardiovascular fitness in aging. Front. Aging Neurosci **5**, 75 (2013)
11. Berryman, N., et al.: Multiple roads lead to Rome: combined high-intensity aerobic and strength training vs. gross motor activities leads to equivalent improvement in executive functions in a cohort of healthy older adults. Age (Dordr) **36**, 9710 (2014)
12. Müller, P., et al.: Evolution of neuroplasticity in response to physical activity in old age: the case for dancing. Front Aging Neurosci **9**, 56 (2017)
13. Borella, E., Carretti, B., Zanoni, G., Zavagnin, M., De Beni, R.: Working memory training in old age: An examination of transfer and maintenance effects. Arch Clin Neuropsychol 1–17 (2013) https://doi.org/10.1093/archin/act020
14. Rizkalla, M.N.: Cognitive training in the elderly: a randomized trial to evaluate the efficacy of a self-administered cognitive training program. Aging Ment. Health. **22**, 1–11 (2015). https://doi.org/10.1080/13607863.2015.1118679
15. Soldevila-Domenech, N., Boronat, A., Langohr, K., de la Torre, R.: N-of-1 clinical trials in nutritional interventions directed at improving cognitive function. Front. Nutr **6**, 110 (2019)
16. Solfrizzi, V., et al.: Nutritional intervention as a preventive approach for cognitive-related outcomes in cognitively healthy older adults: a systematic review. J. Alzheimers Dis. **64**(s1), S229–S254 (2018)
17. Klimova, B., Slaninova, G., Prazak, P., Kacetl, J., Valis, M.: Enhancing cognitive performance of healthy Czech seniors through non-native language learning -a mixed-methods pilot study. Brain Sci. **10**, 573 (2020)
18. Pfenninger, S.E., Polz, S.: Foreign language learning in the third age: a pilot feasibility study on cognitive, socio-affective and linguistic drivers and benefits in relation to previous bilingualism of the learner. JESLA **2**(1), 1–13 (2018)

19. Cheng, K.W., Deng, Y.H., Li, M., Yan, H.M.: The impact of L2 learning on cognitive aging. ADMET & DMPK **3**(3), 260–273 (2015)
20. Corbett, A., et al.: The effect of an online cognitive training package in healthy older adults: an online randomized controlled trial. JAMDA **16**(11), 990–997 (2015)
21. Klimova, B.: Computer-based cognitive training in aging. Front Aging Neurosci. **8**, 313 (2016)
22. Ponce, J., Latín, C., Leiva, V., Cortés, G., Rodríguez, F., Jiménez, C.E.: Non-pharmacological motor-cognitive treatment to improve the mental health of elderly adults. Rev. Assoc. Med. Bras. **65**(3), 394–403 (2019)
23. Pikhart, M., Klimova, B.: Maintaining and supporting seniors' wellbeing through foreign language learning: psycholinguistics of second language acquisition in older age. Int. J. Environ. Res. Public Health **17**, 8038 (2020)
24. Toepoel, V.: Ageing, leisure, and social connectedness: how could leisure help reduce social isolation of older people? Soc. Indic Res. **113**, 355–372 (2013)
25. Mukhtar, S.: Psychological impact of COVID-19 on older adults. Current Med. Res. Prac. **10**(4), 201–202 (2020)
26. Cotton, S.R., Anderson, W.A., McCullough, B.M.: Impact of internet use on loneliness and contact with others among older adults: cross-sectional analysis. J. Med. Internet Res. **15**(2), e39 (2013)
27. Klimova, B.: Use of the Internet as a prevention tool against cognitive decline in normal aging. Clin. Interv. Aging **11**, 1231–1237 (2016)
28. Fan, Q.Y.: Utilizing ICT to prevent loneliness and social isolation of the elderly. A literature review. Cuadernos de Trabajo Soc. **29**(2), 185–200 (2016)
29. Gonzales, A., Ramirez, M.P., Viadel, V.: ICT learning by older adults and their attitudes toward computer use. Current Gerontol. Geriatrics Res. 2015, ID 849308 (2015)
30. Klimova, B., Poulova, P.: Older people and technology acceptance. In: Zhou, J., Salvendy, G. (eds.) ITAP 2018. LNCS, vol. 10926, pp. 85–94. Springer, Cham (2018). https://doi.org/10.1007/978-3-319-92034-4_7
31. González, A., Ramírez, M.P., Viadel, V.: ICT learning by older adults and their attitudes toward computer use. Current Gerontol. Geriatr. Res. **2015**, 849308 (2015)
32. Cox, J.G.: Explicit instruction, bilingualism, and the older adult learner. Stud. Second. Lang. Acquis. **39**(1), 29–58 (2017)
33. Cox, J.G., Sanz, C.: Deconstructing PI for the ages: explicit instruction v. practice in young and older bilinguals. IRAL: Int. Rev. Appl. Linguist. **53**, 225–248 (2015)
34. Lenet, A., Sanz, C., Lado, B., Howard, J.H., Howard, D.V.: Aging, pedagogical conditions, and differential success in SLA: an empirical study. In: Sanz, C., Leow, R.P. (Eds.) Implicit and Explicit Conditions, Processes and Knowledge in SLA and Bilingualism, pp. 73–84. Washington, DC: Georgetown University Press (2011)
35. Marcotte, K., Ansaldo, A.I.: Age-related behavioural and neurofunctional patterns of second language word learning: different ways of being successful. Brain Lang. **135**, 9–19 (2014)
36. Van den Berg, F.A.: Boosting cognition in older adults by means of foreign language learning. Master's Thesis. The Netherlands: University of Groningen (2019)
37. Ware, C., et al.: Maintaining cognitive functioning in healthy seniors with a technology-based foreign language program: a pilot feasibility study. Front Aging Neurosci. **9**, 42 (2017)
38. Wong, P.C.M., et al.: Language training leads to global cognitive improvement in older adults: a preliminary study. J. Speech Lang Hear Res. **62**(7), 2411–2424 (2019)
39. Antoniou, M., Gunasekera, G., Wong, P.C.M.: Foreign language training as cognitive therapy for age-related cognitive decline: a hypothesis for future research. Neurosci. Biobehav. Rev. **37**(1002), 2689–2698 (2013)
40. Roseta Stone. https://www.rosettastone.eu/learn-english/. Accessed 22 Dec 2020
41. Pappas, M., Demertzi, E., Papagerasimou, I., Koukianakis, L., Voukelatos, N., Drigas, A.: Cognitive-based e-learning design for older adults. Soc. Sci. **8**, 6 (2019)

42. Formosa, M.: The University of the Third Age and active ageing. Springer (2019)
43. Klímová, B., Pikhart, M.: Current research on the impact of foreign language learning among healthy seniors on their cognitive functions from a positive psychology perspective – a systematic review. Front. Psychol. **11**, 765 (2020)
44. Singleton, D., Zaborska, D.: Adults learning additional languages in their later years: The ain, the profit, and the pleasure. J. Multilingual Theor. Prac. **1**, 112–124 (2020)

A Human-Machine Interaction Solution for Household Medical Furniture Design

Yunhui Li[1], Jing Luo[1(✉)], Qianqian Jing[1], and Yan Luximon[2]

[1] School of Arts and Design, Shenzhen University, Shenzhen, Guangdong, China
luojng@szu.edu.cn
[2] School of Design, The Hong Kong Polytechnic University, Kowloon, Hong Kong SAR

Abstract. In the current situation of covid-19 pandemic, the supply and demand relationship of medical resources in various hospitals is unstable. However, people's needs for understanding their health status are increasing. The purpose of this project is to assist telemedicine so that people can check their health at home. So, we proposed a civilian medical furniture solution. In the solution, we took the chair design as an example. First, we found out the user's needs and pain points via observation and interview. Based on this, we analyzed the characteristics of chair design and developed a prototype using a flexible contact sensor technology. In a follow-up evaluation experiment, we also added the details of the product according to ergonomic design principles of sitting posture. Moreover, after obtaining the heath data of users, we improved the product quality by visualizing the data. Finally, we tested the interactive effects of data visualization and then received positive feedback from users. The results of this project could help the design and development of civilian medical furniture.

Keywords: Health · Medical furniture · Flexible bionic tactile sensing technology · Human-machine interaction · Visualization

1 Introduction

The advancement of China's medical standards has raised people's health awareness. Therefore, a number of people are undergoing regular physical examinations and this trend is increasing day by day [1]. However, people in some areas where medical facilities are limited, patients have to experience long waiting time in hospitals for outpatient consultations, physical examinations, or re-examinations [2]. Telemedicine and new technology can provide new methods to address the excessive burden to hospitals, especially when the medical conditions are not very critical. One technology, the flexible bionic tactile sensing technology has developed rapidly [3] and this technology has been applied in the medical robot industry as well as in smart homes [4, 5].

Flexible bionic tactile sensing technology has the characteristics of high flexibility, high sensitivity, and wireless signal transmission [3]. It can be easily integrated with existing medical robots [4]. This technology can also be combined with smart homes and smart car applications [5]. Also, the product can detect the movement of every

© Springer Nature Switzerland AG 2021
Q. Gao and J. Zhou (Eds.): HCII 2021, LNCS 12787, pp. 260–276, 2021.
https://doi.org/10.1007/978-3-030-78111-8_18

muscle and tendon of a person through the use of bionic tactile sensing technology, thereby analyzing the person's posture [3]. Therefore, this technology also has broad application prospects in gesture recognition and motion analysis in functional products [4].

For medical examinations in the home environment, the characteristics of flexible technology just make the solution of telemedicine possible [10]. The current era is a smart technology era in which consumers widely use Internet services and Internet enabled products which cater for different user experience [7]. In the smart home environment, compared with traditional electronic sensors, users drag countless wired, hard, and non-fitting medical monitoring equipment to perform various tasks. In this proposed design, users are more inclined to use products that use flexible bionic tactile sensing technology [6, 8]. Therefore, this research uses flexible sensor technology and combines aesthetics and interactive habits to design household medical furniture. *Leisure seat*, a proposed conceptual design, can be used in future smart home environment to initially detect the health problems of each member of the family by initial screening for early diseases at home.

People have considered the design and development of telemedicine from different directions. Some have put a "warm and kind" material shell on the cold medical equipment in the CMF (i.e., Color-Material-Finishing) design to make it commercialized and civilian. Others have removed redundant functions in equipment and only retain functions that have low detection accuracy but can detect important physiological data. Consider medical furniture as an example. The current medical furniture has the most basic functions, but the auxiliary functions are not perfect. For example, hospital beds, infusion chairs, etc. can provide the most basic functions, but they do not significantly help doctors to treat and improve the efficiency of medical staff. In densely populated hospitals, the available space per person is small, and it is particularly important to save space on furniture or to provide multiple functional services on a piece of furniture.

Take Apple's smartwatch as an example. In addition to heart rate testing, Apple Watch also pays attention to people's breathing, sound, healthy drinking, and so on. The latest sixth-generation of smartwatch can measure blood oxygen levels through innovative sensors and apps; it can also monitor the health of the heart; it can also show various fitness data at a glance on an optimized all-weather retina screen. This can well meet the needs of users to understand their health in general. However, because of the area to be measured, the method of measurement and the type of data measured is limited. There is still much room for improvement in the accuracy of the health data [17, 18].

In the furniture field, people have more contact area and spend more time in the chair. So, this study considered the design of the chair. Starting from the interaction mode between the chair and the person, this study explores the design of contact points and interaction of the product. In this research, we have proposed a conceptual design of home medical furniture that can be used for medical testing and can be used as conventional furniture, while also conforming to ergonomics and human-computer interaction. The purpose is not only to better detect physiological data but also to better integrate it into the home environment. First of all, through observation and interviews, in ensuring the basic functions of the furniture, we found out the problems related to ergonomics in furniture and looked for the contact points between the flexible sensor and the furniture that may interact with the human body. Next, based on the above findings and analysis, we formulated the design requirements and propose design concepts. Feedback from users was obtained using a simulation test.

This paper introduces the application of flexible bionic tactile sensing technology and ergonomic principles in the product design process of home medical chairs in detail.

2   User Research

User research consists of two parts: (A) Observe the interaction nodes between people and the chair during the whole process of using the chair by people of different ages, and explore the design touchpoints (i.e. contact points) of the product; (B) Conduct structured interviews on the medical testing habits and personal opinions of users and family members, which will not only prove the insightful design concept of part (A) but also benefit developing novel design concepts.

2.1   Observation

We observed the dynamic process of people in the use of the chair and analyzed the design node diagram of the chair. The armrest is in close contact with the human hand and is an important source of human physiological data; the surface of the chair is the stress point and the main detection part of the flexible pressure sensor; the backrest must fit the curve of the human back to relieve pressure on the lumbar spine and relax the body; the legs of the chair are the supporting part of the entire product, and the strength and performance of its structure need to be considered (see Fig. 1).

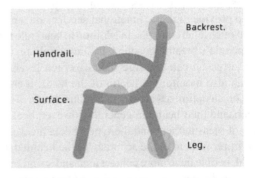

Fig. 1. The design node diagram of the chair.

The results of Bleda et al.'s study show that direct contact between the flexible sensor and the skin will result in more accurate human physiological data [10]. If the direct contact part is the user's palm, wrist and forearm area, then the quality of the human physiological data will be higher [10]. Therefore, we arrange the position of the sensor in the position of the armrest to improve the accuracy.

The product experience process was shown in Fig. 2. The first step is to sit on a telemedicine testing chair or product; the second step is to identify the identity and start the test; the third step is to generate a health report and send it to the remote family doctor; the fourth step is to discuss and summarize a more comprehensive health report by the remote doctors in each department; the fifth step, the attending doctor feeds back the health report and gives health advice (see Fig. 2).

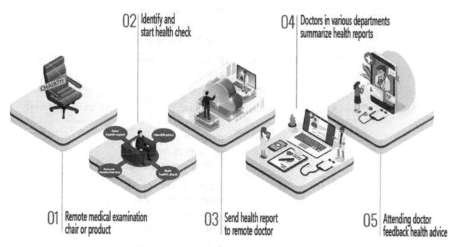

Fig. 2. Product experience process.

2.2 Interview

Interviews with users of different ages and their families (41 different families, 153 people in total) were conducted to understand what types of health testing products they have used. We asked them about their experience and questions about using the product. The following are some common questions collected. First of all, they reported that there are too many types of testing equipment. For example, measuring blood pressure, blood sugar, and body fat require three different instruments. And the interface and product usability are also very different. Some equipment needs to be tied to the arm; for some equipment needs to stand, and others are inconvenient in daily use. Even the use of some equipment does not conform to ergonomic. Secondly, the data can be viewed, but requires manually or separately recording. This creates confusion and is not effective in providing comprehensive understanding of their health status and trends. Finally, they hope that the testing equipment can be easy to use, does not take up more space, and be easy to carry.

3 Design Process and Program Output

The user research results provide an effective reference for the design concept and the program output. It was found that product integration, ergonomics, and data visualization are the most prominent problems that users expect to solve. Therefore, we determined

Table 1. Home self-test equipment.

Equipment category	Device	Features	Equipment iteration
Home self-test equipment	Blood Pressure Monitor	It can measure the blood pressure data indirectly by Oscillographic method	Flexible pressure sensor
	Blood glucose meter	It can measure and evaluate human blood glucose levels	Flexible pressure sensor
	Digital Thermometer	It can use semiconductor temperature sensing resistors to measure body temperature data	Flexible pressure sensor
	Ear thermometer	It can use the infrared spectrum emitted by the eardrum to measure body temperature	
	Pedometer	It can calculate calories or calorie consumption by counting steps, distance, speed, time and other data	
	Human health scale	It can check human health (weight, fat)	Flexible strain sensor
	Smart fat scale	It can measure body weight, fat, water, muscle weight, etc.	Flexible strain sensor
	Body composition measuring instrument	Body composition measurement: body weight, obesity judgment, body age, basal metabolism, muscle mass, estimated bone mass, body fat rate, visceral fat level, exercise mode, etc., which can be accurate to the various health indexes of the hands and feet	Flexible strain sensor

the design principles and designed a new solution. To ensure the basic functions of the furniture, the flexible sensor is etched on the contact point where the furniture and the human body may interact. The advantage of this is that it does not affect the normal use of the furniture, and can accurately detect various physiological data of the user during contact with the human body. Compared with traditional medical furniture in the hospital, it can better integrate into the home environment. And there is the choice of shape, material, and structure for different personality and individual styles. In addition, it does not occupy a lot of space in terms of volume.

First of all, the technical analysis is as follows. The flexible sensors developed at present include flexible gas sensors, flexible temperature sensors, flexible humidity sensors, flexible pressure sensors, and flexible strain sensors (also called flexible bionic tactile sensing technology, which is the main electronic skin Original), a flexible magnetic impedance sensor, and flexible thermal flow sensor. However, due to the limitations of technology, detection methods, and transmission power problems, an analysis of its ability when applied to medical health detection is shown in Table 1, 2 and 3). There is a need to design a human-computer interaction model that matches these flexible sensors.

Table 2. Medical smart wearable equipment.

Equipment category	Device	Features	Equipment iteration
Medical smart wearable equipment	Smart cervical ring	It can monitor cervical spine and body state, including neck posture, posture correction, sedentary reminder	Host system
	Smart monitor	It is easy to carry, can monitor the heart health at any time, accurate diagnosis of heart disease	Flexible strain sensor
	Sensor smart suit	It can monitor our physical condition, exercise status, and metabolism status at all times, and make our dynamic and static life and body characteristics digitized	
	Smart sports shoes	It can measure the user's running distance and other information. It can not only measure the route, but also measure the heart rate while running	

(continued)

Table 2. (*continued*)

Equipment category	Device	Features	Equipment iteration
	Intelligent blood pressure detection	Using a variety of communication methods (Bluetooth, USB cable, GPRS, WiFi, etc.), the measurement data of the electronic sphygmomanometer is uploaded to the cloud through intelligent processing to realize real-time or automatic timing measurement and record the user's blood pressure value, and intelligently analyze blood pressure changes	Flexible pressure sensor
	Smart heart rate detection	It can record real-time data such as exercise, sleep, some food and others in daily life, and synchronize these data with mobile phones, tablets, iPod touch, and play a role in guiding healthy life through data	Flexible strain sensor
	Intelligent ECG monitoring	It can synchronously save and record the user's ECG data in real-time, health trend analysis, and the cumulative data can be formed into a columnar trend analysis chart, which is convenient for users to grasp the law and trend of heart health	Flexible strain sensor

(*continued*)

Table 2. (*continued*)

Equipment category	Device	Features	Equipment iteration
	Intelligent three-high detection	It can monitor the user's blood pressure, blood sugar, blood lipids and other data in real-time, extract and visualize abnormal data	Flexible strain sensor
	Oximeter	It can get the data of blood oxygen saturation and pulse by detecting fingers	Flexible strain sensor
	Smart wearable chip	It is divided into four parts: including two ECG engines, a biometric recognition engine, and a heart rate heart disease recognition engine. Among them, the biometric engine can determine whether the tester is the owner himself or not according to the heart condition	Flexible strain sensor
	Cardiovascular tester	It can obtain a set of 35 cardiovascular function parameters and 64 expert-assisted diagnosis information reflecting heart function, vascular status, blood status and microcirculation function	Flexible strain sensor
	Sweat detection	Instead of blood testing, it can monitor the body's electrolyte imbalance, lactic acid index, sweat glucose level, dehydration and calorie burn value	Flexible strain sensor

(*continued*)

Table 2. (*continued*)

Equipment category	Device	Features	Equipment iteration
	Mobility aids	It can accurately process more complex and digital signals to improve the quality of life of the disabled and the elderly	
	Intelligent diagnostic instrument	It can analyze body data such as body composition, body shape, body function, etc., comprehensively evaluate the health status and exercise ability of the user	Flexible strain sensor
	Smart eye tracker	It can record the eye movement characteristics of people when processing visual information, and study the user's mental health by examining eye movements	Flexible strain sensor
	Dynamic health monitor	It can collect the blood oxygen saturation and pulse volume of the user during the activity, and then analyze the blood oxygen saturation and pulse volume to obtain the user's current health status	Flexible strain sensor

Secondly, ergonomic considerations focus on the seat size and the inclination angle. Because it needs to provide a comfortable experience, and at the same time prevent the users from increasing fatigue by prolonged and constant posture. Also, there is a need to avoid the user's long-term bowing operation, then increase the pressure on the cervical spine. We refer to the ergonomic size of the driving seat of a car with similar needs [12, 13].

Also, the *sinking amount of the chair* is a key consideration [14, 15], where the *sinking amount of the chair* refers to the extent to which the chair is downward when a person is sitting in it. It can make the seat surface and the backrest of a single-curved fit the user's back curve when used. Then make the curvature of the spine in a natural state.

Table 3. Home health equipment.

Equipment category	Device	Features	Equipment iteration
Home health equipment	Massage chair	It can use mechanical rolling force and mechanical force squeeze to perform the massage. Regular massage can dredge the meridians and promote blood circulation	
	Eye massager	It can relieve visual fatigue, prevent myopia and amblyopia, can clear the meridians, improve blood microcirculation in the eyes, promote metabolism, relieve eye fatigue, and restore ciliary muscle elasticity	
	Physiotherapy bed	It can activate the activity of biological macromolecules, promote and improve blood circulation, enhance metabolism, improve human immune function, have anti-inflammatory and swelling effects, and relieve pain	Direct use

The design can avoid abnormal pressure distribution in the intervertebral disc which can damage the spine and increase the fatigue of the user.

Finally, based on the results of the previous product experience process analysis, we set up the following specific usage processes and functional principles: When the user sits on this chair, the flexible temperature, pressure, and strain sensors in the cushion start to operate. Then it can detect the user's metabolic status, body temperature, and other physiological conditions in real-time. The user holds the armrest of the chair with both hands and then triggers the flexible bionic tactile sensor etched on the armrest. It can extract the user's biometric information and various indicators that can reflect the user's physical health from the user's palm prints and sweat. If the neck is leaning on the magnetic cervical spine pillow, it can also detect the information of user's cervical spine and physical condition, and then transmit it to the intelligent processor of the chair.

Using software and hardware with Artificial Intelligent algorithms (AI brain) the data is stored and also compared with previous files and standard human health indicators. The complex human health information is visually display on a flexible screen. Users only need to have basic physiological knowledge to understand their health intuitively. If any data is not within standard, the system can give corresponding suggestions based on the data. These may include possible disease, severity and potential consequences.

The user can also open the telemedicine system and directly communicate with doctors online in the cloud through the high-definition camera and eye tracker in front of the flexible screen display. Alternatively, the physiotherapy pad embedded in the cushion can be used to reduce inflammation and swelling, relieve pain, promote the blood circulation, enhance metabolism, and improve human immunity.

Based on the previously summarized design principles, and combining it with the use process and functional principles, we propose the following conceptual design (see Fig. 3, 4 and 5).

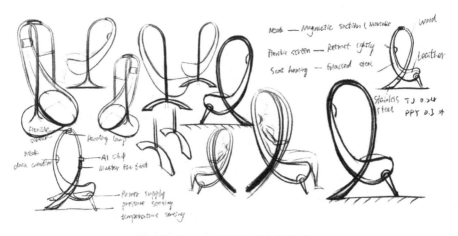

Fig. 3. Concept sketch of chair design.

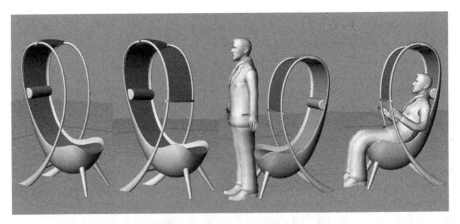

Fig. 4. Computer model diagram.

Fig. 5. 3D printing model diagram.

4 Performance Analysis

The final rendering of the conceptual model is shown in Fig. 6.

Fig. 6. Chair scene diagram.

In addition to its health detection function, it is also a leisure health chair. And it is mainly used in the home environment, such as living rooms, bedrooms, balconies, courtyards and other environments. Due to the unique shape and avant-garde CMF design, it can be integrated into various modern home styles.

Besides, it can also be placed in public places such as the hospital lobby, waiting room, waiting room for relatives, etc. The various soft and sensitive sensors can also be applied to popular VR (Virtual Reality) games. This is an absolutely novel entertainment revolution for us, which not only satisfies the entertainment needs of users, but also extricates users from the bad habit of playing with mobile phones with bowing their heads.

From an ergonomic point of view, referring to the size and the inclination design of the car seat, the overall size of the chair we set is 1065 * 600 * 1780 mm, seat width is 600 mm, the seat depth is 500 mm, and the seat height is 450 mm. The neck pillow is magnetic and can be moved according to user needs. The inclination angle between the seat cushion and the backrest is 95° (see Fig. 7).

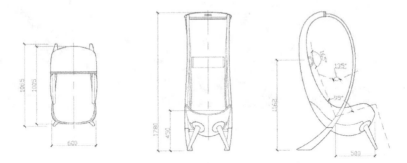

Fig. 7. Seat size and inclination design.

To improve the comfort of the seat, we designed a high-elastic foam with a cushion of 50 mm (i.e., sinking amount) on the seat surface. And based on the previous analysis of the sitting posture, a medium-density sponge with a cushion of 40 mm (i.e., sinking amount) for the shoulders and thighs was set up. The rest is a 10 mm low-density sponge (see Fig. 8).

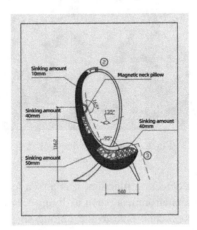

Fig. 8. Seat sponge design.

The evaluation of the innovation points of this design has the following points: First, user needs, people have the awareness of regular physical examinations, people want to know their health conditions, and they require functionally integrated household products; second, technical feasibility, flexible sensing technology is becoming more and more mature, intelligent chip information processing technology is powerful, and the etching technology of flexible sensing sheet is progressing; third, business continuity, the state's support and attention to the medical and health field, users need physical examination services without leaving home and a new software and hardware interactive experience.

Finally, in terms of data visualization, the interface design allows users who do not understand medical knowledge to understand their health through visual design [16]. The functional interface of this system is divided into five sections as shown in the menu bar: telemedicine, member files, health reports, film and television programs, and entertainment games. This article focuses on the visual design of the health report.

In the health report, there are five modules: data list, human body three-dimensional grid display, severe abnormality index, controllable abnormality index, and risk assessment. Among them, the data list mainly displays all the health test data of the identified user, except for basic height, weight and other information. Because standard control data is set in each test item, users can intuitively see the deviation of each health data from the standard data. In the three-dimensional grid display frame of the human body in the middle, the parts with abnormal data will be marked in red. Because the display is a virtual three-dimensional human body model, users can freely zoom in or zoom out the parts marked in red and share screenshots on their smart devices to facilitate communication with doctors.

The first column on the right is the serious abnormality index display column, which shows the prevalence index of large diseases, such as the early preliminary screening of tumors and cancers. The second column on the right is the controllable abnormality index display column, which displays the values of the more abnormal items in the data list on the left, for later reference when consulting a doctor. The third column on the

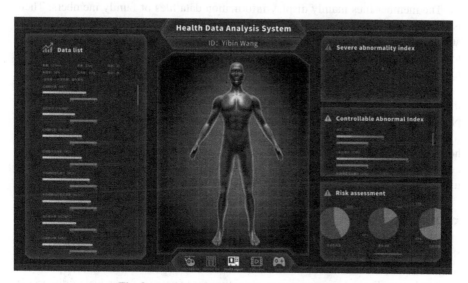

Fig. 9. Health report homepage interface design.

right displays field of risk assessment, showing that the probability of suffering from various diseases calculated based on the controllable index (see Fig. 9).

The main interface of telemedicine matches with cloud platforms such as Alibaba Health and Xiliudata and lists the product profiles of clients such as Doctor Yun, Dingxiang Doctor, and Good Doctor Online for users to choose from (see Fig. 10).

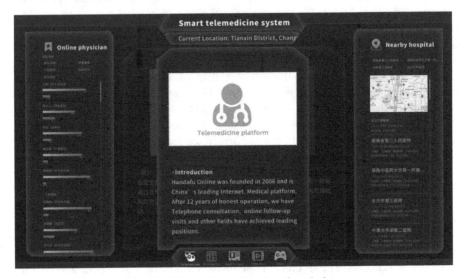

Fig. 10. Telemedicine client interface design.

The member files mainly display information data files of family members. There is a suggestion column on the left, which lists the matters that each family should pay attention to in daily life and recent physical conditions. The interface design of film and television programs and entertainment games is consistent with the interface design of today's major online video platforms.

To test the effect after visualization, we conduct a test on several volunteers via the popular projection technology. Based on the volunteers' feedback, knowledge of physical health, simple disease prediction, and even establish a simple family medical file, is a good realization. Through the chair we designed, the perfect combination of home and medical care can be realized and applied to daily life. This can alleviate the current ubiquitous medical difficulties and expensive medical problems, and lead people to a healthier and smarter medical life.

5 Conclusion

Smart furniture design solves the storage problem of multiple home medical equipment with a single function. Users do not need to leave home to obtain health reports and can conduct preliminary screening for early diseases to prevent the arrival of diseases in advance. There is no need to waste time go to hospital to queue up for routine physical examination.

Although the solution of this research has a certain accuracy limitation when compared with the medical equipment of hospitals. Improvement of the system requires subsequent iterative optimization of technology and several prototype developments. On the level of solving telemedicine problems, it has certain feasibility and potential usefulness. Compared with the smartwatch, although the contact time between furniture and people is not as long as the contact time with the watch [17, 18], it has a wider measurement area, can have accurate sensors, and richer measurement methods to meet the needs of telemedicine data.

References

1. Liu, P.C.: Study on the status and development of integration between china's urban and rural medical security system, p. 08. Chinese Health Service Management (2013)
2. Chen, Y., Yin, Z., Xie, Q.: Suggestions to ameliorate the inequity in urban/rural allocation of healthcare resources in china. Int. J. Equity Health **13**(1), 1–6 (2014)
3. Núñez, C.G., Navaraj, W.T., Polat, E.O., Dahiya, R.: Energy-autonomous, flexible, and transparent tactile skin. Adv. Funct. Mater. **27**(18), 1606287 (2017)
4. Yogeswaran, N., et al.: New materials and advances in making electronic skin for interactive robots. Adv. Robot. **29**(21), 1359–1373 (2015)
5. Nathan, A., et al.: Flexible electronics: the next ubiquitous platform. In: Proceedings of the IEEE 100(Special Centennial Issue), pp. 1486–1517 (2012)
6. Lu, T., Yuan, K., Zou, W., Hu, H.: Smooth path planning for intelligent wheelchair based on human-machine interaction. In: 2006 IEEE International Conference on Information Acquisition, pp. 988–993. IEEE (2006)
7. Katore, M., Bachute, M.: Speech based human machine interaction system for home automation. In: 2015 IEEE Bombay Section Symposium (IBSS), pp. 1–6. IEEE (2015)
8. Tsumugiwa, T., Kamiyoshi, A., Yokogawa, R., Shibata, H.: Position-detecting device for measurement of human motion in human-machine interaction. In: 2007 IEEE/ASME International Conference on Advanced Intelligent Mechatronics, pp. 1–6. IEEE (2007)
9. Foster, K.R., Torous, J.: The opportunity and obstacles for smartwatches and wearable sensors. IEEE Pulse **10**(1), 22–25 (2019)
10. Bleda, A.L., Maestre, R., García, A.: Unobtrusive contactless cardiac monitoring for telemedicine and ambient assisted living. In: 2018 Computing in Cardiology Conference (CinC), vol. 45, pp. 1–4. IEEE (2018)
11. Malone, E.B., Dellinger, B.A.: Furniture Design Features and Healthcare Outcomes. The Center for Health Design, Concord (2011)
12. Fahma, F., Iftadi, I., Putri, N.A.: Customer requirement analysis of driver's seat design using quality function deployment (QFD) case study: city car. In: Proceedings of the Joint International Conference on Electric Vehicular Technology and Industrial, Mechanical, Electrical and Chemical Engineering (ICEVT & IMECE), pp. 173–177. IEEE (2015)
13. Makhsous, M., Hendrix, R., Crowther, Z., Nam, E., Lin, F.: Reducing whole-body vibration and musculoskeletal injury with a new car seat design. Ergonomics **48**(9), 1183–1199 (2005)
14. Vlaović, Z., Grbac, I., Domljan, D., Bublić, A.: Office work chairs–research of deformations and comfort index. Drvna industrija: Znanstveni časopis za pitanja drvne tehnologije **61**(3), 159–168 (2010)
15. Groenesteijn, L., Vink, P., de Looze, M., Krause, F.: Effects of differences in office chair controls, seat and backrest angle design in relation to tasks. Appl. Ergon. **40**(3), 362–370 (2009)

16. Kirk, A.: Data Visualization: A Successful Design Process. Packt publishing LTD (2012)
17. Bai, Y., Hibbing, P., Mantis, C., Welk, G.J.: Comparative evaluation of heart rate-based monitors: Apple watch vs fitbit charge hr. J. Sports Sci. **36**(15), 1734–1741 (2018)
18. Thomson, E.A., et al.: Heart rate measures from the apple watch, fitbit charge hr2, and electrocardiogram across different exercise intensities. J. Sports Sci. **37**(12), 1411–1419 (2019)

System Architecture and User Interface Design for a Human-Machine Interaction System for Dementia Intervention

Miroslava Migovich[1]([⊠]), Ritam Ghosh[2], Nibraas Khan[2], Judith A. Tate[3], Lorraine C. Mion[3], and Nilanjan Sarkar[1,2]

[1] Mechanical Engineering, Vanderbilt University, Nashville, TN 37212, USA
miroslava.migovich@vanderbilt.edu
[2] Electrical Engineering and Computer Science, Vanderbilt University, Nashville, TN 37212, USA
[3] College of Nursing, The Ohio State University, Columbus, OH 42310, USA

Abstract. A growing number of older adults in America face dementia and its associated behaviors. One of the most prevalent behaviors is apathy, which leads to social isolation, reduced quality of life, cognitive decline, increased mortality and caregiver burden. Current interventions are costly and require intensive personnel resources. Given the shortage of qualified care givers, technology may be an effective and complementary approach. Research has shown that multimodal interventions that include social, physical, and cognitive activities have the best outcomes. We propose a novel system combining social robotics and virtual reality to engage older adults in tasks that target all three areas. In this paper, we describe the system architecture, which includes the Virtual system Musical Task, the social robot, the state machine, and the wand that is used as an input device. Five participants tested the system. The virtual reality and robot functioned as expected with no errors. The wand had errors below 10%. The average usability score was 89.5. Overall, this study demonstrated that the system performs as expected per the functional system requirements. Further studies are necessary to explore the functionality and usability of the system with older adults.

Keywords: Interface for disabled and senior people · Mixed reality and environments

1 Introduction

An estimated 14% of adults age 70 and older in the United States have a dementia diagnosis. As the population of older adults (65+) is projected to rise by 32 million over the next 30 years, the number of older adults with dementia is also expected to rise. Dementia results in difficulties with memory, problem-solving, language, everyday activities and often accompanied by behavioral and psychological symptoms [1]. Apathy, a syndrome with cognitive, affective and behavioral dimensions, is one of the most prevalent neuropsychiatric symptoms associated with Alzheimer's and related dementias; individuals with apathy exhibit indifference, lack of interest in activities, lack of initiative

© Springer Nature Switzerland AG 2021
Q. Gao and J. Zhou (Eds.): HCII 2021, LNCS 12787, pp. 277–292, 2021.
https://doi.org/10.1007/978-3-030-78111-8_19

and poor goal-setting. Apathy leads to social isolation, further cognitive and physical decline, reduced quality of life, increased mortality and caregiver burden and frustration [2]. Apathy is difficult to treat and few pharmacologic treatments are available. Current treatments and interventions include physical activity, social engagement, and cognitive activities [3, 4], as well as music and art therapy [5, 6]. It is believed that multimodal strategies that are individualized and include physical, cognitive, and social engagement together are most successful [6]. Physical activity is known to improve voluntary motor control while cognitive activities and social engagement improve attention, visuospatial abilities and overall cognitive function [7, 8]. However, these nonpharmacologic interventions require personnel resources. There is a shortage of both formal (paid) and informal caregivers for older adults [9].

In order to address this problem, various technological intervention techniques, particularly the use of socially assistive robots (SAR) have been explored. The therapeutic baby seal robot PARO has been used to improve mood and foster social engagement [10, 11], but such intervention is passive in nature and dependent on initiative taken by the older adults and requires a trained therapist to be effective. Various SARs have been used as a fitness coach to demonstrate exercises to the older adults and provide feedback on their performance [12–14]. The socially assistive robot Brian 2.1 has been used to assist older adults in a meal eating activity [15]. Though promising, many of these SARs are built and programmed for very specific applications and hence can be limited in terms of type and variety of tasks they can perform. The use of virtual reality to administer guided exercise has also been proposed [16]. But research shows that participants are likely to respond better to instructions from physically present robots than from a virtual avatar on a computer [17, 18].

Keeping all these considerations in mind, we propose a novel system that combines social robotics with non-immersive virtual reality (VR) to create activities that encourage cognitive, physical and social engagement that can be adapted to the abilities of the individual participants. A musical task that focuses on playing a drum is presented in this paper, but the system can be adapted for a variety of multi-domain activities.

2   System Design

2.1   Architecture

Fig. 1. System setup with VR, Wand, and NAO

The system architecture consists of four broad components: (1) a VR system presented through a computer monitor, (2) a humanoid robot as the partner and/or coach, (3) a wand that acts as an input device to interact with the VR system and as a sensor to collect data, and (4) an infrared (IR) marker used as reference for cursor position (only required for tasks that need position data). Figure 1 shows the VR environment with the humanoid robot NAO and two wands. The VR system consists of the interaction layer that interprets the data coming from the wand in the context of the current task, the communications layer that manages communication with the robot, and the state machine that controls the task, the difficulty level, score, and robot messages, encouragement/reward. The system architecture is displayed in Fig. 2.

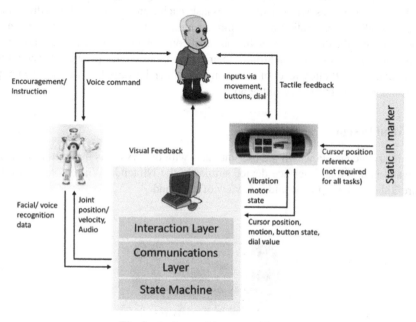

Fig. 2. System architecture with user

2.2 Task Design

The objectives of the task are to provide both physical and cognitive challenges to older adults. To fulfill these objectives the task should have components that require physical movement and cognitive effort that require the user to recognize, memorize, synchronize, sort and/or compute. The task should also have a metric to measure participant's progress and provide reward or positive reinforcement that encourages greater effort and increases focus and interaction during the task. In order to accommodate participants with different abilities, varying levels of physical and cognitive difficulty must be available. Considering the above requirements, we designed a musical task using the Unity game engine (www.unity.com).

The musical task requires the participant to play an instrument along with a song played in the virtual environment. A pre-processing step isolates the notes of a particular instrument in each song using a software-based audio spectrum analyzer. The notes are then displayed along two vertical bars, corresponding to the left and right hand, in sync with the song and NAO announces each note as it is displayed. The bars each have a yellow zone (top), a green zone (middle) and a red zone (bottom). The notes pass through each of the three zones, first entering the yellow zone at the top of the bar and exiting through the red zone at the bottom of the bar. The notes played while in the green zone corresponds to playing correctly, the yellow zone corresponds to playing too early and the red zone corresponds to playing too late. The score is increased when the participant plays in the green zone and is displayed on the upper right corner of the scene.

The participant uses two 'wands' for this task, each wand corresponds to a drumstick. The drumsticks are controlled by a drumming motion of the wands. The movement of the arms to play the drums provide the physical component of the task. The participant has to follow the notes and synchronize their arm motions, which provides the cognitive component. The difficulty level of each component can be varied by varying the tempo of the song and the frequency of the notes.

2.3 Wand Design

The primary means via which the user interacts with the system is through the 'Wand'. The wand is a human interface device similar to the Nintendo Wii remote controller. Figure 3 shows the top view and side view of the wand.

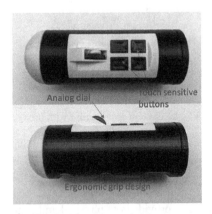

Fig. 3. Wand top and side views

The ergonomics of the wand has been designed keeping the requirements of older adults in mind and to accommodate a wide variety of palm sizes. The guidelines for hand tool designing given by the Canadian Center for Occupational Health and Safety were considered [19]. The length of the wand should be optimum; a short length will place excessive stress at the middle of the palm and if too long it will increase the weight of the device. The recommended width of handle of cylindrical-like objects is between 30 mm and 50 mm. Taking these factors into consideration, the wand has been designed with a length of 110 mm and a diameter of 40 mm. The weight of the wand is 75 g (2.65 oz). The underside of the wand includes a grip design to increase the comfort for prolonged uses and prevent slipping. The surface of the wand is a smooth hard plastic to enable easy cleaning between uses. The structure of the wand has been 3D printed to facilitate rapid prototyping and iterations based on user feedback.

At the core of the wand is an ESP32 based Node-MCU development board. The ESP32 is a dual core 240 MHz microcontroller by Espressif Systems (www.espressif. com). This microcontroller was chosen due to its relatively high processing power and built-in 12 bit analog to digital converters (ADC) and capacitive touch sensors. The wand interface includes an analog potentiometer dial connected to one of the ADC channels and four copper plated buttons connected to four capacitive touch sensors. The wand contains an Infrared (IR) positioning sensor that detects the position of up to four IR sources. The image processing and position calculation is done in hardware by the sensor itself. Using this sensor, the relative position of the wand is calculated with reference to an IR LED mounted on top of the monitor. The sensor sends the position data to the micro-controller using the i2c protocol. The wand also features an inertial measurement unit (IMU) to measure the motion and orientation of the wand. The IMU used here is the MPU9250 by InvenSense (www.invensense.tdk.com) which is a low cost, low power IMU with a three-axis accelerometer, three-axis gyroscope and three-axis magnetometer built in the same chip. The IMU connects to the microcontroller via the i2c protocol and sends raw accelerometer, gyroscope and magnetometer data at 100 Hz. The raw data are used to calculate the absolute orientation using the gradient descent method proposed by Madgwick [20].

We selected this method over other commonly used methods like complimentary filters and Kalman filters because this method is computationally inexpensive and can be computed in relatively low powered microcontrollers and, unlike complimentary filters, orientation obtained by this method remains stable over time. The orientation of the sensor frame with respect to the world frame was estimated by the numerical integration of the rate of change of orientation as measured from the gyroscope values after removal of bias. The gravity vector, known in the world frame, transformed by the orientation should be the same as the one measured by the accelerometer in the body frame. The difference between these two quantities is minimized by a gradient descent algorithm. A tunable parameter β is used as a 'trust' parameter that determines how much trust we will put on the gyroscope values vs the accelerometer values. The detailed mathematical equations and derivations is present in the original paper cited above.

The wand also has a vibration motor to provide tactile feedback to the user. The speed of the vibration motor can be controlled by the BJT-based motor driver using pulse width modulation (PWM). The vibration motor is turned on/off by a flag set by serial command from the computer. The wand was programmed using the Arduino IDE (www.arduino.cc). The hardware architecture of the wand can be seen in Fig. 4.

The wand communicates with the computer via USB and sends data as a string of the form (pitch, roll, yaw, position_x, position_y, button_state_1, button_state_2, button_state_3, button_state_4, potentiometer_value) and receives a single character 'V' to enable tactile feedback.

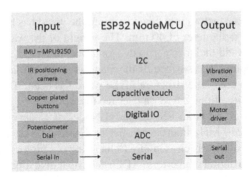

Fig. 4. Hardware architecture of the wand

2.4   State Machine

The basis of the system is interactions among the different components. We chose to use state machines to observe how each component is behaving within another component [21]. For the musical task, we use the machine to understand what errors the user has made within the game. For example, if the user is playing the game at a faster speed than directed, we change states to recognize that error. Within this error state, we can communicate appropriately with the user and the robot.

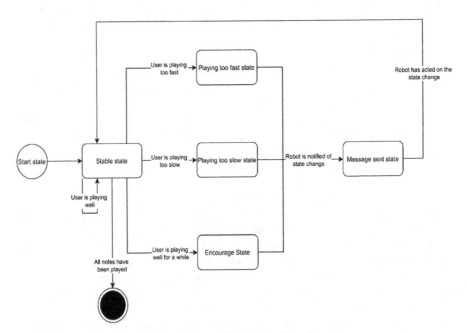

Fig. 5. State Machine for the task

For this paper, we have implemented the following states: StartState (make sure everything in the system is working as expected), StableState (the task proceeds without interruptions), PlayingTooFastState (the user hits the drum when the notes are in the yellow zone), PlayingTooSlowState (the user hits the drum when notes are in the red zone), EncourageState (the user hits the drum when the notes are in the green zone), and MessageSentState (message has been sent to the robot). These states are shown in Fig. 5.

When the system begins, the system is in StartState. In this state, preliminary tests are conducted such as whether the robot is connected, and the wands are connected. As the system is expanded with more sensors and tools, more tests can be added. Once the components are checked, the task moves into the StableState. In this state, notes are generated for the user to play and the robot is notified to alert the user to "PlayLeft" or "PlayRight". Also, the system now starts to pay attention to how the user is playing. If it notices that the user is playing too fast, it moves into the PlayingTooFastState, sends a message to the robot, moves into the MessageSentState, waits to confirm that the robot has notified the user, and then moves back into the StableState. The system moves through a similar path when it detects if the player is playing too slow or the player is playing well with states PlayingTooSlowState and EncourageState, respectively. The system moves into the final state once the song has ended.

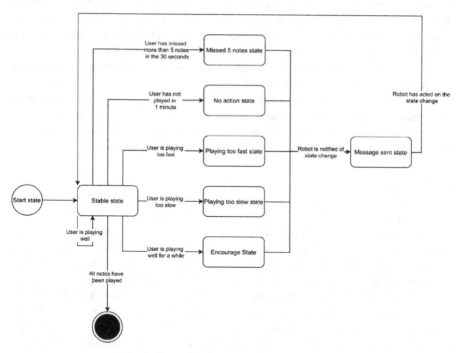

Fig. 6. Example of an expanded state machine

There are several more states that can be added to the system. As an example of how the state machine can be expanded, consider Fig. 6.

The state machine was built with the ability to be easily expanded. In technical terms, the only changes needed in order to add extra states are creating the state and its actions and a transition to the additional state. All other details are handled by the design of the state machine.

2.5 Communication Layer

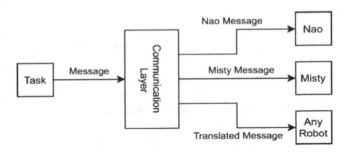

Fig. 7. Communication Layout

While building the system, we kept the expandability of robots (adding more robots in the future) in minds. Within the states, we send messages to the robot; thus, we built an intermediate layer to handle communication for different robots. The intermediate layer allows us to translate the ambiguous message such as "PlayLeft" into robot-specific messages. This design also allows us to add as many different robots as we need with changes only on the robot side and the communication layer without having to modify the task. This design can be seen in Fig. 7.

If the robot connected to the system is NAO, the steps in the communication layer are: translate the ambiguous English message to a code for NAO, send the translated message to a server, and send the message from the server to NAO. With this flow, we only need to modify a minimal amount of code to add additional robots.

3   Testing

System and usability testing was completed by five participants in order to evaluate the performance of the VR system component, the robot component, and the wand component according to their functional requirement specifications (FRS), both subjectively as a user and objectively with comparison to system logs. System usability was measured using the System Usability Scale [21] that has excellent psychometric properties of reliability and validity [22]. Participants rated comfort and confidence with each component using a questionnaire after the interaction. This study was reviewed by the Vanderbilt University Institutional Review Board and was designated as exempt research. COVID-19 precautions, such as face coverings, disinfecting between users, and social distancing, were used in order to keep the researchers and participants safe.

Participants began by completing a demographic and technology use questionnaire. Of the five participants, 2 were female and 3 were male. All of the participants had completed or were enrolled in an engineering based Bachelor's program and rated their technology skills high (above 7/10). After completing the pre-questionnaire, the participant played one song lasting approximately 3 min and 30 s using the wands in the virtual

Fig. 8. Video Recording and View of Testing Setup

task. Participants were asked to purposefully play in the yellow and red zone for a few notes in order to test the state transitions and logging in each section. After the task, they completed the SUS and a post questionnaire about their confidence and comfort level with the system components.

The task was set up and recorded by Flashback Express (www.flashbackrecorder. com) so that the virtual environment and video footage were recorded simultaneously as shown in Fig. 8. A timestamp was also displayed for comparison of video footage to the generated logs. The first set of logs included timestamps and in which colored area the system documented the note was played for both left and right wand. The second set of logs included time stamps when each wand relayed haptic feedback to the user. An example of both log outputs can be seen in Fig. 9. A haptic feedback is expected in the wand when the corresponding drumstick comes in contact with the surface of the drum in the virtual environment. The researchers independently compared the logs to the video recordings to evaluate the accuracy and fulfillment of the FRS.

```
04-02-2021    16:31:31 Right drumstick on green
04-02-2021    16:31:35 Right drumstick on green

04-02-2021    16:31:31 Right drumstick vibrate
04-02-2021    16:31:35 Right drumstick vibrate
```

Fig. 9. Example of log output

The main FRS of the VR system includes the note generation, tracking the user's score, logging colored area when the note was hit, and generating the drum sound at the correct time. The notes should be spawned in such a way that it keeps the user engaged and follow the rhythm of the song. The score tracking and note logging are used to inform the state machine and should be accurate, defined as less than 10% error rate. The drum noise generation should also be in sync with the note playing in order to not distract the user.

The robot is expected to maintain connection with the system at all times, without failure. The accuracy of the robot providing direction was evaluated by comparing when the robot says 'left' and 'right' to which side the note had appeared. For state transition, the robot is expected to say "You are doing great!" after five consecutive hits in the green zone; "You are playing too fast" after five consecutive hits in the yellow zone; or "You are playing too slow" after five consecutive hits in the red zone. The logs and video were used to confirm that the robot changes states correctly.

The wand should provide haptic feedback when the user makes contact with the drum in the virtual world. Logs of vibration were compared to the videos to measure that the haptic feedback occurred when a note was played. There should be no perceptible delay between the user making the drumming motion and the drum being played in the virtual environment. Finally, unintended hits of the drum when the user is not moving or missed hits when the user does move but it is not captured by the system were evaluated with an a priori error rate of 10% considered acceptable.

4   Results and Discussion

4.1   System Testing Results

For testing our system, we focused on the role of the three main components; (1) the VR system; (2) the robot component; and (3) the wand component. For the task, we tested to ensure that the notes were generated correctly, the score was kept accurately, and the task reacted in real time to wand input. The video recordings from the five participants were analyzed and used as ground truth to compare against logs generated by the system to measure the accuracy of all the components of the system.

The VR system was able to generate the notes, track the user's score and accurately log the colored areas in which the note was played. The notes were spawned randomly while still matching the music, which kept the participants engaged and on task. The drumming sound was in sync with the wand. Overall, the functional system requirements of the VR system were met with no adjustments needed.

The robot component was tested based on whether the robot provides correct direction to the user on how to play the notes (either play the left or right note), remain connected to the system and communicate appropriately, and observe the state transitions. This component of the system also behaved with 100% accuracy. The robot was able to provide time and performance appropriate feedback. We would like to highlight that the state transitions were accurately interpreted by the robot without delay or loss of information.

The final component we tested was the wand with the criteria of whether the haptic feedback occurred correctly, the drum was hit without the intention of the user, the user intended to hit the drum but it did not occur, or the drum hit was registered twice instead of once. The haptic feedback did not have any errors; however, we did find errors for the other criteria. With our testing, we know that the drum was hit 362 times with all

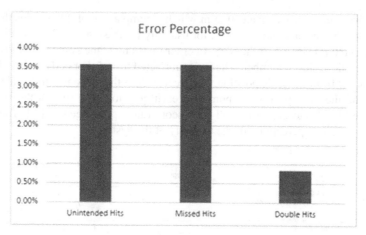

Fig. 10. Overall error percentages for hits on the drum

participants combined. Out of these hits, a total of 13 hits were unintended, 13 were missed, and 3 registered as double. The error percentage is shown in Fig. 10. While there was some error, it was well below our 10% acceptance margin. It should also be noted that no participant had a total wand error percentage above 10%, as can be seen in the Fig. 11 below. While the error level is low, it should be addressed in order to improve overall performance and user experience.

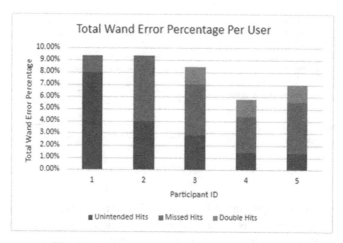

Fig. 11. Total wand error percentage for each user

4.2 Usability Results

The System Usability Scale (SUS) is used to measure the perceived usability of the system. This scale is used across a wide variety of hardware, software, websites and validated with an empirical evaluation in which a comparison of 200 studies that used the SUS as a "robust and versatile tool for usability professionals" [21, 22]. Figure 12 shows the standard version of the SUS. In order to calculate the system usability score, the scale position of even numbered items is subtracted from 5. For odd numbered items, 1 is subtracted from the scale position. This scales all of the responses to a scale of 1–4 with 4 being the most positive response for each question. The sum of the questions is multiplied by 2.5 to get an overall SUS score ranging between 0–100. This score represents the user's perception of the usability of the system.

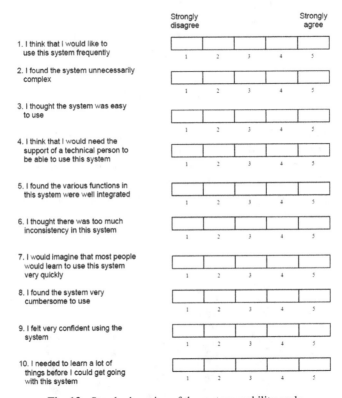

Fig. 12. Standard version of the system usability scale

Participants' SUS scores ranged from 85 to 95 with an average SUS score of 89.5. In general, a score above 68 is considered average while an SUS score above 80.3 is considered excellent [22]. This suggests that the system is very usable compared to other systems that were tested using the SUS. The item results are shown in Fig. 13 and it can be seen that overall, the responses to the questions did not have much variability, suggesting that the system is perceived as usable and not complex. The participants were able to figure out the system with little to no input from the researchers and enjoyed the interaction. Even though they were not the target group, the participants, on average, indicated that they would like to use the system again which suggests that overall the system is engaging. However, it is important to note that the current participants all rated their technology skills as high and therefore may view the system as more easy to use than the target population of older adults. Future studies with the target population are necessary to confirm the SUS results.

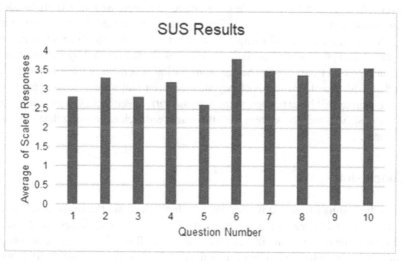

Fig. 13. Average scaled SUS responses per question

4.3 Post Questionnaire Results

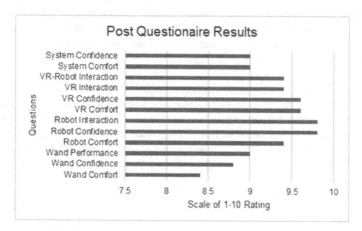

Fig. 14. Post questionnaire average results per question

In the post questionnaire, we tested the comfort and confidence the users felt with our system on a scale of 1–10. We asked the participants for their opinions on their comfort with using the components, confidence on how they felt using them, their interactions with the components, and the intracomponent interactions. The results of the questionnaire are shown in Fig. 14 as averages of the answers from the users. The wand comfort and confidence had the lowest scores, which is consistent with the error percentages as no other system component had errors. For the wand, qualitative feedback included the desire for rubber grippers on the side of the wand and decreased sensitivity to address the unintended and double hits. Missed hits were often caused by two notes spawning too close together. We will include a delay between notes to address this problem. While the overall percentage wand errors were low, it was noticed by participants and will be addressed in future works. Suggestions for improvement of the robot interaction included the addition of new feedback beyond the current states. As discussed previously, the state machine will be expanded to incorporate varied feedback. Overall participants were very positive about the system with the main feedback expressing desire for more song choices.

5 Conclusion

Based on the results of our study, the state machine, the task, the robot, and the wand work well within our margin of acceptable error. User feedback indicates that the system is easy to use, the components interact well, and overall confidence and comfort level with the system is high. There is no component of the system with major problems.

Limitations of this study include small sample size and the fact that the participants are not the target population. Further studies are necessary to explore the functionality and usability of the system with older adults. Overall, this study proved that the system performs as expected per the functional system requirements.

Future work includes further development with the addition of new states and expansion of the task. New tasks will also be added to allow for more utilization of the wand. Natural language processing for the robot, physiological data tracking of the user, and expanded sensors to inform the state machine will also be integrated. This system has opened several possible research routes to be followed.

Acknowledgments. Research reported in this publication was supported by the National Institute on Aging of the National Institutes of Health under award number R01AG062685. The content is solely the responsibility of the authors and does not necessarily represent the official views of the National Institutes of Health. One author was also supported by the National Science Foundation Research Traineeship DGE 19–22697. The authors would like to thank the participants for their time and feedback.

References

1. Alzheimer's Association: Alzheimer's Disease Facts and Figures On the Front Lines : Primary Care Physicians and," 2020. https://www.alz.org/news/2020/primary-care-physicians-on-the-front-lines-of-diag
2. Volicer, L.: Behavioral problems and dementia. Clin. Geriatr. Med. **34**(4), 637–651 (2018). https://doi.org/10.1016/j.cger.2018.06.009

3. Lanctôt, K.L., et al.: Apathy associated with neurocognitive disorders: recent progress and future directions. Alzheimer's Dementia **13**(1), 84–100 (2017). https://doi.org/10.1016/j.jalz. 2016.05.008

4. Brodaty, H., Burns, K.: Nonpharmacological management of apathy in dementia: a systematic review. Am. J. Geriatr. Psych. **20**(7), 549–564 (2012). https://doi.org/10.1097/JGP.0b013e318 22be242

5. Manca, M., et al.: The impact of serious games with humanoid robots on mild cognitive impairment older adults. Int. J. Hum. Comput. Stud. **145** (2021). https://doi.org/10.1016/j. ijhcs.2020.102509

6. Cohen-Mansfield, J., Marx, M.S., Dakheel-Ali, M., Thein, K.: The use and utility of specific nonpharmacological interventions for behavioral symptoms in dementia: an exploratory study. Am. J. Geriat. Psych. **23**(2), 160–170 (2015). https://doi.org/10.1016/j.jagp.2014.06.006

7. McCallum, S., Boletsis, C.: Dementia games: a literature review of dementia-related serious games. In: Ma, M., Oliveira, M.F., Petersen, S., Hauge, J.B. (eds.) SGDA 2013. LNCS, vol. 8101, pp. 15–27. Springer, Heidelberg (2013). https://doi.org/10.1007/978-3-642-40790-1_2

8. Krueger, K.R., Wilson, R.S., Kamenetsky, J.M., Barnes, L.L., Bienias, J.L., Bennett, D.A.: Social engagement and cognitive function in old age. Exp. Aging Res. **35**(1), 45–60 (2009). https://doi.org/10.1080/03610730802545028

9. "Long-Term Services and Supports: Nursing Workforce Demand Projections About the National Center for Health Workforce Analysis" (2015). http://bhw.hrsa.gov/healthworkfo rce/index.html

10. Yu, R., et al.: Use of a therapeutic, socially assistive Pet Robot (PARO) in improving mood and stimulating social interaction and communication for people with dementia: study protocol for a randomized controlled trial. JMIR Res. Prot. **4**(2), e45 (2015). https://doi.org/10.2196/ resprot.4189

11. Šabanovic, S., Bennett, C.C., Chang, W.L., Huber, L.: PARO robot affects diverse interaction modalities in group sensory therapy for older adults with dementia (2013). https://doi.org/10. 1109/ICORR.2013.6650427

12. Görer, B., Salah, A.A., Akın, H.L.: A robotic fitness coach for the elderly. In: Augusto, J.C., Wichert, R., Collier, R., Keyson, D., Salah, A.A., Tan, A.-H. (eds.) AmI 2013. LNCS, vol. 8309, pp. 124–139. Springer, Cham (2013). https://doi.org/10.1007/978-3-319-03647-2_9

13. Fasola, J., Mataric, M.: A socially assistive robot exercise coach for the elderly. J. Hum.-Robot Interact. **2**(2), 3–32 (2013). https://doi.org/10.5898/jhri.2.2.fasola

14. Matsusaka, Y., Fujii, H., Okano, T., Hara, I.: Health exercise demonstration robot TAIZO and effects of using voice command in robot-human collaborative demonstration. In: Proceedings - IEEE International Workshop on Robot and Human Interactive Communication, pp. 472–477 (2009). https://doi.org/10.1109/ROMAN.2009.5326042

15. McColl, D., Louie, W.Y.G., Nejat, G.: Brian 2.1: a socially assistive robot for the elderly and cognitively impaired. IEEE Robot. Autom. Mag. **20**(1), 74–83 (2013). https://doi.org/10. 1109/MRA.2012.2229939

16. Eisapour, M., Cao, S., Domenicucci, L., Boger, J.: Virtual reality exergames for people living with dementia based on exercise therapy best practices. Proc. Hum. Fact. Ergon. Soc. **1**, 528–532 (2018). https://doi.org/10.1177/1541931218621120

17. Mann, J.A., Macdonald, B.A., Kuo, I.H., Li, X., Broadbent, E.: People respond better to robots than computer tablets delivering healthcare instructions. Comput. Hum. Behav. **43**, 112–117 (2015). https://doi.org/10.1016/j.chb.2014.10.029

18. Bainbridge, W.A., Hart, J.W., Kim, E.S., Scassellati, B.: The benefits of interactions with physically present robots over video-displayed agents. Int. J. Soc. Robot. **3**(1), 41–52 (2011). https://doi.org/10.1007/s12369-010-0082-7

19. Canadian Centre for Occupational Health and Safety: "Hand Tool Ergonomics - Tool Design: OSH Answers", Canada, 2020. https://www.ccohs.ca/oshanswers/ergonomics/handtools/tooldesign.html. Accessed 26 Oct 2020
20. Madgwick, S.O.H.: An efficient orientation filter for inertial and inertial/magnetic sensor arrays (2010). Accessed 09 Feb 2021
21. Brooke, J.: SUS-A quick and dirty usability scale (1996). Accessed 26 Oct 2020
22. Bangor, A., Kortum, P.T., Miller, J.T.: An empirical evaluation of the system usability scale. Int. J. Hum.-Comput. Interact. **24**(6), 574–594 (2008). https://doi.org/10.1080/10447310802205776

LifeSenior – A Health Monitoring IoT System Based on Deep Learning Architecture

Maicon Diogo Much[✉] , César Marcon , Fabiano Hessel ,
and Alfredo Cataldo Neto

Pontifical Catholic University of Rio Grande do Sul, Ipiranga Avenue 6681, Porto Alegre, Brazil
maicon.much@edu.pucrs.br

Abstract. This paper proposes an efficient and reliable elderly health monitoring system based on a low power IoT communication service inside a watch type wearable device. The watch senses motion (accelerometer, gyroscope, and magnetometer) and vital signs (heart rate variability, oxygen saturation, breathing rate, and blood volume pressure) to detect falls and other possible risk situations estimated by the EAEWS (Elderly Adopted Early Warning Scores) algorithm. Sense data collected are continuously fed into an embedded bi-LSTM (bidirectional Long Short-Term Memory) deep-learning neural network that bases the LifeSenior AI (Artificial Intelligence) health monitoring system. As there are no databases with motion and vital signs collected in the same environment, we design the LifeSenior Database Project (LDP); a motion-vital signs correlated database explicitly developed to the neural network training phase. Our experimental results in a simulated environment show that this architecture presents a 84,63% of accuracy in fall situations detection and can keep the user alert about his health.

Keywords: Wearable fall detector · IoT · Health monitoring system

1 Introduction

The number of older people living alone is continually increasing. In parallel, advances in diagnosis and treatment of diseases are growing life expectancy and creating a global scenario of older people away from an assisted living. According to the World Health Organization (WHO), between 2015 and 2020, the proportion of the world's population over 60 years will nearly double from 12% to 22% [1]. In a related context, WHO also showed that falls are the second leading cause of accidental or unintentional deaths worldwide [2].

The consumer electronics market is already saturated with wearable devices that intend to detect falls and request help from family members. However, these products have a high rate of false alarms associated with bad user interfaces, high energy consumption, and outdated communication systems, which affect their reliable performance.

Automated fall detection in real-time from data produced by sensors, such as triaxial accelerometers, is considered still an open research problem [3]. The goal of the

© Springer Nature Switzerland AG 2021
Q. Gao and J. Zhou (Eds.): HCII 2021, LNCS 12787, pp. 293–306, 2021.
https://doi.org/10.1007/978-3-030-78111-8_20

fall detectors is to identify real falls and usually notify family or caregivers so that they can intervene as fast as possible. However, fall recognition is challenging from a computational perspective. Falls can be defined as rapid changes like peak values in accelerometers data; still, they cannot be considered a controlled movement because they can happen in innumerable other scenarios that do not represent risk situations [4]. The reliability of a fall detector is based on a high capacity in detecting real falls associated with a low incidence of false alarms.

Over the last few years, many researchers proposed different architectures to overcome these problems. In a timeline scenario, the firsts fall detectors based on wearable devices sensing motion data proposed threshold-based algorithms [5] to identify the peak values from the accelerometer sensor that represents a fall. Still, researchers verified that this topology is not suitable outside a laboratory environment due to the high rate of false positives. Researchers started to aggregate new motion sensors to accelerometers to decrease the high rate of false fall detections, like a gyroscope, magnetometer, and barometric pressure [6]. Other researchers also tried to fuse motion and vital signs data but considering vital signs only as complementary information to the fall detector [7]. With the recent development of deep learning algorithms, the reliability of fall detection has evolved to the desired quality standards, opening up a significant area of research.

Vital signs are among the most critical health indicators in detecting or monitoring medical problems [8]. A change in an individual reference range may indicate an essential warning sign. Information such as fluctuations in skin temperature, a sudden increase in heart rate, decreased oxygen saturation, or blood pressure decrease associated with a specific movement can be used to confirm that a risk situation is in progress. Stress situations, like fall situations in older people, induces changes in vital signs [9]. Unfortunately, the relationship between motion and vital signs has been poorly addressed in the literature; the complete information about how vital signs behave after a fall is open research. However, some studies revealed important relations among falls, blood pressure, temperature, and respiration/heart rate [10]. Integration of vital signs into the fall detection algorithm system gives an enormous advantage to the proposed model in identifying and detecting real falls.

To develop an effective fall detector for older people, we built an embedded Artificial Intelligence (AI) system that processes physiological and motion data using a bi-LSTM deep learning neural network inside LifeSenior wearable. For the training phase, we develop a hybrid database that simulates vital signs in risk situations associated with collected real falls showing that this theory is applicable in a practical way.

The health information collected by LifeSenior wearable is transmitted continuously through SigFox IoT service [11] to a cloud system that processes all data received, enabling it to generate vital signs trends and calculate EAEWS to each aged person. Sigfox network covers many countries, establishing the most extensive Internet of Things (IoT) network in the world, making it possible to communicate directly from the device to the cloud. This topology is more power-efficient, breaking barriers comparing with traditional communication systems.

This paper is organized as follows. Section 2 details the system architecture and describes how LifeSenior works. Section 3 explains the health status detection algorithm developed. Section 4 details the experimental results and the conclusion is summarized at Sect. 5.

2   System Architecture

Figure 1 details our proposed IoT for an efficient health monitoring system; this architecture covers a wearable device, Sigfox network, back-end, LifeSenior cloud system, and application.

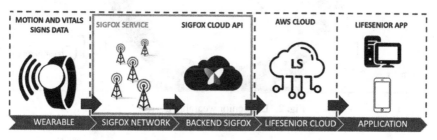

Fig. 1. LifeSenior older health monitoring system.

2.1   Wearable Device

The wearable device detailed in Fig. 2 was designed to be similar to a traditional watch, improving older people's acceptance. However, the wearable is much more complex than a simple watch. Inside the wearable case, dedicated circuits acquire vital user signs through a photoplethysmograph (PPG) sensor; besides, the wearable covers a complete motion system focused on learning the user's biological activity and detecting anomaly situations.

PPG sensor is used as an optical technique for detecting blood volume changes in the microvascular bed of tissue [12]. Our system uses the ADPD1080 PPG sensor from Analog Devices that process periodic data collected from the monitored user. Based on the PPG signal, LifeSenior extracts motion tolerant heart rate frequency [13], enabling the application to draw a trend variance, essential to control the heart rate variability (HRV). HRV is a recognized tool for the estimation of the cardiac autonomic modulations [14].

Processing optic sensor data, the wearable device also estimates the user oxygen saturation (SpO2) [15], filtering noise data to provide clean and trusted SpO2 information. A decrease in SpO2 value can indicate a reduction in oxygen circulation, which can predict respiratory problems. Besides pulse rate and SpO2, we also implemented a way to estimate the user breathing rate (BR) [16], a crucial physiological parameter used in a range of clinical settings, including patient deterioration analysis.

It is essential to regularly monitor the blood pressure to prevent hypertension cases and, as a result, strokes or heart failure. LifeSenior provides a way to continuously monitor blood pressure through an artificial intelligence algorithm that processes optic data estimating systolic and diastolic values [17]. All physiologic information obtained by LifeSenior wearable is not collected in diagnostic character, but to continuously monitor

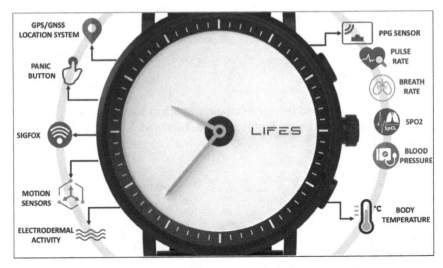

Fig. 2. LifeSenior wearable device.

the information checking for abnormal variations, rapid changes, or other situations that can indicate a risk situation. Vital signs collected help LifeSenior application check the user-health condition and notify family or health system in case of problems.

Elderly motion information is continuously collected using iNEMO [18] solution from STMicroelectronics, a 9-axis accelerometer, 3D gyroscope and 3D magnetometer encapsulated in a single package, named LSM9DS1.

In addition to the technical characteristics of the wearable to detect risky situations, it is essential to take into account its usability. In particular, we dedicate an exclusive research topic to take care of the time between battery charges, which is a problem due to the difficulties that the elderly has with electronic components. To be assertive in our choices, we specify an estimated time between charges of about 30 days. Our premise was to use all components board with low power consumption, which includes the choice of Sigfox IoT communication system, low power display, and the battery with more capacity than could be accommodated in the case (in our case, a rechargeable 100 mAh Lithium-Ion battery).

We choose an e-paper display to show the information in the wearable. The most important advantage of this technology is that it consumes energy only in the refresh process, meaning that static information remains on the screen without consuming energy. We choose the ET011TT3 from the E-INK e-paper manufacturer. In most parts, this display is composed of plastic materials and associated with the possibility of "turn-off" the display without impairing view and meeting some radio frequency communication requirements.

Antenna Design

As the communication system of LifeSenior is on a Sigfox network that works in the 900 MHz ISM frequency band in Latin America (Sigfox RC2 for Brasil), the design of an efficient antenna is a big challenge. It can explain why most smart wearable devices today only have either a Bluetooth or a Wi-Fi antenna that needs less internal space than one for a 900 MHz frequency band with similar efficiencies.

Meanwhile, a low manufacturing cost and a low specific absorption rate (SAR) are also highly desired since the human body is a lossy dielectric medium, the antenna performances must be robust against wrist tissue. The antenna radiation efficiency can be reduced dramatically once the antenna is placed near a human body.

To minimize the occupied space in the LifeSenior device, we proposed a circular ring antenna type made in copper and positioned immediately below the e-paper display with 33 mm (0.1 λ_0) in internal diameter, 2 mm (0.006 λ_0) thickness, and 3 mm (0.009 λ_0) high as shown in Fig. 3. The e-paper display was chosen with minimum metal parts and free of electronic components to reduce the electromagnetic interaction with the antenna, which certainly would degrade the communication performance.

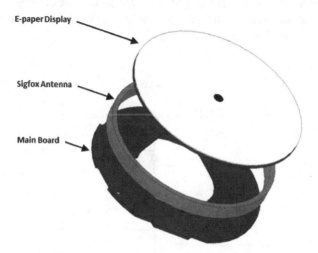

Fig. 3. Location of the SigFox ring antenna.

The ring antenna was designed using a software tool based on a Method of Moments, a computational electromagnetic method. A usual impedance matching circuit was also designed for obtaining the maximum power transfer between the antenna and Sigfox modem. Some significant results are presented in Table 1. It is worth noting that despite the tiny dimensions of the smartwatch for the 900 MHz frequency band, the antenna offers a good radiation efficiency.

The ring antenna was implemented on the LifeSenior device, and laboratory tests performed to measure the radiated power showed promising results, as displayed in Table 1. The experimental result section offers some field tests to confirm the reliable design of the antenna.

Table 1. Ring antenna characteristics.

Parameter	Value
Frequency band (MHz)	900–908
VSWR	<1.5
Radiation frequency (%)	68%
Radiated power (dBm) @ 902.2 MHz	20.2

2.2 Sigfox Network and Backend

Sigfox backend is the central hub where messages and information from each device are stored. To retrieve and use the data and administrate devices, we develop an integration process that creates a link between Sigfox and our LifeSenior Cloud-based in the callback service option, detailed in Fig. 4.

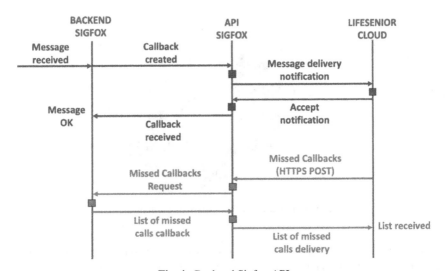

Fig. 4. Backend Sigfox API.

In a typical operation, each message sent is received in the backend, and a callback is generated to Sigfox API that instantly delivers a message to LifeSenior Cloud. A callback return message confirms to the backend that each message was received in the customer's cloud. A downtime situation in any part of this system is managed using a missed callback message that returns all missed messages and the reason why the messages were not received.

2.3 LifeSenior Cloud

We used a cloud service provided by Amazon Web Services (AWS) without any cost, thanks to the Sigfox IoT startups program [19], to manage the received messages from all wearable devices, creating LifeSenior Cloud service. Any new message received in the Sigfox network is identified by a unique device id and correlates with the list of the partners, redirecting it directly to the customer's cloud. In LifeSenior Cloud, we store all messages received from each device, notifying the application whenever is needed.

LifeSenior cloud runs the LifeSenior Health Status Algorithm detailed in Sect. 3 for each user keeping the elderly continuously under care.

2.4 LifeSenior Mobile Application

The LifeSenior application is a mobile and desktop platform dedicated to managing information from a predefined user. LifeSenior mobile application must be installed on the phone of the responsible person that receives notifications in any problem.

3   LifeSenior Health Status Algorithm (LHSA)

Monitoring elderly health status is the main functionality of the LifeSenior system. Figure 5 details that LHSA is divided into three main areas: elderly adopted early warning scores, vital signs trend analysis, and deep learning fall detector.

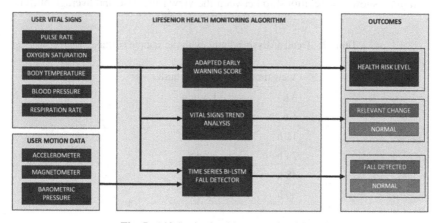

Fig. 5. LifeSenior health status algorithm.

3.1 Elderly Adapted Early Warning Score (EAEWS)

We implemented an adapted early warning score algorithm to predict illness situations in older people based on a joint analysis of user vital signs. EWS was initially created as a hospital bedside tool for alerting the medical staff about the patient situation. Still, the EWS use outside the hospital environment is increasing, and EWS is becoming a standard in the patient health classification. There are many different versions of EWS, and because of that, we implemented an adapted version [20] focused on older people shown in Fig. 6. The sum of each vital sign's results will form the user health score, where higher values denote a health-risk situation.

Vital Signs	SCORES						
	+3	+2	+1	0	+1	+2	+3
Systolic Blood Pressure [mmHg]		71-80	81-100	101-199		≥ 200	
Heart Rate [bpm]		<40	41-50	51-100	101-110	111-129	≥ 130
Respiration rate [rpm]		<9		9-14	15-20	21-29	≥ 30
Temperature [°C]		< 35		35 – 38.4		≥ 38.5	

Fig. 6. Classification standard of early warning score adapted for older people.

3.2 Vital Signs Trend Analysis

Every 30 s, a new sample of vital signs is made and stored for trend analysis. Each sample contains all the essential parameters received, technical conditions (data out of range or artifact), date, and acquisition time. This information is stored in LifeSenior Cloud and serves as the basis for calculating three buffer storage mediums: averages of 1.5, 6, and 12 min. The buffers are selected to provide data depending on the view time base. Table 2 shows the relationship between the view time base and average buffers.

Table 2. Trend analysis relation with the sample buffers.

View time base	Sample buffer
3 h	1.5 min
6 h	1.5 min
12 h	1.5 min
24 h	6 min
48 h	6 min
96 h	12 min

Taking different views of each time base, we can extract relevant changes in elderly health scenarios, filtering small changes associated with daily activities and using this information to detect appropriate changes in vital signs. For reference, we define that changes above or below 20% of the baseline of each vital sign is relevant and deserves attention.

3.3 Deep Learning Fall Detection

A usually fall situation is composed of three primary parameters: impact, posture, and velocity. The impact parameter is associated with four phases:

• Pre-fall - associated with daily living activities followed by some instability;

- Critical - correlated with a sudden movement directed to the ground;
- Post-fall - usually associated with a body rest scenario;
- Recovery - a phase that can exist or not.

As mentioned in Sect. 1, most fall detectors work based on detecting the critical phase, verifying only the instant peak represented by a fall situation in motion sensors. Our proposal is based on analyzing the four phases of a fall situation, combining information from motion and physiological sensors. Figure 7 displays the expected relation between movement and vital signs in a real fall.

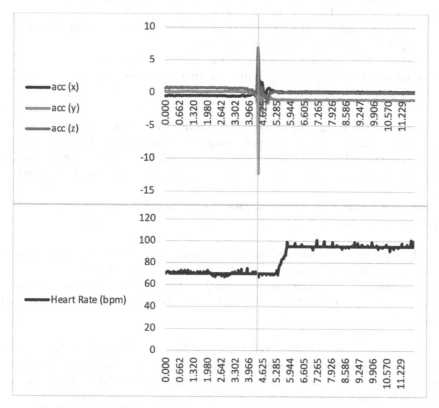

Fig. 7. Typical fall situation with accelerometer and heart rate data correlated.

Including the analysis of vital signs, while a fall is detected in motion sensors, we can take a better "picture" of the environment in which the user is inserted and his health situation, contributing to improving the accuracy and consequently decreasing the false-positive fall rate.

To develop an efficient AI algorithm to detect falls is essential to have a dataset that represents this scenario. There are no available databases in scientific repositories in that motion data was collected together with vital signs, like heart rate and oxygen saturation. In this scenario, we develop a simulated dataset associating real motion sensors in a fall, simulated vital signs that represent changes derived from an advanced stress situation creating the LifeSenior Database Project (LDP).

LifeSenior Database Project (LDP)

We build the LifeSenior database based on a reference dataset made up of real collections of movement data in fall situations and situations composed of daily activities [21]. The dataset collections encompass eight volunteers simulating 13 types of falls and five daily activities, each repeated three times. In detail, the dataset includes:

- Four simulated forward falls (falling on knees ending up lying, ending in a lateral position, ending up lying, ending up lying with recovery);
- Four backward falls (falling sitting and ending up lying, ending in a lateral position, ending up lying, ending up lying with recovery);
- Two lateral right (ending up lying, ending up lying with recovery);
- Two lateral left (ending up lying, ending up lying with recovery);
- One syncope.

Simulated ADLs are: lying on a bed than standing; walking a few meters; sitting on a chair then standing; go up or down three steps; and standing after picking something. Data were acquired using a MARG (Magnetic Angular Rate and Gravity) sensor, a wearable multisensory device, that recorded time-variations of the subject's acceleration and orientation.

For each situation of fall or simulated daily activity, we associate vital sign information consistent with the moment, considering the following criteria:

- Daily activities - we associated the typical physiological values of the adult patient maintaining them before, during, and after the simulated movement;
- Fall situations - we incremented around 20% the baseline values for the heartbeat, breathing, and blood pressure parameters and decreased 20% the temperature parameter.

The basis for this estimation comes from the fact that it is expected that in a risk situation, the physiological signals will change, helping to "validate" the fall that is detected in the motion sensors. The repository with the generated database is available at [22] to be used in other researches.

Deep Learning Architecture

Long-Short Term Memory (LSTM) provides a high capacity of modeling time-series data [23] thanks to its structure containing three gates, namely, input, forget, and output gates. LSTM uses the "input" and "forget" gates to decide which information to remember and drop, respectively. This skill makes it possible to modulate the ratio between remember old data and learn new information as reported in recent articles [24, 25], helping the system identify each user's natural behavior during LifeSenior use. This unique feature from LSTM is decisive to understand the real emergency that is applicable for each user, decreasing the false positive rate hugely.

In terms of the time-dependent classification task, both past and future input features can be useful information for a specific period. Additionally to the LSTM capabilities, the bi-LSTM can learn backward and forward long term dependencies. This architecture was first proposed by Graves [26] and is composed of a sequence input layer, multiple bi-LSTM layers, and one dense layer.

Let A be information from the sensors and B be the time bin (we use 300-time bins in 50 Hz sampling that produces 6 s of window frames), so the deep neural network proposed for this application uses continuous time-series of motion and physiological sensors as A × B input dimension. The dense layer output turns the output vector into an equal-length probability matrix, and the class that receives the highest probability is chosen.

Figure 8 details the proposed architecture, which allows the continuous analysis of the temporary series generated by the sensors without the need to carry out manual feature engineering.

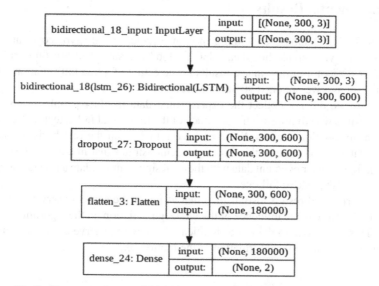

Fig. 8. Deep neural network bi-LSTM architecture proposed in LifeSenior.

The training phase encompasses 432 real movements associated with coherent simulated vital signs; these movements were divided into 120 daily living situations and 312 falls. We used 70% of the dataset for training and 30% for tests; the results can be observed in the next chapter.

Table 3 summarizes the characteristics and hyperparameters of the proposed deep neural network.

Table 3. Hyperparameters and characteristics adopted in bi-LSTM model.

Information	Value
Activation	Sigmoid
Optimizer	Adam
Dropout	0.2
Learning rate	1e−3
Decay	1e−5
Epochs	100
Batch size	300
Trainable parameters	1092000

4 Experimental Results

Using LifeSenior Database combining motion (accelerometer, gyroscope, and magnetometer) and vital signs (heartbeat, SpO2, blood pressure, and breathing rate), we achieved 84.63% of accuracy in test results for detection of a true fall situation. During the training phase, we obtained 90.36% of accuracy.

Although we did not collect the experimental data in older people, this scenario shows a feasible way to improve the accuracy of the traditional fall detectors based only on motion information sensors. We can observe that given the real basis of the vital signs simulated in the dataset, this technique demonstrates that in a true risk situation, the correlation of the movement data with the vital signs can validate a true fall situation, reducing the false positive fall rate.

The experimental results also display that as larger the signal observation window after a fall, the more is the influence of the vital sign variation on the algorithm decision making. This fact is due to the more significant latency to observe a change compared to the almost instantaneous information of the motion sensors.

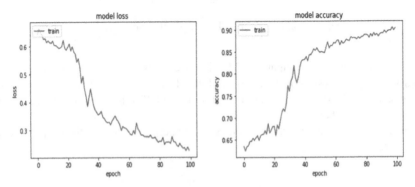

Fig. 9. Live loss and accuracy graph in the training process.

Figure 9 illustrates the loss decreasing during the training phase in line with the increasing of the epochs number, until getting the best result around 100 epochs.

5 Conclusion

This paper introduced an efficient and feasible IoT health monitoring system contributing to technologies that help older people worldwide live alone, preserving their independence, but keeping their family peaceful that no emergency or risk situation occurs without their knowing.

The framework proposed for the elderly health status algorithm allowed to avoid manual segmentation enabling a high-performance time-series verification in near real-time with good accuracy results confirming that this model can represent a true risk situation.

For future work, we will embed the health status algorithm in the wearable device to confirm the simulated environment results and develop a clinical study to update the LifeSenior Database Project with physiological data collected during falls and daily living activities.

Acknowledgment. This work was financed in part by the Coordenação de Aperfeiçoamento de Pessoal de Nível Superior (CAPES) – Finance Code 001, and CNPq.

References

1. World Health Organization: Ageing and health (2018). https://www.who.int/news-room/fact-sheets/detail/ageing-and-health. Accessed 07 Jan 2021
2. Falls (2018). https://www.who.int/news-room/fact-sheets/detail/falls. Accessed 07 Jan 2021
3. Pannurat, N., Thiemjarus, S., Nantajeewarawat, E.: Automatic fall monitoring: a review. Sensors **14**, 12900–12936 (2014)
4. Noury, N., et al.: Fall detection-principles and methods. In: Noury, N., et al. (ed.) 2007 29th Annual International Conference of the IEEE Engineering in Medicine and Biology Society, pp. 1663–1666. IEEE (2007)
5. Bourke, A.K., O'brien, J.V., Lyons, G.M.: Evaluation of a threshold-based tri-axial accelerometer fall detection algorithm. Gait Posture **26**, 194–199 (2007)
6. Huynh, Q.T., et al.: Fall detection system using combination accelerometer and gyroscope. In: Proceedings of the Second International Conference on Advances in Electronic Devices and Circuits (EDC 2013) (2013)
7. Koshmak, G.A., Loutfi, A.: Evaluation of the android-based fall detection system with physiological data monitoring. In: 2013 35th Annual International Conference of the IEEE Engineering in Medicine and Biology Society (EMBC), pp. 1164–1168 (2013)
8. Chester, J.G., Rudolph, J.L.: Vital signs in older patients: age-related changes. J. Am. Med. Dir. Assoc. **12**, 337–343 (2011)
9. Kim, H.G., et al.: Stress and hear rate variability: a meta-analysis and review of the literature. Psychiatry Investig. **15**, 235 (2018)
10. Naschitz, J.E., Rosner, I.: Orthostatic hypotension: framework of the syndrome. Postgrad. Med. J. **83**, 568–574 (2007)
11. Sigfox: A 0G network. https://www.sigfox.com. Accessed 07 Jan 2021

12. Allen, J.: Photoplethysmography and its application in clinical physiological measurement. Physiol. Meas. **28**, R1 (2007)
13. Ishikawa, T., et al.: Wearable motion tolerant ppg sensor for instant heart rate in daily activity. In: International Conference on Bio-Inspired Systems and Signal Processing, pp. 126–133 (2017)
14. Camm, A.J., et al.: Heart rate variability. Standards of measurement, physiological interpretation, and clinical use. Task Force of the European Society of Cardiology and the North American Society of Pacing and Electrophysiology (1996)
15. Mohan, P.M., et al.: Measurement of arterial oxygen saturation (SpO2) using PPG optical sensor. In: International Conference on Communication and Signal Processing (ICCSP), pp. 1136–1140 (2016)
16. Jarchi, D., et al.: Validation of instantaneous respiratory rate using reflectance PPG from different body positions. Sensors **18**, 3705 (2018)
17. Kurylyak, Y., Lamonaca, F., Grimaldi, D.: A neural network-based method for continuous blood pressure estimation from a PPG signal. In: 2013 IEEE International Instrumentation and Measurement Technology Conference (I2MTC), pp. 280–283 (2013)
18. ST MICROLECTRONICS: iNEMO. https://www.st.com/en/mems-and-sensors/inemo-inertial-modules.html. Accessed 29 Jan 2021
19. Sigfox: Sigfox IoT startups program. www.sigfox.com/en/news/iot-startups-sigfox-programs-can-now-benefit-aws-activate-program. Accessed 18 Jan 2021
20. Cei, M., Bartolomei, C., Mumoli, N.: In-hospital mortality and morbidity of elderly medical patients can be predicted at admission by the modified early warning score: a prospective study. Int. J. Clin. Pract. **63**, 591–595 (2009)
21. Cotechini, V., et al.: A dataset for the development and optimization of fall detection algorithms based on wearable sensors. Data Brief **23**, 103839 (2019)
22. Much, M.: LifeSenior Database Project. https://github.com/maicondiogomuch/LifeSeniorDatabase. Accessed 10 Jan 2021
23. Sülo, I., et al.: Energy efficient smart buildings: LSTM neural networks for time series prediction. In: 2019 International Conference on Deep Learning and Machine Learning in Emerging Applications (Deep-ML) (2019)
24. Queralta, J.P., et al.: Edge-AI in LoRa-based health monitoring: fall detection system with fog computing and LSTM recurrent neural networks. In: 2019 42nd International Conference on Telecommunications and Signal Processing (TSP) (2019)
25. Li, H., et al.: Bi-LSTM network for multimodal continuous human activity recognition and fall detection. IEEE Sens. J. **20**, 1191–1201 (2019)
26. Graves, A., Schmidhuber, J.: Framewise phoneme classification with bidirectional LSTM and other neural network architectures. Neural Netw. **18**, 602–610 (2005)

Prediction of Sleep Quality in Live-Alone Diabetic Seniors Using Unobtrusive In-Home Sensors

Barry Nuqoba[✉] and Hwee-Pink Tan

School of Information Systems, Singapore Management University, Singapore, Singapore
barrynuqoba.2019@phdcs.smu.edu.sg, hptan@smu.edu.sg

Abstract. Diabetes, a chronic disease that occurs when the pancreas does not produce enough insulin or when the body cannot effectively utilize its insulin, is increasingly recognized as a significant health burden and affects many older adults. Poor sleep quality in diabetic seniors worsens the diabetes condition, but most seniors are tend to regard poor sleep quality as a usual event and do not seek treatment. This study aims to detect poor sleep quality in diabetic seniors through passive in-home monitoring to inform intervention (e.g., seeking diagnosis and treatment) to improve the physical and mental health of diabetic seniors. We derive sensor-based classification models using data from motion sensors installed in each apartment zone (bedroom, living room, kitchen, and bathroom) and a contact sensor on the main door from 39 seniors. Diabetes and poor sleep quality labeling are done based on psychosocial survey data. Our evaluation of the model reveals that (i) diabetes classification using features related to kitchen activity achieved perfect precision, (ii) sleep quality classification in diabetic seniors achieved the best results using Naïve Bayes and features related to night activity. Correlation analysis also reveals that seniors with diabetes are more likely to have poor sleep quality due to frequently voiding at night. Our findings can help community caregivers to monitor the sleep quality of diabetic seniors.

Keywords: Diabetes · Sleep quality · Sensors

1 Introduction

Diabetes affects around 463 million people globally in 2019 [8]. The rate is similar in both genders [20], but the prevalence is more than two times higher among seniors compared to middle age or young adults [7]. Moreover, the trends show that the rate is continually increasing over time [8]. Around 4.2 million death cases in 2019 are caused by diabetes [8], making it the seventh leading cause of death worldwide [19]. International Diabetes Federation (IDF) defines diabetes as a chronic condition that occurs when the pancreas is no longer able to produce insulin, or when the body cannot make good use of the insulin it provides [15].

© Springer Nature Switzerland AG 2021
Q. Gao and J. Zhou (Eds.): HCII 2021, LNCS 12787, pp. 307–321, 2021.
https://doi.org/10.1007/978-3-030-78111-8_21

Diabetes is a chronic, long-term disease that has a massive impact on the lives and well-being of individuals, relatives, and societies worldwide [18]. Improper treatment of diabetes can cause many complications, such as cardiovascular disease, stroke, chronic kidney disease, foot ulcers, damage to the nerves, damage to the eyes, and cognitive impairment [2,17]. The expenditure related to diabetes was approximately US$727 billion in 2017 worldwide [8]. In the United States, medical cost for diabetes was around US$327 billion in 2017 [6]. [3] showed that people with diabetes have a 2.3 times higher average medical cost than non diabetic people.

According to [12], the most important factor causing the increase of morbidity and mortality in diabetic patients is the lack of self-care. Self-care is an active process that should be used daily by diabetic patients to control their disease more efficiently. One of the most important aspect of self-care is related to sleep quality, as sleep disturbance often appears among patients with diabetes [16]. On the other hand, other studies revealed that sleep helps memory functions [1], emotional regulation [4], and metabolic processes [5]. Ironically, most people, including diabetic seniors, are tend to regard poor sleep as a usual event and do not seek treatments.

SHINESeniors [13] investigated in-home sensors' actual use to enable 100 senior Singaporeans living alone to age-in-place in the community. Analysis of the sensor data, together with psychosocial survey data as well as ad-hoc observations made during home visits by the research team, enables holistic studies to address (i) the immediate and personal safety needs of the seniors (reactive care) and (ii) long-term conditions and social needs of the seniors (preventive care). Previous studies, part of SHINESeniors, have achieved promising results for detecting risk of poor sleep quality [14], social isolation [10], and frailty deterioration [9] on seniors using in-home sensors.

We aim to detect diabetes and poor sleep quality in diabetic seniors through objective and continuous in-home sensor data and psychosocial survey data to inform intervention to improve the physical and mental health of the seniors. We describe the data sources and our approach to data preparation and feature extraction in Sect. 2. We present the results of sensor-based diabetes and poor sleep quality classification using ground truth labeling based on survey data in Sect. 3. Also, we explain the relationship between sensor derived features with diabetes and poor sleep quality in diabetic seniors in Sect. 4. Finally, we conclude the paper and outline possible future research directions in Sect. 5.

2   In-Home Sensors for Poor Sleep Quality Detection in Diabetic Seniors

In this section, we describe our approach towards in-home sensor-based poor sleep quality detection in diabetic seniors as illustrated in Fig. 1. Specifically, we first describe the data sources used in this study. Following this, our approach towards data preparation and feature extraction are described subsequently in the next sections.

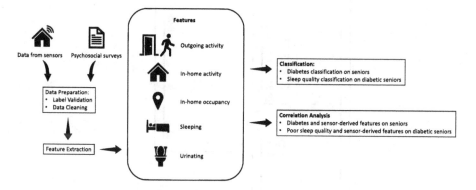

Fig. 1. Framework for in-home sensor-based diabetes and poor sleep quality detection.

2.1 Data Sources

This study used data from the seniors who voluntarily participate in the SHINE-Seniors project. All participants aged 65 years or more, live alone in government-subsidized apartments, and have affiliation with caregiver organizations in local communities. The project deployed passive infrared (PIR) motion sensors in each location of the senior's home and a door contact sensor on the main door to unobtrusively and continuously capture the seniors' activities at home and understand the going out patterns. Moreover, the project also installed a gateway in each senior's home to transfer the sensors collected data to the backend server for further analysis. Figure 2 present an illustration of sensor-enabled home in a typical senior's apartment.

Figure 3 shows an example of raw sensors data collected from in-home sensors. Each row in the sensors' raw data consists of information about the device (device_id, device_loc, reading_type), time and values transmitted by the device (gw_timestamp, value), and the id of the senior (resident_index_list). The motion sensor will transmit a value of 255 (indicating the senior start a motion) if it detects a motion in its location range after a minimum of four minutes of non-motion. Otherwise, it will transmit a value of 0 (indicating the senior ends the motion) if the sensor detects no movement within four minutes after the last movement. The door contact sensor send a signal each time the door is opened (value = 255) or closed (value = 0). The device_loc values in rows 30 and 39 are "NaN" because the values are not related to a specific location of the house. Those rows represent gateway intrinsic information in the senior home (e.g. inactivity period).

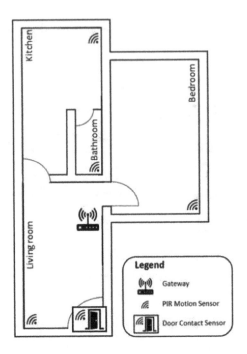

Fig. 2. An illustration of in-home monitoring system in a usual senior's home.

	device_id	device_loc	gw_timestamp	reading_type	resident_index_list	value
26	6005-m-01	living_room	2018-04-01T00:22:58	motion	MP0012	255
28	6005-m-04	toilet_bathroom	2018-04-01T00:25:40	motion	MP0012	0
29	6005-m-03	kitchen	2018-04-01T00:26:41	motion	MP0012	0
30	6005	NaN	2018-04-01T00:27:05	inactivity_ms	MP0012	24095
31	6005-m-01	living_room	2018-04-01T00:29:02	motion	MP0012	0
34	6005-m-04	toilet_bathroom	2018-04-01T00:33:38	battery_percent	MP0012	100
35	6005-m-01	living_room	2018-04-01T00:33:56	motion	MP0012	255
37	6005-m-01	living_room	2018-04-01T00:38:17	motion	MP0012	0
39	6005	NaN	2018-04-01T00:42:05	inactivity_ms	MP0012	227532

Fig. 3. Example of raw sensor data.

This study uses the Chronic Disease Profiling and Management survey of the seniors as the ground truth for diabetes classification. We classify the seniors as diabetic if they answer that they are diagnosed with diabetes in the survey; otherwise, we classify them as non-diabetic. Moreover, we use the Pittsburgh Sleep Quality Index (PSQI) results to calculate the seniors sleeping quality and subsequently classify the seniors based on the calculated sleep quality score. We categorize the seniors as having poor sleep quality if the calculated sleep quality score is equal to or more than 5; otherwise, we classify the seniors as having good sleep quality.

For this study, we considered the results of two psychosocial surveys conducted in around March 2018 and December 2018 to serve as the ground truth. Accordingly, we use the sensor data up to one month before each senior's survey date (see Fig. 4) for the subsequent steps. The reason is that the survey about sleeping habits only relates to the month's sleeping pattern before the survey.

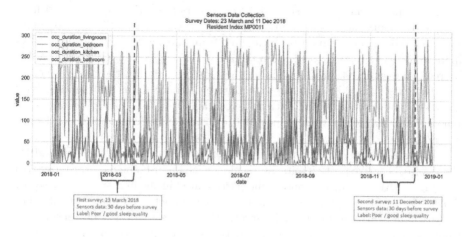

Fig. 4. Sensor data collection timeline.

2.2 Data Preparation

Data preparation in this study aimed to prepare the raw data before being used in feature extraction. We conduct data preparation in two steps (see Fig. 1). First, we validate each senior's label related to diabetes diagnosis by considering the results of the two Chronic Diseases Profiling and Management surveys. If the results of the two survey are different, we apply several rules to validate the survey results as presented in Fig. 5. Moreover, we conduct an additional treatment if the answer is 'NaN' by checking the sensors data one month before the survey took place to ensure that the senior has not dropped out of the project. If the sensors' data are available, we treat 'NaN' the same as 'Not sure' (as rule 3 and 4). Otherwise, we remove the senior from the experiments.

Fig. 5. Validation rules.

The requirements of the study are the seniors must (i) live alone and have complete sensors data during one month before the survey, (ii) have diabetes label derived from the survey, or concluded from another survey and (iii) participate in a survey related to sleep. In the second stage, we conduct data cleaning by removing seniors that do not fulfill the requirements. Furthermore, we clean the raw sensor data by removing the device intrinsic data, such as inactivity duration (row 30 and 39) and battery percentage (row 34) (see Fig. 3), and what remains are only data with values of 0 or 255 comes from motion and door contact sensors.

During the study duration, i.e., between January 2018 to December 2018, there were 39 active participants, i.e., seniors with an in-home monitoring system (see Fig. 6). Among the 39 seniors who participated in the first survey, one senior did not respond to the survey questions about diabetes. We can not inference the diabetes status from another survey. Also, two seniors had no sensor data from the bathroom motion sensor, and two seniors had no sensor data at all in the month preceding the survey. Among the 34 seniors who participated in the second survey, one senior had a helper or long stay visitor. Two seniors had no sensor data from the bathroom motion sensor, and three seniors had no sensor data at all in the month preceding the survey. As the project conducted both surveys eight months apart, we treat the same senior survey results as two independent data points in this study.

Accordingly, we have data set A consisting of 62 data points: 34 data points from the first survey and 28 data points from the second survey. Among them, we labeled 22 data points as diabetic, while 40 data points as non-diabetic. Moreover, prepare data set B by filtering the data set A to contain only diabetic seniors. Among the 22 data points which we labeled as diabetic, 5 data points labeled as having good sleep quality and 17 data points labeled as having poor sleep quality.

As the result of the data preparation, we have (i) two data sets (data set A and data set B) containing only the label for each senior in the data set and (ii) cleaned raw data to be used in the feature extraction.

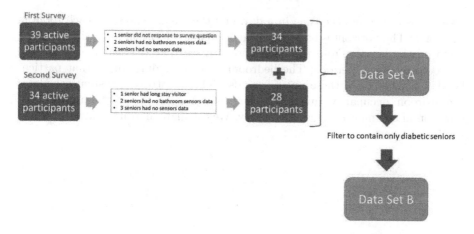

Fig. 6. Removing the seniors who do not fulfill the study requirement.

2.3 Feature Extraction

We extracted several features from the cleaned raw sensors data to depict the seniors' daily living patterns. The features are derived based on three periods: the whole day (24 h), daytime (7 am to 7 pm), and night-time (7 pm to 7 am). Below are the definitions of each generated feature:

1. **Outgoing activity**: Outgoing activity includes away duration and frequency. The system calculates away duration when the door contact sensor is triggered, and it detects no motion inside the house for a minimum duration of 30 min afterward. Away frequency is the number of times the seniors leave the house.
2. **In-home activity**: In-home activity related to the in-home active duration in each location of the house and in-home transitions. The system calculates in-home active duration in each home's part based on the respective area's motion sensor. Furthermore, the system calculates in-home transitions by counting the number of times the seniors move between one place to another inside the house (e.g., move from bedroom to living room).
3. **In-home occupancy**: In-home occupancy related to in-home occupancy duration and frequency. The system calculates the in-home occupancy duration for each house's part based on the time the seniors spent in the corresponding area. Furthermore, occupancy frequency is the number of times the senior occupies the area.
4. **Sleep duration**: sleep duration is the period spent by the senior for sleeping activity.
5. **Urinating**: Urinating is related to the number of times the seniors urinating and spending time in the bathroom.

To better understand how the system extracts the sensor data features, below is an example of how it derives the occupancy duration features. Figure 7 illustrates the occupancy duration in a single day derived from the sensors data.

The x-axis represents the time in a day, and the y-axis represents each room in the home. The horizontal bar shows the occupancy duration for each respective room on the y-axis. From the graph, we can see that the senior occupies the bedroom for seven periods. The bedroom occupancy duration of that particular day is the sum of these seven periods. Subsequently, the system calculates the bedroom occupancy duration feature by averaging the bedroom occupancy duration in one month before the survey. We calculate all other features using a similar approach.

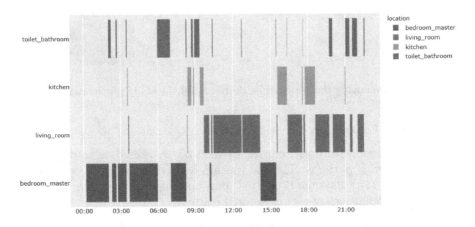

Fig. 7. Occupancy duration in each location in a day.

After feature extraction, we used data set A in the experiments of (i) identifying seniors with diabetes and (ii) correlation analysis between diabetes and features extracted from in-home sensors. Furthermore, we used data set B in the experiments of (i) identifying poor sleep quality in diabetic seniors and (ii) correlation analysis between poor sleep quality in diabetic seniors and features extracted from in-home sensors.

3   Sensor-Based Poor Sleep Quality Detection in Diabetic Seniors

In this section, we utilize the two data sets prepared previously to build sensor-based classification models for detecting diabetes in seniors and poor sleep quality in diabetic seniors. We first calculate the Pearson Correlation Coefficient (r) between the dependent variable (i.e., diabetes or poor sleep quality) and each of independent variables (features derived from in-home sensors). The values of r represent the strength of the correlation. Specifically, the correlation coefficient with absolute values between 0.00 and 0.09 is considered very weak, 0.10 to 0.29 is weak, 0.30 to 0,49 is moderate, and 0.50 to 1.0 is strong. Furthermore, the sign of the r represents the direction of the correlation. Then, we removed less important features ($r < 0.15$). Finally, we applied forward feature selection by selecting one feature that results in the highest classification accuracy, and adding more features until there is no further improvement in accuracy.

3.1 Sensor-Based Classification of Diabetes in Seniors

We randomly split the data set A into training and testing set with a proportion of 80:20, respectively. We added a constraint on the split process that makes the training and testing set have the same distribution of the two classes (diabetic and non-diabetic). We evaluated four machine learning algorithms' classification performance, namely, Decision Tree, Support Vector Machine (SVM), K-Nearest Neighbour (KNN), and Naive Bayes. The evaluation metrics used include precision, recall, accuracy, and F1-score, where the F1-score will be used as the primary performance metric.

Next, Table 1 shows the results of forward feature selection for data set A before the classification. It is interesting to observe that the feature most correlated with diabetes are features related to kitchen activity and occupancy.

Table 1. Features selected (r value) and description for data set A.

Feature (r value)	Description
duration_kitchen_occ_day (−0.369607)	Duration in the kitchen at day time
duration_act_level_kitchen_day (−0.335706)	Activity duration in the kitchen at day time
num_kitchen_occ_day (−0.335706)	Frequency of kitchen visit at day time

Finally, Table 2 show the results of classification with forward feature selection on data set A using features selected in Table 1. The experiments on classifying seniors into diabetic and non-diabetic show that all algorithms performed well by having more than 85% accuracy and perfect precision. Moreover, Decision Tree algorithm outperforms other algorithms with F1-score of 89%.

Table 2. Classification results with forward feature selection on data set A.

Methods	TP	FP	FN	TN	Accuracy	Precision	Recall	F1-Score
Decision Tree	8	0	1	4	0.92	1.00	0.80	0.89
SVM	8	0	2	3	0.85	1.00	0.60	0.75
KNN	8	0	2	3	0.85	1.00	0.60	0.75
Naive Bayes	8	0	2	3	0.85	1.00	0.60	0.75

3.2 Sensor-Based Classification of Sleep Quality in Diabetic Seniors

We randomly split the data set B into training and testing set with the same proportion and constraint as data set A. We also applied the same machine learning algorithms and metrics as in diabetes classification to evaluate the algorithms' performance.

Next, Table 3 shows the results of forward feature selection for data set B before the classification. It is interesting to observe that the feature most correlated with sleep quality in diabetic seniors is bathroom activity level duration at night.

Table 3. Features selected (r value) and description for data set B.

Feature (r value)	Description
duration_act_level_bathroom_night (−0.423131)	Activity duration in the bathroom at night
duration_bedroom_occ_night (0.405703)	Duration in the bedroom at night
duration_act_level_kitchen_night (−0.403440)	Activity duration in the kitchen at night

Finally, Table 4 show the results of classification with forward feature selection on data set B using features selected in Table 3. The experiments on classifying diabetic seniors into diabetic and non-diabetic show that the limited number of data points became an obstacle for the algorithms to perform well, eventhough Naive Bayes able to yield a perfect classification.

Table 4. Classification results with forward feature selection on data set B.

Methods	TP	FP	FN	TN	Accuracy	Precision	Recall	F1-Score
Decision Tree	1	0	1	3	0.80	1.00	0.75	0.86
SVM	0	1	1	3	0.60	0.00	0.75	0.00
KNN	0	1	0	4	0.80	0.00	1.00	0.00
Naive Bayes	1	0	0	4	1.00	1.00	1.00	1.00

4 Correlation Analysis of Sensor-Derived Features

This section observes the strength and direction of the relationship between sensor derived features and diabetes and poor sleep quality in diabetic seniors by calculating the Pearson correlation coefficient (r).

4.1   Correlation Analysis Between Sensor-Derived Features and Diabetes

Figure 8 shows the correlation between diabetes and each feature extracted from sensors. From the results, we observe that diabetes and sensor-derived features are correlated with various strengths and directions. Moreover, the strength span from very weak to moderate. These results support the explanation given by [11] that features extracted from passive data collection (which is our case) may correlate with target diseases, but the strengths are not as significant as features resulting from active data collection which tends to target metrics specific to a disease.

Diabetes positively correlated with bathroom activity features at night, such as duration spent by the seniors in the bathroom at night, number of nocturia, and activity duration in the bathroom at night. The results are in line with the previous research finding that seniors with diabetes are tend to void more, especially at nighttime. In other words, diabetic seniors likely to wake up at night due to urination.

Moreover, diabetes negatively correlated with kitchen activity features in the daytime, such as duration spent by the seniors in the kitchen during the day, activity duration in the kitchen during the day, and the number of times the seniors go to the kitchen during the day. The low energy level of the diabetic seniors possibly leads to the seniors prefer to spend their time in the bedroom rather than doing activity in the kitchen (i.e., cooking).

4.2   Correlation Analysis Between Sensor-Derived Features and Poor Sleep Quality in Diabetic Seniors

Figure 9 shows the correlation between poor sleep quality in diabetic seniors and each feature extracted from sensors. From the results, we observe that the results also support the explanation given by [11].

Poor sleep quality in diabetic seniors positively correlated with features related to bedroom occupancy during day and night. The results signify that diabetic seniors with poor sleep quality are tend to spend most of their time in the bedroom. Also, poor sleep quality in diabetic seniors positively correlated with activity duration in the bedroom day and night. The results imply that eventhough the seniors spend most of their time in the bedroom, the movement is also high. These facts probably because the seniors cannot sleep at ease even though they are already in the bedroom.

The result shows that diabetic seniors with poor sleep quality negatively correlated with the bathroom's activity duration at night. This fact contradicts our previous result mentioned that diabetes is positively associated with bathroom activity at night. The reason for this contradiction probably because diabetic seniors with poor sleep quality are more frailty. Therefore they already wear diapers at night to urinate without needing to go to the bathroom.

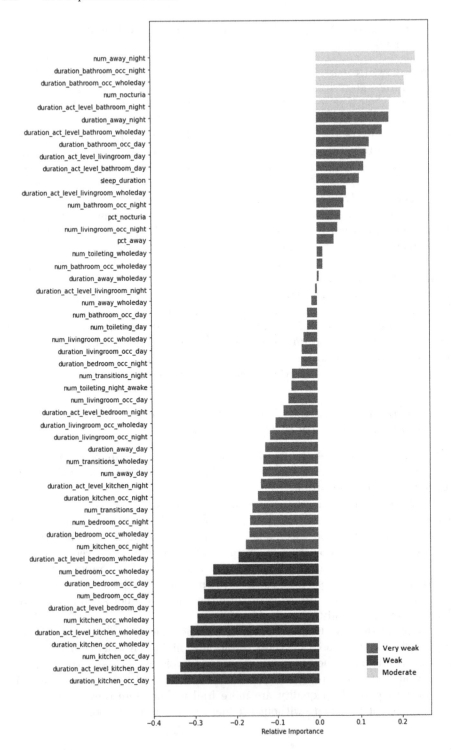

Fig. 8. Correlation between diabetes and features extracted from sensors.

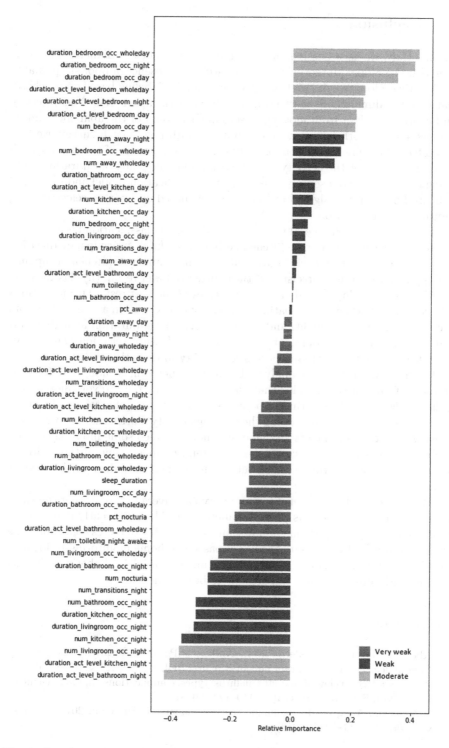

Fig. 9. Correlation between poor sleep quality in diabetic seniors and features extracted from sensors.

5 Conclusion

In this study, we used passive, in-home monitoring to detect diabetes among 39 seniors living alone. Moreover, we also identify the presence of poor sleep quality in diabetic seniors. We did diabetes and sleep quality labeling based on psychosocial surveys administered at two time points 8 months apart. Based on objective and continuous data from motion sensors in each room of the apartment and a contact sensor on the main door up to one month before each survey, we first extracted 52 features consisting of daily behavioral patterns of the seniors, such as room occupancy, the activity level in each room, and going out duration. Subsequently, we derived a sensor-based diabetes classification model and compared four machine learning algorithms' performance based on features selected using forward feature selection.

The results showed several interesting findings: (i) classification based on diabetes using features related to kitchen activity (i.e., kitchen occupancy duration at day, kitchen activity level duration at day, and number of kitchen occupancy at day) achieved perfect precision at the expense of lower recall, (ii) classification based on sleep quality in diabetic seniors achieved the best results using features related to night activity (i.e., bathroom activity level duration at night, bedroom occupancy duration at night, and kitchen activity level duration at night), (iii) Naive Bayes model in combination with forward feature selection can achieve perfect accuracy in identifying poor sleep quality in diabetic seniors.

In addition, correlation analysis between diabetes in seniors and features extracted from sensors revealed that diabetic seniors (i) tend to void more, especially at night, which resulting in poor sleep quality (ii) prefer to spend time in the bedroom, and (iii) rarely doing the cooking activity. Furthermore, correlation analysis of poor sleep quality in diabetic seniors revealed some interesting facts. Diabetic seniors with poor sleep quality (i) tend to spend time in the bedroom at day and night, (ii) rarely go to bathroom at night (use diapers) because of their frailty condition.

The above results can benefit community caregivers in monitoring the sleep quality of diabetic seniors as part of diabetic care. Moreover, early detection of poor sleep quality can prevent the worsening effect of the diabetes condition. The future research will investigate the use of passive in-home monitoring to identify harmful mental disorders (e.g., depression, anxiety, fear) in diabetic seniors as mental conditions have huge impacts on diabetes condition.

References

1. Abel, T., Havekes, R., Saletin, J.M., Walker, M.P.: Sleep, plasticity and memory from molecules to whole-brain networks. Curr. Biol. **23**(17), R774–R788 (2013)
2. Amin, N.: An overview of diabetes mellitus; types, complications, and management. Int. J. Nur. Sci. Pract. Res. **4**(1), 119–124 (2018)
3. Association, A.D., et al.: Economic costs of diabetes in the us in 2012. Diabetes Care **36**(4), 1033–1046 (2013)

4. Baran, B., Pace-Schott, E.F., Ericson, C., Spencer, R.M.: Processing of emotional reactivity and emotional memory over sleep. J. Neurosci. **32**(3), 1035–1042 (2012)
5. Benington, J.H., Heller, H.C.: Restoration of brain energy metabolism as the function of sleep. Prog. Neurobiol. **45**(4), 347–360 (1995)
6. Care, D.: Economic costs of diabetes in the us in 2017. Diabetes Care **41**, 917 (2018)
7. Cowie, C.C., et al.: Full accounting of diabetes and pre-diabetes in the us population in 1988–1994 and 2005–2006. Diabetes Care **32**(2), 287–294 (2009)
8. Federation, I.D.: Idf diabetes atlas ninth edition 2019 (2019)
9. Goonawardene, N., Tan, H.-P., Tan, L.B.: Unobtrusive detection of frailty in older adults. In: Zhou, J., Salvendy, G. (eds.) ITAP 2018. LNCS, vol. 10927, pp. 290–302. Springer, Cham (2018). https://doi.org/10.1007/978-3-319-92037-5_22
10. Goonawardene, N., Toh, X.P., Tan, H.-P.: Sensor-driven detection of social isolation in community-dwelling elderly. In: Zhou, J., Salvendy, G. (eds.) ITAP 2017. LNCS, vol. 10298, pp. 378–392. Springer, Cham (2017). https://doi.org/10.1007/978-3-319-58536-9_30
11. Kourtis, L.C., Regele, O.B., Wright, J.M., Jones, G.B.: Digital biomarkers for Alzheimer's disease: the mobile/wearable devices opportunity. NPJ Digit. Med. **2**(1), 1–9 (2019)
12. Landim, C.A., Zanetti, M.L., Santos, M.A., Andrade, T.A., Teixeira, C.R.: Self-care competence in the case of Brazilian patients with diabetes mellitus in a multiprofessional educational programme. J. Clin. Nurs. **20**(23–24), 3394–3403 (2011)
13. Liming, B., et al.: Shineseniors: personalized services for active ageing-in-place. In: 2015 IEEE First International Smart Cities Conference (ISC2), pp. 1–2. IEEE (2015)
14. Ma, X., Goonawardene, N., Tan, H.P.: Identifying elderly with poor sleep quality using unobtrusive in-home sensors for early intervention. In: Proceedings of the 4th EAI International Conference on Smart Objects and Technologies for Social Good, pp. 94–99 (2018)
15. Organization, W.H., et al.: Definition and diagnosis of diabetes mellitus and intermediate hyperglycaemia: report of a who/idf consultation (2006)
16. Resnick, H.E., et al.: Diabetes and sleep disturbances: findings from the sleep heart health study. Diabetes Care **26**(3), 702–709 (2003)
17. Saedi, E., Gheini, M.R., Faiz, F., Arami, M.A.: Diabetes mellitus and cognitive impairments. World J. Diabetes **7**(17), 412 (2016)
18. Saeedi, P., et al.: Global and regional diabetes prevalence estimates for 2019 and projections for 2030 and 2045: results from the international diabetes federation diabetes atlas. Diabetes Res. Clin. Pract. **157**, 107843 (2019)
19. Sreedharan, R., Abdelmalak, B.: Diabetes mellitus: preoperative concerns and evaluation. Anesthesiol. Clin. **36**(4), 581–597 (2018)
20. Vos, T., et al.: Years lived with disability (ylds) for 1160 sequelae of 289 diseases and injuries 1990–2010: a systematic analysis for the global burden of disease study 2010. Lancet **380**(9859), 2163–2196 (2012)

Development of Smartphone Based Personal Health Tracking System for Older People

Xuan Wang and Qin Gao[✉]

Department of Industrial Engineering, Tsinghua University, Beijing, People's Republic of China
gaoqin@tsinghua.edu.cn

Abstract. With the rapid aging of China's population, the imbalance between the needs and resources in health maintenance for the elderly is getting more and more attention. On the one hand, although most of the elderly are able to take care of themselves, the extremely high prevalence of chronic diseases makes them also need some help. On the other hand, there is a serious "empty nest" phenomenon among the elderly in China, which indicates insufficient home care. It is an effective way to alleviate this imbalance to help the elderly who have self-care ability better carry out healthy self-management. However, there is still a lack of effective interventions to guide the elderly in health self-management. Based on this idea, this study designed a personal health tracking system for the elderly based on smartphone. The system integrates needs of the elderly and medical staff, and its functions involve medical records management, physical index monitoring and daily habits developing. Design features of information products for the elderly were fully considered. After three rounds of iterative design, a high-fidelity prototype was finally proposed and all evaluation indicators performed as expected in the usability evaluation experiment.

Keywords: Elderly health · Health self-management · System design · Smartphone

1 Introduction

China's population aging is becoming increasingly severe. It is predicted that the proportion of the population aged over 65 will exceed 20% in 2034 [28]. Closely related to this is the rapid development of medical and elderly care services. At present, the policy of "combination of medical care and pension" is being implemented steadily. The elderly can already enjoy basic medical treatment, and a large number of related smart products have emerged on the market. Nevertheless, the imbalance between needs and resources in health maintenance for the elderly is getting more and more prominent. On the one hand, although most of the elderly have the ability to take care of themselves [11], studies of older people in both urban and rural areas have found high prevalence of chronic diseases [24, 26]. The number of elderly patients with chronic diseases is expected to reach 300 million by 2050 [27], which also indicates a great demand for health tracking and management of the elderly.

© Springer Nature Switzerland AG 2021
Q. Gao and J. Zhou (Eds.): HCII 2021, LNCS 12787, pp. 322–334, 2021.
https://doi.org/10.1007/978-3-030-78111-8_22

On the other hand, data in 2015 showed that the proportion of "empty-nest" older people reached up to 51.3% [7], which means that home care is inadequate.

To alleviate this imbalance, one of the trends in medical development is to help the elderly who are able to take care of themselves carry out self-health management better. At present, some products such as wearable devices and home care AI robots have focused on this field, but there still lacks a fully effective solution. There are three main problems. First, current products are mainly used by children or caregivers for remote care, and it is difficult for the elderly to obtain and manage their health data. Second, due to physical limitations and incomplete electronic medical record systems (EMRs), older people often encounter difficulties in recording medical information and communicating with doctors. Third, the characteristics and special needs of elderly users are rarely considered in the design of information technology products, therefore the use experience is often unsatisfactory.

Based on the considerations above, this study started by integrating the needs of older people and their caregivers, combining with special design features of information products for the elderly, and designed a personal health tracking system based on smartphone. The system aimed to help the elderly manage their health conditions, promote a healthy lifestyle, facilitate doctor-patient communication and improve treatment accuracy. After multiple rounds of iterative design, the system was finally evaluated by six elderly users using a high-fidelity prototype.

2 Related Work

As people grow old, their body functions gradually decline and many chronic diseases appear. Common chronic diseases in the elderly include hypertension, diabetes, cardiovascular and cerebrovascular disease, arthritis, gastroenteritis, cervical spondylosis and lumbar vertebra disease [24]. Sarcopenia, which is closely related to the loss of muscle strength, quantity and quality, also has a high incidence, but is seldom taken seriously by the elderly. Sarcopenia is a common geriatric syndrome, which is believed to associated with increased likelihood of falls, fractures, physical disability and mortality [9]. One of the most effective ways to prevent sarcopenia is physical exercise, the effects of resistance training, strength training and power training have all been confirmed [23].

Measurement of daily physical indicators for the elderly is helpful to know the changes of their health status and to prevent the disease before it occurs. In addition to routine physiological indicators such as heart rate, blood pressure and blood glucose, some functional indicators such as mid-arm circumferences (MAC), calf circumferences (CC) and grip strength are also closely related to the prediction of health status, especially the prediction of sarcopenia. MAC and CC performed well in predicting the nutritional status, health conditions, and follow-up mortality risk of older adults [20]. However, although some studies [3, 15, 22] explored the cutoff values of MAC and CC of elderly patients with malnutrition and sarcopenia, there is still a lack of universally accepted authoritative data for Chinese older people. Mehta and Fleegler [19] found that in order to meet daily life activities, the minimum grip strength should be at least 20 lb (about 9.1 kg). Many studies have summarized the normal data on grip strength in older adults of all ages in different regions [2, 6]. In terms of the cutoff value of grip strength for sarcopenia, the Asian Working Group on Sarcopenia (AWGS) believes that it should not be less than 26 kg for men and 18 kg for women [5]. Some questionnaire scales also have been verified to be effective in functional monitoring of the elderly [9]. The SARC-F (sluggishness, assistance in walking, rising from a chair, climb stairs, falls) scale proposed by Malmstrom and Morley [17] only requires the elderly to fill out questionnaire subjectively, which can quickly diagnose the risk of sarcopenia. The SPPB (short physical performance battery) test proposed by Guralnik et al. [13] can distinguish the gradient of risk for short-term mortality and nursing home admission, and is one of the most commonly used tools for the elderly's physical performance measurement.

There are many information technologies and related products with great potential to help older people manage their health. Electronic medical record systems (EMRs) allow older patients to participate in personal health management, and can predict their attitude toward health self-management [4]. Mobile health (mHealth) can naturally embed interventions into patients' daily life [18]. Previous studies have shown that mHealth tools have high potential for enhancing compliance in chronic disease management [14]. Wearable wireless health monitoring system (WWHMS) can not only help medical staff and family members to carry out telemedicine, but also help patients to understand their own health status [8]. Combining these technologies may be a cost-effective way to deliver self-management education and support [16].

As the Internet continues to penetrate into the elderly, electronic products for the elderly have a greater market potential. Although there still have many obstacles, researchers are optimistic about the elderly's acceptance and learning of information technology [12, 21, 25]. The limited functional capabilities of the elderly need to be taken into account when designing information products. Czaja and Lee [10] summarized the functional changes of the elderly in three aspects: changes in the sensory process such as visual and auditory decay; changes in motor skills such as longer reaction time, loss of flexibility and increased motor variability; changes of cognitive abilities such as the decrease of semantic understanding ability, information reasoning ability and memory retrieval ability. Based on the above limitations, Czaja and Lee [10] also summarized key points of information product design for the elderly to ensure their adaptation of new technological environment.

3   Product Requirements Gathering

We collected product requirements through user and specialist research. In user research, 14 elderly people including 5 men and 9 women were interviewed, with an average age of 67. They all had financial security, self-care ability and basic smartphone experience. We interviewed them about their health, medical experience, daily care behavior and attitude toward related products. In specialist research, we interviewed two experts in the health of older adults, who were the deputy director of geriatric department of a hospital and the founder of a rehabilitation nursing group. We asked about the difficulties of doctor-patient communication, and suggestions for elderly health care and related products.

There were nine people suffering from chronic diseases such as diabetes, hypertension, cardiovascular and cerebrovascular disease, and need a long-term medication. All the 14 seniors had the consciousness of exercise, some of them had a regular exercise habit while others did not want to be too restrained. Experts recommended using tools to record information and set reminders to improve medication and exercise compliance among older adults.

All the 14 seniors collected medical records after a treatment, but most of them discarded the record after a while because they thought "these were useless" or "have too much material to organize". Some of them imagined that there should be an app which integrates all medical records in the future. Experts mentioned that they might have trouble communicating with older patients due to their memory decline and other physiological limitations.

In addition to the annual national health check-up, daily physiological index testing was also gradually popularized. Most of the elderly paid attention to blood pressure and blood glucose, and eight of them have measuring meters at home. Experts suggested that functional indicators related to muscle and strength are more valuable, but only one person had a preliminary understanding of these indicators. At present, smart bracelets and other products generally lack the interpretation and guidance of data results. Experts proposed to strengthen data visualization and feedback to promote older people's use and form habits.

Most elderly people did not actively search for health knowledge because "I do not know how to search" or "there is no need". Two people had the experience of blindly purchasing irregular health care products. Four expressed a desire for authoritative and personalized guidance. Experts believed that health education for the elderly was not professional and effective enough, so it was suggested to use a higher degree of visualization to popularize health knowledge among the elderly.

Based on above interview results and suggestions, we aim to design a system for the elderly with following goals:

1. Manage medical information, such as prescription, medical record, physical examination report, etc. Users can record and view information easily.
2. Manage daily body index information, such as physiological indicators and functional indicators, and provide feedback and suggestions.
3. Manage daily activity information, such as sports, reminders, etc. Data collection should not interfere with users' daily life.
4. Provide personalized guidance, such as customized health information and regular summary of personal health status, etc.

4 Personal Health Tracking System

To achieve these goals, we proposed a personal health tracking system based on smartphone for the elderly, which contains four main function modules: (1) medical information, (2) health self-test, (3) daily activities, and (4) personalized guidance. After three rounds of iterative design, a high-fidelity prototype was finally obtained. This prototype fully considered the functional limitations of the elderly. To reduce the requirements on cognitive abilities, the information hierarchy was clear; the amount of information on each page was reasonable; a unified page structure and interaction mode were adopted for similar functions. To make up for the shortcomings in perception process, monochrome style was used as overall background; functional modules were clearly divided through color coding; all text information was larger than the standard font size (40 px for the text and no less than 28 px). To adapt to the characteristics of motor skills, multiple input/output formats such as audio, picture and video were provided to replace text, and voice command was used as a supplement to touch operations in some functions.

4.1 Medical Information

This module aims to manage all patients' medical information, and as convenient as possible for the elderly to upload and view (goal 1, see Fig. 1). To clarify visual clues for older users, the color of this module is red. Data formats include picture, audio and text. Medical information is organized in two ways: (1) in reverse order according to the timeline, (2) by the type of information (prescription, examination results, medical records and physical examination reports). Users can search for specific date when viewing medical information, or select only a certain type of information to view. When uploading data, they need to set the type of information first, and can add tags such as hospital, department, doctor, disease to facilitate follow-up search. For diseases that require regular review, users can set the relationship between multiple records and set a reminder time for the next review. System will automatically associate relevant information based on tags, so as to make the retrospective search of elderly users easier.

4.2 Health Self-test

The color of health self-test module is green. This module mainly includes physiological indicators and functional indicators (goal 2, see Fig. 2). Physiological indicators will be personalized adjusted according to the user's illness, such as blood pressure, blood glucose, heart rate, etc. Functional indicators include grip strength, number of falls, SARC-F scale and SPPB test. On the basis of SARC-F scale, which is a preliminary screening tool for sarcopenia in the elderly, SPPB test further evaluates the physical condition of older people. Data of each indicator can be imported from wearable devices and other apps, or entered by users themselves. When the system detects that the user has entered incorrect data, it will remind him/her to check and correct. Changes of each indicator are shown in a dynamic chart, which can be viewed in different time intervals: weekly, monthly and annual. The system provides the average value, health threshold, and ranking among all users for each indicator. Users can also view all historical records of a certain indicator directly. Due to the complexity of SPPB test content, the system will guide users through voice prompts and video tutorials, and users can use voice commands instead of touch operation.

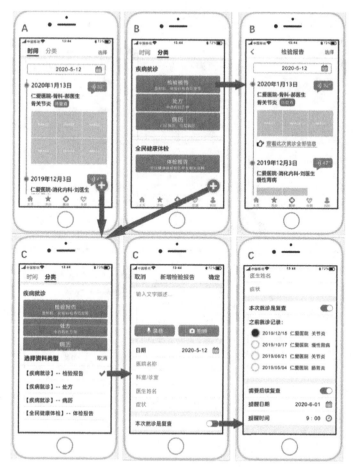

Fig. 1. Overview of medical information. The arrow means "click the button to jump to a new page". (A) Manage records in reverse chronological order. (B) Manage records by information type. (C) Step to add a medical information.

4.3 Daily Activities

The color of daily activities module is blue. This module contains two parts: reminder and exercise record (goal 3, see Fig. 3). Reminder can be set by the user, or by the system based on historical data, such as re-examination reminder, physical examination reminder, self-test reminder and exercise reminder. All items are arranged in order of the reminder time. Completed items are gray, current items are highlighted in blue, and others are black. All items can be modified or deleted. Exercise record include walking, running, swimming, table tennis, square dancing and so on. Data can be imported from wearable devices and other apps, or entered by users themselves. To make it easier for older people to judge how much exercise they have done, the system allows them to enter length of exercise as a rating. The display form of exercise records is also dynamic chart, similar to that of the health self-test module.

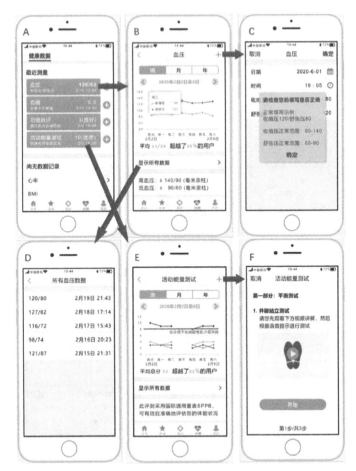

Fig. 2. Overview of health self-test. The arrow means "click the button to jump to a new page". (A) Home page of this module shows the latest results for all indicators. (B) Blood pressure page. (C) Record a new blood pressure record manually. (D) All historical blood pressure data. (E) SPPB test page. (F) Take a SPPB test with audio and video instruction.

4.4 Home Page and Personalized Guidance

To make it more convenient for older adults, home page summarizes the most commonly used information in each module (see Fig. 4). It consists of three parts: the top part is personalized guidance module in the form of notification bar; followed by today's reminders and today's exercise records in the form of card; at the bottom are health records arranged in reverse chronological order, including medical information and self-test results. The presentation form and color of each content in home page are the same as those in each module. Contents in home page are linked to corresponding module page. In addition, home page and each module can also be arbitrarily switched through tab bar at the bottom of each page.

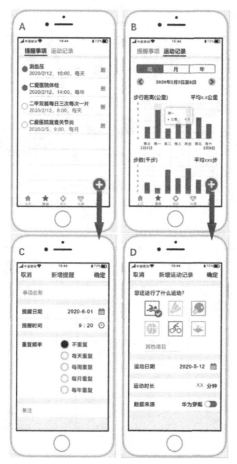

Fig. 3. Overview of daily activities. The arrow means "click the button to jump to a new page". (A) Reminder page. (B) Exercise record page. (C) Set a new reminder manually. (D) Add a new exercise record manually.

Personalized guidance module includes monthly report and health care classes (goal 4, see Fig. 4). Monthly report summarizes monthly medical information, exercise record and self-test data, and gives corresponding evaluation and suggestions. Health care classes regularly push information according to personalized settings about illness and interests, and make flexible adjustments based on recent historical data.

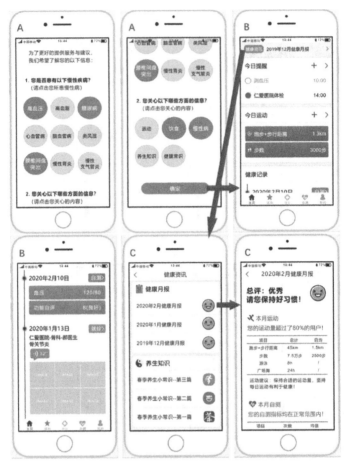

Fig. 4. Overview of home page and personalized guidance. The arrow means "click the button to jump to a new page". (A) Personalization settings page, set illness and interests when logging in for the first time. (B) Home page, the default page when entering the app. (C) Personalized guidance page.

5   Evaluation

In multiple rounds of iterative design, we invited four evaluators with relevant research experience and three real users to participate in the evaluation. A total of 51 feasible suggestions were collected in terms of function logic, page layout, interaction style and visual details. After improving the system, we obtained a final high-fidelity prototype and conducted an experimental evaluation on it.

5.1   Method

The evaluation experiment was conducted on a computer, where participants interacted with a mouse and keyboard. The experiment recruited 6 participants, including 3 males and 3 females, with an average age of 55. All participants had financial security, self-care ability and basic smart product experience. We used 5ES [1] as evaluation standard: (1) efficiency referred to the degree of participants quickly and effectively completed the task, in this experiment we only considered subjective validity; (2) effectiveness referred to the extent to which participants completed tasks accurately; (3) engagement referred to how satisfied the participants were with the overall function and interface; (4) error tolerance referred to the ability to prevent error in error-prone situations, or the ability to help recover after errors occurred; (5) ease of learning referred to the degree of participants understanding of the functions and operations. Efficiency, engagement and ease of learning were measured by Likert seven-point scale, while effectiveness and error tolerance were measured by task achievement and errors.

Each participant needed to complete 10 tasks that covered all main functions of the system (Table 1). Among them, tasks 6, 7, and 9 were used to evaluate error tolerance of the system. After completing each task, participants were asked to score the efficiency and ease of learning of this task, and were interviewed about task experience. After all tasks were completed, participants needed to consider the overall system comprehensively, score the engagement of the system and propose suggestions.

Table 1. Task list of the experiment.

No.	Task description	Function module
1	Choose your chronic disease and interests	Personalized guidance
2	Explore "reminder" and add a new one	Daily activities
3	Explore "exercise record" and add a new one	Daily activities
4	Explore "medical information" and check out records about a disease by timeline and tag	Medical information
5	Check out all information about a treatment (including four information types)	Medical information
6	Add a new medical information	Medical information
7	Explore "health self-test" and add a new blood pressure record	Health self-test
8	Take a SARC-F test	Health self-test
9	Take a SPPB test	Health self-test
10	Explore "home page" and check out monthly report	Personalized guidance

5.2 Results

Efficiency. The efficiency of all the 10 tasks met the expectation. Task 2 "explore 'reminder' and add a new one" and task 10 "explore 'home page' and check out monthly report" had a relatively low score (5/7 for task 2 and 5.33/7 for task 10), while other tasks all scored above 5.67/7. According to the interview, we found that the reason for task 2 was that participants rarely use "add a reminder" function in mobile phone, so they did not understand the meaning of some components such as input box and date selection box. After they became familiar with such functions, the performance in task 3, 6, 7 which involved "add" function improved significantly. Task 10 scored lower because personalized guidance module was placed at the top of home page, which could not be quickly found when participants were not familiar with the whole system.

Effectiveness. According to task achievement, the overall effectiveness of all 10 tasks was in line with expectations. Only tasks 2, 3, 6 were not finished completely and accurately by all participants. The reason why some participants made mistakes in task 2 has been mentioned above. Errors in task 3 "explore 'exercise record' and add a new one" were caused by the neglect of the icon representing sports. Errors in task 6 "add a new medical information" were mainly caused by interaction details, such as been confused by the meaning of check mark.

Engagement. The score of overall engagement met the expectation (6.17/7), and it was generally believed that the function of this system is complete and effective. The use of color coding clearly divided several function modules. Font size and spacing are both reasonable, and the overall visual effect is friendly.

Error Tolerance. There was room for improvement in task 6, while task 7 "explore 'health self-test' and add a new blood pressure record" and task 9 "take a SPPB test" performed well in error tolerance. Some participants failed to fill in all labels and misunderstood the content of some labels in task 6. In task 7, all participants filled in information accurately or corrected the error according to the system prompt. Participants in task 9 generally thought that the test was clear and easy to understand, and they also mentioned that voice command made the test result more reliable.

Ease of Learning. All the 10 tasks scored well in learnability, among which the lowest score was task 3 (5.17/7), and other tasks all scored above 5.5/7.

Suggestions. After deleting the duplicates, participates made 21 usability suggestions and expectations in total. The cumulative number of suggestions tended to be stable with the increasing number of participants. Since the sixth participant did not propose any new recommendations, it could be considered that most of the defects had been found, so system evaluation was completed. These suggestions involved multiple aspects. Some of them were changes in textual expression and interaction details, such as "please use colloquial descriptions rather than medical terms". Some were enhancements to data visualization, such as "maybe I can choose to view it as a histogram or a line chart". Some were further improvements and prospects, such as "I want a more flexible delivery of health information combined with daily data".

6   Conclusion

To alleviate the imbalance between medical care needs and resources of the elderly in China, and help them perform a better self-management, we designed a smartphone-based health tracking system. In order to meet both medical and practical life needs, this study considered the requirements of health care providers and elderly users at the same time. The health tracking system provided help for the elderly from four aspects: medical information management, health self-test management, daily activity management and personalized health guidance. Considering the function limitations of older adults, the system allowed two data input methods (manual input and automatic reading), guided the user through audio and video, and added a voice control function. We invited elder users to participate in iterative design work, and finally get a high-fidelity prototype. The experimental evaluation showed that the system performed well in terms of efficiency, effectiveness, engagement, error tolerance and ease of learning. We believe that older adults can understand and use each function accurately after a short period of learning.

This study has some limitations. First, the results of system evaluation cannot represent all elderly groups. On the one hand, the number of participants was small and the group composition was relatively homogeneous. On the other hand, the evaluation was conducted on a computer, which was different from that of a smartphone in terms of interactive experience. In future work mobile APP may be developed, and the system evaluation can be conducted separately from different elderly groups classified by economy, education, and electronic product experience. Second, the degree of personalization of this system was low. Future research may strengthen the correlation of data among different function modules. For example, exercise programs can be designed according to medical information and health self-test results, and medical resources can be provided for serious health problems.

References

1. Albers, M.J., Mazur, M.B.: Content and Complexity: Information Design in Technical Communication. Routledge, London (2014)
2. Bohannon, R.W., et al.: Average grip strength: a meta-analysis of data obtained with a Jamar dynamometer from individuals 75 years or more of age. J. Geriatr. Phys. Ther. **30**(1), 28–30 (2007)
3. Bonnefoy, M., et al.: Usefulness of calf circumference measurement in assessing the nutritional state of hospitalized elderly people. GER **48**(3), 162–169 (2002). https://doi.org/10.1159/000052836
4. Bzowyckyj, A.S., et al.: Leveraging the electronic medical record to identify predictors of nonattendance to a diabetes self-management education and support program. Diab. Educ. **45**(5), 544–552 (2019). https://doi.org/10.1177/0145721719873066
5. Chen, L.-K., et al.: Sarcopenia in Asia: consensus report of the asian working group for Sarcopenia. J. Am. Med. Directors Assoc. **15**(2), 95–101 (2014). https://doi.org/10.1016/j.jamda.2013.11.025
6. Chen, X., et al.: A survey on senior people's handgrip strength. Health Res. **33**(5), 331–334 (2013)
7. China Research Center on Aging: Sampling Survey on the Living Conditions of the Elderly in Urban and Rural China (Fourth). http://www.crca.cn/sjfw/2019-11-21/1564.html. Accessed 05 Feb 2021
8. Claes, V., et al.: Attitudes and perceptions of adults of 60 years and older towards in-home monitoring of the activities of daily living with contactless sensors: An explorative study. Int. J. Nursing Stud. **52**(1), 134–148 (2015). https://doi.org/10.1016/j.ijnurstu.2014.05.010
9. Cruz-Jentoft, A.J., et al.: Sarcopenia: revised European consensus on definition and diagnosis. Age Ageing **48**(1), 16–31 (2019). https://doi.org/10.1093/ageing/afy169

10. Czaja, S.J., Lee, C.C.: Older adults and information technology: opportunities and challenges. Hum.-Comput. Interact. Handb. Fundam. Evol. Technol. Emerg. Appl. 825–840 (2012)
11. DU, P.: An analysis on the health status of the older persons in China. Popul. Econ. **6**, 3–9 (2013)
12. Fischer, S.H., et al.: Acceptance and use of health information technology by community-dwelling elders. Int. J. Med. Inform. **83**(9), 624–635 (2014). https://doi.org/10.1016/j.ijm edinf.2014.06.005
13. Guralnik, J.M., et al.: A short physical performance battery assessing lower extremity function: association with self-reported disability and prediction of mortality and nursing home admission. J Gerontol. **49**(2), M85–M94 (1994). https://doi.org/10.1093/geronj/49.2.M85
14. Hamine, S. et al.: Impact of mHealth chronic disease management on treatment adherence and patient outcomes: a systematic review. J. Med. Internet Res. **17**(2), e52 (2015). https://doi.org/10.2196/jmir.3951
15. He, X., Liu, X.: The role of upper arm and calf circumferences in nutrition assessment for elderly patients. J. Nursing **6**, 10–13 (2008)
16. Lewinski, A.A. et al.: Addressing diabetes and poorly controlled hypertension: pragmatic mhealth self-management intervention. J. Med. Internet Res. **21**(4), e12541 (2019). https://doi.org/10.2196/12541
17. Malmstrom, T.K., Morley, J.E.: SARC-F: a simple questionnaire to rapidly diagnose sarcopenia. J. Am. Med. Directors Assoc. **14**(8), 531–532 (2013). https://doi.org/10.1016/j.jamda.2013.05.018
18. Marcolino, M.S. et al.: The Impact of mHealth interventions: systematic review of systematic reviews. JMIR mHealth uHealth. **6**(1), e8873 (2018). https://doi.org/10.2196/mhealth.8873
19. Mehta, A., Fleegler, E.: Rehabilitation of the hand: surgery and therapy. Cleveland Clin. J. Med. **59**(5), 554 (1992)
20. Tsai, A.C.-H., et al.: Mid-arm and calf circumferences (MAC and CC) are better than body mass index (BMI) in predicting health status and mortality risk in institutionalized elderly Taiwanese. Arch. Gerontol. Geriatr. **54**(3), 443–447 (2012). https://doi.org/10.1016/j.archger.2011.05.015
21. Vassli, L.T., Farshchian, B.A.: Acceptance of health-related ICT among elderly people living in the community: a systematic review of qualitative evidence. Int. J. Hum.-Comput. Interact. **34**(2), 99–116 (2018). https://doi.org/10.1080/10447318.2017.1328024
22. Wang, Y., et al.: Cutoff values of upper arm circumference and calf circumference in nutrition evaluation for elderly patients with digestive diseases. Mil. Med. J. South China **24**(6), 464–467 (2010)
23. Waters, D., et al.: Advantages of dietary, exercise-related, and therapeutic interventions to prevent and treat sarcopenia in adult patients: an update. Clin. Interv. Aging **5**, 259–270 (2010)
24. Wen, Y., et al.: Health status, health needs and provision of health services among the middle-aged and elderly people: results from a survey in 12 counties, 5 provinces in Mid-western China. Popul. Res. **38**(5), 72–86 (2014)
25. White, H. et al.: A randomized controlled trial of the psychosocial impact of providing internet training and access to older adults. Null **6**(3), 213–221 (2002). https://doi.org/10.1080/136 07860220142422
26. Xu, W.: Health status of elders in urban communities and their demands for health services in China. Chin. Gen. Pract. **13**(25), 2846–2849 (2010)
27. Yushao, W., Junwu, D.: China Report of the Development on Silver Industry. Social Sciences Academic Press (2014)
28. Zhai, Z., et al.: Future trends of China's population and aging: 2015–2100. Popul. Res. **41**(4), 60–71 (2017)

A Novel Mobile Application for Medication Adherence Supervision Based on AR and OpenCV Designed for Elderly Patients

Songlin Yang, Xiaoping Pang, and Xingxi He[✉]

College of Mechanical Engineering, Chongqing University, Chongqing 400044, China
xingxi@cqu.edu.cn

Abstract. Elderly people or individuals diagnosed in the very early stages of Alzheimer's Disease might have difficulty in taking medications according to the doctors' instructions due to the vision problems or memory loss. However, medication adherence can be crucial for good health or cause a major health setback. Traditional apps for medication adherence supervision use time reminders when the doses are supposed to be taken. This paper has developed a novel Android app to track the patient's action of taking medication for avoiding skipping the doses or taking too much medication. The app includes two modules, i.e. the AR medicine packaging box recognition module and the medication adherence supervision module. The former uses the surface of the medicine packaging box as an AR trigger and displays the virtual words of medical prescription to help the elderly patients identify the correct medications. The second module tracks the date and time of taking medications by recognizing the pills in the photo taken by the user. The pill detection is accomplished by applying the OpenCV image processing library to identify the pill contours based on dimensions and shape. Finally the pill detection tests were conducted to measure the detection accuracy and robustness of the app considering lighting conditions, different locations the pills were placed and the pills overlapped with each other.

Keywords: Medication adherence · Pill recognition · AR

1 Introduction

Medication adherence can be defined as the "extent to which a patient acts in accordance with the prescribed interval, and dose of a dosing regimen" [1]. Adherence to medications has always been a problem for elderly people or individuals diagnosed in the very early stages of Alzheimer's Disease due to the vision problems or memory loss. According to the research conducted by Koper et al. [2], 56.2% of the elderly patients with polypharmacy had at least one dosing error including over- or under-dose. Failure to comply with prescription medications leads to a major health setback for patients. Therefore Researchers have presented mobile applications to assist the elderly patients to take their medications through self-management since smart phones have been used widely in our day-to-day lives. Kanno et al. [3, 4] developed an augmented reality mobile

© Springer Nature Switzerland AG 2021
Q. Gao and J. Zhou (Eds.): HCII 2021, LNCS 12787, pp. 335–347, 2021.
https://doi.org/10.1007/978-3-030-78111-8_23

application to help mild Alzheimer patients overcome challenges concerning treatment and the performing of everyday tasks. The application includes time reminders for taking medicine and a feature of identification of which medicine to be taken through a mobile augmented reality interface, developed using Vuforia Software Development Kit (SDK) for Unity and Android features. The evaluation results show that with the AR technology the volunteers spent less time to locate the correct medication.

On the other hand, based on our literature review, there haven't been any application to track whether or not the elderly patient has taken the medicine on time and how many times the action of taking medication has been completed per day. Traditionally, the pillbox dispensers are used as a common strategy by older people to keep medication organized and help avoid missing a dose or doses. A pillbox commonly has seven horizontal compartments labeled Monday to Sunday and four vertical slots for each day, corresponding to the most common times to take pills during a day, such as morning, noon, evening and bed. However, filling the pillbox can be difficult for the elderly due to the complexity in treatment regimens. Therefore, Martin Ingeson et al. [5] developed a smart application of Medication Coach Intelligent Agent (MCIA) implemented in an AR headset, i.e. a Microsoft HoloLens, to assist elder patients when filling a pillbox according to the prescription. Their evaluation results show that using the AR-headset to assist people in filling a pillbox was feasible and acceptable. However, medicines are suggested to be stored in the manufacturer's original packaging/container or the integrity of the medicine can be affected [6]. In some cases medications are packed in special containers to keep out moisture or light which are the conditions a pillbox cannot guarantee. Concerning storage temperatures, there are medications that have to be kept refrigerated while some are supposed to be stored in room temperature. Especially in China most Chinese patent medicines contain sugar, bringing disadvantages to the mixed storage of medicines in the same compartment of a pill box. It also puts a strain on market supervision and inspection to ensure the pillbox dispensers on the market are non-toxic, non-corrosive and can prevent growth of microorganisms.

Therefore, the paper developed a mobile application to track the patient's action of taking medication while the pills can be kept inside the original packaging or containers. The app can analyze one image taken by the patients before they take the pills, recognize the pills in the image and save the dates and time for future inquiry. The research works concerning automatic pill identification have been developed based on image processing on mobile devices. The extracted image features are used to query on-line or built-in databases to find the best match with the closest metric distance for the query image pill. Cunha et al. [7] proposed a mobile based tool HelpmePills and applied computer vision to aid elderly persons on pill identification task considering the usage of both the elderly and the caregiver. After image acquisition, resizing and pre-processing operation are performed in the recognition mode, the pills placed inside a marker can be detected as the most similar ones in database based on the features of shape, dimension and color. To determine a given pill is legal or illegal, Annasaro et al. [8] presented a pill identification system which performed color and shape feature extraction with RGB color histogram for color feature and geometrical gradient vector algorithm for the shape. Lee et al. [9] developed an automatic system called Pill-ID to identify illicit drugs by using a database which includes 1029 illicit drug pill images and 14002 legal drug pill images. Their results show that the pill recognition based on the characteristics of shape, color and imprinting ensures levels of accuracy above 70%. Since the proposed app do not need to retrieve any information related to the pills, the simplified pill recognition can be achieved by using computer vision without visiting any database.

2   Methodology

To effectively assist and monitor the medication compliance of elderly patients, this article proposes an Android application written in Java programming language using the IDE of Android Studio. Figure 1 presents the first screen of the developed app which can lead to the two major modules, i.e. the medication recognition module and the medication adherence module, against the mistakes related with wrong ingestion of medication and forgetfulness respectively.

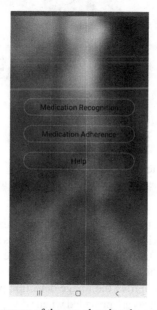

Fig. 1. The first screen of the app showing the major two modules

2.1   Medication Packaging Box Identification Module

In this basic module, the image on the surface of the medicine packaging box is used as an AR trigger which can be added into the local database with the related prescription. When the box is seen through the smart phone's camera, the corresponding virtual words of medical prescription will be displayed. Technically speaking, Google ARCore SDK with Unity was employed for the marker recognition and the generated Unity project was integrated into the native Android app to use some of the android-specific functionalities and to be combined with the second module. In ARCore, a computer vision algorithm is used to extract features from the grayscale information in each image and a representation of these features is stored in one or more Augmented Image databases. Therefore, in the session configuration of the ARCore SDK, the database with the pill packaging images was set as the currently active Augmented Image Database. Each image target has a unique image index and once the image target is detected in the field of view of the camera, the corresponding augmented model will be loaded due to the script in the "ExampleController" object. As shown in Fig. 2. Multiple markers or medicine packaging boxes can be recognized simultaneously with the dosage of medication in virtual words. And the virtual text size was increased for the low-vision elderly patients.

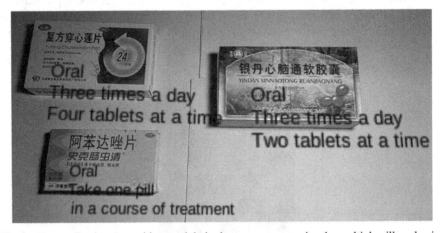

Fig. 2. The medication recognition module in the app can recognize the multiple pill packaging boxes simultaneously and provides the prescription information in virtual words

When detecting the image targets at runtime, ARcore searches for the stored features on flat surfaces in the field of view of camera and it provides estimates for image position and orientation in each frame. Especially if the physical size of the image is not provided, ARCore estimates the size and refines the result over time, which adds some time to the overall initialization. To improve the image detection performance in ARCore, the physical sizes of the image targets are provided when adding an image to the Augmented Image database so that ARCore can estimate the image pose based on the provided size.

12 values of physical size between 0 and 1 were tested, and it is found that as the physical size increases, the recognition speed increases while the size of the displayed augmented content decreases. The image size value of 0.15 was chosen to achieve a better balance and comprehensive performance considering both the detection speed and the displayed text size. ARCore can track up to 20 images simultaneously and can fully meet the needs of elderly patients with polypharmacy.

2.2 Medication Adherence Module

The paper focuses on the second module to track the time when the elderly patients take the medications. As shown in the Fig. 3, after the app initialization and the medication adherence mode starts, the user can either check the medication adherence log or track the time to take the medicine. The user needs to move the pills outside of the packaging box and click one button in the app to take a picture of the pills before having the medicine. For example, the pills can be placed in their hands or in the pill bottle cap. Then the app analyzes the image and if any pill is identified, the current date and time will be saved. When the user forgets how many times the medications have been taken today, the saved data will be shown to avoid over- or under-dose. Instead of allowing users to enter information before having the medicine for supervision, the pill identification used in the paper without any patient input is simpler and more convenient for the elderly. The procedure only takes a couple of clicks while the results provide more reliable medication adherence tracking.

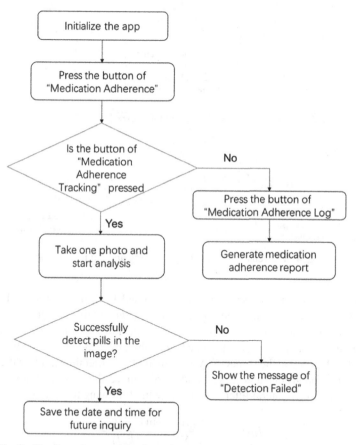

Fig. 3. The flow chart explains how the medication adherence module works

For pill recognition, an image pre-processing operation is performed which includes grayscale, thresholding, bilateral blur, Canny for edge detection and contour finding by using OpenCV image processing library. It is assumed that the area and perimeter of tablets suitable for swallowing should be within a certain range. After the contour is obtained, the area and perimeter of each closed-contour region are calculated and compared with the collected statistical data. The closed contours with proper area and perimeter are chosen for shape recognition. Figure 4 presents the process flow of pill recognition and the details in pre-processing are described as follows.

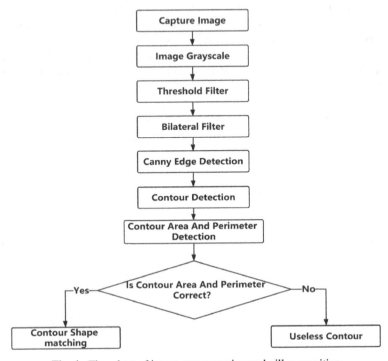

Fig. 4. Flowchart of image preprocessing and pill recognition

At the first step, the grayscale image is obtained from the original color image, it carries intensity information and has the contrast ranges from black at the weakest intensity and to white at the strongest. Next in thresholding, the grayscale image is converted into a binary image, simply black and white by using the simple thresholding and Otsu thresholding in the OpenCV. As shown in Fig. 5, after thresholding the image is segmented into foreground and background. Furthermore, the bilateral blur is conducted to reduce noise. The bilateral filter is defined by the following formula:

$$I_D(i,j) = \frac{\Sigma_{k,l} I(k,l) w(i,j,k,l)}{\Sigma_{k,l} w(i,j,k,l)} \tag{1}$$

where $I_D(i,j)$ is the de-noised intensity of pixel (i,j) and it replaces each pixel value with a weighted average of pixel values from nearby pixels. $w(i,j,k,l)$ denotes the normalization factor and can be calculated as

$$w(i,j,k,l) = \exp\left(-\frac{(i-k)^2 + (j-l)^2}{2\sigma_d^2} - \frac{\|I(i,j) - I(k,l)\|^2}{2\sigma_r^2}\right) \tag{2}$$

where σ_d and σ_r are smoothing parameters; $I(i,j)$ and $I(k,l)$ are the intensity of pixels. $\Sigma_{k,l} w(i,j,k,l)$ is the convolution of the spatial kernel for smoothing differences in coordinates with the range kernel for smoothing differences in intensities. Since $w(i,j,k,l)$ is the multiplication of the spatial weight and the range weight, in the flat area where the pixel values change very little, the filter becomes closer to Gaussian blur because the range weight is almost equal to 1. Across edges the range weight plays a more important role to preserve the image content without averaging. The bilateral filter can be applied to an image by calling the bilateralFilter method in the OpenCV library. The parameters of the method involving the diameter of each pixel neighborhood, the filter sigma in the color space and the filter sigma in the color range are set to 25, 100 and 100 respectively to achieve a better filtering effect.

The next step Canny edge detection in OpenCV is a multi-stage algorithm involving noise reduction with a Gaussian filter, finding intensity gradient and direction for each pixel to find the edges which are always perpendicular to the gradient direction, removing the non-edge pixels and hysteresis thresholding to keep the real edges. To improve the blur effect of Gaussian blur which is a low-pass filter, built in the OpenCV Canny edge detection, the previous step of bilateral blur was added in to smooth an image while preserving its edges. Figure 5 presents the image pre-processing results for pills in the shape of a circle, an oblong and a capsule. The five images in each row are the original color image, the grayscale image, the image after thresholding, the image with a blurring effect and the image with Canny edge detection applied.

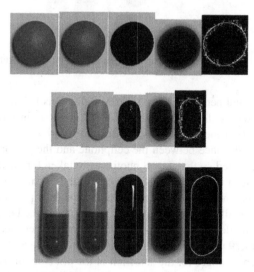

Fig. 5. The image pre-processing for pills in the shape of a circle, an oblong and a capsule

Furthermore, the edges are connected to obtain a closed contour by using the contour detection in OpenCV. In addition, the typical area and perimeter of the contours of the pills are calculated and used to filter out the possible unrelated contours. For shape classification, the OpenCV approxPolyDP function is used to generate a vector of points from which the polygons can be created to approximate the original contours. Based on the number of points obtained and the ratio of length and width of the bounding rectangular, the pills with regular shapes can be classified into triangle, rectangle, circle, ellipse or non-detectable shape. The triangular and rectangular shapes have fixed number of points. The circular and ellipse shapes have the number of points above a threshold value and their ratio of length and width of the bounding rectangular are set within a range. Therefore the pill with an oblong shape is classified as an ellipse.

3   Results and Discussion

3.1   Measurement of Area and Perimeter Ranges

Figure 6 shows 20 types of pills collected on the market with typical dimensions and shapes which are used for pill recognition in the paper. The shapes of circle, triangle, oblong, ellipse etc. are included in the contour of these pills.

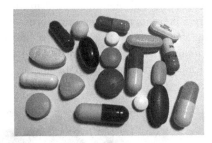

Fig. 6. The pills with typical dimensions and shapes collected on the market for pill recognition

The contour area and perimeter were measured in pixels for the pills shown in the Fig. 6 by applying the contourArea and arcLength methods in OpenCV. Each time a single pill is placed on the table. With the normal position and angle at which the cellphone is held, the distance between the cellphone and the pill on the table and the shooting angle were varied so that 7 or 8 photos were taken for each pill. After image analysis and comparison of these photos in OpenCV, the maximum and the minimum values of contour area and perimeter were obtained for each pill. Figure 7 shows the results in bar chart. For all the sample pills used in this paper, the largest contour area is 5019 pixels and the smallest is 163 pixels; the largest contour perimeter is 319.61 pixels and the smallest is 49.79 pixels. The ranges of pill contour area and perimeter obtained above provide reference ranges for the selection of the pill contour. After the user takes a photo of pills in the app to track the time of taking medications, it is assumed that the area and perimeter of the pill contour should fall within these ranges.

3.2   Pill Recognition

As already stated, the contours satisfying the area and perimeter conditions are selected for shape classification. Generally the pills or tablets have regular geometric shapes,

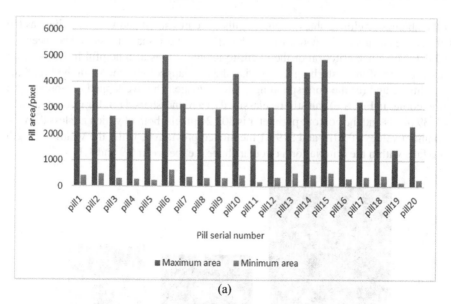

(a)

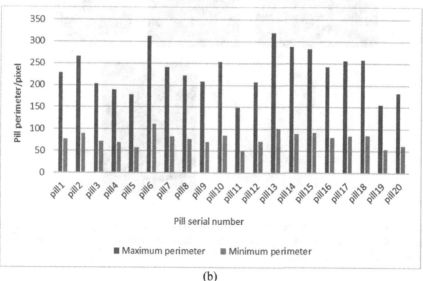

(b)

Fig. 7. The maximum and minimum values of (a) contour area and (b) contour perimeter of each sample pill

therefore the contours classified as triangles, rectangles, circles and ellipse are assumed as pill contours. After the polygon approximation, the shapes of triangle and rectangle are easy to detect due to the fixed vertices. For circles and ellipses, the width-to-length ratio of the contour bounding rectangular determines the shape classification if the number of vertices is greater than the threshold value. For example, the width-to-length ratio of the bounding rectangular of a circle is defined between 0.9 to 1.1. The width and length of the oblong- or ellipse-shaped sample pills were measured and were classified as the same shape category. The width-to-length ratio for ellipse shape is defined between 0.2 and 0.4. The range criterion of the width-to-length ratio is also helpful for identifying pills with one of the disturbing factors, i.e. the overlapped pills shown in the Fig. 8 (d) color image and (e) the corresponding contour image. The overlapped contours at the lower corner in Fig. 8(e) can still be classified as a round-shaped pill for its contour area is 4539 pixels and the contour perimeter is 302.24 pixels, both of which are less than the maximum values of 5019 and 319.61 mentioned previously, while the width-to-length ratio falls within the criteria for a circular shape, i.e. between 0.9 and 1.1.

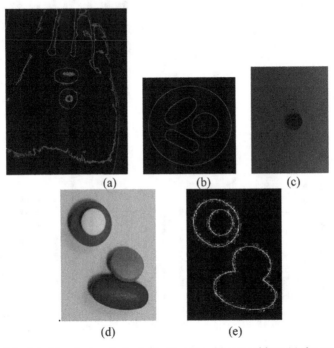

Fig. 8. Possible disturbing factors that might affect the pill recognition: (a) the contours on the finger (b) the contour of bottle cap (c) dim light (d) overlapped pills in color image and (e) overlapped pills in contour image

Another possible disturbing factor is shown in Fig. 8(a). The contours on the fingers might be mistaken as pill contours. The influence can be reduced by adjusting the parameters in the OpenCV methods. On the pill contours in this image, the contours of reflection of light can be observed which also might be mistaken as pill contours. In Fig. 8(b) the tablets are placed in the pill bottle cap whose contour will not affect the pill detection result after applying the contour area condition. However, the pill in Fig. 8(c) is hard to detect due to the dim light for the tuned parameters in grayscale, thresholding and blurring are not suitable anymore.

Therefore 389 times of pill detection tests were conducted to check the robustness of the app in identifying whether or not there is any pill. All the disturbing factors mentioned above or the combination of them were randomly added into the tests. Both the single-pill and overlapped-pill detection were considered, the influence of dim light and strong light were included and the pill/pills were placed in the hand, on the table or in the pill bottle cap. The two overlapped pills were used in the tests for it is assumed that the elderly people might have trouble swallowing three or more tablets at a time. Based on the test results, the pill detection accuracy was calculated by using the F-measure technique as follows

$$\text{Accuracy} = \left((TP + TN)/(TP + TN + FP + FN)\right) * 100$$

where TP is True Positive, TN is True Negative, FP is False Positive and FN is False Negative. The Positive means there is at least one pill and the negative means there is no pill. In another form [8], the accuracy percentage can be written as.

$$\text{Accuracy Percentage} = \left((\text{Matched Pill})/(\text{Matched Pill} + \text{Miss Matched Pill})\right) * 100$$

The results and the calculated detection accuracy were given in Table 1.

Table 1. Accuracy results of the pill detection tests

	TP	TN	FP	FN	Detection Accuracy (100%)
Overall performance	301	44	6	38	88.69%
Single-pill detection	283	N/A	N/A	31	90.13%
Overlapped-pill detection	18	N/A	N/A	8	72%

As shown in Table 1, the overall accuracy rate of 389 pill detection tests is 88.69%, of which the tablets are correctly detected for 301 times and the app can tell there is no pill at all for 44 times. The False Positive error was generated when the contours on the hand or the contour of reflection of light under certain lighting conditions and with certain photo-shooting angles. The False Negative error was caused mostly by dim light. The accuracy rates of the single-pill detection and the overlapped-pill detection were compared when there is at least one pill in the image. It can been seen that the detection accuracy of one pill is 90.13%, higher than that of the overlapped pills. In the help file of the app, it can be suggested that the photo shall be taken under normal lighting conditions, without any overlapped pills and it is better to place the pills in the pill bottle cap or on the table to avoid the impact of palm prints. Finally, after the pill detection, the time of taking the medication can be tracked and displayed in medication adherence log shown in the Fig. 9.

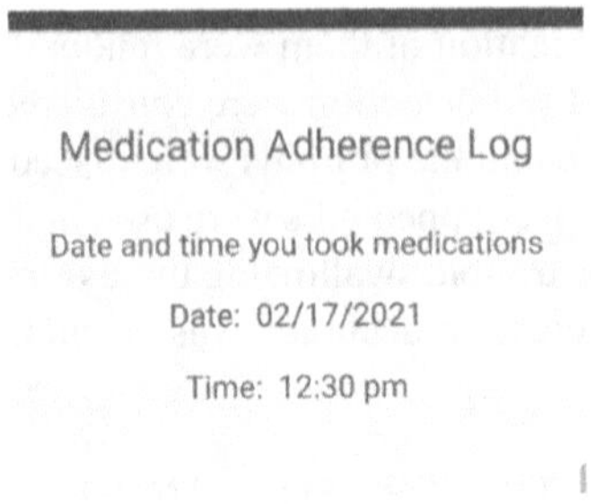

Medication Adherence Log

Date and time you took medications

Date: 02/17/2021

Time: 12:30 pm

Fig. 9. The time tracking of medication adherence

4 Conclusion and Future Work

An Android app was developed to track the date and time when the elderly patients take medications. A photo of pills is supposed to be taken before the user has the medicine and then the pill detection in the image is conducted by the app. The tracked date and time can be displayed in the medication adherence log for inquiry so that the over- or under-dose can be avoided. Since the pills on the market normally have regular and standard shapes and the dimensions of the pills suitable for swallowing are within a certain range, a simple algorithm to detect the existence of pills is proposed based on the pill dimensions and shapes. The overall accuracy of the pill detection tests is 88.69% considering all the disturbing factors, such as lighting, the locations of placing the pills and the overlapped pills. In addition, the AR module in the app can help the elderly patients recognize the correct medications from the multiple pill packaging boxes.

In the future, the app shall adopt a more advanced pill detection algorithm to improve the detection accuracy and reduce the influence of disturbing factors. Furthermore, an evaluation shall be conducted among the elderly patients to investigate the degree of acceptance and convenience of the app and whether it can achieve the expected medication adherence supervision.

References

1. Cramer, J.A., et al.: Medication compliance and persistence: terminology and definitions. Value Health **11**(1), 44–47 (2008)
2. Koper, D., Kamenski, G., Flamm, M., Böhmdorfer, B., Sönnichsen, A.: Frequency of medication errors in primary care patients with polypharmacy. Fam. Pract. **30**(3), 313–319 (2013)
3. Kanno, K.M., Lamounier, E.A., Cardoso, A., Lopes, E.J., de Lima, G.F.M.: Augmented reality system for aiding mild Alzheimer patients and caregivers. In: 2018 IEEE Conference on Virtual Reality and 3D User Interfaces (VR), pp. 593–594. IEEE, March 2018
4. Kanno, K.M., Lamounier Jr, E.A., Cardoso, A., Lopes, E.J., Fakhouri Filho, S.A.: Assisting individuals with Alzheimer's disease using mobile augmented reality with voice interaction: an acceptance experiment with individuals in the early stages. Res. Biomed. Eng. **35**(3), 223–234 (2019)
5. Ingeson, M., Blusi, M., Nieves, J.C.: Smart augmented reality mHealth for medication adherence. In: AIH@IJCAI, pp. 157–168 (2018)

6. https://www.dorsetccg.nhs.uk/wp-content/uploads/2018/04/Standard-E1-storage-safe-custody-of-medicines.pdf.
7. Cunha, A., Adão, T., Trigueiros, P.: Helpmepills: a mobile pill recognition tool for elderly persons. Procedia Technol. **16**, 1523–1532 (2014)
8. Annasaro, E., Hema, A.: Color and shape feature extraction and matching in pill identification systems. Int. J. Comput. Sci. Inf. Technol. **5**(2), 1011–1015 (2014)
9. Lee, Y.B., Park, U., Jain, A.K., Lee, S.W.: Pill-ID: matching and retrieval of drug pill images. Pattern Recogn. Lett. **33**(7), 904–910 (2012)

Elderly Sleep Support Agent Using Physical Contact Presence by Visual and Tactile Presentation

Yaze Zhang$^{(\boxtimes)}$, Xin Wan, and Tomoko Yonezawa

Kansai University, 2-1-1 Ryozenji-cho, Takatsuki-shi, Osaka, Japan
{k800023,yone}@kansai-u.ac.jp

Abstract. In this study, we propose an agent that guides elderly people to bed and supports better sleep through visual, voice, and tactile sense presentation. The system is mainly based on the following: 1) a visual presentation part that shows a agent approaching to bed, and getting into bed, to guide the user go to bed and sleep; and 2) a tactile presentation part that imitates the arm and body of the person lying down and that is equipped in a blanket. To draw the user to the bed in order to sleep, the agent presents a voice-like sound to notify bedtime, guides the user to the bed, and gives the user a tactile sense, such as a hug or a light tap via our blanket-type device, as though someone who cares for the user is actually there. Mental stability and sleep are expected to be drawn by the system. According to the experimental results, both the visual expression and tactile representation of simulated hugs and patting have an effect on the user's mental stability, whereas the tactile stimulation of patting gives the user a sense of healing and comfort. Therefore, the proposed agent is considered effective to make the user comfortable.

Keywords: Elderly care system · Sleep support · Tactile presentation · Virtual agent · User evaluation

1 Introduction

Recently, the increase in the elderly population has become a major problem all over the world [1]. It has been reported that physical, cognitive, and mental function decline with age and that these declines are correlated [2]. On the other hand, some recent studies have also shown that a good night's sleep is essential for maintaining a healthy life and preventing functional decline [3]. Moreover, these declines create various problems; especially due to cognitive decline, people are more likely to develop BPSD (behavioral and psychological symptoms of dementia), such as anxiety, depression, and excitement, with reduced quality of life. In other words, when the elderly patient's sleep is disturbed or he or she wakes up in the middle of the night (nocturnal awakening), caregivers become exhausted during subsequent sessions. If patients cannot improve their sleep, they can develop cognitive problems and BPSD. Therefore, the key to preventing

© Springer Nature Switzerland AG 2021
Q. Gao and J. Zhou (Eds.): HCII 2021, LNCS 12787, pp. 348–362, 2021.
https://doi.org/10.1007/978-3-030-78111-8_24

poor quality of life for people with dementia and their caregivers is to support them in going to sleep and returning to sleep when they awaken during the night.

Sleep disorder includes sleep deprivation and abnormal sleep rhythms. Such disorders are due to 1) aging and lifestyle problems, 2) sleep apnea syndrome, and 3) oversleeping and insomnia. In this study, to support elderly people in their daily life, we propose an agent system that reduces sleep disorder by guiding them to go to bed, fall asleep, and continue sleeping when they have a nocturnal awakening. The agent is associated with a set of visual, tactile, and auditory presentations. The agent is projected on a wall screen and guides the user to bed by visually presenting how the agent approaches and enters the bed. A robotic arm inside of the blanket simulates the tactile sensations of hugs and repetitive touches to ease the user's mood before/during the sleep. If the elderly can gain a sense of trust in the agent through the sleep-support system, the agent can effectively reduce their stress and promote their psychological stability and drowsiness.

In this paper, we evaluated the agent's visual and tactile presentations in the proposed system to discuss how the sleeping environment with the agent influences the user's emotional state.

2 Related Researches

2.1 Relationship Between Sleep and Physical, Cognitive, and Mental Functions

Regarding the relationship between sleep and physical function, it has been reported that the length of sleep time can cause changes in grip strength and the quality of activities of daily living (ADL) and that the quality of sleep leads to physical weakness [4].

As for the relationship between sleep and cognitive function, it has been reported that elderly people who sleep more than 7 h have lower cognitive function than elderly people who sleep less than 7 h [5].

Regarding the relationship between sleep and mental function, it has been reported that it is easy to fall into an emotional state of anxiety, tension, and depression if sleep is too short [6]. In addition to bereavement, physical impairment, and past history of depression being risk factors for depression in elderly people, there was also a decline in sleep quality, suggesting a relationship between sleep and mental state [7].

It can be seen from the above content that the sleep state is closely related to the physiological, cognitive, and psychological functions of the elderly.

2.2 Effect of Human Physical Contact

Previous studies have shown that hugs can lower blood pressure and prevent an increase in the number of pulses when the pulse is pumping [8]. In addition, hugs can relieve stress and boost immunity to the infectious viruses that cause colds [9]. Tactile stimuli, such as skin friction and hugging, also trigger the release of oxytocin, a hormone that promotes social bonding and trusting behavior [10].

Touch affects not only health but also psychological aspects. According to the study of J. D. Fisher et al. [11], women are more inclined to perceive contact than men, and women have a better impression of the object and environment they are in contact with. Thus, social contact, including cuddling, is considered to improve well-being and health as a mental and physical benefit.

2.3   Tactile Interaction Between Humans and Robots

There are various forms of emotional communication between people. In the research field of human-robot interaction (HRI), there have been many discussions so far. In addition to using physical action such as voice, gaze, and gestures to communicate, the research on communication contact is just beginning. As part of understanding body-contact robotics and applied research, a system that detects when a robot is being petted or hugged is currently under development [12]. There are also reported cases of the seal-like pet robot PARO improving the mood of elderly people with dementia [13] and robots encouraging human effort by touching them, enabling them to perform tedious tasks longer and more repetitively [14].

Since the touch between a robot and a human has the same effect as the touch between a human and another human [15], it is possible that the robot's emotional expression can be conveyed to the user. It has also been verified that stimuli combining touch and sound affect the impression of the robot [16].

To sum up, contact has many potential benefits, and it has proven useful in improving mood before sleep. In this study, we propose a sleep-snuggling agent that uses a naked-eye stereoscopic vision system to enhance the sense of virtual agents' coexistence and a tactile presentation to feel physical contact from a robot. The agent usually presents the user with a tactile sensation like physical contact after the user goes to bed as if they are sleeping together, thus improving the user's mood before and after sleep.

3   System Configuration

3.1   System Overview

We constructed the following system that aims to satisfy visual, auditory, and tactile needs in reference to Humanization methods and agent research methods [17].

Our system shows how an agent who is close to the room drawn by autostereoscopic vision is projected on the wall surface: 1) The agent enters the user's field of view, 2) approaches the bed, and 3) enters the bed. After that, 4) when the user follows the agent into bed, the tactile-sensation generator, which imitates a human arm or body, makes physical contact with the user, such as hugging or repeatedly patting him or her, to encourage him or her to fall asleep.

In the current testbed system, PowerPoint animation is used to draw an agent as a visual stimulus. As shown in Fig. 1, an agent with a face, body, and

 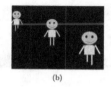 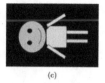

(a)   (b)   (c)

Fig. 1. Visual presentations

limbs is projected onto a wall screen using a projector (EPSON EH-TW5200). The movements of the agent are as follows: 1) The shape of the agent gradually expands and enters the user's field of view from a distance, and 2) it approaches the bed. At this time, the leg length fluctuates interchangeably to represent the agent's walking movement. Then, 3) to express the movement of the agent entering the bed, it is rotated with respect to the x-axis so as to fall counterclockwise. Since the experimental participants do not actually sleep, but the experiment is designed to simulate the conditions for sleep onset, the background is shown in black so that its light intensity does not affect the onset of sleep. The execution time for each movement is 6 s.

3.2   Tactile Presentation Part

In the tactile presentation, we constructed the following system where a blanket hugs and makes repeated physical contact so that the user feels as if the agent is touching him or her on the side. Figure 2 shows the tactile-sense generator. This tactile display device consists of three rectangular, parallel Styrofoam pieces connected as arm bones, imitating the movement of a human arm. The length of each part is 18 cm. The three parts of the arm are connected as joints using hinges at each end of the cubic foam o imitate a bending arm. We made a hole from one end of the arm to the other, connected the bones with a PP string that passes through it internally, and fixed the end with the tip of the arm. The other end is connected to a pulley driven by a servomotor (Fig. 3). The arm bends under the tension of the PP string (Fig. 4). In addition, the upper parts of the arm are fixed with a rubber band so that it can automatically move back to the original position. Additionally, when the servomotor returns to the original angle, the arm is restored by the elastic rope to keep the position (Fig. 5). By adjusting the time and frequency of arm bending, various movements can be displayed, such as hugging and repeated physical contact. The arm is wrapped with a blanket to make the participant feel as if he or she is being touched by the agent under the blanket.

By moving the arm in the blanket, the agent can express the patting and holding haptic motions on the user's body.

Fig. 2. Arm parts

Fig. 3. Servomotor to drive pulley

4 Experiment

4.1 Purpose

To verify the effectiveness of the proposed agent on promoting relieved, satisfied, and familiar emotions of the user, we conducted a subjective evaluation. We focused particularly on the visual and tactile cues.

4.2 Hypotheses

H1: The user feels that the agent is kind based on the agent's expression, as if the agent is close to the user.
H2: The user feels sleepy due to the patting actions of the agent.
H3: The user feels relieved due to the hugging action of the agent.

Fig. 4. Robot arm set in blanket (Bending state)

Fig. 5. Robot arm set in blanket (straight state)

4.3 Experimental Participants

The experiment included 18 participants aged from 20 to 30, of whom 8 were males and 10 were females.

4.4 Experimental Conditions

This experiment employed a within-subjects design, where Factor A was the agent's movement (3 levels, as below) and Factor B was the tactile generator movement (3 levels, as below), so the experiment had 9 conditions. The levels for each factor were as follows.

Factor A: The visual behavior of the agent

A1: Moves toward the bed and disappears
A2: Disappears and does not move
A3: Does not move nor disappear

Factor B: Movement of the tactile generator

B1: Patting
B2: Hugging
B3: No movement

The order of each condition was crossed using the Latin-square method in consideration of counterbalance.

4.5 Experimental Environment

As shown in Fig. 6, a projection screen wall was installed next to the experimental bed. The proposed robot arm was set in the experimental bed. The base of the robot arm was installed 40 cm above the bed to afford the participants space to lie down. In addition, a darkroom environment was designed using black curtains to simulate a sleeping environment with a slight and constant ambient light. Other devices placed in the room were tactile and auditory devices.

4.6 Experimental Procedure

In the experimental process, the bend duration of the arm was set to 1) 6 s only once when indicating "hugging" and (2) 1 s 6 times when indicating "patting."

First, before starting the experiment, we informed the participants that the purpose of the experiment was to verify our agent system for care of the elderly

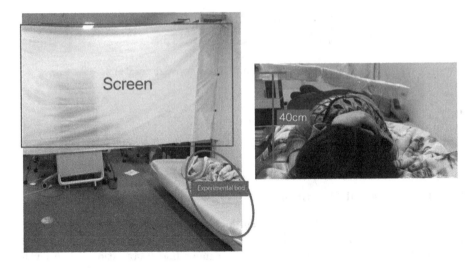

Fig. 6. Experimental environment

with dementia. We also explained that the character projected on the wall was the agent, and that the agent could also go into the bed. The participants were instructed to assume the agent as they met first during the experiment.

Next, before the experiment, the subjects were asked to lie in bed once to adjust their position so that the robot arm could touch their shoulders. In addition, the subjects' heads were set to face the screen at the bedside so that they could see the visual presentation of the agent.

Before the experiment, we asked the participants to go through the procedure once as follows.

First, the participant looked at the visual presentation. Then, he or she went to the bed and laid down. Next, the tactile sensation was presented, and we confirmed the participant's position.

In the actual session (9 times), after a signal to start the experiment, the agent gave a visual presentation and tactile stimulus according to the condition while playing a voice presentation of sleep guidance. After the signal to end the experiment, the participant evaluated the system in the condition.

4.7   Evaluation Items

According to the mean opinion score (MOS) method, the participants provided scores using 5-point scale ratings (1 = Not relevant, 2 = Somewhat not relevant, 3 = Neutral, 4 = Somewhat relevant, and 5 = Relevant to the statement). The statements were as follows. Q1 to Q4 were related to familiarity and kindness, Q5 and Q6 were related to respect, Q7 and Q8 were related to inner peace, Q9 to Q11 were related to favor, Q12 and Q13 were related to presence, Q14 and Q15 were related to naturalness, Q16 and Q17 were related to discomfort, and Q18 was related to sleepiness.

Q1 You felt a familiar attitude from the agent.
Q2 You felt familiar with the agent.
Q3 The agent was kind to you.
Q4 You felt kind toward the agent.
Q5 You felt the agent's respect for you.
Q6 You respected the agent.
Q7 You were relieved by the agent's motions.
Q8 The agent responded politely to you.
Q9 You felt that the agent had emotions.
Q10 You felt that the agent liked you.
Q11 You liked the agent.
Q12 You felt uncomfortable with the agent's behavior.
Q13 You felt that the agent was a close presence to you.
Q14 The agent's behavior was natural.
Q15 The agent's behavior was unnatural.
Q16 You found it unpleasant to be with the agent.
Q17 You felt uncomfortable with the agent.
Q18 You became sleepy compared to before the experiment.

5 Experimental Result

5.1 Analysis of Variance

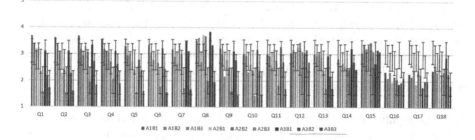

Fig. 7. Mos results for each evaluation item

The mean and standard deviation of the 18 evaluation items are shown in Fig. 7, and the results of analysis of variance are shown in Table 1.

First, for Factor A, visual presentation, Q1–Q6, Q9, and Q13 resulted in {A1, A2} > A3. That is, the evaluation items related to familiarity, kindness, respect, favor, and presence were elevated by the visual presentation that disappeared before the participant moved to the bed. Q10 showed A1 > A2, and the approach to the participant elevated the likeness. Q17 showed A1 > A3, indicating that the visual presentation with movement toward the bed and disappearance might cause the user to feel like the agent was not in the bed. Next, regarding Factor

Table 1. Analysis of variance for Mos results

	Factor A		Factor B		Factor AB		Multiple comparisons		
	F	p	F	p	F	p	A	B	Simple main effects
Q1	15.804	¦0.01*	13.322	0.01*	2.443	0.06	{1,2}>3	1>2>3	-
Q2	14.067	0.01*	15.031	0.01*	3.173	0.02 *	{1,2}>3	1>2>3	A1>A2>A3(b2),A1>A3>A2(b3),B1>B2>B3(a2),B1>B2>B3(a3)
Q3	3.966	0.03 *	15.525	0.01*	1.422	0.24	{1,2}>3	1>2>3	-
Q4	7.121	0.01*	8.107	0.01*	1.256	0.30	{1,2}>3	{1,2}>3	-
Q5	13.179	0.01*	9.787	0.01*	2.580	0.05 *	{1,2}>3	{1,2}>3	A1>A3>A2(b3),B1>B2>B3(a2),B1>B2>B3(a3)
Q6	6.347	0.01*	13.138	0.01*	1.807	0.14	{1,2}>3	1>2>3	-
Q7	0.451	0.64	14.114	0.01*	2.779	0.03 *	-	{1,2}>3	A1>A2>A3(b2),B1>B2>B3(a2),B1>B2>B3(a3)
Q8	0.853	0.44	21.025	0.01*	1.959	0.11	-	{1,2}>3	-
Q9	3.365	0.05 *	11.856	0.01*	0.663	0.62	{1,2}>3	{1,2}>3	-
Q10	3.981	0.03 *	18.734	0.01*	1.418	0.23	1>2	{1,2}>3	-
Q11	1.065	0.36	11.488	0.01*	2.069	0.10	-	{1,2}>3	-
Q12	1.303	0.29	0.536	0.59	0.203	0.94	-	-	-
Q13	6.121	0.01*	9.356	0.01**	2.720	0.04 *	{1,2}>3	1>3	A1>A2,A3(b3),B1>B2>B3(a2),B1>B2>B3(a3)
Q14	1.171	0.32	1.219	0.31	0.583	0.68	-	-	-
Q15	1.808	0.18	0.685	0.51	0.582	0.68	-	-	-
Q16	1.257	0.30	0.232	0.79	0.470	0.76	-	-	-
Q17	4.509	0.02*	1.086	0.35	0.600	0.66	1>3	-	-
Q18	0.507	0.61	3.524	0.04 *	2.216	0.08	-	1>3	-

*p<0.05

B, tactile feedback, there were significant results indicating B1 > B2 > B3 for Q1–Q3 and Q6. The physical contact by patting most strongly elevated familiarity, kindness, and respect. Q4–Q5 and Q7–Q11 showed the significant results of {B1, B2} > B3, indicating that the physical contact elevated kindness, respect, security, and favor. Q13 and Q18 showed B1 > B3. Although there was no significant difference from B2, it was suggested that patting physical contact might be effective to promote presence and sleepiness.

Next, we summarize the interaction results for Q2, Q5, Q7, and Q13.

Q2 showed A1 > A2 > A3 in combination with B2 and A1 > A3 > A2 in combination with B3. In terms of familiarity, the agent's visual presentations of moving toward the bed and only disappearing before the movement to the bed, correspondingly, were effective when combined with the hugging physical contact. On the other hand, the simple disappearance was the least effective when the agent did not touch the participant.

There were also significant interactions and simple main effects of Factor B in Q2. The significant results of B1 > B2 > B3 were confirmed in combination with A2 or A3. These results imply that patting and hugging contacts, correspondingly, were effective even without movement toward the bed or disappearance of the agent and that the tactile expression was effective.

Q5 showed A1 > A3 > A2 in combination with B3. The result indicates that the agent's disappearance after movement toward the bed and disappearance without movement, correspondingly, resulted in an impression of respect when there was no physical contact. There was also a significance of Factor B, B1 > B2 > B3, in combination with A2 or A3. That is, the physical contact itself, especially patting, was effective for promoting a feeling of respect, even if the agent did not move or disappear. Q7 and Q13 showed A1 > A2 > A3 in combination with B3. It can be seen that the proposed animation agent was desirable for the evaluation of security and presence when there was no physical contact. In addition, the significant difference of B1 > B2 > B3 in combination with A2 or A3 implies that physical contact, especially patting, was desirable.

5.2 Factor Analysis

Table 2. Factor analysis

Factor matrix (varimax rotation)				
Factor loading				
	Factor1	Factor2	Factor3	Factor4
paleasant–painful	0.803	0.224	0.012	0.054
interesting–boring	0.652	0.385	0.275	0.028
enjoyable–unenjoyable	0.694	0.310	0.209	0.292
happy–sad	0.612	0.483	0.219	0.167
ambitious–lethargic	0.547	0.459	0.349	−0.311
healthy–tired	0.691	0.183	0.461	0.074
lively–lonelt	0.652	0.291	0.375	−0.281
happiness–unhappy	0.783	0.174	−0.032	0.166
graphic–lifeless	0.557	0.528	0.326	−0.205
kindness–unkind	0.292	0.803	0.189	0.152
friendly–unfriendly	0.352	0.754	0.189	0.109
polite–rough	0.087	0.799	−0.173	0.228
bright–dark	0.440	0.599	0.332	0.011
warm–cold	0.449	0.654	0.265	0.038
positive–negative	0.477	0.516	0.444	−0.274
cheerful–gloomy	0.435	0.598	0.413	−0.010
full–empty	0.562	0.599	0.225	−0.096
strong–weak	0.130	0.123	0.781	−0.090
v iolent–gentle	−0.121	−0.066	0.726	−0.421
lively–feable	0.340	0.199	0.712	−0.049
dynamic–static	−0.010	0.384	0.526	−0.521
diplomatic–introverted	0.269	0.323	0.633	−0.213
bullish–bearish	0.448	0.125	0.730	0.060
stable–unstable	0.343	0.327	0.289	0.634
calm–fidile	0.166	0.339	−0.257	0.634
rational–emotional	−0.072	−0.007	−0.214	0.647

Factor analysis was performed based on the results of the impression evaluation using the SD method with the adjective pairs on a 5-point rating scale. First, the lower eigenvalue limit was set as 1, and the factors were extracted through the IT-iterative principal factor method. Based on the scree plot, the four-factor solution was judged to be appropriate. The result of executing the iterative principal factor method, assuming the four-factor solution again, was a cumulative explanation rate of 69.512%. The commonality of each item, factor load, and interpretation rate of variance of each factor after varimax rotation are shown in Table 2. We focused on the adjective pairs in which factor loads had absolute values over 0.50 to interpret the factors (Table 2).

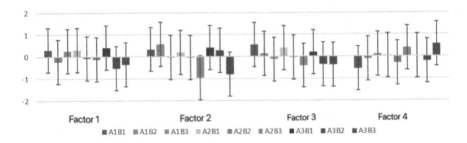

Fig. 8. Standard factor scores for each extracted factor

Table 3. Analysis of variance for standard factor scores

	FactorA		FactorB		FactorAB		Multiple comparisons		
	F	p	F	p	F	p	FactorA	FactorB	Simple main effects
active positiveness	1.30	0.29	6.00	0.01*	0.82	0.52	-	1>{2,3}	-
kind warmth	5.70	0.01*	7.38	0.01*	3.71	0.01*	1>2	{1,2}>3	A1>A3>{A2(b2),A2(b3)},B1>B2>B3{(a2),B3(a3)}
intensity	3.79	0.03*	3.31	0.50+	0.48	0.75	1>3	-	-
rational calm	1.59	0.22	3.11	0.06+	1.87	0.13	-	-	-

^{1}+p<.1,*p<.05

Factor 1 was defined as *active positiveness*, from "fun" and "amusing" to "sprightly." Factor 2 was defined as *kind warmth*, from "bright" and "aggressive" to "warm." Factor 3 was determined as *intensity* based on "strong," "strenuous," and "brisk." Factor 4 was *rational calm*, ranging from "stable" to "rational."

Based on the four factors obtained from the verification results, the following hypotheses were set.

H1: The impression of kind warmth changes depending on the visual presentation of the agent system.

H2: The pleasant impression changes depending on the tactile presentation of the agent system.

H3: The impression of kind warmth changes depending on the tactile presentation of the agent system.

H4: The impression of calmness changes depending on the tactile presentation of the agent system.

Then, we calculated the standard factor scores from the results of factor analysis to compare the impression of each condition with two factors: the visual presentation of guiding the participants to bed and the tactile presentation of patting or hugging.

The results of the analysis of variance are shown in Table 3.

The results showed a significant difference of A1 > A3 in Factor 2, kind warmth. That is, the visual presentation of approaching the bed was interpreted as kind warmth, which supported hypothesis H1. In addition, Factor 3, intensity, showed A1 > A3, which indicates the same result as that of Factor 2. Thus, the proposed visual presentation was effective in the intensity factor. Factor 1 showed B1 > {B2, B3}, and it is conjectured that the tactile presentation of tapping is considered to represent active positivity. Therefore, hypothesis H2 was supported. In addition, Factor 2 showed {B1, B2} > B3; that is, some physical contact is considered important to express warmth. Therefore, hypothesis H3 was supported.

Standard factor scores were then calculated from the results of factor analysis to compare the impression of each condition with the visual presentation of guiding the agent's subjects to bed and the tactile presentation of tapping or hugging. On this basis, analysis of variance was conducted (Table 3).

Furthermore, we summarize the interaction results in Factor 2. Factor 2 showed A1 > A3 > A2 in combination with B2 or B3. The results demonstrate the effectiveness of the proposed visual presentation with hugging or without physical contact. There were also significant interactions and simple main effects of Factor B in Factor 2. Based on the significant results of B1 > B2 > B3 in combination with A2 or A3, it is conjectured that physical contact was particularly effective when the agent did not move.

6   Discussion

In this study, we proposed a sleep-support system to reduce loneliness in the elderly's daily lives through the presence of an agent presenting visual and tactile sensations. The proposed system was expected to convey the familiarity, kindness, respect, security, and stability of the agent to users before they fell asleep, to naturally induce users to go to bed, and to make them relaxed and sleepy. Here, we discuss the effectiveness of our proposed method based on the results of the subjective evaluations using MOS values and the standard factor scores calculated from the extracted factors in the factor analysis.

First, the analysis of variance of the MOS values showed that the proposed movement of the agent to the bed, the disappearance of the agent before the tactile presentation in the bed, and the tactile stimulation of patting on the user's body could promote a sense of familiarity, respect, favor, presence, and sleepiness. In other words, for bedtime care, it is conjectured that our proposed agent approaching the bed and making a patting physical contact is effective, as we assumed, so that users can more easily feel the love, respect, and comfort of the agent and can be prepared for peaceful sleep. As a result of better sleep, it is also expected that the elderly will more easily receive care.

On the other hand, neither visual presentation nor tactile presentation had a significant effect on naturalness. We presumed that the simple animation design to reduce residual valuables would be interpreted to be unnatural, or that the artificial tactile presentation using a robotic arm in the blanket would not provide a natural touch with appropriate strength, like a human touch. To make the visual presentation more natural, it is possible to adopt 3D computer graphics with motion parallax based on the user's viewpoint [18]. The drawing method, appearance, and tactile device expressions such as torques should be discussed in detail.

Second, four factors were extracted through factor analysis: active positiveness, kind warmth, intensity, and rational calmness. Through variance analysis of standard factor scores for these factors, we found that the visual presentation affected kind warmth and that tactile presentation affected active positiveness, kind warmth, and intensity.

There were also significant results of the patting touch when the visual presentation was not the proposed method, as well as significant results of the proposed visual presentation when the tactile expression was hugging or without touch for evaluation of kind warmth. Therefore, either visual or tactile presentation of the proposed method could promote a kind, warm, and polite impression of the agent.

Thus, both the simple main effects in the interaction and the significance of the factors showed the effectiveness of our proposed method in promoting kind warmth.

The analyses using MOS values and factor scores revealed the effectiveness of the proposed method, especially using 1) the agent's visual presentation of moving toward the bed and disappearing before the tactile presentation and 2) the patting tactile expression to make the user feel familiar, comforted, and respected, as we aimed.

As a result of the simple main effects of the interaction, kindness, respect, and presence were elevated by the agent's visual presentation of moving toward the bed when there was no tactile representation and by the agent's patting without the proposed animation. Thus, both the visual and tactile presentations of our proposed method were considered important in expressing the kindness, respect, and presence of the agent. Therefore, the proposed agent is considered to be effective in stabilizing the user's mind, as we aimed.

Finally, some problems remain in the experiment. For example, the settings for the visual presentation, such as the moving speed and display duration before disappearance, intensity of the tactile expressions, and beat frequency of the patting, were set to fixed values; however, the validity of these values was not verified. Therefore, it is necessary to modify and verify each value in further evaluations to determine the best values. Next, our aim to induce elderly people's sleep was not directly evaluated. We should vary sleeping situations to consider appropriate behaviors of the agent corresponding to such situations.

7   Conclusion

In this study, we proposed a system that aims at a gentle induction of the sleep of elderly people with dementia by combining visual presentation with a wall projection-type agent that visually guides the user to the bed and physical contact expressions from the blanket to the user, such as hugging and patting repeatedly. The proposed system was expected to promote the feeling of being loved, respected, and comforted for further sense of trust and relief toward the agent.

The experiment confirmed that both the proposed animation of the agent's induction to the bed and the tactile presentation of the blanket imitating physical contact were effective in promoting the user's positive impression of the agent, such as familiar and respected, whereas the sleep induction effect was not verified. In the future, it is necessary to improve the tactile movement to be felt as natural and acceptable. It is also important to obtain the user's sleeping state using an infrared camera and a pressure sensor on the bed as a physiology measurement system so that physical contact such as hugging and patting can be carried out in various ways corresponding to the user's state. The effect of sleep induction/support using this system should also be evaluated with the users in various sleeping states. Furthermore, the scope and effectiveness of the system on relief and sleep induction should be expanded to not only elderly people but also children and mentally unstable people.

Acknowledgements. This research is supported in part by JSPS KAKENHI 19H04154, 18K11383, and 19K12090. The authors would like to thank the participants in the experiment.

References

1. World Bank staff estimates based on age/sex distributions of United Nations Population Division's World Population Prospects: 2019 Revision. https://data.worldbank.org/indicator/SP.POP.65UP.TO.ZS
2. Hillsdon, M.M., Brunner, E.J., Guralnik, J.M., Marmot, G.M.: Prospective study of physical activity and physical function in early old age. Am. J. Prev. Med. **28**(3), 245–250 (2005)
3. Tamakoshi, A., Ohno, Y.: Self-reported sleep duration as a predictor of all-cause mortality: results from the JACC study, Japan. Sleep-New York Then Westchester **27**(1), 51–54 (2004)
4. Dam, T.T.L., et al.: Association between sleep and physical function in older men: the osteoporotic fractures in men sleep study. J. Am. Geriatr. Soc. **56**(9), 1665–1673 (2008)
5. Tassi, P., Bonnefond, A., Engasser, O., Hoeft, A., Eschenlauer, R., Muzet, A.: EEG spectral power and cognitive performance during sleep inertia: the effect of normal sleep duration and partial sleep deprivation. Physiol. Behav. **87**(1), 177–184 (2006)
6. Lorton, D., et al.: Bidirectional communication between the brain and the immune system: implications for physiological sleep and disorders with disrupted sleep. NeuroImmunoModulation **13**(5–6), 357–374 (2006)
7. Cole, M.G., Dendukuri, N.: Risk factors for depression among elderly community subjects: a systematic review and meta-analysis. Risk **160**(6) (2003)
8. Grewen, K.M., Anderson, B.J., Girdler, S.S., Light, K.C.: Warm partner contact is related to lower cardiovascular reactivity. Behav. Med. **29**(3), 123–130 (2003)
9. Cohen, S., Janicki-Deverts, D., Turner, R.B., Doyle, W.J.: Does hugging provide stress-buffering social support? A study of susceptibility to upper respiratory infection and illness. Psychol. Sci. **26**(2), 135–147 (2015)
10. Bartz, J.A., Zaki, J., Bolger, N., Ochsner, K.N.: Social effects of oxytocin in humans: context and person matter. Trends Cogn. Sci. **15**(7), 301–309 (2011)

11. Fisher, J.D., Rytting, M., Heslin, R.: Hands touching hands: affective and evaluative effects of an interpersonal touch. Sociometry **39**(4), 416–421 (1976)
12. Yonezawa, T., Yamazoe, H.: Analyses of textile pressure-map sensor data of a stuffed toy for understanding human emotional physical contact. In: Proceedings of the 6th International Conference on Human-Agent Interaction, D **92**(1), 191–198 (2018)
13. Yu, R., et al.: Use of a therapeutic, socially assistive pet robot (PARO) in improving mood and stimulating social interaction and communication for people with dementia: study protocol for a randomized controlled trial. JMIR Res. Protoc. **4**(2) (2015)
14. Shiomi, M., Nakagawa, K., Shinozawa, K., Matsumura, R., Ishiguro, H., Hagita, N.: Does a robot's touch encourage human effort? Int. J. Soc. Rob., 1–11 (2016)
15. Takahiro, H., et al.: How do communication cues change impressions of human-robot touch interaction? Int. J. Soc. Rob. **10**(1), 21–31 (2018)
16. Chen, T.L., King, C.-H.A., Thomaz, A.L., Kemp, C.C.: An investigation of responses to robot-initiated touch in a nursing context. Int. J. Soc. Rob. **6**(1), 17954–17958 (2007)
17. Biquand, S., Zittel, B.: Care giving and nursing, work conditions and humanitude Work **41**(Supplement 1), 1828–1831 (2012)
18. Yoshida, N., Yonezawa, T.: Spatial communication and recognition in human-agent interaction using the motion parallax-based 3DCG virtual agent. HAI **2015**, 97–103 (2015)

Technology, Gender and COVID-19. Analysis of Perceived Health in Adults and Older People

Vanessa Zorrilla-Muñoz[1,2]([✉]), María Silveria Agulló-Tomás[1,3], Maria João Forjaz[4], Eduardo Fernandez[5], Carmen Rodriguez-Blazquez[6], Alba Ayala[7], and Gloria Fernandez-Mayoralas[1,8]

[1] University Institute on Gender Studies, University Carlos III of Madrid, Getafe, Spain
vzorrill@ing.uc3m.es
[2] Department of Mechanical Engineering, University Carlos III of Madrid, Getafe, Spain
[3] Department of Social Analysis, University Carlos III of Madrid, Getafe, Spain
msat@polsoc.uc3m.es
[4] National Center of Epidemiology, Institute of Health Carlos III and REDISSEC, Madrid, Spain
jforjaz@isciii.es
[5] Bioengineering Institute, Miguel Hernández University of Elche and CIBER BBN, Elche, Spain
e.fernandez@umh.es
[6] National Center of Epidemiology and CIBERNED, Institute of Health Carlos III, Madrid, Spain
crodb@isciii.es
[7] Department of Statistics, University Carlos III de Madrid, Getafe, Spain
aayala@est-econ.uc3m.es
[8] Institute of Economics, Geography and Demography (IEGD), Research Group on Ageing (GIE-CSIC), Spanish National Research Council (CSIC), Madrid, Spain
gloria.fernandezmayoralas@cchs.csic.es

Abstract. This chapter aims to know the psychosocial impact and social behaviours and related to the perception of technological needs in adults and older persons with diseases, health problems and/or sensory or motor disabilities. This work delves into this reality from a gender, inclusive and, at the same time, technological, biotechnological and/or virtual device approach. This goal includes two secondary objectives: 1) To know the health conditions that affect the adult and older people, whether they suffer from chronic diseases and health problems. In this way, it will be possible to understand if there are specific conditions in which the adult and older persons have felt especially sensitive during the pandemic outbreak in Spain. 2) To understand the needs of older people with sensory or motor disabilities before the pandemic and how this connects with the looking forward to an activity after COVID-19. One conclusion is that new emerging technologies are essential in aspects such as safety, hygiene and other social factors that help to improve autonomy and independence - such as canes and support devices in functional disability type EGARA - of older persons during and after the pandemic times. In addition to the needs of adults and the older persons prior to the pandemic, especially in older women, there are others that require research from a more inclusive and gender perspective.

© Springer Nature Switzerland AG 2021
Q. Gao and J. Zhou (Eds.): HCII 2021, LNCS 12787, pp. 363–379, 2021.
https://doi.org/10.1007/978-3-030-78111-8_25

Keywords: COVID-19 · Perceived health · Technology · Adult and Older people · Gender

1 Introduction

The advances in biomedicine and biotechnology in recent decades have achieved and unstoppable increase in life expectancy at birth, and more so in women. However, concern about COVID-19 has exploded around the world and is generating alarms and problems at all levels. Moreover, the COVID-19 is considered the most important public health disease of the last years for the world population. The high death rate in the pandemic is clouding the future outlook for older people. In turn, this disease is the main cause of hospitalization and death, particularly for older persons, which has reduced life expectancy in all latitudes [1]. Spain is one of the European countries with the highest excess mortality since the beginning of the pandemic. For example, the maximum null peak of 43.15 Z-score[1] was reached during week 14 of 2020 and the maximum value of 11.34 was reached in week 45 [2]. In particular, the high mortality rate due to diseases and complications caused by the SARs-CoV-2 virus in society is leading to a negative change in the future outlook [4], due to the decrease in life expectancy and the impact on people and communities, for example related to attitude, behavior, risk perception or social relationships in this crisis (see [5, 6], among others).

Furthermore, the complications are even greater if persons suffer from chronic conditions such as heart disease, diabetes and/or chronic bronchitis [7–9]. Additionally, people affected - directly or indirectly, for example, women and caregiving entities-residences - by the new disease may be more vulnerable to suffering from certain motor pathologies, for example, caused by thrombi in infected people [10–12] or necrosis [13] due to complications such as avascular necrosis [14], among others of a motor- and sensory-type.

This chapter assumes that COVID-19 should serve as an impetus to the study and, therefore, as a trigger for change and improvement in the most vulnerable groups such as older people. The attention focus should be on the case of dependency, physical and/or sensory disability and as chronic diseases that can affect older people mobility. For these aims, it is first necessary to know in detail the situation, behaviours and main attitudes of older persons. The idea starts from the fact that before the current socio-health crisis, older people (with physical and/or sensory disabilities) were already in a complex and difficult situation and with a questionable quality of life, an indicator that is linked to situation of dependency. In this sense, the United Nations criteria on the Human Development Index [15] indicates that better quality of life - where physical inactivity as morbidity and mortality indicator are identified [16] - as multidimensional concept, is related to health aspects. Currently, these aspects can be questioned from different perspectives in the current socio-health context. For example, the main measure to contain the virus and prevent its spread is to maintain the interpersonal distance. In people with visual or hearing disabilities or, with some mobility limitation, this measure can become an added barrier. In fact, risk factors related to musculoeskeletal disorders have been

---

[1] The Z-Score formula allows the standardization of the data distribution and, therefore, the data normalization. For more information see [3].

frequently analysed in occupational sectors with high accidentability prevalence and associates factors such as construction [17], but gender perspective includes a new sectorial view (i.e. in agriculture [18]). In this sense, adult and older women are especially vulnerable because they live longer than their peers and suffer from more musculoskeletal disorders [19] or are more prone to disabilities [20] and more specifically, sensory impartment [21].

In the context of the current pandemic, numerous researches related to the psychosocial impact of older people are being carried out, for example, some analyses have found emotional distress in older persons [22, 23, among others], i.e. if there are economic loss conditions and when the use of anxiolytics [24]. However, so far there are no studies considering the role of emerging technologies from the health conditions of people with disabilities (with chronic diseases, or susceptible to developing disabling/chronic diseases and in specific relation to mobility) as well as the behaviour health during the first pandemic outbreak. If to this profile is added being older person, and taking into account the gender perspective (women are also indirectly affected, since they are often longer-lived than their peers and develop more musculoskeletal disorders or visual impairment, among others), we find that studies are very scarce.

This chapter aims to know the psychosocial impact of persons with diseases, health problems and/or sensory or motor disabilities addressed to the social and hygiene behaviours and the perception of technological needs. This objective considers the point of view of experts, adults and older people with physical or sensory disabilities, with chronic diseases or susceptible to developing disabling diseases or those who are at risk of suffering from chronic conditions and aftermaths even when they have overcome SARS-CoV-2. This work delves into this reality from a gender, inclusive and, at the same time, technological, biotechnological and/or virtual device approach.

The objectives are the following: 1) To know the health conditions that affect the adult and older people, whether they suffer from diseases or health problems or not. In this way, it will be possible to understand if there are specific conditions in which the adult and older persons have felt especially sensitive during the outbreak. 2) To understand the needs of older people with sensory or motor disabilities before the pandemic and how this connects with the looking forward to an activity after COVID-19. Both will help to connect current conditions and needs with emerging technologies and understand their possible validity in the current context of a pandemic.

2 Methods

This chapter uses the multi-method triangulation strategy based on quantitative data which are complemented by qualitative data. For this reason, two types of information were used.

The first objective is analysed through the 'Survey of Health, Ageing and Retirement' [25], wave 8 (W8, 2020) in Spain (June 11th–August 10th) started as 'SHARE COVID-19 survey'. The accesses to the questionnaire data are free for scientific user purpose. SHARE data are protected by factual anonymity (as defined by the strict norms of the German Federal Statistics Act and the German Federal Data Protection Law). The collection of the data is anonymously registered and never contains identifying

Table 1. Technical data of statistical analysis and information used.

Geographical Score	Spain
Information Collection	Macro-questionnaire SHARE COVID-19 Survey
Population Selected	Women and Men in Spain (=> 49 years)
Sample size calculated (N)	2042 persons (women and men)
Stratified procedure	Classification in relation to health conditions that suggest mobility during the outbreak
Sociodemographics and health conditions variables used	Sex; Age; Diabetes or high blood sugar; Hip fracture; Heart attack or other heart problem; Chronic lung disease; Cancer or malignant tumor; Other illness or health condition
Items analysed which suggests social and hygiene behaviours	Went shopping since outbreak; Went out for a walk since outbreak; Met more than 5 people outside household since outbreak; Visited other family members since outbreak; Wore a face mask in public; Kept distance from others in public; Washed hands more than usual; Used hand Sanitizer or disinfection gel more than usual; Covered coughs and sneezes more than usual
Dependent variable	Looking forward to an activity after COVID-19
Analysis tool	Software STATA IC

information about the participants. A resume of technical data and information of the questionnaire used is presented in Table 1.

The second objective utilized qualitative analysis: Interviews and discussion groups (118 documents) with experts/key informants and older people were analysed through qualitative methodology by using the ATLAS.ti (v9) programme. This data comes from a fieldwork carried out in 2017, in Spain in four contexts: key informants from firms, Civil Society Organizations (CSO henceforth), and Institutions and professionals, as well as older persons. From a total of 124 primary codes, the following were used to the search of discourses: 'technologic'; 'funcfisico' (physical functions); 'care' (aspects related to the provision/receiving of care); 'health'; 'psychologic factors'; 'future'; 'identity'.

3 Results

The birth mean of the total 2,042 people interviewed in Spain is 75.18 ± 0.21 years. This means that the people average age is close to 75 years, which corresponds to a risk population group of COVID-19. If the data related to diseases and health problems are analysed, it can be seen that the people interviewed, in general, could be considered to be of adult age and older people with a high risk of suffering complications in the case of contracting the virus. Regarding women, the profile is highlighted with other diseases or health problems or limitations, for example, osteoarthritis and disorders due to perception of instability - which includes hearing loss, among others.

Table 2. Adults and older people according to sociodemographic and health condition variables of the study.

Sociodemographic and health condition variables		Total (N = 2042) [Med. ± SD]	Women (n = 1173) [Med. ± SD]	Men (n = 869) [Med. ± SD]
		[N (%)]	[N (%)] over n = 1174	[N (%)] over n = 869
Sex	Women	1174 (57,42)	1174 (100)	–
	Man	869 (42.54)	–	869 (100)
Age		75.15 ± 9.51	75.15 ± 9.95	75.16 ± 8.89
Diabetes or high blood sugar	Yes	39 (1.91)	22 (1.88)	17 (1.96)
Hip fracture		8 (0.39)	7 (0.60)	1 (0.12)
Heart attack or other heart problem		42 (2.06)	18 (1.54)	24 (2.77)
Chronic lung disease		22 (1.08)	11 (1.27)	11 (0.94)
Cancer or malignant tumor		29 (1.42)	13 (1.11)	16 (1.85)
Other illness or health condition		135 (6.62)	82 (7.00)	53 (6.11)

Note: *t-Student (p)* = *t-Student test* (probability); *p KW* = *Kruskal-Wallis test probability*. Scales used:

The second analysis (Table 3) reports applicable items related to behaviour health during the pandemic outbreak in Spain. Pearson correlation coefficient is provided for all the items and 'looking forward to an activity after COVID-19'. It is observed that social behaviors are avoided, specifically; social outings and visits to their family. Moreover, there is awareness of the mask use, the maintenance of social distance and the hygiene (washed hands, use gel and coverer coughs or sneezes) items that are related to the item 'looking forward to an activity after COVID-19'.

These restrictions during confinement (Table 3) are associated to the health items conditions observed in Table 2 which have also been found in the situations discussed in the following sections. The qualitative analysis is divided into 3 parts and considers the perception of health from these dimensions: 'Motor and sensory disabilities before the pandemic and aids devices'; 'Demand for higher accidents and falls risk prevention of older person' and; 'Physical limitations persistence in older persons and lack of social and health care programmes'.

Table 3. Statistical analysis for the health behaviours' items in comparison to the possibility to look forward to an activity after COVID-19.

Items		Scale used	Mean ± SD	Pearson correlation coefficient (with 'looking forward to an activity after COVID-19')
Dependent variable: Looking forward to an activity after COVID-19		1: Refusal or I don't' know; 2: Did not name anything; 3: Hesitate to name something; 4: Named something right-away;	3.36 ± 0.02	–
Independent variables	Went shopping since outbreak	0: Not applicable or don't know; 1: Not anymore; 2: Less often; 3: About the same; 4: More often	1.52 ± 1.02	0.32**
	Went out for a walk since outbreak		1.54 ± 1.04	0.20**
	Met more than 5 people outside household since outbreak		1.07 ± 0.84	0.18**
	Visited other family members since outbreak		1.13 ± 0.88	0.20**
	Wore a face mask in public	1: Always 2: Often; 3: Sometimes; 4: Never; 5: Not applicable or don't know	2.07 ± 1.69	– 0.28**
	Kept distance from others in public		2.04 ± 1.68	– 0.26**
			N (%)	
	Washed hands more than usual	0: No or I don't know 1: Yes	No: 140 (6.86) Yes: 1901 (93,14)	0.19**
	Used hand Sanitizer or disinfection gel more than usual		No: 202 (9.90) Yes: 1839 (90.10)	0.16**
	Covered coughs and sneezes more than usual		No: 335 (16.41) Yes: 1706 (83.59)	0.22**

$^{**}p < 0.01$

3.1 Motor and Sensory Disabilities Before the Pandemic and Aids Devices

Physical disabilities are mentioned in all kinds of speeches (by professionals, but especially by the elderly themselves in any context consulted), from mobility disabilities to sensory (visual or auditory, among others) and other types of chronic diseases functional type.

[...]My brother is 81 years old. He is diabetic, his sight was caught and he has gone blind. Then he also had to put a pacemaker [...] D5, GD, older man, 80 years[2]

[...]I was distracted a lot reading or doing crosswords, word searches that were bigger now because I see less and less... until now they have to... they don't know what they will have to do to me in this other eye. I mean, I see it a bit like that, everything as blurry... [...] D1, GD, older woman, 81 years

[...]I have hip pain because I have osteoarthritis in the joints [...] D74, VC, older woman, 80 years

From the speeches of key informants, the resources or products that can be used in these diseases must (already should and nowadays even more) be understood as basic needs.

[...]I believe that the basic needs are well taken care of [...]the subject of orthodontics, glasses, assistive devices, such as canes. Also headphones... That it is an important issue, and that it is good, because, logically, that they are very expensive, and that it is good because some have difficulties to buy it [...] D17, INS-RES, key informant

Sometimes, there is a refusal to accept that when suffering from diseases or disabilities (physical and sensory) vitality is being lost and it is necessary to use this type of product. In addition to that, this negation generates a feeling of frustration for not being able to deal with the disability and there is no remedy to return to an earlier stage in life.

[...]The other day I saw one women crying, I approached "but what's wrong with you?", because I'm already talking with her for a while and of course, everything is the physical problem. Here the big problem that older people have is to see that we are running out of being able to do what we wanted, today's detail, right? 'I like to go down the stairs', I say: 'I would like to go too without cane'. [...] D113, VC-RES, older woman

3.2   Demand for Higher Accidents and Falls Risk Prevention of Older Person

The criticism of safety in the environment, whether rural or urban, is noteworthy in the speeches, since they are not prepared for the use of technological devices that generate a greater sense of independence. On the contrary, the elements designed for older persons are not conceived to reduce the risks of the surroundings.

---

[2] In order to maintain the anonymity of each interviewee, the information collected in the quotes is identified as follows: D# (number of document), type of interview of discussion group (GD-RES: Discussion group in residence or day center; GD-CM: Discussion group in older people center; VC: Collaborative residence; VC-RES: Collaborative housing responsible person; VF: Family housing; INS-RES: Institutional key informant of residence or day center; INS: Institutional key informant; EPQ-CM: Professional of center team; EPQ-RES: Professional of residence), person (older woman, older man or key informant) and age (in the case of older person).

[…]I understand that if the person goes with the cane or with the walking aid and a bike passes and maybe… oh! You get scared because the bike passes, but the bike has not done anything to you. […] D102, VF, older woman, 77 years

[…]Older people are cannon fodder. We need road safety to elude accidents, due to vision and hearing problems. We want active people, to go out, to socialize and such, but the we have to teach and train, because their vision and hearing problems prevent them from going out, the traffic lights, the cities are often not prepared for older persons. It is an important effort, to make cities… today a concept of friendly cities, accessible cities. […] D11, INS, key informant

[…]Regarding safety, we did have an initiative that was to prevent accidents and social isolation, because they are two variables that are quite related… to see a little the situation of these people, how was the accident rate, especially in the home environment and others, and establish the protocols that already exist, to facilitate how people have to have their home to avoid accidents, what they have to have, what they do not have to have… both in the physical aspect purely (the furniture) as well as the facilities and others, and avoid all that… in short, that security is not only outside (which we also promote, avoid barriers) […] D13, INS, key informant

One of the greatest resources used by older people with motor disabilities is the use of the cane. In addition, there are speeches that indicate cane as a preventive product to avoid falls and support when muscular strength is lacking, which could also be applied to other types of problems or functional disabilities.

I have a lot of imbalance because I have to… let's say… not support myself, but stabilize myself, to have an order to walk, right? I use them, the cane. […] D61, VC, older man, 79 years

[…] I have difficulty moving around, it seems that I have a lack of muscular strength, which makes me function very well here, within an order. But if I go out to the street I already have to carry one of those elbow crutches because it offers you more security than a cane. I'll end up with a chair… but for the moment I move alone… it's hard for me to walk, so… […] D62, VC, older man, 79 years

It is even commented in some speeches that the cane combined with socio-cultural animation or attention of older carers, invites older people to participate in activities in which they had not been included previously. In this sense, experts in residential and occupational older people care guide them to carry out activities that improve and enhance their physical condition and, at the same time, allow them to participate in leisure.

[…]Or she makes us even dance. I say: 'I can't, Amanda, I can't dance!' Well, I pick up the cane and say, 'Come on, come on.' With my legs and my can, I try to dance!'. […] D1, GD-RES, older woman, 81 years

[…]We have a process of physical activity for the prevention of aging that is done every two days a week in this center, and that other centers for the disabled attend […]we have many sports activities, many, something incredible. Well, we have

from soccer, hockey with envelope with envelope eh is called indoor jockey, indoor hockey, basketball, swimming, dice, darts, hiking, we do hiking very frequently. Hiking there are two outings every month: one for occupational centers, that is, for the most valid, and another for the most assisted or the most dependent, who are easier routes, as you will understand. But all these are aimed at preventing the aging of pathologies and functional disabilities. [...] D25, INS, key informant

In any case, it follows that there should be a greater awareness of the ageing process, in participating in it, of the need to prevent accidents and falls in this vital stage.

[...]We and older persons will be aware of prevention of falls or risks that can be had because the body is already turning years and a series of changes are taking place at all levels. The person should be aware of changes [...][...] How to prevent falls at home and how to adopt proper habits at home...D10, EPQ-CM, key informant

[...]In any active aging programme, a fall prevention programme must be implicit. Because women have a risk, and the risk of falling, that we all have because of the clumsiness in the march that we have, the loss of vision [...]A fall in an older woman is followed by a fracture. 30% do not regain their previous functional level that they had. Then, due to an excess of medication, a hypnotic not well prescribed, not well selected, or the selection of a hypnotic with a long-half life, or a hypnotic that is potentiated with a hypertensive one that the next day causes that hangover and such, makes that the person falls and that we have had a fracture, and that perhaps by checking we had avoided. [...] D11, INS, key informant

By summarizing, the need for a social-health environment that prevents diseases and empowers the elderly is also considered. From another sense, the speeches mention that any type of viral process (for example, flu, since at the time of doing interviews and discussion groups there were no cases of COVID-19, but it could be extrapolated to it), however slight it may seem, can cause neuromotor problems in older people.

[...]And you are going to tell me: 'Well that is a simple flu...' No no, that is not a simple flu. In an older person, a flu process lasts 7–9 days, and for each day that that person is bedridden, they lose 3% of their muscle mass. If we multiply 9–10 by 3, 30% of his/her muscle mass. What are we talking about? That a person, who roamed well, who was almost autonomous, can become not autonomous. Well we have lost the most precious asset we have. [...] D11, INS, key informant

3.3   Physical Limitations Persistence in Older Persons and Lack of Social and Health Care Programmes'

Despite the fact that the care and attention are oriented to the person and resources have been increased, sometimes, there is concern and fear of ageing, stopping performing activities at this stage of life and the disease and losing their autonomy and independence.

[...]When you get older you are afraid: that you will become ill, that they might take you away... The older ones feel a virile disability, saying 'What if I get this,

what if...?', But no, in this town you are well covered. [...] D92, VF, older man, 78 years

[...]*Well, on safety issues, they clearly say that they can fend for themselves because they feel fear. The fear of losing autonomy, because it is the fear of losing freedom. So, from there... That's why sometimes when they talk in terms of health, how they are doing, they give us a percentage of positivity higher than the average population, which is striking. That is, let's say the felt needs do not coincide with the needs perceived by the professionals. There is a clear distortion in that sense. So that, the suspicion is because they want to pretend an autonomy that they sometimes lack, and that implies that of course, they are afraid, afraid of losing that status of autonomy and of living freely for something they do not know. So that is logically an issue to watch on our part.* [...] D13, INS, key informant

[...] *When they start to have physical problems, that also makes it difficult for them to grow old because it limits them a lot. Depending on someone, in this case, the Nursing Assistant, the Nurse, because it makes them feel worse and sometimes they stop relating to others, wanting to go out, not wanting to do activities in the center. I mean, I think the physical issue limits them a lot.* [...] D18, INS, key informant

In other discourses, older people feel aware of their limitations; accept them, despite the existence of mobility or sensory disability that increases with age and in these stages. However, it is also observed that they empower themselves and experience a more participatory old age.

[...]*What I have to know are my limitations. And from my limitations, playing with my possibilities, which is called: being safe. There are things that I don't do, sometimes I apologize and say: 'I don't do that', other times I can't, and from those limitations that I know, I don't tell anyone, I tell myself... I don't have to drool it. I look for what possibilities I have. And in those possibilities I feel safe.* [...] D6, GD-CM, older woman, 72 years

[...]*that I fell, I fell and, they say, it was due to failure of the brain. And I fell again and the same thing, thank goodness [laughs] the vertebra was welded. But, when now I notice myself very diminished in speaking and moving my hand, and my feet also go... I'm dragging my feet a lot but hey, I have times, better times, worse times, but I... well I accept it... From trembling, from walking, but not that at the moment. My motor form is limited.* [...] D66, VC, older woman, 84 years

[...] *I have just had my knee operated, I have a knee replacement, well I would like to do more things, sometimes they go hiking here, but I cannot because I am very limited. So with what I do in the gym and hanging around here in the group is fine. The crafts that I also attend them and on Fridays at bingo.* [...] D98, VC, older woman, 59 years

From the speeches of experts it is concluded that disabilities and diseases which reduce mobility influences and hinders the active and healthy aging that the WHO and other organizations recommend. In this sense, physical activity should be valued both as a preventive aspect throughout the ageing process.

[...] *I think that the issue of diseases overwhelms people a lot, makes them go down a lot. They usually say: 'It's that I... it's that my leg hurts a lot, I'm not feeling well.'* [...] D7, EQP-RES, key informant

[...]*By having to overcome a physical discomfort is not the same as not having to go through it, right? The humor that suffers with pain, fatigue and others, it limits, right? That's clear. But I don't know, I still see the motivation for contact by others or at least for interest in a subject more decisive than the physical subject.* [...] D8, EPQ-RES, key informant

[...]*Physical activity is a pending issue among the older population. Yes well it is in the form of playful participation, this deficit is beginning to be alleviated, it is I mean, they don't understand what pure and simple promotion is to be better, but to do something.* [...] D13, INS, key informant

4 Discussion

The results expose that before the appearance of COVID-19, older people suffered from physical disabilities of a motor or sensory type, which, in one way or another, generate fear and frustrations in the face of active and participatory ageing. This matches recent data from the disability survey [26]. For this reason, results suggest that the current pandemic situation is affecting even more the emotions and sense of safety of adults and the older people with some type of functional disability, chronic disease or dependence situation.

Another aspect related to dependency and care is that before the pandemic, there was already the need to carry out socio-cultural and leisure programmes, as well as other types of programmes focused on the needs of the people themselves, whether dependents or caregivers. These programmes before COVID-19 were already little evaluated [27]. The demand continues in the current situation, it is obviously not less than before. It would be about increasing them in number and quality and also their evaluation. These programmes should be readapted to the new situation (e.g. from a more online offer or from the inclusion of new technological proposals). All of this should be consistent and in favor of a better active and participatory aging at the psychosocial level and, supporting the constant reduction of the digital divide [28].

In this sense, it is observed how older people in situations of dependency, disability or chronic diseases have been changing with respect to past decades and are experiencing an increasingly active and participatory ageing [29], where women have also taken the big step and have become increasingly empowered and with greater control and leadership [30]. However, due to the current pandemic, socio-educational programmes have been slowed down by reducing attendance and support for essential services is being limited, leaving in the background all the psychosocial and leisure activities that for the elderly and caregivers who also was and is 'essential', but is being put off by basic care. COVID-19, instead of being a catalyst to adapt and promote new programmes at the moment, is serving as a brake and justifying other reductions that could also be compatible, with more resources and efforts, in all kinds of health support. The 'essential' debate also moves here and harms, once again, the groups that already before the pandemic could not be served.

The results also depict the need for technological devices that generate a greater sense of older people independence and help to reduce environment risks in this vital stage. In addition, in the current pandemic situation with reduced mobility and outbreak, both the need for a safe environment, as well as physiological care, have become evident, even more, it is from the need to create a positive image, especially in the case of women, where it is more accentuated.

In the context of disabilities, not being able to return to previous stages in life generates frustration and helplessness in the older person. This should be understood from the current pandemic context, where helplessness has been emphasized by increasing control over behaviours - such as, safety distance, wearing a mask, washing hands and not being able to continue enjoying social and family life with the intensity that was done in the past -. Hence, there appears the need to develop emerging technologies adapted to the person - for example, artificial intelligence, machine learning and neurosciences adapted in social robots and mobile or social support devices, among others -, which in turn improve images on the old age and allow a better perception (and real experience) of physical and psychosocial health of the older persons.

The fear of ageing and the negative perceptions of ageing are evident in the context before the pandemic. In some way, it is confirmed, but the technological and psychosocial resources are still insufficient or not adequate. In return, it is also observed how certain socio-health stereotypes are changing. For example, from the rural environment, more and better care resources are being reached than decades ago. In a way, the current situation is forcing the technological gap to disappear (from any perspective, not only age, but also socio-spatial). Consequently, emerging technologies must be increasingly focused on offering resources adapted to the person, their environment, their individuality, in short, improve their usability and ergonomics and, from an innovative aspect, relate their emotions to respond to the person's needs. In this sense, it is worth highlighting the progress in emerging technologies related to the valence of emotions at the cortical level (see, i.e. [31]).

In general, it is evidenced in the results that older people are or may worsen at multiple levels of dependency and disability, which connects with recent studies of active ageing and reveal the importance of the biocognitive component - referring to cognitive function, health conditions or pain - [32]. In this sense, there is concern about the environment and the prevention of accidents, especially in the case of falls, which can generate multiple disabilities. This connects with the study by Bang et at. which evidences the impact in the case of postural instability related to hearing loss [33]. In the same way, instability is also related to the fact that people who suffer from dizziness can generate an unconscious worry that increases the perception of instability [34]. In general, the results outline that there is a need for prevention of falls and accidents that could be configured through programmes oriented to this key objective such as participation, but the need to promote safe environments, where the role of emerging technologies is the key.

Following this context, products adapted to older persons are a part of the ageing process with disabilities and, as such, should be recommended, investigated and evaluated. These products can be used for the entire older population in general, with more or less limitations, physical or sensorial disabilities. For example, in the case of visual impairment, great advances have been known in cortical visual prosthesis [35, 36, 37, among others].

From other aspects, this chapter reports greater support necessary for older people with mobility problems, but not only from social and support services, but also through the development of assistive devices to maintain social distance in people with different disabilities - physical, visual and/or hearing -. For example, this is the case of the handle for the traditional white cane, known as EGARA[3] that avoids collision with impacts from the waist up in visually impaired or blind people. Specifically, technological products address to design devices allowing older persons to maintain their autonomy, in order to the chapter results and in turn, into a positive image in the whole of society [29].

All the new systems developed in the COVID-19 era should include the hardware and software necessary to allow their programming and adaptation to the specific characteristics of each user. With all this, a greater biotechnological transfer and its advantages to society would be facilitated from the development of devices that allow improving mobility in this group or profile of the most affected people in this context of pandemic and, in turn, maintaining the social distance. The new technological devices could be a positive change from the *internet of things* applied to everyday life, as well as facilitate the selective and positive use of digital platforms for the most vulnerable and less mobile groups - as in the case of adults, older people with physical and/or sensory disabilities, and/or with chronic diseases -. An improvement in usability, ergonomics and further training is necessary in new technological devices addressed to older people to reduce the different digital gaps - related to age, training level, sex or the residential space where older people lives - as suggested Criado-Quesada et al. in the case of ICT for health aspects - such as medical prescription – [38]. In other contexts, the development and design or eco-sustainable ICT and aid devices is required to connect new behaviours of older persons with environmental, land and, sustainability for leisure and health, beyond agriculture that has characterized and still stereotypes images of older people.

On the other hand, RNA based vaccines are being considered as the solution by nature to the transmission of the disease, but the sample used in clinical studies have evidenced to be effective in healthy people [39], However, the population necessary for global immunity has not yet been reached either state or worldwide, so the risk of contagion continues to exist. To this, we could add the discussion that is being generated about the possibility of dysfunctional immune response [40], the adverse effects derived of the administration [41] - i.e. in the case of allergies [42] - and particularly especially if a group of population has been excluded of the clinical trials, such as fragility older persons [43] and, the accessibility and acceptance for the vaccines [44]. Therefore, there is a need to continue designing and researching medical devices and aids for older people with emerging technologies by supporting contributing to the regulation of certain hygiene and safety functions during the pandemic.

---

[3] http://bastonegara.es/.

Undoubtedly, chronic diseases and disabilities have been accentuated since the arrival of SARS-CoV-2, which could lead to general socio-political disinterest in the needs of dependent and fragile older people by, limiting the socio-health to cover only palliative care. In this regard, there is still an unresolved debate on euthanasia related to the need to care for and seek a higher quality of life at these ages, but also a higher quality of death and the right to choose in this final phase. The promotion of health, both physical and psychosocial - even more so, due to the growing loneliness not chosen during the pandemic - continues to be the pending issue in the socio-health area.

Among limitations of the results, it is worth mentioning the specificity lack or invisibility masks or disabilities and chronic diseases which are related to autonomy and dependency and compromise the motor abilities in older women, such as arthritis or instability. For Eldesouky et al., some of these diseases can predict other diseases, such as depression [45], so it would also be interesting to consider them together with cognitive diseases or cognitive symptoms.

In summary, there is a need to continue researching psychosocial questions about the impact of the SARS-CoV-2 virus. The adoption of a gender, socio-spatial, technological and intergenerational approach could be a key factor to better understand the perception of health and point towards programmes and policies in favor of better health and social sustainability, satisfaction and quality of life during and after COVID-19 for the older people and moreover, in the case of older people with disabilities, chronic diseases, mobility problems and/or dependency situations.

5 Conclusion

New emerging technologies are more and more essential during and after the pandemic. The social and hygiene behaviours and restrictions are forced to design more inclusive, adaptative, functional, usable and ergonomic devices and medical devices. In this design it is important to highlight the consideration of aids to improve autonomy and independence - such as canes and support devices in functional disability type EGARA - of older persons.

As this chapter is suggested, for adults and older people it is still unpredictable how future behaviors will develop. However, older people with chronic diseases and at risk of complications from COVID-19 look cautiously to the social behaviours in future. In this sense, technology could be a favorable element that helps social participation. Moreover, the influence of technology and gender on the older people perceived health is clear, but needs more research and assessment, especially in the current pandemic context.

Fundings and Grants. This work is part of the QASP (Quality of life, Ageing in Sweden, Spain, and Portugal) research project, funded by the Institute of Health Carlos III, Intramural Strategical Action in Health AESI 2018, Ref: PI18CIII/00046, PR: MR Forjaz). We appreciated the support of: ENCAGEn-CM R&D Activities Program (Active Ageing, Quality of Life and Gender. Promoting a positive image of old age and ageing against ageism) (Ref. H2019/HUM-5698) (Community of Madrid-FSE. PR: G. Fernandez-Mayoralas, C Rodriguez-Blázquez, M.S. Agulló-Tomás, M.D. Zamarrón, and M.A. Molina).

Moreover, this contribution takes parts of the grant PROMETEO/2019/119 from the Generalitat Valenciana and the Bidons Egara Research Chair of the University Miguel Hernández to

Eduardo Fernández. The fieldwork for the qualitative analysis was financed by the ENVACES R&D + i project (MINECO-FEDER, ref. CSO2015- 64115-R. PR: F. Rojo-Perez) and the ENCAGE-CM R&D Activities Program (Community of Madrid-FSE, ref. S2015/HUM-3367. LR: G. Fernandez-Mayoralas).

References

1. Marois, G., Muttarak, R., Scherbov, S.: Assessing the potential impact of COVID-19 on life expectancy. PLoS ONE **15**(9), e0238678 (2020). https://doi.org/10.1371/journal.pone.023 8678
2. EUROMOMO. Graphs and maps (2020). https://www.euromomo.eu/graphs-and-maps
3. EUROMOMO. What is a Z-Score (2020). https://www.euromomo.eu/how-it-works/what-is-a-z-score/
4. Ruiz Cantero, M.T.: Las estadísticas sanitarias y la invisibilidad por sexo y de género durante la epidemia de COVID-19. Gac. Sanit. **35**(1), 95–98 (2020). https://doi.org/10.1016/j.gaceta. 2020.04.008
5. Majid, U., Wasim, A., Bakshi, S., Truong, J.: Knowledge, (mis-)conceptions, risk perception, and behavior change during pandemics: a scoping review of 149 studies. Public Underst. Sci. **29**(8), 777–799 (2020). https://doi.org/10.1177/0963662520963365
6. Knowles, K.A., Olatunji, B.O.: Anxiety and safety behavior usage during the COVID-19 pandemic: the prospective role of contamination fear. J. Anxiety Disord. **77**, 102323 (2021). https://doi.org/10.1016/j.janxdis.2020.102323
7. Chudasama, Y.V., et al.: Impact of COVID-19 on routine care for chronic diseases: a global survey of views from healthcare professionals. Diabetes Metab. Syndr. **14**(5), 965–967 (2020). https://doi.org/10.1016/j.dsx.2020.06.042
8. Jordan, R.E., Adab, P., Cheng, K.K.: Covid-19: risk factors for severe disease and death. BMJ **368**, m1198 (2020). https://doi.org/10.1136/bmj.m1198
9. Schett, G., Sticherling, M., Neurath, M.F.: COVID-19: risk for cytokine targeting in chronic inflammatory diseases? Nat. Rev. Immunol. **20**(5), 271–272 (2020). https://www.nature.com/articles/s41577-020-0312-7
10. Connors, J.M., Levy, J.H.: COVID-19 and its implications for thrombosis and anticoagulation. Blood J. Am. Soc. Hematol. **135**(23), 2033–2040 (2020). https://doi.org/10.1182/blood.202 0006000
11. Hashemi, A., Madhavan, M.V., Bikdeli, B.: Pharmacotherapy for prevention and management of thrombosis in COVID-19. Seminars in thrombosis and hemostasis. Semin. Thromb Hemost **46**(7), 789–795 (2020). https://doi.org/10.1055/s-0040-1714273
12. McFadyen, J.D., Stevens, H., Peter, K.: The emerging threat of (micro) thrombosis in COVID-19 and its therapeutic implications. Circ. Res. **127**(4), 571–587 (2020). https://doi.org/10. 1161/CIRCRESAHA.120.317447
13. Feldmann, M., et al.: Trials of anti-tumour necrosis factor therapy for COVID-19 are urgently needed. Lancet **395**(10234), 1407–1409 (2020). https://doi.org/10.1016/S0140-6736(20)308 58-8
14. Hu, B., Huang, S., Yin, L.: The cytokine storm and COVID-19. J. Med. Virol. **93**(1), 250–256 (2021). https://doi.org/10.1002/jmv.26232
15. United Nations. United Nations Development Programme. Human Development Reports (2020). http://hdr.undp.org/en/content/human-development-index-hdi
16. Higuita-Gutiérrez, L.F., Cardona-Arias, J.A.: Índice de desarrollo humano y eventos de salud pública: revisión sistemática de la literatura 1990–2015. Revista Facultad Nacional de Salud Pública **36**(1), 5–16 (2018). https://doi.org/10.17533/udea.rfnsp.v36n1a02

17. Zorrilla-Muñoz, V., Petz, M., Agulló-Tomás, M.S.: Ergonomic risk factors analysis with multi-methodological workers' activities in buildings under construction. Dyna **94**(3) (2019). https://doi.org/10.6036/8764

18. Zorrilla-Muñoz, V., Agulló-Tomás, M.S., Garcia-Sedano, T.: Socio-ergonomic analysis in agriculture. Evaluation of the oleic sector from a gender and aging perspective. ITEA-INFORMACION TECNICA ECONOMICA AGRARIA, **115**(1), 83–104 (2019). https://doi.org/10.12706/itea.2019.005

19. Cimas, M., Ayala, A., Sanz, B., Agulló-Tomás, M.S., Escobar, A., Forjaz, M.J.: Chronic musculoskeletal pain in European older adults: cross-national and gender differences. Eur. J. Pain **22**(2), 333–345 (2018). https://doi.org/10.1002/ejp.1123

20. WHO. World Report on Disabilities (2011). https://www.who.int/disabilities/world_report/2011/report.pdf

21. Lyu, J., Kim, H.Y.: Gender-specific associations of sensory impairments with depression and cognitive impairment in later life. Psychiatr. Investig. **15**(10), 926 (2018). https://doi.org/10.30773/pi.2018.06.28.2

22. Bui, C.N., Peng, C., Mutchler, J.E., Burr, J.A.: Race and ethnic group disparities in emotional distress among older adults during the COVID-19 pandemic. Gerontologist gnaa217 (2020). https://doi.org/10.1093/geront/gnaa217

23. Yang, H., Ma, J.: How an epidemic outbreak impacts happiness: factors that worsen (vs. protect) emotional well-being during the coronavirus pandemic. Psychiatr. Res. **289**, 113045 (2020). https://doi.org/10.1016/j.psychres.2020.113045

24. García-Fernández, L., Romero-Ferreiro, V., López-Roldán, P.D., Padilla, S., Rodriguez-Jimenez, R.: Mental health in elderly Spanish people in times of COVID-19 outbreak. Am. J. Geriatr. Psychiatry **28**(10), 1040–1045 (2020). https://doi.org/10.1016/j.jagp.2020.06.027

25. Survey of Health, Ageing and Retirement (2020). http://www.share-project.org/home0.html

26. Silván, C., Quífez, L.E.: Efectos y consecuencias de la crisis de la COVID-19 entre las personas con discapacidad (2020). https://www.odismet.es/sites/default/files/2020-07/Informe_Estu dioCOVID_19_v3_0.pdf

27. Agulló-Tomás, M.S., Zorrilla-Muñoz, V., Gómez-García, M.V.: Aproximación socio-espacial al envejecimiento ya los programas para cuidadoras/es de mayores. Revista INFAD de Psicología. Int. J. Dev. Educ. Psychol. **2**(1), 211–228 (2019). https://doi.org/10.17060/ijodaep.2019.n1.v2.1433

28. Agulló-Tomás, M.S., Zorrilla-Muñoz, V.: Technologies and images of older women. In: Gao, Q., Zhou, J. (eds.) HCII 2020. Human Aspects of IT for the Aged Population, pp. 163–175. Springer, Cham (2020) https://doi.org/10.1007/978-3-030-50232-4_124

29. Fernández-Mayoralas, G., Schettini del Moral, R., Sánchez-Román, M., Rojo-Pérez, F., Agulló-Tomás, M.S., Forjaz, M.J.: El papel del género en el buen envejecer. Una revisión sistemática desde la perspectiva científica. Prisma Social: revista de investigación social (21), 149–176 (2018). https://revistaprismasocial.es/article/view/2422

30. Agulló-Tomás, M.S., Zorrilla-Muñoz, V., Gómez-Díaz, M.V., Criado, B.: Liderazgo, envejecimiento y género. In: Alonso, A., Langle De Paz, T. (eds.) The Time is Now. Feminist Leadership in a New Era. Published by Red Global de Cátedras UNESCO en Género y por la Organización de las Naciones Unidas para la Educación, la Ciencia y la Cultura, pp. 112–122 (2019). https://eprints.ucm.es/id/eprint/57166/1/art.%20unesco.pdf

31. Sorinas, J., Fernandez-Troyano, J.C., Ferrandez, J.M., Fernandez, E.: Cortical Asymmetries and Connectivity Patterns in the Valence Dimension of the Emotional Brain. International journal of neural systems, 2050021–2050021 (2020). https://doi.org/10.1142/S01290657205 00215

32. Hijas-Gómez, A.I., et al.: The WHO active ageing pillars and its association with survival: findings from a population-based study in Spain. Arch. Gerontol. Geriatr. **90**, 104114 (2020). https://doi.org/10.1016/j.archger.2020.104114

33. Bang, S.H., Jeon, J.M., Lee, J.G., Choi, J., Song, J.J., Chae, S.W.: Association between hearing loss and postural instability in older Korean adults. JAMA Otolaryngol. Head Neck Surg. **146**(6), 530–534 (2020). https://doi.org/10.1001/jamaoto.2020.0293

34. Ellmers, T.J., Kal, E.C., Young, W.R.: Consciously processing balance leads to distorted perceptions of instability in older adults. J. Neurol. **268**(4), 1374–1384 (2020). https://doi.org/10.1007/s00415-020-10288-6

35. Fernandez, E., et al.: Development of a cortical visual neuroprosthesis for the blind: the relevance of neuroplasticity. J. Neural Eng. **2**(4), R1 (2005). https://doi.org/10.1088/1741-2560/2/4/R01

36. Martínez-Álvarez, A., Crespo-Cano, R., Díaz-Tahoces, A., Cuenca-Asensi, S., Ferrandez Vicente, J.M., Fernández, E.: Automatic tuning of a retina model for a cortical visual neuroprosthesis using a multi-objective optimization genetic algorithm. Int. J. Neural Syst. **26**(07), 1650021 (2016). https://doi.org/10.1142/S0129065716500210

37. Lozano, A., Suárez, J.S., Soto-Sánchez, C., Garrigós, J., Martínez-Alvarez, J. J., Ferrández, J.M., Fernández, E.: Neurolight: a deep learning neural interface for cortical visual prostheses. Int. J. Neural Syst. 2050045–2050045 (2020). https://doi.org/10.1142/S0129065720500458

38. Criado-Quesada, B., Zorrilla-Muñoz, V., Agulló-Tomás, M.S.: El uso de internet de la población mayor para la asistencia sanitaria desde una perspectiva de género. Teknokultura. Revista de Cultura Digital y Movimientos Sociales (2021)

39. Oliver, S.E., et al.: The advisory committee on immunization practices' interim recommendation for use of Pfizer-BioNTech COVID-19 vaccine—United States, December 2020. Morbidity and Mortality Weekly Report **69**(50), 1922–1924 (2020). https://doi.org/10.15585/mmwr.mm6950e2

40. Talotta, R.: Do COVID-19 RNA-based vaccines put at risk of immune-mediated diseases? In reply to "potential antigenic cross-reactivity between SARS-CoV-2 and human tissue with a possible link to an increase in autoimmune diseases". Clin. Immunol. (Orlando, Fla.) **224**, 108665 (2021). https://doi.org/10.1016/j.clim.2021.108665

41. Cirillo, N.: Reported orofacial adverse effects of COVID-19 vaccines: the knowns and the unknowns. J. Oral Pathol. Med. Off. Publ. Int. Assoc. Oral Pathol. Am. Acad. Oral Pathol. (2021). https://doi.org/10.1111/jop.13165

42. Ortega Rodríguez, N.R., et al.: The century of mRNA vaccines: COVID-19 vaccines and allergy. J. Investig. Allergol. Clin. Immunol. **31**(1) (2021). https://doi.org/10.18176/jiaci.0665

43. Soiza, R.L., Scicluna, C., Thomson, E.C.: Efficacy and safety of COVID-19 vaccines in older people. Age Ageing (2020). https://doi.org/10.1093/ageing/afaa274

44. Prüß, B.M.: Current state of the first COVID-19 vaccines. Vaccines **9**(1), 30 (2021). https://doi.org/10.3390/vaccines9010030

45. Eldesouky, L., Thompson, R.J., Oltmanns, T.F., English, T.: Affective instability predicts the course of depression in late middle-age and older adulthood. J. Affect. Disorders **239**, 72–78 (2018). https://doi.org/10.1016/j.jad.2018.06.038

Supporting Communication, Social Participation and Everyday Activities

MR System to Promote Social Participation of People Who Have Difficulty Going Out

Yanjiao Ao, Masayuki Kanbara$^{(\boxtimes)}$, Yuichiro Fujimoto, and Hirokazu Kato

Nara Institute of Science and Technology, Ikoma, Nara 6300192, Japan
{ao.yanjiao.av1,kanbara,yfujimoto,kato}@is.naist.jp

Abstract. This paper proposes a promotion system of social participation for people who have difficulty in going out with mixed reality collaboration technique. More than one billion population in the world are tortured by disabilities, and a majority of them have difficulties in social participation due to the unsatisfied transportation demanding. Therefore, in this paper, we propose to use a remote collaboration system based on mixed reality to help people with disabilities to join in social activities. Specifically, our system employs a pair of VR and AR HMDs as well as a 360° camera to create a virtual environment, where physically separated users can interact with each other immersively. Furthermore, we also equip our system with a branch of functions which can further facilitate the communications. In order to test our system, we also design a remote shopping scenario to simulate the condition where people with disabilities want to go shopping at home. The user study shows that our system can satisfy most requirements without triggering obvious discomfort.

Keywords: Disability · Social participation · Remote collaboration · Mixed reality · 360° camera

1 Introduction

Participation refers to the involvements of people in life. According to the International Classification Function, Disability and Health (ICF) [8], participation plays as a key factor in measuring health condition. Concretized to the definition of social participation, it characterizes how people are engaged in activities that provide interactions with others in society or community [12]. Suggested by Levasseur, social participation can be divided into six levels according to social intimacy or distance between people with disabilities and others. In general, it is encouraged to reach level 4, which requires to do interactions among people.

It is reported that the social life of a majority of individuals with disabilities is hindered by the unsatisfied transportation demanding [2], which prevent them from going outsides and taking part in social activities. This is especially a problem in low-income countries due to the lack of facilities for the disabled.

© Springer Nature Switzerland AG 2021
Q. Gao and J. Zhou (Eds.): HCII 2021, LNCS 12787, pp. 383–402, 2021.
https://doi.org/10.1007/978-3-030-78111-8_26

Fortunately, the flourish of virtual reality (VR) [5], augmented reality (AR) [7], and their combination of mixed-reality (MR) [3] offers another choice to cope with this tough problem. That is, these techniques provide an opportunity for the disabled to experience the world they desire in an immersive manner with no need to physically reach the places [6]. Moreover, owing to the unique interaction methods of VR, people with disabilities can not only "see" the environment, but also interact with it and get feedback.

In this paper, we propose to use the remote collaboration system based on MR to help people with disabilities to join in social activities. Specifically, it can facilitate the disabled to participate in community activities with others, such as go shopping for groceries with their friends or family members. In specific, remote collaboration system can free people with physical disabilities from the restriction of transportation and the shortage of facilities. Furthermore, the company of friends or family members can also encourage people with disabilities to join in social activities; and hence improving their social participation to some extent.

Existing literatures mainly focused on developing the remote collaboration systems for general scenarios, which lacks the feedback from the perspective of social participation. Therefore, In this paper, we develop a prototype based on MR to enable people with physical disabilities to remotely participate in social activities together with others. Furthermore, through a user study, we also provide extensive evaluations of the feasibility of our prototype on assisting people with disabilities to take part in social activities.

2   Related Work

In this section, we introduce two fields of related work. The first part focuses on approaches and applications that aiming at facilitating people with disabilities in AR, VR, and MR. The second part consists of similar remote collaboration systems based on MR as we proposed.

2.1   Techniques for Tele-Presence and Remote Collaboration

Nowadays new techniques have been widely developed in tele-presence and remote collaboration. Sharing the ambient environment of a remote person via telecommunication is becoming one of the most popular applications. In this section, we review related work in live 360° panorama video sharing and remote collaboration based on MR, and compare the differences between the existing methods and our approach.

Owing to the natural properties of the VR technique, the VR HMDs are employed recently for creating an immersive and seamless experience for users to watch panorama images or videos. With the recent developments of hardware devices, panorama 360° cameras and VR HMDs have become affordable for common customers. This increases the demands of applications in the field of tele-presence. Recently, live-streaming 360° panorama videos is even supported by some commercial social network platforms. For example, on YouTube, there are some live streaming 360° videos for audiences to watch on mobile phones or even VR HMDs.

Tang [14] presents suggestions on refinements for 360° video chat by conducting a study to simulate a guided tour in the campus. The user who walks in the campus carries a bag with a streaming 360° camera fixed on a monopod. Simultaneously, the remote user is required to observe the characteristics of the environment by watching the videos streamed through a tablet, following which it needs to direct the local participant to landmarks for taking pictures. They point out the challenges in the system is the insufficiency of orientation by verbal communication and the lack of visual contexts. They conclude that adding some virtual clues like remote gestures as well as mutual gaze hints would be helpful to improve the quality of 360° video chat systems.

The panorama video capture devices can be put on users other than the remote one, some work also proposes to rely on robots for tele-presence. For example, Oh [13] propose an intuitive robot tele-presence system with a VR-based interface for a remote tour scenario. Specifically, this work focuses on the development of a system that integrates together a 360° video streaming device, a mobile robot for navigating the remote environment, and VR based user interface. Different from the aforementioned two systems in which the navigation is affixed to the local participant, the robot-based system requires the remote user to navigate the system by themselves. Consequently, it is not suitable for people with disabilities to use.

Users in exiting live panorama video sharing systems are in a asymmetric condition. That is, the interaction is in a one-way mode that stream from the remote end to the panorama camera end. Therefore, the panorama camera end cannot get feedbacks from the remote end. On the other hand, we add a AR HMD to realize a two-way communication and interaction.

2.2 Remote Collaboration Based on Mixed Reality

Optical see-through AR HMDs are advantageous in remote collaboration such as work assistant since the user can see the annotations in a seamless way, such as Microsoft HoloLens. With these devices, people can share their real-time view with the experts in distant location. However, for the remote user, using smartphone or 2D display is limited when the shared ambient surrounding is a large-scale environment. Take the maintenance work in a factory as an example, it is particularly important for experts to see the ambient environment while the working area is colossal. For solutions, Lee [11] created an MR collaboration system that allows to share communication cues, in which the "guest user" watches a shared live panorama scene which is captured from the host user who wears an AR-HMD with a helmet-mounted a 360° camera. Hand gestures and view awareness can also be shared by displaying on both HMDs. They also implement an independent view that the guest user can freely navigate the omnidirectional video without following the host user's view direction. In their following work [10], they change the previous optical-see through AR HMD to Microsoft HoloLens and conduct a user study to evaluate non-verbal communication including hand gestures and view awareness, and compare the independent view and dependent view. Teo [16] conducts a series of user studies using a similar MR remote collaboration system [10] to compare the effects of different combinations of three visual cues including hand gestures, ray pointing and drawing in both asymmetric and symmetric remote collaboration tasks. In general, their work focus on implement and enrich the non-verbal communication functionalities.

In addition to 360° video which can provide a panoramic scene of the remote ambient environment, 3D reconstruction is also popularly used in MR remote collaborations to virtually represent the physical environments. With this method, the remote user can freely walk and explore the local user's workplace. Teo [15] explore mixing 360 video and 3D reconstruction together for remote collaboration. They compare the benefits and problems of using 3D reconstruction and 360° video separately, and merge the two techniques to enhance the experience in MR remote collaboration. They study is conducted only in one-to-one collaboration scenario. Lee [9] first attempt to evaluate view-sharing techniques including 2D video. 3D video and 3D model in one-to-many collaborative MR environment. There are one remote expert wearing the VR HMD and two local users wearing an AR headset. They compare three types of view-sharing techniques. 2D Video is the live streaming video from HoloLens camera. 3D video is as same as the live streaming panorama 360° video in the prior work. 3D model is a static 3D reconstruction of the workplace where the remote user can walk around, the 3D table of the workplace is replaced by 2D video for updating changes. Unlike the 360° video, static 3D reconstruction can capture the dynamic real-time changes of the real environment. Bai [1] use a dynamic 3D reconstruction captured by a live 360° panorama sensor cluster that can update the changes in real-time. They investigate the performance of visual cues including eye gaze, hand gestures and pin arrow in 3D collaborative MR environment. In general, 3D reconstruction technique can only be used in a small-scale environment. Therefore, in our research, we choose the panorama 360° video to provide the real environment for more flexible usages.

3   Development of MR Remote Collaboration System

In this section, we introduce in detail how the AR HMD, the VR HMD, and 360° camera are used in our system, as well as the developments of related algorithms.

3.1   System Overview

Our system consists of three main components: the HoloLens 2 AR HMD with a 360° camera sticking on the top of it for receiving visual instructions and capturing the real-world scenarios; the VR HMD for watching the videos streamed from the 360° camera; and the related software to make the interaction smooth. The pipeline is plotted in Fig. 1. In application, the local user wears the HoloLens 2 AR HMD and the 360° camera in the real world and streams its surroundings in real-time to the VR HMD, which is used by the remote user. Therefore, the

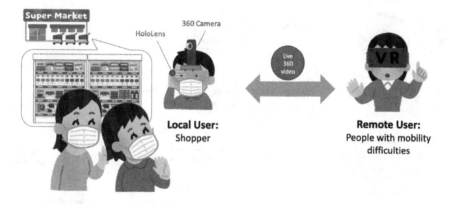

Fig. 1. System overview.

remote user can experience within the virtual environment and accordingly send instructions to the local user for further exploration. Moreover, with our system, the remote user can not only communicate with the local user but also the other people that show up in the 360° scene.

3.2 Software Development

We develop our software with the Unity 3D engine (version 2019.5.15f1)[1]. The application run by HoloLens 2 AR HMD and the project run on the PC for controlling the VR HMD are developed with different Software development kits (SDK), therefore there are two individual unity projects for developing the system. The one for HoloLens 2 is companied by the development toolkit of Mixed Reality Toolkit for Unity (MRTK-Unity, version 2.4.0)[2], and the other one is with the virtual reality SDKs of Unity and the Oculus integration SDK (version 23.1)[3]. As shown in Fig. 2, there are two main types of data that are collected. The first one is the panorama 360° video which is live-streamed by the 360° camera, visualized in Unity, and watched through the VR HMD, and the second type of data is the head motions obtained from the HoloLens 2 VR HMD and the VR HMD. Photon Unity Networking (PUN)[4] is used as the networking platform to transfer the head motions between the two HMDs. Details are given in the following sections.

---

[1] https://unity.com/.
[2] https://github.com/Microsoft/MixedRealityToolkit-Unity.
[3] https://developer.oculus.com/downloads/package/unity-integration/.
[4] https://www.photonengine.com/ja/PUN.

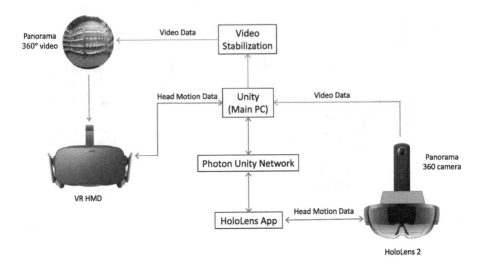

Fig. 2. Pipeline of our entire system. The VR HMD is used by the remote users with physical disabilities. The AR HMD and 360° camera are for the local user to receive instructions and live stream its surroundings. Softwares for handling the interactions among the devices are based on Unity.

3.3   Functions of Communication Improvement

Our remote collaboration system not only allows the local user and the remote one to act as a broadcaster and a live show watcher but also provides more functions to enhance the quality of interaction. In this section, we introduce 3 functions of our system that can facilitate communications between the users.

Hints of View Direction. Verbal communication for describing the orientation is ambiguous. For example, when users are sharing the same panorama video and searching for some objects, they may look in different directions. Since movements of the panorama 360° video is fixed by video stabilization, it is hard for the VR user from the remote place to distinguish the direction that the AR user is facing now. Therefore, in order to let them aware of where the other user is looking at, we visualize the view direction as the red or green rectangles with a cursor in the center of them, which indicates an approximate field of view of the other user.

The interface in the system is a first-person view as shown in Fig. 3. Hence how to let the user see the view direction of the other user continuously across different devices is one of the challenges we face. As a solution, we choose PUN as the networking platform for sending and receiving data in real-time between two different types of devices. With it, the two users can access the same networking room while keep the projects running on their respective individual devices. The PUN room can not only determine the initial position and rotation of the two users, but also instantiate objects for users to interact with. Therefore, the view

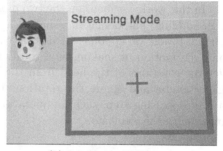

(a) Interface of HoloLens 2 user   (b) Interface of VR user

Fig. 3. The virtual head is on the upper left of the interface. Beside it, there is a red text to indicate whether the current mode is the "Streaming Mode" or "Image Mode". The green or red rectangle shows the view direction of the other user, respectively.

direction of the user can be set as the direction that the user is facing while wearing HMDs. In implementation, we set the initial position of the remote user as the same as the local user and let them be relatively fixed. And by sending and receiving the transformation data of the HMD of the other user, we apply the rotations of the two HMDs on the red and green rectangles, respectively. Consequently, the red and green rectangles which stand for the rotation of the head of two users can be seen by both users through the PUN platform.

Virtual Head for Confirmation. People do not always use languages for expression. Sometimes for simple words, we prefer body language as a substitution. This is especially true when we want to admit or deny. Therefore, in order to make the communications between the local user and the remote one more smooth, we also insert a virtual head icon on their respective screen to show the head motions of their partners.

A simple implementation is to first obtain head motions from the embedded inertial measurement unit (IMU) sensors of the AR and VR equipments and directly apply them to the virtual heads. However, such a solution may trigger misunderstandings since it is difficult to distinguish meaningful expressions from unintentional movements. In general, since we desire the virtual head to only reflect common body languages rather than recording any tiny body movements, it should be designed to satisfy the following two conditions:

- The orientation of the users should not affect the expression. In specific, no matter to which directions the user is looking at, its partner should always be able to understand its body language clearly.
- Random body movements should be filtered out and only meaningful expressions are recorded.

In this work, we focus on the two most common body languages of admission (i.e. nodding) and denial (i.e. shaking). Specifically, given the coordinates of the virtual heads, we appoint the motion of nodding as a rotation along the X-axis and the motion of shaking as a rotation along the Y-axis. Therefore, once we get the rotations of the head from the IMU sensor, we first decompose it into Euler angles and ignore the rotations that are associated with the Z-axis. As a pre-processing step, such an operation can effectively help us to ignore some meaningless movements.

Snapshot for Revisiting. People take photos to help to memorize. Take shopping as an example, if we cannot immediately decide whether to purchase a certain product or not, it is natural for us to take a photo and use it later for comparison. We also equip our remote collaboration system with a similar function. This is important since our system is not consistent with translations. Therefore, with such a function, the remote user can rapidly switch between two scenes in different positions and make comparisons.

We desire our function to maintain the immersive experience of the remote user. Therefore, instead of only capturing the field of view rendered on the VR HMD, we save the entire 360° image as the snapshot when receiving the saving command. Therefore, once the remote user wishes to use the snapshot for references in the future, exactly the same virtual environment can be recreated for exploration without harming the feeling of immersion.

In the implementation, we define 2 different modes named the "streaming mode" and the "image mode". The former one stands for the aforementioned condition where the surroundings of the local user are live-streamed to the remote user, and the latter one represents the mode where the remote user can re-visit an explored scene. In the image mode, the video stream is temporally terminated and hence the movements of the local user have not effect on the virtual environment. For switching from the streaming mode to the image one, we render the latest snapshot in default and enables the user to switch among all of them in a loop sorted by timestamps.

4   User Study

4.1   Research Questions

Our system aims are facilitating people with mobility difficulties (the remote user) on social participation. In order to test our proposed MR remote collaboration system, we setup a remote shopping scenario and conduct a user study on it to investigate the following research questions:

Q1. *Is it feasible for an MR collaboration system to assist the remote user in a remote shopping scenario?*
    When the remote user and the local user are shopping together for groceries, their shopping purpose and behavior can be divided into several tasks:

1) Searching Task: The remote user wants to buy a product but neither the remote user nor the local user know where the product is.
2) Navigation Task: The local user doesn't know the location of a certain product while the remote user knows, hence the remote user can navigate him to find it out.
3) Exploration Task: The remote user can make its final decision by comparing similar products together.

Besides, there are two sub-tasks of each main tasks:

1) Confirming task: The local user confirms with the remote user if the product is the target one.
2) Examining task: The remote user checks the detailed information of a product, such as the price, description, raw materials, maker, etc.

We desire to figure out whether the remote user and the local user can collaborate together to complete these shopping tasks through an MR collaboration system. For the previous work [1,10,16], they more focus on enriching the functionalities of the MR collaboration system, however, they didn't mention the specific application scenarios. We need to first confirm the feasibility of the MR collaboration system in the shopping scenario in our research.

Q2. *How useful are the two functions of the virtual head and revisiting snapshots?*

In common face-to-face communication, in addition to verbal communication, there are body language and facial expressions as well. Especially when people express "Yes" or "No", they usually have some head movements. We want to investigate that whether it is important to use the function of the virtual head and if it can improve the speed of confirming products. Besides, the shopping supermarket is generally very large and products are divided into different categories displayed in different areas. If the remote user can only watch live streaming panorama video, it means that his view is always dependent on the local user's position, in other words, they are in the same position at all times. It can also be seen as two users working dependently. However, if one user struggles with which product to choose, the other user may wait for a long time. In this case, they may also want to work independently, which means while one user is shopping for products, the other user may search for other different products separately to make the shopping procedure more efficient. So we propose that taking static photos so that the remote users can buy from panoramic photos, and the local users can find other things. We want to investigate whether this function is useful and if it can shorten the shopping time.

Q3. *How effective is the communication between the remote and the local user? How effective is the communication between the remote user and other shoppers in the store?*

As mentioned in the introduction of Chap. 1, doing activities with others is one of the ways of social participation. In our case, we choose shopping with others as a research scenario. Interaction and communication with others play a key role in ensuring that people with mobility difficulties are participating in social activities, instead of mechanically commanding another user to buy things for them. We want them to use this system to greet, chat and share thoughts or moods. In this research, we focus on communications of two relationships, one is the communication between people with mobility difficulties and their friends or family members who assist them to buy products, the other communication relationship is that people with mobility difficulties communicate with other friends they accidentally meet in the same shopping store through the panorama 360 video.

Q4. *Is it feasible for an MR remote collaboration system to facilitate the remote user in social participation?*

Using MR collaboration system as a support tool to help people with mobility difficulties in improving their social participation has never been done before. It is challenging to define whether this system can facilitate people with disabilities in their social participation or not. We expect to comprehensively evaluate this problem through the above assumptions.

4.2   Experimental Design

The experiment is intended for people with mobility difficulties, however, we can also conduct with normal people with a simulation that is let the participants sit on the chair to simulate the state of limited mobility. Moreover, one of the goals of conducting the user study is to evaluate two types of communication relationship. Therefore, there are three participants as a team, each playing a different role. The experiment is divided into two sessions. There are three evaluations:

1. Evaluation of the system usability for the first session. We evaluate usefulness of functions of "virtual head" and "revisiting snapshots". For how extent two users feel they are together, we evaluate the presence of two users. The acceptability of the system is assessed as well. We also measure the completion time of the first session.
2. Evaluation of communication and the social participation for the second session. In this evaluation, we evaluate the effectiveness of communications for discussing and recommending products, chatting and inviting others than the local user for social activities.
3) Evaluation of cyber-sickness of the remote user by Simulated Sickness Questionnaire (SSQ) [1]. This evaluation is assessed for the video stabilization, and the usability for the VR system.

The experimental workplace is approximately 3.5 m × 3.5 m. A simulated shopping store which is approximately 3.5 m × 2 m placed four 120 cm × 45 cm × 180 cm shelves is used for the local user. Two shelves are placed in vertical row and the other two shelves are placed horizontally at both ends of the vertical row as shape "C" as shown in Fig. 4. 202 types of products are placed on shelves by categories. Each product is attached with a tag including price and number. The price is randomly 50 JPY or 100 JPY. The number is randomly from 1 to

(a) Products placed on the shelf

(b) Products with tags

Fig. 4. Products with tags is placed on the shelf.

202. A 120 cm × 50 m "L" shape partition is placed to separate the workplace of the remote user and the local user. The remote user wearing the VR HMD is seated on a office swivel chair and in front of a 150 cm × 60 cm × 70 cm desk.

4.3 Profile of Participants

24 participants divided into 8 groups are recruited for the user study. There are 3 participants in each group. Members in most groups know each other before as friends or colleagues. The sample consisted of 14 males and 10 females. Average age of the participants was 27.7 (*agemin:* 22, *agemax:* 33, *stdev:* 3.87). Participants were gathered from various laboratories at Nara Institute of Science and Technology, Japan. Each participant was given 1000 JPY remuneration (approximately 9 USD) per hour for the participation in the user study.

Since the participants were in the same room, they were only separated by partitions during the experiment. If two people communicate directly, the presence of stereo will interfere with the participant's judgment on the presence of another user in the remote environment. So we used the smartphone for communication, and the participants put on earphones to block the live sound.

4.4 Experimental Procedure

In the user study, participants are asked to conduct two rounds of experiments. Each round includes two sessions of experimental trials. Participants are assigned to three roles, then they swapped their roles after finishing the first round to ensure all of them can experience different roles in the second round. The differences of three roles are as follows:

1) The remote user: wearing VR HMD and siting on the chair. Shopping from the remote place, instructing the AR user in the simulated shopping store to buy products.
2) The local user: wearing AR HMD and shopping in the simulated shopping store. Assisting the remote user to buy products.

Fig. 5. Interface with a shopping list

3) Shopper: wearing nothing. The shopper appears as the friend of the remote
   user in the second session of the experiment.

For the first session in each round of the experiment, there are two conditions:
with functions and without functions. The order of the condition is counter
balanced between different group to avoid order effectiveness. Before and after
the experiment, the remote user are asked to fill out a SSQ. After finishing each
session, participants are asked to answer a questionnaire.

Session 1: Evaluation for the System Usability. The remote user and the
local user are asked to conduct a searching task in the simulated shopping store.
There are 5 random products with numbers, names, and categories showing in
the interface. The remote user is asked to find out all the five products. The AR
User assists the remote user to search for products. They can share names and
categories. Only remote users can use the number for searching for products,
they can not tell or ask the number to the local user (Fig. 5).

Session 2: Evaluation for Improving Social Participation. The remote
user and the AR user are asked to spend a 600 JPY shopping budget to buy
the products for a party. These products need to contain the favorite foods of
the remote user, favorite foods of the local user, and recommended foods for
each other. The budget should be used out. After finishing shopping, the remote
user is asked to find out the shopper, who is shopping in the simulated shopping
store. A photo of remote user is pasted on the camera holder which indicates the
remote user is watching videos through the camera. The remote user needs to
greet the shopper and send an invitation. There are two conditions of invitation,
one is for having dinner in a restaurant, the other is for sightseeing in KANSAI
area. The condition changes in each round of experiments. The remote user needs
to make an appointment that including four components with the shopper. The
four components are date, time, location, transportation.

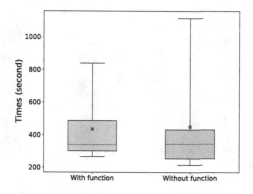

Fig. 6. Results of completion time.

4.5   Results

In this section, we analyze the statistical results of the user study and summarize the feedback gathered from the participants. A 5-point Likert scale is used for rating items in each questionnaire.

Task Completion Time. Results of completion time is showing in Fig. 6. Comparing the completion time of with function condition (*Mean* = 435.3, *Standard Deviation* = 218.6) and without function condition (M = 450.7, SD = 336.7), there is no significant difference between the two conditions. Participants took marginally longer time in the condition of without functions. The result indicates that the two functions of "virtual head" and "revisiting snapshot" make hardly any contributions for shortening the shopping time.

System Usability for Remote User. We evaluate the system usability from three aspects: presence, usability and functionalities as showing in Fig. 7.

Question 1 to 3 are for evaluating the presence. The result of the first question between two conditions has no difference according to the rating score. (with function: M = 4.375, SD = 0.744; without function: M = 4.375, SD = 0.744). For evaluating the tele-presence of "being there" (question2), with function condition (M = 4.25, SD = 0.463) is slightly higher than without function condition (M = 4, SD = 0.756). Participants also gave a tiny higher rating to the with function condition (M = 4.25, SD = 0.463) compared to the without function condition (M = 3.875, SD = 0.835) in the aspect of the social presence of "being there together" (question3). Nevertheless, the difference is not statistically significant. It shows that functions of "virtual head" and "revisiting snapshot" can help the remote user increase their feeling of presence in the remote place to a slight degree.

Usability is weighed by question 4 to 6. Among them, question 4 and 5 are taken from SUS questionnaire [4]. Participants rated a small higher point to the with function condition (M = 4.25, SD = 0.707) which they thought the system is slightly easier to use than the without function condition (M = 3.625,

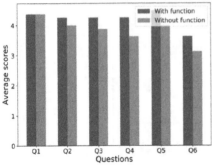 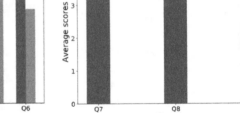

Q1: I can aware my partner's presence.
Q2: I feel I'm being there where my partner is.
Q3: I feel I'm with my partner.
Q4: I thought the system is easy to use.
Q5: I would imagine that most people would learn to use this system very quickly.
Q6: I prefer to use this system to buy products than shopping on the website.

Q7: I think the function of taking pictures and watching pictures in image mode is useful
Q8: I think the system with the function of virtual head is useful.
Q9: I feel I can aware my partner is shaking head or nodding head by watching the virtual head

Fig. 7. Results of system usability questionnaire for the remote user (1: strongly disagree 5: strongly agree).

$SD = 1.061$) (question 4). Question 5 and 6 is used for acceptability checks. The result of question 5 indicates that this system can be popularized with function ($M = 4.5$, $SD = 0.756$) than without function ($M = 4$, $SD = 1.414$). However, comparing online shopping and our system, participants gave an average medium rating in both with function condition ($M = 3.625$, $SD = 0.916$) and without function condition ($M = 3.125$, $SD = 0.991$).

These questions are answered only by participants who experienced "virtual head" or "revisiting snapshot" in the condition of with function as questions 7 to 9 showing in Fig. 7. Participants gave a slightly positive rating for the function of "revisiting snapshot" ($M = 3.556$, $SD = 1.013$). The results of assessing the function of "virtual head" is minor positive rating as well ($M = 3.875$, $SD = 0.835$). Participants can determine the meaning of the movement of the "virtual head" as shaking or nodding to a certain extent ($M = 4.167$, $SD = 0.753$).

4.6 System Usability for the Local User

Aspects of evaluation for system usability of the local user is identical to the evaluation for system usability of the remote user. Results are showing in Fig. 8.

We ignore the question of "being there" since the local user is already in the physical environment. The result of "awareness of the remote user's presence here" shows a trend of participants giving a higher rating in the without function condition ($M = 4.25$, $SD = 0.463$) than in the with function condition ($M = 3.625$, $SD = 0.744$). A similar trend is found in the question of "being with the remote user", the rating of without function condition ($M = 4.375$, $SD = 0.744$)

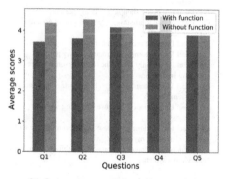
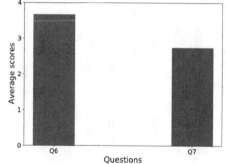

Q1: I can aware my partner's presence here.
Q2: I feel I'm with my partner.
Q3: I thought the system is easy to use.
Q4: I would imagine that most people would learn to use this system very quickly.
Q5: I prefer to use this system to buy products than shopping on the website.

Q6: I think the system with the function of virtual head is useful.
Q7: I feel I can aware my partner is shaking head or nodding head by watching the virtual head.

Fig. 8. Results of system usability questionnaire for the local user (1: strongly disagree 5: strongly agree).

is higher than the rating of with function condition ($M = 3.75$, $SD = 0.886$). The results are opposite to those in the remote user questionnaire.

The questions in the part is as same as those in the remote user questionnaire. For question 4 and 6, the results of with function condition (question 3:$M = 4.125$, $SD = 1.126$; question 5: $M = 3.875$, $SD = 1.356$) are equal to the results of without function condition (question 3:$M = 4.125$, $SD = 0.991$; question 5: $M = 3.875$, $SD = 0.835$). For the question of popularizing the system, participants gave a minor lower rating in the with function condition ($M = 4$, $SD = 1.309$) than in the without function condition ($M = 4.5$, $SD = 0.535$). This result is to be the contrary to the results in the remote user questionnaire.

As the "revisiting snapshot" function is used only for the remote user, the local user does not need to answer this question. The result of the usability of "virtual head" shows that participants gave a minor positive rating ($M = 3.545$, $SD = 1.179$). Nevertheless, the results of question 7 is slightly negative ($M = 2.75$, $SD = 1.389$), which shows a trend of participants expressing slight disagreement of "Being conscious of the meaning of head movements".

Social Participation. The results of the evaluation of social participation in the second session were generally rated high ($M = 4.417$, $SD = 0.743$). We evaluate the social participation of remote users from two aspects. One is interaction and communication with local users, and the other is interaction and communication with shoppers.

There are six questions for the remote user as showing in Fig. 9 are corresponding to the questions 1 to 6 for the local user as showing in Fig. 10. Participants gave a relatively high point to the experience of shopping with each other

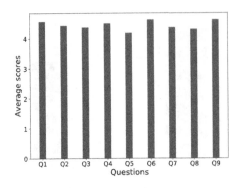

Q1: I feel I'm going shopping with my partner.
Q2: I would like to use this system if I cannot go outside for shopping easily.
Q3: I feel I can get recommendation from my partner.
Q4: I feel I can recommend products to my partner.
Q5: I feel I can easily notice the other person who are shopping in the same scene.
Q6: I feel I can communicate with my partner by using this system.
Q7: I feel I'm not lonely because I'm being with my partner.
Q8: I feel I'm not lonely because I can communicate with person others than my partner.
Q9: I can make an appointment with the third person through this system.

Fig. 9. Results of evaluation of social participation for the remote user.

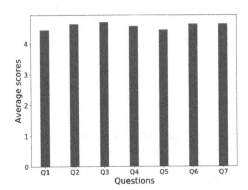

Q1: I feel I'm going shopping with my partner.
Q2: I feel I can get recommendation from my partner.
Q3: I feel I can recommend products to my partner.
Q4: I would like to use this system if I cannot go outside for shopping easily.
Q5: I feel I can communicate with my partner by using this system.
Q6: I feel I'm not lonely because I'm being with my partner.
Q7: I feel I can help my partner to buy products by using this system.

Fig. 10. Results of evaluation of social participation for the local user.

(Q1 for the remote user: $M = 4.562$, $SD = 0.629$; Q1 for the local user: $M = 4.438$, $SD = 0.814$). Not only the communication (Q6 for the remote user: $M = 4.625$, $SD = 0.5$; Q5 for the local user: $M = 4.438$, $SD = 0.629$), but also the experience of recommending products to each other is highly rated (Q1 and Q4 for the remote user: $M = 4.438$, $SD = 0.716$; Q2 and Q3 for the local user: $M = 4.656$, $SD = 0.545$). Moreover, there is a feeling of company between them, because they do not feel alone (Q7 for the remote user: $M = 4.375$, $SD = 0.619$; Q6 for the local user: $M = 4.625$, $SD = 0.5$). For participants of local users, the feeling of being able to assist the remote is a high rating (Q7 for the local user: $M = 4.625$, $SD = 0.5$). Participants rated highly of their willingness to use the system (Q2 for the remote user: $M = 4.438$, $SD = 0.727$; Q4 for the local user: $M = 4.563$, $SD = 0.629$) (Fig. 11).

Participants of remote users can easily notice their friends in the same shopping store (Q5 for the remote user: $M = 4.188$, $SD = 0.75$). Also, the shopper can notice the existence of the remote user (Q1 for the shopper: $M = 4$, $SD = 0.966$), but is relatively less aware of the remote user shopping with others (Q2 for the shopper: $M = 3.875$, $SD = 1.147$). Participants agreed with the effectiveness of communication with each other (Q8 for the remote user: $M = 4.313$,

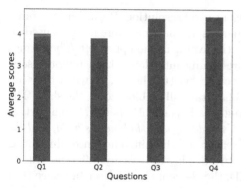

Q1: I can realize he/she (Remote user) is here.
Q2: I can aware of he/she's shopping with the person
Q3: I can communicate with him/her through this system.
Q4: I can make an appointment with him/her through this system.

Fig. 11. Results of evaluation of social participation for shopper.

$SD = 0.727$; Q3 for the shopper: $M = 4.5$, $SD = 0.894$) and the effectiveness of inciting others for an appointment (Q9 for the remote user: $M = 4.625$, $SD = 0.5$; Q4 for the shopper: $M = 4.563$, $SD = 0.814$).

4.7 Discussion

Overall the experimental results indicate that this system is useful, and it can help people who have difficulty going out can shop remotely with others at home. The interaction and communication between them and the local user or shopper at the supermarket is reasonably effective. Participants think the system is handy *"The communication is smooth."* *"The system is easy to use"* *"The operation is simple"*, they also mentioned *"It is very useful for disable people, they can experience realistic shopping at home."* *"Overall the experience is smooth and the technology is very useful for people who cannot going out to do their own shopping."* We can expect that for people who have difficulty going out, participating in social activities of going shopping with others is active and effective and it can promote the social participation of people who have difficulty going out to some extent.

In addition, there are many details in the experimental results that are worthy of discussion. The functions of the "revisiting snapshot" and the "virtual head" do not have much impact on the completion time. We observed that in the first session of the experiment, participants were more inclined to voice communication for the searching task, and the "revisiting snapshot" function was hardly used. They mentioned *"Voice communication is faster"* *"It takes time to switch modes of "streaming mode" and "Image mode".* Another reason why they didn't use the "revisiting snapshot" function was that the area of the experimental site was somewhat small, so they didn't need massive movements. Two people could search at the same position and could see most of the products.

Participants gave a slightly high rating for both functions. For the "revisiting snapshot" function, they think *"It's good to go back and forward to confirm the order of pictures."* *"It is easy to notice items and find their names."*. However, most of them complained about insufficient pixel resolution. Regarding the function of the "virtual head", most participants said that they were more focused on the task of searching and did not notice the avatar in the upper left. The ratings of local users for the "virtual head" are significantly lower than remote users. Many of them said that they cannot see the "virtual head", or when they are particularly close to the shelf, the virtual avatar will be blocked by the shelf. The evaluation of remote users for the "virtual head" is slightly better. Some participants said *"I can clearly feel the partner's nodding and shaking his head, and the sense of immersion is stronger"*. The reason for the difference in evaluation is because the Field of View (FoV) of the two display devices are different. Due to the limited FoV of HoloLens 2 AR HMD, the elements in the User Interface (UI) are not effortlessly noticeable. With an immersive environment in VR, the sight will not be disturbed by the external environment, making it easier to notice and feel the presence of the "virtual head". In addition, HoloLens 2 AR HMD uses a depth sensor to generate the surrounding environment, hence some errors lead to occlusion. Some participants complained *"The head-mounted display is too heavy"*, which may also make it difficult for them to turn their heads, making the effect of the "virtual head" less obvious.

We observed that in the SSQ results, the ratings of two symptoms are higher than the other results. The first one is difficulty concentrating. This is because the UI design in VR is not perfect and there is too much content on the screen. Some participants suggested *"make the font of the shopping list easier to read"* *"add transparent background to the shopping list to distinguish it from the video."* In addition, the resolution of the video is a big challenge for focusing on watching the video. Most of the participants mentioned that their vision was blurred, and the video was too blurred to clearly see.

We noticed an interesting phenomenon. Most of the participants applied as a group. However, there are few individual applicants, and these applicants need to be assigned to form a group to participate in the experiment. Experimental results show that the evaluation of the acquaintance team is significantly better than the stranger team. The acquaintance team had a relatively active atmosphere during the experiment, and the tend of evaluation results were positive. Conversely, the evaluation of the stranger team tends to be more negative. This also indicates that those who have difficulty going out participate in social activities with friends or family members will be more beneficial in terms of increasing their social participation.

We also interviewed the feelings of local users who acted as intermediaries between shoppers and remote users. Their feelings are divided into two levels. Some participants found *"It is a little bit embarrassing"* to be an intermediary, and some thought *"It's kind of nice to be a channel between the remote user and the shopper, as the local user, I think that it is pne of the stronger points of the system."*

5 Conclusion

This paper has investigated usability of the mixed reality collaboration system for social participation through the experiments. The transmission resolution of the live streaming 360° video is low, so the image resolution is insufficient. This problem is the biggest obstacle encountered in the entire experiment because the products on the shelves cannot be clearly seen, and it greatly affects the experience of the participants. In addition, the 360° camera of the current system uses USB for transferring videos. Due to the existence of the cable, the participants are restricted by the scope of their activities. In the initial experimental settings, we plan to divide the shelves into several rows so that participants can shuttle back and forth in the aisle. But the data cable will prevent participants from moving between different rows of the shelf. Therefore, due to the problem of the site setting, the "revisiting snapshot" function cannot be commendably applied. In terms of experimental design, the first experiment only evaluated the difference between the existence of two functions and the absence of two functions, but for each function, about its effectiveness and role in the experiment, our experimental results cannot draw any conclusions. Therefore, more detailed experiments are needed to test the effectiveness of each function.

References

1. Bai, H., Sasikumar, P., Yang, J., Billinghurst, M.: A user study on mixed reality remote collaboration with eye gaze and hand gesture sharing. In: Proceedings of the 2020 CHI Conference on Human Factors in Computing Systems, pp. 1–13 (2020)
2. Bascom, G.W., Christensen, K.M.: The impacts of limited transportation access on persons with disabilities' social participation. J. Transp. Health **7**, 227–234 (2017)
3. Billinghurst, M., Kato, H.: Collaborative mixed reality. In: Proceedings of the First International Symposium on Mixed Reality, pp. 261–284 (1999)
4. Brooke, J.: SUS: a quick and dirty usability. In: Usability Evaluation in Industry, vol. 189 (1996)
5. Burdea, G.C., Coiffet, P.: Virtual Reality Technology. Wiley, New York (2003)
6. Desai, P.R., Desai, P.N., Ajmera, K.D., Mehta, K.: A review paper on oculus rift-a virtual reality headset. arXiv preprint arXiv:1408.1173 (2014)
7. Furht, B.: Handbook of augmented reality. Springer, New York (2011). https://doi.org/10.1007/978-1-4614-0064-6
8. Krahn, G.L.: Who world report on disability: a review. Disabil. Health J. **4**(3), 141–142 (2011)
9. Lee, G., Kang, H., Lee, J., Han, J.: A user study on view-sharing techniques for one-to-many mixed reality collaborations. In: 2020 IEEE Conference on Virtual Reality and 3D User Interfaces (VR), pp. 343–352. IEEE (2020)
10. Lee, G., Teo, T., Kim, S., Billinghurst, M.: A user study on MR remote collaboration using live 360 video. In: 2018 IEEE International Symposium on Mixed and Augmented Reality (ISMAR), pp. 153–164 (2018)
11. Lee, G.A., Teo, T., Kim, S., Billinghurst, M.: Mixed reality collaboration through sharing a live panorama. In: SIGGRAPH Asia 2017 Mobile Graphics & Interactive Applications, pp. 1–4 (2017)

12. Levasseur, M., Richard, L., Gauvin, L., Raymond, É.: Inventory and analysis of definitions of social participation found in the aging literature: proposed taxonomy of social activities. Soc. Sci. Med. **71**(12), 2141–2149 (2010)
13. Oh, Y., Parasuraman, R., McGraw, T., Min, B.C.: 360 VR based robot teleoperation interface for virtual tour. In: Proceedings of the 1st International Workshop on Virtual, Augmented, and Mixed Reality for HRI (VAM-HRI) (2018)
14. Tang, A., Fakourfar, O., Neustaedter, C., Bateman, S.: Collaboration in 360 videochat: challenges and opportunities. University of Calgary, Technical report (2017)
15. Teo, T., Lawrence, L., Lee, G.A., Billinghurst, M., Adcock, M.: Mixed reality remote collaboration combining 360 video and 3D reconstruction. In: Proceedings of the 2019 CHI Conference on Human Factors in Computing Systems, pp. 1–14 (2019)
16. Teo, T., Lee, G.A., Billinghurst, M., Adcock, M.: Investigating the use of different visual cues to improve social presence within a 360 mixed reality remote collaboration. In: The 17th International Conference on Virtual-Reality Continuum and its Applications in Industry, pp. 1–9 (2019)

A Synthetic Elderly Companion Named Lois

Ron Fulbright[✉]

University of South Carolina Upstate, 800 University Way, Spartanburg, SC 29303, USA
fulbrigh@uscupstate.edu

Abstract. Described is a synthetic elderly companion named Lois, short for Loved One's Information System, able to tend to an elder's needs, monitor overall well-being and progress, detect decline and signs of further medical problems, and in general, 'be there' for an elder. Lois is a cognitive system comprised of computer displays, cameras, speakers, microphones, and various sensors placed throughout the home facilitating both non-invasive monitoring and highly interactive collaboration. Lois maintains a set of models enabling the recognition of events and changes of condition as well as the compiling of a historical record for later use by medical personnel and family members. Since Lois lives with the elder over an extended period of time Lois becomes tailored specifically to the elder learning their schedule, likes, dislikes, and tendencies. By working with the elder, the elder's family members, and medical personnel, Lois is at the center of a synthetic elderly caregiver ensemble capable of performance superior to any human caregiver.

Keywords: Cognitive systems · Human cognitive augmentation · Synthetic expertise · Artificial intelligence · Health monitoring · Assistance for the ageing

1 Introduction

According to the World Health Organization, the world's population over sixty years of age will exceed two billion by the year 2050 [34]. As we get older, we naturally encounter cognitive and physical degradation often requiring the assistance of another person. Common is hiring a caregiver to visit on a daily basis or live-in on a full-time basis. Also common is elderly moving in with younger family members or entering a nursing home/assisted living facility. However, the elderly wish to remain independent and continue to live in their own homes as long as possible. There is a tremendous need for in-home artificial and synthetic caregiver technology for the elderly. In the United States alone, elder care is projected to be worth over $400 billion with in-home healthcare services being the second largest and fastest growing segment [2]. The requirements of elder care are extensive and building a synthetic expertise for elder care pushes and tests the state of the art in cognitive systems and artificial intelligence.

This paper presents some details of the architecture for a synthetic elderly companion named Lois (short for Loved One's Information System.) Physically, Lois is embodied in a number of display screens, microphones, speakers, cameras, and other sensors located throughout the home. Logically, Lois is a cognitive system (a "cog") with which the elder

© Springer Nature Switzerland AG 2021
Q. Gao and J. Zhou (Eds.): HCII 2021, LNCS 12787, pp. 403–417, 2021.
https://doi.org/10.1007/978-3-030-78111-8_27

works with and relies on as an assistant, confidant, and friend. Together, the elder, Lois, family members, and medical professionals form a human/cog ensemble—a synthetic elderly companion—capable of performance exceeding that of a human caregiver.

2 Literature and Previous Work

2.1 Existing Robotic Elderly Assistants

Robotic assistants for the elderly are available today. However, none are comprehensive elderly caregivers as we envision.

Desktop Assistants. Catalia Health's Mabu is designed to be a personal healthcare companion with the ability to socially interact and assist patients with the medication portion of their treatment (http://www.cataliahealth.com) [3, 22]. JIBO is a family companion able to send messages, take pictures, communicate with others, and be a "friend" with a personality (https://jibo.com). Intuition Robotics' ElliQ is aimed at keeping older adults active and engaged by connecting them to their families and the outside world [10]. ElliQ is a friendly, intelligent, inquisitive presence in the elder's daily life able to offer tips and advice, respond to questions, and surprise with suggestions. Pillo Health's Pria is a voice-activated assistant designed to help maintain a mediation schedule (https://www.okpria.com).

Artificial Companion Pets. Blue Frog Robotics' emotional companion, Buddy, is able to wander around the home like a pet and express emotions through a screen mounted on an articulated neck (https://buddytherobot.com/en/buddy-the-emotional-robot/). Companion pets in form of furry dogs and cats are offered by Ageless Innovations, a spinoff of Hasbro (https://joyforall.com). Similarly, the PARO Therapeutic robot has the form of a soft baby seal and is able to respond to actions while being held and stroked (http://www.parorobots.com).

Semi-humanoid Robots. Pepper is a semi-humanoid robot manufactured by SoftBank Robotics. It is designed with the ability to read emotions by analyzing expressions and voice tones (https://www.softbankrobotics.com/emea/en/pepper). Lynx, by UB Tech, has Amazon's Alexa built into it for voice activation, speech synthesis, and enables Lynx to act as a smart home hub (https://ubtrobot.com/products/lynx-with-amazon-alexa?ls=en). Aido is a modular service robot by InGen Dynamics, able to assist in home security and entertainment (http://aidorobot.com).

Full-Sized Robots. Asia Robotics' Dinsow is a service robot designed for elderly care service (https://www.dinsow.com) [9]. Riken's Robobear is an experimental nursing care robot capable of performing tasks such as lifting a patient from a bed into a wheelchair or providing assistance to a patient who is able to stand up but requires help to do so (https://www.riken.com) [27].

The synthetic caregiver described in this paper, Lois, is designed from a different perspective than these existing systems. We do not envision Lois to be encased in a single physical unit. Rather, Lois sensors and interface devices are distributed throughout every room in the elder's home and therefore is more of a "smart home" solution.

2.2 Intelligent Software Agents

At the heart of any synthetic elderly companion is software able to assist the elder—a software agent—capable of acting deliberatively to accomplish tasks on behalf of its user. Dating back to Hewitt's Actor Model describing a self-contained, interactive and concurrently-executing objects [18, 19], the idea of autonomous, goal-driven software agents has evolved in the fields of multi-agent systems (MAS), distributed artificial intelligence (DAI), distributed problem solving (DPS), and parallel artificial intelligence (PAI). Nwana identifies types of software agents [26]:

- **Collaborative Agents** agents cooperating with other agents to perform tasks
- **Interface Agents** personal assistants in collaboration with a user
- **Mobile Agents** capable of roaming networks (such as the Internet)
- **Information Agents** managing/collating information from distributed sources
- **Reacting Agents** lacking internal knowledge representation/ reasoning
- **Hybrid Agents** a combination of two or more agent types
- **Heterogeneous Agents** a collection of different agent types
- **Smart Agents** agents capable of human-level cognition

When these types of agents were identified in the mid-1990s, the idea an agent could perform high-level cognition (smart agents) seemed futuristic. Now, some 25 years later, this future has arrived. The synthetic elderly companion we envision in this paper is a smart hybrid interface agent capable of collaboration and human-level cognitive processing. We view Lois as not only a personal assistant, but also a friend and confidant for the elder.

2.3 Cognitive Systems

In the 1960s. Licklider and Engelbart described humans and computers working together, each complementing the other and ultimately becoming mutually interdependent [11, 25]. However, Licklider and Engelbart envisioned the artificial elements as being merely assistive aids leaving the high-level thinking to the human. With recent advances in cognitive systems, we envision Lois to be more on a peer level with the elder and other humans it interacts with.

In 1987, Apple, Inc. envisioned an intelligent assistant and collaborator called the Knowledge Navigator [1]. The Knowledge Navigator was an artificial executive assistant capable of natural language understanding, independent knowledge gathering, and high-level reasoning. The Knowledge Navigator concept was well ahead of its time and not taken seriously at the time. However, many of its features are seen today in current voice-controlled "digital assistants."

In 2014, IBM released a video showing two humans interacting with and collaborating with a cognitive system based on Watson technology—technology originally built to play the game *Jeopardy!* [15, 20, 21, 35]. The similarity between the IBM Watson video and the Knowledge Navigator video is striking with the exception everything in the IBM video is real whereas everything in the Apple video is faked. As we do, IBM envisions systems acting as partners and collaborators with humans. John Kelly (IBM) describes the coming revolution in cognitive augmentation as follows [23]:

"The goal isn't to replace human thinking with machine thinking. Rather humans and machines will collaborate to produce better results—each bringing their own superior skills to the partnership."

In 2016, Google's AlphaGo defeated the reigning world champion in Go [6, 30]. In 2017, a version called AlphaGo Zero learned how to play Go by playing games with itself and not relying on any data from human games [7]. AlphaGo Zero exceeded the capabilities of AlphaGo in only three days. Also in 2017, a generalized version of the learning algorithm called AlphaZero was developed capable of learning any game. While Watson and other machine learning systems coming before required a large amount of knowledge engineering and supervised training, AlphaZero achieved expert-level performance in the games of Chess, Go, and Shogi after only a few hours of unsupervised self-training [5].

These recent achievements herald a new type of artificial entity—cognitive systems—able to achieve expert-level performance in a domain using unsupervised learning. Lois will likewise learn the art and science of elderly caregiving as it gains experience. We also envision millions of Lois installations across the world sharing learned knowledge with each other allowing Lois to evolve quickly and exceed human capability. In fact, there are cognitive systems already better than humans in many domains including: predicting mortality [33], detecting signs of child depression [24], detecting lung cancer [29, 32]. Systems can even find discoveries missed by humans in scientific papers [17].

Fulbright [12, 13] believes these kinds of cognitive systems—cogs—will lead to a multitude of mass-market apps and intelligent devices able to perform high-level cognitive processing. Millions of humans around the world will work daily with and collaborate with multiple cogs much like they use apps today. This future will belong to those of us better able to collaborate with these systems to achieve expert-level performance in a domain—something we call synthetic expertise.

2.4 The Model of Expertise

What it means to be an expert has been debated for decades. Traditional definitions of expertise rely on *knowledge* (the know-that's) and *skills* (the know-how's) with Gobet offering a more general definition: *"an expert obtains results vastly superior to those obtained by the majority of the population"* [16]. De Groot established how experts perceive the most important aspects of a situation faster than novices [8]. Formally, experts are goal-driven intelligent agents where a set of goals, *G,* and a set of utility values, *U,* drive the expert's perceiving, reasoning and act cycles over time [14, 28]. Intelligent agents perceive a subset, *T,* of possible states, *S,* of the environment and perform actions from set of actions, *A,* to effect changes on the environment.

Chase and Simon found experts compile a large amount of domain-specific knowledge from years of experience—on the order of 50,000 pieces [4]. Steels later described this as *deep domain knowledge* and also identified: *problem-solving methods,* and *task models* as needed by an expert [31]. Experts match the current situation to their enormous store of deep domain knowledge and efficiently extract knowledge and potential solutions from memory. Furthermore, an expert applies this greater knowledge to the

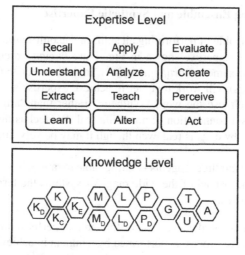

Knowledge
K   declarative knowledge statements
K_D domain-specific knowledge
K_C common-sense knowledge
K_E episodic knowledge   **G** goals to achieve
M/M_D world models   **U** utility values
L/L_D task models   **T** perceivable states
P/P_D problem-solving models   **A** actions

Skills
Perceive   sense/interpret the environment
Act   perform action affecting environment
Recall   remember; store/retrieve knowledge
Understand classify, categorize, discuss, explain, identify
Apply   implement, solve, use knowledge
Analyze   compare, contrast, experiment
Evaluate   appraise, judge, value, critique
Create   design, construct, develop, synthesize
Extract   match/retrieve deep knowledge
Learn   modify existing knowledge
Teach   convey knowlege/skills to others
Alter   modify goals

Fig. 1. Model of expertise

situation more efficiently and quicker than a novice making experts superior problem solvers.

Fulbright [12, 13] extended the description of experts by including fundamental skills identified in Bloom's Taxonomy. These skills, described at the Expertise Level, and the knowledge stores, described at the Knowledge Level, form Fulbright's Model of Expertise shown in Fig. 1. Lois' architecture is based on this model.

2.5   The Human/Cog Ensemble and Synthetic Expertise

Biological systems capable of performing all skills and acquiring/possessing all knowledge in the Model of Expertise shown in Fig. 1 are *human experts*. Non-biological systems capable of the same are *artificial experts*. In the immediate future, humans and artificial systems (cogs) will work together to achieve expertise as an ensemble—*synthetic expertise*. We choose the word "synthetic" rather than "artificial" because the word artificial carries a connotation of not being real. We feel as though the cognitive processing performed by cogs is real even though it may be very different from human cognitive processing.

Cogs are certainly intelligent agents—entities able to rationally act toward achieving a goal [28]. However, instead of the wide range of systems the term intelligent agent refers to we define cog as:

> *cog:* an intelligent agent, device, or algorithm able to perform, mimic, or replace one or more cognitive processes performed by a human in achieving a goal.

Therefore, cogs are more than merely reactive devices (like a thermostat) but do not have to be fully intelligent either. As shown in Fig. 2, the human and cog form an Engelbart/Licklider-style system with the human component performing some of the cognitive work, WH and the cog performing some of the cognitive work, WC with the total cognitive work performed by the ensemble being W*. When the cognitive performance of the ensemble reaches or exceeds that of a human expert in the domain (W* > WExpert), the ensemble has achieved synthetic expertise. The difference between Fig. 2 and Engelbart/Licklider's vision is cogs are capable of high-level human-like cognitive processing and act as peer collaborators working with humans rather than mere tools.

Because the human and the cog are physically independent agents, both must *perceive, act,* and *collaborate*. To achieve expertise, the human/cog ensemble must perform all skills and maintain all knowledge stores shown in Fig. 1. Skills performed solely by the human correspond to Engelbart's human-explicit processes. Skills performed solely by the cog correspond to Engelbart's artifact-explicit processes. Many skills will be performed by a combination of human and cog effort corresponding to Engelbart's composite processes. To the outside world, it does not matter which entity performs a skill as long as the skills are performed by the ensemble. For the immediate future, cogs will perform lower-order skills and humans will perform higher-order skills. However, as cognitive systems evolve, they will be able to perform more of the higher-order fundamental skills themselves.

3   The Loved One's Information System - Lois

3.1   The Lois Ensemble

As stated earlier, synthetic expertise is the result of the collaborative work of one or more artificial systems and one or more humans—a human/cog ensemble. For the elderly caregiver domain, Fig. 3 shows the Lois ensemble consisting of Lois (the cog), the

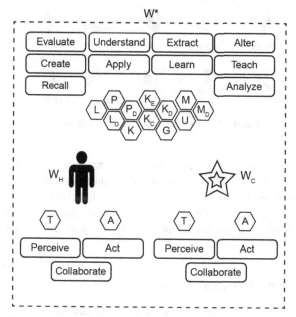

Fig. 2. A human/cog ensemble achieving synthetic expertise

elderly person Lois is tasked with observing and assisting, various medical/professional personnel, and family members.

Lois is embedded in the elder's home communicating directly with the elder on a daily basis as well as continually receiving data from the wealth of sensors throughout the home. Lois's overall purpose is to assist the elder and monitor the elder's overall well-being. Figure 4 is representative of the areas of the elder's life Lois monitors.

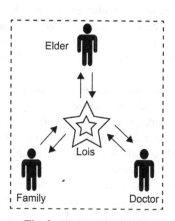

Fig. 3. The Lois ensemble

Fig. 4. Areas of the elder's life Lois monitors

Communication with medical/professional personnel and family members is initiated either by Lois, when the situation dictates, or by the medical/professional personnel themselves when desired or necessary. Upon request, Lois makes information relating to any of these areas available if the requestor has proper clearance to receive the information. These communications can happen locally inside the elder's home or remotely over the Internet.

3.2 Models, Events, States, and Tokens

Lois maintains several sets of *models* to permit it to determine when certain events happen (event models), when certain states are in effect (state models), and to document the elder's progress and history (dossier models). A model contains static information necessary to enable Lois to differentiate between one situation and another. A model also contains dynamic information—the historical record relating to the model.

Events are instantaneous occurrences not persisting over a significant period of time, such as a knock on the door or the ringing of the telephone. *States* are conditions of being persisting over a significant period of time, such as being asleep or being awake. Models can "fire" and "clear" events and states. An event is fired when the onset of an event or state is detected. Some events and states are cleared after a specific period of time, others are cleared by the firing of other events or states.

As shown in Fig. 5, all currently active events and states are placed on a *blackboard*. The blackboard is accessible by all models, states, and events and serves as a means for intercommunication. Lois detects events, states, and coordinates its response by interaction via the blackboard.

Tokens are the result of processing raw sensory input. Sensors detect physical disturbances in the environment and event models classify them putting a token on the blackboard for each. For example, when a microphone detects a sound, the event model $M_{doorbell}$ may recognize the sound and classify it as a doorbell. As a result, a doorbell token is placed on the blackboard allowing other event and state models to process the fact a doorbell sound has been detected.

Tokens represent low-level occurrences in the physical environment. Recognizing higher-level events and states involve more sophisticated processing of tokens, events, and state models. As an example, consider how Lois determines the elder is asleep. The $M_{isAsleep}$ state model contains information about what Lois can look for to determine if the elder is asleep. Taking into consideration observed characteristics such as: eyes being closed for a lengthy time, body in a lying or sitting position, elder is in the bed, head is slumped to one side, forward, or backward, mouth slightly open, regular/deep breathing, snoring, rapid eye movement, and the current time allows Lois to determine the elder has fallen asleep. These defining characteristics are captured in the static information within the $M_{isAsleep}$ model.

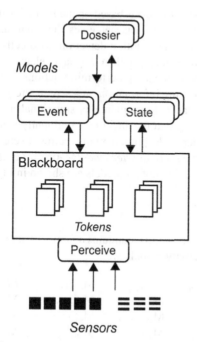

Fig. 5. How event, state, and Dossier models interact

Other state models relating to being asleep, such as the $M_{isInBed}$ model and the $M_{eyesClosed}$ model, will have already fired and those states would be currently active on the blackboard. When the $M_{isAsleep}$ model sees these and knows the elder is in bed and his or her eyes are closed (for a relatively long time) and also notices the current time is within the elder's normal bedtime, it can make the determination the elder is asleep and therefore fires the *isAsleep* state in turn placing it on the blackboard. Once there, other models may observe and respond to the fact the elder is now asleep. In similar fashion, the $M_{isAwake}$ model determines when the elder is awake thereby setting the *isAwake* state and clearing the *isAsleep* state.

One such model interested in responding to the isAsleep state would the Msleep model. The Msleep model is a dossier model meaning it captures and retains historical information about the elder's sleep patterns. The Msleep model logs when the elder goes to sleep and when the elder wakes, noting duration and other quality-of-sleep metrics. The dossier information stored in a model persists indefinitely (until explicitly cleared for some reason). Therefore, any dossier model can be queried at any time to see the historical information. In this way, medical professionals and family members can always query Lois by asking questions such as "How did they sleep last night?" Lois can answer this query by displaying the information logged and maintained in the Msleep model.

3.3   Overall Architecture of Lois

As shown in Fig. 6, the design of Lois is based on the Formal Model of Expertise shown in Fig. 1. As an intelligent agent, Lois perceives the environment through a variety of sensors (cameras, microphones, motion detection, load cells, temperature, etc.) and interfaces (screens, keyboards, mice, spoken language, electronic communication, etc.) and interacts with the environment by performing actions (turning a light on or off, speaking to the elder, displaying information on a screen, etc.).

As with a human caretaker, Lois maintains situational awareness and contextual awareness of the elder throughout the day. Lois continually determines the state of the elder such as when the elder is sleeping, napping, eating, exercising, etc. Lois captures this historic information in a set of *dossier models*—one for each area of the elder's life Lois monitors. Note, for brevity, not all models are shown in Fig. 6.

3.4   Models in Lois

To monitor the elder's activities, Lois maintains a family of activity and behavior models ($M_{activity}$). Examples of activity models are:

$M_{appointment}$	$M_{bathing}$	$M_{cleaning}$	$M_{cooking}$
$M_{dressing}$	M_{eating}	$M_{emergency}$	M_{gaming}
$M_{excursion}$	$M_{exercising}$	$M_{gardening}$	$M_{grooming}$
$M_{medicating}$	M_{online}	$M_{reading}$	$M_{resting}$
$M_{restroom}$	$M_{sleeping}$	$M_{socializaing}$	$M_{swimming}$
M_{tv}	M_{waking}	$M_{walking}$	$M_{washing}$
$M_{working}$	$M_{yardwork}$		

Activity models contain descriptions of each activity the elder is likely to engage in allowing Lois to recognize the activity based on observations. Since models are dynamic data stores, over time, Lois is able to learn idiosyncrasies of the specific elder being cared for by continually updating the activity models using the evaluation, analyze, and learn skills. Also, Lois will be able to learn the elder's routines allowing Lois to calculate expectations such as "on a weekday, the elder wakes about 8AM." Learning the elder's normal pattern of behavior allows Lois to detect departures from the norm—a key capability of an elderly caregiver—since departures can signal further decline or the onset of new problems.

Likewise, Lois maintains a family of emotional and mood models (M_{mood}) allowing Lois to monitor the elder's emotional state. Sample emotional models are:

Mangry	Masleep	Mdistant	Mhappy
Mlonely	Mmanic	Mnostalgic	Mpain
Mpanic	Mreflective	Mrestless	Msad
Mworried	Mdanger		

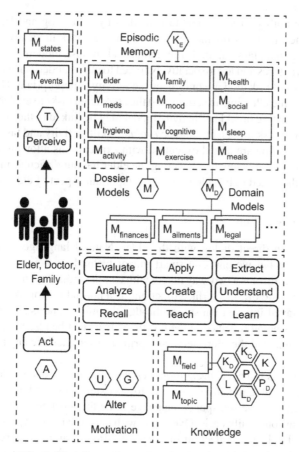

Fig. 6. How Event, State, and Dossier Models Interact

Behavioral and emotional models represent states the elder can be in at any point of the day and the elder may be in multiple states simultaneously. For example, the elder could be eating, reading, and watching television all at the same time. Likewise, the elder could be lonely, worried, and restless at the same time.

During an activity, the elder is likely to perform one or more tasks. Indeed, executing a series of tasks constitutes an activity. Lois maintains a family of task models allowing it to both monitor the elder's activity but also assist with the activity when needed. Sample task models are:

Lbed	Lcoffee	Ltoast
Leggs	Lgrits	Lbacon
Ldishes	LwaterPlants	Lnewspaper
Ltv	Lfacebook	Lmail
Lbathe	Ldress	Lmeds

Lois has the ability to *learn* new task models by observing and being taught by the elder. Via the Internet, Lois may also download new task models when necessary. We expect Lois to maintain hundreds if not thousands of task models. Since models are dynamic data structures and are associatively linked to other models, an activity model is linked to a number of task models comprising the activity as appropriate. This association can change over time allowing an activity and the associated tasks to evolve as necessary. For example, an "eating breakfast" activity model may be linked to the "grits," "coffee," "eggs," and "toast" task models. Using the *evaluate* skill, activity and task models gives Lois the ability to compare actual execution with expectations allowing Lois to detect departures from normal behavior. Detecting the elder having difficulty in performing a task or activity they used to be able to do is an important aspect of elderly caregiving.

3.5 Interaction with Lois

Lois can engage in direct dialog with the elder. Natural language is a major mode of communication, but we envision smart mirror technology being a primary visual interface. A smart mirror is a two-way mirror with computer displays mounted in the rear. When the displays are off, the surface functions as a normal mirror. When the displays are on, the displayed information shines through the mirror and is superimposed onto whatever image is being reflected in the mirror. Mirrors can be placed unobtrusively in any room of a home and therefore serve as a primary user interface any time of the day or night.

We envision Lois to be a *conversational chatbot* meaning Lois is able to carry on a verbal (or textual) dialog in natural language for an extended period of time (essentially continuously). In fact, we see spoken language to be the most common way the elder interacts with Lois on a daily basis. Over time, with episodic memory, Lois accumulates an extensive and valuable collection of diagnostic information. As a result, Lois can detect emotional and cognitive problems early. Departures from normal behavior and the onset of new and different idiosyncrasies can alert Lois to problems such as: depression, loneliness, dementia, stroke, brain seizures, etc. To recognize signs of cognitive, emotional, and mental abnormalities, Lois maintains a collection of models ($M_{ailments}$) including:

Mmemloss	Mcomm	Mvisiospatial	Mreasoning
Mtaskex	Morganization	Mcoordination	Mconfusion
Mpersonality	Mdepression	Manxiety	Mbehavior
Mparanoia	Mhallucination	Mloneliness	Mdespair
Mstroke	Mheart	Mseizure	Mdementia

For example, one sign of cognitive decline in the elderly is loss of memory ($M_{memloss}$). By comparing current experiences and knowledge to past experiences, Lois is able to detect lapses in memory.

Lois employs wearable interface devices. For example, a "smart ring" worn by the elder monitors the elder's location, movements and vital signs (e.g. heart rate, blood pressure, blood sugar, and body temperature). All information gathered by the ring is transmitted to Lois wirelessly via Bluetooth or local WiFi shared by Lois. The smart ring can also vibrate and display different colors to communicate caution or alarm and an embedded speaker/microphone combination allows the elder to communicate via voice interaction with Lois. Besides a ring worn on a finger, such interface devices could take on the form of any kind of accessory such as: bracelet, necklace, arm band, watch, etc.

Many elderly wear eyeglasses so the use of "smart glasses" is a natural one for Lois. By communicating with smart glasses worn by the elder, Lois can superimpose digital information onto the elder's field of view. Thus, via augmented reality, Lois can assist the elder in activities and tasks such as: cooking, medication, and finding misplaced items.

4 Conclusion

We have described a cognitive system, named Lois, which by continually monitoring and observing an elderly person in their own home and by working with medical personnel and family members achieves a level of elderly caregiving exceeding that of a human caregiver. We have noted how Lois is a fusion of contributions from several different fields including: artificial intelligence, intelligent agents, cognitive systems, machine learning, and cognitive psychology. Lois is a comprehensive caregiver maintaining a large set of models enabling it to detect, classify, and keep track of events, states, activities, and performance metrics in all facets of the elder's life, health, and well-being. The ensemble consisting of Lois, medical personnel, and family members is an example of a synthetic expert able to maintain all sets of knowledge and perform all skills required of an expert. Alone, neither of these three elements are expert caregivers. However, the combined effort of these biological and artificial elements achieves expertise in the elderly caregiving domain.

References

1. [Apple]. Knowledge Navigator, You Tube video (1987). https://www.youtube.com/watch?v=JIE8xk6Rl1w. Accessed Jan 2021
2. Buitron, C.: Rise of the $300 Billion Senior Care Industry, Huffington Post Internet site (2017). https://www.huffpost.com/entry/rise-of-the-300-billion-senior-care-industry_b_58b0c35ce4b0e5fdf61971ee. Accessed Jan 2021
3. [Catalia Health]. How Mabu Works, Catalia Health Internet site (2019). http://www.cataliahealth.com/how-it-works/. Accessed Dec 2019. Video. https://www.youtube.com/watch?v=A3XwzlvOW7k. Accessed Jan 2021
4. Chase, W., Simon, H.: Perception in chess. Cogn. Psychol. **4**, 55–61 (1973)
5. [ChessBase]. AlphaZero: Comparing Orangutans and Apples, ChessBase Internet site (2018). https://en.chessbase.com/post/alpha-zero-comparing-orang-utans-and-apples. Accessed Jan 2021
6. [DeepMind]. The story of AlphaGo so far, DeepMind Internet site (2018a). https://deepmind.com/research/alphago/. Accessed Jan 2021
7. [DeepMind]. AlphaGo Zero: learning from scratch, DeepMind Internet site (2018b). https://deepmind.com/blog/alphago-zero-learning-scratch/ Accessed Jan 2021
8. De Groot, A.D.: Thought and Choice in Chess. Mouton, The Hague (1965)
9. [Dinsow]. CT Asia Robotics Internet site (2019). https://www.dinsow.com. Accessed Jan 2021

10. [ElliQ]. Hi, I'm ElliQ, Intuition Robotics Internet site (2019). https://elliq.com. Accessed Jan 2021
11. Engelbart, D.C.: Augmenting human intellect: a conceptual framework. Summary Report AFOSR-3233, Stanford Research Institute, Menlo Park, CA, October (1962)
12. Fulbright, R., Walters, G.: Synthetic expertise. In: Schmorrow, D.D., Fidopiastis, C.M. (eds.): HCII 2020. LNCS (LNAI), vol. 12197. Springer, Cham (2020). https://doi.org/10.1007/978-3-030-50439-7_3
13. Fulbright, R.: Democratization of Expertise: How Cognitive Systems Will Revolutionize Your Life, 1st edn. CRC Press, Boca Raton (2020)
14. Genesereth, M., Nilsson, N.: Logical Foundations of Artificial Intelligence. Morgan Kaufmann, San Francisco (1987)
15. Gil, D.: Cognitive systems and the future of expertise, YouTube video (2019). https://www.youtube.com/watch?v=0heqP8d6vtQ. Accessed Jan 2021
16. Gobet, F.: Understanding Expertise: A Multidisciplinary Approach. Palgrave, UK (2016)
17. Gregory, M.: AI Trained on Old Scientific Papers Makes Discoveries Humans Missed, Vice (2019). https://www.vice.com/en_in/article/neagpb/ai-trained-on-old. Accessed Jan 2021
18. Hewitt, C., Bishop, P., Steiger, R.: A universal modular actor formalism for artificial intelligence. WorryDream Internet site (1973). http://worrydream.com/refs/Hewitt-ActorModel.pdf. Accessed Jan 2021
19. Hewitt, C.: Viewing control structures as patterns of passing messages. J. Artif. Intell. **8**, 232–364 (1977)
20. Isaacson, W.: The Innovators: How a Group of Hackers, Geniuses, and Geeks Created the Digital Revolution. Simon & Schuster, New York (2014)
21. Jackson, J.: IBM Watson Vanquishes Human Jeopardy Foes, PC World. Internet site (2011). http://www.pcworld.com/article/219893/ibm_watson_vanquishes_human_jeopardy_foes.html. Accessed Jan 2021
22. Kidd, C.: Introducing the Mabu Personal Healthcare Companion, Catalia Health Internet site (2015). http://www.cataliahealth.com/introducing-the-mabu-personal-healthcare-companion/. Accessed Jan 2021
23. Kelly, J.E., Hamm, S.: Smart Machines: IBMs Watson and the Era of Cognitive Computing. Columbia Business School Publishing, Columbia University Press, New York (2013)
24. Lavars, N.: Machine learning algorithm detects signals of child depression through speech, New Atlas, published May 7, 2019 (2019). https://newatlas.com/machine-learning-algorithm-depression/59573/. Accessed Jan 2021
25. Licklider, J.C.R.: Man-computer symbiosis. IRE Trans. Hum. Factors Electron. HFE-1, March (1960)
26. Nwana, H.S.: Intelligent tutoring systems: an overview. Artif. Intell. Rev. **4**(4), 251–277 (1990)
27. [Riken]. The strong robot with the gentle touch, Riken Internet site (2015). https://www.riken.jp/en/news_pubs/research_news/2015/20150223_2/. Accessed Jan 2021
28. Russell, S., Norvig, P.: Artificial Intelligence: A Modern Approach, 3rd edn. Pearson, London (2009)
29. Sandoiu, A.: Artificial intelligence better than humans at spotting lung cancer. Med. News Today Newslett. (2019). https://www.medicalnewstoday.com/articles/325223.php#1. Accessed Jan 2021
30. Silver, D., et al.: Mastering the game of Go with deep neural networks and tree search. Nature **529**, 484–489 (2016)
31. Steels, L.: Components of expertise. AI Mag. **11**(2), 28 (1990)
32. Towers-Clark, C.: The Cutting-Edge of AI Cancer Detection, Forbes, published April 30, 2019 (2019). https://www.forbes.com/sites/charlestowersclark/2019/04/30/the-cutting-edge-of-ai-cancer-detection/#45235ee77336. Accessed Jan 2021

33. Wehner, M.: AI is now better at predicting mortality than human doctors, *BGR* Internet site (2019). https://bgr.com/2019/05/13/ai-is-now-better-at-predicting-mortality-than-human-doctors/. Accessed Jan 2021

34. [WHO]. Mental health of older adults. World Health Orgainzation Internet site (2017). https://www.who.int/news-room/fact-sheets/detail/mental-health-of-older-adults. Accessed Jan 2021

35. Wladawsky-Berger, I.: The era of augmented cognition. The Wall Street Journal. CIO Report. http://blogs.wsj.com/cio/2013/06/28/the-era-of-augmented-cognition/. Accessed Jan 2021

Topic-Shift Characteristics of Japanese Casual Conversations Between Elderlies and Between Youths

Youtaro Iida and Yumi Wakita(⊠)

Osaka Institute of Technology, Osaka, Japan
yumi.wakita@oit.ac.jp

Abstract. To support senior citizens' smooth conversations, we have developed a conversation support system that provides several topics for speakers. To effectively support conversation, the system should select suitable topics and speaking styles for the speakers while observing topic-shift situations regarding their previous conversations. In this study, we discuss the differences in conversation styles and topic-shift characteristics between elderlies and those between youths. A comparison of conversations of elderly people and youths revealed two distinct characteristics. The casual conversations of elderlies tended to include long utterances with the speakers firmly expressing their knowledge or opinion. By contrast, the conversations of youths did not reveal long utterances and they tended not to express their opinions at once, but only gradually, after watching the reaction of the other person. Further, elderly speakers tended to talk on a topic more in-depth and did not get sidetracked compared with young speakers. Moreover, the boundary of topics in the case of elderly people tended to be clearer than in the case of youths. As a result of generation identification experiments using "the number of utterances by each topic," "the number of content words in each utterance," and "the deviation of word similarity," the precision rate for youths is 90.5% but that for elderlies is 42.2%. This suggests that these parameters are effective to extracting the young speakers with certainty.

Keywords: Conversation support system · Generation identification · Topic-shift characteristics · Word similarity

1 Introduction

With the recent increase in the number of senior citizens living either alone or in reclusive situations, many communities, companies, and schools have realized the importance of human-to-human communication. To support senior citizens' smooth conversations, we have developed a conversation support system that provides several topics. The current system selects and provides new topics from recent news. However, sometimes the conversations do not change smoothly even after the system provides a topic because the system cannot understand the speakers' characteristics. Occasionally, speakers feel uncomfortable about the topic provided by the system as well as its expression and

© Springer Nature Switzerland AG 2021
Q. Gao and J. Zhou (Eds.): HCII 2021, LNCS 12787, pp. 418–427, 2021.
https://doi.org/10.1007/978-3-030-78111-8_28

the talking style, and thus, are unable to continue their conversations. To support the conversations more effectively, the system should select suitable topics and speaking style while observing topic-shift situations for their previous conversations.

Several studies describing the topic-shift characteristics of casual conversations have already been reported. The relationship between expressions that encourage topic change and the content of the next topic and the timing of the topic change was analyzed in [1–3]. In [4], the differences in topic-shift expressions because of differences in the mother tongue were also investigated. The topic-shift characteristics of casual conversations could be dependent on the speaker's generation. To offer the next suitable topic for conversation, the support system should understand the topic-shift characteristics of each generation in addition to the characteristics examined in these previous studies.

In this study, we describe the results of our analysis on the differences in topic-shift characteristics between elderly and young speakers and discuss the possibility of topic estimation for casual conversation considering generational differences.

2 Our Conversation Support System

Figure 1 illustrates the process of the conversation support system. The text within the blue rectangle shows our current system. The system extracts fundamental frequency values from input utterances and calculates their standard deviation. When these values of some utterances in the conversation are detected to be under the threshold value, the system decides that the conversation is not progressing smoothly and provides a new topic to liven up the conversation.

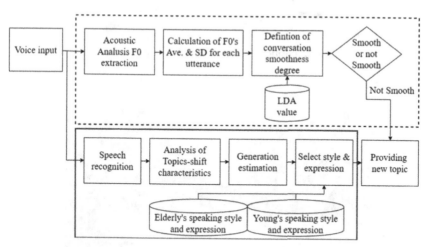

Fig. 1. Process of the conversion support system (Color figure online)

The text inside the red rectangle in Fig. 1 shows the decision part of the topic and speaking style that is provided by the system. When the speakers begin their conversation, the system analyzes their topic-shift characteristics from their conversations and predicts their generations. After deciding the speaker's generation, the system creates sentences for providing new topics to speakers by selecting the suitable topic and speaking style.

3 Casual Conversation Database

3.1 Free Conversation Recording

We recorded several sets of 3-min dyadic conversations. Figure 2 depicts the schematic positional setup of these recordings. We used two microphones and a video camera for this purpose. As an example, Fig. 3 illustrates a photo extracted from the video data. The conditions of the recordings are listed in Table 1. Although the participating speakers were not meeting for the first time, they never had a mutual conversation before. We used fourteen conversation sets for the study, of which, seven sets were conversations between elderlies aged between 62 and 82 years, and the other seven sets were conversations between youths aged between 21 and 23 years. We did not set any conditions regarding the topics and the participants conversed freely. After recording, we created a database of transcript text from all the recorded conversations.

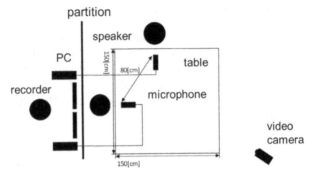

Fig. 2. Positional setup of recording conversation

Fig. 3. Example photo extracted from the video data

Table 1. Conditions of conversation

Number of Speakers	6 elderly speakers 7 young speakers
Ages	Elderly: 62–82 years old Young: 21–23 years old
Number of conversations	Each of 7 conversations
Conversation periods	Three minutes/conversation
Conversation condition	Free dyadic conversation

3.2 Transcription of Conversation Speech Database

After recording, we created a transcript database watching the video recording data. Morphological analysis was performed on the transcript text database using "Mecab," which is a Japanese morphological analyzer engine.

3.3 Difference in Conversation Characteristics Between Elderlies and Youths

Tables 2 and 3 present the number of topics for each conversation. These tables indicate that the number of topics in the conversations between youths is greater than that of conversations between elderly people. The results demonstrate that the casual conversation of elderlies shows a greater tendency to dwell on one topic and talk longer when compared with the conversation of youths.

Table 2. Number of topics for each elderly conversation

Conversation No.	1	2	3	4	5	6	7	Ave.
Number of topics	2	3	4	2	2	1	2	2.29

Table 3. Number of topics for each young person conversation

Conversation No.	1	2	3	4	5	6	7	Ave.
Number of topics	5	5	4	5	3	5	1	4

Next, we compared the conversation contents between elderly people and those between youths. Tables 4 and 5 present the number of utterances for each topic and the number of content words for each utterance.

These tables indicate that the number of utterances in conversations between elderly people is fewer than those in conversations between youths, and the number of content words in the utterances of the former is greater than those in the utterances of youths. The

Table 4. Number of utterances and content words for each older adults conversation

Conversation No.	1	2	3	4	5	6	7	Ave.
Total of number of utterance	25	25	24	20	25	16	21	22.3
Average of number of content words for each utterance	2.16	1.92	1.88	2.95	1.64	3.44	2.38	2.34

Table 5. Number of utterances and content words each young people conversation

Conversation No.	1	2	3	4	5	6	7	Ave.
Total of number of utterance	49	84	45	58	36	68	45	55
Average of number of content words for each utterance	1.73	1.17	2.02	1.50	0.67	1.34	1.76	1.45

results show that the casual conversations of elderly people tended to include one long utterance with the speakers firmly expressing their knowledge or opinion. By contrast, the conversations of youths did not reveal long utterances and they tended not to express their opinions at once, but only gradually, after watching the reaction of the other person.

Table 6 shows the number of utterances that include each number of content words. In the case of youths, 36.3% of their utterances did not include a content word. It seems that youths often progress their conversation only through back-channel feedbacks.

Table 6. Number of utterances that include each number of content words

Number of content words	0	1	2	3	4	5	6	7	8	Over 8
Number of older adults utterances	35	46	27	16	12	7	1	2	3	7
Number of young people utterances	140	107	72	21	18	12	7	4	2	2

3.4 Word Similarity Calculation

For topic-shift analysis, "word similarity" is defined as an expression of similarity based on how similar the word senses are and where the synsets occur relative to each other in the hypernym tree of the WordNet [5]. Formula (1) expresses the degree of word similarity. The values of A and B describe the depths of the two synsets in the WordNet taxonomies and the C value describes the depth of the least common subsumer, which is the most specific common ancestor of the two concepts found in a given ontology [6].

$$\text{Word Similarity degree} = \frac{C \times 2}{A + B} \qquad (1)$$

3.5 Deciding the Boundary of Topics

We asked three individuals to read the 14 transcripts to decide the various topic boundaries for each conversation. After deciding the boundaries, the individuals selected the most important word that expressed the topic for each part of the conversation separated by the boundary. The difference in boundaries given by the three individuals were all within three utterances. This result explains that the changing point of the topics is clear. We decided the boundary according to the answers of the three individuals. After determining the boundaries, we asked them to choose the most important word for each topic.

3.6 Analysis of Topic and Topic-Shift Features

We calculated the average values (Ave-WS) and deviation values (Dev-WS) of word similarity of all content words in the same topic. The word similarity values were calculated using formula (1). Figure 4 depicts the relationship between Ave-WS and Dev-WS.

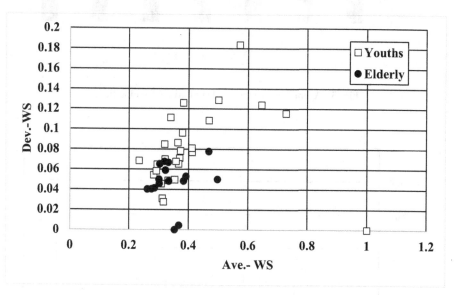

Fig. 4. Relationship between Ave-WS and Dev-WS for each topic

Both the Ave-WSs and Dev-WSs of utterances by elderly people were mostly smaller than those of youths. The result of T-tests shows that Dev-WSs are significant when the significance level is 5% ($p = 0.0027 < 0.05$) but Ave-WSs are not significant. This indicates that the range of topics by elderlies is narrow and organized compared with that of youths.

We also selected the most important word for each topic using Term Frequency and Inverse Document Frequency (TD-IDF) values. The word for which the TD-IDF value was the highest was regarded as the "most important word." Further, we calculated the word similarity value between the important word of the current topic and that of the next topic in the same conversation. Figure 5 and 6 presents the average of word similarity values of each conversation in the database.

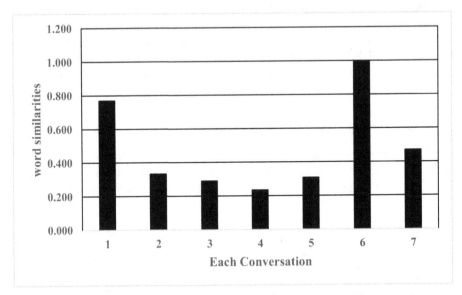

Fig. 5. Average values of word similarities for elderlies

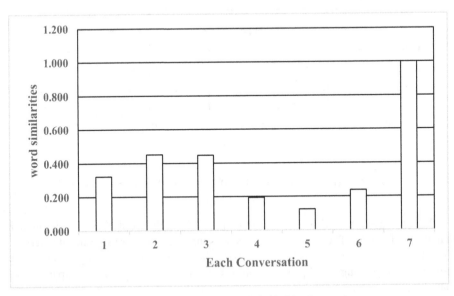

Fig. 6. Average values of word similarities for youths

The average values of word similarity for elderlies are mostly higher than those for youths, although the difference in the average of all conversations of elderlies and those of youths is not substantial. The extent of difference between elderlies and youths is dependent on the conversation. The result of the T-test shows that the difference was significant for certain conversations.

Figure 4 and Figs. 5, 6 illustrate that elderly speakers tend to talk on a topic more in-depth and do not get sidetracked compared with young speakers. Moreover, the boundary of topics in the case of elderly persons tends to be clearer than in the case of youths.

4 Evaluation of Generation Identification

We evaluated that the probability of generation estimation using each word similarity in a topic. The generation estimation performances were confirmed using the following parameters:

1. The number of utterances by each topic;
2. The number of content words in each utterance; and
3. The deviation of word similarity.

The performance in the case of elderlies is especially important for our conversation support system. We used the SVM package, LIBSVM, for identifying the generation of both elderlies and youths. The function of the kernel is RBF and the cost is 1,000.

We divided the transcription database for learning and evaluating and used five conversation transcriptions for learning and two for evaluating. These transcriptions were evaluated in conversation-open conditions.

Table 7 shows the youths estimation performance. The precision rate of 90.5% is high. But the recall rate of 42.2% is low. This suggests that these parameters are effective to extracting the youths speakers with certainty, but some youths' utterances are regarded as elderly's mistakenly.

Table 7. The youths identification performance

	Recall	Precision
Ave.	0.422	0.905

5 Discussion

The identification experiment in Sect. 4, which was evaluated using "the number of utterances by each topic," "the number of content words in each utterance," and "the deviation of word similarity" as parameters, it revealed that the precision rate of youths is high. This means that those who are judged to be young are highly reliable, but the characteristics of the elderly also mean that they are often mistaken for youth. However in practical use, the identification process is not done for each utterance. The generation are identified using several utterances spoken until current time.

By consideration of the results in Sect. 4, when all utterances which are spoken until the current time are judged as elderly's, the speakers can be identified as elderly, when if even one utterance is judged as youth's, the speakers could be identified as young person.

According to this idea, we confirmed the identification performance using seven conversations each for youths and elderly people. The accuracy rate for the youths' conversations was 85.7% and that for elderly people was 100%. This result suggests that it is possible to identify the generation from the topic-shift characteristics by observing a period which includes several utterances, for example, a period in which one topic continues.

6 Conclusion

To support senior citizens' smooth conversations, we have developed a conversation support system that provides several topics for speakers. To effectively support conversation, the system should select suitable topics and speaking styles for the speakers while observing topic-shift situations regarding their previous conversations. In this study, we discussed the differences in conversation styles and topics and topic-shift characteristics between elderlies and those between youths.

A comparison of conversations of elderly people and youths revealed two distinct characteristics. The casual conversations of elderlies tended to include long utterances with the speakers firmly expressing their knowledge or opinion. By contrast, the conversations of youths did not reveal long utterances and they tended not to express their opinions at once, but only gradually, after watching the reaction of the other person. Further, elderly speakers tended to talk on a topic more in-depth and did not get sidetracked compared with young speakers. Moreover, the boundary of topics in the case of elderly people tended to be clearer than in the case of youths. As a result of generation identification experiments using "the number of utterances by each topic," "the number of content words in each utterance," and "the deviation of word similarity," the precision rate for youths is 90.5% but that for elderlies is 42.2%. This suggests that these parameters are effective to extracting the youths speakers with certainty, but some youths' utterances are regarded as elderly's mistakenly. However, in practical use, the identification process is not done for each utterance. The generation are identified using several utterances spoken until current time. According to this idea, we confirmed the identification performance using seven conversations each for youths and elderly people. The accuracy rate for the youths' conversations was 85.7% and that for elderly people was 100%.

In the future, we should confirm identification performance using more speakers and casual conversation databases. Further we will improve the identification performance by adding processing for unknown words.

Acknowledgment. This work is supported by JSPS KAKENHI Grant Number 19K04934.

References

1. Arguello, J., et al.: Topic segmentation of dialogue. In: HLT-NAACL Workshop on Analyzing Conversations in Text and Speech, pp. 42–49 (2006)
2. Afantenos, S., et al.: Discourse parsing for multi-party chat dialogues. In: EMNLP, pp. 928–937 (2015)
3. Ryuichi, T., et al.: A weakly supervised method for topic segmentation and labeling in goal-oriented dialogues via reinforcement learning. In: 27th IJCAI-18, pp. 4403–4410 (2018)
4. Bai, P.S., et al.: Topic shifts in conversations: Focus on Malaysian Chinese teenagers. SARJANA, **26**(2), 101–118 (2011)
5. Wu, Z., Palmer, M.: Verbs semantics and lexical selection. In: Proceedings of the 32nd Annual Meeting on ACL, pp. 133–138 (1994)
6. Batet, M., Sánchez, D.: A review on semantic similarity. In: Encyclopedia of Information Science and Technology Third Edition, vol. 10, pp. 7575–7583 (2015)

An Expert Interview Study of IoT Wearable Technologies for an Aging Population from Product, Data, and Society Dimensions

Sheng-Hung Lee[1,3]([✉]), Ziyuan Zhu[2,4], Chaiwoo Lee[1], Fabio Duarte[2], and Joseph F. Coughlin[1]

[1] MIT AgeLab, Cambridge, USA
{shdesign,chaiwoo,coughlin}@mit.edu
[2] MIT Senseable City Lab, Cambridge, USA
{zyzhu,fduarte}@mit.edu
[3] MIT Integrated Design & Management, Cambridge, USA
[4] MIT School of Architecture and Planning, Cambridge, USA

Abstract. This research focuses on investigating the product, data, and society dimensions around IoT (Internet of Things) wearable technologies with insights and empirical knowledge from exploratory expert interviews. The purpose is to find implications around future designs of IoT wearable technologies for the aging population. Quantitative and qualitative data were collected through in-depth expert interviews and pre-surveys to explore topics and insights related to the design and development of IoT wearable technologies. Through synthesizing findings from expert interviews and pre-surveys, insights and concerning issues were summarized into three dimensions: product, data, and society. The implications from this research can help overcome the obstacles that impede the inclusiveness and adaptability of IoT wearable technologies. This study concludes that it is essential for designers, engineers, and researchers to consider these non-technological issues when designing and developing future IoT wearable technologies for the aging population.

Keywords: IoT wearable technology · Data ethics · Design with data · Aging population · Expert interview

1 Introduction

IoT (Internet of Things) wearable technologies have become increasingly prevalent and been used in a wide range of scenarios [1, 2]. In this study, IoT wearable technology is defined as a type of electronic product that can be used as a hands-free device with the feature of internet connectivity to transmit data and information. There are increasing needs for IoT wearable technologies in the field of healthcare, fitness, entertainment, education, and communication. IoT wearable technologies can reduce the nursing demand and cost in expensive healthcare institutions, but more importantly, they monitor real-time health conditions of the aging population to help maintain their independence and

© Springer Nature Switzerland AG 2021
Q. Gao and J. Zhou (Eds.): HCII 2021, LNCS 12787, pp. 428–437, 2021.
https://doi.org/10.1007/978-3-030-78111-8_29

well-being [3]. The application of healthcare IoT wearable devices make it possible for aging population to stay in their home longer, and to help mitigate the workload and stress experienced by healthcare providers [4]. However, with design opportunities brought by the flourishing of IoT wearable technologies in the aging market, there are also innumerable challenges, among which are user acceptance, such as data-related issues include data relevance, security and privacy, and possible bias associated with programs and algorithms used [5–7].

This research utilizes qualitative and quantitative methods to explore, analyze and synthesize insights gathered from exploratory expert interviews and surveys on IoT wearable technologies. The purpose is to find design implications, and identify opportunities and challenges that the design team, including designers, researchers, and engineers, may come across in the process of designing and improving IoT wearable technologies [8, 9]. Our approach includes the discussion of data ethics issues related to IoT wearable technologies for aging population [10]. The in-depth exploratory expert interview outcome as the fundamental of research materials. We harnessed the expert pre-survey result and its qualitative analysis as auxiliary materials to support the qualitative result and conclusion from the expert interview [11]. The interview process sought to collect the experts' perceptions about smart home, related professional experiences, examples of interacting with IoT wearable technologies at home, interpretation of the relationship between design and data, discussion about data ethical issues, and perspectives around how they view IoT wearable technologies can help people in the future. The utilization of expert interviews in this research aimed at resolving three key questions:

1. From the three dimensions, product, data, and society, what should be emphasized in detail in the IoT wearable technologies design process?
2. What other dimensions should be considered during the product design and development of IoT wearable technologies?
3. As for designing IoT wearable technologies for aging population, what are the other considerations?

This research also aims to address issues around the use of data associated with IoT wearable technologies. While past research has included experts' perspectives in utilizing human-centered design approach to understand people's needs, designing for elderly adults [12], addressing psychological demands faced by elderly adults, and mitigating the stress of healthcare workers [13], issues around data collection and use have been neglected. As additional discussions designers, researchers, and engineers over responsible and ethical use of data becomes increasingly essential [14], this study sought to include discussions around data-related design considerations. The social issues including technological bias, inclusiveness, sustainability, and acceptance of technologies are taken into consideration in this paper. Synthesized from the interview insights, what positive and negative impacts IoT wearable technologies will bring to society is a consideration that designers, researchers, and engineers need to take in the process of design and improvement.

2   Data Collection: Expert Interview and Pre-survey

In order to better understand the importance of IoT wearable technologies for the aging population, as well as apply the evaluation framework of collecting, generating, analyzing, and utilizing users' data properly and ethically in the process of design and improvement of IoT wearable device, we recruited experts of different backgrounds to leverage their professional perspectives and well-thought-out considerations. Recruited experts participated in 1-on-1 interviews, as well as a pre-survey with questions complementing the interview contents.

2.1   Preparation and Expert Recruitment

A literature review and secondary research were conducted to develop relevant and specific interview questions. A survey of existing papers and publications spanned related topics such as "ethical issues in wearable technologies [15]", "data and wearable device [16]", "wearable device design [17]", among other themes. Based on findings from the literature review, we developed questions to be used in a qualitative interview method combined with a quantitative pre-survey, with the purpose of securing a more objective, clear, and balanced findings [18].

Expert interviews have been adopted as a tool of qualitative research as widely discussed in social research [15–17]. In order to get diverse perspectives in the study, we selected and recruited thirty-one experts from the field of industrial design, user-experience design, education, healthcare and medicine, cognitive science, IoT, software engineering, electronics engineering, and aging research. Experts were invited to participated in in-depth interviews around what needs to be considered in the process of IoT wearable technologies design and development. Recruited experts represented diverse backgrounds across different disciplines and included technological entrepreneurs (18%), people in leadership roles (24%), consultants (18%), designers (16%), technologists (4%), educators (16%), and extreme users[1] (4%) (Fig. 1).

To better highlight the individual perspective and insights from experts [19], as well as quantify the expert interview result based on the expertise and credibility of experts, we started the evaluation of experts based on their professional knowledge and experience in IoT wearable product design, understanding of IoT wearable technologies and the comfort level of talking IoT wearable device related topics). This evaluation is a subjective framework for us to make a high-level evaluation based on the interviewees' empirical and fact-based knowledge, and meanwhile, it serves as a tool eliminating the bias of experts due to their personal experience with IoT wearable technologies [20]. The three criteria cover: adaptability—understanding the comfort level of the interviewee when facing IoT products and their challenges; expertise—understanding how knowledgeable the interviewee is about the IoT industry; responsibility—understanding the perception of the interviewee about the ethics of IoT and data-privacy-related issues, which reflect the three dimensions of knowledge which experts can contribute to resolving the problem [21].

---

[1] In the study, we define an extreme user as one type of expert.

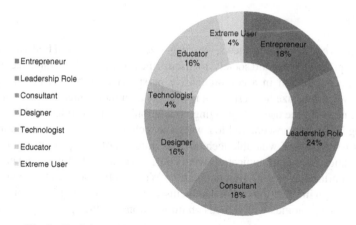

Fig. 1. Participants' backgrounds of the expert interview (n = 31)

2.2 Expert Interview Procedure

An interview guide and a pre-survey was developed to curate the interview in a systematic and structural way. Each expert interview lasted about 45 min and was conducted online. Additionally, a 3-min online pre-survey was completed prior to the interview. Figure 2 illustrates the overall procedure of the mixed-methods approach, as well as contents and topics covered in each stage of research. As shown in Fig. 2, five main steps were taken throughout the research process, including (1) recruiting; (2) interview pre-survey: a quantitative survey asked experts to share their perspectives on wearable technologies in a pre-defined format; (3) semi-structured interview: open-ended questions were posed to allow experts to share and express their views and knowledge in their own terms across the product, data and society dimensions, such as cases of IoT wearable device design to obtain detailed insights around specific dimensions of IoT wearable technology design and development [22]; (4) interview material review: after each interview, the interview team quickly reviewed the contents and completed notes to find lessons and insights.

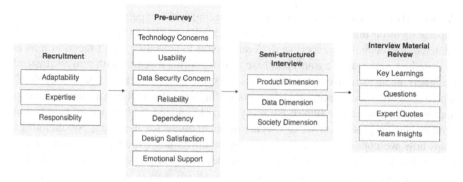

Fig. 2. Expert interview flow and key considerations

3 Result

From the thirty-one expert interviews, we categorized and synthesized findings into three dimensions: product, data, and society, to discuss the topic of IoT wearable technologies for the aging population in a comprehensive perspective (Table 1). For the product dimension, we emphasize how critical it is to apply a human-centered design process to address the needs of the users' (e.g. aging population), their lifestyles, and life routines for creating better human-centered IoT wearable technologies. For the data dimension, data ethics issues of IoT wearable technologies in terms of data privacy, data security, data clarification, and communication were considered not only for the general public but more importantly, for the aging population. Whereas for the society dimension, we considered design implications related to inclusiveness and social responsibility beyond IoT wearable technologies with a focus on implications for the aging population.

Table 1. Dimensions of IoT wearable technologies in product, data, and society

Product	Data	Society
– Human-centered approach and framework – Design considerations based on users' needs, behavior, and ritual – User-friendly interface across touchpoints of the user journey – Intuitive design in product, service, and experience	– Personal data privacy concerns – Data security in digital and physical assets – Data awareness of users – Data communication among devices – Proper distribution of secondary data	– Inclusiveness of product feature – Social and environmental responsibility of design teams – Social acceptance of the technology – Potential bias caused by technology

3.1 Product

Apply a Human-Centered Approach. According to the expert interview study, some experts mention that a great IoT wearable technologies design results from a human-centered approach. One expert said "A successful IoT product won't mention it as an IoT product, since people won't purchase an extra coffee machine with sensors. Instead, designers need to reinvent the overall user experience for using a coffee machine.", which reinforces the importance of understanding users by applying a human-centered approach [23]. A further step of the study is to (1) understand how we refine a typical product design process of an IoT wearable technology for the aging population. (2) learn how we conduct a user (e.g. aging population) and expert interview integrated into an IoT wearable technology design and development process. (3) apply a human-centered approach to clarify users' the core needs of users (e.g. aging population) by understanding users' behavior, knowing users' rituals, and identifying users' purpose of why or why not use IoT wearable technology at home.

Understand Users' Needs, Behavior, and Ritual. "I only want my IoT product to show the things, the functions that you (product) promise and I don't want to have any surprises," said an expert who talked about his viewpoints as an end-user. Understanding users' needs are critical and essential from the expert interviews, as one expert said "Any other kind of design: you have to understand your customer and you must have a vision. Data alone will not yield great products and services." Some experts mentioned that IoT wearable technologies should respond to the users' needs precisely and they can offer many options. It can also predict users' behaviors and know their rituals in order to help users explore themselves from different angles. While others said that understanding users' needs through IoT wearable technologies is a tricky issue, because it is often used to serve the purpose of companies that own the IoT wearable technologies rather than meeting the core needs of end-users.

According to the pre-survey result (Fig. 3), expert interviewees hoped that IoT wearable technologies could make life convenient (75.9%), which echoed by some of the experts' responses: "When I choose IoT products, I consider three aspects: (1) efficiency—it can make my life convenient; (2) the pace of my life—It can help me control my life pace; (3) cost—this is the least critical one since every product has its price.", "I want every smart IoT device in my home to be seamlessly connected and they can have the conversation so that I don't even need to bring and use my phone at home.", and "IoT products can easily predict people's daily behavior, move, and trajectory, but it's hard to read what's on people's minds. The time of "I know what you think" is yet to come." In the interviews, it was revealed that the experts' interpretation of convenience included offering customized services based on an understanding of user habits, daily rituals, and individual needs.

Since we didn't specifically mention the aging population as our target user in the pre-survey, the result of Fig. 3 reflects more about the needs of the general public through the lens of the experts. For further study, we can define the aging population as the target users and make a comparison with diagram 2 result to probe into what are the goals and requirements that the aging population want to achieve according to their core needs.

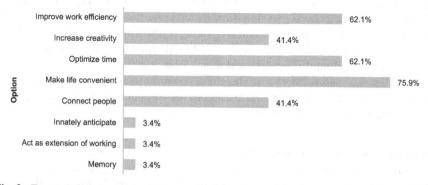

Fig. 3. Experts' choices on what IoT wearable technology may help users with (n = 31, multiple selections)

3.2   Data

Data issues were frequently highlighted during the expert interviews, as much of the related literature indicated that disclosure of data collection, data interpretation, and cybersecurity is significant for keeping personal information private and consent. Among all the topics we looked up from the interviews, the most commented are using data as design research tools, concerns on data privacy, proper usage of data, ethical considerations, and the waste of data were among the most heavily discussed. The following part shows the three key dimensions of using and deploying data in the process of designing and developing IoT wearable technologies: (1) leverage data in the iterative design process properly; (2) consider personal data privacy and security; (3) enhance users' data awareness.

Leverage Data in the Iterative Design Process Properly. "The more we can understand all aspects of data and all the various touchpoints, the more that we can develop systems and opportunities for greater and more ethical products," emphasized an expert from the design industry. On the one hand, data collected through IoT wearable technologies serve as sources for ubiquitous and context-aware computing [17], on the other hand, it also contributes to the iterative design process for enhancing the experiences of users (e.g. aging population) and understanding their needs. However, in the process of leveraging data for research purposes, it is critical to consider secondary data distribution and privacy issues for individual users.

As discussed by an expert in the interview, data is "an essential ingredient for intelligence, but hard to trust that it's handled responsibly," indicating concerns users' trust and awareness of data collecting during the use of IoT wearable technologies. Thus, it is worth emphasizing and being mindful of creating a transparent data-processing mechanism, designing an interpretable process, and conceiving an understandable and user-friendly interface for delivering data usage information as well as building trust between IoT wearable technologies and users.

Consider Personal Data Privacy and Security. According to the pre-survey results (Fig. 4), experts were divided in their degrees of comfort with having data collected through IoT wearable technologies stored and shared in the cloud. Only 13.8% of experts indicated that they feel comfortable and are willing to share and store their data on the cloud via IoT wearable technologies. Synthesized from expert interview outcomes, most IoT wearable technologies need data and inputs from users to understand behaviors, routines, lifestyles, and preferences. Therefore, capturing user data in an ethical and transparent way, and utilizing non-invasive and secure ways of collecting and using data are becoming increasingly important.

Enhance Users' Data Awareness. "Due to the enormity of this issue, we need to learn better ways to collect and extract data that will enable us to develop greater rubrics and or opportunities to identify problems that need to be solved that would not fall into the same category as what marketing entities call innovation," said one expert. Data awareness has been discussed by nearly one-third of the experts. Helping users to better understand the use of data, including questions about what types of data will be captured, where

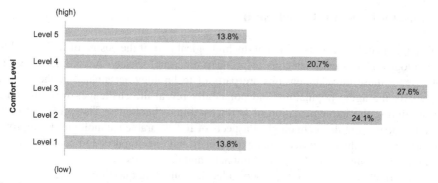

Fig. 4. The result of the experts' comfortable level for data to be shared and stored on the cloud through IoT wearable technologies (n = 31)

the data will go, if the data will be further distributed, if their data is treated securely, as well as data ethical issues are all crucial in the design of IoT wearable technologies, especially for the aging population. "Data should be used in a more human-centered way, and not make users think they are tracked or their data is collected for the business purpose". It is significant to design and deploy user-friendly ways of informing the usage and distribution of data to ensure user's right to know where their data will go and how it will be used.

4 Society

Inclusiveness of Product Features. As shown earlier in Fig. 3, when asked to indicate the ways in which the experts think IoT wearable technologies can help them achieve in life, the top choices were to make life convenient (75.9%), to improve work efficiency (62.1%), and to optimize time (62.1%), which are all connected to the functional aspects of IoT wearable technologies. In the interviews, experts discussed that using IoT wearable technologies can streamline people's work and life in terms of convenience, efficiency, and optimization. Whereas the emotional side such as users' feeling, a feature of inclusiveness of product for the aging population is lacking, which experts were also emphasized less.

Design for Sustainability. Applying a human-centered approach needs to not only consider the lens of users but also design IoT wearable technologies in the context of the industry. One expert who's a design entrepreneur shares his view that "Every time I will consider the consequences if I need to create a new IoT device. We need to think about the issue in the context of the global environment since we only have one earth." Currently, most IoT wearable technologies design is based on its platform/system different from brands to brands. As for designers, when we create a new type of IoT wearable technologies for the aging population, we need to consider its product lifecycle and eco-system in order to make not only the business but also the environment sustainable.

5   Discussions and Conclusion

This paper mainly focuses on the non-technological part of the design of IoT wearable technologies from the dimensions of product, data, and society. According to expert interviews, these three dimensions are parts of technology acceptance of the public, especially the aging population, and potentially reveal the challenges we will come across during the implementation of IoT wearable technologies. Thus, it is not only vital to know about the technological aspects of IoT wearable technologies to improve the design of products, services, and experiences, but also important to consider issues related to individuals' needs, societal impacts, and data ethics.

For further study, we want to re-consider the following questions in the process of conducting interviews: How do people use IoT wearable technologies to increase the interaction among people? How do users such as the aging population feel being cared for with the help of IoT wearable technologies? How do we value the design team's role and responsibilities while creating human-centered IoT wearable technologies for people and with people? For the next generation of IoT wearable technologies design, it helps the design team think comprehensively in planning, designing, executing, and refining in regard to target users, especially for the aging population.

Future research can apply the result of this study as fundamental resource and conduct more expert interviews targeted to specific fields with our interview flow (Fig. 2). Also, the methodology can be applied to interviewing potential end users' interviews to get more practical insights and perspectives toward IoT wearable technologies. From the practice perspective, the study can be interpreted from three angles: (1) the results can serve as a checklist for the IoT wearable technology design team, including designers, developers, and engineers to consider the non-technological and human-centered aspects; (2) the results related to data privacy, security and societal implications can serve as resources for policymakers and regulatory bodies to set up ethical standards around the collection and use of data; and (3) the results can be utilized by generally target users (e.g. aging population) to evaluate the positive and negative impacts of IoT wearable technologies on their life.

Since IoT wearable technologies consist of a relatively wide range of products, service, and techniques as well as methodologies, future research can take a more comprehensive approach to address dimensions and aspects of IoT wearable technologies design. A possible approach is to invite experienced industry experts from diverse fields and target discussions in specific domains, such as wearable devices to enhance aging population well-being or wearable products for communication. Moreover, interviews and surveys with a larger group of diverse stakeholders, including end users, need to be conducted to incorporate different perspectives and voices into the research process and obtain deeper insights into IoT wearable technologies design and application.

Acknowledgement. The authors appreciate all the invited experts who shared their invaluable experiences, meaningful ideas, and constructive suggestions, as well as support provided by the MIT AgeLab and the MIT Senseable City Lab.

References

1. Lee, I., Lee, K.: The Internet of Things (IoT): applications, investments, and challenges for enterprises. Bus. Horiz. **58**, 431–440 (2015). https://doi.org/10.1016/j.bushor.2015.03.008
2. Çiçek, M.: Wearable technologies and its future applications. Int. J. Electr. Electron. Data Commun. **3**, 2320–2084 (2015)
3. Wiles, J.L., Leibing, A., Guberman, N., et al.: The meaning of "aging in place" to older people. Gerontologist **52**, 357–366 (2012). https://doi.org/10.1093/geront/gnr098
4. PeerCare: Supporting Awareness of Rhythms and Routines for Better Aging in Place | SpringerLink. https://link.springer.com/article/10.1007/s10606-009-9105-z. Accessed 26 Jan 2021
5. Google PAIR AI+Design tool. https://pair.withgoogle.com. Accessed 17 Nov 2020
6. Healy, B., Fulton Suri, J., Freaner, J., et al.: IDEO AI Ethics Cards (2019)
7. Gispen, J.: Ethics for Designers. In: Ethics for Designers (2017). https://www.ethicsfordesigners.com. Accessed 26 Nov 2020
8. Sewell, M.: The Use of Qualitative Interviews in Evaluation. https://cals.arizona.edu/sfcs/cyfernet/cyfar/Intervu5.htm. Accessed 31 Jan 2021
9. Expert Interviews for Qualitative Data Generation. https://ecpr.eu/Events/Event/PanelDetails/4920. Accessed 1 Feb 2021
10. Ethics of Wearables: Health Data and Wellness Technology. In: UIC Online Health Informatics (2020). https://healthinformatics.uic.edu/blog/ethics-of-wearables/. Accessed 2 Feb 2021
11. Bogner, A., Littig, B., Menz, W.: Interviewing Experts. Palgrave Macmillan, London (2009)
12. White, G.: Towards wearable aging in place devices. In: Proceedings of the 7th International Conference on Tangible, Embedded and Embodied Interaction, pp. 375–376. Association for Computing Machinery, New York (2013)
13. Lee, C., Ward, C., Ellis, D., Brady, S., D'Ambrosio, L., Coughlin, J.F.: Technology and service usage among family caregivers. In: Zhou, J., Salvendy, G. (eds) Human Aspects of IT for the Aged Population. Applications, Services and Contexts, pp. 420–432. Springer, Cham (2017). https://doi.org/10.1007/978-3-319-58536-9_33. Accessed 3 Feb 2021
14. Shilton, K., Porter, A., Winter, S., Heidenblad, D.: Finding Practices that Cultivate Ethical Computing in Mobile and Wearable Application Research and Design - Privacy by Design Card Game (2014)
15. Habibipour, A., Padyab, A., Ståhlbröst, Å.: A social, ethical and ecological issues in wearable technologies, p. 10 (2019)
16. Radin, J.M., Wineinger, N.E., Topol, E.J., Steinhubl, S.R.: Harnessing wearable device data to improve state-level real-time surveillance of influenza-like illness in the USA: a population-based study. Lancet Digital Health **2**, e85–e93 (2020). https://doi.org/10.1016/S2589-7500(19)30222-5
17. Casale, P., Pujol, O., Radeva, P.: Human Activity Recognition from Accelerometer Data Using a Wearable Device (2011)
18. Lapan, S.D., Quartaroli, M.T., Riemer, F.J.: Qualitative Research: An Introduction to Methods and Designs. Wiley, Hoboken (2011)
19. Döringer, S.: 'The problem-centred expert interview'. Combining qualitative interviewing approaches for investigating implicit expert knowledge. Int. J. Soc. Res. Methodol. 1–14 (2020). https://doi.org/10.1080/13645579.2020.1766777
20. Bogner, A., Littig, B., Menz, W.: Introduction: Expert Interviews - An Introduction to a New Methodological Debate, pp. 1–13 (2009)
21. Van Audenhove, L.: Expert Interviews and Interview Techniques for Policy Analysis (2011)
22. Edwards, R., Holland, J.: What is Qualitative Interviewing? A&C Black (2013)
23. IDEO: The Field Guide to Human-Centered Design: Design Kit, 1st edn. IDEO, San Francisco (2015)

Towards Representation of Daily Living Activities by Reusing ICF Categories

Satoshi Nishimura$^{(\boxtimes)}$ (iD) and Ken Fukuda (iD)

National Institute of Advanced Industrial Science and Technology (AIST), Tokyo, Japan
satoshi.nishimura@aist.go.jp

Abstract. The study of commonsense reasoning and robotic agents in home environments is trending considering artificial intelligence. Handling the contexts of human daily living is crucial for the system to achieve, for example, the detection of risky situations in a care facility and long-term natural dialogue with other individuals. This study aims to construct an ontology to represent daily living activities by reusing the International Classification of Functioning, Disability and Health (ICF) categories. We extracted relevant categories from the ICF, introduced new classes, and defined an "is-a" hierarchy to provide a common vocabulary for the annotation of the context of multiple sensor data obtained in home environments. As a result, the constructed ontology consists of 284 classes. The evaluation of its coverage is performed using the following two resources related to commonsense reasoning: ATlas Of MachIne Commonsense (ATOMIC) and STAIR Actions captions. We sampled 100 sentences from each resource and described the context of the samples using the constructed ontology, which resulted in 63% and 84% of each sample being covered by our ontology. This demonstrates that our ontology has the competency to describe the context in a daily living environment. In addition, we found the types of contexts that are lacking in the ontology via the evaluation.

Keywords: Daily living activities · Ontology · International classification of functioning · Disability and health

1 Introduction

Daily living activity is recorded for various purposes, such as evaluating the changes in an individual's daily activity over time, comparison of daily activities among multiple individuals [2, 6], detection of risky-situation, and providing reminders to individuals with memory problems in a smart home [9, 10]. In any case, controlled vocabulary is beneficial to describe the interpretation of sensing data consistently. In a previous study [10], vocabulary to describe daily living activities was developed as an ontology, but its common vocabulary remains limited.

The International Classification of Functioning, Disability, and Health (ICF) [20] is one of the well-known vocabularies available that includes the terms for describing human activities. The ICF divides the concepts related to human health and health-related

© Springer Nature Switzerland AG 2021
Q. Gao and J. Zhou (Eds.): HCII 2021, LNCS 12787, pp. 438–450, 2021.
https://doi.org/10.1007/978-3-030-78111-8_30

states into the following four major categories: "Body functions", "Body structures", "Activities and participation", and "Environmental factors". It was designed to provide a common vocabulary to improve communication between different domains, such as clinical practitioners, co-medical staff, care managers, etc.

While the ICF provides a comprehensive vocabulary for daily living activities, it does not suffice for an ontology. Kumar and Smith indicated seven shortcomings of the ICF, such as incongruent classification, confusion between classes of activities and their qualities or features, and over-emphasis on subsumption [7]. The first shortcoming is due to the fact that the ICF does not provide clear criteria for classification. The second and third shortcomings are due to the fact that the ICF does not distinct the relationships with "is-a" relationship and others such as "has-quality" relationship. These shortcomings cause inconsistent annotation or misuse of the term to describe daily living activities.

We aim to construct a comprehensive vocabulary to describe daily living activities by reusing the ICF categories. First, in Sect. 2 we present related work involving a knowledge graph for commonsense reasoning and cognitive robotics in a home environment to review the knowledge resources related to daily living. Second, we provide the notion to reuse the categories in ICF in Sect. 3. Based on the notion, we constructed the ontology including the description of major concepts in Sect. 4. We evaluated the coverage of the ontology using two commonsense knowledge resources. We also used the constructed ontology for annotating one video file to verify its coverage. Sections 5 and 6 provide the discussion of the evaluation and conclusion of this study.

2   Related Work

Sap et al. proposes the Atlas Of MachIne Commonsense (ATOMIC) as a dataset for commonsense reasoning [13]. Each record of this dataset has one central sentence to represent an event, such as "PersonX repels PersonY attack." The event sentence has nine properties that describe the past and future of the event, such as "because X wanted to", "before, X needed to", "attributes of X", "as a result, X wants", "as a result, X feels", "has an effect on X", "as a result, Y feels", "as a result, Y wants", and "has an effect on Y". Each value of the properties is annotated as natural language text by three crowd workers. As a result, they have 877,108 if-event-then triples and 245,905 base events. After training a model using the dataset, they can infer the unseen events in the dataset.

Tandon et al. developed WebChild 2.0 [16], which is a large and fine-grained commonsense knowledge base that can disambiguate terms, such as "hot" in the sense of temperature or being trendy. They proposed a method to generate the knowledge base to make property semantics clear, extract comparative properties (such as smaller than), make part-whole relationships detailed, and extract knowledge of activities. As a result, the WebChild 2.0 contains over 2 million concepts and activities, connected by over 18 million assertions.

For caption generation, Yoshikawa et al. provided STAIR Actions as a video dataset for human action recognition in the home environment [21]. It contains 109,478 video clips with activity labels. In addition, STAIR Actions captions [14] is a caption dataset adherent to the STAIR Actions and contains 399,233 captions for 79,922 video clips in STAIR Actions. The caption describes an action that occurred in a video clip and consists of the following three properties: a person performing the action, place where the action occurred, and the action itself. Each value of the property is described in natural language in Japanese.

Efforts were made to handle daily living activities in the robotics and simulation domain. Everyday Activity Science and Engineering (EASE) is a collaborative research center led by the University of Bremen [4], which aims to enable robots to perform everyday activities, such as preparing a meal, doing laundry, and moving in complex situations in a home environment while cooperating with people. Kümpel et al. [8] proposed an ontology to provide linkage between household objects and activities related to the objects under the EASE project, which aims to infer the appropriate activities of robotic agents in a specific situation. They developed an ontology of products including barcodes that contain the European Article Number to identify an object type. They also generated linkages from the object type to the entity in Wikidata. The Wikidata dataset provides the property of the related activity to the object. In the end, their ontology can provide the object and related activities.

VirtualHome is a multi-agent platform to simulate activities in a household environment [18]. Vassiliades et al. [17] proposed a knowledge retrieval framework by extracting the VirtualHome dataset. They aimed to determine how the robotic system should behave towards a household object. Their proposed framework helps retrieve the object information by using external knowledge bases, such as DBpedia [1], ConceptNet [15], and WordNet [11]. Their evaluation demonstrated that the answer of the framework satisfied a large percentage of the subjects.

3   Construction of Ontology

We reuse the ICF categories to obtain a comprehensive vocabulary to describe daily living activities. First, we reviewed all subcategories of "Activities and participation" in the ICF. After the review, we extracted categories that are relevant to representing daily living activities. We constructed an "is-a" hierarchy of the extracted categories by comparing similar categories, removing the inadequate categories, and adding abstract concepts.

3.1   Reused Categories

The ICF divides the concepts related to human health and health-related states into the following four major categories: "Body functions", "Body structures", "Activities and participation", and "Environmental factors." Among the four categories, we reused "Activities and participation" for describing daily living activities and reviewed its subcategories. During the process, we chose not to include the categories including "other specified XX" or "unspecified XX", such as "Acquisition of goods and services, other specified." For instance, this category has "Shopping" and "Gathering daily necessities" as its co-hyponym in the ICF hierarchy. According to the definition of "Gathering daily necessities," the classification criterion of these two categories determines whether to obtain goods or services by exchanging with money. This criterion is logically disjoint;

therefore, we do not import the category "Acquisition of goods and services, other specified." Furthermore, we do not import concepts that do not represent activities, such as "Human right."

3.2 Construction of is-a Hierarchy

After extracting the categories, we specified each extracted category and their definitions, which are provided in the natural language. They were then manually compared and abstract categories were created to organize similar concepts. We referred to the original hierarchy and concepts in the same level that are arranged in a manner that they disjoint each other, and their abstractions are at the same degree. Abstract concepts were added when the degree of abstraction was different. For instance, there is a category named "d335. Producing nonverbal messages" in the ICF. However, there is no category to represent the opposing concept with the same abstraction level. Therefore, we added a class "Producing verbal messages" and classified the other three categories, that is, "d330. Speaking," and is placed in the same level as "d335. Producing nonverbal messages."

4   Result

4.1   Overview

Figure 1 presents the first level classification of daily living activities. The ontology is composed of 284 concepts. We extracted 226 concepts from the ICF categories. We created 58 additional new classes to describe the abstract concept to classify the terms in the ICF.

4.2   Detail

Sixteen major classes were categorized according to the similarities and differences in the ICF. The description of each class is defined as follows:

- Acquiring goods or services.
  This class denotes the activity of acquiring goods or services regardless of the means, such as buying, gathering, and renting. Its subclasses are divided by criteria based on how the items are acquired and whether these items are a daily living necessity.
- Caring.
  This class denotes the activity of a person taking care of something. The criteria of diving the subclasses aim to determine whether a person is taking care of oneself or others. Most of the housework, such as preparing a meal, eating, drinking, and toileting, are subsumed under this class.
- Changing and maintaining body position.
  This class denotes an activity of a person changing or maintaining a body position. This class was created to represent an abstract class of the ICF categories, "d410. Changing basic body position" and "d415. Maintaining a body position."

- Communicating.
  This class denotes an activity of a person communicating with others. It is classified into "conversation," "discussion," "producing communication," and "receiving communication," according to the classification of the ICF categories.
- Creating or maintaining relationship.
  This class denotes an activity involving a person creating or maintaining a relationship with others, such as "creating relationships with employers," "maintaining relationships with cousins," and "creating relationships with strangers," when asking a direction. It is mainly classified by two criteria, indicating whether the relationship is created or maintained and lasting or temporal. A more detailed classification is based on the types of opponents with whom one relates.
- Having leisure.
  This class denotes an activity of a person experiencing leisure, such as "playing a game," "playing soccer," "playing guitar," "painting," and "collecting stamps".
- Interacting.
  This class denotes an activity of a person interacting with others. It includes an activity on how to express one's thoughts and a general activity, such as interacting according to social rules.
- Learning.
  This class denotes an activity related to learning. It includes an activity of detailed learning techniques, such as "copying" and "rehearsing," and a coarse-grained activity, such as "acquiring skills."
- Maintaining asset.
  This class denotes an activity of a person maintaining assets. It subsumes only "economic self-sufficiency" that is extracted from ICF categories in the current ontology.
- Moving.
  This class denotes an activity related to moving. The criterion of classification determines whether the moving target is oneself or others. After this classification, there is more fine-grained classification according to the distance of moving, such as "walking short distance" and the manner in which one moves, such as "walking" and "using transportation."
- Participating community.
  This class denotes an activity of a person participating in a community, which includes informational, formal, ceremonies, socializing, and political and religious communities. In the ICF categories, political and religious communities are classified into individual categories. However, we unite these concepts into the same class in this ontology. That is, we focus on classifying the activity required to participate in the communities rather than the types of community.
- Transacting.
  This class denotes an activity related to an economic transaction. It specifies basic and complex economic transactions according to the ICF categories.
- Using devices.
  This class denotes an activity of a person using devices and does not specify the objective of using them. It specifies the activity by the device that is used, such as communication devices, transportation devices, and household appliances. A few of the classes are also located under the other major classes.

- Using mental functions.
  This class denotes an activity of a person using mental functions, such as "thinking," "calculating," and "making decisions." This class represents fine-grained actions rather than the context of daily living activity.
- Using sensory functions.
  This class denotes an activity of a person using sensory functions, such as "watching" and "listening." The granularity of this class is similar to that of the class "using mental functions."
- Work related activity.
  This class denotes an activity related to working. It includes activities related to remunerative and non-remunerative employment. It also covers the steps of working including preparation, seeking, maintaining, and termination of a job.

Fig. 1. First level classification of daily living activity

4.3   Coverage Evaluation

We evaluated the coverage of our ontology by applying it to two datasets, as indicated in Sect. 2. The ATOMIC [13] and STAIR Actions captions [14] are used in the evaluation. We also applied our ontology to a video archive called the Elderly Behavior Library [12] for annotating the actions performed in the video data.

Comparison with ATOMIC

As indicated in Sect. 2, the ATOMIC contains the "if-then" information centered on an event. The event information is provided in one sentence, such as "PersonX takes the ferry." We randomly sampled 100 events from the ATOMIC dataset. We selected one class from the constructed ontology to represent the context of each sampled event. If a relevant class was found in the ontology, it was determined to cover the context of the sampled event. For instance, we selected "d470. Using transportation" as a context of the event "PersonX takes the ferry."

As a result, 63 events are represented by our ontology. Table 1 presents a list of classes that we used and their frequency. The classes labeled with "d" and the digits are the reused categories from ICF. The following are examples of the ontology covering the context in the form of "event text; class": "PersonX asks ___ for a recommendation; d330. Speaking," "PersonX drives home from work one ___; d475. Driving," "PersonX is trying to lose weight; d570: Looking after one's health." The "___" symbol in the text denotes a placeholder of any type of operand. On the other hand, the following are examples of the ontology not being able to cover the context: "PersonX feels very depressed," and "PersonX looks stupid."

Comparison with STAIR Actions Captions.

We conducted the same coverage evaluation on the STAIR Actions captions dataset. As indicated in Sect. 2, the dataset provides information regarding a person, place, and action in a short sentence to describe each video data. We sampled 100 sentences of the action and evaluated the coverage of our ontology to determine whether it represents the context of the sentence. For instance, we selected the class "d9201. Sports" as a context of the sentence "腹筋をしている" (He is doing sit-ups.).

As a result, 84 sentences are represented by our ontology. In this dataset, a few of the action sentences contain multiple contexts. Therefore, we determined that our ontology can represent the context of the sentence if all of the contexts can be represented. For instance, the sentence "カゴの中で寝転んで泣いている" ((A baby) is lying down in the basket and crying) contains two contexts, including "lying down" and "crying." Our ontology has a class to represent "lying down," but does not have a class to represent "crying"; therefore, this case cannot be represented by our ontology. Table 2 presents a list of classes that we used and their frequency.

The following are examples of the ontology covering the context in the form of "action text (English translation); class": "椅子に座って、雑誌を読んでいる ((A person) sits on a chair and read a magazine.); d4103. Sitting and d166: Reading", "ギターを弾いている ((A person) plays the guitar.); d9202. Arts and culture", and "椅子に座りドライヤを髪にあてている ((A person) sits on a chair and dries his hair with the dryer.); d4103. Sitting and d5202. Caring for hair". On the other hand, the following

Table 1. List of classes and frequencies to represent 100 samples in the ATOMIC

Class	Frequency	Class	Frequency
Caring_other	3	d170. Writing	1
Caring_things_ other_than_person	2	d330. Speaking	1
Communicating	2	d335. Producing nonverbal messages	1
Creating_relationship	1	d350. Conversation	1
Educate_other	2	d4103. Sitting	1
Having_leisure	3	d445. Hand and arm use	1
Interacting	5	d470. Using transportation	1
Learning	1	d475. Driving	1
Learning_to_solve_problems	1	d550. Eating	1
Moving_oneself	5	d570. Looking after one's health	1
Moving_other	6	d630. Preparing meals	1
Producing_communication	4	d650. Caring for household objects	1
Using_sensory_functions	1	d7100. Respect and warmth in relationships	2
Work_related_activity	2	d7101. Appreciation in relationships	1
d110. Watching	4	d7103. Criticism in relationships	1
d115. Listening	1	d810-d839. Education	1
d163. Thinking	1	d845. Acquiring, keeping and terminating a job	2

are examples of the ontology not covering the context: "地面に腕をついている ((A person) places his hands on the ground)", "黒い服を着た男性の手を殴っている ((A person) hits hands of a man who wears a black shirt)" and "カゴの中で寝転んで泣いている ((A baby) is lying down in the basket and crying)".

Annotating a Video in the Elderly Behavior Library

We used the constructed ontology to annotate daily living activities for the video retrieved from the Elderly Behavior Library [12], which is a video archive of older people living in care facilities and houses. The library was developed for business use in the manufacturing industry related to home appliances, especially to develop safe products. The library contains 2,243 videos that are manually annotated with 136 tags from 14 categories. We used a video from the library that displays a scene of two caregivers supporting a care receiver's move from the toilet to a chair. It was 1.1 min long with a rate of 30

Table 2. List of classes and frequencies to represent 100 samples in STAIR Actions captions

Class	Frequency	Class	Frequency
Having_leisure	3	d4701. Using private motorized transportation	1
Moving_oneself	1	d5201. Caring for teeth	2
Using_devices	5	d5202. Caring for hair	3
d166. Reading	2	d5203. Caring for fingernails	2
d170. Writing	2	d5204. Caring for toenails	1
d3350. Producing body language	4	d5400. Putting on clothes	10
d350. Conversation	9	d5401. Taking off clothes	3
d4100. Lying down	2	d5402. Putting on footwear	1
d4103. Sitting	10	d550. Eating	2
d4104. Standing	7	d560. Drinking	1
d4300. Lifting	1	d6300. Preparing simple meals	1
d440. Fine hand use	1	d6400. Washing and drying clothes and garments	2
d4401. Grasping	1	d6401. Cleaning cooking area and utensils	1
d445. Hand and arm use	1	d650. Caring for household objects	1
d4454. Throwing	1	d6506. Taking care of animals	1
d4550. Crawling	1	d6600. Assisting others with self-care	10
d4551. Climbing	1	d9200. Play	5
d460. Moving around in different locations	1	d9201. Sports	2
d465. Moving around using equipment	2	d9202. Arts and culture	10
d4700. Using human-powered vehicles	1	d9204. Hobbies	1

frames/second. One caregiver (caregiver 1 hereafter) mainly supports the care receiver in walking by holding his/her body. We annotated the actions of the caregivers and the care receiver by using ELAN [3], which is a community standard tool for video and dialogue annotation. Figure 2 presents an example of the annotation in ELAN. The annotator presented the actions in the tiers at the bottom of the video, as shown in the upper right. Each annotation contains information regarding the individual performing an action, in addition to the type of action performed as well as to what/whom during a specific time slot. Details regarding the notation are presented in our previous study [19].

As a result, we annotated 15 actions throughout 10 tiers and used 6 types of actions from the ontology: d110. watching, d4154. maintaining a standing position, d4451. pushing, d4455. catching, d4503. walking around obstacles, d4508. walking, others specified, d4601. moving within buildings other than home.

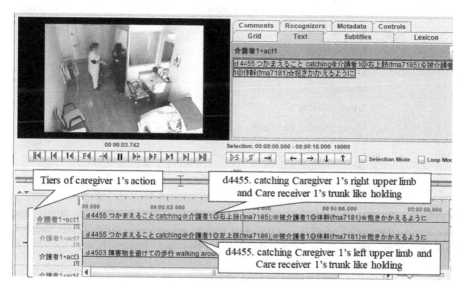

Fig. 2. Example of annotation by using ELAN tool

5   Discussion

5.1   Abstraction Competency

In this section, we discuss the abstraction competency of our ontology and the coverage of the used dataset considering daily living activities. We abstracted the used classes in the evaluation and aggregated them into the "major class," as indicated in Sect. 3. Tables 3 and 4 present the list of the major classes and their frequency in the coverage evaluation with the ATOMIC dataset and STAIR Actions captions dataset, respectively.

The ATOMIC dataset covers 12 classes of the 16 major classes in our ontology. The results show that events related to "Moving" and "Caring" occurred in the dataset. On the other hand, "Acquiring goods or services," "Maintaining asset," "Participating community," and "Transacting" did not occur in the dataset. These activities tend to be intangible, thus may less frequently occur in the dataset.

The STAIR Action captions dataset covers 7 classes of the 16 major classes in our ontology. The results show that the action data related to "Caring" and "Having leisure" occur frequently compared to other activities. There are no classes related to "Creating

Table 3. List of DLE major classes and frequencies for representing ATOMIC samples

Major class	Frequency
Caring	12
Changing_and_maintaining_body_position	1
Communicating	9
Creating_or_maintaining_relationship	1
Having_leisure	3
Interacting	9
Learning	2
Moving	14
Using_devices	3
Using_mental_functions	2
Using_sensory_functions	6
Work_related_activity	4

or maintaining relationship," "Interaction," "Learning," "Using sensory functions," and "Work related activity," other than the classes that do not appear in the ATOMIC dataset. This dataset is connected to a video dataset, which causes intangible activities not to occur in the dataset.

5.2   Remaining Issues

Table 4. List of DLE major classes and frequencies for representing STAIR Actions captions samples

Major class	Frequency
Caring	41
Changing_and_maintaining_body_position	19
Communicating	13
Having_leisure	21
Moving	13
Using_devices	5
Using_mental_functions	4

Regarding the remaining issues of this study, we should consider the distribution of the sampled data in the daily life domain. We conducted coverage evaluation using random sampling. However, the question of how the sampled dataset from the resource and the original resource covers the daily life domain remains inconclusive. As indicated in Section 5.1, the STAIR Actions captions lack 9 types of contexts that are contained in our ontology. We consider that the cause is derived from the objective of the dataset. STAIR Actions captions are developed for describing the actions that occurred in the video dataset. The video dataset aims to cover activities in the daily life domain; however, it is difficult for a short video to describe intangible activities, such as participating in a community. On the other hand, the ATOMIC dataset consists of natural language sentences without a connection to any video datasets. We consider that this small restriction causes high expressiveness; the results show that the ATOMIC dataset covers 12 contexts, as indicated in Section 5.1. We note that our ontology does not cover all the contexts in daily life and improving it comprehensiveness is an ongoing challenge. We also plan to apply this ontology to annotate daily living activity for the indexing of video archives [5] as part of our future work. Our ontology can be used in the task of video retrieval. The ontology provides the subsumption hierarchy with other relationships, such as "part-of" to describe detailed activities. The user can retrieve the video by using these transitive relations. The structural information will be encoded using graph embedding to improve the performance of information retrieval.

6 Conclusion

This study takes the first step in constructing the ontology to represent the context of daily living. The expected contribution of this work is to provide a common and comprehensive vocabulary to annotate the context of daily living activities. We constructed the ontology by reusing the ICF categories related to "Activity and participation." We included 226 categories from the ICF, and the resulting ontology contains 284 classes. The coverage of the ontology was evaluated by annotating two commonsense knowledge resources: ATOMIC and STAIR Actions captions. We sampled 100 sentences from each knowledge resource and attempted to represent their context using our ontology. As a result, we found 63 and 84% of each sample is covered by our ontology. We also discussed the coverage of the extracted samples using the major classes of our ontology and determined that these resources do not cover intangible concepts, such as "Participating community." The ontology was also used for the annotation of a video file that shows the activity in a care facility. Future work will concentrate on extending this annotation to additional videos for indexing video archives [5].

Acknowledgment. This paper is based on results obtained from a project, JPNP20006, commissioned by the New Energy and Industrial Technology Development Organization (NEDO).

References

1. Bizer, C., et al.: Dbpedia - a crystallization point for the web of data. J. Web Seman. **7**(3), 154–165 (2009)
2. Bolger, N., Davis, A., Rafaeli, E.: Diary methods: capturing life as it is lived. Ann. Rev. Psychol. **54**(1), 579–616 (2003)

3. Brugman, H., Russel, A.: Annotating multi-media/multi-modal resources with ELAN. In: Proceedings of the Fourth International Conference on Language Resources and Evaluation (LREC 2004). European Language Resources Association (ELRA), Lisbon, Portugal (2004)
4. Everyday activity science and engineering. https://ease-crc.org/
5. Fukuda, K., Vizcarra, J., Nishimura, S.: Massive semantic video annotation in high-end customer service. In: Nah, F.-H., Siau, K. (eds.) HCII 2020. LNCS, vol. 12204, pp. 46–58. Springer, Cham (2020). https://doi.org/10.1007/978-3-030-50341-3_4
6. Gurrin, C., Smeaton, A.F., Doherty, A.R.: Lifelogging: personal big data. Found. Trends Inf. Retr. 8(1), 1–125 (2014)
7. Kumar, A., Smith, B.: The ontology of processes and functions: a study of the international classification of functioning, disability and health. In: Proceedings of the AIME 2005 Workshop on Biomedical Ontology Engineering, Aberdeen, Scotland (2005)
8. Kumpel, M., de Groot, A., Tiddi, I., Beetz, M.: Using linked data to help robots understand product-related actions. In: Hammar, K., Kutz, O., Dimou, A., Hahmann, T., Hoehndorf, R., Masolo, C., Vita, R. (eds.) JOWO 2020 The Joint Ontology Workshops. CEUR Workshop Proceedings, CEUR-WS.org (2020)
9. Martinez-Santiago, F., Garcia-Viedma, M.R., Williams, J.A., Slater, L.T., Gkoutos, G.V.: Aging neuro-behavior ontology. Appl. Ontol. 15, 219–239 (2020)
10. Meditskos, G., Kompatsiaris, I.: iKnow: Ontology-driven situational awareness for the recognition of activities of daily living. Pervasive Mob. Comput. 40, 17–41 (2017)
11. Miller, G.A.: WordNet: An electronic lexical database. MIT press (1998)
12. National Institute of Advanced Industrial Science and Technology: Elderly behavior library. http://www.behavior-library-meti.com/behaviorLib/homes/about (2017)
13. Sap, M., et al.: ATOMIC: an atlas of machine commonsense for if-then reasoning. In: The Thirty-Third AAAI Conference on Artificial Intelligence. pp. 3027–3035. AAAI Press (2019)
14. Shigeto, Y., Yoshikawa, Y., Lin, J., Takeuchi, A.: Video caption dataset for describing human actions in Japanese. In: Proceedings of the 12th Language Resources and Evaluation Conference. pp. 4664–4670. European Language Resources Association, Marseille, France (2020)
15. Speer, R., Chin, J., Havasi, C.: Conceptnet 5.5: an open multilingual graph of general knowledge. In: The Thirty-First AAAI Conference on Artificial Intelligence. pp. 4444–4451 (2017)
16. Tandon, N., de Melo, G., Weikum, G.: WebChild 2.0: Fine-grained commonsense knowledge distillation. In: Proceedings of ACL 2017, System Demonstrations. pp. 115–120. Association for Computational Linguistics, Vancouver, Canada (2017)
17. Vassiliades, A., Bassiliades, N., Gouidis, F., Patkos, T.: A Knowledge Retrieval Framework for Household Objects and Actions with External Knowledge. In: Blomqvist, E., et al. (eds.) SEMANTICS 2020. LNCS, vol. 12378, pp. 36–52. Springer, Cham (2020). https://doi.org/10.1007/978-3-030-59833-4_3
18. VirtualHome. http://virtual-home.org/
19. Vizcarra, J., Nishimura, S., Fukuda, K.: Ontology-based human behavior indexing with multimodal video data. In: IEEE 15th International Conference on Semantic Computing (ICSC), p. 6 (2021)
20. World Health Organization: ICF: International classification of functioning, disability and health (2001)
21. Yoshikawa, Y., Lin, J., Takeuchi, A.: Stair actions: a video dataset of everyday home actions. arXiv preprint arXiv:1804.04326 (2018)

COVID-19 Impact of Virtual Communication During Social Isolation on Bulgarian Society

Lilia Raycheva$^{(\boxtimes)}$ ⓘ, Nadezhda Miteva, Neli Velinova, and Mariyan Tomov

The St. Kliment Ohridski Sofia University, Sofia, Bulgaria
lraycheva@yahoo.com

Abstract. The topic of virtual communication in the context of social isolation during the spread of the new corona virus strain (SARS-CoV-2) and its associated disease COVID-19 is an extremely important scientific problem with paradigmatic dimensions and fundamental consequences for society. As a technologically mediated way of communication, it proved that during a pandemic, the virtual communication is the only alternative to traditional face-to-face communication, and its use was inevitable to partially or completely overcome the social restrictions imposed. In order to examine some of the effects of the virtual communication during the social isolation in Bulgaria, an academic research team from the Faculty of Journalism and Mass Communication at The St. Kliment Ohridsky Sofia University undertook a study in the declared two month's period (13.03.–13.05.2020) of the state of national emergency in the country. The researchers conducted a three-folded study: on the sociological polls and the media coverage during the pandemics; on the activities of the telecommunication industry; and on the impacts of virtual communication during the social isolation, using mixed methodology: quantitative and qualitative survey with three groups of respondents: media users, media professionals and media experts. The results of the effects of virtual communication in social isolation were indicative.

Keywords: Virtual communication · Social isolation · COVID-19 · Media ecosystem · Telecommunications

1 Introduction

The COVID-19 pandemic has led to drastic changes in people's lifestyle around the world, including those related to the natural way in which individuals interact and communicate. It was the World Health Organization (WHO) which declared the corona virus infection a pandemic and a critical public health situation of international concern (PHEIC). Throughout the pandemic period, the WHO had periodically issued a number of recommendations to address the global situation. Thus, in March 2020, at a joint virtual press conference, the UN, the UNICEF and the WHO announced a coordinated global plan to combat COVID-19, with the aim of helping the most financially vulnerable countries in the world [1]. The WHO pointed as well that infodemic management should be considered a pillar of an integrative approach to public health in complex

© Springer Nature Switzerland AG 2021
Q. Gao and J. Zhou (Eds.): HCII 2021, LNCS 12787, pp. 451–464, 2021.
https://doi.org/10.1007/978-3-030-78111-8_31

knowledge societies [2]. The European Commission's revised Work Program for 2020 stated, that what started with isolated cases quickly turned into a public health crisis, an economic shock of unprecedented scale and a pandemic of global and tragic proportions [3]. The Commission also mobilized significant funds from its program for research and innovation *Horizon 2020* for urgently needed corona virus research.

Though a plethora of research topics worldwide would be well fit for analyzing the effects of the pandemics in general, of significant importance is the societal segment. COVID-19 pandemic exposed people to psychological distress, fatigue, occupational burnout, fear, combined with the economic insecurity and the forced social isolation, has potentially dangerous consequences for the individual [4]. The COVID-19 outbreak has also provoked social stigma and discriminatory behavior against people of certain ethnic backgrounds as well as anyone perceived to have been in contact with the virus [5]. Therefore it is of utmost importance that effective communication should be ensured at workplace, in families and at communities. In light of the COVID-19 crisis it is significant to assess how information forms and sources influence the public's information-seeking behavior and the perception of government's crisis response strategies during the pandemic [6–8]. The ECLB-COVID-19 consortium of researchers of the effects of social isolation on the health and mental state of people living on four continents recommended the urgent introduction of modern technology-based solutions to promote an active and healthy lifestyle. Among them was virtual communication as a technologically mediated way of communication [9]. During a pandemic, it proved to be the only alternative to traditional face-to-face communication, and its use was inevitable to partially or completely overcome the social restrictions imposed.

This paper focuses on the situation in Bulgaria. The country reacted relatively quickly at the institutional level to the public health emergency announced by the World Health Organization regarding the disease COVID-19. On February 26, 2020, by order of the Prime Minister, a National Crisis-Management Staff was established. Among its responsibilities were to organize, coordinate and monitor all actions of the competent authorities in relation to the prevention of the spread of COVID-19, as well as to collect, summarize and analyze all information on the development of the situation in order to inform the media and the public. Lack of social activity (interpersonal communication, participation in public life, and economic employment) was considered to be among the leading reasons for the deterioration of the mental and emotional state of people in the affected by the infection country. [10]. The National Assembly passed a law on measures and actions during the state of national emergency, declared by its decision of March 13, 2020 [11]. Up to that date out of 696 tested people (since March 8 – the day of the first reported case), 31 cases of corona virus have been reported and 3 deaths declared. The state of national emergency in the country lasted exactly two months and was lifted on 14.05.2020 (over 30 000 tested people, 2100 reported cases, and 102 declared deaths altogether for the period), when it was replaced by a state of an emergency epidemic situation until the end of June [10].

The strict measures taken at that time in Bulgaria, as well as the economic actions of the government were among the most adequate in the European Union and helped to meet the first challenges of the situation. No matter that nowadays the health system in the country is much more prepared to fight the challenges of COVID-19, the danger of infection is still very strong and the future developments of the pandemic are difficult to determine. Thus, six months after the first wave of the infection, the death rate of COVID-19 in Bulgaria is currently among the leading member-states of the European Union.

Dealing with the pandemic not only in medical and economic, but also in social and communication terms posed significant challenges to the institutions and the population in the country during the state of national emergency. In this sudden and unprecedented situation, the crisis response systems and the capacity to make balanced decisions were subjected to a kind of a stress test in a real situation. In order to limit the spread of the corona virus in Bulgaria, the state institutions issued a number of measures and recommendations to citizens, companies and organizations. The appeal to the people was to observe the three D: discipline, disinfection, and distance [12]. The traditional understandings of labour, physical communication, and working space were transformed ad hoc. Online education was introduced at all levels. The means of virtual communication, including the introduction of specialized training software, "saved" students for completing the school year on a regular basis. The so-called "home office" became increasingly important and popular. However, in this extraordinary situation people experienced the professional deficits in the field of digital infrastructure and connectivity at national and international level.

2 Aim and Research Methods

Undoubtedly, the COVID-19 pandemic will probably have a long-lasting influence on how individuals, employees, customers and organizations will work, produce and interact with each other. The transformations of human contacts during the pandemic towards intensive e-communication in a number of social spheres, institutions, communities and even individuals have fundamental scientific importance because it had caused and continues to cause a change of paradigms, concepts, social practices and policies.

The aim of the undertaken research is to focus on a fundamentally specific societal segment: tracking of the effects of virtual communication in the situation of social isolation in Bulgaria so that the structured and analyzed information be utilized into patterns for policy support for decision makers, academia, media, telecommunications, general publics, and private sector in possible future crises, similar to the present one.

The study is interdisciplinary and it uses mixed research methods, among them:

- Comparative analysis of the derived data from academic sources, sociological surveys, regulatory frameworks and media and telecommunications practices;
- Qualitative research, conducted with three groups of respondents: media ecosystem (traditional media; social media, and social networks) users, media professionals and media experts. The qualitative research techniques included semi-structured interviews with 185 respondents in Bulgaria and analysis of texts and documents, such as government reports, media articles, and websites in the country;
- Quantitative research, conducted via an individual direct poll.

In addition, cross-combining technique for data collection and analysis was applied in order to compensate some of the inherent limitations.

Major findings of the research have been disseminated to decision makers, media companies, and academia [13].

3 Results

3.1 Sociological Polls and Media Coverage During the Pandemics

The declared state of emergency and the accompanying restrictive measures unequivocally displayed that the media environment with its timely and constant information about the development of the disease in the country was crucial for the normal functioning of the economy and the society. The media also had to readjust ad hoc because they had the heavy responsibility to participate in the national management of the pandemic and in alleviating the stress in society caused by the imposed profound and sudden changes.

The national representative surveys of Alpha Research [14], Trend [15], and Gallup International [16] sociological agencies, conducted during the state of national emergency (13.03.–13.05.2020) in Bulgaria showed an overall acceptance and support by the publics for the health quarantine measures and restrictions. Critical sentiments were present only towards the still unclear economic measures. Most of the participants answered, that increased amount of time spent at home had a negative effect on their mental and physical health. Many Bulgarians realized that the fight against the corona virus would take a long time until the return to their normal lifestyle.

An express telephone snap poll conducted by *Gallup International* (4–7.06.2020) confirmed the high public assessment of the measures taken by the authorities. Bulgarian society was divided into two groups regarding the fear/non fear of the corona virus infection with a small predominance of the people who were afraid of it (51%:48%). 51% declared also that their incomes had been significantly decreased because of COVID-19. Almost two thirds of the participants were expecting a normalization of their lives till the end of the year [17].

Although the behavior of the media was not tackled in these sociological surveys, the practices have shown the unprecedented activity of the media in covering the state of national emergency and the information that has been promptly reported by the National Crisis-Management Staff and the institutions involved in controlling of the spontaneous extreme situation.

The point of the public debate in the media about the corona virus, however, was not so much to challenge the constitutional right of the executive power to vital measures during the pandemic, nor to instruct people on how and whether to comply with the undertaken restrictive measures. The important issue was to protect people from "infodemia", i.e. from the disproportion in their access to other important information, in order to they do not fall prey to unreliable messages, rumors and fake news that were spread mostly via social networks. For example, 43% of the Bulgarians right after the emergency epidemic situation was lifted in June believed that the pandemic was caused by the pharmaceutical companies seeking for profit and 40% were convinced of COVID-19 being a bio-weapon for reduction the number of humans [18].

Thus, on March 2, even before the state of national emergency in Bulgaria was declared, the Council for Electronic Media (the program broadcasting regulator) issued a Position on the radio and TV coverage of the extreme situation regarding the spread of the COVID-19 virus. The Council addressed media service providers with a call to inform citizens responsibly, in a timely and accurate manner, avoiding sensationalism in presenting information and not disseminating unverified facts. The broadcasting regulator called on media service providers to adhere to high professional ethical standards [19].

On April 15 the Council for Electronic Media published the Press Release of the European Regulators Group for Audio-visual Media Services (ERGA) on the systemic importance of media in times of crisis. It provided that the Group will assess how the platforms were responding to the challenges posed by the "infodemia" that accompanied the pandemic [20]. In line with ERGA's initiative that the role of the media in critical and complex situations is to contribute to citizens' awareness of public health and tranquillity, the Council for Electronic Media has prepared a report on the behaviour of the nationally distributed media service providers during the pandemic.

The Association of the European Journalists in Bulgaria (AEJ) was particularly active in defending professional standards during the pandemic. On March 17 it published the standpoint COVID-19: Guidelines for Responsible Reporting. This document has brought together some of the most useful guidelines for work in the ongoing crisis, covering its various aspects - from ethics and journalistic responsibility to countering misinformation and protecting personal physical and mental safety, with an emphasis on expertise and compliance with professional standards [21].

In order to assist journalists when covering COVID-19, AEJ-Bulgaria organized various initiatives for journalists and media professionals, such as: an online course for journalists "Corona Virus Coverage" (April 10), a free webinar "Statistics, Data and Lies" (April 24), etc. The training presented practical tools and advice necessary to deal with the "infodemia" and to reliably reflect on the problems associated with COVID-19, such as: the ways misinformation was disseminated; monitoring of COVID-19-related information on social networks; basic tools and techniques for online content verification; good practices for handling fake news, etc. [22].

The Union of the Bulgarian Journalists (UBJ), a professional media organization uncompromising about the existence of fake news, has expressed its readiness to contribute with concrete proposals for the development of a special European program of support and protection, including financial, of media independence and social and professional rights for journalists. This position was expressed in a special letter sent by the President of the Management Council of the Union on 10.04.2020 to the Heads of the European Council, the European Commission, the European Parliament and all national governments of the Member-States of the European Union insisting to include support for the media, journalists and freedom of speech in the recovery plans for Europe after the corona virus crisis [23].

3.2 The Unexpected Challenges and Opportunities for the Telecommunications Companies

For many sectors in the economy (e.g. tourism, restaurant services, retail trade, transport and logistics, media, entertainment industry and film production) during the period of forcibly imposed anti-epidemic measures had adverse effects such as temporary or even permanent termination of activities, lay-offs and furloughs, financial losses, re-organizing the supply and distribution chains, even filing for bankruptcy. However, for the telecommunications industry in Bulgariathose challenges had just the opposite effect. From the very first days of social isolation mobile operators and internet providers enjoyed peak consumption of their services. A sharp increase in phone calls (32% rise compared to the average data from the previous Sundays) was registered on March 8 when the news of the first infected people with corona virus broke. The explanation for this was the compulsively introduced social isolation and the attempts to continue casual activities online (e.g. work and education from home; shopping, payment of bills, and medical consultations, etc.). High levels of distress in people as a result from the abrupt changes in their way of living, as well as the ban to travel without a valid reason also contributed to overloading the capacity of mobile and fixed transmission networks. Their service had to ensure not only the connectivity of their subscribers, but also the ability to operate the entire education system, public administration, all digital services and the work of a huge number of people from home. At the same time, however, networks and mobile operators got higher income and faced surge in consumption of digital services due to the pandemic. The Communications Regulation Commission – the regulatory body for postal services and electronics communications in the country, monitored with anxiety the functioning of the transmission networks and called for reasonable usage of capacities and traffic prioritization in order to avoid possible collapse [24].

The process of adaptation of the Bulgarian mobile operators to the new situation was characterized with speedy flexibility of adapting to the changes in societal and economic life. Thus, the following dimensions of their reaction can be outlined:

– Ensuring the safety of company employees and customers and encouraging the usage of existing and the development of new digital services. Providing for additional opportunities for communication, connectivity, entertainment, and education was the unifying policy of the three leading mobile operators in Bulgaria (A1, Vivacom and Telenor). Telecommunications companies used the period of forcibly imposed social isolation to promote online purchases of devices, gadgets and accessories by using just mobile apps, or discounts, or gifts, or other incentives. Besides, it was a favourable period to promote their own mobile platforms for payment services of all kinds (A1 Wallet, Pay by Vivacom). Thus, the efforts to promote online the mobile operators' online services paid off. In April (compared to February) Telenor doubled the amount of purchases via its electronic shop and got 59% increase of payments via the mobile app MyTelenor [25]. Another mobile operator - A1, reported a 300% increase in video store calls and a 200% increase in users connecting with company employees via chat and social media [26].
– Social solidarity and online security in times of isolation. All mobile operators, in cooperation with the National Crisis-management Staff, maintained free of charge the mobile application ViruSafe. It has been used for uncovering clinical symptoms and tracking down ill patients. Besides, efforts were made to raise awareness of users by useful topical articles, such as „How to Disinfect My Mobile Phone", „How to Identify Fake News", „Is 5G Harmful" (A1) [27]. Digital services were developed to serve business clients how to run and manage work from home, for example virtual phone switchboard for servicing clients from a distance, an app for invoice and documents

exchange named Hartii.online, an app for online submission and approval of requests for leave of absence named Otpuski.com (Telenor) [28]. Vivacom offered access to the cloud service Viva Cloud [29] for developing its own virtual database centre for preferential prices till the end of May 2020. In April A1 came up with an application for prevention of telephone fraud – first of a kind in Bulgaria. A1 Guard could be used free of charge by clients of all mobile operators and users of fixed telephone lines owned by A1 [30]. Its release was in line with the warnings of the Ministry of Interior for activating telephone fraudsters.

- Donation during quarantine - shared responsibility. Telecommunications companies in Bulgaria started wide-scale donations activity during the state of national emergency. They were very active in the direct assistance to health authorities and hospitals to effectively deal with corona virus infection and support for schools and students in adapting to distance learning from home. The overall amount of the reported donations by the telecommunications companies to fight against COVID-19 amounted to 1 320 000 BGN (Euro 660 000) [31]. The donation campaigns, which have raised impressive sums in support of the healthcare system, were built on the principle of shared responsibility. Consumers "invested" funds in the company, which in turn "shared" the gains with the society to overcome the crisis. The amount of donated funds was an indirect indicator of the increase in revenues of telecommunications companies during the forced social isolation.

During the state of national emergency, the telecommunications companies operated under the increased control of the Communications Regulation Commission and in the shadow of the re-opened legal possibility to use mobile data for mass and uncontrolled monitoring of the publics.

3.3 Virtual Communication During the Social Isolation

In order to examine some of the effects of virtual communication in the conditions of social isolation, an academic team from the Faculty of Journalism and Mass Communication at The St. Kliment Ohridski Sofia University undertook a survey during the two-month's period of the state of national emergency in the country (13.03.2020–13.05.2020). Among the objectives of the survey was to monitor the level of adaptability and the way in which respondents coped socially, psychologically, communicatively and healthily during the isolation associated with the corona virus pandemic, as well as to check which channels of information and communication, work and training online have been used by the interviewees during this period. The level of trust in the media (traditional media, social networks, and social media) was also examined, checking in quantitative terms the frequency of their usage, and as a qualitative dimension - the preferences of the respondents and the degree of their trust in media.

The respondents (N = 185) of various age, gender, educational level, and employment were asked 28 questions. Complementary techniques for information gathering and analysis were also used. The survey was conducted in the declared two month's period (13.03.–13.05.2020) of the state of national emergency in the country. The total share of answers of all respondents in percentage exceeded one hundred, as each of them had the right to indicate more than one answer, and the majority of respondents took advantage of this opportunity.

As many as 86% of the respondents were satisfied with the opportunity to work and/or study online. 65% of the interviewees gave positive answer to the question whether employers/teachers supported distance work. 11% indicated, however, that they did not have the technological possibility to work/study online from home. Among them were a salesman in a grocery store in a metropolitan mall, a business manager, and a bank employee.

The survey also aimed to investigate whether since the beginning of the emergency measures in the country employers/teachers have supported distance work/training. 65% of the interviewees responded with a positive answer. 15% answered "Occasionally", while for 13% working/studying distantly was impossible. Only 0.5% of the respondents indicated that the employer did not support them working from home, although they had such an opportunity.

Although 67% claimed that they were not worried of losing their job or of education failure, 59% felt that the pandemic situation negatively affected their work. The prevailing opinion of the respondents was that dealing with the situation, which changed the status quo, required solidarity, empathy and care for the weaker and riskier groups of our society. Thus they saw the crisis as an opportunity for the Bulgarian society to look at these problems in depth.

Another objective of the survey was to study which channels of information the interviewees had used. 78% of all respondents pointed out the traditional media as the most used information source during the COVID-19. The prevailing part of them stated that they prefer to watch television, then - listen to the radio. Most of the interviewees specified that combine their sources of information, as they wanted to compare the data with more than one media channel.

The third objective of the survey was to analyze the level of trust in traditional, online, social networks, and social media of the participants in the survey. More than half of the respondents – 65.9% - were adamant that they trusted the traditional media at most. Again, television was the preferred medium - 22.1%, followed by radio – 12.2%, and press - 9.8%. Merit deserved the comparison between consumption (62.2%) and trust (23.7%) in the online news agencies and websites. Similar was the situation with the social networks. Close to half of all respondents (48.1%) were regular users of Facebook, Tweeter, Instagram, LinkdIn, etc., but only 12.4% stated that they trusted social networks. Although only 9.2% used as main source of information social media (blogs, YouTube, etc.), the trust in them was higher than in social networks (14.5%).

Curious was the explanation of those 3.7% of all respondents who categorically did not trust traditional media. For them these media were "illiterate", "incompetent" and reported what "came down from above". Some pointed out that years ago, journalists were conducting their own in-depth investigations, while nowadays they simply broadcasted the government information. Other close opinions were that the television stations with national coverage did not always communicate the whole truth about the corona virus, and that they did not present alternative opinions. Some respondents believed that traditional media tended to exaggerate the information or presented only this small part of it, which was more influential. Others shared that they mostly trusted the documentaries presenting specific facts, as well as the opinions of experts interviewed on the topic of corona virus.

When asked whether there were discrepancies in data presentation regarding the situation with the infection, disseminated via different information channels (traditional media, electronic news agencies and sites, social media, social networks, and eyewitness accounts), 38.3% of the respondents were adamant that there were such discrepancies, and 27.5% rather supported such a finding. There was no consensus on the reasons for these allegations. Some respondents believed that the media were to a varying degree dependent on the institutional point of view and those in power. Another group of respondents pointed out that in some TV channels the data was intentionally inflated to scare people. Some underlined that some of the platforms were trying to gain more popularity, visits and likes, taking advantage of the critical situation and "embellishing" information, distorting it or exaggerating it. The insufficiently clear and specific information and the presence of contradictions and discrepancies in the presented data gave rise to a number of conspiracy theories, supported by a small part of the respondents. The number of respondents who were convinced that there were no discrepancies in the information was much smaller. Only 7% were of this opinion, and another 25.9% believed that there were rather no discrepancies in the data. Only 21% of the participants in the survey were convinced that the media in Bulgaria were objectively covering the situation with the corona virus, and 27.5% were more inclined to trust their objectivity. According to them, the media, which were of high professional standards and largely independent, were objective, while others showed subjectivism and a tendency to manipulate. On the other hand, 31.3% backed the opinion that the Bulgarian media were not objective, and 9.7% were categorical about this. According to them, a number of journalists did not ask adequate questions, important for the audiences, during the briefings of the National Crisis-Management Staff and not all of them checked their sources of information, thus tending to impose their biased opinion on the audiences. In addition, some of the participants in the survey had the feeling that information on the corona virus threat was transformed into an ersatz reality show focused on the negative and scandalous.

Some of the respondents explained that the media concentrated mainly on the spread of the corona virus and did not pay enough attention to other factors following the pandemic, such as the economic challenges in Bulgaria and throughout the world. When asked how they assessed the media coverage of the COVID-19 pandemic, the largest percentage of the respondents claimed that negative news prevailed (e.g., for people who have fallen ill or died, but not for those who have recovered), and that they were shocking for the people (51.6%). For 46.2% of the interviewees, the media paid too much attention to the situation with the corona virus and became intrusive, seeming to exhaust their responsibility with repeating the slogan "Stay at home!".

The most unpleasant impression for some of the respondents was the search for sensations at any cost, which often led to incitement to hatred - to the church, to the Roma, to the Bulgarian guest workers returning from abroad, etc. By doing so media helped to instill fear in society. Regarding the psychological impacts, the largest number of respondents - 59.7% answered that the over saturation with information about COVID-19 depressed them. 16% claimed that the information was contradictory and confused them. Only a smaller share (13.4%) was of the opinion that the information was timely and useful and that they felt informed.

Most of the respondents were impressed by the level of mobilization of the Bulgarian media and by their responsiveness to the emergency. Among the negative opinions about the media coverage of COVID-19 was the pyramidal paramilitary model of information, as well as the lack of criticism of the official information and the limited debate with various opinions about the corona virus.

4 Conclusion

The crisis with COVID-19 might be considered as the biggest social experiment that will happen in our lives [32]. Among the main factors for a country's success in controlling the COVID-19 pandemic could be listed the previous experience of governments in managing crises, the level of social trust, and the state capacity [33].

After the first wave of the spread of COVID-19, nearly half of Bulgarians believed that governmental measures against the infection were sufficient. The obligatory wearing of masks in public places met the greatest support. In November, the people in the country felt more secure about their jobs than in spring. There were noticed lower levels of fears among Bulgarians of shortages of food, household supplies, medicines and fuels compared to April. However, an increase in the share of people who were left without savings has been indicated [34].

In democratic countries, the public is highly responsive to management cues sent by political elites whose messages can encourage unity or deepen social cleavages. Because the public leans on these cues for reliable information, it is especially important that elites present a unified message during a crisis [35].

Bulgaria met the second wave of COVID-19 politically divided, facing both parliamentary and presidential elections in 2021. Currently there is lack of creative and constructive opposition. The president, instead of unifier of the nation by default, turns to be the constant critic of the prime minister. The aspiring for power non-parliamentary political forces are striving to gain public visibility by organizing various street protests against the ruling coalition for six months now, accusations of corruption and discrediting incumbent politicians, public burning of masks, etc. Quality journalism, alas, in many cases gives way to marketplace temptations for sensationalism. Failure to observe strictly the three D: discipline, distance, disinfection has led to an increase in the severity of the infection. Thus many people tested positive, among them – the Bulgarian Prime Minister Boyko Borisov. As of December 10, 2020 171 483 corona virus cases have been reported in the country, with 5 283 deaths and 72 028 recovered [10]. The health system is suffocating because plenty of dedicated medics is infected with COVID-19 and quarantined. The economic problems are increasing, despite the flexible and timely reaction of the government to introduce a number of measures for retirees, working people and businesses suffering from the extreme situation.

Slowing viral transmission during pandemics caused significant shifts in individual and collective behavior. The crisis required large-scale communication change and placed significant psychological burdens on individuals and organizational difficulties to institutions and businesses.

The study of the virtual communication in the social isolation of the two-month state of national emergency regarding COVID-19, led to some major conclusions:

- The restructuring of the communication in the situation of social isolation caused a variety of challenges to the media system and telecommunications sector, which requires new approaches to their management and regulation;
- The period of forced social isolation provided an opportunity for media and telecommunications companies to gain audiences' trust in their social responsibility and solidarity;
- The effects of virtual communication during the social isolation presupposed the importance of the media system and the telecommunications industry as core determinants in the social management of the processes in extraordinary situations.

The research was based on the idea that insights from the social and behavioral sciences can be used to help align human virtual communication with the recommendations of the epidemiologists and public health experts during social isolation. In crisis situations, such as the one with COVID-19, the effects of virtual communication in social isolation are indicative.

Acknowledgements. The paper has been developed within the framework of COST Action CA16226 *Indoor Living Space Improvement: Smart Habitat for the Elderly* (SHELD-ON) of the European Commission, supported by the research projects КР-06-COST/5-18/06/2019 and КР-06-М35/4-18/12/2019 of the National Scientific Fund of Bulgaria.

References

1. United Nations. Global Humanitarian Response Plan COVID-19. United Nations Coordinated Appeal (2020). https://www.unocha.org/sites/unocha/files/Global-Humanitarian-Response-Plan-COVID-19.pdf
2. World Health Organization: Infodemic management: Infodemiology. World Health Organization (2020). https://www.who.int/teams/risk-communication/infodemic-management
3. European Commission: Communication from the Commission to the European Parliament, the Council, the European Economic and Social Committee and the Committee of the Regions. Adjusted Commission Work Programme 2020. Brussels, 27.5.2020 COM (2020) 440 final (2020). https://ec.europa.eu/info/sites/info/files/cwp-2020-adjusted_en.pdf
4. Venkatashiva, R.., Gupta, A.: Importance of effective communication during COVID-19 infodemic. J. Family Med. Prim. Care **9**(8) 3793–3796 (2020). https://www.ncbi.nlm.nih.gov/pmc/articles/PMC7586512/
5. World Health Organization: A Guide to Preventing and Addressing Social Stigma Associated with COVID-19 (2020). https://www.who.int/publications/m/item/a-guide-to-preventing-and-addressing-social-stigma-associated-with-covid-19
6. Moreno, Á., Fuentes-Lara, C., Navarro, C.: COVID-19 communication management in spain: exploring the effect of information-seeking behavior and message reception in public's evaluation. El profesional de la información **29**(4), e290402 (2020). https://doi.org/10.3145/epi.2020.jul.02
7. Zarocostas, J.: How to fight an infodemic. Lancet **395**(10225) (2020). https://doi.org/10.1016/S0140-6736(20)30461-X

8. Cuan-Baltazar, J.Y., Muñoz-Perez, M.J., Robledo-Vega, C., Pérez-Zepeda, M.F., Soto-Vega, E.: Misinformation of COVID-19 on the Internet: infodemiology study JMIR Public Health Surveill. **6**(2), e18444 (2020). https://doi.org/10.2196/18444 https://doi.org/10.2196/18444

9. Ammar, A., Brach, M., Khaled, T.: Effects of Home Confinement on Mental Health and Lifestyle Behaviours during the COVID-19 Outbreak: Insight from the "ECLB-COVID-19" multi countries survey (2020). https://www.medrxiv.org/content/10.1101/2020.05.04.200910 17v1.full.pdf+html

10. COVID-19. Edinen informatsionen portal. Unified Information Portal (2020). https://web cache.googleusercontent.com/search?q=cache:WYbmUQ_RSyQJ:https://coronavirus.bg/ bg/231+&cd=8&hl=en&ct=clnk&gl=bg

11. Dŭrzhaven vestnik. Zakon za merkite i deĭstviyata po vreme na izvŭnrednoto polozhenie, obyaveno s reshenie na Narodnoto sŭbranie ot 13 mart 2020 g. br. 28, 24. 03. 2020 g. (In Bulgarian). State Gazette. Law on Measures and Actions during the State of Emergency, announced by a decision of the National Assembly of March 13, 2020, 28 March 2020 (2020). https://dv.parliament.bg/DVWeb/showMaterialDV.jsp?idMat=147150

12. Kantardjiev, T.: To Observe the Three D: Discipline, Disinfection, Distance, 10 June 2020. https://bntnews.bg/news/prof-todor-kantarjiev-da-se-spazvat-trite-d-disciplina-dezinf ekciya-distanciya-1059151news.html

13. Raycheva, L., Velinova, N., Miteva, N., Tomov, M.: Impacts of virtual communication during social isolation of Covid'19. In: Karwowski, W., Ahram, T., Etinger, D., Tanković, N., Taiar, R. (eds.) Human Systems Engineering and Design (IHSED 2020): Future Trends and Applications, 22–24 September 2020, pp. 63–68. Springer, Cham (2020). https://doi.org/10. 1007/978-3-030-58282-1_11

14. Alpha Research: Otrazhenie na pŭrviya etap ot krizata s koronavirusa vŭrkhu politicheskata kartina v stranata. Impact of the First Stage of the Corona Virus Crisis on the Political Picture in the Country, 05 2020. https://alpharesearch.bg/post/969-otrajenie-na-purvia-etap-ot-krizata-s-koronavirusa-vurhu-politicheskata-kartina-v-stranata.html. (in Bulgarian)

15. Novini.bg: "Trend": 68% ot bŭlgarite imat pritesnenie da poseshtavat mesta s mnogo khora. Trend: 68% of the Bulgarians Are Worried about Visiting Places with Many People, 08 May 2020. https://novini.bg/bylgariya/obshtestvo/597366. (in Bulgarian)

16. Gallup International. Center for Public and Political Studies. Masovite naglasi kŭm situat-siyata s koronavirusa: Belezi na normalizatsiya. (In Bulgarian). Mass Attitudes towards the Coronavirus Situation: Signs of Normalization, 20 May 2020. https://www.gallup-internati onal.bg/43323/%d0%b0ttitudes-towards-the-coronavirus-situation/

17. Gallup International. Center for Public and Political Studies. Aktualni danni za obshtestvenoto mnenie po otnoshenie na koronavirusa. Current Data for the Public Opinion about the Coronavirus, 10 June 2020. https://www.gallup-international.bg/43390/public-opinion-cor onavirus-crisis/. (in Bulgarian)

18. Trend. Naglasi na bulgarite kum korona virusa i konspirativnite teorii. Attitudes of Bulgarians towards the Corona Virus and Conspiracy Theories, 06 2020. https://rctrend.bg/project/% D0%BD%D0%B0%D0%B3%D0%BB%D0%B0%D1%81%D0%B8-%D0%BD%D0% B0-%D0%B1%D1%8A%D0%BB%D0%B3%D0%B0%D1%80%D0%B8%D1%82%D0% B5-%D1%81%D0%BF%D1%80%D1%8F%D0%BC%D0%BE-%D0%BA%D0%BE% D0%BD%D1%81%D0%BF%D0%B8%D1%80%D0%B0/. (in Bulgarian)

19. Council for Electronic Media. Positziya. Position, 02 March 2020. https://www.cem.bg/actbg/ 5882. (in Bulgarian)

20. Council for Electronic Media. Pressŭobshtenie: Evropeĭskite regulatori prizovavat Evropeĭskata komisiya: Sistemno znachenie na mediite vŭv vremena na kriza. Press Release: European Regulators Call on the European Commission: Systemic Importance of the Media in Times of Crisis, 15 April 2020. https://www.cem.bg/displaynewsbg/657. (in Bulgarian)

21. Association of European Journalists – Bulgaria. Cheresheva Mariya. COVID-19: Nasoki za otgovorno otrazyavane. Guidelines for Responsible Reporting, 17 March 2020. http://new. aej-bulgaria.org/covid-19-resources/. (in Bulgarian)

22. Association of European Journalists – Bulgaria. First Draft provezhda onlaĭn kurs za "infodemiyata" ot koronavirus. First Draft Conducts an Online Course on the "Infodemia" of Corona Virus, 10 April 2020. https://new.aej-bulgaria.org/first-draft-covering-coronavirus/. (in Bulgarian)

23. Union of the Bulgarian Journalists SBZH s pismo do ES: Vklyuchete i mediite, zhurnalistite i svobodata na slovoto vŭv vŭzstanovitelnite planove. Involve the Media, Journalists and Freedom of Speech in the Recovery Plans, 10 April 2020. https://sbj-bg.eu/index.php?t= 45956. (in Bulgarian)

24. Communications Regulation Commission Komisiyata za regulirane na sŭobshteniyata preporŭchva na potrebitelite da se sŭobrazyat s tendentsiite v internet trafik. The Communications Regulation Commission Recommends that Consumers Take into Account Trends in Internet Traffic, 02 April 2020. https://crc.bg/bg/novini/1304/komisiqta-za-regulirane-na-syo bshteniqta-preporychva-na-potrebitelite-da-se-syobrazqt-s-tendenciite-v-internet-trafika. (in Bulgarian)

25. Telenor. Mrezhata na Telenor izdŭrzha na predizvikatelstvata i otnovo be sertifitsirana Best in Test v Bŭlgariya. .. Telenor's Network Withstood the Challenges and Was Again Certified Best in Test in Bulgaria, 20 May 2020. https://www.telenor.bg/bg/news/%D0% BC%D1%80%D0%B5%D0%B6%D0%B0%D1%82%D0%B0-%D0%BD%D0%B0-% D1%82%D0%B5%D0%BB%D0%B5%D0%BD%D0%BE%D1%80-%D0%B8%D0% B7%D0%B4%D1%8A%D1%80%D0%B6%D0%B0-%D0%BD%D0%B0-%D0%BF% D1%80%D0%B5%D0%B4%D0%B8%D0%B7%D0%B2%D0%B8%D0%BA%D0%B0% D1%82%D0%B5%D0%BB%D1%81%D1%82%D0%B2%D0%B0%D1%82%D0%B0-% D0%BD%D0%B0-%D0%BA%D1%80%D0%B8%D0%B7%D0%B0%D1%82%D0% B0-%D0%B8-%D0%BE%D1%82%D0%BD%D0%BE%D0%B2%D0%BE-%D0%B1% D0%B5-%D1%81%D0%B5%D1%80%D1%82%D0%B8%D1%84%D0%B8%D1%86% D0%B8%D1%80%D0%B0%D0%BD%D0%B0-best. (in Bulgarian)

26. A1: A1 daryava po 1 lev na MZ pri vsyako plashtane na smetka onlain. A1 Donates BGN 1 to the Ministry of Health for Each Payment of an Online Bill, 24 March 2020. https://www.a1.bg/ medien-tsentar-informatsia-za-mediite/mc/index/ma/view/infoblock_id/2731. (in Bulgarian)

27. See Vivacom (2020). https://www.vivacom.bg/bg/home

28. Telenor: Telenor udŭlzhava gratisniya period za uslugi na biznesa. .Telenor extends the grace period for business services, 02 Apr 2020. https://www.telenor.bg/bg/news/%D1%82%D0% B5%D0%BB%D0%B5%D0%BD%D0%BE%D1%80-%D1%83%D0%B4%D1%8A% D0%BB%D0%B6%D0%B0%D0%B2%D0%B0-%D0%B3%D1%80%D0%B0%D1%82% D0%B8%D1%81%D0%BD%D0%B8%D1%8F-%D0%BF%D0%B5%D1%80%D0%B8% D0%BE%D0%B4-%D0%BD%D0%B0-%D1%83%D1%81%D0%BB%D1%83%D0% B3%D0%B8-%D0%B7%D0%B0-%D0%B1%D0%B8%D0%B7%D0%BD%D0%B5% D1%81%D0%B0. (in Bulgarian)

29. Vivacom (2020). https://www.vivacom.bg/bg/home

30. Investor Tehnologiite v borba s telefonnite izmamnitsi. . Technologies in Fight against Telephone Fraud, 01 April 2020. https://www.investor.bg/telekomunikacii/457/a/tehnologiite-v-borba-s-telefonnite-izmamnici-301664/. (in Bulgarian)

31. See A1 (2020). https://www.a1.bg/medien-tsentar-informatsia-za-mediite/mc/index/ma/ view/infoblock_id/2744; https://www.telenor.bg/bg/news/; https://www.vivacom.bg/bg/ home

32. Krastev, I.: Is It Tomorrow Yet? Sofia: Obsidian (2020)

33. Rachel, K.: Do Authoritarian or Democratic Countries Handle Pandemics Better? CEIP, 31 March 2020. https://carnegieendowment.org/2020/03/31/do-authoritarian-or-democratic-countries-handle-pandemics-better-pub-81404
34. Trend: Naglasi na bulgatite za razprostranenieto na korona virusa. (In Bulgarian). Attitudes of Bulgarians towards the Spread of COVID-19, 11 2020. https://rctrend.bg/project/%D0% BD%D0%B0%D0%B3%D0%BB%D0%B0%D1%81%D0%B8-%D0%BD%D0%B0-% D0%B1%D1%8A%D0%BB%D0%B3%D0%B0%D1%80%D0%B8%D1%82%D0%B5-% D1%81%D0%BF%D1%80%D1%8F%D0%BC%D0%BE-%D1%80%D0%B0%D0%B7% D0%BF%D1%80%D0%BE%D1%81%D1%82/
35. Green, J., Edgerton, J. Naftel, D., Shoub, K., Cranmer, S.J.: Corona Virus Elusive Consensus: Polarization in Elite Communication on the COVID-19 Pandemic (2020). https://advances. sciencemag.org/content/6/28/eabc2717

Effect of Different Secondary Tasks Types on the Driving Safety of Older Drivers

Jinjun Xia[1]([✉]), Yi Liu[1], Yingjie Wang[1], and Na Xu[2]

[1] Department of Industrial Design, Chongqing University, Chongqing, P.R. China
design@cqu.edu.cn
[2] School of Design, Sichuan Fine Arts Institute, Chongqing, P.R. China

Abstract. This paper studies the impact of different types of secondary tasks on older drivers' driving safety. The study used a dual-task experimental design, the older participants need to perform three different secondary tasks while performing driving tasks on the simulated driver, including touch tasks, reading tasks, and conversation tasks. The study collected various metrics of older drivers in various distraction types of tasks, such as vehicle position, speed, acceleration, brake pedal force, distraction times and reaction time to emergencies. Results showed that the touch task has the longest reaction time and the most possibility of collision; the reading task has the largest lane offset and lateral acceleration. The indicators of the conversation task perform better than the other two tasks.

Keywords: Older drivers · Driving distraction · Driving performance · Secondary tasks · Safety

1 Introduction

Distracted driving can lead to decreased driver performance in both lateral and vertical handling [1]. With the increase in distract-related driving accidents, studies focusing on driver distraction have grown rapidly recently. Driving distraction mainly includes visual distraction, manual distraction and cognitive distraction (lack of reference). Visual distraction refers to the fact that when a driver is engaged in a visual secondary task, his/her sight spans from the external road to the display device in the vehicle, thereby distracting attention and increasing cognitive load [2, 3]. Manual distraction refers to driving in which the driver's hands are removed from the steering wheel for other actions, which will occupy the driver's action resources during the driving's primary task operation, resulting in driving interference [4, 5]. Cognitive distraction refers to the processing, encoding and memory retrieval of visual or auditory information acquired by drivers in the execution of secondary tasks, which will occupy the cognitive resources of drivers in the execution of primary tasks and affect the perception of driving situation and the processing of surrounding information [6].

Previous studies have shown that drivers engaged in secondary tasks (operating on-board information systems and similar devices) while driving will cause visual and manual distraction, resulting in impaired driving performance and increased collision

© Springer Nature Switzerland AG 2021
Q. Gao and J. Zhou (Eds.): HCII 2021, LNCS 12787, pp. 465–477, 2021.
https://doi.org/10.1007/978-3-030-78111-8_32

risk [7, 8]. In driving, when the second task is visual-tactile, the left hand needs to control the steering wheel to stabilize the stability of the vehicle running laterally, and the right hand needs to complete the click, slide and other operations of the second task. In this case, the motion state of hands will conflict with each other and inhibit each other. The driver will cause abnormal fluctuations of the steering wheel during the touch control task (lack of reference). With the growth of age, the muscle strength of older drivers will be greatly reduced, and the movement speed will also be reduced [9]. Age-related movement changes may also affect driving ability and overall mobility [10]. Especially in complex driving tasks, older drivers may have more significant effects due to age-related sensory and motor functions decline, cognitive resources decrease, and attention control ability is weakened [11, 12].

Many studies have also explored the effects of distraction on driving older drivers from different types of tasks, such as phone task interference and auditory/visual distraction task interference [13, 14]. Thompson et al. [15] also found that distracted attention during audio-verbal tasks affected steering and speed control in older drivers. However, it is worth exploring whether there are differences in older drivers' performance on different types of distraction secondary tasks, especially which type of distraction secondary tasks have more adverse effects on driving safety.

The main purpose of this paper is to explore whether older drivers engaged in different types of distraction tasks in the process of driving simulation will have different effects on driving safety. For the judgment of driving safety, we mainly consider the duration of each type of distraction and the response time to dangerous events in the case of distraction. On the other hand, the relevant data of drivability, including the vehicle's lateral and longitudinal control. We set an emergency in distracted driving. The hazardous incident response time reflects when it takes the driver to react to the emergency when he encounters the road during the second task. For the above considerations, we put forward the following hypotheses: (1) the duration of older drivers in various types of distraction is different. (2) Different types of distracting secondary tasks have different impacts on the driving performance of older drivers. (3) There are differences in the response time of older drivers to dangerous events when they perform various types of distraction tasks. Therefore, it can be inferred which type of distracting secondary task has a greater impact on driving safety for middle-aged and older drivers. To solve the above problems, we conducted a driving simulator experiment.

2 Methods

2.1 Participants

Ten older drivers were recruited to voluntarily participate in the simulation driving experiment (2 male, 8 female), with an average age of 55.80 years (SD = 4.87). They all have valid driver's licenses and drive regularly. All participants had normal visual, auditory, tactile and cognitive abilities. After the driving simulation, none of the participants showed obvious dizziness Table 1.

Table 1. Information of participants

Age		Driving experience		Driving mileage per year/10^4 km	
Mean	SD	Mean	SD	Mean	SD
55.80	4.87	28.10	11.37	3.11	2.77

2.2 Apparatus

This experiment using REAL-TIME RDS-MODULAR simulation driving device, including the steering wheel, the brake pedal, seat, and LED car dashboard. The simulator can output real-time simulation of the vehicle running status data, including speed, coordinates, lane-keeping performance, Yaw angles, steering wheel movements, pedal force. These data can evaluate driver safety performance and driving risk, and the sampling frequency is 60 Hz. The driving environment's view is projected by three high-definition projectors onto three screens, creating a 180-degree view. A camera is installed in front of the driver's seat and in the rear of the vehicle to record behavioral data, Apple iPad (6th generation) tablet computer is used to simulate the central control screen, as shown in Fig. 1.

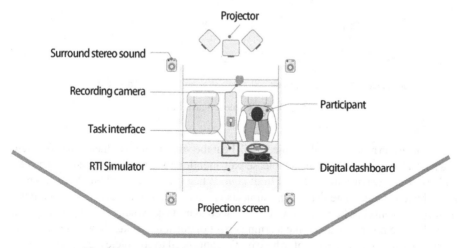

Fig. 1. Experimental equipment and environment construction

2.3 Driving Scenario and Tasks Design

The road scene of simulated driving is an urban road scene with two-way four lanes, no red street lights on the road, and city buildings on both sides of the road. The lane is 3.5 m wide and has a 60 km/h speed limit sign at 250 m from the starting point, as shown in Fig. 2.

Fig. 2. Simulated driving scenario

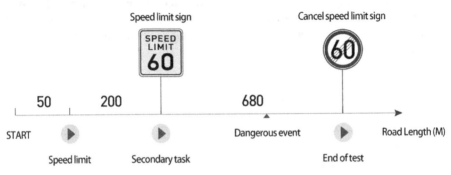

Fig. 3. Experimental task flow

In the urban road scene, the subjects will hear the voice prompt of the main task "there is a speed limit after 200 m ahead, please pay attention to control the speed between 50 and 60" when driving to the speed limit sign. When the limit speed has been reached, the vehicle running state data of the subjects is collected. The triggering of potentially dangerous events has been set between the "Secondary task" voice prompt and the "End of test" voice prompt to avoid the learning effect of participants, as shown in Fig. 3. We designed a dual-task experiment, where participants need to complete the secondary task while driving. The driving task requires participants to drive straight along the current lane in the scene and keep the speed between 50 km/h and 60 km/h.

Three types of secondary tasks were set up in the experiment, touch task, reading task, and conversation task. In the touch task, participants were asked to click a button on the screen in the central control position after hearing the task voice prompt. The interface reading task required the participants to read the information from the navigation interface on the screen in the central control position and give an oral answer after hearing the voice prompts. The conversation task required participants to give oral answers after hearing the voice prompts, as shown in Table 2.

Table 2. Three types of task settings

Task type	Secondary task interface	Secondary task voice
Touch		Please click the button that appears on the screen after hearing the voice (random multiple times)
Reading		(1) Please find out the number of kilometers from the destination (2) Please find out the number of traffic lights from the destination (3) Please find out how many minutes it takes to the destination
Conversation		(1) Please answer what is your favorite food (2) Please answer what day is today (3) Please answer what is the result of 25 plus 38

2.4 Procedure

Before the experiment began, the participants were first introduced to the experiment environment and the overall process. After learning about the experiment, they signed the experimental consent form and filled in the basic information questionnaire. Before the formal experiment, all participants completed a 5-min driving exercise and secondary task operation exercise on the simulated driving to familiarize themselves with the experimental scene, tasks and equipment. After the exercise, we adjusted the behavior observation camera and calibrated all the equipment to ensure that the data could be recorded properly. All participants were asked to complete three types of secondary tasks, which were randomly assigned to them, including interface reading, conversation and touch manipulation. Participants filled out the NASA-TLX scale to assess subjective workload after completing each task type, and were given a five-minute break at the end of each task. It takes about an hour to complete all the procedures.

2.5 Data Analysis

During the experiment, the total duration of each type of distraction (visual distraction, cognitive distraction, manual distraction) was determined by analyzing the cognitive activities and secondary task behaviors in the driving videos using the backward labeling method. The image frame rate of video analysis is 5 fps, 5 frames of still images are taken from video per second for analysis.

Relevant data of drivability are derived from the simulated driving platform, including braking response time, steering wheel angle, pedal force, lateral speed, vertical speed, lateral acceleration, longitudinal acceleration, yaw angle and other vehicle movement data. After calculation, the following metrics to measure the safety of driving are extracted, as shown in Table 3.

The risk coefficient $R_{b,s}$ is to characterize the driver's safety when performing secondary tasks [16]. Many previous studies have verified this formula and related models [17, 18]. This formula can predict the collision probability and expected collision energy between the vehicle and the road boundary in the future time period, the calculation formula is as follows:

$$R_{b,s} = \begin{cases} 0.5 \, km(V_{s,b})^2 \cdot \max(e^{-|r_{s,b}|/D}, \, 0.001) \,, & if \, |r_{s,b}| \in [0, \, |r_L|) \\ 0 & , \, if \, |r_{s,b}| \in [|r_L|, \, \infty) \end{cases} \quad (1)$$

Table 3. Metrics description

Metrics	Description	Units
Distraction Times (DT)	The time interval between the task beginning and the participant's completing the task	s
Reaction Times (RT)	The time interval between the onset of a stimulus and the participant's first response to that stimulus	s
Maximum collision probability (MPR)	Estimated the collision probability with Road boundary during the process of one secondary task	–
Speed deviation (SpDev)	The mean deviation between the target and driving speeds during the process of a secondary task	–
Standard deviation of the lane position (SDLP)	The standard deviation of the lateral distance between the car center and the lane center	–
Maximum lateral acceleration (MLA)	The maximum lateral acceleration during the secondary task phase	m/s^2
Maximum deceleration (MD)	The maximum deceleration during the avoidance of dangerous events	m/s^2
NASA task load index (NASA-TLX)	Measure the overall mental workload of the participants through the various dimensions and weights of the NASA task load index	Point

The parameter k representing the road boundary object's rigidity, with range [0–1], in this paper we set k = 0.5; M denotes the mass of the vehicle, we set M = 1000. $r_{s,b}$ and r_L are vectors that denote the shortest distance between b and s (the center of gravity) and lane center respectively; In $V_{s,b} = v \cdot \sin(yaw)$ the parameter Vs,b denotes the velocity of the vehicle along $r_{s,b}$; $|r_{sb}| = |y - y_b|$, y_b is the abscissa of the road edge, the right side of the road $y_b = 7$, the left side of the road $y_b = -7$, the parameter y is the coordinate of the vehicle's lateral position, and this term attains the maximum of 1 at $r_{s,b} = 0$ and depicts a decrease in crash probability with an increase in $r_{s,b}$, because a road object further away offers more possibility for the driver to avoid the collision. The coefficient D determines the steepness of descent of the potential risk field, in $D = \frac{|r_L|}{7}$ we set D = 1 in this paper.

After processing the collected vehicle data, the homogeneity of variance test is used to test the three secondary task types and different metrics (Distraction Times, Reaction Times, Maximum collision probability, Speed deviation, Standard deviation of the lane position, Maximum lateral acceleration, Maximum deceleration, NASA-TLX). If the result is not significant (p > 0.05), different task types are consistent with the metrics' volatility. Whether there is a significant difference between the direct ANOVA variance test, and compare the difference; If the result is significant (p < 0.05), use Welch ANOVA for non-parametric test and study the difference relationship.

3 Results

3.1 Distraction Times

For different secondary tasks, no significant difference in the distraction time of the participants was found (F = 0.045, p = 0.956). Distraction times were 41.88 s, 41.66 s, 41.80 s for the touch task, reading task and conversation task.

3.2 Reaction Times

The reaction time reflects the time it takes for the participant to give a brake response after encountering a sudden dangerous situation during one secondary task. Reaction times differed significantly across the different task type (F = 5.681, p = 0.005). As shown in Fig. 4, participants' reaction time to dangerous events when performing touch tasks (M = 2.50 s, SD = 0.55 s) was longer than the reading tasks' reaction time (M = 2.34 s, SD = 0.85 s). Simultaneously, it was significantly longer than the reaction time to dangerous events when performing a conversation task (M = 1.99 s, SD = 0.78 s), indicating the participants' speed of responding to danger when performing a touch task significantly slower than a reading task or a conversation task, as shown in Fig. 4.

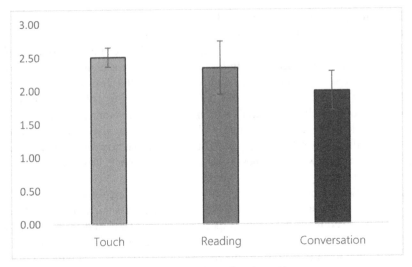

Fig. 4. Result of reaction times (s)

3.3 Maximum Collision Probability

The data has been chosen from the beginning of the task to 50 m after the dangerous event to calculate maximum collision probability. Three different secondary tasks showed significant differences in the maximum risk factor ($F = 3.514$, $p = 0.033$). The results showed that the maximum collision probability of the touch task ($M = 0.17$, $SD = 0.05$) was significantly higher than the maximum collision probability of the conversation task ($M = 0.14$, $SD = 0.05$) and is higher than the maximum collision probability when performing a reading task ($M = 0.16$, $SD = 0.06$), as shown in Fig. 5.

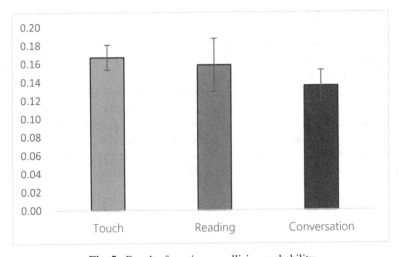

Fig. 5. Result of maximum collision probability

3.4 Speed Deviation

No effects on speed deviation were found for the different types (F = 0.106, p = 0.899). Speed deviation were 12.18, 12.57, 12.40 for the touch task, reading task and conversation task.

3.5 Standard Deviation of the Lane Position

The standard deviation of the lane position (SDLP) reflects the fluctuation of the vehicle's lateral position, directly reflects the effect of participants on the vehicle's lateral control, and can characterize the lane departure risk. Figure 6 shows the statistical SDLP under different types of secondary tasks. The SDLP was significantly different across different task types (F = 5.928, p = 0.004). The results showed that the SDLP of the reading task (M = 0.22, SD = 0.13) was significantly higher than the SDLP of the conversation task (M = 0.13, SD = 0.06) and was higher than the SDLP of touch task (M = 0.18, SD = 0.10).

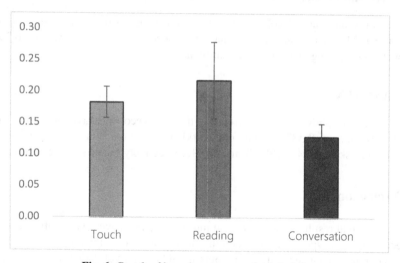

Fig. 6. Result of lane departure standard deviation

3.6 Maximum Lateral Acceleration

Welch ANOVA was used to analyze the influence of different secondary tasks on the vehicle's maximum lateral acceleration. The result showed three different secondary tasks have significant differences in the maximum lateral acceleration (F = 3.716, p = 0.034). The reading task (M = 0.45, SD = 0.39) resulted in significantly higher maximum lateral acceleration compared to both the conversation task (M = 0.19, SD = 0.26) and the touch task (M = 0.26, SD = 0.16) Fig. 7

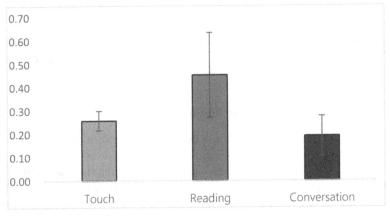

Fig. 7. Result of maximum lateral acceleration (m/s^2)

3.7 Maximum Deceleration

No effects on maximum deceleration were found for the different type of task (F = 0.294, p = 0.746). The result showed maximum deceleration were 5.95, 5.85, 6.25 for the touch task, reading task and conversation task.

3.8 NASA-TLX

The results did not show significant effects of different secondary tasks on mental workload (F = 0.958, p = 0.387). The mental workload of the touch task, reading task, and conversation task were 24.76, 29.38, and 28.91, respectively, but no statistical difference.

4   Discussion

The experimental results have shown that multiple metrics have related influences with the secondary task types, such as reaction times, maximum collision probability, standard deviation of the lane position, and maximum lateral acceleration. Drivers' driving performance metrics (such as speed, reaction time, changes in the lane position, etc.) can be used to analyze the consequences of driving distraction. The impact of distraction varies with the type of distraction source. For example, visual distraction can lead to increased lane position changes, while it is improved in cognitive distractions (such as conversation).

In this study, we found the SDLP of the conversation task is significantly lower than the other two types of secondary tasks. This is probably because the driver focuses on the center of the road ahead when the driver is cognitively distracted, and steering wheel operation increases frequency [19]. This will directly lead to a reduction in the lane position's standard deviation, leading to a better lane-keeping [20]. The driver's point of view is more concentrated on the center of the road ahead, which leads to increased perception of lane deviation, thereby increasing the frequency of steering wheel correction and ultimately improving lane-keeping performance [21]. The reason is that the conversation task does not need participants to watch the central control screen, which can pay more attention to road keeping and consume less attention on the central control screen. On the contrary, in the touch task and reading task driver is visually distracted. At the same time, the point of view leaves the road, which results in the inability to obtain the road and vehicle information in time [22]. Meanwhile, the steering wheel can not be corrected according to the lane deviation, and the lane deviation can be caused.

Conversation task produces less visual distraction than touch and recognition tasks. This result is in line with previous studies in this context, the non-visual distraction tasks showed lower SDLP and higher gaze concentration towards the center of the road [23, 24]. Previous studies have shown that lane positioning is not affected by cognitive distraction (such as talking), while driving speed or speed changes are affected by cognitive distraction [21]. In this study, the speed offset did not significantly differ between different tasks because the driver may dynamically adjust the driving task's difficulty by changing the speed (such as decelerating). However, the lack of driving performance of older drivers in real traffic cannot be fully characterized by driving metrics such as lane-keeping and steering. In fact, dealing with emergencies is a serious problem for older drivers when they occur in complex environments or situations [12]. The result showed that the touch task has the longest reaction time in an emergency among the three secondary tasks. The reason is that the touch task requires a manual response, which must be performed with the steering movement and requires more cognitive resources to control and prepare for the movement response. Related studies have shown that task difficulty and potentially distracting stimuli can affect the response to sudden events [25]. Among the three types of secondary tasks, the conversation task's reaction time that does not need to divert attention from the lane is the shortest. Meanwhile, this result could further prove that distraction will affect the driver's reaction time to sudden events.

Distraction is considered a form of lack of attention because it can lead to a lack of attention. However, lack of attention is not always caused by distraction. Inattention caused by distracted driving may lead to lateral and longitudinal driving performance deterioration and subsequently increase collision probability. The impact of distracted driving on collision probability is assessed by establishing the relationship between distraction and the collision observed during driving. The three types of secondary tasks in the research results show consistency in maximum collision probability and reaction time. This is due to the lack of attention caused by different degrees of distraction, and collision probability can be used as a metrics to reflect this degree of distraction.

The variance analysis of distraction times, maximum deceleration, and NASA-TLX showed no significant direct impact on different types of secondary tasks. Although the results of NASA-TLX did not show any difference from the task type, the mean value of the recognition task and the conversation task was significantly higher than the mean value of the touch task. The possible reason was that the participants had more cognitive distractions to secondary tasks in the process, which leads to an increase in the mental workload for driving. In the course of the experiment, we found that some older participants had difficulty filling in the NASA-TLX scale, which may also be why the data did not show significant differences.

In conclusion, the distraction of older drivers caused by different types of secondary tasks has different degrees of impact on driving performance, especially the possibility of collision and the response to dangerous incidents on the road. Besides, lateral acceleration and lane departure reflect the impact of visual distracted driving safety, and the results are consistent in different secondary tasks. A single secondary task's distraction may include multiple types, such as visual distraction, manual distraction, and cognitive distraction. Therefore, when evaluating the impact of secondary tasks on road safety, this interaction's consequences should be considered to ensure older drivers' driving safety.

References

1. Greenberg, J., et al.: Driver distraction: evaluation with event detection paradigm. Transp. Res. Rec. **1843**(1), 1–9 (2003). https://doi.org/10.3141/1843-01
2. Summala, H., Nieminen, T., Punto, M.: Maintaining lane position with peripheral vision during in-vehicle tasks. Hum. Factors **38**(3), 442–451 (1996). https://doi.org/10.1518/001 872096778701944
3. Noy, Y.I., Lemoine, T.L., Klachan, C., Burns, P.C.: Task interruptability and duration as measures of visual distraction. Appl. Ergon. **35**(3), 207–213 (2004). https://doi.org/10.1016/ j.apergo.2003.11.012
4. Wickens, C.D.: The structure of attentional resources. Attention Perform. VIII **8**, 239–257 (1980)
5. Strayer, D.L., Drews, F.A.: Cell-phone–induced driver distraction. Curr. Dir. Psychol. Sci. **16**(3), 128–131 (2007). https://doi.org/10.1111/j.1467-8721.2007.00489.x
6. Goodsell, R., Cunningham, M., Chevalier, A.: Driver distraction: a review of scientific literature (2019)
7. Klauer, S.G., Dingus, T.A., Neale, V.L., Sudweeks, J.D., Ramsey, D.J.: The impact of driver inattention on near-crash/crash risk: an analysis using the 100-car naturalistic driving study data (2006)
8. Ziakopoulos, A., Theofilatos, A., Papadimitriou, E., Yannis, G.: A meta analysis of the impacts of operating in-vehicle information systems on road safety. IATSS res. **43**(3), 185–194 (2019). https://doi.org/10.1016/j.iatssr.2019.01.003
9. Stelmach, G.E., Nahom, A.: Cognitive-motor abilities of the elderly driver. Hum. Factors **34**(1), 53–65 (1992). https://doi.org/10.1177/001872089203400107
10. Zagaria, M.A.E.: Vision, cognition, and mobility challenges for elderly drivers. US Pharmacist **32**(1), 36 (2007)
11. Chaparro, A., Wood, J.M., Carberry, T.: Effects of age and auditory and visual dual tasks on closed-road driving performance. Optom. Vis. Sci. **82**(8), 747–754 (2005). https://doi.org/10. 1097/01.opx.0000174724.74957.45
12. Karthaus, M., Falkenstein, M.: Functional changes and driving performance in older drivers: assessment and interventions. Geriatrics **1**(2), 12 (2016). https://doi.org/10.3390/geriatrics10 20012
13. Shinar, D., Tractinsky, N., Compton, R.: Effects of practice, age, and task demands, on interference from a phone task while driving. Accid. Anal. Prev. **37**(2), 315–326 (2005). https:// doi.org/10.1016/j.aap.2004.09.007
14. Rizzo, M., Stierman, L., Skaar, N., Dawson, J.D., Anderson, S.W., Vecera, S.P.: Effects of a controlled auditory–verbal distraction task on older driver vehicle control. Transp. Res. Rec. **1865**(1), 1–6 (2004). https://doi.org/10.3141/1865-01

15. Thompson, K.R., Johnson, A.M., Emerson, J.L., Dawson, J.D., Boer, E.R., Rizzo, M.: Distracted driving in elderly and middle-aged drivers. Accid. Anal. Prev. **45**, 711–717 (2012). https://doi.org/10.1016/j.aap.2011.09.040
16. Mullakkal-Babu, F.A., Wang, M., He, X., van Arem, B., Happee, R.: Probabilistic field approach for motorway driving risk assessment. Transp. Res. Part C: Emerg. Technol. **118**, 102716 (2020). https://doi.org/10.1016/j.trc.2020.102716
17. Aven, T., et al.: Society for risk analysis glossary. In: Society for Risk Analysis, August 2018
18. Zou, Y., Tarko, A.P., Chen, E., Romero, M.A.: Effectiveness of cable barriers, guardrails, and concrete barrier walls in reducing the risk of injury. Accid. Anal. Prev. **72**, 55–65 (2014). https://doi.org/10.1016/j.aap.2014.06.013
19. Son, J., Lee, Y., Kim, M.H.: Impact of traffic environment and cognitive workload on older drivers' behavior in simulated driving. Int. J. Precis. Eng. Manuf. **12**(1), 135–141 (2011)
20. Engström, J., Markkula, G., Victor, T., Merat, N.: Effects of cognitive load on driving performance: the cognitive control hypothesis. Hum. Factors **59**(5), 734–764 (2017). https://doi.org/10.1177/0018720817690639
21. Engström, J., Johansson, E., Östlund, J.: Effects of visual and cognitive load in real and simulated motorway driving. Transp. Res. F: Traffic Psychol. Behav. **8**(2), 97–120 (2005). https://doi.org/10.1016/j.trf.2005.04.012
22. Kountouriotis, G.K., Spyridakos, P., Carsten, O.M., Merat, N.: Identifying cognitive distraction using steering wheel reversal rates. Accid. Anal. Prev. **96**, 39–45 (2016). https://doi.org/10.1016/j.aap.2016.07.032
23. Reimer, B.: Impact of cognitive task complexity on drivers' visual tunneling. Transp. Res. Rec. **2138**(1), 13–19 (2009). https://doi.org/10.3141/2138-03
24. Victor, T.W., Harbluk, J.L., Engström, J.A.: Sensitivity of eye-movement measures to in-vehicle task difficulty. Transp. Res. F: Traffic Psychol. Behav. **8**(2), 167–190 (2005). https://doi.org/10.1016/j.trf.2005.04.014
25. Karthaus, M., Wascher, E., Falkenstein, M., Getzmann, S.: The ability of young, middle-aged and older drivers to inhibit visual and auditory distraction in a driving simulator task. Transp. Res. F: Traffic Psychol. Behav. **68**, 272–284 (2020). https://doi.org/10.1016/j.trf.2019.11.007

Data Cleaning of Binary Sensor Events in Activity Recognition by Cluster-Based Methods

Chunyang Zhao[1,2], Xia Que[1,2], Yue Yin[1,2], Xiaoman Xing[3], Jiaoyun Yang[1,2(✉)], and Ning An[1,2]

[1] Key Laboratory of Knowledge Engineering with Big Data of Ministry of Education, Hefei University of Technology, Hefei, China
jiaoyun@hfut.edu.cn
[2] School of Computer Science and Information Engineering, Hefei University of Technology, Hefei, China
[3] Medical Imaging Department, Chinese Academy of Sciences, Suzhou, China

Abstract. The Ambient Assisted Living (AAL) systems use sensors to detect the daily behavior of older adults and provide necessary assistance based on changes in their cognitive status and physical functions, thus enabling older adults to maintain their independence at home. However, the effectiveness of the AAL systems depends on the accuracy of the data provided by sensors. Namely, when a human error or a hardware failure occurs, the activity recognition model can become inaccurate. This inaccuracy hinders the identification of critical and potentially life-threatening activities. Although there are many methods for cleaning sensor data, there is no method for binary sensors deployed in smart homes. By considering noisy sensor events and unintentional forgetting of turning off the device, this paper proposes two clustering-based methods for denoising and splitting binary sensor events to address possible inaccuracy due to the two mentioned problems. The effectiveness of the proposed methods is verified by the experiments using four machine learning models and three real-world smart home datasets and adopting different sensor configurations. The experimental results demonstrate that compared to the original unprocessed datasets, by combining the two proposed methods, the average accuracy and F-measure are improved by 15.00% and 17.25%, respectively.

Keywords: Data cleaning · Activity recognition · Cluster-based methods · Sensor events

1 Introduction

With the rapid development of economy, science, and medical treatment, the world population has been continuously aging. According to recent estimations, in 2025, 13.7% of the Chinese population will be 65 or more years old, and this percentage will increase to almost a quarter of the Chinese population in 2050, which will be about 329 million

© Springer Nature Switzerland AG 2021
Q. Gao and J. Zhou (Eds.): HCII 2021, LNCS 12787, pp. 478–495, 2021.
https://doi.org/10.1007/978-3-030-78111-8_33

people [1]. Compared to young adults, older adults are susceptible to the consequences of dementia due to physical function factors, which significantly affects their physical and mental abilities [2]. This can even cause a reduced ability to speak, write, memorize, and perform activities [3]. Moreover, due to the cognitive decline, older adults lose their self-care ability and thus require help from caregivers.

There is a correlation between the cognitive level of older adults and their ability to perform activities of daily living (ADL); namely, cognitive impairment affects the independence of older adults. Recent studies have shown that the ADL is an important indicator in life quality assessment [4, 5]. The activity recognition technology has been used to monitor older adults performing the ADL at home to maintain their independence. The Ambient Assisted Living (AAL) systems collect data from sensors to monitor the interaction between residents and the surrounding environment. These systems obtain the status of residents' performing their ADLs by analyzing both the current data and historical records. Activity recognition is the foundation of many applications intended for elderlies, including fall detection [6], Alzheimer's disease symptoms detection [7], thermal comfort monitoring of older adults [8], intention recognition [9], and abnormal behavior detection [10].

Different methods (e.g., Naive Bayes, Support Vector Machine, Hidden Markov Model) and devices (e.g., cameras, smartphones, and sensors) have been used to identify activities of residents accurately. The activity recognition was realized by fitting the ADL of residents based on various sensor data, daily time, and relationships with activities. However, regardless of the adopted method, sensors are required to provide reliable information. Unfortunately, raw sensor data may include errors [11]. According to the report in [12], when hundreds of sensors are used in the smart home systems for a long period, there will be at least one sensor failure per day on average. On the one hand, sensors are likely to produce error readings due to low battery state, sensor aging, module failure, and environmental interference. On the other hand, human errors denote another major factor of sensor anomaly; for instance, devices can be mistakenly switched on or off by residents. The presence of error data in a sensor dataset reduces its quality, which further leads to a decrease in the activity recognition performance of a model. Besides, a high failure rate can result in inaccurate identification of residents' activities, especially in life-threatening situations, causing a failure in timely addressing of residents' needs. Therefore, the sensor data should be pre-processed.

Most of the existing data cleaning techniques use sensor-values-based methods (e.g., range, change gradient, distribution, and other adjacent sensor values) for anomaly detection and data cleaning, which is designed for continuous sensors. However, the readings of most sensors deployed in smart homes are binary (0 or 1) [13], so only calculating the relationship between binary values may not help to judge whether sensor data are abnormal. Namely, it is difficult to determine the validity and correct values of binary data by only determining whether sensor readings or the data change rate exceed the predefined thresholds. Besides, in some cases, some rooms only deploy one single sensor [14], and so the spatial correlation methods based on neighboring nodes' data cannot be applied to this situation. There is currently no data cleaning method for binary sensors. Considering the regularity of residents' daily activities, and based on the fact that each sensor has its implicit semantic features, the spatio-temporal correlation of binary sensors should be considered form another perspective to develop an efficient data cleaning method.

In order to address the above-mentioned problems, this paper proposes two cluster-based data cleaning methods for binary sensors deployed in smart homes, called Sensor Noise Event Removal (SNER) method and Sensor Event Group Split (SEGS) method, respectively. By using these two methods, the binary sensor dataset can be optimized, which can help to improve the performance of the activity recognition model. The SNER method calculates the outlier factor of each sensor event according to the time concentration of sensors triggering by residents. The higher the outlier factor value is, the more likely the sensor event is to be a noisy event. The SEGS method detects and splits abnormal sensor events caused by residents forgetting to turn off devices in order to reduce the negative impact of such events on the activity recognition model. The proposed methods are verified by three publicly available smart home datasets from Kasteren et al. [15] and four machine learning models. The evaluation results show that the average accuracy and F-measure of SNER and SEGS combined methods reached 75.95% and 54.53%, respectively, which are 15.00% and 17.25% higher than those without data cleaning.

The rest of the paper is organized as follows. Section 2 introduces the related work of sensor data cleaning. Section 3 describes the proposed methods for sensor event data cleaning. Section 4 presents experimental datasets and the effectiveness validation of different strategies combining the two solutions. Finally, Sect. 5 concludes the paper and presents future work.

2 Related Work

Data cleaning is an essential step in data pre-processing, and it detects data validity and repairs errors if there are some of them. Several methods have been used for sensor data cleaning in order to improve data quality [16], including the probability-based, statistic-based, and correlation-based cleaning methods.

The probability-based cleaning methods have often been applied to estimate noisy sensor data. Elnahrawy and Nath [17] introduced a Bayesian-based cleaning method to calculate the confidence of sensor data collected in noisy environments. This method is used to reduce the uncertainty of sensor readings caused by random noise. A sensor data cleaning method based on the Kalman filter was proposed in [18] to correct sensor data by comparing and analyzing the predicted and observed values. Both of these methods belong to supervised data cleaning, but their main disadvantage is that the prior knowledge about noise characteristics and sensor readings are required, which can be relatively difficult to obtain in practice.

The statistical-based methods determine whether data need to be processed based on the data deviation degree from the normal data range. Hu et al. proposed a training data cleaning strategy based on the Euclidean distance and Z-score [19] to reduce the negative impact of outlier sensor data values on the training model. This method is highly effective for data that deviates from the normal sensor value. However, this method requires the sensor data to conform to the Gaussian distribution.

The model-based methods use machine learning models for data cleaning. Qu et al. [20] presented a data cleaning algorithm based on the Support Vector Machine (SVM) and random sub-sampling verification. The outlier data points were removed one by one by calculating the classification error rate. Wang et al. [21] introduced a data cleaning method based on bootstrap sampling. The data cleaning was performed according to the classification of the samples by several weak SVM classifiers. The number of weak SVM classifiers was positively correlated with the elapsed time and consumed system resources.

Since the sensor values are statistically correlated and can be verified by nearby sensor values, the correlation-based methods have been increasingly applied to the sensor data cleaning. For instance, these methods have been used to monitor the correlation between multiple sensor readings in adjacent spaces [22–25], variation rule of sensor readings within a certain period [22, 25], and the correlation between different physical phenomena of the same object (e.g., temperature and humidity) [24]. This type of method usually judges whether the sensor value fits the regression curve or conforms to the predefined rules. If the sensor value does not conform to the rules or deviate from the regression curve, these methods determine which of the sensors has an error and then correct its data.

3 Proposed Method

In smart homes, sensors may experience noisy events at incorrect times due to malfunctions or environmental interference. Also, some residents may forget to turn off their devices, which can cause sensors to be turned on over a long period. Both of these factors challenge the activity recognition performance of a model. In order to address these two issues, a data cleaning framework for binary sensor events is designed, and it is shown in Fig. 1. The proposed framework consists of two primary methods, SNER and SEGS methods. Next, we introduce two proposed methods, respectively.

3.1 SNER Method

Under normal circumstances, residents commonly perform particular activities within a specific time range during the day; for instance, bathing in the morning, going out at noon, sleeping during the night, and many others. The corresponding sensors are triggered when a particular activity is performed by residents, so the sensor triggering also shows certain time regularity. This means sensors will be triggered centrally during the normal-use period. However, sensors may experience abnormal noisy events at the wrong time due to their malfunctions and other reasons. Although noisy outlier events have a lower triggering probability than usual events, they can cause incorrect recognition results of the activity recognition model. For instance, the sensor located in a toilet is highly correlated with the activity "use toilet", and once a resident leaves the home, the sensor can generate an error signal due to interference. Therefore, the noisy sensor data should be detected and removed.

By considering residents perform activities following a fixed pattern every day, this paper assumes that sensors will be triggered intensively during several periods of the day, that is, events of each sensor concentrated in several clusters. Besides, when a sensor fails, it will be triggered when deviating from the normal time with a high probability,

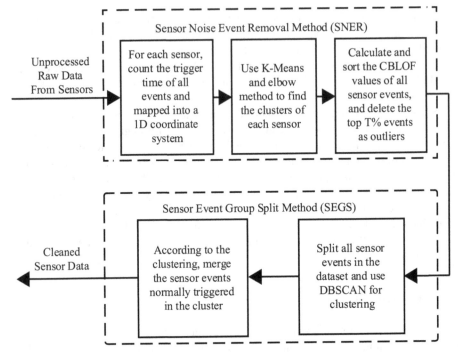

Fig. 1. The framework for data cleaning.

and the frequency is usually lower than that of the normal use. Therefore, the clustering-based methods are used to detect and remove noisy events. The following steps are performed for each sensor.

First, the trigger time distribution is determined for each sensor. For each sensor, the trigger time in one day of events related to the sensor is calculated and mapped to a 1D coordinate system. Under normal circumstances, a fixed time has been commonly used as a segmentation criterion (e.g., in [15], 3 am was used as the boundary), but the main disadvantage is the laws of sensors' trigger can differ; namely, some sensors may frequently trigger near the boundary time, and events with the same distribution will appear at both ends of the coordinate axis due to time segmentation. If this situation is not processed, these sensor events will be mistaken for two smaller clusters in the next clustering algorithm. For instance, assuming the boundary time is 00:00, and the trigger time of a sensor is from a set {00:05, 07:55, 08:00, 08:05, 22:45, 23:00, 23:30, 23:45, 23:55, 23:59}, although the node 00:05 is close to 23:59 in terms of time, this time point is not in the same cluster as the time before midnight because of the set time boundary. As a result, the probability that these events are misjudged as abnormal will be increased. In order to solve this problem, considering that the nodes on both sides of the largest gap are often separated into two different clusters in the clustering process, it is needed to find the largest time gap to set a boundary. Therefore, the sensor triggering times in one day are sorted in the ascending order, and these time values are represented by T_i^j respectively, where i denotes the sensor's number, j denotes the sequence number of triggering time after sorting, and m represents the total number of events triggered by the ith sensor. Then, the triggering time gap TG_i^j between the sensor events of the ith sensor is defined as:

$$TG_i^j = \begin{cases} T_i^{j+1} - T_i^j, & j \neq m, \\ T_i^1 + 1 - T_i^j, & j = m. \end{cases} \tag{1}$$

Then, position P_i of the largest time gap of the ith sensor is calculated by:

$$P_i = \underset{j \in \{1,2,\ldots,m\}}{\arg\max} \ TG_i^j, \tag{2}$$

For all event numbers with a trigger time sequence less than or equal to P_i of the ith sensor, the trigger time in the coordinates will be shifted to the right by one day so that the proximity sensor events in time can be concentrated into the same cluster.

After the sensor triggering time distribution processing, the K-Means algorithm is employed to divide the event nodes into several clusters. Determination of the parameter k value is crucial for the K-Means algorithm performance. The elbow method is one of the common methods for establishing the k value. This method observes the changing trend of the k value and uses the sum of squared errors (SSE) to select the optimal number of clusters, i.e., the optimal k value. However, the main disadvantage of the elbow method is that it is needed to identify inflection points by human observation. Therefore, the method for automatic selection of the k value based on the elbow method proposed in [26] is adopted in this work. By utilizing the characteristic of the SSE that it first descends fast and then slowly, this method determines the optimal k value by calculating the maximum difference between the SSE value of each k (in this case, k is from 1 to 10) and the line connected with the first and the last k. The SSE trend and the straight line of the sensor's triggering time distribution under different k values are shown in Fig. 2, where the largest difference is at $k = 3$, so this value is chosen as optimal k value, and the corresponding clustering result of the sensor triggering time is shown in Fig. 3.

In order to determine whether the sensor event is a noisy event, it is needed to calculate the outlier factor of the sensor event using the clustering result. Next, the previously obtained sensor clustering results are applied to the cluster-based outlier detection algorithm, the FindCBLOF [27]. The FindCBLOF considers that the normality of nodes is positively related to the similarity of large clusters, which is similar to the assumption used in this work. The algorithm separates large clusters (LCs) from small clusters (SCs) according to the cluster size order. For the cluster set $C_i = \{C_{i,1}, C_{i,2}, \ldots, C_{i,k}\}$ of the ith sensor, the CBLOF value of the sensor event node t is expressed as:

$$CBLOF(i, t) = \begin{cases} |C_{i,a}| \times similar(t, C_{i,a}), & \\ \quad \text{if } t \in C_{i,a}, C_{i,a} \in LC, & \\ |C_{i,a}| \times \max(similar(t, C_{i,b})), & \\ \quad \text{if } t \in C_{i,a}, C_{i,a} \in SC, C_{i,b} \in LC. \end{cases} \tag{3}$$

However, the triggering frequencies of sensors can differ. If the similarity is calculated considering the cluster size, for a sensor with a lower triggering frequency, the

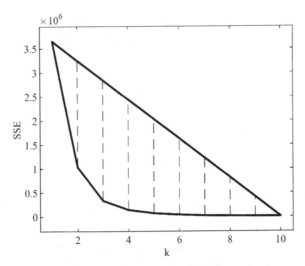

Fig. 2. Elbow method line chart under different k values.

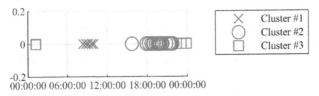

Fig. 3. Clustering result of the sensor trigger time ($k = 3$).

sensor's event corresponds to a lower CBLOF value. Therefore, (3) is modified to include the total number of events triggered by the ith sensor $|D_i|$ into the CBLOF calculation, and the improved formula for calculating the CBLOF is given by:

$$
CBLOF(i, t) = \begin{cases} |C_{i,a}|/|D_i| \times similar(t, C_{i,a}), \\ \quad \text{if } t \in C_{i,a}, C_{i,a} \in LC, \\ |C_{i,a}|/|D_i| \times \max(similar(t, C_{i,b})), \\ \quad \text{if } t \in C_{i,a}, C_{i,a} \in SC, C_{i,b} \in LC. \end{cases} \quad (4)
$$

After performing the above-presented steps for each sensor, the CBLOF values of all sensor events are obtained and then sorted in the ascending order. Since a noisy sensor event tends to get a lower CBLOF value, the threshold T is set, and sensor events in the top $T\%$ of the CBLOF values are regarded as noise events and removed from the dataset.

3.2 SEGS Method

After removing the noisy events, the remaining sensor events reflect the real-life situation more accurately. However, some sensors can be turned on for a long time due to residents' forgetting to turn off them and other reasons. For instance, consider a series of sensor and activity events of a particular period in the Kasteren House A dataset shown in Fig. 4 and Fig. 5.

```
11-Mar-2008 09:18:17    11-Mar-2008 09:18:18    'ToiletFlush'          1
11-Mar-2008 09:18:32    11-Mar-2008 09:18:33    'Hall-Toilet door'     1
11-Mar-2008 09:18:38    11-Mar-2008 09:18:51    'Hall-Toilet door'     1
11-Mar-2008 09:26:38    11-Mar-2008 09:26:39    'Hall-Toilet door'     1
11-Mar-2008 09:26:42    11-Mar-2008 18:28:57    'Hall-Toilet door'     1
11-Mar-2008 09:33:50    11-Mar-2008 09:33:54    'Frontdoor'            1
11-Mar-2008 17:57:20    11-Mar-2008 17:57:24    'Frontdoor'            1
11-Mar-2008 17:58:11    11-Mar-2008 17:58:19    'Freezer'              1
11-Mar-2008 18:02:32    11-Mar-2008 18:02:36    'Plates cupboard'      1
11-Mar-2008 18:12:24    11-Mar-2008 18:12:25    'Freezer'              1
11-Mar-2008 18:12:29    11-Mar-2008 18:12:35    'Freezer'              1
11-Mar-2008 18:16:05    11-Mar-2008 18:16:07    'Cups cupboard'        1
11-Mar-2008 18:16:09    11-Mar-2008 18:16:22    'Fridge'               1
11-Mar-2008 18:29:01    11-Mar-2008 18:29:52    'Hall-Toilet door'     1
11-Mar-2008 18:30:35    11-Mar-2008 18:30:36    'ToiletFlush'          1
```

Fig. 4. A segment of the sensor events in Kasteren House A dataset.

```
11-Mar-2008 09:15:39    11-Mar-2008 09:18:24    'use toilet'
11-Mar-2008 09:18:39    11-Mar-2008 09:29:06    'take shower'
11-Mar-2008 09:33:30    11-Mar-2008 17:57:51    'leave house'
11-Mar-2008 17:58:06    11-Mar-2008 18:12:51    'prepare Dinner'
11-Mar-2008 18:16:03    11-Mar-2008 18:16:30    'get drink'
11-Mar-2008 18:29:55    11-Mar-2008 18:30:44    'use toilet'
```

Fig. 5. A segment of the activity events in Kasteren House A dataset.

According to the activities described in Fig. 5, the fifth sensor event in Fig. 4 indicates that the resident forgot to close the door until the next use (nine hours later) after taking a shower. During this period, the resident did a total of three activities: "leave house," "prepare dinner," and "get drink." By observing three of Kasteren datasets, it is found that such forgetting actions often happen, and some sensors are often turned on continuously for a week. Therefore, if such sensor events are not examined and processed in the pre-processing step, the constructed activity recognition model is likely to summarize incorrect knowledge. For instance, users occasionally forget to close the toilet door when they leave their home, and the sensor "Hall-Toilet door" is the only sign to judge the activity "take shower." Suppose there is a scenario in which the sensor "Hall-Toilet door" is triggered more frequently during the activity "take shower" than the activity "leave house." In a probability-based model, the period when a user forgets to close the bathroom door and go out will be mistaken for the period when the user takes a bath.

In the model that considers the recognition accuracy, since the time for the user to go out is generally longer than the bathing time, the model will recognize that the user is going out when the sensor "Hall-Toilet door" is triggered. But in either case, there will be a misjudgment of the activity recognition model. Considering that the sensor state has a relatively significant impact on the activity recognition model's performance, it is needed to detect and separate long-term sensor events caused by residents' forgetting.

This work assumes that residents perform particular activities only in one specific room (e.g., they take a bath only in the bathroom and sleep in the bedroom), and activities in one area do not overlap with those in other areas. During the activity execution, residents turn on or off only sensors in the room corresponding to the activity they perform at that moment. Under normal circumstances, all sensors are turned off when residents start or end their activities. When the residents finish activities but forget to turn off devices, the related sensors will stay turned on until the next use. That is, the opening and closing of the sensors do not occur for the same activity.

For a given sensor event set S in the dataset, each sensor event is characterized by four features: *start*, *end*, *id*, and *val*, which represent the start time, end time, sensor ID number, and signal value of the current sensor event, respectively. First, sensors are grouped according to the room location of sensor deployment provided by the dataset. Next, each record of the sensor event set S is split into two events in terms of the start time and end time, whose *val* values are set to 1 and 0, respectively, and the separated sensor event set S' is sorted in time sequence. If a sensor is triggered normally, the events of the sensor occur in the same activity in the order of first on and then off, and will be recombined into one event in the following merging algorithm. Otherwise, the algorithm will consider them as two events. Although the duration and triggering frequency of each activity performed by residents are different, it is considered that, when residents do activities, the sensor events of the same group are closer in terms of temporal, spatial, and event record distance than those of different groups. On this basis, a density-based clustering algorithm DBSCAN [28], which does not need to pre-defined the cluster size but requires parameter values ε and *MinPts* to automatically cluster the data, is used to group sensor events. However, the problem of how to determine the distance between two sensor events should be solved. In order to solve this problem, the distance of sensor events is defined from the above three aspects as follows.

As previously mentioned, this paper assumes that residents' activities in one area do not overlap with those in other areas. Hence, sensors in different areas are responsible for identifying different activities. For the two sensor events S_i' and S_j', their ID numbers are $S_i'.id$ and $S_j'.id$ respectively, and the area correlation between then is given by:

$$AC(S_i', S_j') = \begin{cases} 1, & \text{if } S_i'.id \text{ and } S_j'.id \text{ in same area,} \\ 0, & \text{otherwise.} \end{cases} \tag{5}$$

When residents perform certain activities, sensors in the activity-related areas will be triggered frequently, and sensor events have a local correlation regardless of event or time distance. The event correlation and time correlation of sensor events S'_i and S'_j are respectively expressed as:

$$EC(S'_i, S'_j) = \exp(-E_{dist}(S'_i, S'_j)/E_{range}), \tag{6}$$

$$TC(S'_i, S'_j) = \exp(-\chi \left| S'_i.time - S'_j.time \right|), \tag{7}$$

where $E_{dist}(S'_i, S'_j)$ denotes the entry distance of sensor events S'_i and S'_j, and when events S'_i and S'_j are adjacent, then $E_{dist}(S'_i, S'_j) = 1$; E_{range} denotes the radius of the event distance to be detected; $S'_i.time$ and $S'_j.time$ represent the triggering times of S'_i and S'_j, respectively; and lastly, χ represents the time decay rate. The influence of χ on sensor events at the time level was analyzed by Krishnan and Cook in [29].

Finally, the distance between two sensor events S'_i and S'_j can be calculated by:

$$dist(S'_i, S'_j) = 1 - AC(S'_i, S'_j) \times EC(S'_i, S'_j) \times TC(S'_i, S'_j), \tag{8}$$

After determining the distance between two sensor events, considering that the traditional DBSCAN algorithm needs to operate on the entire dataset, significant system resources are needed, and the sensor trigger has locality based on the previously mentioned assumptions about residents' activities. Therefore, the DBSCAN algorithm is improved. Namely, each event in the sensor event set S' is detected in time order, and the sliding window method is employed to check whether there are available events in the range with the radius of E_{range}. Further, each detected cluster is assigned with a cluster number, and sensor events with the same numbers occur during the same activity performed by residents. For outlier sensor events smaller than *MinPts*, according to the previously mentioned assumptions, it is considered that residents turn on or off a device only once during the activity performing. In this work, it is set that $\varepsilon = 0.2$, *MinPts* = 2, $E_{range} = 30$, $\chi = 0.1$.

For a cluster set $C = \{C_1, C_2, \ldots, C_n\}$ and an outlier number set $O = \{O_1, O_2, \ldots, O_l\}$, Algorithm 1 is used to combine the separated sensor event sets $S' = \{S'_1, S'_2, \ldots, S'_m\}$ to generate the processed sensor event set S^{new}. Each event cluster is detected in the time order after the improved DBSCAN algorithm is used to partition clusters. If a sensor has an off signal first or is still on after the cluster traversal ends, it means that another signal of the sensor is in another cluster, and in that case, it is regarded as two events; otherwise, when the sensor normally triggers in the cluster, that is, a sensor in the same event cluster had an turn on event first, and then had a turn off event, merge both into a sensor events that occur within this interval.

Algorithm 1 Combine Sensor Events Algorithm

Input: S', C and O
Output: S^{new}

1: $S^{temp} \leftarrow \emptyset, S^{new} \leftarrow \emptyset$
2: **for** $i \leftarrow 1$ to n **do**
3:     $G \leftarrow C_i$
4:     **for** $j \leftarrow 1$ to $length(G)$ **do**
5:         $k \leftarrow G_j$
6:         **if** $S'_k.val = 1$ **then**
7:             **if** $S^{temp} = \emptyset$ or $S'_k.id \notin S^{temp}.id$ **then**
8:                 $S^{temp} \leftarrow S^{temp} \cup S'_k$
9:             **else**
10:                 $k' \leftarrow find(S^{temp}.id, S'_k.id)$
11:                 $S^{new} \leftarrow S^{new} \cup [S^{temp}_{k'}.time, S^{temp}_{k'}.time, S^{temp}_{k'}.id, 1]$
12:                 $S^{temp} \leftarrow (S^{temp} - S^{temp}_{k'}) \cup S'_k$
13:             **end if**
14:         **else**
15:             **if** $S^{temp} = \emptyset$ or $S'_k.id \notin S^{temp}.id$ **then**
16:                 $S^{new} \leftarrow S^{new} \cup [S'_k.time, S'_k.time, S'_k.id, 1]$
17:             **else**
18:                 $k' \leftarrow find(S^{temp}.id, S'_k.id)$
19:                 $S^{new} \leftarrow S^{new} \cup [S^{temp}_{k'}.time, S'_k.time, S'_k.id, 1]$
20:                 $S^{temp} \leftarrow S^{temp} - S^{temp}_{k'}$
21:             **end if**
22:         **end if**
23:     **end for**
24:     **if** $S^{temp} \neq \emptyset$ **then**
25:         **for** $i \leftarrow 1$ to $length(S^{temp})$ **do**
26:             $S^{new} \leftarrow S^{new} \cup [S^{temp}_i.time, S^{temp}_i.time, S^{temp}_i.id, 1]$
27:         **end for**
28:         $S^{temp} \leftarrow \emptyset$
29:     **end if**
30: **end for**
31: **for** $i \leftarrow 1$ to l **do**
32:     $k \leftarrow O_i$
33:     $S^{new} \leftarrow S^{new} \cup [S'_k.time, S'_k.time, S'_k.id, 1]$
34: **end for**
35: $S^{new} \leftarrow sort(S^{new})$

---

4 Experiment and Results

4.1 Experimental Setup

The proposed methods were verified on the publicly available datasets provided in [15]. The Kasteren's datasets includes information on three real-world houses denoted as House A, House B, and House C that are instrumented by several wireless sensor networks. Within each house, a single resident is conducting regular ADL. The sensors deployed in each room record the details of the resident's life and his interactions with the objects. For instance, reed switches detect whether doors and cabinets are open or closed; float sensors measure flushing toilets. The information about the three datasets is provided in Table 1.

Table 1. Details of the datasets

Dataset	House A	House B	House C
Age	26	28	57
Gender	Male	Male	Male
Setting	Apartment	Apartment	House
Rooms	3	2	6
Duration	25 days	14 days	19 days
Sensors	14	23	21
Sensor events	1,229	19,075	22,700
Activities	10	13	16
Activity events	259	112	234

The sensor data were divided into multiple time slices using a sliding window at 60-s intervals, as suggested in [14]. Each time slice generated a feature vector $X = (X_1, X_2, \ldots, X_N)^T$, where N represented the total number of sensors deployed in a smart home, and X_i represented the signal of the ith sensor. In terms of the feature representation of sensor data, a binary representation was used; when the ith sensor was turned on in the current time slice, the eigenvalue value X_i was marked as one; otherwise, it was marked as zero.

Two metrics were used to evaluate the effectiveness of the proposed methods, accuracy and F-measure. The accuracy was calculated to evaluate the correct rate of the machine learning model at each time slice, and F-measure was calculated to evaluate the machine learning model's ability to identify each of the activities.

The leave-one-day-out strategy [14] was adopted, and the data of a single day was used for testing, while the data of remaining days for used for training. This process was repeated until each day of the dataset has been used at least once as the test data. Then, the average results were calculated.

In order to evaluate the effectiveness of two methods, several different activity recognition classifiers were used, including the Naive Bayes (NB), Hidden Markov Model (HMM), Hidden Semi-Markov Model (HSMM), and Long Short-Term Memory (LSTM). As for the LSTM model, Matlab Deep Learning Toolbox was used to implement a two-hidden-layer LSTM network, where both hidden layers consisted of 50 neurons, and the learning rate, time step, batch size, and the maximal number of epochs were initialized to 0.0004, 60, 10, and 500, respectively. In order to prevent overfitting in the training phase, a dropout layer, which was set at a rate of 0.2, was added to the network after the input layer and each hidden layer.

4.2 Determine the Noise Events Proportion

In the SNER method, it is needed to determine a threshold T and delete the top $T\%$ of the CBLOF values of all sensor events that are considered as noisy events. However, in different smart homes, the number, type, deployment location, and triggering frequency of sensors are not the same, so their probabilities of noisy events are also different. When a low T value is used, the remaining noisy events will still mislead the activity recognition model; on the contrary, when a high T value is used, higher than the true noise rate, the method will consider the events that residents occasionally do as noise and thus delete them, thereby reducing the model recognition performance. In the experiments, different T values were used (0%, 0.5%, 1%, 2%, 3%, and 5%) for three datasets and four classifiers. The obtained results are shown in Table 2.

Table 2. Impact of threshold on different models and datasets (Accuracy/F-measure)

Dataset	T	NB	HMM	HSMM	LSTM
House A	0%	77.13/46.42	59.29/43.20	59.56/45.24	84.97/55.22
	0.5%	77.15/47.29	59.38/43.31	59.57/45.40	**87.11/57.16**
	1%	77.15/**47.63**	59.16/44.63	59.58/46.34	86.52/55.92
	2%	77.13/46.73	59.41/**44.72**	59.83/**46.46**	86.29/54.93
	3%	**77.19**/46.71	**59.45**/44.53	**59.86**/45.81	85.34/55.02
	5%	**77.19**/46.78	58.78/44.58	59.75/45.97	84.36/54.80
House B	0%	80.74/38.47	**65.42/44.60**	**65.37**/43.70	**84.47**/43.15
	0.5%	**81.39/41.75**	63.80/43.76	63.80/**43.83**	84.05/**43.91**
	1%	71.88/40.72	53.91/42.89	54.10/43.78	83.27/42.84
	2%	71.72/41.33	54.63/42.61	54.62/43.46	80.09/43.29
	3%	67.68/40.60	55.15/41.94	54.45/42.44	75.04/41.59
	5%	67.86/40.11	55.32/41.99	54.65/41.83	72.60/40.26
House C	0%	47.46/23.66	33.28/22.54	38.17/24.84	35.59/**16.37**
	0.5%	**63.98**/32.14	**34.69/25.78**	**44.80/29.68**	37.77/16.25
	1%	57.77/26.29	27.60/19.04	33.28/21.47	29.39/14.23
	2%	63.82/**34.68**	34.60/24.35	44.46/28.52	**38.38**/16.05
	3%	53.21/29.10	35.12/25.40	37.97/27.76	33.95/14.96
	5%	52.42/28.65	33.61/24.79	37.73/26.99	33.79/14.40

According to the results obtained for House A dataset, the best accuracy was achieved at $T = 0.5\%$, and an average accuracy was 70.80%. In terms of average F-measure, $T = 1\%$ provided the best results, and an average F-measure was 48.63%. The LSTM had the highest accuracy and F-measure at $T = 0.5\%$, while the other three models, the NB, HMM, and HSMM, had the best accuracy at $T = 3\%$. In terms of the F- measure, the NB reached its maximum value at $T = 1\%$, and HMM and HSMM reached their maximum values at $T = 2\%$. From the trend of each model's performance, the noisy events of House A accounted for at least 0.5% of the dataset.

The results of the House B dataset show that there was no clear winner between $T = 0\%$ and 0.5% in all models' performances. Further, in terms of average accuracy, $T = 0\%$ (74.00%) was slightly higher than $T = 0.5\%$ (73.26%), but the latter's average F-measure was the highest among all T values, reaching the value of 43.31%. However, the accuracy values of the NB, HMM, and HSMM models all significantly decreased at $T = 1\%$. As for the LSTM model, this trend started at $T = 2\%$. The accuracy of the four models did not return to the previous level when T increased; F-measure showed a downward trend after T was greater than 0.5%.

As for the House C dataset, most models achieved the best performance at $T = 0.5\%$, with the average accuracy and F-measure of 45.31% and 25.96%, respectively, but there was a significant decrease in performances at $T = 1\%$. It was found that the outlier events of some sensors provided a background for certain activities. At a specific range of T values, the SNER method could only clean a part of the outlier events, and since the outlier events were not entirely cleaned, inconsistent backgrounds were caused, and some common activities could not be recognized, which further reduced the performance of the activity recognition model. At $T = 2\%$, due to the elimination of enough number of outliers, the performances of the four models returned to the levels close to those at $T = 0.5\%$, achieving the average accuracy and F-measure of 45.32% and 25.90% respectively. The recognition ability of the models started to decline as T continued to increase. In the LSTM model, even at T of 0.5% and 2%, F-measure was slightly lower than that without noise reduction; the accuracy was improved, and the highest accuracy was achieved at $T = 2\%$, and it was equal to 38.38%.

The performances of all the models were compared in terms of average accuracy and F-measure at different T values, and from the results are presented in Table 2. The average accuracy and F-measure values for all the models and datasets were: 60.95% and 37.28% for T of 0%, 63.12% and 39.19% for T of 0.5%, 57.80% and 37.15% for T of 1%, 60.42% and 38.93% for T of 2%, 57.87% and 37.99% for T of 3%, and 57.34% and 37.60% for T of 5%. Consequently, at $T = 0.5\%$, the results were better than at all other T values, and this value was the only one at which the average accuracy and F-measure both exceeded those of the original unprocessed datasets. Therefore, $T = 0.5\%$ was set as the threshold for detecting noise events and applied to the next experiment.

4.3 Activity Recognition Results

The following schemes for data cleaning were used on the three Kasteren datasets:

- *SNER*—Only use the Sensor Noise Event Removal method where $T = 0.5\%$.
- *SEGS*—Only use the Sensor Event Group Split method.
- *SNER+SEGS*—both methods were used, first the SNER method and then the SEGS method.

After processing the datasets by the previous three mentioned schemes, they were input to the machine learning model for the purposes of modeling and testing. The comparison results are given in Table 3. According to the results in Table 3, the SNER+SEGS achieved the best results for scenarios of House B and House C. In terms of the mean accuracy and F-measure of all datasets and models, the SNER+SEGS obtained the best performance among all the schemes, achieving the average accuracy and F-measure of 75.95% and 54.53%, respectively. In other words, by using the SNER+SEGS scheme for data cleaning, the model performance was improved significantly; in comparison to the original datasets, the improvements in the average accuracy and F-measure were 15.00% and 17.25%, respectively.

Table 3. Accuracy and F-measure of activity recognition in different schemes (Accuracy/F-measure).

Dataset	Scheme	NB	HMM	HSMM	LSTM
House A	Original	77.13/46.42	59.29/43.20	59.56/45.24	84.97/55.22
	SNER	**77.15**/47.29	59.38/43.31	59.57/45.40	**87.11**/57.16
	SEGS	55.92/**50.15**	**89.32/68.89**	89.33/**69.66**	82.87/61.83
	SNER+SEGS	55.91/49.50	89.31/68.78	**89.33**/69.51	85.47/**62.75**
House B	Original	80.74/38.47	65.42/44.60	65.37/43.70	84.47/43.15
	SNER	**81.39**/41.75	63.80/43.76	63.80/43.83	84.05/43.91
	SEGS	69.37/46.99	80.27/57.88	80.59/57.29	83.49/47.11
	SNER+SEGS	69.41/**47.54**	**80.35/58.41**	**80.62/58.06**	**88.78/51.82**
House C	Original	47.46/23.66	33.28/22.54	38.17/24.84	35.59/16.37
	SNER	**63.98**/32.14	34.69/25.78	44.80/29.68	37.77/16.25
	SEGS	60.68/42.87	76.28/57.93	76.31/56.65	58.76/26.33
	SNER+SEGS	60.75/**44.29**	**76.30/58.75**	**76.41/58.19**	**58.80/26.70**

As for the House A dataset, although the generative performances of the NB, HMM, and HSMM models by using the SNER+SEGS scheme were better than those on the original dataset, they were slightly lower than those when the SEGS was used alone. On the one hand, this was related to the "get drink" activities. The majority of "get drink" activities occurred in the afternoon and evening, but there were three occurrences in the morning. Therefore, sensor events triggered during this period were more likely to be regarded as noisy events by the SNER. On the other hand, other outlier sensor events detected by the SNER method were relatively misleading in the activity recognition on the original dataset. After using the SEGS method, the negative impact of these events on the model performance was lower than on the original dataset. Removing these events could only slightly improve the recognition performance. The above two factors were the reasons for this phenomenon.

When the NB classifier was used, the accuracy of the SEGS was lower than that of the SNER because the NB classifier modeled the sensor feature vector and activity of the current time slot. For activities with prolonged duration and a low triggering frequency of related sensors, the NB model might treat the sensors that were previously forgotten to be turned off as the background to perform the relevant activity, and thus obtained the incorrect knowledge. Although such knowledge could help improve the recognition accuracy, if the forgotten sensors were essential for identifying certain activities, this could reduce the activity identification ability. After the SEGS method was used to split the forgotten sensor events, the NB model output only the activity with the highest possibility for the time slot without sensor triggering. However, since a sensor will not remain on when residents do other activities after splitting, the F-measure of the NB model can be further improved.

5 Conclusion and Future Work

By providing accurate and reliable information, sensors play an essential role in activity recognition systems. Therefore, in order to increase the recognition ability, abnormal sensor data detection and cleaning are necessary. This paper introduces two cluster-based data cleaning methods, the SNER and SEGS methods, for binary sensors to improve the quality of activity recognition. The proposed methods are verified by the experiments using several models and publicly available datasets. The experimental results show that the combination of the SNER and SEGS methods provides the best overall results. Compared to the original unprocessed datasets, the average accuracy and F-measure are improved by 15.00% and 17.25%, respectively. Thus, using the SNER+SEGS scheme for data cleaning can significantly improve the performance of activity recognition models. However, the proposed methods are unable to deal with the abnormal sensor events that occur during the normal time and the missing sensor events. In future work, we will design solutions to solve these problems.

Acknowledgements. This work was partially supported by the Anhui Provincial Key Technologies R&D Program (No. 1804b06020378), the National Natural Science Foundation of China (No. 61701159, No.61673156), and the National "111 Project" (No. B14025).

References

1. Chen, F., Liu, G.: Population aging in China. In: Uhlenberg, P. (ed.) International Handbook of Population Aging, pp. 157–172. Springer, Dordrecht (2009) https://doi.org/10.1007/978-1-4020-8356-3_8
2. Albert, M.S., et al.: The diagnosis of mild cognitive impairment due to Alzheimer's disease: recommendations from the national institute on aging-Alzheimer's association workgroups on diagnostic guidelines for Alzheimer's disease. Alzheimers Dement. 7(3), 270–279 (2011)
3. Alzheimer's Association: 2019 Alzheimer's disease facts and figures. Alzheimer's Dementia 15(3), 321–387 (2019)
4. Sikkes, S.A., et al.: Do instrumental activities of daily living predict dementia at 1-and 2-year follow-up? Findings from the development of screening guidelines and diagnostic criteria for predementia Alzheimer's disease study. J. Am. Geriatr. Soc. 59(12), 2273–2281 (2011)
5. Torisson, G., Stavenow, L., Minthon, L., Londos, E.: Reliability, validity and clinical correlates of the Quality of Life in Alzheimer's disease (QoL-AD) scale in medical inpatients. Health Qual. Life Outcomes 14(1), 90 (2016)

6. Chandra, I., Sivakumar, N., Gokulnath, C.B., Parthasarathy, P.: IoT based fall detection and ambient assisted system for the elderly. Clust. Comput. **22**(1), 2517–2525 (2018). https://doi.org/10.1007/s10586-018-2329-2

7. Pedro, S., Quintas, J., Menezes, P.: Sensor-based detection of Alzheimer's disease-related behaviors. In: Zhang, Y.-T. (ed.) The International Conference on Health Informatics. IP, vol. 42, pp. 276–279. Springer, Cham (2014). https://doi.org/10.1007/978-3-319-03005-0_70

8. Yu, J., Hassan, M.T., Bai, Y., An, N., Tam, V.W.: A pilot study monitoring the thermal comfort of the elderly living in nursing homes in Hefei, China, using wireless sensor networks, site measurements and a survey. Indoor Built Environ. **29**(3), 449–464 (2020)

9. Rafferty, J., Nugent, C.D., Liu, J., Chen, L.: From activity recognition to intention recognition for assisted living within smart homes. IEEE Trans. Hum. Mach. Syst. **47**(3), 368–379 (2017)

10. Arifoglu, D., Bouchachia, A.: Detection of abnormal behaviour for dementia sufferers using convolutional neural networks. Artif. Intell. Med. **94**, 88–95 (2019)

11. Ni, K., et al.: Sensor network data fault types. ACM Trans. Sens. Netw. (TOSN) **5**(3), 1–29 (2009)

12. Hnat, T.W., Srinivasan, V., Lu, J., Sookoor, T.I., Dawson, R., Stankovic, J., Whitehouse, K.: The hitchhiker's guide to successful residential sensing deployments. In: Proceedings of the 9th ACM Conference on Embedded Networked Sensor Systems 2011, pp. 232–245 (2011)

13. Cook, D.J., Crandall, A.S., Thomas, B.L., Krishnan, N.C.: CASAS: a smart home in a box. Computer **46**(7), 62–69 (2012)

14. Van Kasteren, T., Noulas, A., Englebienne, G., Kröse, B.: Accurate activity recognition in a home setting. In: Proceedings of the 10th International Conference on Ubiquitous Computing 2008, pp. 1–9 (2008)

15. van Kasteren, T.L., Englebienne, G., Kröse, B.J.: Human activity recognition from wireless sensor network data: Benchmark and software. In: Chen, L., Nugent, C., Biswas, J., Hoey, J. (eds.) Activity Recognition in Pervasive Intelligent Environments, pp. 165–186. Springer, Dordrecht (2011) https://doi.org/10.2991/978-94-91216-05-3_8

16. Karkouch, A., Mousannif, H., Al Moatassime, H., Noel, T.: Data quality in internet of things: a state-of-the-art survey. J. Netw. Comput. Appl. **73**, 57–81 (2016)

17. Elnahrawy, E., Nath, B.: Cleaning and querying noisy sensors. In: Proceedings of the 2nd ACM International Conference on Wireless Sensor Networks and Applications 2003, pp. 78–87 (2003)

18. Kenda, K., Mladenić, D.: Autonomous sensor data cleaning in stream mining setting. Bus. Syst. Res. J. **9**(2), 69–79 (2018)

19. Hu, Y., Chen, H., Li, G., Li, H., Xu, R., Li, J.: A statistical training data cleaning strategy for the PCA-based chiller sensor fault detection, diagnosis and data reconstruction method. Energy Build. **112**, 270–278 (2016)

20. Qu, J., Zuo, M.J.: Support vector machine based data processing algorithm for wear degree classification of slurry pump systems. Measurement **43**(6), 781–791 (2010)

21. Wang, S., Li, Z., Zhang, X.: Bootstrap sampling based data cleaning and maximum entropy SVMs for large datasets. In: 2012 IEEE 24th International Conference on Tools with Artificial Intelligence 2012, pp. 1151–1156. IEEE (2012)

22. Jeffery, S.R., Alonso, G., Franklin, M.J., Hong, W., Widom, J.: A pipelined framework for online cleaning of sensor data streams. In: 22nd International Conference on Data Engineering (ICDE 2006), p. 140. IEEE (2006)

23. Narkhede, P., Deshpande, S., Walambe, R.: Sensor data cleaning using particle swarm optimization. In: Abraham, A., Gandhi, N., Pant, M. (eds.) IBICA 2018. AISC, vol. 939, pp. 182–191. Springer, Cham (2019). https://doi.org/10.1007/978-3-030-16681-6_18

24. Lei, J., Bi, H., Xia, Y., Huang, J., Bae, H.: An in-network data cleaning approach for wireless sensor networks. Intell. Autom. Soft Comput. **22**(4), 599–604 (2016)

25. Shao, B., Song, C., Wang, Z., Li, Z., Yu, S., Zeng, P.: Data cleaning based on multi-sensor spatiotemporal correlation. In: Zhai, X.B., Chen, B., Zhu, K. (eds.) MLICOM 2019. LNIC-SSITE, vol. 294, pp. 235–243. Springer, Cham (2019). https://doi.org/10.1007/978-3-030-32388-2_20

26. Wu, G., Zhang, J.-L., Yuan, D.: Automatically Obtaining K value based on K-means elbow method. Comput. Eng. Softw **40**, 167–170 (2019). (in Chinese)

27. He, Z., Xu, X., Deng, S.: Discovering cluster-based local outliers. Pattern Recogn. Lett. **24**(9–10), 1641–1650 (2003)

28. Ester, M., Kriegel, H.-P., Sander, J., Xu, X.: A density-based algorithm for discovering clusters in large spatial databases with noise. In: Kdd 1996, vol. 34, pp. 226–231 (1996)

29. Krishnan, N.C., Cook, D.J.: Activity recognition on streaming sensor data. Pervasive Mob. Comput. **10**, 138–154 (2014)

Author Index

Printed in the United States
by Baker & Taylor Publisher Services